TEACHING, LEADING, AND LEARNING

TEACHING, LEADING, AND LEARNING

BECOMING CARING PROFESSIONALS

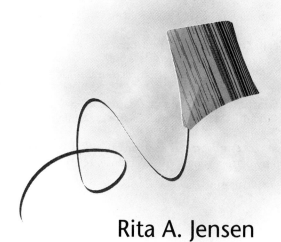

Rita A. Jensen

Bradley University

Therese J. Kiley

Bradley University

Houghton Mifflin Company   Boston   New York

We lovingly dedicate this book to our first teachers:

Myrtle L. Shipp Jensen	*Lorene M. Hubbard Kiley*
John W. Jensen	*John B. Kiley*

Senior Sponsoring Editor: Loretta Wolozin
Associate Editor: Lisa A. Mafrici
Senior Project Editor: Christina M. Horn
Editorial Assistant: Leah Y. Mehl
Senior Production/Design Coordinator: Jennifer Meyer Dare
Senior Designer: Henry Rachlin
Senior Manufacturing Coordinator: Marie Barnes
Associate Marketing Manager: Jean Zielinski DeMayo

Cover image: Excerpt from *Arlene Alda's 1-2-3's*. Copyright © 1998 by Arlene Alda. Reproduced by permission of Writers House, LLC.

Cover design: Catherine Hawkes, Cat & Mouse

Text credits begin on page A-27.

Printed in the U.S.A.

Library of Congress Catalog Card Number: 99-71968

ISBN: 0-395-76524-2

2 3 4 5 6 7 8 9-DOC-03 02 01 00

CONTENTS

PART TWO   TEACHING AND LEARNING IN CONTEXT   55

PART THREE   INSTRUCTION IN LEARNING COMMUNITIES   157

- Teachers as leaders (leadership skills and roles, leadership development)
- The intangibles of teaching (hidden curriculum, emotional literacy, ethics)
- Parents and families as collaborators (parents' roles, parent and family involvement, individual family differences)
- Working creatively within the system (collaboration, change, the change process)

With regard to the microview of the teaching/learning process, this book offers a focus on best practice, developmentally and culturally appropriate practice, appropriate use of technology, provision for individual differences, and the impact of professional standards on curricular reform and teacher preparation. In addition to focusing on the *how* of teaching, we address the *why* or rationale for the approaches we advocate. This book provides guidance on the importance of integrated curriculum and the effects that an integrated-curriculum approach can have on the instructional planning process, as well as guidance relevant to assuring that objectives and assessment are linked directly.

THEMES OF THIS BOOK

Four recurring themes appear throughout this book:

- Leadership and Decision Making
- Diversity
- Technology
- Collaboration

Because these themes relate to numerous concepts and issues that cross a variety of contexts, we chose to discuss them within the contexts in which they naturally appear. The focus of each chapter determines the extent to which we highlight particular themes.

■ Leadership and Decision Making: Teachers as Leaders and Decision Makers

We believe that every effective teacher leads and that effective teaching emerges from informed decision making. As our preceding comments regarding leadership indicate, for us, *leader* is the most important role that teachers play.

■ Diversity: Learners' Varying Needs and Characteristics

All learners bring with them unique understandings, experiences, abilities, skills, and attitudes when they enter those places called schools. This diversity results from their various cultures, races, communities, and family environments, as well as from exceptionalities and special learning needs they may possess. Therefore, teachers first must learn to appreciate learner diversity and then must learn strategies for accommodating and responding to that diversity.

■ Technology: Using Technology to Support the Teaching/Learning Process

The many recent advances in technology offer means for increasing the ways teachers can help students learn and the ways students can show what they know and can do. However, if teachers are to take advantage of these opportunities, they must first be aware of the variety of technology options available to them and must be open to continually updating their technological knowledge and skills. Most important, teachers must plan how to make technology an integral component of the teaching/learning process and must incorporate it appropriately to meet learners' diverse needs.

■ Collaboration: Working Together to Support the Teaching/Learning Process

Teaching is a difficult enterprise, but you don't have to face its many challenges alone. Both learners and teachers benefit when attempts to address learner needs involve collaboration. Just as learners can work collaboratively, teachers, families, agencies, and support personnel can collaborate to provide a comprehensive, integrated-services approach to responding to learner needs.

FEATURES OF THIS BOOK

This book includes several features that we designed to create opportunities for you to reflect on, and respond to, the ideas and concepts presented.

■ Beginning-of-Chapter Features

Each chapter begins with **intended outcomes** designed to help focus your reading. For example, knowing that an intended outcome of the chapter is that you will be able to describe steps you can take now to prepare for a teaching career, you can read with that outcome in mind. That way you'll be more likely to recognize such steps when you "trip over them."

The **Reflect & Respond** box focuses your attention on a particular concept by inviting you to keep a journal and write in it regularly. When this feature appears at the beginning of a chapter, we want to help you as a reader connect what you're about to learn with what you already know or have experienced.

■ Within-Chapter Features

The **Reflect & Respond** box often appears in the middle of a chapter, as well. We recommend that you actually write down your responses in some sort of organized fashion so that you can return to them at a later date. Preservice teachers who make journal writing a habit early in their preparation programs find that the process of putting their responses on paper offers one way of "thinking out loud" about the concepts profiled. Just as important, the written record allows them to return to their original responses at a later point in time so they can rethink their responses if they choose to and can reflect on the variables that may have contributed to changes in their thinking.

New Teachers Talk appears in every chapter. As its title suggests, it highlights responses from new teachers who are either in the process of completing their preservice preparation or are in their first years of practice. In addition to profiling the responses novice teachers have made to particular prompts, each **New Teachers Talk** includes our synopses and analysis of the new teachers' responses and then asks for your thoughts on the same topics.

■ End-of-Chapter Features

This book includes several end-of-chapter features designed to extend your understanding of chapter concepts and provide options for further study. **Summarizing What You've Learned** reviews major chapter points, **Key Terms** highlight chapter concepts that may be new to you, and **Your Professional Teaching Portfolio** suggests components you may wish to include in a portfolio that showcases your work.

The feature called **Relevant Resources for Professionals** provides a variety of information sources that relate to the focus of each chapter. These resources offer several ways for you to extend your knowledge and understanding of chapter concepts and include some or all of the following: books and articles, professional journals, professional organizations, videos, and Web sites.

■ End-of-Book Features

An additional feature of this book is the **extensive, current research base** that supports the book's themes and major points. We don't think you should believe something just because we say so—or just because a particular person whose name you might recognize states that something is so. Educators should build their knowledge bases and inform their instructional decisions by consulting credible, reliable research sources. Teachers as leaders and decision makers use theory and research in a way that improves their own teaching effectiveness and, in turn, benefits learners.

Consequently, at the end of this book you'll find a fairly lengthy compilation of the sources and research we've referenced in our attempt to assist you in blending theory, research results, and practice in meaningful and productive ways that will serve to inform your instructional decision making. In addition to the reference list, at the end of the book you'll also find a **Glossary** that defines the key terms we identified in each chapter.

ANCILLARIES

The **Instructor's Resource Manual** developed to accompany *Teaching, Leading, and Learning: Becoming Caring Professionals* offers additional ways to use the book, as well as ideas for extending your learning. These include resources for you to consult (such as Web sites, books, videos, professional organizations), recommendations for you to consider (for example, specific items to include in different types of learning centers), cooperative learning activities, and a case analysis of a change initiative designed to provide comprehensive, integrated services to young special needs learners.

The Instructor's Resource Manual also provides instructors with a variety of assessment prompts, including project descriptions, integrative unit guidelines, professional development plan components, process portfolio assessment criteria, and multiple choice and essay questions.

A set of colorful **Overhead Transparencies** are available on adoption of the text to present key concepts in a graphic format. The package includes text art and additional representations to support the book .

WAYS TO USE THIS BOOK

Although we're certain you could think of many alternative uses for this book (such as paperweight, leaf presser, bug smasher), *we'd really like you to read it.* We'd like you to put down your highlighter and just read. This is your resource, not just for now, but for later on. It will have multiple uses, only to be fully recognized as your needs emerge in classroom contexts.

In writing this book, we attempted to take an informal, conversational approach and flavor it with appropriate and judicious use of humor and actual teaching scenarios. In addition, we incorporated a variety of visuals that we hope will assist you in identifying organizational structures, main ideas, and significant connections between concepts. In other words, we wanted the book to be functional, fun, and user-friendly.

After you read particular chapters or sections, *we'd also like you to respond to and reflect on what you've read.* As we explained earlier, we've built in opportunities for you to do that and to make connections between what you already know and what you're learning. Although at this point you may be groaning in protest and adopting a classic "in your dreams" posture, we hasten to assure you that these opportunities to respond to and reflect on what you're reading and to make connections between what you know and what you're learning are not busywork designed to keep you confined to quarters and off the streets. Instead, they're designed to help you begin to formulate responses to some of the questions you'll need answers to when you're standing in your own classroom. If you're interested in taking responsibility for your own professional development, we think you'll welcome opportunities to reflect on what you believe about teaching, learners, learning, and principles of effective instruction.

Finally, *we'd like you to talk about what you're reading*—with other preservice teachers, practicing teachers, professors, your former teachers, parents, grandparents, your future in-laws, and even with kids. We want you to practice saying out loud what it is you think you believe about teaching and learning. We want you to listen to what other people believe about teaching and learning. We want you to ask questions about teaching and learning. And we want you to use this book as one tool to assist you in the lifelong process of teacher preparation. So go ahead, read.

ACKNOWLEDGMENTS

Even when a single author writes a book, the process involves a great deal of collaboration. In addition to our own collaboration, this book is the product of the collaborative efforts of several individuals whom we wish to acknowledge.

First of all, we wish to thank the following preservice and inservice teachers, most of whom we have had the pleasure of mentoring and teaching, who allowed us to incorporate their original contributions in this publication.

These individuals include Michael Alm, Lara Beaver-Medina, Karen Bensinger, Sarah Berman, Jennifer Bernitt, Ann Bond, Bradley Cohen, Helen Gehrenbeck, Lee Ann Isbell, Marni Lehtman, Lisa Podowski, Tina Pronschinske, Shana Savitz, Pamela Scranton, Emily Swanson, Robin White, and Angela Williams.

In addition to his original contributions, Michael Alm also assisted us with our literature searches and our efforts to include relevant and current resources. His investment of time and energy earned him the title of "literature boy," as well as our sincere gratitude.

Bradley University offered technical support to this project. In particular, we acknowledge the dean of our college, Joan L. Sattler, and our department chair, Barbara Penelton. Our special thanks go to Cathy Sherlock, whose secretarial support, competence, and kindness consistently saw us through a myriad of deadlines and dilemmas. We greatly appreciate the high quality of her contributions to this project.

We also appreciate the useful suggestions and feedback offered by the following manuscript reviewers: Bobbette M. Morgan, University of Texas at Arlington; Marlene Rosenbaum, Fairleigh Dickinson University; Jane B. Swiderski, Le Moyne College; and Mary Carol Turner, Indiana State University.

There are also those individuals who, although they may not have contributed directly to this project, certainly influenced its development and direction by virtue of shaping us and influencing our thinking. We extend our sincere appreciation to the following friends, mentors, and former teachers: Michael Alm, Raymond Bartholemew, Lara Beaver-Medina, Barbara Brown, Marjorie Crestodina, Robert Dean, Larry Ebbers, Philip Gammage, Helen Gehrenbeck, Genevieve Hanson, Carol Rocklin Kay, Sylvia Klingman, Sister Mary Catherine, Sherrie Pardieck, Dianne Portfleet, Pat Romance, and Sue Stroyan.

Speaking of people who influenced and shaped us, both authors gratefully acknowledge the love and support of their families—especially their parents, to whom this book is dedicated. Rita's parents, Senator John W. Jensen and Myrtle L. Jensen, patiently listened to five years of trials and tribulations related to this project, as did Therese's parents, John B. Kiley and Lorene M. Kiley.

Therese also wishes to thank her daughters, Shauna and Megan Shepston, for their tolerance of her often onerous work schedule. She appreciates their acknowledgment of the fact that work overloads function to offset some of the costs associated with college and assorted professional development opportunities related to her efforts to support them in pursuit of their goals and dreams.

Finally, we would like to acknowledge individuals at Houghton Mifflin for their collaboration in this project. We thank Loretta Wolozin for giving us the opportunity to write this book. In addition, we are grateful for the collaborative efforts of Lisa Mafrici, Ann Greenberger, Christina Horn, and Bruce Carson, who contributed their expertise to this project.

R. A. J.
T. J. K.

BEGINNINGS

In Part One, we consider what it takes to be a teacher. As you focus on the profession of teaching, it's important for you to reflect on your strengths and recognize challenges you may encounter along the way. Begin by taking a memory walk through your school days. What was your school experience like? Which teachers are the most memorable? In what ways do you want to be different from some of the teachers you had in school? As you begin to learn about teaching and begin to discover what your strengths are, you'll map out a direction to follow, a direction that will lead you toward your goal.

1

BECOMING A TEACHER

— OR —

Reflections on Connections

SCHOOL DAZE: WHAT DO YOU REMEMBER ABOUT SCHOOL?

Most people's school recollections include at least a few bad memories. Were you the shy second grader who cried when your teacher told you your answer was wrong? Perhaps you remember being teased or picked on by other students. Did you ever misread the directions on a test, and your entire row knew you got an F before you did because they looked at your grade as they passed your paper back to you? Most people have school memories they'd like to forget, and many people had at least one teacher they'd like to forget.

YOUR EXPERIENCES AND ATTITUDE MATTER

If you were to ask a group of preservice teachers to describe their memories of school, our prediction is that few of them would mention curriculum content, writing skills, or mathematical concepts. Rather, their school memories would primarily involve emotions, attitudes, and experiences. Most people tend to remember how it felt to succeed or to fail, not the exact skills or concepts with which they were experiencing success or having trouble. By way of illustration, we offer the following examples.

Fortunately, we both hold fond memories of our school days, memories that flow from a goodly number of positive experiences and a handful of near epiphanies that occurred in that place called school. For Rita, there was her supporting role as the duchess in Mrs. Demro's fourth grade play, all the singing in Ms. Moon's class (perhaps explained in part by the fact that Ms. Moon later married the music teacher, whose room was just across the hall

"School doesn't have to be the way you remember it."

—Howard Gardner

Everybody remembers something about school. What do you remember? Maybe your positive memories include the special field trip you took to the state capitol at the end of sixth grade, sliding down the fire pole during your visit to the fire station in kindergarten, sharing one of your favorite books with a classmate, or the feeling of satisfaction you experienced when you finally conquered those multiplication tables.

For the first entry in your teaching journal, make a list of positive recollections from your own days as a student. Include the names of at least three teachers who truly made a difference in your life and served as significant role models for you. What did they do that made them so special?

from hers), and Mrs. Crestodina's saying, "You have the ability to do whatever you want to do." And for Therese there was staying after school to perform important functions such as clapping erasers and cleaning blackboards, winning the class spelling bee, walking home for a lunch of tomato soup and a grilled cheese sandwich, and taking a special trip to visit a favorite former teacher.

Unfortunately, time has not erased some not-so-pleasant school memories, which for Therese include rulers used for purposes other than measuring to the

Perhaps sharing one of your favorite books with friends is among your positive school recollections.
(© Michael Zide)

nearest sixteenth of an inch, reading above grade level yet receiving a below-average grade in reading, and conjuring up something to confess on a monthly basis. (Yes, Therese attended a Catholic school!) As for Rita, she loved school until her first day of kindergarten. She finds solace in Howard Gardner's reminder that "School doesn't have to be the way you remember it." Therese, by contrast, does remember enjoying music class a great deal. The fact she was an accomplished pianist; that her teacher, Sister Mary Catherine, expressed confidence in her and her abilities; and that Therese truly liked her teacher all contributed to her positive experiences.

YOUR PRIOR EXPERIENCES CAN HELP YOU BECOME A BETTER TEACHER

What purpose does this little trip down memory lane serve? We have prompted you to resurrect your school-years recollections—both good and bad—to illustrate the basic premise undergirding our thinking regarding the teaching/learning process. That premise, simply stated, is that the affective dimension of teaching and learning pervades all others. Discussions of learning theories, cognition, and pedagogy are incomplete when we fail to acknowledge the role attitudes and emotions play in the teaching/learning process. Consequently, we'll frequently revisit this premise throughout the following chapters.

What contribution, then, will your school memories make to your teaching preparation? Are you aware of how your recollections color your attitudes, and can you predict how they might affect your teaching style? For example, Rita lets this principle guide the teacher-student relationship: "I'll trust you until you show me I shouldn't." Rita demonstrates this principle in her practice of giving students the benefit of the doubt, and her adherence to it is a direct result of her being accused of a crime she didn't commit! The year was first grade; the alleged crime was the dreaded offense of gum chewing. The incident made an impression on Rita—and not a positive one. It also made a small but lasting contribution to shaping the teacher she would someday become. Additionally, it serves to remind her that even well-intentioned teachers make mistakes and that they need to be willing to acknowledge those mistakes, especially when they negatively impact students' self-concepts.

On a more positive note, three of Rita's favorite teachers in junior high and high school were English teachers, and as an undergraduate she chose to major in English. We'd venture to say that, in Rita's case, at least, there's reason to believe a significant correlation exists between those two variables: choice of undergraduate major and subject matter taught by favorite teachers.

Your school-years recollections may shape your teaching in another important way. In the absence of different models, teachers tend to teach in the same ways as they themselves were taught. In fact, sometimes teachers will use the same methods and strategies used to teach them, even after they've been presented with different teaching models. This seems to be especially true in situations where teachers don't know what else to do. In moments of panic or as the result of inadequate planning, they revert to what they know best—their personal experiences as students.

What activities and strategies did your teacher use? List those that were most helpful to you. Then list those that were the most fun for you. What methods and strategies would you like to use as a teacher?

WHY CHOOSE TEACHING?

If you already have made the decision that you want to be a teacher, what brought you to that decision? Why do you "want to be a teacher when you grow up"? If you have not yet decided whether you want to teach, what factors are you considering in attempting to make that decision? Some teachers' coffee mugs proclaim "I teach for three reasons: June, July, and August!" but we find such reasons invalid as rationales.

Another reason often cited as the call to teaching is the proverbial "I just love children." Although we view appreciating and truly enjoying children or adolescents as a necessary precondition for choosing teaching as a profession, it does not prove sufficient in and of itself. If liking children were enough to teach, every loving, caring parent and grandparent would make great teachers. Our collective experiences and observations prompt us to conclude that it's just not so. Bearing in mind that we have disallowed "June, July, and August" and "liking children" as possible responses, please take a moment to respond to the following prompt.

On a scale from 1 to 10, with 1 being low and 10 being high, how would you rate your commitment to pursuing teaching as a career at this point in time?

In your teaching journal, record and explain the rationale for your rating.

Several studies (such as Covert, 1986; Daniel & Ferrell, 1991; Green & Weaver, 1992; Holt-Reynold, 1991; Marso & Pigge, 1994; Roberson, 1983; Serow, 1994; Snyder, 1995) have focused on the question of why people decide to teach. Generally, findings reveal that preservice teachers are motivated by idealistic factors, such as a desire to work with young people, a love of children, and a need to make a difference (Green & Weaver, 1992; Snyder, 1995). But those same individuals who enter the teaching profession for altruistic reasons make it clear from the beginning that they will remain in the profession only if they derive the expected satisfaction from working with children

(Young, 1995). This lack of commitment to lifelong teaching accounts, at least in part, for the profession's high attrition rate (Su, 1994).

Not surprisingly, preservice teachers rarely cite income potential as a rationale for choosing teaching as a career (Snyder, 1995), and the majority of teacher candidates recognize that teaching should not be viewed as a way to make an easy living until something better comes along (Daniel & Ferrell, 1991). However, the prospect of a favorable work schedule (remember "June, July, and August"?) did rank fifth among the six most frequently cited reasons for selecting teaching as a career (Marso & Pigge, 1994). Seventy-five percent of the teacher candidates who participated in Marso and Pigge's study identified the same six reasons for entering teaching:

1. Influences of other people or experiences with people
2. Liking children
3. Former teachers
4. Prior experience with children
5. Favorable work schedule
6. Love of subject field

Late-entry teachers tend to be attracted to teaching because of its intrinsic rewards. They cite socioeconomic and self-fulfillment concerns as reasons for leaving their previous occupations (Serow & Forrest, 1994).

WHO CHOOSES TEACHING?

According to one study (Roberson, 1983), twenty years ago most high school seniors who aspired to teach were white females who were not motivated by job security, were less concerned than those who chose other professions with earning a good income, and were intellectually less able than their classmates (Roberson, 1983). Ouch! Does that mean that teaching was simply "Plan B" for a number of young women who went to college with the "Plan A" of meeting and marrying a future physician, engineer, or MBA?

THE ISSUE OF DIVERSITY

Today men and minorities still are underrepresented in the teaching profession, and the changing demographics of the United States mean educators will need to recruit even more minorities to teacher preparation programs in the future than they do today (Green & Weaver, 1992; Su, 1994; Zapata, 1988). What reasons do minorities identify for not choosing teaching as a career? The themes that emerge from the research on this question focus on negative experiences in school, social and economic obstacles, and cultural and community concerns (Gordon, 1994). Over half of 140 teachers of color who participated in a 1993 study (Gordon, J.) indicated that teaching had been their second career choice and that they had been unable to pursue their first choice because of poverty, sexism, racism, or lack of adequate preparation. Throughout

Today men and minorities still are underrepresented in the teaching profession.
(© Michael Weisbrot)

this book, we will address issues of cultural and ethnic diversity pertaining to students, teachers, and families. Chapter 5 focuses on these issues in detail.

THE NEED FOR QUALITY

Changing demographics and an anticipated teacher shortage make it tempting to issue a "you all come" invitation to the teaching field. Although temporary teaching certificates and alternative teacher preparation programs may serve as partial solutions to these problems, if teachers are to be prepared adequately for the challenges that await them, then education policy makers, teacher educators, and PreK–12 administrators must be willing to address issues of quality and standards in both preservice and inservice teacher education.

Long ago, researchers and practitioners identified the two most important variables in the teaching/learning process—learners and teachers. Although administrators and teacher educators have little or no control over the initial preparedness of the former, they must exercise control over the preparedness and quality of the latter. In fact, both preservice and inservice teachers indicate that teacher attributes (for example, intelligence, personality, background, preparation program) contribute more to the overall effectiveness of teachers than do learner attributes (intelligence, personality, background) or institutional factors related to other personnel (other teachers, principals, support staff) (Ganser, 1996). After years of focusing on instructional strategies, technology, different teaching approaches, curriculum redesign, and organizational restructuring as means of reforming education, teachers and teacher preparation have become the new reform agenda. The National Commission on Teaching and America's Future (1996) concluded that capable teachers should be every child's birthright. At the same time that the public is demanding significant improvements in student learning, *schools are facing unprecedented challenges, including the breakdown of family and community structures, increasing levels of violent behavior among young people, the rapid creation of new knowledge, and advances in technology which can literally transform traditional teaching and learning processes. The most critical variable in determining whether the schools will be able to succeed in meeting these demands and challenges will be the competencies and commitments of their teachers.* (Spagnolo, 1997, p. 7)

WHAT CHALLENGES DO TEACHERS FACE?

If the prospect of entering your own classroom for the first time sounds daunting, that's only because it should. Effective teaching is one of the most difficult of all occupations.

SURVIVAL CONCERNS

Even the most qualified, best prepared novice teachers may spend much of their first teaching year preoccupied with survival concerns and plagued by self-doubt stemming from unrealistic expectations they have set for themselves (Jensen & Kiley, 1997b). Their survival concerns may result from the school environments that first-year teachers encounter. In fact, administrators and their supervision of first-year teachers influence the ways teachers perceive their initial teaching experience. However, the personal qualities that beginning teachers bring to their profession also serve as important indicators of both the attitude and the competencies they will demonstrate during their first year of teaching. For example, motivation to teach constitutes an essential condition for the professionalization of teachers (Covert, 1986).

Effective teachers are much more likely than other teachers to convince all of their students to do quality work. "The few teachers who can consistently persuade almost all their students to do quality work are, without doubt, succeeding at the hardest job there is" (Glasser, 1992, p. 15). Part of what makes teaching difficult is the simple fact that not everyone involved in the teaching/learning process wants to be there. Unlike the world of work, where employees who don't like their jobs can quit, most students don't have that option. For those who aren't motivated to learn, school can become a form of socially appropriate incarceration.

Another variable that sometimes makes teaching difficult, or at least frustrating, concerns compensation. Basically there is no direct relationship between how effective teachers are and the level of pay they receive.

OUTSIDE INTERFERENCE

Others have suggested that another variable that makes teaching exceptionally difficult is the fact that everybody thinks he or she knows what's wrong with education (Glasser, 1992; Zemelman, Daniels, & Hyde, 1998). Neurosurgeons rarely are second-guessed by casual observers, and the work of chemical engineers seldom is scrutinized and critiqued in the popular press, yet we are hard-pressed to find people who don't have an opinion—informed or other-wise—about how best to educate the youth of today. Why, then, are educators so overly blessed with uninformed critics? Part of the answer lies in virtually everyone's having had firsthand experience with schools and schooling. Personal experience with the system sometimes leads to statements such as "They should just teach like they did when I was in school. I didn't have all of the frills they want these days, and I turned out okay."

Another part of the reason that educators hear more rhetoric than they know what to do with rests in the vested interests that different groups have in public education. Obviously, parents of school-aged children have a legitimate interest in the education their children receive. However, taxpayers also have a legitimate interest in the quality of publicly funded education. Simply put, there are few people whom public education does not affect in some way. One of the many important roles teachers must assume is that of educating the public regarding the critical importance of investing in the education of children and youth so that they can become contributing members of society.

LACK OF RESPECT

Although many people are willing to argue about the best way to educate children, few are willing to argue with the notion that teachers fulfill an important function. However, some teachers fall into the habit of disparaging their own profession, saying, for example, "I'm *just* a teacher." We sometimes hear the parallel of this statement at the undergraduate level: "I'm *just* an education major." It's nothing short of audacious to expect the general public to respect teaching as a profession when preservice and inservice teachers fail to respect themselves and their occupational choice. Thus it is our hope that those who drift into teaching as a nonchoice of sorts ("I don't know what else to do") will drift a bit further and choose an occupation where there is less opportunity for their apathy and disinterest to affect children and young people.

We also dare to hope that the individuals who select teaching as a career do so as the result of making an informed decision regarding the potential for a good fit between the demands of teaching and the strengths and assets they can bring to the profession.

HOW CAN YOU PREPARE FOR A TEACHING CAREER?

Now is the best time to begin taking responsibility for your development as a preservice teacher. In addition to enrolling in a teacher preparation program, there are other steps you can take to better prepare yourself for entry into the field of education.

TAKE A PERSONAL STRENGTHS INVENTORY

If you have not yet conducted a personal strengths inventory, we encourage you to do so at this juncture. As you learn more about what effective teaching requires of those who aspire to teaching, you should begin to identify the strengths you possess that you can apply to the teaching field. Although you may find the process of identifying your strengths an uncomfortable one, do it anyway! To improve and continue to grow, you need to build on your strengths; building on your weaknesses doesn't have quite the same effect. Be specific in your responses (for example, "I can attend to details without losing sight of the big picture" rather than "I'm pretty organized"). Then after—and only after—you've identified the strengths you bring to the teaching profession, list a few areas you need to target for improvement.

Your academic adviser or campus career counseling center can suggest formal inventories you can complete to assess your strengths, profile your personality, and identify careers for which you may be well suited. In addition, a simple list of prompts, such as the ones included in Figure 1.1, can help you identify the strengths you have to offer the field of education. Remember that such self-assessment aids are truly effective and valid only if you complete them honestly, after engaging in focused reflection about and analysis of your skills, characteristics, and attitudes.

FIND WAYS TO INCREASE YOUR LIKELIHOOD OF SUCCESS IN YOUR FIRST YEAR

What other steps can you take now to begin preparing for your first year of teaching? You can start by attempting to be the kind of student you hope to have the opportunity to teach someday! We sometimes wonder quietly to ourselves what particular preservice teachers will do when they eventually have the opportunity to teach students in whom they observe some of their own less positive traits. We encourage you to begin with the following basics:

- Attend class regularly and be on time.
- Come to class prepared.
- Display a positive attitude.
- Acknowledge that you have a lot to learn.
- Participate actively and positively in class activities and discussions.
- Read assigned material.
- Ask relevant questions.
- Make connections between what you know and what you're being asked to learn.
- Apply what you're learning to your experiences in those places called schools.
- Take responsibility for your own professional development.

These may seem like obvious points for any student, but even those studying to become teachers themselves occasionally overlook their importance! If you're willing to extend yourself a bit, then we suggest the following additional steps you can take now to prepare for your first year of teaching:

(continued on page 13)

Figure 1.1
A Self-Assessment Tool

PERSONAL STRENGTHS INVENTORY
(Jensen & Kiley)

Using the scale provided, assess your performance, attitudes, and abilities in the following areas.

UNDEVELOPED (1–3)			DEVELOPING (4–6)			WELL DEVELOPED (7–9)		
1	2	3	4	5	6	7	8	9

1. Honesty _____
2. Trustworthiness _____
3. Dependability _____
4. Responsibility _____
5. Self-awareness _____
6. Resilience _____
7. Energy _____
8. Task commitment _____
9. Organization _____
10. Attention to detail _____
11. Ability to see the big picture _____
12. Ability to see and make connections between concepts _____
13. Creativity _____
14. Appropriate use of humor _____
15. Positive attitude _____
16. Open-mindedness _____
17. Ability to take intelligent risks _____
18. Overall wellness _____
19. Desire for personal growth _____
20. Listening skills _____
21. Interpersonal communication skills _____
22. Public speaking _____
23. Written communication skills _____
24. Ability to bend _____
25. Empathy _____

(cont.)

Figure 1.1
**A Self-Assessment
Tool** (*cont.*)

26. Ability to give   _____

27. Goal setting   _____

28. Ability to read with understanding   _____

29. Ability to understand and apply mathematical concepts   _____

30. General knowledge   _____

31. Appreciation of visual and performing arts   _____

32. Ability to provide effective and appropriate leadership   _____

33. Ability to appreciate and accommodate diversity   _____

34. Ability to collaborate effectively with a variety of
    people and personalities   _____

35. Ability to use technology   _____

Provide complete and thoughtful responses to the following prompts.

36. If I were describing myself to someone who's never met me,
    I would say _____ .

37. Other people see me as _____ .

38. My most positive characteristics are _____ .

39. The qualities I like about myself include _____ .

40. I find it easy to do the following things: _____ .

41. My main strength is _____ .

42. The things I value most deeply include _____ .

43. During my lifetime, I hope to accomplish the following goals: _____

    _____ .

44. When I face a problem, I _____ .

45. When I am upset with others, I _____ .

46. I am most confident and secure when _____ .

47. I hide my ability when _____ .

48. I tend to feel insecure when _____ .

49. The most difficult thing for me to do is _____ .

50. My first impressions of people tend to be _____ .

51. Most people think I _____ .

52. When I don't like people, I tend to _____ .

53. The quality I dislike about myself is _____ .

54. My number one priority to target for personal growth is _____

    _____ .

55. If I were a historical personality, I would be _____ .

- Begin thinking of yourself as a professional and conducting yourself as one.
- Find a mentor—even as a preservice teacher.
- Keep a journal in which you reflect on what you're learning (both in and out of class).
- Set personal development goals for yourself (more about this process in Chapter 2).

We began the previous section by asserting that the prospect of entering your own classroom for the first time *should* sound daunting, because teaching is one of the most difficult of all occupations. Now we'd like to offer you some encouraging news as well. Please let us assure you that there are three things you can do right your very first year of teaching. Whether you're a preprimary, primary, middle school, or secondary school teacher, if you wish to succeed as a first-year teacher:

- *Read to your students.* When we say *read,* we mean whole pieces of connected text, or "real books," rather than the directions at the tops of worksheets. We could give you at least twenty-four reasons to read aloud to your students. For the moment, however, we'll limit ourselves to five reasons. Reading aloud to children and adolescents

  1. Is the most important motivating factor in helping them become readers, along with allowing time for them to read books on their own
  2. Encourages them to read for themselves
  3. Generates further interest in books and reading
  4. Leads to writing
  5. Improves their linguistic development, aptitude for listening, attention span, narrative sense, reading comprehension, vocabulary development, and ability to recognize newly learned words that appear in other contexts

- *Give your students opportunities to read.* Children and adolescents learn to read and improve their reading ability by reading whole pieces of connected text. To reach the level of automaticity—the point where reading as a skill becomes automatic—children and adolescents must do more reading than most of them currently do in school.

- *Help your students make connections between what they know and what you're asking them to learn.* Doing so makes new concepts and skills more meaningful to students, so they're more likely to learn them. Also, students who succeed at making meaningful connections between information that's new to them and experiences they already have are more likely to remember the new information.

ACKNOWLEDGE THE CRITICAL ROLE OF TEACHER PREPARATION

Building on another premise we've already introduced, we acknowledge that what teachers know and can do is the most important influence on what students learn. This brings us back to the notion of recruiting, preparing, and retaining competent teachers as the central strategy for improving schools and making teaching more effective. However, this strategy cannot succeed unless it also focuses on creating conditions in which teachers can teach well. How can U.S. education get from here to there and reach this goal of reforming schools by focusing on teacher quality? The National Commission on Teaching and America's Future (1996) offers the following recommendations:

1. Get serious about standards for both students and teachers.
2. Reinvent teacher preparation and professional development.
3. Focus on teacher recruitment and put qualified teachers in every classroom.
4. Encourage and reward teacher knowledge and skill.
5. Create schools that are organized for learner and teacher success.

What Is Your Teaching Credo?

Your **teaching credo** should succinctly articulate your fundamental beliefs about teaching and learning. If it's well formulated and carefully thought out, it can serve as a set of guiding principles that will inform the instructional decisions you make and the actions you take. **Instructional decision making,** when guided by fundamental beliefs about teaching, involves critical thinking, if-then logic, and reflection on the needs of learners—all of which combine to create the best practices that are informed by research as well as personal experiences.

The Power of Reflection

Just as a mirror enables you to see and assess your appearance, when used as a tool for self-analysis, contemplative **reflection,** or self-analysis, enables teachers to see and assess the attitudes, dispositions, knowledge base, and performances that together make up the whole picture of who they are and how effective they are as teachers (see Figure 1.2). Reflection plays a particularly critical role in the teaching profession, since teachers operate fairly autonomously on a day-to-day basis, often without much interaction with or observation by other teachers or administrators. Consequently, teachers who cannot or do not honestly and accurately assess their own practice on a regular basis are not contributing to the goal of ensuring there's a competent and qualified teacher in every classroom.

When conducting postobservation conferences with student teachers, we often begin with questions designed to allow them the opportunity to identify their strengths and acknowledge areas for improvement (for example, "What do you think the students learned from the lesson?"). Student teachers' responses also help us measure their ability to use reflection to accurately assess their current competencies. Sometimes, after we've squirmed and winced our way through an observation of what we considered to be a less-than-stellar

Figure 1.2
The Reflective Practitioner

Look in the mirror on a regular basis to discover how you can become a competent teacher. Are you contributing to the goal of putting a competent teacher in every classroom?

© Robert Llewellyn

The Mirror
Shows reflection of self—
your attitudes, dispositions,
knowledge base, and performances

Reflection of You
Self-analysis; provides whole
picture of who you are and how
effective you are as a teacher

performance, the student teacher will respond to our request for a bit of self-assessment by beaming at us and stating emphatically that "the lesson went great." Those occasional experiences make us even more resolute in our belief that we must begin early in the teacher preparation process to encourage the development of **reflective practitioners.**

Indeed, teacher educators often attempt to weave the theme of teachers as reflective practitioners throughout the fabric of teacher preparation programs. Thus prospective teachers may first discover the concept of reflection in their introductory education courses and then continually "rediscover" it throughout their course of study. They also learn to use the paradigm of reflection to help them develop and examine their teaching philosophies and to guide their field experiences as they begin to make connections between theory and practice (Kasten, 1996; Leahy & Corcoran, 1996).

LEARNING AND USING REFLECTION SKILLS

For example, we asked education majors to analyze videotapes of teaching segments from their junior-level field experiences. On different occasions, these students evaluated their own competencies in the following three areas: interpersonal skills, instructional management and organizational skills, and questioning skills. We found that students' attempts at reflection and self-assessment yielded more reliable, specific, and helpful information when their observations and analyses focused on specific aspects of their teaching than when no particular focus guided their attempts to assess their overall teaching competency (Jensen, Kiley Shepston, Connor, & Killmer, 1994). A combination of self-analysis of videotapes, case studies, journals, and portfolios also can be used to help preservice teachers develop reflection skills (Kasten & Ferraro, 1995), as can analyses of different types and functions of reflection (Fairbanks, 1995; Hatton & Smith, 1994).

Reflection also can prove beneficial in helping preservice teachers understand their reading and discuss course work, field experiences, and issues relevant to their reading (Kasten, 1996). How do teachers learn to be reflective about their professional and personal decisions and actions? The process must begin in courses that prepare students to teach (Eby & Kujawa, 1994). Both preservice and inservice teacher education programs must promote teaching practices that facilitate students' construction of their own understanding (Brooks, 1984; Brooks & Brooks, 1987; Loucks-Horsley, et al., 1990). That is, they must provide opportunities for teachers to draw on their own experiences and prior knowledge to make sense of and re-create the knowledge, skills, and strategies they are learning. Teachers more readily understand and apply concepts and methodologies when they are exposed to specific programs and approaches and have experiences based in real classrooms with practicing teachers. Therefore, it makes sense for teacher educators to design collaborative opportunities that bring preservice and inservice teachers together. If preservice teachers are not given ample opportunities to learn in authentic settings, to critically reflect on educational practice, and to construct their own visions, the instruction they receive may be trivialized to a "cookbook" approach (Brooks & Brooks, 1993).

Reflective teaching focuses on skills and attitudes that teachers must develop. These include

1. *Empirical skills,* concerned with collecting data and describing situations, processes, causes, and effects with care and accuracy

2. *Analytical skills,* needed to interpret descriptive data

3. *Evaluative skills,* used to make judgments about the educational consequences of the results of practical inquiry

4. *Strategic skills,* directly related to planning for action and anticipating its consequences

5. *Practical skills,* needed to implement the action planned

6. *Communication skills,* necessary because critical and reflective practitioners are concerned about aims and consequences, as well as means (Pollard & Tann, 1987)

COLLABORATIVE REFLECTION AMONG PEERS

Discussion and collaborative reflection provide preservice teachers with an authentic context in which to develop the skills and attitudes that support reflective teaching. Developing the link between reflection and professional practice is a process in which "the learners interrogate practice and, in doing so, clarify their thoughts about what they do and their feelings about their practice" (Ghaye, Cuthbert, Danai, & Dennis, 1996, p. 5). Furthermore, collaborative exchanges foster personal and professional relationships between preservice and inservice teachers, often leading to collaborative modeling, coaching, supervision, and, occasionally, mentoring between these two groups of professionals. (Collaboration is one of the themes of this book. You'll be encouraged to work collaboratively in many arenas. Chapter 13 focuses on collaboration in great detail.) Unfortunately, most teachers have not been prepared to engage in reflection, especially during their preservice teacher preparation programs. Because collaboration provides the foundation for connecting theory with practice and can play a key role in enhancing the reflective skills and attitudes of preservice teachers, we routinely ask our education students to combine collaboration and reflection (Jensen & Kiley, 1997a). Thus we have the students in our teacher preparation program participate in field experiences throughout their undergraduate career, beginning in their freshman year. In the process of completing these field experiences, they work with a variety of practicing teachers in a variety of settings.

We also want to provide structured opportunities for our preservice teachers to discuss with practicing teachers the concepts, teaching strategies, and theories they are reading about and learning about in class, so we create opportunities for our students to discuss their course readings with practicing teachers. We ask our students to "recruit" inservice teachers who are willing to discuss the concepts and topics they are exploring in specific courses. The result is an intervention we call **collaborative reflection.** Before our students use collaborative reflections, we often ask them to write summaries and reflections in response to the reading they have been doing or to keep learning logs in which they chronicle their thoughts and questions regarding their reading. Although such requirements, for the most part, motivate students to complete their assigned reading in a timely fashion, sometimes they question if what they have read has anything to do with the "real world" of teaching and learning. Completing collaborative reflections allows our students to answer this question.

■ Using Technology to Collaborate

When preservice teachers indicate that they need assistance in connecting with practicing teachers, we provide them with the names and locations of likely prospects. We also give students the latitude to choose the means by which they will communicate with their collaborating teachers (by phone, by mail, by e-mail, by fax, in person, and so on). (Using e-mail to contact a collaborating teacher is only a small example of the uses you will find for technology in your career as a teacher. Technology will be discussed throughout this book. You might find the Web sites provided at the end of each chapter particularly useful for your professional growth. Consider sharing these with other teachers.) Approximately once every ten days, the preservice teachers contact their

Preservice and inservice teachers collaborate to share their reflections on the teaching/learning process.
(© Elizabeth Crews)

collaborating teachers to discuss their readings and course activities. In addition, we invite our students to pose questions motivated by their own interests.

Following their discussions with their self-selected inservice teachers, our students then write descriptions of their collaborative reflection experiences, consisting of the following three components: summaries of the assigned readings, synopses of their discussions with their collaborating teachers, and their own reflections regarding the readings, their class activities, and their collaborations. Predictably, in our students' first few attempts at writing collaborative reflections, the reflective component is consistently the weakest of the three required components. Although students generally provide complete summaries of assigned readings and describe their discussions with their collaborating teachers in some detail, they often falter when it comes to clearly articulating their own thoughts and analyses regarding their reading and discussions. In fact, initially some students' papers do not even include a reflection component. However, as they begin to realize that we really do want to know what they think and that we really do expect them to respond thoughtfully to what they are reading and hearing, the reflection components of their papers increase in length and depth. The skills and attitudes of reflection can be learned and can be taught!

COLLABORATIVE REFLECTION TO SUPPORT LEARNERS AND LEARNING

Typically, students who take collaborative reflection seriously find the process beneficial. Many of them find examples of best practice in the "real world," and those who do not find examples of best practice at least learn to distinguish between examples and non-examples of best practice and less effective practice. Feedback from the preservice and inservice teachers who have participated in this collaborative venture indicates that most of them find the experience beneficial. Even those students who initially are skeptical of the requirement indicate that it is worth the time and effort they invest in the process, and students' comments often convey their amazement on discovering that theory and practice do connect. The following excerpts are typical of such comments:

> "I am really enjoying my conversations with Monica. They make the entire process seem like it is actually culminating in something attainable."

> "I am starting to get a grasp for the responsibilities that I will have to my students and their parents, and I find that talking with Maureen is helpful. The things that she says are right out of my books—proof that this isn't just a bunch of baloney!"

> "When I read our text, I think everything sounds so wonderful, but can it really work? Then I go visit Jolyn's classroom and see her implementing everything the book advocates. I get excited because I see that it really can work!"

Although on-site visits aren't a requirement for collaboration, many students make at least one visit to their collaborating teachers' classroom sometime during the course of the semester. Their involvement ranges from simply observing to conducting whole-group activities. Some preservice teachers read books to their collaborating teachers' class, and others help individual students with their work. All but one of our students who visited their collaborating teachers' classroom reported that their interactions with their collaborating teachers increased afterward.

Feedback from our students also indicates that the benefits of participating in this intervention outweigh the frustrations. When we ask students to identify specific benefits of the intervention, they often cite the personal relationships they develop with their collaborating teachers. They report that their collaborating teachers become mentors, role models, friends, and professional contacts that they intend to maintain. The following are representative of other benefits identified by participating preservice teachers:

> "I learned how to incorporate children's literature into subjects."

> "The chance to discuss how certain teaching strategies work in a real classroom environment."

> "Learning how a teacher actually uses integration of curriculum."

> "Seeing or hearing application of what we have been learning."

> "I realized that teachers really care about students' well-being—sometimes more than their education."

> "She helped me understand the classroom environment of special education."

> "Because Jen and I often disagreed, I learned how to deal with conflicting ideas."

COGNITIVE DISSONANCE: WHEN REALITY GOES BUMP IN THE NIGHT

As the preceding quotation suggests, some students experience **cognitive dissonance** in the course of completing their collaborations with practicing teachers: their version of truth and reality bumps into a different, conflicting version that conflicts with their own. We view such collisions as positive learning opportunities that cause students to rethink what they know and believe, to analyze why they think and believe as they do, and to clearly articulate what they believe and why they believe it.

When we asked her to identify challenges or frustrations that resulted from collaborating with her chosen practicing teacher, one student stated, "Although I value his teaching style, we had a lot of disagreements." Another commented, "I was quite frustrated with her feelings about Ritalin." One student apparently experienced more frustrations than benefits. She concluded, "Even though my collaborating teacher is young, her ideas about education are quite old-fashioned. . . . It seemed as if she just didn't care. Her classroom was out of control, and she didn't have a good classroom management system, but she thought all of her problems were the kids."

Fortunately, such experiences are not representative of what participants most commonly cite. Both preservice and inservice teachers indicate that scheduling times to meet or talk is the greatest challenge inherent in collaborating with other teachers.

An important secondary result of this intervention involves the collaborating teachers. Through their interactions with preservice teachers, some of them become more familiar with best practice and update their own knowledge base. Others report that the experience provides them with an opportunity to articulate the rationale and theory behind their practice. Many inservice teachers indicate that it has been some time since they last reflected on their personal response to the question "Why am I doing what I'm doing?"

The following quotations are representative of specific responses to a prompt asking inservice teachers to identify the benefits of their collaborations with preservice teachers:

> "It helped me touch base with what I was utilizing as a classroom management plan and also why I use it."

> "New and interesting views given on different issues helped to reinforce the need to look at the whole child."

> "I appreciated Mike's feedback on my current teaching techniques."

> "I like hearing what's being taught in college these days. The exchange of ideas benefited me."

> "I'm flattered that someone wants to hear what I do in my class."

In the papers they write about their collaborations, students also relate ways in which inservice teachers report benefiting from their collaborative experiences. One preservice teacher wrote: "Sheryl and I are really learning from each other. Today I brought in our text and showed her the sample lessons for agriculture. Sheryl is taking her class on a field trip to a farm and found those lessons extremely helpful." Regarding their collaborating teachers, other preservice teachers related the following two comments:

> "My collaborating teacher is giving me great ideas and is open to learning from me as well."

> "She stated that she enjoys this project [collaborating], because it gives her the chance to stop and remember the key essentials that are necessary for the teaching process."

PHILOSOPHICAL PERSPECTIVES ON TEACHING

Experiences such as those described above also can contribute to your developing philosophical perspectives on teaching (Grene & Campbell, 1993; Reagan, 1993; Telease, 1996). As one preservice teacher reflected: "I have learned that I must be able to articulate my philosophy readily and recall theorists for support." If you've taken a philosophy course or an educational foundations course, you likely have at least a vague recollection of terms such as *behaviorism, essentialism, existentialism, perennialism,* and *progressivism*. For those of you whose recollections are vaguer than you'd like them to be, please refer to Figure 1.3 for brief descriptions of five different philosophical theories.

Although it isn't essential to identify yourself as an essentialist, an existentialist, or a progressive, it can prove helpful to analyze your developing views of the teaching/learning process by comparing them to "textbook categories" of philosophical thought. For example, on a scale from 1 to 4, where

> 1 = "I totally disagree with this philosophy,"
>
> 2 = "I somewhat disagree with this philosophy,"
>
> 3 = "I somewhat agree with this philosophy," and
>
> 4 = "I totally agree with this philosophy,"

you could rate each philosophy based on the degree to which you agree or disagree with its main tenets. Many people identify their thinking as some combination of philosophies. However, please note that it would seem inconsistent to describe yourself as ascribing simultaneously to opposing views (for example, saying that you believe both in perennialism's view of human nature as constant and existentialism's view of the universe as unordered).

PERSPECTIVES ON THE ROLES OF TEACHERS

You might find it helpful to use analogies to reflect on different views or perspectives of teachers. For example, we sometimes emphasize the dichotomy between content and process by referring to a teacher as "a sage on the stage" rather than "a guide on the side." You can create your own analogies to assist you in clarifying your thinking about the roles you want to play as a teacher, or you can consider the perspectives on teaching offered by Bennett (1995):

- *Teacher as Inculcator:* Transmission of academic content knowledge as central to teaching
- *Teacher as Empowerer:* Teaching as social action or change

Figure 1.3
Philosophies of Education

Behaviorism
A theory that equates learning with changes in observable behavior.

Essentialism
An educational philosophy that asserts there is a core body of knowledge and skills that an educated person must have and that all children should be taught.

Existentialism
A philosophical doctrine that asserts that individuals are not part of an ordered universe and that they therefore must create their own meaning and purpose in life. In education, an existentialist believes that each student must ultimately make meaning through individual learning, not group learning.

Perennialism
A particular view of philosophy that sees human nature as constant, changing little over time. Perennialism in education promotes the advancement of the intellect as the central purpose of schools. The educational process stresses academic rigor and discipline.

Progressivism
A form of educational philosophy that sees nature as ever-changing. Because the world is always changing and new problems require new solutions, learners must develop problem-solving skills and strategies.

(Adapted from Telease, 1996)

- *Teacher as Friendly Pedagogue:* Teaching as lesson preparation and teacher personality characteristics
- *Teacher as Facilitator:* Thinking and lifelong learning as the principal goals of teaching
- *Teacher as Nurturer:* Teaching primarily as interactions with students
- *Teacher as Friendly Scholar:* Transmission of academic knowledge balanced with a desire to make knowledge relevant and learning fun
- *Teacher as Scholar Psychologist:* A mix of all perspectives

A WORK IN PROGRESS: QUESTIONS TO GUIDE YOUR REFLECTIONS ON DEVELOPING YOUR PERSONAL TEACHING CREDO

Closely related to the question of why you want to teach is the question of your personal teaching mission. The following are representative of questions that may help you clarify that mission:

- What is most important to you in the teaching/learning process?
- What qualities and skills do you want to characterize you and your teaching?
- What do you want your students to remember about you and your teaching?
- How do you want your students to describe you to others?

- What beliefs, attitudes, and values do you bring to the teaching/learning process?
- At the end of the school year, what skills, attitudes, and knowledge do you want your students to possess that they didn't have when they began their year with you?

NEW TEACHERS TALK

We asked some of the preservice and inservice teachers we have had the pleasure of working with to respond to six questions, and we've included some of their responses throughout this book in the New Teachers Talk feature of each chapter. As you consider their responses, see if you can detect any differences between the responses of teachers at different stages of their professional development. It's quite common for preservice teachers' attitudes and philosophies to change as they gain experience. For example, an analysis of one group of student teachers' field journals revealed that they moved from teacher-centered to student-centered views of instruction, from personal to professional views of teacher-student relationships, and from controlling to holistic views of instructional management as they advanced in their preservice programs (Wilson & Cameron, 1996).

At this point in your teaching preparation, perhaps you haven't spent much time reflecting on questions such as those we have posed here. If not, we encourage you to begin formulating responses to those questions as you read this book and reflect on its contents. You may find it difficult to provide clear-cut answers at first, and this may be due in part to your being in the initial stages of your teacher education program. However, it's likely also attributable to the fact that many aspects of the teaching/learning process reveal it to be an activity filled with uncertainty. We hope that your preservice teacher preparation will introduce you to some of the uncertainties you're likely to encounter in teaching and help you become comfortable with—or at least tolerant of—the ambiguity you'll routinely face as a teacher and a learner (Floden & Buchmann, 1992).

WHY DOES INSTRUCTIONAL DECISION MAKING NEED TO BE SITUATION-SPECIFIC?

As we mentioned in the preface, our students occasionally demand unequivocal solutions from us for hypothetical cases they invent. They want to know exactly what they should do if a certain event transpires in their classrooms. Although we understand and appreciate their longing for a "cookbook" approach to teaching that clearly identifies what steps to take and in what order to take them, we find such approaches unrealistic and inauthentic. Consequently, we typically respond to demands for unequivocal solutions with the answer, "It depends." After students' groans have subsided, we go on to explain that teaching is a complex act that requires situation-specific decision making from teachers—a point that takes us back to the conceptual framework of teachers as educational leaders and informed decision makers and provides us with another opportunity to emphasize the critical role that reflection plays in the teaching/learning process.

Speaking of reflection, before you proceed to Chapter 2, we encourage you to record your answers to the six mission-clarifying questions we posed earlier. We also encourage you to use your responses, along with your other teaching-journal entries, as a way of reflecting on what you're reading about and discussing with others. Then, after you've read the entire book, revisit your original answers. You may find you'll want to modify some of them. Generally that's a good sign, because it means your teaching philosophy is developing right along with you. Once you've put your current responses aside for safekeeping, continue on to Chapter 2 for more about planning for your professional development.

SUMMARIZING WHAT YOU'VE LEARNED

■ In the absence of different models of teaching, teachers tend to teach in the same ways that they themselves were taught. In fact, teachers sometimes use

New teachers talk

What is most important to you in the teaching/learning process?

In order for the student to learn, I feel that it is crucial to build a trusting relationship between the student and the teacher. Since people naturally organize information into chunks or groups, I feel that it is necessary to teach in this manner. This means that teachers must provide connections between the material and the children's lives. Authenticity is key and will lead to interest in the learning process.

—KAREN, Preservice Teacher

I think it is most important to accept responsibility for one's own learning and to foster that excitement and passion for learning in others. Learning is an active pursuit. One can be cajoled

through a variety of extrinsic motivators to perform, to answer questions, or to complete a task. However, I believe that learning is a choice, and we as educators must empower students to choose to learn, and we must support the enthusiasm that will most certainly accompany the pursuit of knowledge. I believe that the most important "skill" I will ever teach is how to be a learner. Children need guidance to become researchers and experimenters, anthropologists and architects, and, given these opportunities, they will become lifelong learners by nature.

—SARAH, Preservice Teacher

The most important thing to me in the teaching/learning process is exactly that—the process. The process of gaining knowledge and experience is the most crucial thing. I want to learn the same methods and strategies they experienced as students even when they are presented with different instructional models as student teachers.

■ Research findings reveal that preservice teachers generally are motivated to teach because of idealistic factors such as a desire to work with young people, a love of children, and the need to make a difference (Green & Weaver, 1992; Snyder, 1995). But even individuals who choose teaching for altruistic reasons make it clear that they will remain teachers only if they derive the satisfaction they expect from the profession (Young, 1995).

■ If teachers are to be prepared adequately for the challenges that await them, then education policy makers, teacher educators, and PreK–12 administrators must be willing to address issues of quality and standards in both preservice and inservice teacher education.

■ Even the most qualified, best prepared novice teachers spend much of their first teaching year preoccupied with survival and plagued by self-doubt stemming from unrealistic expectations they have set for themselves (Jensen & Kiley, 1997b). Survival concerns also may result from the school environments first-year teachers encounter.

about methods of teaching and gain insight as to how to work with children in various situations.

—ANN, Preservice Teacher

I feel the comfort level of my students is most important. I strive to ensure my students feel valued and challenged by the learning environment presented to them. I rely upon humor to create a learning environment that is flexible and student oriented. If the students themselves don't feel comfortable enough to take risks and learn, how is real, authentic learning going to occur?

—MIKE, Third-Year Teacher

Authors' Analysis

We find it interesting—but not surprising—to note that each teacher's response focuses on the emotions and attitudes involved in teaching and learning. When students are asked to reflect on what's important to them in the teaching/learning process, they also focus on affective components. For example, in one study the four themes that emerged from students' reflections regarding what they wanted from their teachers all focused on affective characteristics: gentleness, caring, understanding, and a love of fun (Thomas & Montgomery, 1998).

Now It's Your Turn

 In your teaching journal, provide your own response to the given question: What is most important to *you* in the teaching/learning process?

- Part of what makes teaching difficult is the simple fact that not everyone involved in the teaching/learning process wants to be there. Unlike the world of work, where employees who don't like their jobs can quit, most students don't have that option.

- Begin to identify the strengths you possess that you can apply to the teaching field. List a few areas you need to target for improvement.

- What teachers know and can do is the most important influence on what students learn. Recruiting, preparing, and retaining competent teachers are the central strategies for improving schools and making teaching more effective.

- Your teaching credo should succinctly and clearly articulate your fundamental beliefs about teaching and learning.

- Reflection enables teachers to assess the attitudes or dispositions, knowledge base, and performances that make up the whole picture of who they are and how effective they are as teachers. Reflection plays a particularly critical role in the teaching profession, since teachers operate fairly autonomously.

- Collaborative discussions and reflection provide preservice teachers with an authentic context in which to develop the skills and attitudes that support reflective teaching. Developing a link between reflection and professional practice helps teachers clarify their thoughts and feelings about their practice (Ghaye, Cuthbert, Danai, & Dennis, 1996).

- Teaching is a complex act that requires situation-specific decision making from teachers—a point that leads to the conceptual framework of teachers as educational leaders and informed decision makers and provides an opportunity to emphasize the critical role that reflection plays in the teaching/learning process.

YOUR PROFESSIONAL TEACHING PORTFOLIO

- Draft a philosophy of teaching that clearly articulates your personal teaching credo. Within this draft, identify the established teaching philosophy that most closely resembles your own (behaviorism, essentialism, existentialism, perennialism, or progressivism), and describe your beliefs about learners, learning, and teaching. At regular intervals during your preservice teacher preparation, revisit this draft of your teaching philosophy, revise it as necessary, and record your reflections regarding what led to the changes in your philosophy.

Key Terms

cognitive dissonance (p. 20)
collaborative reflection (p. 17)
instructional decision making
   (p. 14)

reflection (p. 14)
reflective practitioners (p. 15)

teaching credo (p. 14)

Relevant Resources for Professionals

Books and Articles

- Jensen, R. A., & Kiley, T. J. (1997). Significant connections: Mentoring relationships and processes. *Eastern Education Journal, 26*(1), 37–44.

- National Commission on Teaching and America's Future. (1996). *What matters most: Teaching for America's future.* New York: National Commission on Teaching and America's Future.

- Zemelman, S., Daniels, H., & Hyde, A. (1998). *Best practice: New standards for teaching and learning in America's schools* (2nd ed.). Portsmouth, NH: Heinemann.

Professional Organizations

- American Federation of Teachers.
  A national professional organization for teachers.

  http://www.aft.org/index.htm

- National Education Association.
  The larger of two national professional organizations for teachers.

  http://www.nea.org/

Web Sites

- **Fifty States' Certification Requirements**
  This page, maintained by the University of Kentucky College of Education, is a collection of links to the teacher certification requirements of all fifty states.

  http://www.uky.edu/Education/TEP/usacert. html

- **Education Index**
  An annotated guide to the best education-related sites on the Web.

  http://www.educationindex.com

- **ERIC Clearinghouse on Teaching and Teacher Education**
  One of sixteen ERIC clearinghouses. Collects, abstracts, and indexes education materials for the ERIC database. This site also includes links to information about becoming a teacher and to Internet sites for teachers.

  http://www.ericsp.org

- **Internet Resources for Networking Preservice Teachers**
  This page was designed for educators and preservice teachers. It provides a list of Internet resources for educators who are interested in incorporating electronic networking and telecommuting into their preservice teachers' methods courses. This page also provides preservice teachers with access to resources that will help them incorporate Internet resources into their lesson plans and provide opportunities for communication with peers and instructors to aid in the exchange of ideas.

  http://www.tapr.org/~ird/Mathew/main.html

2

CHARTING YOUR PROFESSIONAL DIRECTION

— OR —

"If you don't know where you're going you'll probably end up somewhere else."

(Campbell, 1974)

IT'S GOOD TO HAVE A PLAN!

Real-life experiences with getting lost can give you an idea of why it is good—indeed, critical—to have a plan, for your career as well as for your next car trip. If you don't know where you're going, you'll probably never get there. Or, if you do get there, you might not even realize it! We all know people who seem to drift through life with no direction. We also know people who are always running, but never getting anywhere, because they have no established goals to help them chart their course.

PLANNING FOR PROFESSIONAL DEVELOPMENT

Because teaching is the heart of education, the single most important action the United States can take to improve schools is to strengthen teaching. How can a nation strengthen teaching? We would like to begin by suggesting a strategy for designing **professional development plans (PDPs).** To be an effective and developing teacher, you must have a plan. Both preservice and

"Cheshire-Puss," . . . said Alice, "would you tell me, please, which
way I ought to go from here?"

"That depends a good deal on where you want to get to," said the
Cat.

"I don't much care where—" said Alice.

"Then it doesn't matter which way you go," said the Cat.

"—so long as I get somewhere," Alice added as an explanation.

"Oh, you're sure to do that," said the Cat, "if you only walk long
enough."

—Lewis Carroll, *Alice's Adventures in Wonderland*

Have you ever set off for a destination with no directions and no real idea how
to get there? Or have you ever been a passenger held hostage by a lost driver
with a "good sense of direction" but no map? Maybe after missing an important
job interview, party, or meeting, you vowed never to be caught without a map
or directions again! Or perhaps you vowed always to be in the driver's seat
rather than the passenger's seat.

In your teaching journal, write down your ideas about what you want to
do as a teacher, why you want to do it, and how you plan to go about
getting there.

inservice teachers are expected to set **goals** and **objectives,** and then determine how they are going to reach them. The objectives, rationales, procedures,
materials, and assessment and evaluation strategies that teachers define and
develop constitute their PDPs. As you progress through this chapter, we'll work
with you to help you create a PDP.

The chapter also includes some "think-alouds." A **think-aloud** is a strategy designed to make observable the thinking processes involved in a particular task. Teachers often use think-alouds to model for their students the
cognitive strategies they use to solve complicated problems with many steps.

PLANNING TO BECOME A REFLECTIVE EDUCATOR

The decision to enter the world of teaching carries with it a commitment to becoming a lifelong learner and reflective practitioner. That means taking responsibility for identifying your professional goals and designing strategies
(maps) to help you reach those goals. As Chapter 1 suggested, many educators
embrace the concept of the reflective educator (Brubacher, Case, & Reagan,
1994) or the scientist practitioner (Barlow, Hayes, & Nelson, 1984). **Reflective
educators** are individuals who carefully examine their own and others' pro-

Figure 2.1
Charting Your Own Direction

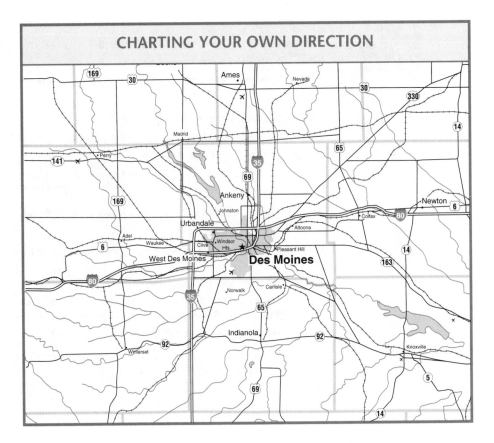

CHARTING YOUR OWN DIRECTION

fessional practice and engage in school-based action research with fellow researcher-teachers (Calhoun, 1993; Johnson, 1993). **Researcher-teachers** analyze their teaching and their students' learning to find out if certain strategies they're using are making a difference in their students' achievement and performance. Such teachers must design systematic ways of assessing the results of implementing those strategies. Consequently, they take on the role of researcher-teachers, whose attempts to assess the effectiveness of their teaching practices are called **school-based action research.**

Teachers who want to improve their professional practice must think carefully about what is taking place in any given situation, correctly identify the options available to them, and make conscious choices about how to act. "Reflective educators are constantly testing the assumptions and inferences they have made about their work as teachers" (Brubacher, Case, & Reagan, 1994, p. 131). Teachers must make numerous decisions each day about what to say, what to do, when to intervene, and when to step back and encourage students to take the lead. Consequently, teachers' abilities to simultaneously reflect, analyze, and make appropriate judgments are critical to both teacher and student success.

Unfortunately, many studies have found educators to be more reactive than reflective (Brubacher, Case, & Reagan, 1994). Teachers who are continually "putting out fires" or seem to be "roller-skating through a buffalo herd" characterize the reactive mode of instruction. If you've ever been a student of a reactive teacher, you understand how disconcerting it can be. Your experiences in classrooms where reflection and inquiry were valued were probably much more fruitful. In schools that have a culture of inquiry, teachers, administrators, and other professionals collaboratively seek to better understand and thereby improve the educational experience (Brubacher, Case, & Reagan, 1994; Johnson, 1993). Indeed, the school culture significantly influences the value placed on reflection (Zins, Travis, & Freppon, 1997).

■ Peer Support Is Part of the Plan

Peer support groups provide an example of organizational structures that invite teachers to take active roles in leadership and decision-making processes. In peer support groups, a small number of professionals with similar areas of interest meet regularly to learn from one another, solve problems, and provide support for one another's professional development. An atmosphere of trust and support is established so that members can share their professional challenges; learn new ideas; and help one another deal with stress, isolation, and burnout (Zins, Maher, Murphy, & Wess, 1988). These teachers "are never satisfied that they have all the answers. By continually seeking new information, participants constantly challenge their own practices and assumptions. In the process, new dilemmas surface and teachers initiate a new cycle of planning, acting, observing, and reflecting" (Ross, Bondy, & Kyle, 1993, p. 337). Peer support groups are appropriate for preservice teachers, as well as inservice teachers. We certainly hope that throughout your initial teacher preparation you will engage in many collaborative learning experiences that will provide opportunities for you to learn from other preservice teachers and in turn support their professional development.

In peer support groups, a small group of teachers meets regularly to learn from one another.
(© Susie Fitzhugh)

In education, professional development is an ongoing process, as it is in professions such as medicine and law. As a teacher, you will continually set goals for yourself, as well as for your students. Your ability to develop and successfully achieve your goals will directly impact your success in the field of teaching—today and in the future.

PRINCIPLES OF EFFECTIVE PROFESSIONAL DEVELOPMENT

Committing yourself to a career that is grounded in professional development may seem a bit overwhelming. Just as you've been dreaming about how you'll never take another class after you graduate, we wake you up to remind you that as a teacher you are, and always will be, a learner. That means you'll be growing, changing, learning, risking, and writing PDPs for the rest of your teaching life. To help you understand the role professional development will play in your career, we include here (in Figure 2.2) a set of principles extrapolated from research on effective professional development (Epstein, 1993; Modigliani, 1993). Since the final principle states that students and professionals should be involved in designing their professional development plans, in the next section we focus on providing you with a blueprint for writing a PDP.

Figure 2.2
Professional Development Principles

- Professional development is an ongoing process.
- Professional development experiences are most effective when grounded in a sound theoretical and philosophical base and structured as a coherent and systematic program.
- Professional development experiences are most successful when they respond to an individual's background, experiences, and current role.
- Effective professional development opportunities are structured to promote clear links between theory and practice.
- Providers of effective professional development experiences must have an appropriate knowledge and experience base.
- Effective professional development experiences take an active, hands-on approach and stress interaction to encourage participants to learn from one another.
- Effective professional development experiences contribute to participants' self-esteem by acknowledging the skills and resources they bring to the educational process, as opposed to creating feelings of self-doubt or inadequacy by immediately calling into question their current practices.
- Effective professional development experiences provide opportunities for application and reflection and allow for individuals to be observed and to receive feedback about what has been learned.
- Students and professionals should be involved in the planning and design of their professional development programs.

(National Association for the Education of Young Children, 1994)

THE FIVE-QUESTION PROFESSIONAL DEVELOPMENT PLAN

At this point you're ready to write a PDP for yourself. How will you begin? Think about the purpose of your PDP. Will it outline your professional goals for the next school year, or will its focus be much broader (for example, a goal that you will attain only once you've completed your teacher preparation program)? Is this a PDP that must be completed in the next few months for a specific class or committee assignment? You can develop PDPs to assist you in setting goals and mapping strategies in a variety of situations and for a variety of purposes. The five questions remain the same, but the breadth and depth of the plans vary, depending on their purpose (see Figure 2.3).

PDP QUESTION 1: WHAT DO I WANT TO DO? (GOALS AND OBJECTIVES)

The key to writing a PDP is to define a specific objective that relates to and emerges from a broader goal. To return to the previous analogy of a traveler, if you were on a trip, you might consider your goal to be the general direction in which you'd like to head (south, New England, the Midwest) and your objective the exact point where you want to end up or what you want to accomplish

Figure 2.3

Writing a Professional Development Plan: Five Questions for Goal Setting and Goal Attainment

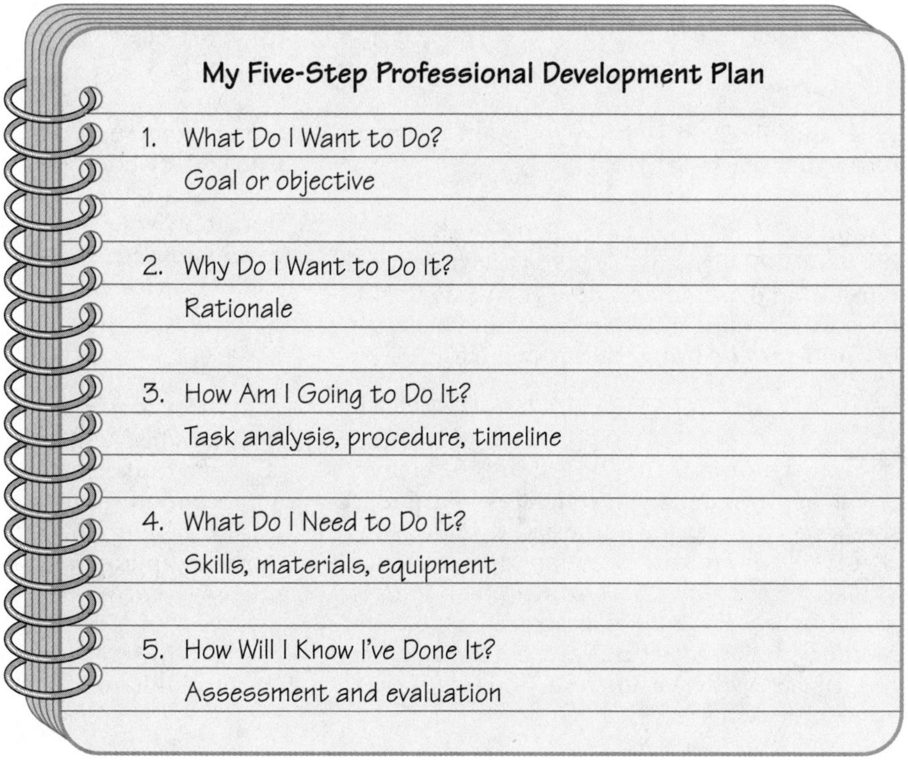

My Five-Step Professional Development Plan

1. What Do I Want to Do?
   Goal or objective

2. Why Do I Want to Do It?
   Rationale

3. How Am I Going to Do It?
   Task analysis, procedure, timeline

4. What Do I Need to Do It?
   Skills, materials, equipment

5. How Will I Know I've Done It?
   Assessment and evaluation

while you're there (visit Boston to take the historic walking tour, travel to Grand Island to visit your aunt and uncle, go to Minneapolis to explore the Mall of America).

The goals and objectives in a PDP follow the same pattern: the goals indicate the general direction you'd like to head (for example, learn more about question-asking strategies, increase your teaching strategies repertoire), and one or more specific objectives relate to and emerge from each goal (examples follow). Our collective experience has demonstrated that "What do I want to do?" is the most difficult question to answer, the one that requires the greatest amount of energy. Consequently, we'll share a few examples to help you get the idea. The first two are examples of objectives that preservice teachers might include in a PDP, whereas the final one is an objective that inservice teachers might have.

Marjorie's Objective: By December 15, I will have completed at least five sections of my professional teaching portfolio (a type of portfolio we explain later in this chapter).

Jen's Objective: Over the next semester, I will work with my six-year-old niece, Lauren, using alphabet flashcards and phonics games to enhance her love of reading.

New teachers talk

What qualities and skills do you want to characterize your teaching?

I want my teaching to be challenging, and I want to be nonjudgmental, patient, flexible, open-minded, understanding, and a good listener. I believe in providing a balance between challenging my students and being realistic and fair.

—KAREN, Preservice Teacher

I want to be a facilitator of learning. Therefore, I will be open to input and ideas—flexible, responsive, creative, and enthusiastic. I also believe that I will be very kind and supportive of the individuals with whom I have contact. In addition, I want to be very knowledgeable about teaching methods, the needs of children and families, and the subject matter of interest. However, perhaps

more importantly, I do not believe in limiting my teaching to the confining scope of my own knowledge base. I want to be able to find out information when needed, and to help others discover knowledge for themselves, whether they are students, parents, or colleagues.

—SARAH, Preservice Teacher

I want to be a fair, respectful, and flexible teacher. I want to use my knowledge about the project approach, integrated curriculum, and appropriate learning environments to teach children in the most age-appropriate and developmentally appropriate ways. I want people to think of me as the teacher who is on the cutting edge. I want them to ask, "How does she do it? She sure is brave to let the children do that!" I will be known for em-

Jorge and the Primary Assessment Committee's Objective: The Primary Assessment Committee will submit a draft of the proposed primary report card, integrating all content areas, to the Metcalf Curriculum Committee by May 31, 2000.

■ The SAM Principle for Effective Objectives

To assist you in writing effective objectives, we suggest you evaluate your objectives by using a strategy we call the SAM principle—as in Specific, Attainable, and Measurable. We have found this principle to be helpful to preservice teachers and inservice teachers alike as they formulate objectives to guide their professional development. A well-written objective is the key component of a PDP that successfully guides your efforts in the direction you have chosen. Consequently, be prepared to rethink and revise your objective a number of times. Figure 2.4 outlines five important criteria that will help you frame your objectives appropriately.

■ Think-Alouds: One Way to Create a PDP

Because writing effective PDPs is a task many preservice teachers find challenging, we've decided to use think-alouds to guide your efforts. A think-aloud is

powering my students to use their reasoning and critical-thinking skills.

—ANN, First-Year Teacher

Humor and rationality. I attempt to portray myself in a light-hearted fashion. This models the flexibility I believe is central to the learning process. I also attempt to provide a model of a "self-learner." Even though I am the teacher, I learn along with the kids. I don't know everything, but I know how to challenge myself into finding what I need to know at a given time. That's what I want my students to do as well.

—MICHAEL, Third-Year Teacher

Authors' Analysis

These beginning teachers are describing what they value in teaching, what strengths they bring to the teaching/learning process, and what they hope will set them apart from other teachers. Ann wants to be on the cutting edge and take risks; Mike values a sense of humor; Karen wants to challenge learners appropriately; Sarah wants to approach teaching with creativity and flexibility. As developing teachers, they might approach their goals by seeking feedback from more experienced or mentor teachers and by making lists of tasks that will help them achieve their goals. What is your response to this same question?

Now It's Your Turn

 What qualities and skills do you want to characterize your teaching? Record your answer in your teaching journal, and prepare a list of potential mentors who might be willing and able to help you reach that goal.

Figure 2.4
The SAM Principle for Effective Objectives: Specific, Attainable, Measurable

- The objective is stated positively.
- There is one task per objective.
- There is an observable behavior.
- There is a condition.
- There is a performance criterion.

an instructional strategy in which teachers model their thinking by talking out loud about the kind of thinking they are using to approach a problem or answer a question. It is our hope that our attempts to "think out loud" here, in a written format, will help you better understand the process of creating PDPs.

The think-alouds are based on authentic experiences we have had over the years as teacher educators. We intend them to provide an opportunity for you to discuss the questions we pose, in or out of class, before you read on for "the rest of the story." Our responses and experiences may be quite different from yours—and that's okay! We just want you to be an engaged learner who reads, responds to, and reflects on the contents of this book—and who is willing to share your own ideas and experiences as you develop as a teacher and learner!

Let's review the example objectives we've provided to determine if they are written effectively. Remember that objectives must meet the SAM criteria, meaning they must be specific, attainable, and measurable. Thinking through each of the characteristics outlined in Figure 2.4 will help you assess whether the objectives merit the "SAM Seal of Approval." The following excerpts show our responses to Marjorie's, Jen's, and Jorge's PDP objectives. First, Marjorie, Jen, and Jorge state their objectives. Then we review each of the SAM principle characteristics to check the effectiveness of their objectives. The responses in italics are the results of our putting ourselves in Marjorie's, Jen's, and Jorge's shoes. We are thinking aloud as a way to help you assess their PDPs. Did they come up with effective objectives?

THINK-ALOUD: Marjorie's Objective for Her PDP

OBJECTIVE: By December 15, I will have completed at least five sections of my professional teaching portfolio.

Does this objective satisfy the SAM principle?

Let's review the characteristics of effective objectives outlined in Figure 2.4 to decide.

SAM Characteristic 1: The objective is stated positively.
Yes. It does say that I will be proactive in completing part of my professional teaching portfolio.

SAM Characteristic 2: There is one task per objective.
Well, yes, even though this overall task needs to be broken down into five smaller parts. Since I have a format for the professional teaching portfolio (see pages 46–51), I have decided to

1. Rewrite my teaching philosophy

2. Request, in writing, letters of recommendation from two of my professors and two of my cooperating teachers

3. Edit the case study from my assessment class

4. Prepare captions for the photographs that I will include from my novice teaching experience

5. Request transcripts from the Registrar's Office

SAM Characteristic 3: There is an observable behavior.
Sure! As the sections of my portfolio are completed, they certainly will be observable.

SAM Characteristic 4: There is a condition.
Yes. The condition is in the form of a deadline—December 15.

SAM Characteristic 5: There is a performance criterion.
Yes, again. The performance criterion is "at least five sections." If I get ambitious or have some extra time, I may be able to rework my résumé and edit my project web, in addition to completing the five subtasks I've already identified.

Let's go back to the SAM principle now that we've reviewed the characteristics of effective objectives from Figure 2.4. Since we've answered *yes* to all the questions posed, we can be assured that this objective meets the SAM principle.

THINK-ALOUD: Jen's Objective for Her PDP

OBJECTIVE: Over the next semester, I will work with my six-year-old niece, Lauren, using alphabet flashcards and phonics games to enhance her love of reading.

Does this objective satisfy the SAM principle?

Bear with us while we once again walk through the characteristics of effective objectives, using this example.

SAM Characteristic 1: The objective is stated positively.
Yes, this objective does focus on what I will do rather than what I won't do.

SAM Characteristic 2: There is one task per objective.
Mmmm—this gets a little trickier. The overall task is to enhance my niece's love of reading. The supporting tasks that I have chosen to meet this objective are to use flashcards and play phonics games with her. This is where my professor steps in, to ask why I have made these choices. She shares with me some articles on teaching reading and shaping primary students' attitudes toward reading. I discover that sharing literature with children is much more effective, both for promoting reading acquisition and for encouraging a positive attitude toward reading, than is either flashcard work or phonics games. I decide to develop some literature-based extension activities that incorporate letter, sound, and word identification. I also decide to focus on encouraging a positive attitude toward reading by determining Lauren's interests (she is intrigued by ballerinas and wolves) before choosing literature and by making the time we spend together reading very pleasurable.

With these ideas in mind, let's take a look at a second draft of this objective.

> **REVISED OBJECTIVE**: Over the next semester, I will work with my niece, Lauren, to enhance her love of reading and support her reading acquisition by sharing literature with her for at least one hour per week.

SAM Characteristic 3: There is an observable behavior.
Well, now that the tasks involved in the objective have been changed, I must also recognize that the observable behaviors will change. The behavior now focuses on sharing literature rather than on using phonics games and alphabet flashcards. I will want to specify tasks and behaviors when I get to the question "How am I going to do it?"

SAM Characteristic 4: There is a condition.
Yes, the condition is "over the next semester." If I wanted to be more specific, I could identify the semester.

SAM Characteristic 5: There is a performance criterion.
We're on a roll! The performance criterion is "at least one hour per week."

This scenario actually happened with one of our students. She went on to learn a great deal about literature-based teaching and is now a strong advocate of literature-based reading instruction. She teaches a summer class for gifted students entitled "Hooked on Books" and is a successful fourth-grade teacher.

THINK-ALOUD: Jorge's Objective for His PDP

> **OBJECTIVE**: The Primary Assessment Committee will submit a draft of the proposed primary report card, integrating all content areas, to the Metcalf Curriculm Committee by May 31, 2000.

Since we know that we can't determine if this objective meets the SAM principle until we review the characteristics of effective objectives, let's proceed with that assessment.

SAM Characteristic 1: The objective is stated positively.
Yes. Again, this objective states what the committee will do.

SAM Characteristic 2: There is one task per objective.
Once again, the answer seems to be yes. Although the task may need to be broken down into subsequent parts, there is still one overall task—that of submitting the draft of the primary report card.

SAM Characteristic 3: There is an observable behavior.
Well, this seems a little more complicated. Since this is a committee effort, it is important to identify who is responsible for the development of specific components of the draft report card. The completed draft is certainly observable, but preliminary steps along the way will need to be defined further.

SAM Characteristic 4: There is a condition.
Yes, the condition is again in the form of a deadline date.

SAM Characteristic 5: There is a performance criterion.
The performance criterion is "integrating all content areas." Although this criterion is clearly stated, it may be difficult to obtain agreement among all members of the

committee as to what this means. The committee needs to decide collectively how it will meet this criterion.

Although Jorge's objective does satisfy the SAM principle, you may find that group objectives require negotiation and additional refinement when compared with individuals' objectives. Group objectives also may be more difficult to achieve, because the more people that are involved in the process, the less control you as an individual have over the outcome. This is a good example of how your ability to be a team player will affect your future as a teacher.

These think-aloud activities help you focus on the process of writing effective objectives. Develop an objective and then discuss it with other preservice teachers in cooperative learning groups. Use the characteristics we've suggested, and you'll be able to determine whether your objective is stated effectively or needs to be reworked. After you've decided that your objective is specific, attainable, and measurable, move on to the second PDP question: "Why do I want to do it?"

QUESTION 2: WHY DO I WANT TO DO IT? (RATIONALE)

This part of your PDP is critical, because you must come to terms with the question "Why?" If you've spent much time around two-year-olds, you know that this question seems to be the central core of their existence. *Why is the sky blue? Why do ants make ant hills? Why do birds fly?* Children are natural-born scientists, anthropologists, and researchers who learn through observation and investigation.

Unfortunately, many learners seem to lose the thirst for knowledge that once characterized them as two-year-olds. And, even more unfortunately, sometimes schools and inappropriate educational systems contribute to this loss of motivation and passion to learn. But if you have decided to be a teacher, then you must begin to open doors in your mind and heart that may have been closed. One key to opening those doors is to allow yourself, once again, to ask "Why?" If you're hoping to be an effective teacher, you must model and promote a questioning spirit and engaging mind for each of your students. We've chosen to focus on the revised version of Jen's objective for a think-aloud on the question "Why do I want to do it?"

THINK-ALOUD: Jen's Rationale

> **OBJECTIVE:** Over the next semester, I will work with my six-year-old niece, Lauren, to enhance her love of reading and support her reading acquisition by sharing literature with her for at least one hour per week.

The rationale for this objective actually emerged from a very tragic family circumstance that one of our students encountered. Six-year-old Lauren, the niece of our student Jen, had recently lost her father in a fatal car accident. The effect on Lauren, her mother, and Lauren's younger sibling had been devastating, and Lauren's opportunities for shared pleasurable reading experiences had been severely curtailed. Experiencing the upheaval of grief and loss as a six-year-old just beginning first grade, she understandably suffered acute separation anxiety whenever her mother left her. Thus, school became a place where Lauren felt insecure and anxious, and learning to read was not a priority for her.

> *When Lauren's mother (my sister-in-law) called me after receiving a report from Lauren's teacher that Lauren was having trouble with reading, I began to search for ways in which I could help. I was, in fact, preparing to be a teacher and really wanted to know how to "teach reading." But most of all, I wanted to intercede in the life of my sensitive niece before both school and reading became permanently characterized as negatives in Lauren's mind.*
>
> *I was highly motivated to make a difference for Lauren because I cared about her, cared about my sister-in-law, and understood the importance of enhancing a love of reading in young children. Through the realization of this objective, I was able to support Lauren's love of reading, and her reading competence improved. I also benefited tremendously as a preservice teacher, because I was able to experience Lauren's responses to literature and witness how those responses impacted her literacy development. Lauren emerged as a better reader, writer, talker, listener, and thinker. I emerged as a much more sensitive and competent preservice teacher.*

Motivation comes in many forms and formats. It may stem from a personal situation, from a topic you are intensely interested in (for example, brain-integrated learning), or from another class or area of study. It is imperative that the objective you select for your PDP centers on something you want to do. You need to care about whether you accomplish the objective. If you find that you do not care, write another objective. Now that you have written a rationale that unquestionably supports your objective, let's move on to the third question, "How am I going to do it?"

QUESTION 3: HOW AM I GOING TO DO IT? (PROCEDURES)

This is a question that will lighten the hearts of those of you who enjoy making lists! Now we get to the nitty-gritty—the specific steps you need to complete to attain your objective. Answering the question "How am I doing to do it?" really entails answering three subquestions:

1. What steps are involved in the task?
2. What procedure will I follow to complete those steps?
3. When will I complete each step along the way?

Your response to the last question depends on the length of time you have to attain your objective. If you're a preservice teacher, you're probably working within the context of a semester or part of a semester. If you're an inservice teacher, your time line may extend for a year or even five years (especially if you're engaged in a project that involves the change process). An extended time frame probably will require a more involved task analysis, as well as a more definitive procedure. Designing a time line can help you answer the question of when you'll complete the specific steps involved and can help you successfully accomplish your objective. Let's revisit Jen's revised objective to think through how you might set up a three-part response to the question "How am I going to do it?"

THINK-ALOUD: **Jen's Procedures**

OBJECTIVE: Over the next semester, I will work with my six-year-old niece, Lauren, to enhance her love of reading and support her reading acquisition by sharing literature with her for at least one hour per week.

Looking back at the third characteristic of effective objectives (from Figure 2.4), I ask, "Is there one task to be completed?" I find that I've already thought through the subtasks that need to be a part of the overall task of enhancing Lauren's love of reading. I've suggested the following subtasks:

1. Determine Lauren's interests before choosing literature to share with her.

2. Develop some literature-based extension activities that incorporate letter, sound, and word identification.

3. Share literature and literature-based extension activities with Lauren at least one hour per week throughout the semester.

4. Make the time spent sharing literature with Lauren very pleasurable.

Now I need to go back to my subtasks and add procedures and a time line to support each of the subtasks. I'll plan on beginning this project by the fourth week of the semester. Since I'll need a few weeks to organize the portfolio I'll turn in at the end of the semester to answer the last question—"How will I know I've done it?"—I'll plan on ten weeks of the sixteen-week semester to complete my plan.

1. Determine Lauren's interests before choosing literature to share with her.

   Procedures:
   * *Interview Lauren using the reading interest survey shared in class.*
   * *Prepare interview responses for inclusion in the portfolio.*

Jen shares a favorite book with her niece, Lauren.
(© Michael Zide)

- *Take Lauren to the public library to choose books that focus on her interests—ballerinas and wolves.*
- *Revisit the library every other week to select new books.*

Time line:
- *Reading interest survey—Week 1*
- *Library visits—Weeks 1, 3, 5, 7, and 9*

2. *Develop some literature-based extension activities that incorporate letter, sound, and word identification.*

Procedures:
- *Begin by developing at least two literature extensions that support the books selected during Week 1. Continue to develop at least one additional activity every time we visit the library.*
- *Collect at least four work samples for the portfolio from shared literature extension activities.*

Time line:
- *Two literature extensions—Week 1*
- *At least one additional literature extension activity—Weeks 3, 5, 7, and 9*
- *Collect at least four work samples by Week 9.*

3. *Share literature and literature-based extension activities with Lauren at least one hour per week throughout the semester.*

Procedure:
- *Set up a calendar outlining which hour we will spend sharing literature and activities each week.*

Time line:
- *Weeks 1 through 10*

4. *Make the time spent sharing literature with Lauren very pleasurable.*

Procedures:
- *Discuss with Lauren pleasant locations for shared reading activities—under a tree in the back yard, at a favorite park, on the porch, and so on.*
- *Discuss with Lauren things that make her feel comfortable when reading—a beanbag chair, a pillow, a teddy bear, and so on.*

Time line:
- *Add special locations and "comforts" to the calendar for Weeks 1 through 10.*

Now Jen has a very detailed plan that offers many opportunities to collect evidence for a portfolio. (The importance of "evidence" will become clearer to you when we get to question five, "How will I know I've done it?") For now, Jen has a great start on specific steps that will help her attain her objective.

QUESTION 4: WHAT DO I NEED TO DO IT? (RESOURCES)

This question focuses on skills, materials, and equipment you will need to attain your objective. It is important to consider this question when you're formulating your objective. If the resources you need to accomplish the objective—time, money, a child, a car, computer expertise, mechanical expertise, and so on—are not available to you, then you need to establish a different objective. Remember—your objective must be attainable. Don't try to do in a semester what will take a year to accomplish. As a preservice teacher, your time is a precious commodity, and you must use it wisely. Do not overpromise and underdeliver. Be realistic about what you can accomplish, and do it to the best of your ability.

Since we've done such a thorough job of answering the question "How am I going to do it?" we can look back at our response and start developing a list. (The work you've done previously really pays off when you get to this question.) For example, Jen found she needed the following resources to complete her plan.

THINK-ALOUD: Jen's Resources

> **OBJECTIVE:** Over the next semester, I will work with my six-year-old niece, Lauren, to enhance her love of reading and support her reading acquisition by sharing literature with her for at least one hour per week.
>
> *After reviewing my procedures, I developed the following list of resources that answers the question "What do I need to do it?"*
>
> - *Reading interest survey—a written survey that asks Lauren to identify specific topics of interest to her*
> - *Children's literature*
> - *Transportation to the public library*
> - *Transportation to Lauren's home or school*
> - *Library card*
> - *Materials to develop literature extension activities—paper, glue, stapler, markers, poster board, and so on*
> - *Calendar for Lauren and me*
> - *Work samples*
> - *"Comforts" (such as a teddy bear, pillow, beanbag chair)*
> - *Portfolio holder*

You may need to add some additional items to the list as you proceed, but at least you will now have an idea of the cost and time required to reach your objective. It might be interesting for you to estimate the length of time you think it will take to attain your objective. Since time management is such an important skill for teachers, it's good for you to begin developing an awareness of how you actually spend your time (as opposed to how you would prefer to spend your time) when working toward achieving a professional objective.

QUESTION 5: HOW WILL I KNOW I'VE DONE IT? (ASSESSMENT AND EVALUATION)

To assess and evaluate your success in implementing your PDP, ask yourself the following:

- What evidence have I collected to support the assertion that I have met my objective?

- To what degree did I attain my objective?

- Am I satisfied with my achievement?
- If not, what would I like to do differently?

To answer these questions, consider developing a porfolio. (See the next section for a discussion of portfolio design, development, and use.) A portfolio will help you both in assessing and in evaluating your progress. Use the example provided in the following think-aloud to begin thinking about the purposes of portfolios.

THINK-ALOUD: Jen's Assessment and Evaluation

OBJECTIVE: Over the next semester, I will work with my six-year-old niece, Lauren, to enhance her love of reading and support her reading acquisition by sharing literature with her for at least one hour per week.

The portfolio I will submit to provide evidence that I have completed my objective will contain the following:

1. *Table of contents*

2. *My PDP*

3. *The following documentation:*
   - *Artifacts: A research paper on literature-based teaching*
   - *Reproductions: A videotape that includes at least three of the shared literature experiences*
   - *Attestations: Notes from my professor, included in my language development learning log, that document my interest in emergent literacy*
   - *Productions: Work samples that Lauren develops throughout our ten-week intervention (child-made books, sequence charts, word strips, language charts, and so on)*

4. *Captions attached to each piece of evidence stating why it is included in the portfolio*

5. *A short narrative statement focusing on what I learned from this process*

6. *A conclusion that focuses on the process of completing a portfolio*

PORTFOLIOS: DOCUMENTING YOUR PROFESSIONAL GROWTH

The design and implementation of a PDP requires some method of documenting growth toward accomplishing a self-selected goal or objective. A portfolio offers one way of doing so.

WHAT IS A PORTFOLIO?

A **portfolio** is an organized collection of documents that provides evidence of a person's knowledge, skills, and development. In your case, the portfolio will provide documentation of your professional growth and achieved competence in the complex act called teaching. In the future, both as a preservice teacher and as an inservice teacher, you will no doubt be required to help your students develop portfolios as a means of assessment. Portfolio-based assessment of students is usually considered to have two main purposes: to chart student progress and to document evidence, including student reflections, that show what students know and can do. We will explore the concept of portfolios as an assessment strategy in Chapter 11, which focuses on assessment and evaluation.

WORKING PORTFOLIOS AND PROFESSIONAL TEACHING PORTFOLIOS

There are two kinds of portfolios that you will become familiar with during your preservice education: a working (or process) portfolio and a professional teaching (also known as product or showcase) portfolio. "A *working portfolio* is characterized by your ongoing systematic collection of selected work in courses and evidence of community activities" (Campbell, Cignetti, Melenyzer, Nettles, & Wyman, 1997, p. 3). After developing your working portfolio, you'll analyze and evaluate the many pieces of evidence in it as you select key documentation for your **professional teaching portfolio.** A professional teaching portfolio may be required for graduation from your university's teacher preparation program. Also, you can present your professional teaching portfolio to prospective employers as you interview for teaching positions.

WHY SHOULD YOU CONSIDER DEVELOPING A PORTFOLIO?

When we introduce preservice teachers to portfolios as a means of reflection and assessment, we always attempt to articulate our rationale for exposing them to portfolios and to explain how learning about and creating portfolios contributes to their professional development. Creating portfolios allows preservice teachers to do two things:

1. Demonstrate growth toward accomplishing a self-selected objective related to their teacher preparation program. For example, in the scenario you reviewed earlier in this chapter, Jen used a portfolio to provide evidence that she had reached her objective of working with Lauren to enhance her love of reading and support her reading acquisition.
2. Experience one way to use portfolios in the teaching/learning process.

WHAT SHOULD YOUR PORTFOLIO CONTAIN?

Both your working portfolios and your professional teaching portfolio will benefit from careful organization, structure, and design. Following are some suggestions for portfolio content, as well as organization.

DESIGNING A WORKING PORTFOLIO

Working, or process, portfolios are most effective when they clearly and completely document the progress and growth you've made toward attaining your self-selected objective. A logical organizational structure is essential to clearly communicate the results of your efforts. Consequently, consider including the following components in your portfolio:

1. A table of contents or some alternative form of "road map" for directing the reader through the portfolio.

2. Your PDP. As you now know, your PDP should address the following five questions:

   - What do I want to do?
   - Why do I want to do it?
   - How am I going to do it?
   - What do I need to do it?
   - How will I know I've done it?

3. Relevant and appropriate documentation of your progress and growth toward attaining your stated objective. Evidence of change may take the form of

   - *Artifacts:* Pieces of work that you have produced in your development as a preservice or inservice teacher. Remember that artifacts usually don't look "pretty."
   - *Reproductions:* Material produced when learning to teach (for example, videotapes or audiotapes of your teaching).
   - *Attestations:* Documents produced by someone else that provide evidence of your knowledge and skill (for example, a memo from a professor or a cooperating or fellow teacher; see Figure 2.5).
   - *Productions:* Evidence that you produce explicitly for your portfolio.

4. *Captions* attached to each piece of evidence, stating what it is and your rationale for including it in your portfolio. These captions should be concise and extremely well written. Your role as a reflective practitioner is high-

Figure 2.5
An Attestation for a Working Portfolio

Well-written reflection that clearly articulates your emerging philosophy of education. Thank you for the careful thought it demonstrates. — Dr. Kiley, 10-4-2000

lighted in these captions. Your caption insights are likely to set you apart from other students.

5. Your assessment of the degree to which you feel you have reached your objective—a statement in which you reflect on the substance of your portfolio and what you have learned.

6. A summary or conclusion in which you comment on the experience of completing your combined PDP and portfolio.

DESIGNING A PROFESSIONAL TEACHING PORTFOLIO

Although there are many differing views on this topic, we have synthesized them into a plan that we think will be most helpful (see Figure 2.6). Your input as a reflective practitioner is the most important variable. Only you know what pieces of evidence best illustrate your competencies as a future teacher.

■ Selecting Items to Include in Your Portfolio

More is not necessarily better when it comes to deciding what to include in your portfolio. If you've not yet broken yourself of the habit of asking professors to tell you exactly what they want and how many pages a paper should be, creating a portfolio provides a belated opportunity to do so! Which items to include will depend on whether you're developing a working portfolio or a professional teaching portfolio. If you're preparing a working portfolio to serve as the assessment component of your PDP, begin by selecting the most compelling piece of evidence regarding your objective. Then look at the remaining pieces of evidence to determine what value is added by each. It's helpful to arrange the evidence in some order, such as chronologically or by theme.

In addition, consider documenting not only that you have achieved your objective but also how you went about doing so. For example, if you used technology (such as creating a CD-ROM presentation, developing a Web site, researching a topic on the Internet) in the course of implementing your PDP, it's important for your portfolio to reflect that. If your PDP featured collaboration (for example, working with other teachers, parents, community agencies) as an implementation strategy, that also should be reflected in your portfolio.

Although we can't tell you exactly what to include in your professional teaching portfolio (and we wouldn't tell you if we could), we can offer you the following questions to use in guiding your decisions regarding what—and how much—to include.

Questions to Guide Your Selection of Items to Include in Your Portfolio

- What do I want prospective employers to notice immediately about me?
- What are my strengths, and how can I best showcase them?
- What differentiates me and my qualifications from the other one hundred applicants and their qualifications?
- How can I demonstrate that I interact well with parents, colleagues, and administrators, as well as with children and adolescents?

Figure 2.6
Professional Teaching Portfolio Components

A professional teaching portfolio is a collection of your highest-quality work that demonstrates your professional growth and interest in ongoing development. Suggestions for items to include in your portfolio:

Cover Page
Include your name, the date, and the title—Professional Teaching Portfolio.

Table of Contents
Index all the items you have chosen to include in your portfolio, and put those items in a logical order. Your portfolio should be user-friendly and attractive.

Résumé
Make certain your résumé is current and reflects cocurricular and extracurricular activities, along with pertinent academic and work experiences.

State Certification Document
If you are applying for teaching positions prior to receiving your teaching license or certificate, include a notation that clearly explains when you will be receiving your license or certificate and exactly what the document will allow you to teach.

Philosophy Statement
Clearly articulate your beliefs about the teaching/learning process, the purpose of education, and the mission of schools. If you wrote a philosophy statement early in your preservice program, you may want to include that in your portfolio, along with the updated version and a reflection statement that focuses on the differences between the two versions and the growth those differences indicated.

Letters of Recommendation
Include letters from individuals who can speak to your qualifications and experiences with children (cooperating teachers, university supervisors, professors, directors of child care programs or camps where you have worked).

Official Transcripts
Keep your transcripts updated. Once you have completed your degree, be sure to include a copy of the transcript that indicates that you have met all requirements for the degree you are seeking.

Practica Evaluations
Include evaluations relating to significant field experiences (for example, novice teaching, student teaching, internships).

Instructional Plans
Carefully select examples of your best achievements in the areas of integrated units and daily lesson plans. Include lessons you have taught, along with photographs and your assessment regarding the effectiveness of those lessons and what you might do differently next time. Lesson plans should look professional (typed, standard usage and spelling, neat, well organized).

Assessment
Provide examples of a variety of assessment strategies, both informal and formal, that you have used successfully.

Figure 2.6
**Professional
Teaching
Portfolio
Components**
(cont.)

Visual Display of Your Strengths

Add photographs of learning activities you have implemented (such as bulletin boards, puppet shows, learning centers, parent night, small group work).

Videotape

You may choose to include a videotape of one of your best lessons that displays your natural teaching style, or you may decide to include a series of teaching segments that demonstrate your growth and feature a variety of settings and instructional purposes. In either case, also include your reflections on and assessments of the instructional scenarios.

Instructional Materials

Showcase materials you have created and describe how you used or would use them.

Case Study

Demonstrate your ability to profile the strengths and needs of a learner through the use of multiple data sources, including informal and authentic assessment strategies.

Technology

Demonstrate and describe your competency in using technology to facilitate and support instruction (software evaluation, computer-assisted instruction, Internet or Web-based activities).

(Based on "Designing a Professional Teaching Portfolio," developed by Rita A. Jensen, Therese J. Kiley, Heljä Robinson, and Celia Johnson [1998])

- How can I demonstrate my understanding of learners, their needs, and developmentally appropriate practice?
- How can I demonstrate my interest in teaching and my commitment to ongoing professional development?
- How can I demonstrate that I am a reflective practitioner, educational leader, and informed decision maker who willingly and successfully engages in self-evaluation?
- How can I demonstrate that I am a team player who can collaborate successfully with others?
- If I include this particular item in my portfolio, what value or information will it add?

■ Suggestions for Additional Materials

Your professional teaching portfolio provides an opportunity for you to showcase your personal strengths, creativity, and individuality. What additional items might you choose to include? The following suggestions offer a few ideas:

- Consider using a CD-ROM or Web page to showcase your teaching knowledge and expertise. Technology enables you to scan photographs and include video and sound. Certainly this is one way to convince potential employers of your computer literacy.

- A research paper could document your written communication skills as well as demonstrate your interest in and appreciation of the important link between theory and practice.

- Selected journal entries could provide evidence of your ability to engage in reflection as a tool for assessing and improving your own teaching performance.

- PDPs and portfolios you completed as a preservice teacher could attest to your experiences with those processes and could document your professional growth over time.

- Other materials you have created throughout the course of your preservice program can demonstrate your unique talents, strengths, and ideas (for example, multimedia presentations, instructional computer programs, a children's book).

■ Electronic Portfolios

Exciting developments are on the horizon with respect to storing portfolios. A number of computer software programs have been developed to help you compile **electronic portfolios.** Many peripherals, such as scanners and CD-ROM drives, make storing and retrieving your work electronically a real possibility. In addition, you can post your portfolio on the Web for prospective employers to view.

Advantages and Challenges of Electronic Portfolios After extensively reviewing the literature on electronic portfolios, we've developed a fairly lengthy list of advantages and a much shorter list of challenges. Since the advantages outweigh the challenges, we recommend that you invest some time and energy in contemplating using electronic portfolios to showcase your teaching competencies.

Advantages: Electronic portfolios allow you to
- Import large quantities of information and data quickly and easily
- Attach endless work samples
- Tie your work to professional teaching standards
- Easily locate your work
- Cross reference your work
- Collect work over a number of semesters
- Engage in self-reflection
- Store and retrieve your work
- Make your work accessible to others
- Review your performance
- Make decisions regarding your performance

Challenges: At the same time, electronic portfolios

- Require a certain level of technological expertise to create
- Require a great deal of time to create
- May present software and hardware compatibility challenges when shared with prospective employers

WHAT TEACHING STANDARDS SHOULD BE REPRESENTED IN YOUR PROFESSIONAL TEACHING PORTFOLIO?

When preparing your professional teaching portfolio, use the outline provided in the previous section, as well as the following model standards, developed by the **Interstate New Teacher Assessment and Support Consortium (INTASC).** Your professional teaching portfolio should include evidence that you meet the expectations outlined in each of the ten standards. For further detail regarding organizing your portfolio around the teaching standards, we refer you to a book entitled *How to Develop a Professional Teaching Portfolio: A Manual for Teachers* (Campbell, Cignetti, Melenyzer, Nettles, & Wyman, 1997). This resource describes and explains each of the INTASC standards, includes a teaching scenario for each standard, and provides a sample cover sheet to illustrate how you can document achieved competence in a particular area. These statements can serve as models for you as you develop your rationale statements. You also may wish to visit the INTASC standards Web site at: **http://www.CCSSO.org/corestan.html.**

MODEL STANDARDS FOR BEGINNING TEACHERS' LICENSURE AND DEVELOPMENT

Some states, perhaps including yours, have developed their own standards for beginning teachers. For example, Illinois has adopted eleven standards, which closely mirror the INTASC standards. We encourage you to become familiar with the standards that appear in Figure 2.7 and begin to consider how you can demonstrate your performance with regard to each standard.

WHERE DO YOU GO FROM HERE?

We hope you'll go on to use PDPs and portfolios throughout your preservice teacher preparation, as well as throughout your entire teaching career. PDPs and portfolios can serve as a focal point for your professional development and can provide a method for documenting your growth and progress. Using a combination of PDPs and portfolios also offers a high degree of individualization in your teacher preparation program, by allowing you to identify goals for continued professional development and areas of personal interest for further exploration.

Figure 2.7
Model Standards for Beginning Teachers' Licensure and Development

Standard #1: Knowledge of Subject Matter
The teacher understands the central concepts, tools of inquiry, and structure of the discipline(s) he or she teaches and can create learning experiences that make these aspects of the subject matter meaningful for students.

Standard #2: Knowledge of Human Development and Learning
The teacher understands how children learn and develop and can provide learning opportunities that support their intellectual, social, and personal development.

Standard #3: Adapting Instruction for Individual Needs
The teacher understands how students differ in their approaches to learning and creates instructional opportunities that are adapted to diverse learners.

Standard #4: Multiple Instructional Strategies
The teacher understands and uses a variety of instructional strategies to encourage students' development of critical thinking, problem solving, and performance skills.

Standard #5: Classroom Motivation and Management Skills
The teacher uses an understanding of individual and group motivation and behavior to create a learning environment that encourages positive social interactions, active engagement in learning, and self-motivation.

Standard #6: Communication Skills
The teacher uses knowledge of effective verbal, nonverbal, and media communication techniques to foster active inquiry, collaboration, and supportive interaction in the classroom.

Standard #7: Instructional Planning Skills
The teacher plans instruction based on knowledge of subject matter, students, the community, and curriculum goals.

Standard #8: Assessment of Student Learning
The teacher understands and uses formal and informal assessment strategies to ensure the continuous intellectual, social, and physical development of the learner.

Standard #9: Professional Commitment and Responsibility
The teacher is a reflective practitioner who continually evaluates the effects of his or her choices and actions on others (students, parents, and other professionals in the learning community) and who actively seeks out opportunities to grow professionally.

Standard #10: Partnerships
The teacher fosters relationships with school colleagues, parents, and agencies in the larger community to support students' learning and well-being.

(Campbell, Cignetti, Melenyzer, Nettles, & Wyman, 1997; Interstate New Teacher Assessment and Support Consortium, 1992)

You can count on hearing more about PDPs and portfolios. In fact, you may be required to use a portfolio approach to demonstrate your initial teaching competencies and knowledge base. Some teacher preparation programs and states require a portfolio for graduation or certification, and many school districts request to review portfolios as part of their interviewing process. In addition, some states are recommending, or already are using, portfolios and PDPs as vehicles to guide and document teachers' continuing professional development to qualify them for continuing licensure. If that isn't enough to convince you that portfolios and PDPs have important roles to play in both your preservice and inservice teacher preparation, we'll be exploring the role of portfolios in PreK–12 education when we come to Chapter 11, which focuses on assessment and evaluation. In addition, at the end of each chapter, in the feature entitled Your Professional Teaching Portfolio, we'll include some suggestions for items and documentation to include in your professional teaching portfolio.

SUMMARIZING WHAT YOU'VE LEARNED

- If you want to be an effective teacher, you'll take responsibility for your own professional development. You'll learn to plan, set goals, and develop strategies for reaching your self-selected goals. You'll also engage in reflection as part of the professional development process.

- Professional development efforts should be ongoing, systematic, and personalized to the learner's experiences and background.

- The first and most critical step in designing effective PDPs is the creation of an objective that is specific, attainable, and measurable and answers the question, "What do I want to do?" Once that step has been completed, the learner then must answer the four following questions: "Why do I want to do it?" (rationale), "How am I going to do it?" (procedures), "What do I need to do it?" (resources), and "How will I know I've done it?" (assessment and evaluation).

- Think-alouds are an instructional strategy teachers sometimes use to model their thinking by "thinking out loud" about a particular problem or question. Think-alouds can serve as a useful tool for making observable the thought processes involved in the design of professional development plans.

- Portfolios are organized collections of documents that provide evidence of a person's knowledge, skills, and development.

- Working, or process, portfolios can serve as vehicles for systematically documenting and demonstrating growth and learning over time. After developing a working portfolio, you can analyze and evaluate the many pieces of evidence in it as you select key documentation pieces for your professional teaching portfolio, which sometimes is referred to as a product or showcase portfolio. Both state and national standards for teacher licensure and development can guide you in selecting items to include in your professional teaching portfolio.

YOUR PROFESSIONAL TEACHING PORTFOLIO

■ Write a statement describing your evolving philosophy of teaching at this stage of your preservice teacher preparation. You can then compare it to descriptions of your teaching philosophy that you create at different stages of your preservice preparation and professional practice.

■ Develop a career goal as well as a description of where you'd like to be and what you'd like to be doing five years into your teaching career.

Key Terms

electronic portfolio (p. 50)
goal (p. 29)
Interstate New Teacher Assessment and Support Consortium (INTASC) (p. 51)
objective (p. 29)

portfolio (p. 44)
professional development plan (PDP) (p. 28)
professional teaching portfolio (product or showcase portfolio) (p. 45)

reflective educator (p. 29)
researcher-teacher (p. 30)
school-based action research (p. 30)
think-aloud (p. 29)

Relevant Resources for Professionals

Books and Articles

• Burke, K. (1997). *Designing professional portfolios for change.* Arlington Heights, IL: Skylight Publishing.

• Burke, K. (1997). *Professional portfolios: A collection of articles.* Arlington Heights, IL: Skylight Publishing.

• Campbell, D. M., Cignetti, P. B., Melenyzer, B. J., Nettles, D. H., & Wyman, R. M., Jr. (1997). *How to develop a professional portfolio: A manual for teachers.* Boston: Allyn & Bacon.

• Lyons, N. (1998). *With portfolio in hand: Validating the new teacher professionalism.* New York: Teachers College Press.

Professional Journals in Education

• *Educational Leadership.* 2000 Washington Blvd., Washington, DC 20001
http://www.edleader.org

Professional Organizations

• Association for Supervision and Curriculum Devel-

opment. 1250 N. Pitt St., Alexandria, VA 22314-1453
http://www.ascd.org/

• National Board for Professional Teaching Standards. 26555 Evergreen Rd., Suite 400, Southfield, MI 48076, 800-228-3224
http://www.nbpts.org/

Videos

• A Teacher Portfolios Video Series:
Program 1: Portfolios for Teachers in Training
Program 2: Portfolios for Beginning Teachers
Available from the Association for Supervision and Curriculum Development, 800-933-2723
http://www.ascd.org/

Web Sites

• **Interstate New Teacher Assessment and Support Consortium (INTASC) Standards:** This Web site includes the INTASC standards, as well as background information on the organization itself.
http://CCSSO.org/corestan.html

TEACHING AND LEARNING IN CONTEXT

PART TWO

In Part Two we focus on teachers as leaders and decision makers. We also explore the qualities that make teachers leaders and decision makers. Teachers who are leaders do more than just make it through the day—they know content, guide students' learning, and understand the attitudes and emotions involved in learning and leading. An important leadership component involves the ability to understand the range of family situations students come from and the diverse cultures and ethnic groups that make up each classroom.

3

TEACHERS AS LEADERS AND DECISION MAKERS

— OR —

"If I'm in charge here, why is everybody laughing?"

(Campbell, 1980)

WHAT MAKES TEACHERS LEADERS AND DECISION MAKERS?

Teachers must wear many different hats throughout the course of a typical school day: manager, motivator, instructor, evaluator. But regardless of the hat they are wearing at any particular time, effective teachers always are engaged in the processes of leading and making decisions (Eggen & Kauchak, 1992). Unfortunately, some teachers fail to acknowledge their leadership and decision-making roles and therefore give little or no conscious thought to the types of leaders or decision makers they are. Consequently, they may not be as effective as they could be as leaders or decision makers.

When PreK–12 teachers neglect their leadership and decision-making roles, the result is what Doyle and Hartle referred to in 1985 as a dearth of educational leadership. Doyle and Hartle identified classroom teachers as the real leaders in education and recognized—as we do—that lasting change cannot be accomplished without the active participation and leadership of those people who make the day-to-day decisions that are an integral part of the teaching/learning process. In the decade following Doyle and Hartle's pronouncement, teachers' involvement in the school reform debate has spurred

"Every great leader is teaching, and every great teacher is leading."

—John Gardner, 1989

Take yourself back to a time when you were in charge of an athletic club fundraiser, a book fair, or some other school event. How would you characterize your leadership during that event: conflicted chaos, quiet questioning, purposeful procrastination, or creative competence? What variables impacted your leadership performance, either positively or negatively? Where on the effective-ineffective continuum would you place that particular personal leadership experience?

In your teaching journal, respond to these questions and describe what you would do to improve on your original leadership performance if you found yourself in that same situation again.

an unprecedented focus on the need for teacher leadership (Urbanski & Nickolaou, 1997).

Without decisive leadership from teachers, even the most responsive reform measures and the most insightful instructional plans will be ineffective. Consequently, we've dedicated this chapter to a discussion of a moral imperative that comes with the job of teacher—to serve as a leader and a decision maker. Someone will serve as the leader and decision maker in your classroom, and we'd like it to be you.

LEADERSHIP AND DECISION MAKING DEFINED

Some define **leadership** and **decision making** in terms of getting people to do what they would not otherwise do or what a leader wants them to do. We invite you to consider an alternative perspective on leadership. Think of leadership and decision making in terms of leaders influencing followers "to act for certain goals that represent the values and the motivations—the wants and needs, the aspirations and expectations—of both [the] leaders and [the] followers." Then consider that "the genius of leadership lies in the manner in which leaders see and act on their own and their followers' values and motivations" (Burns, 1995, p. 100).

Finally, think about how that perspective on leadership and decision making relates to the teaching/learning process and to your experience as a student and a preservice teacher. For example, did you ever have teachers who could get you to do just about anything? You worked harder for them than you ever worked before, and there's nothing you wouldn't have done for them. Perhaps such teachers possessed the genius of leadership, which allowed them to

Effective teachers always are engaged in the processes of leading and making decisions. (© Michael Newman/ PHOTO EDIT)

unlock the key to what motivated you and to what was important to you. Remind yourself that you need a different key for every learner, and you'll realize that it requires a measure of true leadership genius to tap the learning potential of all students.

CONNECTIONS BETWEEN TEACHING, LEADING, MANAGEMENT, AND DECISION MAKING

Great teachers, like other great leaders, make measurable differences in people's lives. However, in the case of teachers those differences may be difficult to detect and may not come to fruition for years (Bolman & Deal, 1993). In spite of John Gardner's assertion (1989) that great leaders teach and great teachers lead, some teachers see no connections between teaching, leading, and decision making and don't see themselves as leaders. Others may tend to agree, but the false assumption that teaching is for teachers but leading is for principals has worked to the disadvantage of American education for a very long time. Teaching inherently involves leading and decision making. It is a complex process that requires many leadership skills and decision-making processes, such as setting goals, establishing objectives, selecting and implementing strategies for achieving those objectives, evaluating the entire process, and motivating and inspiring reluctant learners (Pellicer & Anderson, 1995).

Just as teaching inherently involves leading, leadership inherently involves managing and making decisions. Therefore, every discussion about teaching is also a discussion about **management** and decision making. We invite you to think of teaching, leadership, management, and decision making as barrels nested one inside the other, with decision making at the center. Decision making is a necessary prerequisite of both effective management and leadership, which in turn are prerequisites of effective teaching.

Classrooms are complex, dynamic workplaces that require management by executives of considerable talent. Although teachers are not often thought of as executives, it's time they became recognized as such (Berliner, 1983). There are nine executive functions that teachers, like corporate leaders, must perform to be successful:

1. Planning
2. Communicating goals
3. Regulating activities of the workplace
4. Creating a pleasant environment for work
5. Educating new members of the work group
6. Relating the work of the site to other units in the system
7. Supervising and working with other people
8. Motivating those being supervised
9. Evaluating the performance of those being supervised

Leadership—like teaching—is a complex concept with a multitude of meanings and purposes. Combining these two concepts into a third, teacher leadership, further increases their complexity. At their core, both leadership and teaching are about relationships. They involve processes "of mutual influence between leaders and those they hope to lead. Good leaders, like good teachers, are as good at listening and sensing as they are at persuading and teaching. What distinguishes leadership from other kinds of relationships is that when it works well, it enables people to collaborate in the service of shared visions, values, and missions" (Gullat, 1997, p. 13).

WHY TEACHERS SHOULD BE LEADERS AND DECISION MAKERS

Leadership is the single most important element of an effective school. Teachers tend to be highly educated, dedicated, hard-working people. However, for centuries they have been told how to do their jobs. They have been told this by bureaucrats, administrators, politicians, parents, businesspeople, students—even college professors. In spite of—(or perhaps because of) all of the advice classroom teachers have received, school achievement levels have not improved (Schargel, 1994). Just as teachers sometimes neglect to ask students for their input when attempting to figure out how best to meet their learning needs, would-be educational reformers often neglect to ask teachers for their input and involvement when attempting to design and implement curricular innovations.

Policy makers and administrators know that teacher leadership and decision making play key roles in developing curricula and school climate. They know that when schools restructure, teachers' roles also undergo redefinition. All involved in school renewal must act on what they know and ask for teachers' leadership and active participation in reforming the instructional process.

What researchers, effective administrators, and informed policy makers know is that teacher leaders stimulate change and empower those they lead, in contrast to teachers who resist change. They also know that teacher leaders tend to be involved with innovation, can motivate students of a variety of abilities, and make themselves available to other teachers (Mooney, 1994).

TWO KINDS OF LEADERSHIP

Although there are many ways to describe leadership, for the moment we'll focus on two types: **transactional leadership** and **transforming leadership**. Transactional leadership occurs when one person takes the initiative to contact others for the purpose of exchanging something of value (such as when a political candidate campaigns for citizens' votes with the promise to support certain policy initiatives). Transforming leadership occurs when leader and follower interact in such a way that they raise one another to a higher level of motivation and morality. Transforming leadership has the potential to raise the moral level of human conduct and the ethical aspirations of both the leader and the led and can have a transforming effect on both (Burns, 1995).

Mohandas Gandhi, for example, was a transforming leader. Through his words and his examples, Gandhi communicated his passion for human rights and freedom and transformed his followers. However, you don't have to be a leader of Gandhi's stature to practice transforming leadership. We've both had the privilege of having teachers who in some way, large or small, changed our lives for the better. We hope you've had similar experiences. We've also had the privilege of working with students who changed us in some way, even as we were in the process of attempting to make a positive difference in their lives. We hope you will have that experience, too.

LEADERSHIP AND DECISION MAKING VERSUS MANAGEMENT

We begin this section with a clarification of terms. What is leadership, and what is management? Do leaders and managers do different things?

■ When to Lead and When to Manage

At various points in the ongoing discussion regarding the differences between leadership and management, some people have proposed that leadership is what individuals do under conditions of change, whereas management is what people do under conditions of stability. For example, Kotter (1995) views leadership and management as two distinctive yet complementary systems of action. For him, managing is about coping with complexity, whereas leadership is about coping with change. More change always demands more leadership.

Others have made a distinction between the two concepts by saying you lead people but manage things. Still others have suggested that effective leadership and effective management are inseparable and that "effective managers and leaders do exactly the same things" (Whetten & Cameron, 1995, p. 17). We suggest that the concepts of leadership and management interrelate and overlap. For us, leadership serves as the umbrella concept, with management as a subset of it. As such, we begin with the premise that effective leaders and decision makers possess effective management skills, and we concur that effective leadership and management are indeed inseparable.

LEADERSHIP AND DECISION-MAKING TRAITS

Is there such a thing as a natural-born leader? Are you one? The evidence shows that there are identifiable leadership traits and that they do matter. Six traits leaders exhibit are drive, the desire to lead, honesty and integrity, self-confidence, cognitive ability, and knowledge of their business or profession. Other traits that differentiate leaders from nonleaders on a smaller scale include charisma, creativity and originality, and flexibility (Kirkpatrick & Locke, 1995).

Factors that have been found to be associated with leadership can be classified under these general headings (Stogdill, 1995):

1. *Capacity:* intelligence, alertness, verbal facility, originality, judgment
2. *Achievement:* scholarship, knowledge, athletic accomplishments
3. *Responsibility:* dependability, initiative, persistence, aggressiveness, self-confidence, desire to excel
4. *Participation:* activity, sociability, cooperation, adaptability, humor
5. *Status:* socioeconomic position, popularity

SITUATIONAL LEADERSHIP

However, we need to add another significant variable to this list. Successful leadership is situation-specific. *Situational leaders* are effective leaders and decision makers who know how to apply their leadership skills and decision-making ability appropriately in different situations. Every situation brings with it followers who possess unique skills and interests, unique objectives to be achieved, and unique needs to be met. Thus, an adequate analysis of leadership must include not only a study of leaders but also a study of situations. Effective leadership is situation-specific, just as effective instructional decision making is situation-specific. It depends.

Some leadership tasks lend themselves to collaborative efforts (such as planning a workshop or coordinating an all-school event), whereas others are more effectively addressed by a single decision maker (such as determining when to introduce a new concept in a unit of study or choosing a starting point for a discussion of class rules). **Situational leadership** entails the ability to distinguish whether group or individual leadership is preferable in a specific circumstance.

Situational leadership also considers the characteristics and needs of individual followers. Some followers require very little external guidance or direction; what they may need most from leaders is to be left alone. Other followers may need specific step-by-step directions. Still others may need more in the way of encouragement and less actual assistance with the task at hand (Hersey, Blanchard, & Johnson, 1996).

Earlier in this chapter we explored the premise that both leading and teaching are about relationships. Effective engagement in both processes requires some degree of active personal involvement with and emotional investment in those you are attempting to lead and/or teach. Transforming leadership possesses the potential to magnify the payoffs that result from such involvement and investment. Which type of leadership should or do teachers engage in—transactional or transforming? Which type of leadership will characterize you as an instructional leader?

 In your teaching journal, record your responses to these two questions.

WHAT ARE THE SKILLS OF TEACHER LEADERSHIP AND DECISION MAKING?

Even if teacher educators and administrators identify individuals who exhibit traits associated with effective leaders, that doesn't guarantee that those individuals will develop into leaders. Leadership traits alone are not enough to ensure successful leadership; they're only preconditions. With that important point in mind, we present in Figure 3.1 three specific skill groups required for leadership and management. These originated with Hersey and Blanchard's theories of managing organizational behavior. Each group contributes significantly to overall leadership effectiveness, and you can learn to apply each group of skills to the teaching/learning process.

| Figure 3.1 **Leadership and Decision-Making Skills** | **Interpersonal Skills**
Ability and judgment in working with and through people, including an understanding of motivation and an application of effective leadership.

Technical Skills
Ability to use knowledge, methods, techniques, and equipment necessary for the performance of specific tasks acquired from experience, education, and training.

Conceptual Skills
Ability to understand the complexities of the overall organization and where one's own operation fits into the organization. This knowledge permits one to act according to the objectives of the total organization rather than only on the basis of the goals and needs of one's own immediate group.

(Hersey, Blanchard, & Johnson, 1996) |

Our discussion begins with what we consider the most important skill group, interpersonal skills. We then move on to the group that tends to receive the majority of attention in preservice teacher preparation programs, technical skills. Finally, we conclude our discussion of leadership skills with the group that includes the most variables yet receives the least attention, conceptual skills (Hersey, Blanchard, & Johnson, 1996).

INTERPERSONAL SKILLS

Of the three groups of leadership skills highlighted here, the interpersonal skills group is by far the most crucial. J. D. Rockefeller, an individual whose oil empire gave him, as well as his heirs, a lifetime of financial security, once said, "I will pay more for the ability to deal with people, than any other ability under the sun!" Obviously, Rockefeller felt strongly about the importance of effective people skills. Part of what makes interpersonal skills so critical to any leader's or decision maker's success is the fact that they are essential at every level of leadership and for the successful completion of almost any work that involves more than one person, whether that work is a grandiose enterprise or a simple task. In short, effective interpersonal skills serve as the common denominator that connects all leaders and decision makers—from the assembly line supervisor to the CEO in the executive suite, and from the lunchroom supervisor to the state superintendent of schools.

Simply stated, individuals who possess effective **interpersonal skills** know how to work with and through people to achieve desired results. This ability includes an understanding of the principles of motivation, as well as an appreciation for individual differences. Certainly, effective teachers recognize that they need to use different leadership styles with different students. Some students require higher levels of guidance and direction; other students prefer to focus on tasks as opposed to relationships. Effective teachers tailor their interpersonal interactions and leadership styles to particular students' needs.

TECHNICAL SKILLS

Effective leaders also possess the **technical skills** they need to do their jobs. Their past experiences and education have taught them how to use the knowledge, methods, strategies, and equipment necessary to perform the specific tasks their jobs require. Teachers must make use of a vast array of technical skills that go far beyond knowing how to use audiovisual equipment. We discuss a few of these in the following sections.

■ Pedagogy

As you progress in your teacher preparation program, your teaching/learning knowledge base will grow. You'll learn a variety of instructional strategies and how to select methods and materials appropriate for particular styles of teaching and learning. You'll acquire what we hope will be a considerable understanding of **pedagogy,** which will provide you with a window into the needs of learners at different developmental stages and help you determine how best to meet those learners' needs. In addition to all that, you'll explore variables such as curricular integration, culturally appropriate practice, learning environments, questioning strategies, providing for special needs, and instructional guidance.

■ Technology

Teachers must identify appropriate technologies and effectively integrate them into instruction. The technology skills teachers need go far beyond being computer literate and keeping current with ever-evolving technologies; they include understanding how both teachers and learners can design and use multimedia presentations in the instructional process. Computer programs offer multiple platforms for learning, and tools such as optical scanners, video equipment, and digital cameras offer multiple ways for students to show what they know and can do. Of course, the Internet opens up many additional instructional avenues for teachers and learners to explore. The challenge lies in finding the time to discover what's out there and then effectively applying it to instruction. Teachers' attempts to become—and remain—technologically current certainly can benefit from collaboration.

CONCEPTUAL SKILLS

The last skill group we'll discuss is also the "fuzziest." By **conceptual skills,** we mean leaders' abilities to understand the complexities of the overall organi-

Teachers and students can collaborate with each other to learn about current technology.
(© Michael Zide)

zation where they work (for teachers, their school) and where and how they and their actions fit into that organization. Leaders who possess such knowledge are able to act according to the objectives of the total organization, rather than only on the basis of their own goals and the needs of their immediate groups (Hersey, Blanchard, & Johnson, 1996). What does all of that mean to you as a prospective teacher? It means that closing the door to your classroom and pretending that no greater reality exists outside it will not work forever. That strategy will serve only as a short-term solution and will, in fact, cause problems in the long run.

When newer teachers engage in the rather painful process of analyzing the errors they made in their first years of teaching, they often find that the majority of their mistakes stemmed from lack of attention to the conceptual skill group. That's not surprising, given the fact that the conceptual skill group is the most abstract, the most encompassing, and the most difficult to observe skill group and that ignoring it has less immediate consequences than does neglecting the other skill groups. Since most first-year teachers live in a survival mode, they tend to concern themselves with the day-to-day realities of their classrooms. Some days, conducting an accurate lunch count, collecting money, taking attendance, and getting students to and from their appointed rounds in a timely manner requires the majority of novice teachers' time and energy. Consequently, the "big picture" may escape their attention.

Take a moment to consider what teachers miss when they fail to use conceptual skills to understand the overall organization in which they work. First of all, they have no idea about "how we do things here." This includes such points as how the principal interacts with teachers, how teachers interact with one another, if teachers at the same grade levels plan collaboratively, how resources are allocated, how the work load is distributed, how curriculum decisions are made, how change is initiated, if and how site-based management is utilized, the degree of parent involvement, the importance placed on student achievement scores, how teachers are evaluated, and what ramifications there may be if teachers dismiss students from their classes for disciplinary reasons. Obviously teachers overlook a great deal when they neglect the conceptual skill group!

Our portrayal of teacher leaders as individuals who possess and apply a combination of interpersonal, technical, and conceptual skills is not just a theoretical construct. Their peers recognize them as teacher leaders by the behaviors they exhibit. For example, one group of secondary-school teachers described teacher leaders as warm, dependable, and self-effacing, with a genuine commitment to the work of their colleagues and their schools. Teacher leaders display well-honed interpersonal skills, as well as the technical skills required for program improvement. They are able to apply their interpersonal and technical skills within the broader contexts of educational policy, the subject matter they teach, their local community, and their entire school. In other words, their conceptual skills help them make effective use of their interpersonal and technical skills (Leithwood, 1997).

WHAT ARE THE ROLES OF TEACHER LEADERSHIP AND DECISION MAKING?

Effective leaders apply their interpersonal, technical, and conceptual skills to fulfill the different roles of leadership and management, which are summarized in Figure 3.2. As you may suspect, the roles leaders play overlap and interrelate. Those roles that likely will sound most familiar to you are planning and organizing. However, just as important to leaders' effectiveness are the roles of motivating and ensuring quality.

PLANNING

Perhaps you've heard the somewhat worn axiom "Teachers who fail to plan, plan to fail." What exactly does planning entail? In the broadest sense, *planning* begins with the process of setting goals and objectives for an organization. Remember the SAM principle from Chapter 2? After articulating objectives that are specific, attainable, and measurable, effective leaders develop work maps that illustrate how those objectives will be met.

When you think of planning in the context of teaching, you probably think of lesson planning. Certainly lesson planning is one important form of planning that teachers do. In fact, teachers tend to be best at short-term planning, such as that involved in writing daily lesson plans. However, they also need to engage in other types of planning that involve mid-range and long-range goals.

As a new teacher, you may find it difficult to imagine what your students will be like at the end of their year with you. How can you predict what and

Figure 3.2 **Leadership and Decision-Making Roles**	**Planning** Setting goals and objectives for an organization and developing work maps illustrating how these goals and objectives will be met.
	Organizing Integrating resources (such as people, equipment, capital) in the most effective way for the purpose of achieving organizational goals and objectives.
	Motivating Providing the situations and circumstances people need to be productive. Everyone is motivated; however, the direction and degree of motivation vary.
	Ensuring Quality Comparing accomplishments with plans and providing feedback on results to ensure appropriate adjustments are made where outcomes have deviated from expectations.

(Adapted from Hersey, Blanchard, & Johnson, 1996)

how much they will have learned by the year's end? During her first year of teaching, one of our former student teachers would conclude each day by running down the hall to ask a fellow second-grade teacher exactly what she and her students had accomplished that day. As a first-year teacher, one of her greatest stressors with regard to her own performance came in the form of mid-range and long-term planning.

In addition to planning instruction for students, whether for the short term or the long term, teachers must plan for curriculum development, textbook adoption, and curricular innovation. Of course, they also must plan for their own professional development, as you discovered in Chapter 2. You'll read much more about instructional planning in Part Three.

ORGANIZING

Closely related to planning is the important leadership role of organizing. *Organizing* involves integrating resources in the most effective way for the purpose of achieving organizational goals and objectives. What do we mean by resources? Resources include variables such as people, time, equipment, and space. Effective teachers generally are very well organized, and effective organization and effective teaching tend to go hand in hand.

Perhaps you recall instances when a teacher asked a roomful of students to wait quietly while he or she went to the office to retrieve supplies needed to conduct an activity already in progress. Can you also remember students' collective response to such requests for cooperation? In the role of student teacher supervisor, Rita had the opportunity to witness one such scenario. It unfolded as follows.

> Shortly after I entered a first-grade classroom for a scheduled observation of a preservice teacher in the midst of completing her student teaching experience, her cooperating teacher and she engaged in an exchange that began with, "I thought you were going to do that" and continued with, "And I thought you were going to do that." Obviously, whatever "that" was, it was a detail to which neither the student teacher nor the cooperating teacher had attended. The cooperating teacher bade farewell to the student teacher; the student teacher smiled weakly in my direction, attempted to collect her thoughts, and then delivered the following address to the congregation of first graders who were intent on watching this drama play out before their eyes. "I need to run to the office for just a second, so what I need you to do is sit quietly and wait patiently." Having completed her plea for cooperation, the student teacher sped out the door, the sound of her short, quick steps echoing down the hallway.
>
> By way of an aside to those not acquainted with the rules by which students interact with university supervisors, let me simply say that generally students deal with university supervisors by not dealing with them. Except for the fact that they take up space, basically university supervisors are invisible to students. Consequently, I awaited the students' responses to their student teacher's exit with great anticipation. I didn't have long to wait. She was seated right in front of me, this little girl in perfect white tights, black patent leather baby-doll shoes,

and a spotless frilly dress complete with Peter Pan collar. Even before the echo of the student teacher's footsteps began to fade, this seven-year-old was on her feet, arms outstretched. With a shimmy that made Elvis's gyrations pale by comparison, she proclaimed to her young colleagues, "Let's party!"

What all of that means, of course, is that organization plays a critical role in effective teaching and effective leading. Attention to detail does pay, as a kindergarten student teacher once discovered. Her first words to her university supervisor after being observed were, "I know! I know! I should have passed out the pencils *after* I gave the directions!" A little drum playing quickly had brought her to that discovery.

MOTIVATING

At some time or another, you've probably sighed, "I just don't feel motivated!" Or perhaps, based on your firsthand observations of family members, friends, acquaintances, or children you've worked with, you've concluded that they're unmotivated. We suggest to you that if you're not motivated, you're dead! You always are motivated; however, the direction and degree of your motivation vary. For example, some mornings when the alarm goes off you may be more motivated to stay in bed than to get up and go to work or to class. On those mornings, you still possess motivation; it's just that you're motivated more strongly in a direction (sleep) that may interfere with your stated goals (completing a degree, maintaining employment) than you are in the direction of getting up and beginning your day.

For what we hope are obvious reasons, effective leaders understand and apply the principles of motivation. Effective leaders consistently succeed at helping people reach high but reasonable expectations. They do so by figuring out

Effective teachers create learning environments and situations that students find motivating.
(© Susie Fitzhugh)

what different individuals find motivating and then attempting to meet those motivation needs. Of course, not everyone is motivated by the same things. Think about that fact with regard to how the teaching/learning process is structured. For example, students are more likely to "buy into" the learning process when they feel they have some say in it. In what ways can teachers help students develop a feeling of ownership in their own learning? What opportunities do students have for making choices and designing some of their own learning opportunities?

As is the case with many of the concepts presented in this general overview of the teaching/learning process, we will further explore the topic of motivation in later chapters. For the moment, ponder how you would respond, as a beginning teacher, to a student who vehemently asserts, "You can't make me!" Would such a student in fact be correct? We suggest that the answer is yes. Those who have had the opportunity to compare the experience of trying to teach students who do not choose to learn with teaching those who do choose to learn will attest to the significant differences between those experiences.

What effective teachers can do is to create learning environments and situations that students find motivating. They can invite students to join the teaching/learning process. What even the most effective teachers cannot do is to force individuals to learn. Although teachers can demand that work be completed, they cannot guarantee that students will learn anything from doing it. Compliance does not equal learning.

ENSURING QUALITY

The final major leadership role we'll discuss here is that of ensuring quality. It's a role that Hersey, Blanchard, and Johnson (1996) label "control"—as in quality control. However, we have found that teachers—even preservice teachers—when they hear the word *control* think of disciplining and controlling students. That certainly isn't what Hersey, Blanchard, and Johnson had in mind when they wrote of controlling quality as a leadership role, and it certainly isn't what we have in mind as we write about appropriate leadership roles for teachers. In fact, when we discuss instructional guidance in Chapter 7, we'll share with you the notion that such control is merely an illusion—and certainly not a valid instructional goal.

Ensuring quality assurance embodies the notion of valuing productivity rather than just activity. As such, it flies in the face of the infamous axiom "Keep them in their seats and quiet." Effective leaders compare accomplishments and outcomes with intended goals and plans, for the purpose of making appropriate adjustments where outcomes have deviated from expectations. For teachers, this means determining if students have met stated objectives and criteria for success in their work, as opposed to simply recording whether or not students have completed and handed in assigned work.

It also means taking the time and the necessary steps to assess your own productivity as a teacher. Going through the motions and putting in the minimum time and effort required are not acceptable standards for either students or teachers. Why is it, then, that schools sometimes seem to value task completion more than outcomes that match expectations?

Effective leaders and managers succeed in creating environments in which those around them can be productive. Leaders who create cultures of productivity

- Value productivity and results—not activity
- Facilitate an environment of trust and openness
- Act with reliability so others will know how to act
- Have high standards and expectations but achieve results without bossing
- Communicate the mission
- Learn from others, as well as about them, by listening, observing, and asking questions (adapted from Akin & Hopelain, 1986)

In Chapter 6, we'll revisit this notion of creating cultures of productivity and explore the challenge of creating organizational environments that facilitate students' and teachers' productivity.

Another important issue related to ensuring quality involves how to respond when students demonstrate that they have met stated objectives without completing all of the tasks or problems assigned. Must those students spend additional time "learning" what they already know? For example, a fifth grader once announced to his teacher that he had no intention of finishing his math assignment. He explained that he had successfully completed fifteen of the assigned problems, and the teacher already had sufficient evidence to document that he had met the stated objective. Consequently, he saw no justifiable reason to do another fifteen problems of the same type. Although this student could have presented his case in a more socially appropriate manner, we believe he has a legitimate point. To those who suggest that "Students can never get enough practice," we say, yes, they can. Ensuring quality involves teachers' making good use of students' time, as well as their own.

TEACHERS LEADING TEACHERS

Teachers often are reluctant to acknowledge themselves as leaders of other teachers. In one study, less than 10 percent of teachers identified themselves as teacher leaders (Vance, 1991). "Most teachers do not recognize that a broader role of teacher leadership is open and available to those who wish to assume the responsibilities. . . . Even teachers who already are active teacher leaders do not see themselves that way" (Katzenmeyer & Moller, 1996, p. 2). The egalitarian norms of teaching's professional culture don't encourage teachers to draw attention to themselves. In an environment that historically has valued treating all teachers the same, teachers may hesitate to allow themselves to be singled out. However, when teachers do see and acknowledge themselves as leaders of other teachers, they discover the potential this has to influence their own students' learning. This belief that they can make a difference is known as **teacher efficacy,** and it influences student achievement and encourages teachers to place less blame on factors beyond their control (such as students' home environments).

WILL YOU BE A TEACHER LEADER?

Researchers who study recent teacher education graduates' perceptions regarding leadership have found that graduates are sometimes less willing to describe themselves as leaders or change agents than are the principals with whom they work (Kull & Bailey, 1993). Although those who have been teaching for four or five years perceive themselves to be leaders more often than do those who have been teaching for only one to three years, they still report a low incidence of what they consider leadership behavior. Those studied reported exhibiting informal leadership behaviors more often than taking on traditional teacher leader roles. When graduates described themselves as standing out from their peers, they attributed it to loving, caring about, and relating well to children; trying new ideas and strategies in the classroom; having excellent rapport with colleagues, parents, and administrators; and being enthusiastic about teaching.

COLLABORATION: TEACHERS HELPING TEACHERS

Any kind of leadership is concerned with helping. Teacher leaders are concerned with helping other teachers so that they can, in turn, better help their students. Teacher leadership is about helping teachers work together to establish and achieve the goals and objectives of the school (Pellicer & Anderson, 1995). Teachers who are leaders lead within and beyond their classrooms, influence others to improve educational practice, and identify with and contribute to a community of teacher leaders (Katzenmeyer & Moller, 1996).

■ Within and Beyond the Classroom

Teacher leaders maintain their connections to the classroom, as opposed to leaving the classroom and possibly the school to become administrators. "The irony is that getting ahead in teaching means leaving it. Moving into administration, however, is not the only way to lead in schools. Countless leadership opportunities exist for teachers who do not wish to leave the work they love— teaching students" (Katzenmeyer & Moller, 1996, p. 6).

■ Influencing Others

It is not necessary for teachers to hold formal leadership positions to influence others. "Motivating colleagues toward improved practice relies on the personal influence of a competent teacher who has positive relationships with other adults in the school. Easily identified in any school are teacher leaders who show initiative, willingly experiment with new ideas, and then share their experiences with others" (Katzenmeyer & Moller, 1996, p. 7).

■ Community of Leaders

Teacher leadership is not limited to a select group. All teachers must develop professional expertise—including leadership skills. Superintendents and principals—as well as teachers—need to check their assumptions about teachers as

New teachers talk

Using the three skills (interpersonal, technical, conceptual) and four roles (planning, organizing, motivating, ensuring quality) of leadership and decision making, identify at least three leadership and decision-making strengths you bring to the teaching/learning process and one area for growth and improvement.

Three leadership and decision-making strengths

Although I am a novice teacher, I possess many years of experience working with preschool age children, infants with disabilities, and families needing financial assistance to pay for child care expenses. Because of such experiences, I have developed a strong sense of responsibility to those whom I am asked to serve. I feel that I must do my absolute best to meet the needs of the program and of individuals using the program.

First, I possess strong organizational skills. Without this, I would not be effective in fulfilling my responsibilities. I plan ahead, write short-term and long-term goals, and am prepared. I often exceed what is expected of me. Through such activities, I am told that I serve as a role model for others.

Second, I am effective in interacting with a variety of individuals. These individuals come from different economic, educational, cultural,

and ethnic backgrounds. I am always accepting of, and look for the good in, each and every person. I am guiding, empowering, and supportive toward those that need me. I encourage teamwork and, at the same time, individuality.

Finally, I am a lifelong learner. I feel that everyone should be open to learning new techniques and approaches. Professional development is the only way to stay current in the field. I often employ self-evaluation, thus guiding the direction of my future professional development.

One area for growth and improvement

Currently, I am working toward increasing my repertoire of teaching strategies. I have the theory and technique; now I need to make learning more interesting for the students. My cooperating teacher says that I need to develop a "bag of tricks." Consequently, I've become this collector of all things—looking at them for a use or idea. This is where being organized comes in handy!

—LEE ANN, Preservice Teacher

Three leadership and decision-making strengths

I am a teacher in a school that depends on its families to support and be actively involved in

leaders and rethink those assumptions if necessary. We invite you to do the same. For example, when you think of teachers as leaders, do you think of

- All teachers or selected teachers?
- A set of functions or formal leadership positions?
- Classroom-based leadership or administrative-based leadership?
- Teaching and learning or organizational issues?
- Reflective practitioners or teachers as technicians?

their children's education. One of my strengths lies in finding ways to support learners and their families and providing circumstances that motivate them to participate in school activities. For example, I use appropriate interpersonal skills to communicate the knowledge I've gained through experience and education.

I also feel I do a good job of planning. To stay organized, I always write lesson plans. In addition, it's not unusual to find me writing short-term and long-term goals and objectives for both the children and myself.

Another strength I have is my ability to reflect and take suggestions. Every night I write in my journal about the day. I reflect on what went well, what I can do better, and who needs extra help. I also ask for feedback from the parents about the days' activities. When taking all this into consideration, I am assured of the quality of my plans and accomplishments.

One area for growth and improvement

I am growing in my ability to use resources that will help learners achieve goals and objectives. I am just now learning about all the skills, knowledge, and occupations of my children's parents. I have had a few parents come in and share their knowledge on such things as snakes, bugs, and soybeans. I hope to encourage more parents to share their knowledge with the children in the future.

—SHANICA, First-Year Teacher

Authors' Analysis:

Lee Ann and Shanica both have positioned themselves to continue their professional development. They have done so by making planning, organization, self-evaluation, and reflection routine parts of their professional lives. These healthy and productive habits will enable them to expand their already considerable knowledge base and enhance their leadership and decision-making skills.

Now It's Your Turn

 From the three skills (interpersonal, technical, conceptual) and four roles (planning, organizing, motivating, ensuring quality) of leadership and decision making, identify at least three leadership and decision-making strengths you bring to the teaching/learning process and one area for growth and improvement.

- Long-term staff development or a menu of short-term options?
- Accountability for outcomes or powerlessness? (adapted from Katzenmeyer & Moller, 1996)

BENEFITS OF TEACHER LEADERSHIP

When teachers are willing to develop the skills and assume the roles of leadership, potential payoffs exist for students, schools, and the teachers themselves. Perhaps most significant among those potential benefits is teacher efficacy—the extent to which teachers believe they can affect student learning. As Katzenmeyer and Moller (1996, p. 3) explain, "If teachers feel confident in their abilities to be leaders, they will assume responsibility for the learning of all students. This single outcome from teacher leadership can affect teaching and learning throughout the school. Linking teacher leadership to efficacy in their classrooms can help teachers understand how they can touch the lives of more students."

Retention of excellent teachers is another potential benefit of teacher leadership. If administrators want to keep excellent teachers in education, they need to develop new roles for them that extend beyond the classroom. Fifty percent of new teachers remain in the profession five years or less. Teacher isolation, absence of career ladders, low salaries, and lack of leadership responsibilities contribute to this situation. For high-ability teachers, teacher leadership is generally appealing—if it influences student learning.

Teachers who view themselves as leaders help overcome resistance to change. When teacher leaders participate in shaping and leading change, there's less resistance to it. Creating teacher ownership in the change process allows teachers to participate actively in decision making, thereby decreasing their resistance to change. After all, it's more difficult to criticize something when you're a part of it.

Teacher leadership can provide a form of career enhancement by offering opportunities for teachers to expand their areas of influence. The challenge of leadership roles can revitalize teachers and keep them actively involved and experiencing professional growth and development. In leading others, teachers learn about their own practice. Taking on leadership roles can encourage teachers to engage in reflection, thereby helping them improve their own performance. Influencing other teachers is another potential benefit of teacher leadership. Teachers are influenced by colleagues they respect, and this is one way to get less-skilled teachers to improve their performance.

Finally, engaging in leadership roles can increase teachers' feelings of accountability. As teachers become involved in decision making and assume authority for making curriculum and instructional decisions, they understand that they'll be held accountable for student outcomes (Katzenmeyer & Moller, 1996). One professional development program was designed to improve student learning outcomes by improving teachers' leadership performance. The sixteen-month program was built on the following three key premises (Donaldson & Marnik, 1995):

Figure 3.3
Leadership Styles and Gender

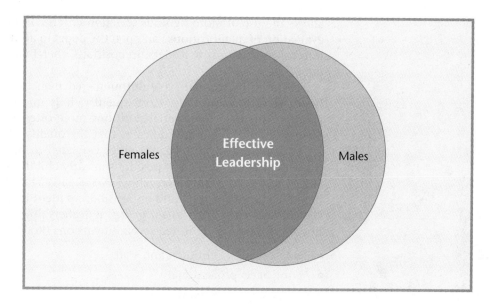

- School leadership is a matter of a person's professional ambition rather than a function of his or her position.
- Leadership effectiveness requires behavioral change.
- Change is the leader's personal responsibility

THE RELATIONSHIP BETWEEN GENDER AND STYLE OF LEADERSHIP AND DECISION MAKING

If women are from Venus and men are from Mars, do their leadership styles differ along with their communication styles? The research does suggest that some differences exist between the leadership styles of males and females. However, as Figure 3.3 demonstrates,their leadership styles overlap more than they differ. That is, "the differences among women (or men), considering variations in background, experience, and so on, are greater than the differences between women in general and men in general. . . . Evidence suggests few differences in the actual behaviors of men and women leaders. Effective leaders, male or female, seek to implement their visions, vary their behaviors contingent upon the situational requirements, and in general grapple successfully with the ever-changing and complex internal and external demands upon their organizations. Ineffective leaders, male or female, do not" (Schein, 1995, pp. 163, 167).

Effective leadership is difficult. Both the public and private sectors admit to a leadership shortage. The increasing attention leadership garners demonstrates its importance and the high priority organizations place on improving the quality of leadership. If society truly wants the most capable individuals to lead its major institutions—schools included—then society should welcome a larger pool of qualified candidates, because a larger leadership candidate pool allows the use of more rigorous selection criteria. Implementing gender-blind evaluation of qualifications can open the doors to allow more women entrants into the race for future leadership positions, thereby increasing the leadership pool.

Historically, women have outnumbered men in the field of early childhood education and care. Consequently, it is one of the few fields where women have held managerial positions more often than men have. A compelling body of literature indicates that the quality of programs and services for young children and their families is related to the effective leadership of those holding management positions in early childhood centers (Rodd, 1996). However, few of the women who serve as early childhood coordinators with broad management roles and responsibilities identify personally with the concept of "leader." When asked to define leadership, one hundred early childhood coordinators identified seven dimensions (Rodd, 1996):

- Being a guide to children and staff
- Acting like a professional
- Being a good communicator
- Being able to meet people's needs
- Being a multifaceted and flexible person
- Taking responsibility
- Being visionary

Their composite definition contains elements similar to H. Gardner's definition (1996), which presents leadership as the use of words and personal examples to influence the behaviors, thoughts, and feelings of a significant number of people. However, their definition also omits some key dimensions, such as the need to articulate their vision with an awareness of political realities, hidden tensions, and power struggles that occur in the early childhood field. The abilities to serve as change agents and to take intelligent, calculated risks are other key dimensions of leadership that are conspicuous by their absence from the early childhood coordinators' definition of leadership. The personal and professional ability to cope with uncertainty in times of accelerating political, social, and economic change appears to be a critical attribute that early childhood leaders need to develop. The good news is that the skills and roles of leadership can be learned!

ESTABLISHING A CULTURE OF TEACHERS AS LEADERS AND DECISION MAKERS

Those in leadership positions must institutionalize a leadership-centered culture, where people value strong leadership and strive to create it. Administrators who wish to create cultures of leadership must begin by demonstrating that they are comfortable with the notion of sharing leadership responsibilities with teachers; communicate the expectation that teachers will serve in leadership capacities; and communicate to teachers that their input, feedback, and professional judgment are both sought and welcomed.

WHAT IS A CULTURE OF LEADERSHIP?

School cultures that value teacher leadership acknowledge the importance of the change process and share the following features and characteristics (Katzenmeyer & Moller, 1996):

1. *A Developmental Focus:* Teachers are supported in learning new knowledge and skills. They are encouraged to facilitate the learning of others.

2. *Recognition:* Teachers are respected and recognized for their professional roles and the contributions they make.

3. *Autonomy:* Teachers are encouraged to take the initiative to make improvements.

4. *Collegiality:* Teachers collaborate on instructional and student-related matters.

5. *Participation:* Teachers are actively involved in making decisions and contributing to important matters.

6. *Open Communication:* Teachers communicate with one another openly and honestly.

7. *Positive Environment:* Teachers experience a positive climate and effective administrative leadership.

PLANNING FOR TEACHER LEADERSHIP DEVELOPMENT

Administrators who facilitate cultures of leadership consciously and purposefully plan for the development of teachers' leadership potential. They create leadership-centered organizational environments and make a concerted effort to identify people with great leadership potential early in their careers and to identify what their development needs are. They then plan for that development and recognize and reward people who successfully develop leaders. These administrators also take responsibility for managing the career patterns of young employees they've identified as having leadership potential (Kotter, 1995).

Prominent leaders often share a number of career experiences, such as a significant challenge early in their career. Later, something else important happens—a lateral career move or an unusually broad job assignment—that broadens their knowledge base. The breadth of knowledge they develop seems to be helpful in all aspects of leadership, as does the network of relationships that they often acquire. Decentralization is the key to creating challenging opportunities for relatively young employees. It pushes responsibility lower in an organization and in the process creates more challenge at lower levels (Kotter, 1995). Unless school districts' organizational hierarchies are flattened, the best and the brightest may be discouraged from entering the teaching field (Coyle, 1997).

EDUCATIONAL VARIABLES THAT SUPPORT OR HINDER TEACHERS' LEADERSHIP DEVELOPMENT

Teacher leadership depends on a supportive organizational culture, is enhanced by gaining a voice in decision making, and is constrained by lack of time and the egalitarian ethic among teachers. Teacher leaders at the elementary, middle, and high school levels share a number of similarities, in spite of the fact that their perceptions of teacher leadership—its activities and responsibilities—differ. For example, teacher leaders at all levels have more years of teaching experience than do nonleaders. They assume leadership roles for personal and professional reasons, as well as for increased involvement in decision making. Teacher leaders are supported by encouraging individuals, decision-making and teaching empowerment, and professional opportunities and are constrained by time, power, and politics. They believe that teacher leadership improves their practice by encouraging collaboration and decision making and advances school improvement efforts by heeding teachers' views and voices (Stone, 1997).

Given the many potential benefits of teacher leadership, it makes sense to identify variables that support its development and those that hinder it. Conditions within the institutional context, conditions outside it, and conditions within teachers themselves can act as sources of support or barriers to teacher leaders. For example, within the institutional context, strong colleague and administrative support can facilitate teacher leaders' development. Principals play a critical role in supporting or hindering teacher leaders. If principals recognize that they can increase their power by sharing it, they will help. However, if they feel threatened and intimidated by teachers who lead, think, and have their own ideas, they will hinder teacher leadership.

Other organizational constraints that can hinder the involvement of teachers in leadership activities include time to meet, how the school day and year are organized, and a lack of opportunities to participate in leadership activities without leaving their students. Outside the institutional context, family and friends often support individual teachers' leadership activities, but family commitments, personal health problems, and other variables can act as barriers that compete with leadership roles (Zinn, 1997).

Teachers themselves can get in the way of their own leadership development. They're concerned about their peers' reactions, afraid of encountering opposition to their ideas, afraid of being criticized, and afraid of standing out—and thereby violating teaching's traditional egalitarian ethic. Somewhere along the line, they've also discovered at least a remnant of truth in the maxim that if you keep your mouth closed and keep moving, you're less likely to get shot at. After all, silent moving targets are more difficult to hit.

A CAUTIONARY WORD ABOUT TEACHER LEADERSHIP

Although most teacher leaders enjoy the challenge of performing two roles, as you might suspect, they sometimes become overwhelmed with the responsibilities of their dual roles. That fact relates to the methods schools use to reward teacher competence. How are teachers rewarded for exemplary performance? Competent teachers are given more responsibility and more work. At some point, the reward becomes a punishment.

For example, an attorney who once taught a course about law and higher education employed a question-asking strategy that resembled cross-examining the opposition's star witness. He would select a victim, stand in close physical proximity to him or her, and proceed to ask his first question. If the victim responded correctly, the attorney asked a second, more challenging question. If the victim answered the second question correctly, the attorney asked a third, even more challenging question. This would continue until the victim responded incorrectly, at which point the attorney would select his next victim and repeat the procedure. The students in the class soon detected this pattern, and in a classic pain-avoidance response learned to answer incorrectly when first questioned by the attorney.

A similar phenomenon occurs in teaching. We call it the "kill the volunteer" syndrome. When people in formal leadership positions discover individuals who repeatedly and consistently perform high-quality work in a timely fashion and with minimal guidance, they wear a path to their doors. They enter their e-mail addresses into their computers and put their phone numbers on speed dial. In short, administrators learn they can rely on those individuals to deliver, and sometimes that reliance becomes overreliance. In worst-case scenarios, high-performing people learn it's best to keep their ideas to themselves rather than risk being rewarded with yet another committee assignment or project to implement.

This "kill the volunteer" phenomenon serves as an example of a negative reward structure—when people are expected to implement tomorrow's organizational values without the necessary preparation to be effective in the new environment. Put another way, someone changes the rules of the game after the game has started but neglects to tell the players that they've changed the rules and what the new rules are.

THE EFFECTS OF CHANGE ON TEACHER LEADERSHIP DEVELOPMENT

Schools and administrators have an obligation to provide planned, organized, systemic professional development for teachers that will enable them to adapt to their changing environment (Patterson, 1993). After all, change cannot simply be mandated; for institutional change to occur, individuals must change. Teachers influence change because they're at the center of the learning process and play a major role in establishing "how we do things here." Consequently, schools can improve only when individual teachers change their behaviors, their attitudes, and their beliefs to take on leadership roles (Fullan, 1993).

For example, inclusion creates opportunities for teachers to function as leaders and decision makers, but it requires a different way of thinking about learning—it involves change. Teachers need to be actively involved in the change process if their behaviors, attitudes, and beliefs regarding inclusion are to change. In Chapter 13, we'll focus on change as a developmental process that individuals participate in and respond to at varying levels and in different ways.

WHEN TO START BECOMING A LEADER AND DECISION MAKER

When should you begin this process of becoming an educational leader and decision maker, in terms of assuming responsibility for your own professional development? Now! A quick review of Chapter 2 will demonstrate that active engagement in your own professional development includes planning, organizing, motivating yourself, and ensuring that your results match your anticipated outcomes. Those processes are all leadership roles.

When should you begin this process of becoming an educational leader and informed decision maker, in terms of assuming responsibility for providing leadership for students? The time to begin is during your first practicum that involves actual teaching. Of course, the teaching/learning process requires you to apply the roles and skills of leadership, which include planning, organizing, motivating, ensuring quality, interpersonal skills, technical skills, and conceptual skills. Remember: If you don't lead in your classroom, someone else will.

As a beginning or novice teacher, can you serve as a teacher leader? It depends. Your first responsibility is to *listen* (you can learn a lot that way) about the school culture, "how we do things here," where the real power and influence lie, and so on. However, teachers new to the field can lead through example—by modeling new practices, participating in new initiatives, using the technical skills they possess, and taking responsibility for their own professional development. We know one teacher who in his second year of teaching became a teacher leader by virtue of his technology expertise. Another teacher we know, a recent graduate, possesses a current knowledge base relating to early childhood and special needs education. This knowledge base, coupled with her willingness to take risks and engage in continuing professional development, resulted in her leading an integrated therapy team composed of experienced education and health care professionals.

APPLYING THE SKILLS AND ROLES OF LEADERSHIP AND DECISION MAKING

In what ways will you as a teacher make use of the leadership and decision-making skills and roles depicted in Figure 3.4? How will you apply interpersonal, technical, and conceptual skills to the teaching/learning process? What contributions will planning, organizing, motivating, and ensuring quality make to your attempts to facilitate instruction? The balance of this book explores plausible answers to these and other related questions. For example, as a teacher, how will you use the roles and skills of leadership and decision making to

Figure 3.4
The Skills and Roles of Leadership and Decision Making

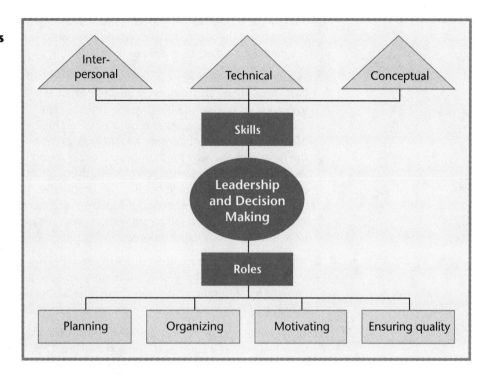

- Identify and analyze the effects of the hidden curriculum on the teaching/learning process?
- Involve learners' parents positively in the teaching/learning process?
- Accommodate learners' individual differences?
- Integrate and create connections across the curriculum?
- Incorporate technology appropriately in the teaching/learning process?
- Anticipate, adapt to, and act on change initiatives?

SUMMARIZING WHAT YOU'VE LEARNED

- Great teachers, like other great leaders, make measurable differences in people's lives. Teaching inherently involves leading and decision making. It's a complex process that requires many leadership skills and decision-making processes, such as setting goals, establishing objectives, selecting and implementing strategies for achieving objectives, evaluating the entire process, and motivating and inspiring reluctant learners.

- Leadership and decision making involve the application of interpersonal, technical, and conceptual skills. Effective leaders apply interpersonal skills when they work with and through people to accomplish organizational goals. They apply technical skills when they appropriately use knowledge, methods, techniques, and equipment to perform specific tasks. They apply conceptual skills when they demonstrate the ability to understand the complexities of the overall organization and where their own operation fits into the organization.

■ Leadership and decision making consist of the four roles of planning, organizing, motivating, and ensuring quality. When leaders engage in the planning role, they set goals and objectives for an organization and develop work maps illustrating how these goals and objectives will be met. When they engage in the organizing role, they integrate resources (such as people, equipment, capital) in the most effective way for the purpose of achieving organizational goals and objectives. When leaders engage in the motivating role, they provide the situations and circumstances people need to be productive. When leaders engage in the role of ensuring quality, they use feedback and results to compare accomplishments with goals, and follow up with appropriate adjustments where outcomes have deviated from expectations.

■ When teachers are willing to develop the skills and assume the roles of leadership, potential payoffs exist for students, schools, and the teachers themselves. Perhaps most significant among those potential benefits is teacher efficacy—the extent to which teachers believe they can affect student learning.

■ Those who occupy formal leadership positions within organizational cultures view teachers as leaders and decision makers. They institutionalize a leadership-centered culture, where people value strong leadership and strive to create it.

YOUR PROFESSIONAL TEACHING PORTFOLIO

■ Reflect on two of your successful leadership experiences. Write a short paper about these experiences. Include at least five attributes that characterize your leadership style.
■ In a small group, create a list of contributions that collaborative decision making can make to effective leadership.

Key Terms

Conceptual skills (p. 64)
Decision making (p. 57)
Interpersonal skills (p. 63)
Leadership (p. 57)

Management (p. 58)
Pedagogy (p. 63)
Situational leadership (p. 61)
Teacher efficacy (p. 71)

Technical skills (p. 63)
Transactional leadership (p. 60)
Transforming leadership (p. 60)

Relevant Resources for Professionals

Books and Articles

- Anderson, S., Rolheiser, C., & Gordon, K. (1998). Preparing teachers to be leaders. *Educational Leadership, 55*(5), 59–61.

- Katzenmeyer, M., & Moller, G. (1996). *Awakening the sleeping giant: Leadership development for teachers.* Thousand Oaks, CA: Corwin Press.

Professional Journals in Education

- *Education Week* on the Web: American Education's On-line Newspaper of Record
  http://www.edweek.org/

- *Leadership Studies Journal*
  http://www.colorado.edu/SLI/LSJ/lsjhome.html

Professional Organizations

- Center for Educational Leadership and Technology. The Center for Educational Leadership and Technology (CELT) is a nonprofit educational service agency whose primary mission is to integrate current education reforms and research with effective uses of technology.
  http://www.celt.org/

- National Foundation for the Improvement of Education.

The National Foundation for the Improvement of Education (NFIE) provides grants and technical assistance to teachers, education support personnel, and higher education faculty and staff to improve student learning in the nation's public schools.
http://www.nfie.org/

- National Staff Development Council. The NSDC's mission is to ensure success for all students by serving as the international network for those who improve schools and by advancing individual and organizational development.
  http://www.nsdc.org/

Web Sites

- **Educational Research Network**
  The Educational Research Network is dedicated to providing easy access to the best print and electronic research information available in education.
  http://www.ernweb.com/

- **A Leadership Guide for Future Leaders**
  This Web site profiles self-management and leadership in private and public sectors.
  http://www.srg.co.uk/index.htm

4

EFFECTIVE TEACHING: KNOWLEDGE, PERFORMANCES, AND DISPOSITIONS

— OR —

Chalk and talk were never enough.

WHAT DO EFFECTIVE TEACHERS LOOK LIKE?

When you recall the best teachers you ever had, your perceptions emerge from some combination of the knowledge base, classroom performances (that is, teaching skills), and dispositions (that is, attitudes) that they displayed on a consistent basis. These three dimensions of teacher competence can be more fully described as follows (Cooper, 1994):

1. *Effective teachers possess a strong knowledge base, both in regard to the subject matter they teach and in regard to pedagogy.* Subject matter knowledge, of course, relates to *what* you teach—the content. Pedagogical knowledge relates to knowing *how* to teach—it involves an understanding of learners, theories of learning, human development, and human behavior.

2. *Effective teachers possess a broad array of teaching skills and the ability to apply them appropriately, and this translates into effective performance in the classroom.* They understand and appreciate the necessity of using a variety of strategies to connect successfully with different learners. Having more than one approach frees teachers from relying on the "plan B" approach of simply repeating whatever they said the first time, only louder and slower.

"What happens in the classroom between people is more important than any assignment, curriculum, procedure, or content. If the people relate to each other in an environment of acceptance and trust, content and competence will grow."

—Children Are People Curriculum

Take a few moments to think about the three best teachers you've ever had, from preschool through your university days. How would you describe these three teachers to others? What was it about them that made them good teachers in your eyes? As you think about these teachers, can you identify any ways in which they were similar? What about ways in which they were different? What specific events do you remember as a learner in their classrooms? How did these experiences differ from those you remember having with teachers you would characterize as the worst you've ever had?

In your teaching journal, write three short paragraphs, each describing one of the three best teachers you have identified. After you write your descriptions, make a list of attributes that characterize these teachers. Share your list of attributes with a group of four or five other preservice teachers. As you share, create an expanded list entitled "Characteristics of Effective Teachers." After you read this chapter, review your list to see how many of the attributes you identified were discussed throughout the chapter.

3. *Effective teachers exhibit a disposition that fosters learning.* Their positive attitude flows from their positive self-image, which allows them to approach students, parents, administrators, colleagues, and their subject matter with the same confident demeanor. Consequently, a warm, welcoming, positive climate permeates effective teachers' classrooms.

CRITICAL COMPETENCIES OF EFFECTIVE TEACHERS

The Interstate New Teacher Assessment and Support Consortium (INTASC), a program of the Council of Chief State School Officers, has crafted model standards for licensing new teachers (1992). These standards define a common core of competencies in regard to knowledge, classroom performances, and attitudes that will help all teachers, both preservice and inservice, in their goal of becoming more effective. An important attribute of these standards is that they are performance-based; that is, they describe what teachers should know and be able to do rather than just list courses teachers must take to become licensed. This shift toward performance-based standards is in line with the National Board for Professional Teaching Standard's approach to developing standards. One of the features of this book, Your Professional Teaching Portfolio, is designed to help you focus on recording and assessing your performance

What do you remember about your best teachers? What was it about them that made them good teachers in your eyes?
(© Elizabeth Crews)

throughout your teacher preparation program. The evidence you compile in your portfolio should focus on showing what you know and can do. Your familiarity with the INTASC standards will help you provide pertinent, convincing documentation of your ability to function as an effective teacher.

You'll read more about the INTASC standards and the National Board for Professional Teaching Standards (NBPTS) in Chapter 12, "Professional Standards for Teaching, Learning, and Curricula." Since the focus of this chapter is on effective teaching, here we share some specific expectations in each of the three key areas: knowledge base, classroom performances (teaching skills), and dispositions (attitudes). As you examine the following expectations, begin thinking about personalizing these competencies: How will you meet these expectations, and what role will they play in your professional development? What goals might you develop to ensure that you emerge from your teacher preparation program an effective teacher?

■ Knowledge Expected of Effective Teachers

The following list of competencies represents some of the INTASC standards related to the knowledge teachers must possess and apply to be effective practitioners:

1. The teacher understands major concepts, assumptions, debates, processes of inquiry, and ways of knowing that are central to the disciplines he or she teaches.

2. The teacher understands that students' physical, social, emotional, moral, and cognitive development influence learning and knows how to address these factors when making instructional decisions.

3. The teacher understands how students' learning is influenced by individual experiences, talents, and prior learning, as well as language, culture, family, and community values.

4. The teacher understands principles and techniques, along with advantages and limitations, associated with various instructional strategies (such as cooperative learning, direct instruction, discovery learning, whole-group discussion, independent study, interdisciplinary instruction).

5. The teacher uses knowledge about human motivation and behavior drawn from the foundational sciences of psychology, anthropology, and sociology to develop strategies for organizing and supporting individual and group work.

6. The teacher understands communication theory, language development, and the role of language in learning.

7. The teacher understands learning theory, the subject matter he or she teaches, curriculum development, and human development and knows how to use this knowledge in planning instruction to meet curriculum goals.

8. The teacher understands the characteristics, uses, advantages, and limitations of different types of assessments (such as criterion-referenced and norm-referenced instruments, traditional standardized and performance-based tests, observation systems, and assessments of student work) for evaluating how students learn, what they know, and what they are able to do, and what kinds of experiences will support their further growth and development.

9. The teacher is aware of major areas of research on teaching and resources available for professional learning (such as professional literature, colleagues, professional associations, and professional development activities).

10. The teacher understands schools as organizations within the larger community context and understands the operations of the relevant aspects of the system within which he or she works. (INTASC, 1992)

■ Performance and Skills Expected of Effective Teachers

The following list of competencies represents some of the INTASC standards related to the classroom **performances** or teaching skills teachers must display and apply as effective practitioners.

1. The teacher creates interdisciplinary learning experiences that allow students to integrate knowledge, skills, and methods of inquiry from several subject areas.

2. The teacher assesses individual and group performance to design instruction that meets learners' current needs in each domain (cognitive, social, emotional, moral, and physical) and that leads to the next level of development.

3. The teacher creates a learning community in which individual differences are respected.

4. The teacher varies his or her role in the instructional process (such as instructor, facilitator, coach, audience) in relation to the content and purposes of instruction and the needs of students.

5. The teacher analyzes the classroom environment and makes decisions and adjustments to enhance social relationships, student motivation and engagement, and productive work.

6. The teacher knows how to use a variety of media communication tools, including audiovisual aids and computers, to enrich learning opportunities.

7. The teacher creates lessons and activities that operate at multiple levels to meet the developmental and individual needs of diverse learners and to help each progress.

8. The teacher maintains useful records of student work and performance and can communicate student progress knowledgeably and responsibly, based on appropriate indicators, to students, parents, and other colleagues.

9. The teacher seeks out professional literature, colleagues, and other resources to support his or her own development as a learner and a teacher.

10. The teacher participates in collegial activities designed to make the entire school a productive learning environment.

■ Dispositions or Attitudes Expected of Effective Teachers

The following list of competencies represents some of the INTASC standards related to the dispositions or attitudes teachers must display as effective practitioners.

1. The teacher realizes that subject matter knowledge is not a fixed body of facts but is complex and ever-evolving. He or she seeks to keep abreast of new ideas and understandings in the field.

2. The teacher is disposed to use students' strengths as a basis for growth and their errors as an opportunity for learning.

3. The teacher appreciates and values human diversity, shows respect for students' varied talents and perspectives, and is committed to the pursuit of "individually configured excellence."

4. The teacher values the development of students' critical thinking, independent problem solving, and performance capabilities.

5. The teacher takes responsibility for establishing a positive climate in the classroom and participates in maintaining such a climate in the school as a whole.

6. The teacher values many ways in which people seek to communicate and encourages many modes of communication in the classroom.

7. The teacher values both long-term and short-term planning.

8. The teacher values ongoing assessment as being essential to the instructional process and recognizes that many different assessment strategies, accurately and systematically used, are necessary for monitoring and promoting student learning.

9. The teacher recognizes his or her professional responsibility for engaging in and supporting appropriate professional practices for himself or herself and for his or her colleagues.

10. The teacher is concerned about all aspects of a child's well-being (cognitive, emotional, social, and physical) and is alert to signs of difficulties.

The INTASC standards and competencies emerged from five major philosophical and professional tenets:

- Teachers are committed to students and their learning.
- Teachers know the subjects they teach and know how to teach those subjects to diverse learners.
- Teachers are responsible for managing and monitoring student learning.
- Teachers think systematically about their practice and learn from experience.
- Teachers are members of learning communities.

Keep these tenets, and the competencies that have emerged from them, in mind as you continue focusing on your professional development goals.

CHARACTERISTICS OF EFFECTIVE TEACHERS

Although the lists of effective-teacher characteristics you will encounter in your teacher preparation program might at times seem endless, remember that every item on every list relates somehow to one of the three dimensions of teaching competence: knowledge, classroom performance or teaching skills, and dispositions or attitudes. We encourage you to use those dimensions as a means of helping you organize and analyze the compilation of effective-teacher characteristics presented in Figure 4.1.

PRINCIPLES OF EFFECTIVE TEACHING AND LEARNING

To function as an effective teacher, you must serve as an educational leader and informed decision maker, acknowledge and provide for the **whole learner** (including social, emotional, physical, and cognitive dimensions), encourage student collaboration, and apply best-practice principles. As you do so, you'll discover that each of these principles underpins many of the effective-teacher competencies discussed earlier in this chapter.

Figure 4.1
Characteristics of Effective Teachers

Effective teachers:

1. Take personal responsibility for students' learning and communicate high but reasonable expectations for all learners.
2. Match the difficulty of the lesson with the developmental level of their students and vary the difficulty when necessary so learners can attain moderate to high success rates.
3. Structure lessons to let learners know what is expected of them and what procedures to follow.
4. Plan and provide developmentally appropriate instruction that facilitates on-task, engaged learning.
5. Provide learners with mental strategies for organizing and learning the concepts being taught.
6. Gradually shift some of the responsibility for learning to their students—encouraging independent thinking, problem solving, and decision making.
7. Implement a variety of instructional materials and verbal and visual aids to foster use of student ideas and engagement in the learning process.
8. Present material in small steps, with opportunities for students to practice newly learned concepts and to receive timely feedback on their performance.
9. Maximize instructional time to provide students with the greatest opportunity to learn.
10. Monitor learners' independent work, checking on their progress and providing appropriate feedback to maintain a high level of student engagement with the task at hand.
11. Pace instruction appropriately to match learners' individual needs.
12. Use naturally occurring classroom dialogue to encourage students to elaborate, extend, and comment on the concepts and skills they are learning.
13. Ask questions that require learners to analyze, synthesize, or evaluate; expect answers at the same levels as the questions; and wait a minimum of three seconds for students to respond to questions.
14. Elicit responses from learners each time a question is asked before moving to the next question.
15. Capitalize on the instructional and motivational use of assessment and evaluation.
16. Provide an organized, friendly, emotionally and physically safe learning environment that promotes intelligent risk taking and creativity.

(Adapted from Berliner, 1985; Borich, 1996)

■ The Effective Teacher as Decision Maker

In Chapter 3, "Teachers as Leaders and Decision Makers," you explored with us the concept of teachers as leaders. Recall from that discussion that effective teachers are continuously engaged in the processes of leading and decision making. As a teacher, you will make critical decisions every day. The decisions that you make must be dynamic and must serve to integrate your knowledge of a variety of disciplines while building bridges between your students, their families, your community, and the curriculum. As a professional, you will be responsible for planning and pursuing your own ongoing learning, for reflecting with colleagues on your practice and theirs, and for contributing to the profession's knowledge base. Your ability to make decisions and to follow through on them will empower you to be an effective teacher.

■ Acknowledging and Providing for the Whole Learner

Building on a premise we've already introduced, we acknowledge that effective education emphasizes affective education and that affective education acknowledges the whole learner—his or her attitudes, values, and emotions as well as social, physical, and cognitive development. Therefore, learning has the potential of being most effective when it occurs "in wholes" rather than in disjointed, decontextualized parts. What does that mean? It means that students need more of the real world in their learning and less of the compartmentalized, the trivialized, and the standardized. It means that students should read "real" books and talk to "real" people to discover answers to their own questions. (They can, for example, surf the Web to find out what other learners around the world are doing to get involved in conservation efforts.) It means that effective teachers can and do provide their students with viable alternatives to reading the next chapter in the social studies textbook, answering the questions at the end of the chapter, and completing the next two worksheets in the series.

Effective teaching and learning occur when

- *Learners have opportunities to apply what they are learning in authentic ways.* Effective learning opportunities are real to students and have meaning that extends beyond the school context (such as exploring real ecological problems in their community versus completing a worksheet on ecosystems).

- *The social nature of learning is valued.* Effective teachers provide learning opportunities that emphasize cooperation rather than competition; they not only tolerate students' talking to one another, they acknowledge it as one way in which students learn.

- *Learners have some control over what, when, and how they learn.* Effective teachers build in opportunities for student choice (such as "You may decide which one of these three projects you'd like to complete.").

- *Learners have the opportunity to* **reflect** *on what they're learning.* Effective teachers invite students to think about learning processes as well as learning outcomes and to analyze their own thinking as well as their own performance (Hornstein, 1992).

■ Students Working Collaboratively

Community engagement is one way to provide **holistic, authentic, collaborative learning experiences** for students, in which the community becomes a resource for students to use in creating knowledge and constructing meaning for themselves. For example, if your second graders, during the course of their unit on water, wonder aloud about how safe their water is to drink, you could help them develop a plan for finding out about the quality of their community's water supply. That plan might include researching exactly where the tap water they drink comes from, interviewing people at the waterworks, collecting and testing water samples, and figuring out how best to present the results of their investigation.

If you attempted to present each skill as a separate and isolated component disconnected from the context that the students provided (safety of drinking water), those skills no longer would have as much purpose or meaning for the students. For example, students might learn how to prepare for and conduct interviews, but they'd have no authentic purpose for using these skills.

■ Principles of Best Practice

Zemelman, Daniels, and Hyde's thirteen **principles of best practice** (1998) provide a synopsis of what researchers and practitioners know about effective teaching and learning (see Figure 4.2). If you're familiar with the work of John Dewey, an individual whom you assuredly discussed in your Introduction to Education course, perhaps you'll recognize what Zemelman, Daniels, and Hyde readily acknowledge—what they have dubbed best practice has its origins in Dewey's Progressive Education Association and his theory of "learning by doing." Embedded throughout these thirteen principles is a focus on the whole learner that includes provisions for social, emotional, cognitive, and physical development. As you analyze teaching—whether your own or someone else's—we encourage you to use these principles as benchmarks. Our contention is that the more elements of best practice you can identify in a particular teaching scenario, the more likely it is that learning is being effectively facilitated.

THE CRITICAL ROLE OF TEACHER PREPARATION

Building on another premise we've already introduced, we acknowledge that what teachers know and can do is the most important influence on what students learn. This brings us back to the notion of recruiting, preparing, and retaining competent teachers as the central strategy for improving schools and making teaching more effective. School reform so conceived cannot succeed, however, unless it focuses on creating conditions in which such teachers can teach well. How can U.S. education reach the goal of reforming schools by focusing on teacher quality? The National Commission on Teaching and America's Future (1996) offers the following recommendations:

1. Get serious about standards for both students and teachers.
2. Reinvent teacher preparation and professional development.

Figure 4.2
Principles of Best Practice

Learning experiences should be

1. *Student centered.* The best starting point for schooling is students' real interests; all across the curriculum, investigating students' own questions always should take precedence over studying arbitrarily and distantly selected content.

2. *Experiential.* Active, hands-on, concrete experience is the most powerful and natural form of learning. Students should be immersed in the most direct possible experience of the content of every subject.

3. *Holistic.* Students learn best when they encounter whole, real ideas, events, and materials in purposeful contexts, not by studying isolated, out-of-context parts.

4. *Authentic.* Real, rich, complex ideas and materials are at the heart of the curriculum. Lessons or textbooks that water down, control, or oversimplify content ultimately disempower students.

5. *Expressive.* Students must use the entire range of communicative media to fully engage ideas, construct meaning, and remember information. They need opportunities and invitations to express themselves through speech, writing, drawing, poetry, drama, dance, music, movement, and visual arts.

6. *Reflective.* Balancing the immersion in direct experience must be opportunities for learners to look back, reflect, debrief, and abstract from their experiences what they have felt, thought, and learned.

7. *Social.* Learning is always socially constructed and often interactional; teachers need to create classroom interactions that "scaffold" learning.

8. *Collaborative.* Cooperative learning activities tap the social power of learning better than competitive and individualistic approaches do.

9. *Democratic.* The classroom is a model community; students learn what they live as citizens of the school.

10. *Cognitive.* The most powerful learning for students comes from developing true understanding of concepts and higher-order thinking associated with various fields of inquiry and self-monitoring of their thinking.

11. *Developmental.* Learners grow through a series of definable but not rigid stages, and schooling should fit its activities to the developmental levels of students.

12. *Constructivist.* Learners do not just receive content; in a very real sense, they re-create and reinvent every cognitive system they encounter, including language, literacy, and mathematics.

13. *Challenging.* Students learn best when faced with genuine challenges, choices, and responsibility in their own learning.

(Zemelman, Daniels, & Hyde, 1998, p. 8)

3. Focus on teacher recruitment and put qualified teachers in every classroom.

4. Encourage and reward teacher knowledge and skill.

5. Create schools that are organized for learner and teacher success.

EFFECTIVE TEACHING: BECOMING EMOTIONALLY LITERATE

How can you make critical decisions about the norms, values, and behaviors that will shape and color your teaching? We suggest that you begin with some introspection. Focus on your emotional health and your ability to create a classroom community that consistently supports and nurtures appropriate norms, values, and behaviors. We call this ability **emotional literacy.**

WHAT IS EMOTIONAL LITERACY?

The question of what emotional literacy is can be answered, at least in part, by assessing the costs of emotional *illiteracy*. One in five children in the United States lives in extreme poverty—a ratio that has doubled since 1975. Substantiated cases of child abuse or neglect and the homicide rate for teens also have risen (Goleman, 1995). As more and more parents find themselves unable to deal with the demands of parenting in today's world, more and more children are experiencing abuse, neglect, and violence. Add teen pregnancy, eating disorders, drug and alcohol abuse, depression, and mental illness to the litany of risk factors, and you can see that both parents and schools face depressing new challenges. When parents and care providers of young children fail to help children develop skills for identifying and coping with stress, emotional illiteracy thrives.

Attempts to address emotional illiteracy must begin with an understanding of what emotional literacy involves. Although a comprehensive definition of emotional literacy seems difficult to compose, Goleman (1995) provides some direction with his definition of what he calls **emotional intelligence.** According to Goleman, having emotional intelligence means

- Being able to identify, express, and manage one's feelings
- Being self-aware
- Being able to control one's impulses and delay gratification
- Being able to handle stress and anxiety
- Being able to read social and emotional cues
- Being able to listen
- Being able to resist negative influences
- Being able to take the perspective of another
- Understanding what behavior is acceptable in a certain situation

Recent research results (Pool, 1997) identify emotional well-being as the strongest predictor of achievement in school and on the job. Unfortunately, today's children are down on all indicators of emotional health. Since emo-

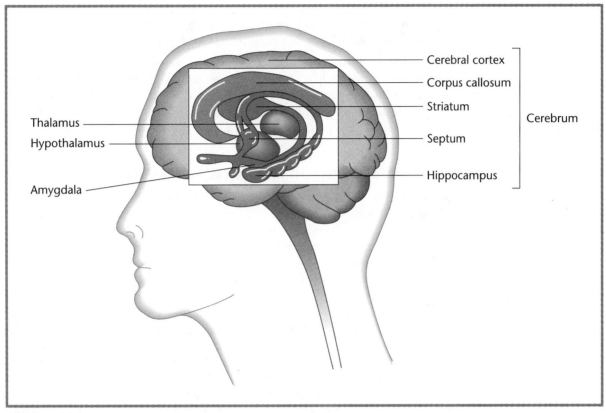

Figure 4.3
Illustration of the Limbic Brain

tional well-being is so critical to success in school and life, teachers must develop responsive learning environments and curricula that support and promote emotional well-being.

WHAT IS THE EMOTIONAL BRAIN?

Understanding the **emotional brain** and how it functions can inform teachers' efforts to enhance learners' emotional literacy. The limbic brain, which is situated between the cortex and the brain stem, controls emotions (see Figure 4.3). In the middle of the limbic area, behind the eyes, are two **amygdalae.** Recent neurological research indicates that these almond-shaped organs receive and send all emotional messages. Of course, nothing in the brain occurs in isolation; the amygdalae are constantly communicating with the cortex, the part of the brain that controls analytical and verbal tasks and where working memory resides (Goleman, 1995):

> *The emotional brain scans everything happening to us from moment to moment, to see if something that happened in the past that made us sad or angry is like what is happening now. If so, the amygdala calls an alarm—to declare an emergency and mobilize in a split second to act. And it can do so, in brain time,*

more rapidly than the thinking brain takes to figure out what is going on, which is why people can get into a rage and do something very inappropriate that they wished they hadn't. It's an emotional hijacking. (Pool, 1997, p. 13)

Analytical thinking is always influenced by emotions. However, people who have mature, healthy connections can control their responses to the messages from the amygdalae. Everyone gets angry, but not everyone acts violently when they get angry. People who are chronically sad, angry, or anxious experience constant interference by the amygdalae; it's hard for them to concentrate and to learn.

WHAT SKILLS ARE ESSENTIAL TO EMOTIONAL LITERACY?

Neglecting the emotional brain can have negative consequences for both your students and you (Goleman, 1995). To face life's challenges and come out on top, children and adolescents need opportunities to develop skills and strategies that will support their emotional health. They need to acquire competencies in the following five dimensions of emotional literacy (Pool, 1997): self-awareness, handling emotions, motivation, empathy, and social skills.

■ Self-Awareness

To become self-aware, children need to learn at a young age what feelings are, why they feel the way they do, and what sorts of actions they can take in response to their feelings. Consider, for example, the OK Bear Touches Program that operates in the Midwest. This program focuses on helping children identify bad touches from good touches. Children talk about their fears, discuss why they're afraid of certain touches, and actually practice saying no to adults that they fear may touch them in inappropriate ways.

■ Handling Emotions

Recent research has focused on impulsiveness and violence (Pool, 1997). The social consequences of impulsiveness are far-reaching for students. Boys who are impulsive as four-year-olds are three to six times more likely to be violent by adolescence. Girls who are impulsive as four-year-olds are three times more likely to get pregnant during adolescence. Visualize the following "Marshmallow Test" in progress:

Four-year-old kids from the Stanford University preschool are the subjects. The experimenter puts a marshmallow in front of each kid and says: "You could have this marshmallow now, if you want, but if you wait until I run an errand, and don't eat it until I get back, you can have two then." The videotaped results are hilarious. Some kids go up to the marshmallow, smell it, then leap back like it's dangerous. Some go off in a corner and sing and dance to distract themselves. Some kids just grab it. About a third of the kids grab it and eat it, about a third wait just a while, and the rest wait an endless 10 minutes until the experimenter comes back, and they get two. (Pool, 1997, p. 13)

When researchers revisited these children sixteen years later (at age twenty), the "grabbers" were still impulsive, quick to anger, and not very popular. The waiters were popular and well-balanced emotionally. But the most astonishing finding was that the "waiters" had higher scores on their SATs than the "grabbers"—by a full 210 points!

As you reflect on your childhood, do you think you would fit the "grabber" or the "waiter" category? What impact has your impulsiveness, or lack of it, had on your development? How will this affect you as a future teacher?

■ Motivation

Motivation involves hope and the ability to follow through when an individual settles on a goal. As we discussed in Chapter 2, goal setting is a critical dimension of your professional development. Goal setting, motivation, and the persistence to follow through on a goal by taking the small, manageable steps that are needed to realize goals are important for teachers, as well as for students. How can you teach and transmit hope to your students? The modeling you will provide is eminently important.

■ Empathy

Empathy is reading other people's feelings by assessing their tone of voice or their facial expression. Children are naturally empathetic if they have been nurtured. Two-year-olds from a loving family will try to comfort a friend who is crying, but young children who have been abused or neglected in the first years of life tend to yell at or hit crying children (Goleman, 1995).

■ Social Skills

All children need opportunities to develop appropriate social skills in the context of a caring community, both at school and at home. Relationships with peers, as well as relationships with adults, provide the building blocks for healthy relationships as children embark on adolescence. Those who have not developed social competence by the age of six will be at risk for the rest of their lives. Waiting until children have reached the age of eleven to intervene makes

Children are naturally empathetic if they have been nurtured themselves.
(© Susie Fitzhugh)

Figure 4.4.
Emotional Intelligence: Key Social and Emotional Skills

1. **Self-Awareness**
   - Recognizing and naming one's emotions
   - Understanding the reasons and circumstances for feeling as one does
2. **Self-Regulation of Emotion**
   - Verbalizing and coping with anxiety, anger, and depression
   - Controlling impulses, aggression, and self-destructive, antisocial behavior
3. **Self-Monitoring and Performance**
   - Focusing on tasks at hand
   - Setting short- and long-term goals
   - Modifying performance in light of feedback
   - Mobilizing positive motivation
   - Activating hope and optimism
   - Working toward optimal performance states; managing the relationship between anxiety and performance
4. **Empathy and Perspective Taking**
   - Learning how to increase these capabilities and how to develop feedback mechanisms to use in everyday life
   - Becoming a good listener
   - Increasing empathy and sensitivity to others' feelings
   - Understanding others' perspectives and feelings
5. **Social Skills in Handling Relationships**
   - Managing emotions in relationships and harmonizing diverse feelings and viewpoints
   - Expressing emotions effectively
   - Exercising assertiveness, leadership, persuasion
   - Working as part of a cooperative learning group
   - Showing sensitivity to social cues
   - Exercising social decision-making and problem-solving skills
   - Responding constructively and in a problem-solving manner to interpersonal obstacles

(Elias, et al., 1997, p. 30)

it virtually impossible to break negative patterns of social interaction (L. G. Katz, personal communication, June 6, 1995).

WHAT DO SOCIAL AND EMOTIONAL COMPETENCE LOOK LIKE?

The synopsis of key social and emotional skills in Figure 4.4 summarizes the five dimensions of emotional intelligence and suggests specific behaviors and skills that support each dimension. Teachers and parents should focus on providing a number of opportunities to help children and adolescents develop these behaviors and skills, because these behaviors and skills will facilitate a child's acquisition of social competence.

WHEN DOES EMOTIONAL LITERACY BEGIN?

Researchers have pondered various pieces of the emotional literacy puzzle, including the origin or source of emotional literacy. For example, some researchers have focused on the importance of developing dispositions for learning (Katz, 1993). **Dispositions** are habits of mind or tendencies to respond to certain situations in certain ways. Curiosity, friendliness or unfriendliness, bossiness, and creativity are all examples of dispositions that parents and teachers can strengthen or diminish by setting learning goals for children.

CHILDREN AND EMOTIONAL LITERACY

For young children, lessons in empathy begin in infancy. A University of Washington team found that when parents are emotionally adept, their children get along better, show more affection toward their parents, and experience less tension with their parents. These children also are better at controlling their own emotions, are more effective at soothing themselves when they become upset, and get upset less often. In addition to these positive emotional outcomes, children of emotionally adept parents are also more relaxed biologically, with lower levels of stress hormones and other physiological indicators of emotional arousal. This constitutes a pattern that, if sustained throughout life, might well enhance physical health. Other advantages are social; these children are more popular with, and better liked by, their peers and are seen by their teachers as more socially skilled. Parents and teachers alike rate such children as having fewer behavioral problems such as rudeness or aggressiveness (Goleman, 1995).

Because the first four years of children's emotional experiences hold significant consequences for their emotional literacy, parents, in particular, need to understand how their actions can help generate the confidence, curiosity, pleasure in learning, and understanding of limits that help children succeed in life. Children who cannot focus their attention, are suspicious rather than trusting, are sad or angry rather than optimistic, are destructive rather than respectful, are overcome with anxiety, are preoccupied with frightening fantasies, and are generally unhappy about themselves will have little opportunity at all—let alone an equal opportunity compared with their peers—to claim the possibilities of the world as their own (Brazelton, 1992).

Toddlers and preschoolers throughout the country exhibit the seeds of emotional ineptitude. Compare the following vignette, taken from child care observations and findings (Goleman, 1995), to a situation you may have experienced:

> *In the rough-and-tumble play of the day care center, Martin, just two and a half, brushed up against a little girl, who began to cry. He reached for her hand, but when the sobbing girl moved away, he slapped her on the arm. As her tears continued, Martin looked away and yelled, "Cut it out! Cut it out!" over and over, each time faster and louder. When Martin made another attempt to pat the girl's*

hand, she resisted again. This time he bared his teeth like a snarling dog and hissed at the sobbing girl. Then Martin started patting the crying girl, but the pats on the back quickly turned into pounding. He went on hitting the little girl, despite her screams.

Abusive patterns of behavior modeled by parents and caregivers are indelibly carved into the hearts and minds of children like Martin. Children, of course, treat others the way they have been treated. This vignette portrays an empathy that quickly sours into abuse. This child, who seems to lack the most primitive sort of empathy, has learned this behavior from a parent or caregiver who harbors the aggression brought on by emotional illiteracy. How many times must people witness similar scenarios played out in the lives of young children, whether at home, in caregiving situations, or in educational programs, before they understand that emotional literacy must become a priority if there is to be any hope of reversing the spiraling incidence of abuse, neglect, and violence in this country?

DEVELOPING AND ASSESSING EMOTIONAL LITERACY

Little is gained if parents, teachers, and caregivers only assess the emotional literacy of children and adolescents. To produce positive change, they also must plan and implement both prevention and intervention strategies. We begin with the obvious—but sometimes overlooked—point that prevention is preferable to intervention. When learners with inappropriate emotional responses are simply removed from the learning situation, they may no longer have the opportunity to unlearn inappropriate responses and learn appropriate ones. Consequently, the optimal goal is to facilitate the development of emotional literacy, beginning at infancy and continuing throughout adolescence and into adulthood.

FACILITATING LEARNERS' DEVELOPMENT OF EMOTIONAL LITERACY

How can teachers facilitate learners' acquisition of emotional literacy? "Raising Healthy Children" is a five-phase staff development program that focuses on key teacher competencies (Cummings & Hagerty, 1997) needed to promote emotional literacy among students. As you review the program's phases and topics, you'll recognize many of the skills for social and emotional learning that we discussed earlier in this chapter.

Topic One: Proactive Classroom Management. During the first phase of the staff development program, teachers learn how to help students become self-managers who can regulate their own behavior and monitor their learning.

Topic Two: Motivating At-Risk Learners. During the second phase of the program, teachers learn how to help students develop strategies that promote success. Students set weekly goals and complete daily reports on the progress they make toward achieving those goals.

Topic Three: Teaching Social Skills. Throughout the third phase, teachers learn strategies for direct instruction in both intrapersonal and interpersonal skills. For example, they may have students role-play difficult situations to increase their personal repertoire of appropriate responses, or they may have students display compliment trees on the bulletin board to help them learn how to give and receive compliments.

Topic Four: Teaching Strategies. As they move into the fourth phase, teachers learn strategies for maximizing student involvement. These include cooperative learning exercises where students practice social and emotional skills by working together.

Topic Five: Reading Instruction. During the final phase, teachers learn how to integrate social and emotional learning with literature instruction (such as teaching self-awareness and empathy through character trait analysis).

INSTRUCTIONAL STRATEGIES FOR PROMOTING SOCIAL AND EMOTIONAL LEARNING

As the preceding section implies, efforts to facilitate learners' acquisition of emotional literacy benefit from planning and from systematic approaches. As we discuss in much greater detail in Chapter 9, using a variety of instructional approaches is critical to successful teaching and learning. The same holds true for attempts to provide emotional and social learning opportunities. Consider the following strategies for promoting social and emotional learning in your classroom (Elias, et al., 1997):

Storytelling and biography	Self-reflection and goal setting
Group discussion	Artistic expression
Rehearsal and practice (role-playing)	Play
Self-awareness and self-regulation	Cooperative and small-group learning

As a result of our many years of teaching experience, we have become familiar with, and excited about, children's literature and have utilized it in our teaching for a number of years. We've also discovered that preservice teachers are able to apply many of the concepts we discuss in class more effectively when they have a tool, such as an appropriate piece of literature, that provides a context for doing so. Therefore, in the following section we include some literature-based activities for each of the teaching strategies just listed.

However, first we feel the need to emphasize two basic, but sometimes overlooked, points for you to remember when using literature-based instructional strategies:

- The books, stories, and poems you select should be examples of high-quality literature. In Chapter 10 we discuss criteria to guide your selection of literature.

- Picture books are not just for young children. Books such as Judith Viorst's *Alexander and the Terrible, Horrible, No Good, Very Bad Day* (1972), Jon Scieszka and Lane Smith's *Math Curse* (1995), and Ann McGovern's *The Lady in the Box* (1997) can be revisited and used effectively at many different grade levels and with a variety of learners.

STORYTELLING AND BIOGRAPHY

Ask intermediate or middle school students to create time lines of their lives, from the day of their birth to their present grade in school. They can create these time lines by interviewing family members and choosing favorite photographs that help the students focus on major events in their lives. After they have created the time lines, ask the students to write autobiographies that include the major events featured on their time lines. Students also could illustrate or dramatize their autobiographies. Then, read a biography aloud to the whole class. Some biographies for your consideration are Adler's *A Picture Book of Martin Luther King* (1991), Lown's *Langston Hughes* (1997), and Freedman's *Lincoln: A Photobiography* (1989). Engage students in comparing and contrasting their autobiographies with the biography that you select to share in class. Discuss how the individual featured in the biography is an exemplar of certain social and emotional skills or attributes.

GROUP DISCUSSION

Group discussion provides opportunities for students of all ages to learn how to express themselves and their points of view in socially appropriate manners. Just as important, group discussion helps individuals learn to listen attentively, critically, and empathetically and to show others that they are listening to them (by eye contact, reflective listening, relevant questions, and so on). Books that feature particular issues can function as vehicles for launching group discussions. *Just Plain Fancy* by Patricia Polacco (1990) and *The Witch of Blackbird Pond* by Elizabeth George Speare (1958) are examples of books that focus on particular groups of people. Polacco's book provides a window into the Amish culture and the practice of shunning, whereas Speare's time-tested classic takes readers back to the New England of the Puritans and the manner in which they dealt with diversity and differences.

REHEARSAL AND PRACTICE (ROLE PLAYING)

Just as rehearsal, practice, and role playing provide opportunities for learners to engage in what-if and if-then kinds of thinking, the characters they read about allow them to experience different situations from a risk-free place of safety. For example, George Orwell's *Animal Farm* (1946) provides a context against which secondary students can inventory their own leadership skills and wonder aloud about the kinds of leaders they are—or would be—in different situations.

SELF-AWARENESS AND SELF-REGULATION

Individuals who are in tune with their own emotional needs and dispositions often can accurately predict how they will respond or react in particular situations. That ability proves advantageous to their attempts to monitor their emotions and avoid strong displays of emotion that may be inappropriate in particular contexts (such as yelling during a religious service) or in any context (such as hitting or hurting others to express anger).

Literature can serve as one way for individuals to become aware of their own attitudes, feelings, opinions, perspectives, and biases.
(© Susie Fitzhugh)

Literature can serve as one way for individuals to become aware of their own attitudes, feelings, opinions, perspectives, and biases. For instance, *Encounter* by Jane Yolen (1992) offers a retelling of Columbus's "discovery" of America from a Native American's point of view. Yolen's story invites readers and listeners to consider the possibility that not everything about Columbus's feat was positive and that perhaps little about his "discovery" was positive for the people whose land he discovered.

The title character in *Wilfrid Gordon McDonald Partridge* by Mem Fox (1985) becomes aware that, even though he's very young, he has something to offer a much older friend. Wilfrid lives next door to a retirement home, and he often visits with many of the people who live there. One of his particularly good friends has trouble remembering things, so Wilfrid figures out a way to help her find her memories. En route to doing so, Wilfrid reminds readers that they have something to offer others as well—even if they haven't yet discovered what that is.

Meg, Charles Wallace, and Calvin—the main characters in *A Wrinkle in Time* by Madeleine L'Engle (1962)—are given the task of turning their weaknesses into strengths so they can use those strengths to help them find their way back home. To do that, they must first become aware of what their weaknesses are, and Meg, in particular, must learn to control her anger and impulsiveness. Through the experiences of its main characters, this entry in L'Engle's Time Trilogy offers several insights related to the topics of self-awareness and self-regulation.

SELF-REFLECTION AND GOAL SETTING

Begin by reading aloud to your upper-primary or intermediate-level students Hoffman's book *Boundless Grace* (1995), which is the sequel to *Amazing Grace*. *Boundless Grace* is a story about a child who lives with her mother—a divorced,

African American single parent. Grace, who is angry about not having a dad like her friends do, is invited to go to Africa to visit her father. When she embarks on this journey, Grace encounters a stepmother and stepsiblings, as well as an unfamiliar, but intriguing, culture.

Ask students to write in their reflection journals at least three feelings that Grace shared during the story. Then, ask them to write about times in their lives when they have had the same feelings (that is, anger, frustration, disappointment, jealousy). Invite students to share their journals with one person they trust (it may be you) and to ask that person to write a short note in their journals. Finally, suggest that the students write one goal or action plan for dealing with a specific feeling that they have had.

ARTISTIC EXPRESSION

Just as there are several forms of artistic expression, there are several books that feature artistic expression. Two of our favorites are *Emily* by Michael Bedard (1992), which features music and poetry, and *Nutcracker Noel* by Kate McMullan (1993), which, as the title implies, features ballet. Both books focus on their main characters' experiences with, and responses to, the types of artistic expression featured, and both books invite a response from their readers.

Of course, picture books are themselves a vehicle for artistic expression of the visual sort. You can guide learners' comparisons of one illustrator's work in several different books and formats. Chris Van Allsburg's *The Polar Express* (1985), *Two Bad Ants* (1988), *The Widow's Broom* (1992), and *The Wretched Stone* (1991) and Jon Scieszka and Lane Smith's *Math Curse* (1995) and *The Stinky Cheese Man and Other Fairly Stupid Tales* (1992) lend themselves to this purpose. Readers also can compare and contrast the styles and media used by different illustrators in a variety of contexts.

PLAY

All children know how to play, don't they? We still remember the time we observed this interaction between a couple of three-year-olds: Pointing to a table, one warned the other, "Don't touch the stove! It's hot." Without hesitation, the other promptly laid her hand on the table and proclaimed contemptuously, "No, it's not!" Apparently she had missed the day trip to Mr. Rogers's Land of Make Believe.

Whereas some children fail to grasp the concept of pretending or will wait for something or someone else to entertain them instead of finding some way to entertain themselves, other children may engage in play that is harmful to themselves or to others. Then there are the children, of all ages, whose perpetual lament is, "I'm bored. There's nothing to do around here." Aside from asking these "bored" individuals what they can do to improve their own plight, as a teacher you can turn to books that provide examples of different kinds of play—examples that then can provoke discussion regarding the appropriateness of the play featured in the books.

Perhaps one of the most classic examples of a book that features play is Dr. Seuss's *The Cat in the Hat* (1957). Ask students what they would have done if

Thing 1 and Thing 2 had paid a visit to them. Another example of play taken a bit too far is Konigsburg's *From the Mixed-Up Files of Mrs. Basil E. Frankweiler* (1967). Konigsburg tells the story of a brother and sister whose cure for boredom includes an unscheduled and unchaperoned trip to New York City with no return tickets.

COOPERATIVE AND SMALL-GROUP LEARNING

Several books feature the collaboration and teamwork central to cooperative and small-group learning. Included among our favorites are *Mrs. Katz and Tush* by Patricia Polacco (1992), *The Patchwork Quilt* by Valerie Flournoy (1996), and *The View from Saturday* by E. L. Konigsburg (1996).

Polacco tells the story of an African American family that sort of "adopts" Mrs. Katz after her husband dies. Mrs. Katz lives alone with her cat Tush and enjoys having a family with whom to share her Jewish customs and holidays. Working together, they all learn something about each other and about themselves.

Flournoy tells the story of a quilt that, in turn, tells one African American family's story. The quilt provides a pictorial family history that is the result of a collective and collaborative labor of love.

Finally, Konigsburg tells the story of four very different middle school students who are brought together by one very different teacher. They learn to work together as a problem-solving team, and in that process also learn to appreciate their differences as strengths.

WHY SHOULD TEACHERS BE CONCERNED ABOUT THEIR OWN EMOTIONAL LITERACY?

Although the research on emotional literacy has far-reaching implications for parent education and the creation of caring communities, the focus here is on your role as a preservice and inservice teacher. As the number of women in the work force continues to increase and the number of children needing both care and education continues to overwhelm a country whose first national education goal is that all children entering school be ready to learn, teacher educators must take very seriously the professional preparation of teachers in the area of emotional literacy. If emotional literacy is the backing that must be woven to support the richness of each individual's tapestry, then teacher educators must ask, How are we preparing teachers for this critical task? What goals are being established to develop the emotional literacy of teachers?

Although teacher educators have long recognized the importance of developing both teachers' and students' affective dimensions, this goal often is overshadowed by the emphasis on students' cognitive dimensions that dominates educational programs. One explanation for this domination is simply that it's easier to teach and assess skills and knowledge that are directly demonstrable or that contain elements that can be objectively measured. For example, learners can demonstrate in very tangible ways their knowledge of the Louisiana Purchase or their ability to write a business letter. However, often the most difficult concepts, principles, and skills to teach and assess are also the most important. In addition, if cognitive ability emerges from emotional well-being, then aren't teacher educators and educators who neglect the emotional dimension of their students' lives somehow guilty of not focusing on a key missing piece (or shall we spell it *peace*, as Shel Silverstein proposed in his book *The Missing Piece*, 1995)?

How Do Teachers Develop Their Own Emotional Literacy?

A child's readiness for school, which we think of as a child's "best shot for a productive and happy life," depends on the most basic knowledge of all—the knowledge of how to learn (Goleman, 1995, p. 193). School success is not predicted by a child's fund of facts or precocious ability to read so much as by emotional and social measures: being self-assured and interested; knowing what kind of behavior is expected and how to rein in the impulse to misbehave; being able to wait, to follow directions, and to turn to teachers for help; and expressing needs while getting along with other children. Almost all students who do poorly in school lack one or more of these elements of emotional intelligence (Goleman, 1995).

Likewise, teachers' readiness for teaching depends most on their ability to transmit their emotional literacy to every child and parent with whom they have the opportunity to interact. Therefore teachers, both preservice and inservice, must assess and nurture their own emotional literacy. Were they successful in school because they knew how to learn? Have they entered teacher preparation programs without the motivation, positive self-concept, and passion necessary to meet the challenges of teaching in the twenty-first century? "Emotional literacy implies an expanded mandate for schools, taking up the slack for failing families in socializing children. This daunting task requires two major changes: that teachers go beyond their traditional mission and that people in the community become more involved with schools" (Goleman, 1995, p. 279).

Although teachers' emotional literacy development begins when they are infants, teacher educators cannot dismiss their responsibility for including emotional literacy in teacher preparation programs. So where does this process of preparing teachers to go "beyond their traditional mission" begin? It begins with dialoguing, researching, analyzing, and synthesizing strategies that promote emotional literacy among and within preservice and inservice teachers and caregivers. Many different points could serve as the "starting line" for this process. One possibility we're piloting evolved from seven key ingredients of emotional literacy suggested by a report from the National Center for Clinical Infant Programs (see Figure 4.5). These provide the launching pad for our initial attempts to assess both program competence and preservice or inservice teacher or caregiver competence. These competencies can also serve as a framework for developing curricular goals and supporting activities that enhance the emotional literacy of teachers.

Figure 4.5 **Framework for the Development and Assessment of Emotional Literacy**	**1.** *Confidence.* A sense of control and mastery over one's body, behavior, and the world; the child's or teacher's sense that he or she is more likely than not to succeed at what he or she undertakes and that adults or colleagues will be helpful. **2.** *Curiosity.* The sense that finding out about things is positive and leads to pleasure. **3.** *Intentionality.* The wish and capacity to have an impact and the ability to act on that wish with persistence. This is related to a sense of competence, of being effective. **4.** *Self-control.* The ability to modulate and control one's own actions in age-appropriate ways; a sense of inner control. **5.** *Relatedness.* The ability to engage with others based on the sense of being understood by and understanding others. **6.** *Capacity to communicate.* The wish and ability to verbally exchange ideas, feelings, and concepts with others. This is related to a sense of trust in others and of pleasure in engaging with others, including adults. **7.** *Cooperativeness.* The ability to balance one's own needs with those of others in group activity. (Competencies suggested by the Report of the National Center for Clinical Infant Programs, 1992; cited in Brazelton, 1992.)

ASSESSING THE EMOTIONAL LITERACY OF TEACHERS

Many vignettes, sentence completion activities, role-playing situations, discussions, questionnaires, and interview formats can be designed to assess the seven competencies outlined in Figure 4.5. As teacher educators prepare to meet the challenge of assessing the emotional literacy of educators and parents, it's critical that they view the culture of the individual, team, or program being assessed as the context within which they craft their assessment.

We are piloting the following questionnaire as one means of assessing the emotional literacy of teacher candidates. Read through the questions and respond to them yourself before reviewing responses from other preservice students in the New Teachers Talk feature on page 108.

Teacher Candidate Questionnaire

1. On a scale of 1–10, with 10 being high, how would you rate your teaching competence at this point in time? Provide a rationale for your rating.

2. On a scale of 1–10, with 10 being high, how would you rate the effectiveness of your interpersonal skills? Provide a rationale for your rating.

3. On a scale of 1–10, with 10 being high, predict the level of teaching competence you will have achieved in five years. Provide a rationale for your rating.

4. Describe three concepts that you are curious about, and discuss how you plan to act on your curiosities.

5. Describe three situations in which you have cooperated with another individual or group of individuals.

6. Describe three situations with adults in which you have reacted in a way that surprised you.

7. Describe three situations with children in which you have reacted in a way that surprised you.

8. Discuss in one paragraph what you would like to be doing five years from now.

Because our emotional literacy questionnaire is in its inception phase, please understand that we share it with you as our attempt to begin. As we share it with diverse audiences, we'll continue to revise and rework our plan and will continue to remind ourselves that "There is nothing so dangerous as

New teachers talk

In this feature, three preservice teachers—Lisa, Tina, and Paula—assess their emotional literacy using the questionnaire that begins at the bottom of page 107. All three are junior-level preservice teachers.

Lisa

Question 1 ("How would you rate your teaching competence at this point in time?") At this time, I would rate my teaching competence a 7. I feel that my field experiences, beginning with initial observations and continuing to novice teaching, have provided me with opportunities to see teachers in action and to begin teaching lessons. Education courses prior to advancement to teacher candidacy gave me some foundational theoretical knowledge, while also allowing me to explore my own topics of interest. Methods courses helped me to make connections between theory and practice, as I began writing and actually teaching lessons in the classroom. I feel that I have a basic foundation, and now I need to gain experience in implementing my ideas. As I gain classroom experience, I think I also will gain confidence in my abilities as a professional educator.

Question 3 ("Predict the level of teaching competence you will have achieved in five years.") In five years, I expect that my level of teaching competence will be a 9. After gaining five years of experience, I will have favorite lessons, will have developed numerous units, will have become familiar with the school system, and will have developed a rapport with parents. Over those five years, I will strive to establish a reputation for myself as a caring, fair, hard-working, and enthusiastic teacher.

Question 6 ("Describe three situations with adults in which you have reacted in a way that surprised you.") At an awards banquet, I spoke with a professor from another department about the educational system, best-practice methods, and my philosophy of education. As I gain more experience in talking with people, I feel that I am growing in my ability to intelligently discuss education. I always strive to speak precisely and clearly, so I enjoy opportunities to discuss my perceptions and ideas.

When I attended a field trip with my third-grade novice teaching class, I sat next to a parent on the bus. We discussed her child's strengths and weaknesses, and she shared her other children's abilities. Because we had a long bus ride, we continued

an idea if it's the only one you have!" Assuredly, there are many ways to approach the question of how to assess the emotional literacy of preservice teachers, and this questionnaire is but one piece of the puzzle. We use it in concert with multiple modes of assessment that are documented in our preservice teachers' professional teaching portfolios.

CREATING THE CONTEXT FOR EMOTIONAL LITERACY PROGRAMS

Nothing occurs in isolation. This principle certainly applies to attempts to facilitate learners' development of emotional literacy. Consequently, in

talking to the point where she began to speak of personal topics like leaving an abusive marriage and now being remarried. I was surprised that she shared such personal things, and I wonder if the situation would have been different if I had been the actual teacher.

Tina

Question 4 ("Describe three concepts that you are curious about, and discuss how you plan to act on your curiosities.") I'm curious about how to handle a chronic behavior problem in the classroom, using whole language in the classroom, and making math and science enjoyable to students. In reference to the chronic behavior problem, I hope to learn methods of dealing with this situation in a course I'll take called "Guiding Learners and Organizing Instruction." I also will look for research that has been done on this topic. I would like to visit whole-language classrooms to pick up some pointers on how to use whole language myself someday. I'm sure there is also lots of literature available that deals with whole language. I've already found some books that deal with fun ways of teaching math and science at the elementary

level. I need to collect and organize some of these ideas and put them in my professional file.

Question 6 While I was in a former supervisor's office, I heard him make a derogatory comment about Koreans. I was standing right next to him, so hearing the comment was unavoidable. I took offense to the comment because my mother is Korean. Instead of walking out of his office and fuming about the comment, I called him on it. What surprised me was that I maintained an even tone and didn't cry. I was angry enough that I easily could have yelled and started to cry out of anger. I think my point was better taken because I remained as outwardly calm as I did.

Question 7 ("Describe three situations with children in which you have reacted in a way that surprised you.") When I first started working as a teacher's assistant, I allowed a sixth grader to lure me into a yelling match. I couldn't believe that I would let myself get angry enough to get into an argument with a child. What was worse was that I took this anger home and took it out on my husband.

I used to work with a second grader who has emotional and behavioral problems. He likes to get his

your attempts to plan and implement emotional literacy programs, you'll need to consider the role that other, related key variables play in the process.

THE ROLE OF HOME AND SCHOOL COLLABORATION

Emotional learning begins during life's earliest moments and continues throughout childhood and adolescence. All the daily exchanges between parents and children have an emotional context. The father who responds with "Don't bother me—I've got work to do" to his child's escalating frustration as the child tries to fix a loose wheel on his tricycle gives his child a very clear message about the father's priorities. The emotional risks are greatest for children whose parents are immature, abusing drugs, depressed or chronically ill, or living in extreme poverty.

Since more and more emotionally at-risk students are entering schools, teachers must be prepared to support both the students in their classrooms and the students' families. Many resources are available to assist teachers and schools as they collaborate with families to meet their needs. Childhood represents a unique window of opportunity for promoting emotional literacy, but it takes both the home and the school to maximize this opportunity to ensure a child's emotional health.

own way, and if he doesn't, he throws terrible tantrums. What surprised me was the way that I learned to interact with him. I told him from the start (in a nice way) that I would not be affected by his tantrums. He and I eventually formed a very cooperative and workable relationship, based on mutual respect. . . .

Paula

Question 2 ("How would you rate the effectiveness of your interpersonal skills?") I rate my interpersonal skills as an 8. I feel that one of my strengths in working with children has been my ability to speak effectively with young children and with their parents. I very much enjoy that important aspect and have always felt competent in my abilities to communicate with children and adults alike. However, I am still working to overcome my occasional fear of speaking to groups of peers, particularly in a learning setting.

Question 5 ("Describe three situations in which you have cooperated with another individual or group.") I have cooperated with other individuals in a teaching setting at the preschool where I have worked. I gained an understanding of the importance of a group's diversity. Our basic philosophies and practices were varied, and not always complementary, but everyone's input was important to the collaborative effort of providing the best possible care and educational experiences for the children.

I also have collaborated with many people in college coursework. However, given the choice, I usually work alone, as I find my schedule and work pattern best support this. Additionally, and perhaps unfairly, I am always slightly concerned about the quality of other individuals' work, especially if I'm not familiar with their personal standards. I have more than once done more than my share, because my "share" was not equivalent to the effort I felt the project deserved.

THE IMPLICATIONS OF CULTURAL DIVERSITY

Prejudice and stereotypical thinking are learned in an emotional context, usually quite early in childhood. The beliefs used to "justify" or rationalize prejudices develop somewhat later. As a teacher, it is important for you, first of all, to be aware of your own prejudices. Only after you've recognized and identified them can you make a concerted effort to delete the filters through which you view certain people or groups of people. Accept the fact that it will take some time; a one-time "diversity training" session is merely a first step.

Involve yourself in teams or committees with people who will challenge your prejudices. When individuals work together toward a common goal of eliminating their own stereotypical thinking, they often find that their prejudices break down. Take advantage of the diversity that exists within your school or organization, and celebrate opportunities to develop harmonious relationships with a rich variety of people.

WHAT HAVE YOU LEARNED ABOUT EMOTIONAL LITERACY?

It is our hope that this brief discussion of emotional literacy has provided you with an opportunity to update your knowledge base, take stock of your own

I also have collaborated with professionals that I hold in high regard for the purpose of analyzing my own learning processes. I enjoy asking questions of, challenging, and conversing with people who have opinions and knowledge to offer me for consideration, and I seek out relationships and friendships with anyone who will challenge and benefit me as an individual.

Question 7 Most of my experiences with children that have surprised me have involved spontaneous changes in my usual patterns, during which I found another tactic to be more effective. Once, I was faced with an argument between two bright five-year-olds. Instead of my usual tactic of working with both to solve the conflict, I simply asked them if they could handle their dispute fairly together. To my surprise, they certainly could! My influence as a mediator was not needed at all in this case, and it really turned around my usual response pattern to such situations.

Question 8 ("Discuss what you would like to be doing five years from now.") Five years from now, I hope to be studying for a higher degree in education. I'm not exactly sure how to plan my future, as I am relatively unfamiliar with graduate schooling, and I'm not sure how long I should practice in the field before pursuing my master's. However, in five years I want to have established myself somewhere as a practicing professional and hopefully as a student of education again by then. I look forward to continuing my study, even if just gradually at first as I gain the experiences I will need.

Authors' Analysis

 The questions these preservice teachers responded to involve many of the dimensions of emotional literacy. Their responses reveal information regarding their abilities and skill levels with regard to self-awareness, self-regulation of emotional responses, social skills, empathetic responding, self-reflection, and goal setting.

emotional health, focus on key components of a social and emotional learning program, and think about ways in which you can apply what you have learned here in your future classroom. Emotional intelligence and social and emotional literacy are not the latest educational fads. Educators must come to realize how powerful the school is as a protective influence in the lives of children (Elias, Bruene-Butler, Blum, & Schuyler, 1997). Teaching social and emotional skills can result in long-term positive effects on academic achievement (Elias, Gara, Schuyler, Brandon-Muller, & Sayette, 1991). But more importantly, the development of emotional and social competence promotes and celebrates the minds and spirits of learners—and teachers—and empowers all of them to be successful!

THE CONNECTIONS BETWEEN EMOTIONAL LITERACY, EFFECTIVE TEACHING, AND ETHICS

What connects emotional literacy, effective teaching, and professional ethics? All three involve the affective domain, and all three rely on teachers' abilities to manage simultaneously with both their heads and their hearts. Effective teachers exhibit high degrees of emotional literacy and exemplify impeccable professional ethics.

Reflect & Respond

We begin our discussion of professional ethics with a brief activity.

In your teaching journal, write down five values or beliefs that you have about education. Then, working collaboratively with four or five other preservice teachers, combine your lists. How many values or beliefs are on your combined list? Are there values or beliefs that are similar? Are there values or beliefs that are quite different? What five shared values or beliefs can you agree on? Now compare your combined list with the compiled lists of other groups in your class. Is this process starting to seem somewhat complicated? Are you, within the context of your class, able to agree on at least five shared values or beliefs that unite teachers?

PROFESSIONAL ETHICS FOR EDUCATORS: WHAT ARE THEY AND WHY ARE THEY IMPORTANT FOR EFFECTIVE TEACHING?

DEFINITION OF PROFESSIONAL ETHICS

Your ability to put yourself in another's place, to feel someone else's pain or share their happiness, is at the heart of your **professional ethics.** Empathy underpins your moral judgment and actions. Your professional ethics are composed of your beliefs and values. These beliefs and values empower you to make decisions and engage in activities that are in the best interests of the students you teach, the families you touch, and the profession you have embraced.

THE CONNECTION BETWEEN PROFESSIONAL ETHICS AND CARING LEARNING COMMUNITIES

By now it must be fairly obvious that you can't be an effective teacher unless your decisions and actions are grounded in professional ethics that support and value your students, their families, and your profession. In Therese's experience as a classroom teacher at a university laboratory school (Metcalf School), she participated in an activity similar to the Reflect & Respond activity you've just completed. The project, entitled "Creating a Caring Metcalf Community," was spearheaded by one of Therese's mentors, Dr. Bob Dean—a long-time friend and colleague. However, instead of focusing on the values and beliefs of preservice teachers, the goal was to develop a list of the top ten shared beliefs or core values of the entire school community. Due to the complexity of the task and the divergent views of the participants, this became a multiyear project.

The process began with interested groups of parents and teachers who were invited to informal coffees at parents' homes to discuss their ideas concerning which beliefs and values were most important for their children in the school context. School administrators facilitated these focus group discussions. During faculty meetings, horizontal meetings (meetings that include teachers at the same grade levels, such as primary teachers), and parent sessions, Metcalf teachers also shared their perceptions. In addition to involving adults in this process, Metcalf School students—kindergartners through eighth graders—developed a list of classroom values, as well as a list of rules that reflected those values. After much discussion and soul searching, the Metcalf project produced a list of ten core values. The school community then began developing a curriculum to support and enhance those values throughout the school culture. Through this fascinating process, a tapestry of caring and collaboration was created for this very special school.

One of the greatest challenges in discussing ethics lies in the fact that your beliefs and values are very personal—a mirror of who you are. Although we understand that you bring your personal beliefs and values to your preservice program, how do we ensure that your personal beliefs align with professional ethics that support and promote effective learning and teaching? Professional ethics must be shaped, defined, and shared throughout your preservice program. Since you will emerge from your preservice program as a professional, you will be held accountable for your judgments and actions. Those judgments and actions will be a result of your professional ethics.

HOW CAN YOU BEGIN DEVELOPING YOUR PROFESSIONAL ETHICS?

You don't have the option of waiting until you become a teacher to develop and articulate your professional ethics. In fact, the development of your professional ethics began years ago, because your professional ethics originate with, and emerge from, your emotional literacy. But what professional ethics are important for teachers? Who decides? No teacher preparation program can—or should—deliver your professional ethics to you. However, teacher preparation programs can—and should—involve you in a variety of activities and reflective opportunities that help you develop your own professional ethics (Luckowski, 1996). Although professional organizations or specific disciplines often have a code of professional ethics, teachers need to develop their professional ethics in a collective context.

■ Reflective Opportunities

The purpose of the Reflect & Respond features in this book is to provide you with structured opportunities to thoughtfully consider issues and variables related to the teaching/learning process. Every individual, whether an adolescent facing peer pressure or a teacher receiving, processing, and responding to a multitude of competing and conflicting stimuli, must make difficult decisions. When people haven't given any prior thought to what they might do or how they might react when placed in a specific situation, they often make poor decisions (or nondecisions) that they later regret.

Consequently, it's imperative for you as a preservice teacher to engage in what-if and if-then kinds of thinking. You need opportunities to respond to situation-specific challenges that require you to demonstrate the knowledge, classroom performance, and attitudes of an effective teacher. Such opportunities facilitate the evolution and development of your system of professional ethics. As an inservice teacher, you will continue to develop your professional ethics as you collaborate with others in the educational community to

1. Develop a shared vision based on community values

2. Organize for, focus, and maintain an ongoing learning dialogue

3. Interpret and protect community values, ensuring both a focus on and a congruence with them in your teaching and learning approaches

4. Work with all participants to implement collaborative decisions that affect teaching and learning (Darling-Hammond, 1993b)

PRINCIPLES FOR A MORAL SCHOOL COMMUNITY

As a starting point for the process of formalizing and developing your professional ethics, review the following list of principles for a moral school community (Berreth & Berman, 1997) and begin to think about the professional expertise and ethical framework you will bring to the school context. Discuss this list with your peers and with your cooperating teachers and administrators, and consult it often as you work toward articulating your professional philosophy. Remember that your understanding and awareness of your own professional ethics are critical to matching your teaching philosophy with an appropriate school culture.

Principles for a Moral School Community

1. The school community collaboratively develops, clearly states, and celebrates core moral values. (These might include values such as trustworthi-

ness, respect, responsibility, justice, fairness, integrity, caring, tolerance, and honesty.)

2. Adults exemplify positive moral values in their work with one another and with students.
3. The school functions as the hub of the neighborhood community.
4. Students develop skills in goal setting, problem solving, cooperation, conflict resolution, and decision making.
5. Students are involved in decision making within their classroom and school.
6. Educators use a problem-solving approach for discipline. Students are involved in developing classroom rules and consequences.
7. School communities provide opportunities for service—within and outside the classroom.
8. Students and staff members appreciate diversity in cultures and beliefs through both study and direct experience.
9. At least one caring adult is personally connected with each child.

KEY CONCEPTS IN THE DEVELOPMENT OF YOUR PROFESSIONAL ETHICS

As you continue to explore the role of professional ethics in your development as a teacher, think about the ethical responsibilities that you'll be called upon to accept and support. We encourage you to focus your energies on ethical *responsibility* rather than on ethical *accountability*. (See Figure 4.6.)

Because you as a preservice teacher need multiple and varied opportunities to study, understand, and apply professional ethics in a variety of situations, case studies, and real-life teaching experiences, we'll continue to share personal experiences, teaching vignettes, and case reviews that will provide you with many contexts for framing and extending your professional ethics.

In Chapter 4, we purposefully tied together the intangibles of teaching to remind you that effective teaching, emotional literacy, and professional ethics

Figure 4.6 **Key Concepts in the Development of Your Professional Ethics**	Replace	With
	produce	process
	reactive	proactive
	authority	leadership
	isolation	collaboration
	explanations	understandings
	manipulation	facilitation
	external reward	internal motivation
	conversation	discourse
	short-term	long-term
	(Sirotnik, 1985).	

all share a common denominator—you! Your desire to take seriously your role as an educational leader demands that you deal effectively with the intangibles of teaching. Be aware of the intangibles of teaching, continually assess their influences, and begin to think about how the learning environments you'll create and the organizational cultures you'll support can be most productive for the learners you'll soon encounter.

SUMMARIZING WHAT YOU'VE LEARNED

- Effective teachers possess attitudes that foster learning, strong subject matter and pedagogical knowledge bases, and a broad array of teaching skills and the ability to apply those skills appropriately. Effective teachers demonstrate knowledge, classroom performances, and dispositions that enable them to serve as educational leaders and informed decision makers, acknowledge and provide for the whole learner, encourage student collaboration, and apply best-practice principles.

- Your own emotional literacy will serve as a major determinant of your ability to create a learning community that consistently supports and nurtures appropriate norms, values, and behaviors. Because they recognize emotional well-being as a variable critical to success in school and life, effective teachers use their own emotional intelligence to develop responsive learning environments and curricula that support and promote emotional competence.

- The first four years of children's emotional experiences hold significant consequences for their emotional literacy. Therefore, parents in particular need to understand how their actions can help generate the confidence, curiosity, pleasure in learning, and understanding of limits that help children succeed in life. To produce positive change, they also must plan and implement both prevention and intervention strategies.

- The use of high-quality literature can enhance your implementation of the following strategies for promoting social and emotional learning in your classroom: storytelling and biography, group discussion, rehearsal and practice (role playing), self-awareness and self-regulation, self-reflection and goal setting, artistic expression, play, and cooperative and small-group learning.

- School success is not predicted by a learner's fund of facts or a precocious ability to read so much as by emotional and social measures. Just as children's readiness for school depends to a large extent on their emotional literacy, teachers' readiness for teaching depends most on their ability to transmit their emotional literacy to every learner and parent with whom they interact. Prior to facilitating students' development of emotional literacy, both preservice and inservice teachers must first come to terms with their own emotional literacy.

- Every piece of emotional learning occurs within an emotional context. Childhood represents a unique window of opportunity for promoting emotional literacy, but it's a process that must involve both the home and the school in order to maximize this opportunity to ensure the child's emotional health.

■ Effective teaching emerges from decisions and actions that are grounded in your professional ethics. The beliefs and values that compose your professional ethics empower you to make decisions and engage in activities that are in the best interests of the students you teach, their families, and the profession you have embraced. Your professional ethics originate with—and emerge from—your emotional literacy.

YOUR PROFESSIONAL TEACHING PORTFOLIO

■ Using as benchmarks the knowledge base, performances, and dispositions of effective teaching that you read about in this chapter, as well as the Model Standards for Beginning Teachers' Licensure and Development (which appear in Figure 2.7), prepare a self-assessment of your teaching competencies. Later in your professional development (just prior to completing your initial teacher preparation program), reassess your teaching competencies using these same benchmarks. Analyze and reflect on the differences and similarities between the two self-assessments.

■ Outline your plan for facilitating learners' social and emotional literacy development. Include at least two original examples of literature-based instructional strategies you would use to address particular dimensions of social-emotional literacy.

Key Terms

Amygdalae (p. 95)
Authentic learning experiences (p. 92)
Collaborative learning experiences (p. 92)
Dispositions (p. 99)

Emotional brain (p. 95)
Emotional intelligence (p. 94)
Emotional literacy (p. 94)
Holistic learning experiences (p. 92)

Performances (p. 87)
Principles of best practice (p. 92)
Professional ethics (p. 112)
Reflect (p. 91)
Whole learner (p. 89)

Relevant Resources for Professionals

Books and Articles

• Adler, D. (1991). *A picture book of Martin Luther King, Jr.* New York: Scholastic.

• Bedard, M. (1992). *Emily.* New York: Bantam Doubleday Dell.

• Freedman, R. (1989). *Lincoln: A photobiography.* New York: Clarion.

• Hoffman, M. (1995). *Boundless grace.* New York: Scholastic.

• Hoffman, M. (1994). *Amazing grace.* New York: Dial Books.

- Konigsburg, E. (1996). *The view from Saturday*. New York: Atheneum Books.
- Konigsburg, E., (1967). *From the mixed-up files of Mrs. Basil E. Frankweiler*. New York: Bantam Doubleday Dell.
- L'Engle, M. (1962). *A wrinkle in time*. New York: Farrar, Straus and Giroux.
- Lown, F. (1997). *Langston Hughes*. Portland, ME: J. Weston Walch.
- McGovern, A. (1997). *The lady in the box*. New York: Turtle Books.
- McMullan, K. (1993). *Nutcracker Noel*. New York: HarperCollins.
- Orwell, G. (1946). *Animal farm*. New York: Harcourt Brace Jovanovich.
- Polacco, P. (1990). *Just plain fancy*. New York: Bantam Doubleday Dell.
- Scieszka, J. (1992). *The stinky cheese man and other fairly stupid tales*. New York: Penguin.
- Seuss, T. (1957). *The cat in the hat*. Boston: Houghton Mifflin.
- Speare, E. G. (1958). *The witch of Blackbird Pond*. New York: Dell.
- Van Allsburg, C. (1992). *The widow's broom*. Boston: Houghton Mifflin.
- Van Allsburg, C. (1991). *The wretched stone*. Boston: Houghton Mifflin.
- Van Allsburg, C. (1988). *Two bad ants*. Boston: Houghton Mifflin.
- Van Allsburg, C. (1985). *The Polar Express*. Boston: Houghton Mifflin.
- Viorst, J. (1972). *Alexander and the terrible, horrible, no good, very bad day*. New York: Macmillan.
- Yolen, J. (1992). *Encounter*. Orlando: Harcourt Brace Jovanovich.

Professional Journals in Education

- *Language Arts*
  National Council of Teachers of English
  1111 W. Kenyon Road
  Urbana, IL 61801–1096
  http://www.ncte.org

- *The Reading Teacher*
  International Reading Association
  800 Barksdale Road
  P.O. Box 8139
  Newark, DE 19714–8139

Professional Organizations

- Best Practices in Education: A not-for-profit organization whose mission is to work with American teachers to find effective educational practices from other countries to adapt to and apply in U.S. schools. This searchable site includes information about their current and featured projects, as well as grant information.

  http://www.bestpraceduc.org/

- The National Center for Research on Teacher Learning (NCRTL). The NCRTL's mission is to be the leader in the field of teacher education research. The center is based in the College of Education at Michigan State University.

Web Sites

- **The Awesome Library**

  http://www.neat-schoolhouse.org/awesome.html

  The Awesome Library organizes your exploration of the World Wide Web with twelve thousand carefully reviewed resources.

- **Developing Educational Standards**

  http://putwest.boces.org/Standards.html

  Developing Educational Standards is a list of annotated links to sites at the international, national, state, and local levels that contain information on educational standards. There are also links to clearinghouses, labs, and other organizations that include standards information, as well as newspapers and magazines. This page is maintained by Charles Hill of the Putnam Valley, New York, schools.

- **Education World**

  www.education-world.com/

  This site is dedicated to educators and students and contains education news, chat forums, education site reviews, and links to commercial sites.

FAMILY INVOLVEMENT IN A DIVERSE SOCIETY

5

— OR —

Partnering with parents

INVOLVING PARENTS AS EDUCATIONAL PARTNERS

A chapter that focuses on actively involving parents in the teaching/learning process is somewhat unusual in a teaching strategies book. We included this chapter because we feel it is extremely important for you to begin preparing—at the preservice level—for the opportunities you will have once you begin teaching to promote parents as partners in the teaching/learning process. Many teachers view working with parents as the most challenging aspect of their profession.

One reason that collaborating with parents can be so arduous for teachers is that the topic of parent education and involvement often is ignored in preservice teacher preparation programs. Consequently, many teachers enter the profession with limited knowledge and skills related to positively involving parents in their children's education. Avoidance, rather than collaboration, can become teachers' primary mechanism for dealing with parents.

If you were a fly on the wall in many teachers' lounges during a coffee or lunch break, you might hear stories, gossip, and rumors that engender negative attitudes and prejudices about families and, consequently, children. We hope that, if this happens to you, knowledge about the importance of parent involvement will empower you to deflect and defuse such talk. Knowledge of family systems and family communication strategies can help you start *today* to develop an attitude that will enable you to collaborate with parents rather than be intimidated by them. Therefore, we begin this chapter with some critical information about families and family involvement that will prepare you

"Home is the first classroom. Parents are the first and most essential teachers."

—*Boyer, 1991, p. 33*

Think back to times during your school days when your parents visited your classroom or school. Were they seated in the front row when you starred in the school play or chorus concert? Did you look forward to their arriving home after the fall or spring parent-teacher conference? Were they involved in the PTA, or did they ever volunteer to be your classroom's room parents? Were they ever invited to any of your classrooms to read a story, discuss their occupations, or share a special talent?

 In your teaching journal, create a PMI chart that looks like this:

P   M   I

Under the *P,* write at least five *positive* memories you have of your parents' involvement during your school days; under the *M* (for *minus*), write at least five not-so-positive memories of your parents' involvement; and under the *I,* write at least five *interesting* memories (not necessarily positive or negative). Share your PMI chart with a peer, and discuss the similarities and differences between your PMI charts.

for many of the challenges and opportunities that await you. We then move on to discussing parent communication, parent-teacher conferences, and volunteer programs in an attempt to share specific ideas and strategies you can employ in your work with parents and families.

SEEING PARENTS AS THEIR CHILDREN'S FIRST TEACHERS

A view of parents as their child's "first and foremost teacher" has dominated social reform movements since the 1600s. Gordon and Gordon's translation (1951) of Pestalozzi's work from the 1700s and 1800s emphasizes the paradigm "parents as teachers." Furthermore, Pestalozzi argued that "for children, the teaching of their parents will always be the core, and the role of the teacher is to provide a decent shell around the core" (p. 26).

Family involvement has been a prominent feature of early childhood education programs for centuries. The emphasis on parent participation during the settlement house movement of the 1880s, the nursery school movement of the 1920s, and the early intervention movement of the 1960s illustrates that parent involvement has historically been viewed as a key component of early childhood education (Kiley Shepston, 1991). Researchers in the 1960s and 1970s concluded that family variables were more powerful than school variables in predicting academic performance (Coleman, et al., 1966; Jencks, et al., 1972). More recently, additional studies have clearly validated that when parents are involved in their children's education, student achievement improves (Walberg, 1984).

During a 1990 meeting of the National Governor's Association, President Bush and the nation's governors developed six national education goals. The first of these goals states that by the year 2000, all children in America will start school ready to learn. Obviously, this goal involves parent education. How can educators ensure that all children in America will begin school ready to learn if they don't promote the importance of education and involvement with American parents? "Before America asks, 'How ready are children for school?' it must ask the dependent question, 'How ready are parents to parent?' While we tacitly acknowledge that parents are the first and most important teachers of children, America has done little to support parents in that role" (Kagan, 1990, pp. 277–278).

What memories do you have of your parents' involvement during your school days? Was your school a place that welcomed parents, made them feel comfortable, encouraged them to participate in the teaching/learning partnership, and respected and valued their relationship with you? Or was your school a place where parents were invited only to attend once-a-semester, fifteen-minute parent-teacher conferences and beginning-of-the-year open houses? Perhaps you are a parent yourself or will be one day. What role will you play as your child's first teacher? What will you expect from your child's teachers?

CLARIFYING WHAT PARENTS AND TEACHERS EXPECT FROM EACH OTHER

The literature on parent and teacher expectations is imbalanced. Many researchers have focused on what teachers expect from parents (for example, see Chrispeels, 1996; Daniels, 1996; Epstein, 1995; Huffman, Benson, Gebelt, & Phelps, 1996; Griffith, 1996; Mantzicopoulos & Neuharth-Pritchett, 1996; Moore & Brown, 1996; Rosenthal & Sawyers, 1996; Sanders, 1996; Thompson, 1996; Vacha & McLaughlin, 1992; Vickers, 1994; Wescott Dodd, 1996; Zeldin, 1990); fewer have focused on parents' expectations of teachers (a few that have include Allen, 1997a, 1997b; Glover, 1992; Kiley Shepston, 1991; Lindle, 1989). Therefore, we'll begin with a review of some of the perceptions and expectations parents have of schools and teachers, and then we'll turn our attention to what teachers expect from parents.

In an article examining the relationship between schools and families, Lindle (1989) reported that most parents feel teachers and principals are too businesslike or even patronizing toward them. The parents in Lindle's study were especially affected when teachers were condescending, stating that they were very uncomfortable when teachers "talked down" to them. Parents found "a personal touch" to be the most enhancing factor in their relationship with their children's teachers. An important consideration for teachers, then, seems to be balancing professionalism with the "personal touch" appreciated by parents.

What other expectations and desires have been voiced by parents? Allen (1997b) notes that parents consistently have shared the following expectations:

- They want to feel welcome in their children's classrooms.
- They want to be kept informed of their children's progress.
- They want to be able to share concerns with their children's teachers.
- They want teachers to listen to them and respect their opinions.
- They want to receive positive information, not just negative reports, from teachers.
- They want more frequent communication from teachers.
- They want teachers to mail notes home instead of sending them with children.
- They want teachers to work together.
- They want teachers to ease their children's transitions.
- They want to be given specific times when they can routinely visit classrooms.
- They want coordination between teachers, school boards, and administrators.
- They want to be treated as equals.

Do any of these parental expectations surprise you? How will you be able to accommodate these parental expectations and desires when you enter the classroom? Later in the chapter, we recommend a number of parent involvement strategies that we hope will get you started off in a positive direction.

To help you assess the similarities and differences that exist between both groups, it's also important to consider what teachers expect from parents. Review the following list of what teachers have said they want from parents, also from Allen's study, 1997b, and decide whether you think you would agree with most or all of these statements. Teachers want parents to

- Provide for their children's basic needs
- Have good parenting skills (discipline—or, preferably, guide—their children properly)
- Be involved in their children's educational experiences at home and school
- Support, encourage, and listen to their children
- Show up for conferences when scheduled
- Be good role models
- Promote and support education at home
- Support the schools
- Communicate regularly with them
- Feel comfortable in their classrooms

■ Foster and encourage independence in their children

■ Be aware of their very important role in their children's education

Though these may seem like roles and attributes you would expect any parent to demonstrate, many parents have not had life experiences that enable them to meet these expectations without your intervention. You, the teacher, are responsible for supporting parents and making it possible for them to meet your expectations.

FINDING THE COMMON GROUND BETWEEN FAMILIES AND SCHOOLS

Let's begin by defining the common ground that exists between the expectations of parents and teachers:

■ Both parents and teachers want children to be successful in school.

■ Both parents and teachers want to be respected.

■ Both parents and teachers value and desire increased communication between homes and schools.

■ Both parents and teachers want parents to feel welcome and comfortable in their children's classrooms.

With regard to differences, the most apparent difference is that although teachers say that they want parents to become more involved in their children's education, parents often don't feel welcome or valued in the school or in their children's classrooms. In addition, although many teachers may think that parents are not involved enough in their children's education, most parents feel that they are very involved. "By their own estimation, American parents are deeply involved in their children's education—at least to the extent that involvement is defined in terms of activities that take place within the home, such as reading and checking on homework" (Marttila & Kiley, 1995, p. 2).

Since such disparity seems to exist between teachers' and parents' perceptions of parent involvement, perhaps teachers need to become more aware of how parents are involved in their children's education at home. Teachers could then promote more home-based educational opportunities that extend the curriculum, by sending home family activities, recipes, surveys, and homework that requires the involvement of another family member in an enjoyable activity (such as reading a book, discussing a current event, or creating a family time line).

As the search for common ground between families and schools continues, so does the ongoing challenge to figure out what to call the family-school connection (Coleman, 1997). Some prefer the label "family involvement," because it reflects the diversity of family structures and lifestyles. Others prefer "parent involvement," which emphasizes the primary role of mothers and fathers in children's education. Still others, instead of using the key term "involvement," prefer the term "parent or family education," because this focuses on the educational needs of parents and families. Other professionals prefer "family-school involvement," to emphasize the mutual responsibility of families and schools in maintaining positive family-school relationships. What label do you believe is most appropriate, based on your perception of the family-school connection?

■ Shared Responsibilities

To focus the energies of the family-school connection, Epstein (1987) suggested five obligations that link families and schools: child rearing and children's health and safety, family-school communication, parent participation within the school, support and reinforcement of children's learning, and leadership and advocacy efforts to advance children's development and education. This list of obligations provides a place to begin the process of defining goals and objectives for the family-school connection.

Epstein's list aside, there is no one "correct" family-school connection—and no "one best way" to deliver a family involvement program. Rather, there are many successful approaches to family involvement that offer many alternatives to consider (Comer & Haynes, 1991; Epstein, 1991; Epstein & Dauber, 1991; Gage & Workman, 1994; Olmstead, 1991; Powell, 1991; Rosenthal & Sawyers, 1996; Swick, 1984). To build successful home-school partnerships, teachers and administrators should consider the following recommendations (Rosenthal & Sawyers, 1996):

- Demonstrate an understanding of and respect for the diversity of attitudes about family involvement held by families and school staff.
- Assess existing barriers to family involvement in your school, as well as current strengths in your school's programs.
- Focus on family strengths (as opposed to family weaknesses) and respect for the choices families make regarding school policies and practices that affect their children.
- Make a commitment to involving all families by adopting alternative program-delivery schedules (mornings, evenings, lunchtimes, weekends) and methods (community-based, workplace-based, or "virtual" meetings, as well as activities and meetings that vary in size from one-on-one to large groups; transportation services for those who need them; interpreters when needed; communication with families by means of face-to-face conferences as well as more innovative communication strategies like videos and audiotapes, radio and television spots, newspaper articles, newsletters, and pamphlets).
- Use visits in students' homes or at other sites outside the school (community centers, churches, workplaces) to involve parents who may feel uncomfortable entering a school environment.
- Provide families with a variety of family involvement activities based in the home, the school, and the community.
- Involve parents and school staff of different cultural backgrounds in school governance.
- Allocate appropriate resources to support family involvement strategies and practices.

- Clarify family-school roles regarding family involvement strategies and practices, while also allowing flexibility in modifying roles as situations demand.
- Maintain close ties and open lines of communication with community agencies that serve children and families.
- Provide ongoing evaluation of the family involvement program, including its impact on children, school staff, families, and the community.

These recommendations can serve as a place to begin to review your school's policies and to focus on the needs and interests of your community of families.

■ Goals 2000 and the National Emphasis on School-Family Partnerships

Recent major legislation—the **Goals 2000: Educate America Act** and the reauthorized **Elementary and Secondary Education Act (ESEA)**—has made parents' involvement in their children's education a national priority. Eligibility for Title I money is now contingent on the development of **school-family compacts** in which families and schools declare their mutual responsibility for children's learning. To receive ESEA monies, at least 1 percent must be allocated for parent involvement programs (Baker, 1997). Partnerships are to be forged between homes, schools, and communities, with an unparalleled level of contact and communication between parents and educators (U.S. Department of Education, 1994). How can schools and communities make these partnerships work? Where should they begin? Where should *you* begin?

■ Five Steps to Developing School-Family Partnerships

Step 1: Develop a family involvement philosophy. Begin by developing a family involvement philosophy for your program or school. Both teachers and parents should collaborate in the development of this philosophy, and you should expect numerous rewrites. It takes a lot of time and shared energy to create a philosophy statement that all parties can accept. Your goal is to write a statement that briefly synthesizes why family involvement is an important component of your program.

An example of a family involvement philosophy statement follows (the following examples are all adapted from Coleman, 1997):

> *Family and school are two of the most important social institutions in the lives of children. Within families and schools, children learn about their world, develop a sense of social responsibility, and acquire social-interpersonal skills. These dispositions and skills are important for a healthy, productive, and enjoyable life.*

Step 2: Develop a goal statement. An example of a goal statement follows:

> *The goal of the [name of school] family involvement program is to establish family-school continuity by providing mutually supportive and inviting environments that challenge children to learn and practice positive life skills. Goal statements should be based on beliefs and assumptions.*

Step 3: List belief statements that provide the foundation for your program. Examples of belief statements follow:

- Children grow and develop best when parents and teachers communicate with each other on a routine basis.
- Parents and teachers are most effective when they respect each other's views.
- Parents and teachers have a responsibility to build on children's learning experiences that occur in the home, school, and community.

Step 4: Write a brief statement that explains the development of classroom objectives and the program evaluation process. Develop family involvement objectives for each classroom. Parents, teachers, and children should work together to develop the objectives. All objectives will reflect the school's family involvement goal and belief statements. Parents, teachers, and children should evaluate the family involvement objectives each year and provide a summary report to the parent-teacher advisory committee.

Step 5: Clearly define role expectations. These role expectations must emanate from the family involvement philosophy statement. Families and teachers have joint responsibility for selecting, defining, modifying, extending, and carrying out the roles. Suggested roles for family involvement personnel include cultural ambassador, educator, family services coordinator, and advocate.

COLLABORATING WITH YOUR SCHOOL'S FAMILY SERVICE COORDINATOR

More and more schools are employing family service coordinators (FSCs) to facilitate the home-school connection. In fact, schools that use FSCs have been described by parents as being "more open" and as helping parents feel "more comfortable in classrooms" (Allen, 1997a). What is the role of the FSC? Mainly, the FSC functions as a liaison between families and schools and in that role supports parents, teachers, and administrators. FSCs support parents by communicating with them about classroom and school activities, dealing with social service agencies on their behalf, organizing meetings between parents and school personnel on topics of interest to parents, and generally keeping the lines of communication open between the school and the home. FSCs support school staff by making teachers and principals aware of potential family problems or family challenges and needs, helping teachers and principals arrange classroom and school activities that involve parents, helping with parent-teacher conferences and home visits, and focusing on acclimating parents to classrooms and teachers to homes. As you can surmise, FSCs can make a significant difference in your partnership efforts. If you are fortunate enough to be employed in a school that has an FSC, be sure to create a strong connection early on with him or her.

UNDERSTANDING MIDDLE SCHOOL STUDENTS AND THEIR FAMILIES

Although much of the literature on dropout prevention emphasizes the importance of nourishing positive relations between home and school, little information is available on involving parents at the middle school level. As students move into **transescence**—the transition phase between childhood and adolescence—positive support that bridges home and school may be the essential link students need to make that transition successfully. Problems faced by students "in the middle" must be addressed by both parents and schools.

Many studies have emphasized the importance of parental involvement for young children, but because of the uniqueness of the middle school–age child and the high risk factors associated with transescence, parental involvement appears to be equally important to the success and well-being of the middle school child. The intense pressure brought on by the physical, social, and emotional changes experienced by the transescent often result in changed attitudes, values, and behaviors that rebuke both parental and school authority. It is of vital importance that teachers and parents cooperate to help the transescent in the journey toward maturity (Roach, Bell, & Salmeri, 1989).

UNDERSTANDING PARENTING STYLES

The manner in which families socialize their children varies. Family theorists have identified three major parenting styles—**authoritative, authoritarian,** and **laissez-faire.** Table 5.1 outlines characteristics common to families that exhibit these three parenting styles, as well as some common characteristics of dysfunctional families, in which the parenting style may be either authoritative, authoritarian, or laissez-faire.

Which type of parenting style is most effective for socializing children? If you guessed the authoritative style, you're right. Why is it the most effective style? In a later chapter we will explore the importance of appropriate guid-

Table 5.1 **Parenting Styles**	Parenting Style	Family Characteristics
	Authoritative	Democratic decision making
		Guidelines and parameters
		Effective communication
		Problem solving
		Self-discipline and responsibility
	Authoritarian	Demanding parent
		Absolute rules
		Restrictive environment
		Punitive control
		Inappropriate expectations
	Laissez-faire	Anything goes
		Neglectful parent
		No one cares
		Withdrawal from parental responsibilities
	Dysfunctional (may be authoritative, authoritarian, or laissez-faire)	Alcohol- or drug-addicted family members
		Neurotic or mentally ill family members
		Abusive family members

(Adapted from Berger, 1995)

ance. For the time being, think about the kind of behaviors and responses that influenced you positively when you were a child. Chances are, they were the kind exemplified by the authoritative style of parenting.

Many resources are available to help you understand parent education and create programs that will involve and meet the needs of each family; we can provide only some highlights in this chapter. But perhaps more important, you need to come face to face with your own biases about families to accept and appreciate all the children and families you will have an opportunity to touch as a teacher. Some families will present unique challenges that will necessitate your intervention. You will be most effective in meeting those challenges if you operate from a knowledge base that provides you with the ability to make appropriate, and sometimes heart-wrenching, decisions that are in the best interests of children and their families. The next section attempts to provide you with information about the many types of family structures that you will encounter as a new teacher in the twenty-first century. Although the statistics will change over time, it is important that you recognize and be responsive to the current trends and issues that affect families and children.

Based on the three different parenting styles described in Table 5.1, identify the parenting style your parents used when raising you.

In your teaching journal, discuss how the parenting style your parents employed might have affected your development. Also, respond to the following two questions:

• Did your parents' parenting style have anything to do with your decision to become a teacher?

• If you could change one thing about how your parents raised you, what would it be?

UNDERSTANDING TRADITIONAL AND NONTRADITIONAL FAMILIES

If you walked down a street in Anytown, U.S.A., and knocked on the door of any house, would you find a family that included a mother, a father, and 2.4 children and in which Mom stayed at home and Dad went to work? Probably not. In 1992, this idealized "traditional family" represented only about 10 percent of all U.S. households (U.S. Bureau of the Census, 1992a).

There has been a gradual, steady increase in the percentage of adults and children residing in single-parent, blended, or other households, which frequently include nonrelated individuals (U.S. Bureau of the Census, 1992a). Married-couple households accounted for more than 55 percent of all households in 1992, but a majority of these (53 percent) did not include any children under eighteen years of age. Never-married persons make up the largest share of unmarried adults (58 percent) and a sizable portion of the total adult population (23 percent).

KIDS RAISING KIDS

After rising for years, the teen birth rate in the United States has begun to decline. Many attribute the drop in teen pregnancy to the growing effectiveness of education and prevention campaigns. Nevertheless, American teens aged fifteen to nineteen have far more babies than do their counterparts in Japan, Australia, Canada, or Europe (Children's Defense Fund, 1998), and the proportion of teen births that occur outside of marriage has climbed year after year, growing from about 30 percent in 1970 to 75 percent in the mid-1990s.

Numerous problems are associated with teen parenting. Children of teenagers are more likely than those born to older mothers to be poor, to suffer health problems in infancy, and to do poorly in school. Teen pregnancy is a major contributor to, as well as a consequence of, the poverty that victimizes more than 14 million American children. Two-thirds of teenage mothers are high school dropouts. About one-quarter drop out before they become pregnant (Children's Defense Fund, 1998).

The issues of poverty, health, and school achievement are the chief concerns of the schools, families, and communities attempting to help and support "kids raising kids." Later in this section we will provide you with some more information related to these concerns.

SINGLE-PARENT FAMILIES

A **single-parent family,** also called a one-parent, lone-parent, or solo-parent family (Hanson & Sporakowski, 1986), is one in which a mother or father is single-handedly raising dependent children living in the same household. Single parents are not a homogeneous group. They include all social classes, all racial and ethnic groups, and all age groups. Divorces, separations, desertions, out-of-wedlock births, incarcerations, hospitalizations, military duties, out-of-state employment, and single-parent adoptions result in single-parent families (Hammer & Turner, 1996).

Newly divorced parents are faced with a number of changes, including decreased financial resources, changes in residence, new roles and responsibilities, new patterns of intrafamilial interaction, reorganized routines and schedules, and, eventually, the introduction of new relationships into the existing family. Usually these changes demand resources beyond those immediately accessible to individual family members (Hetherington, 1992).

■ Single Mothers

The vast majority of single-parent households—more than 83 percent—are maintained by mothers. The figure is even higher—93 percent—for African American single-parent families. Of all children living in single-parent families, 88 percent live with their mothers (U.S. Bureau of the Census, 1992a).

Researchers, policy makers, and educators have responded to the rise in the single-parent family with interest and concern. Some view the single-mother family as an indicator of social disorganization, signaling the "demise of the family." Others regard it as an alternative family form, consistent with the emerging economic independence of women. However one views the change, the mother-only family has become a common phenomenon that promises to alter the social and economic context of family life for future generations (McLanahan & Booth, 1991). As a teacher, how will you view single-mother families? Your perceptions are sure to influence your interactions with both the students in your class and with their mothers.

Single mothers experience higher rates of life stress than do married women (Olson & Banyard, 1993). Sources of stress include

- *Role overload*—single mothers are their children's only support system.
- *Parenting and child care*—single mothers have twenty-four-hour-a-day responsibility, with no relief.
- *Social isolation*—single mothers are often alone and isolated from their peers.
- *Emotional and psychological problems*—single mothers are at high risk for these, across many dimensions. In addition, being poor places single mothers at extremely high risk for anxiety, depression, and other health problems. Feelings of helplessness and despair are common and understandable (Olson & Banyard, 1993).

■ Single Fathers

A *single-father family* consists of an unmarried male and his minor child or children living in the same household. Single fathers include widowers, divorced or separated fathers, never-married males, and single adoptive fathers who have primary responsibility for the care of their children. The number of single-parent fathers has increased in recent years and constituted about 10 percent of all single-parent families in 1992.

Sources of stress for single fathers include unhappiness, conflicts between job and family, financial concerns, and parenting issues. Though single fathers do experience financial problems, they are better able to achieve economic security than are single mothers. It is estimated that the income of divorced men averages 90 percent of their predivorce income. Although many noncustodial fathers pay child support, the amount is generally low and much less than either the actual cost of rearing a child or the expenses borne by custodial mothers (McLanahan & Booth, 1991).

When comparing the social and emotional well-being of single custodial parents, Buehler (1988) found some differences between single mothers and single fathers. Fathers were more bothered than mothers by high blood pressure and frequent drinking and drug use, whereas mothers seemed more bothered than fathers by insomnia, fatigue, and crying spells. The synchronization of work, supervision of children, and household management seems to be a major problem for most single fathers (Hammer & Turner, 1996).

The coordination of work, supervision of children, and household management is a major challenge for most single fathers.
(© Susie Fitzhugh)

BLENDED FAMILIES

The **blended family** is one in which either or both parents bring with them children from a previous marriage (Coleman & Ganong, 1991). By definition, a blended family cannot exist without children. The phenomenon of stepfamilies is certainly not new, but in the last decade a quantitative increase and qualitative changes have taken place in this family system (Ambert, 1986; Teachman & Heckert, 1985). As a child, perhaps you enjoyed stories such as "Hansel and Gretel," "Snow White and the Seven Dwarfs," and "Cinderella," all of which depict a wicked and cruel stepmother. The stepfamily concept dates at least to Greek mythology, and stories about this family structure are found worldwide (Visher & Visher, 1989).

To avoid the negative connotations of the label "stepfamily," this family form has been referred to as the reconstituted, blended, merged, remarried, multimarried, sequential, recoupled, or combined family (Coleman & Ganong, 1991). The most frequent combination is a mother, her children, and a stepfather. Many variations of blended families provide complex family environments—structurally, interpersonally, and emotionally.

The dramatic increase in the number of blended families today is attributable to the high rate of divorce, the increasing numbers of children affected by divorce, and the large percentage of people who remarry. According to the

1990 census, there were approximately ten times as many stepfathers as step-mothers in the United States. The fact that more mothers than fathers retain custody of their children after divorce accounts for the predominance of blended households composed of mothers, their children, and stepfathers. In 1990, a total of 72 percent of divorced women and 80 percent of divorced men had remarried (Hetherington, 1992; Wilson & Clarke, 1992). The average interval from divorce to remarriage was 3.6 years for men and 3.9 years for women (Wilson & Clarke, 1992). Approximately 40 percent of marriages are a remarriage for one or both partners (Coleman & Ganong, 1991).

Perhaps the most difficult interpersonal challenge stepfamilies face is that of developing a constructive relationship between parents and children. The child must renegotiate his or her relationship both with the noncustodial parent and the custodial parent, as well as establish a new relationship with the stepparent. Parents must establish new relationships with stepchildren and redefine relationships with biological children. Family members experience considerable confusion and ambivalence about what the stepparent role should be (Hetherington, 1992).

A number of factors have been found to be important to children's adjustment in stepfamilies. The marital adjustment of the husband and wife is important. One study showed that the quality of the marital relationship affected the quality of both the mother's and the father's relationships with their children (Anderson, Linder, & Bennion, 1992). Satisfaction with remarriage and low marital conflict have been found to be positively associated with the quality of stepparent-stepchild relationships (Coleman & Ganong, 1991).

Stepparents' parenting style is another important factor in children's adjustment. An authoritative style (see Table 5.1) has been shown to have pervasive beneficial effects in blended as well as traditional families (Anderson et al., 1992). Warmth, support, involvement, and monitoring are consistently associated with high levels of social competence in children, and the absence of coercion, conflict, and negativity are associated with lower levels of externalizing behavior and higher social and scholastic competence. Thus, warm, supportive, noncoercive parents who monitor their children's behavior but grant them considerable autonomy have the most well-adjusted children.

The way children respond to their current family situation also depends on their previous family relationships. Children who enter a stepfamily face yet another in a series of family transitions. Many such children, particularly boys, may still be having adjustment problems associated with previous transitions, such as from life in a two-parent family to life in a single-mother home (Hetherington, 1992).

The number of blended families is increasing so rapidly that it is essential for both the social sciences and the helping professions (including teachers) to focus significant attention on the many ramifications of this social trend. There is a need to provide continuing services to these families. Providing opportunities for them to share their experiences with others experiencing the same feelings and problems appears to be helpful. Professionals who work with blended families need to focus on the needs of each individual family member. Blended families are more dissimilar than similar to traditional nuclear families. It seems important for children in blended families to continue relationships with noncustodial biological parents. If stepparents do not compete with natural parents but attempt to establish their own roles with stepchildren, stepparenting will be more effective and more rewarding.

DIVORCED FAMILIES

The largest proportional increase of any family structure has been in the number of *divorced families,* which quadrupled from 4.3 million in 1970 to 16.3 million in 1992 (U.S. Bureau of the Census, 1992b). Recent predictions indicate that two-thirds of new marriages will end in divorce (Kennedy, 1991). Children of divorce make up the largest share of children living with a single parent (37 percent), followed by children born to a parent who has never married (34 percent). African American women have the highest rate of divorce of any sex or racial group (391 per 1,000 persons in 1992), followed by African American men (232 per 1,000 persons) (U.S. Bureau of the Census, 1992a).

The proportion of divorced persons who remarry is high—72 percent of women and 80 percent of men; however, the rate of remarriage declined sharply in the 1970s and continued to decrease during the 1980s. Women with children, women over thirty-five years of age, and African Americans are much less likely to remarry than are younger, Anglo, childless, divorced women (Hetherington, 1992).

Conditions that affect a child's ability to adjust to divorce include the following (adapted from Shaw, 1992, p. 182):

- The tone of his or her parents' relationship following the divorce—are the parents amicable, or do they use their children as ammunition against each other?
- Separation from a parent who is significant to the child.
- The parenting skills of the custodial parent and the strength of his or her relationship with the child.
- The child's relationship with his or her nonresident parent.
- The parents' ability to maintain a certain standard of living.

Every teacher must be prepared to work with students affected by the divorce or remarriage of their parents. Consequently, we would like to offer a few suggestions for your consideration.

■ Separate but Equal Parent Conferences?

Both custodial and noncustodial parents have the right to participate in parent-teacher conferences. It is not your place to determine who is the better parent; it is your responsibility to promote a positive partnership with both parents and to attempt to treat them equitably. Some divorced parents may be comfortable meeting together in parent-teacher conferences; others may not. Arrange your schedule so that you can accommodate the needs and interests of both divorced mothers and divorced fathers. Remember that they did not get divorced just to inconvenience you and to make unreasonable demands on your time.

■ **Attitudes Toward Divorced Parents**

We'd also like to suggest that you excise the term *broken home* from your vocabulary. Don't assume that divorced or blended families are dysfunctional. In a country in which one of every four children lives with only one parent and one in two children will live in a single-parent family at some point during his or her childhood (Children's Defense Fund, 1998), teachers cannot continue to favor the image of the "traditional" family. One of a teacher's greatest assets is his or her ability to positively affect students and their family members by developing relationships with them that promote caring and responsive behaviors. As a teacher, your caring, proactive stance will ripple across the generations. Be a teacher who positively affects eternity. By strengthening families' ability to nurture children physically, emotionally, and intellectually, teachers increase the likelihood that all children will grow up to be adults who are healthy, safe, and successful.

INTERETHNIC FAMILIES

During the twentieth century the population of the United States, once overwhelmingly western European and Caucasian, has grown to include numerous other ethnic and cultural groups. In this chapter, we use the term **ethnicity** to refer to the physical characteristics that can be attributed to both individuals and groups. By contrast, we use the term **culture** to refer to the linguistic, societal, and nonphysical characteristics that distinguish societies and groups.

Since **interethnic** and **intercultural marriages** are becoming more common (Estrada, 1993; Smolowe, 1993), an increasing number of children with parents of different ethnic or cultural backgrounds attend American schools today. Some families have a multiethnic makeup that can be attributed to remarriage. In addition, some families have adopted children from cultures that differ from one or both of the parents' native cultures. Adoptive parents are often interested in preserving features of the adopted child's heritage. If students from various ethnic groups are to succeed in American schools, teachers and other family support professionals must be prepared to expand their knowledge of, and ability to communicate with, children and families of various cultures.

IMMIGRANT AND MIGRANT FAMILIES

As you reflect on the impact that projected demographic changes will have on the composition of your classes, we invite you to take a moment to reflect on **immigrant** and **migrant families.** It is quite likely that you will encounter such families, especially if you teach in certain states or regions. What types of challenges might students from these families face? Certainly continuity is a major issue. Since migrant families are required to move as a condition of their employment, and immigrant families often are highly mobile as well, their children may be hampered and frustrated by varied, inconsistent curricula and assessment programs as well as fractured, inconsistent relationships with teachers and school and program personnel. One way to provide some continuity for such children and their families is to communicate with individuals that played a role in their previous school experiences. It's also important to understand that illegal immigrants may be uncomfortable communicating with the school or program since anonymity is critical to their existence.

ADOPTIVE FAMILIES

Approximately 2 percent of children under eighteen years of age are adopted by adults to whom they're not related (Brodzinsky, 1993). Slightly more children in the United States are adopted by related than by unrelated adults (Stolley, 1993). The majority of *adoptive families* function as traditional nuclear families, except that some of the family's children are not biological offspring of either parent (though they may be related to one parent) (Barbour & Barbour, 1997). Single parents also head adoptive families, and some single-sex families (gay and lesbian partners) adopt children. As you are no doubt aware, many families in the United States contain both biological and adopted children.

ALTERNATIVE LIFESTYLE FAMILIES

Between 6 million and 14 million children in the United States are being raised by parents who are not heterosexual, in **alternative lifestyle families** (Crosbie-Burnett & Helmbrecht, 1993; Patterson, 1992). Because the legal system is still somewhat hostile to the concept of gay parenting, gay men and women usually pursue parenthood without telling others about their true sexual orientation (Patterson, 1992; Unger & Crawford, 1992). As of 1995, eight state supreme courts had ruled that sexual orientation should not be a factor in adoption cases. Five had ruled the opposite (Cavaliere, 1995).

The main problems facing gay parents include doubts voiced by their own parents, misgivings on the part of society in general, social isolation, and ambivalence about their ability to raise children in a "straight" world (Jaffe, 1997). Studies of children of gay and lesbian parents reveal that they are not noticeably different from children in families with heterosexual parents in terms of their sexual orientation, personality development, and social relationships (Golombok & Tasker, 1996; Javaid, 1993; Patterson, 1992; Tasker & Golombok, 1995). To date, the research has not revealed any reason to assume that quality of parenting is related to a parent's sexual orientation.

FOSTER FAMILIES AND GRANDPARENTS RAISING GRANDCHILDREN

More than half a million children are estimated to be in **foster care** today, a 25 percent increase from 1990 (Children's Defense Fund, 1998). As children victimized by abuse and neglect have come to make up a larger share of agency caseloads, agencies are finding it difficult to serve the growing numbers of children who need foster care. The most recent growth in foster care placements has primarily involved children placed with relatives. Infants and young children are entering foster care in greater numbers than any other age group and are remaining in care longer than older children are.

When abuse or neglect occurs or when financial pressures, health problems, mental illness, immaturity, or other problems leave parents unable to care for their children, family members often step in. Data from the National Survey of Families and Households (reported by Esme Fuller Thomson, Meredith Minkler, and others in the June 1997 issue of the *Gerontologist*) reveal that more than 10 percent of grandparents assume primary responsibility for raising a grandchild for six months or more, most often during the child's infancy or a preschool year. The Census Bureau reported that in 1996, a total of 2.14 million children lived in households headed by a relative with no parent present; two-thirds of these children lived with grandparents. The number of children living with relatives and no parent in the home grew 59 percent between 1989 and 1996. These arrangements are often referred to as "kinship" care. Most kin caregivers never have contact with the formal child protection or foster care systems.

How can you effectively prepare to meet the needs of children in foster care that you will someday teach? To begin, we suggest that you familiarize yourself with the social services agencies in your community that coordinate foster care services and foster parent education.

New teachers talk

Describe how your cultural heritage and family structure might color your instructional decisions. Develop a plan for expanding your experience of different cultures or enhancing your knowledge of differing family structures.

Being of a minority religion and having faced much discrimination as a result, I have learned to be open-minded and accepting of various types of differences. These experiences affect my instructional decisions, in that I consciously provide a classroom environment that not only accepts differences but encourages them as well. In terms of my curriculum, I incorporate different viewpoints and opinions to teach about an event.

My . . . cultural heritage and family structure . . . influence my instructional decisions in terms of [my] valuing cooperation over competition. I have seen the effects of both and have found that cooperation yields a much more positive learning environment. I may allow healthy competition in some instances, but I make most of my instructional decisions in favor of a cooperative environment. Also, coming from a two-parent family, I force myself to [remember] that not all families are of that structure.

The first step in developing a plan to expand my cultural experience base is to accept the fact that everyone has biases. It is crucial to recognize one's own biases . . . to overcome them. Another step is to have discussions on these topics within the school faculty, as well as brainstorm a list of school programs designed to enhance students' cultural knowledge and experiences (such as African storyteller). Students also may write about

What special challenges are faced by grandparents and other relatives who step up to care for a family member's child? Obviously, for grandparents, the age disparity can be significant. Economic concerns are also prevalent. Begin thinking now about how you can accommodate the needs of relatives and grandparents in your upcoming family involvement program.

LEGAL GUARDIANS

Parents in any of the various family structures we've described may function as **legal guardians** of the children they're raising. When a child is born, in most cases his or her biological parents receive guardianship rights. Adoptive parents are also guaranteed legal guardianship rights, which can only be terminated by court order or voluntary relinquishment. As legal guardians, parents have the right and responsibility to socialize their children; choose and provide health services for them; provide shelter, nourishment, and care; and decide whether they will be educated in private or public schools.

By virtue of their legal guardianship, parents of students under the age of eighteen have the right to see and control their children's school records, except for information placed in the file before January 1, 1975. The law that ensures this right, the **Family Educational Rights and Privacy Act (FERPA),** also known as the **Buckley Amendment,** was passed in 1974.

these issues and share them with their classes if they agree to do so. An open and accepting classroom environment helps to promote such lessons. Each of these ideas can expand not only my knowledge but also that of other teachers and students.

—KYLIE, Student Teacher

Authors' Analysis

After reflecting on her own life experiences, Kylie has successfully put a positive spin on the unfortunate discrimination that affected her personal development. Her plans to accept and encourage diversity and different points of view, to emphasize cooperation over competition, and to accept the reality that everyone has biases will likely significantly improve her future students' awareness, acceptance, and appreciation of individual and cultural diversity. Kylie's collaborative spirit, which underpins her willingness to discuss diversity issues and curricula with her colleagues, will also facilitate the professional development of her fellow teachers.

Now It's Your Turn

 Describe how your own cultural heritage and family structure might color the instructional decisions you will make. Develop a plan for expanding your experience of other cultures or enhancing your knowledge of different family structures. Record your responses in your teaching journal.

FERPA guarantees access to all pertinent school records—including health files, grades, and other documents—for every student. These records must be kept on file by schools and be made available to students (or parents, for students under eighteen) within forty-five days of their requesting them. Schools must permit eligible students or parents to inspect student records and allow them to correct any misleading or false information. When you join the teaching staff at your future school, inquire about the written procedures and policies that are shared with parents regarding their rights under the Buckley Amendment. Schools must inform eligible students and parents of their rights in regard to record disclosure and privacy.

HELPING AT-RISK CHILDREN AND FAMILIES

One in four Americans is a child. Children are the life, future, and hope of this country. Unfortunately, they are also the poorest group of Americans today. Look over the list of key facts about American children in Figure 5.1. Which facts do you find most troubling? Which of these facts will likely affect your teaching career? We would predict that most, if not all, of these realities will touch you as a teacher. Your commitment to making a difference in the lives of the children and families you will encounter over your years of teaching will have a powerful impact on your effectiveness as an educator. The following paragraphs discuss some specific problems faced by at-risk children and families.

POVERTY

The United States of America—the wealthiest nation in history—allows its children to be its poorest group. The overall numbers of children living in poverty are deplorable. Poor children numbered almost 14.5 million in 1996. Even more disturbing is the number of children living in extreme poverty (that is, in households with an income less than half the federal poverty level, or less than about $6,250 for a family of three). No racial group is immune: 40 percent of Hispanic children, 40 percent of African American children, and 16 percent of Caucasian children were poor in 1996. Poverty afflicts children in every region of the country—in suburbs and rural areas as well as in the cities, and in households headed by couples and single parents alike (Children's Defense Fund, 1998).

Child poverty is associated with a host of ills. Children living in extreme or prolonged poverty tend to suffer disproportionately from conditions such as stunted growth and tend to have lower test scores. Children who live in poverty during their preschool years are less likely to complete school many years later, even if their situation has improved, and older children who are poor are twice as likely to drop out of school as are middle-income youths (Children's Defense Fund, 1998).

Figure 5.1
Key Facts About American Children

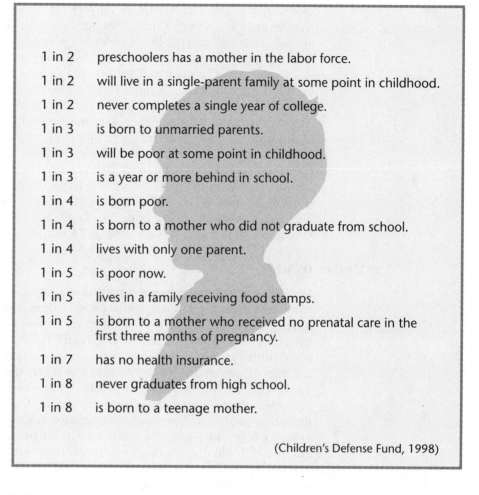

1 in 2	preschoolers has a mother in the labor force.
1 in 2	will live in a single-parent family at some point in childhood.
1 in 2	never completes a single year of college.
1 in 3	is born to unmarried parents.
1 in 3	will be poor at some point in childhood.
1 in 3	is a year or more behind in school.
1 in 4	is born poor.
1 in 4	is born to a mother who did not graduate from school.
1 in 4	lives with only one parent.
1 in 5	is poor now.
1 in 5	lives in a family receiving food stamps.
1 in 5	is born to a mother who received no prenatal care in the first three months of pregnancy.
1 in 7	has no health insurance.
1 in 8	never graduates from high school.
1 in 8	is born to a teenage mother.

(Children's Defense Fund, 1998)

HUNGER

Poverty is the root cause of inadequate nutrition in the United States. During the 1997 school year, 26.9 million children received free or subsidized lunches, and almost 7.1 million received a daily breakfast at school. Unfortunately, millions of children are not being served by the school breakfast or summer food service programs. In twenty-nine cities nationwide, requests for emergency food aid jumped an average of 16 percent in 1997. Most of the requests came from families with children, and nearly one in five of those requests went unmet (Children's Defense Fund, 1998).

HOMELESSNESS

For the past two decades, according to the Department of Housing and Urban Development (HUD), homelessness has increased faster among families with children than among any other group of Americans. In the thirty cities surveyed by the U.S. Conference of Mayors for its *Status Report on Hunger and Homelessness in America's Cities: 1994,* families with children accounted for, on average, about 39 percent of the homeless population. One in every four individuals reported as homeless was a child younger than eighteen.

Wasting America's Future: The Children's Defense Fund Report on the Costs of Child Poverty (Children's Defense Fund, 1994) documents that many children without permanent housing suffer physically, emotionally, and educationally. Among the many problems they face, homeless children have higher rates of infant mortality, more severe health problems, and a reduced chance of being immunized than do other poor children. Homeless children also are at greater risk of missing school (Children's Defense Fund, 1995). Separation from their families is perhaps the most devastating impact of poor housing and homelessness on children. In more than half of the cities surveyed by the U.S. Conference of Mayors in 1994, homeless families had to break up to stay in emergency shelters (Children's Defense Fund, 1995).

UNEMPLOYMENT

In 1997, the national unemployment rate dropped to less than 5 percent, but the unemployment rate for teenagers was three times as high—15 percent. Among Hispanic teenagers, unemployment reached 15.9 percent; among African American teens, unemployment affected 28.6 percent. The job market was tight for young adults as well, with one of every twelve Americans between the ages of twenty and twenty-four (8.4 percent) out of work (Children's Defense Fund, 1998). Significant disparities remain between minorities and Caucasians. Young African Americans are more than twice as likely to be unemployed as their Caucasian counterparts, and young Hispanics are almost twice as likely as young Caucasians to be unemployed (Children's Defense Fund, 1995). Finally, although education improves teens' and young adults' chances of finding employment, 11 percent of sixteen- to twenty-four-year-olds have dropped out of school.

HEALTH CARE AND HEALTH INSURANCE

In 1996, a total of 11.3 million U.S. children under eighteen had no health insurance—the highest number ever recorded by the Census Bureau. Seventy percent of all Americans added to the ranks of the uninsured in 1996 were eighteen or younger. Ninety-two percent of uninsured children have at least one parent who works full-time, year-round (Children's Defense Fund, 1998).

PREVENTION AND IMMUNIZATIONS

Children's immunization levels remain at levels far below acceptable standards, although rates have increased in the past few years. In 1996, a total of 78 percent of American two-year-olds were fully immunized against preventable childhood diseases, up 55 percent from 1992. Unfortunately, more than 1 million two-year-olds who still are not immunized are vulnerable to a host of preventable diseases, such as measles, tetanus, polio, and hepatitis B.

Vaccination levels are lowest among low-income, urban, and non-Caucasian children (Children's Defense Fund, 1998).

SUBSTANCE ABUSE

An estimated 40 to 80 percent of the families in which child protective services agencies intervene have problems with alcohol and other drugs. In a 1997 study, the Child Welfare League of America found that at least half of all foster care placements were due in part to parental alcohol or drug use. Substance abuse is believed to contribute particularly to the number of very young children entering foster care (Children's Defense Fund, 1998).

Two separate surveys released in 1994 documented an increase in teen drug and alcohol use between 1992 and 1993. Over 18 percent of twelfth graders reported they had used an illicit drug within the previous thirty days, with marijuana use showing the sharpest increase. More than one in four (26.2 percent) eighth graders and more than half (51 percent) of high school seniors reported that they consume alcohol (Children's Defense Fund, 1995).

VIOLENCE

An average of fourteen children die each day from gunfire in America—approximately one every one hundred minutes. Violent crime by young people peaks between 3:00 and 7:00 P.M. (Children's Defense Fund, 1998). Each school day, about sixteen thousand thefts and violent crimes occur on or near campuses. Study after study shows that the violence ravaging American cities is taking a toll on American schools as well. In nearly 83 percent of cities surveyed by the Council of Great City Schools, violence and gang-related activity topped the list of worries.

A 1993 study by the National School Boards Association found that of 720 school districts, 82 percent reported an increase in violence in their schools in the past five years. According to the U.S. Department of Education, each year about 3 million thefts and violent crimes occur on or near school campuses. Forty percent of students surveyed in ten inner-city high schools said they have a male relative who carries a gun (Children's Defense Fund, 1995).

CHILD ABUSE, NEGLECT, AND ENDANGERMENT

Estimates of the number of children abused or neglected each year range as high as nearly 3 million. Eighty percent of the child welfare cases served in 1994 involved allegations of abuse or neglect, compared with 45 percent in 1977 (Children's Defense Fund, 1998).

What is child abuse? According to the Child Abuse Prevention and Treatment Act of 1974, or Public Law 93–247 (1977), child abuse is "the physical or mental injury, sexual abuse, negligent treatment or maltreatment of a child under the age of 18 by a person who is responsible for the child's welfare under circumstances which indicate that the child's health or welfare is harmed or threatened thereby" (p. 1826).

■ Mandatory Reporting

School personnel and child care staff not only have a moral responsibility to report suspected child abuse or neglect, they also are required by laws in each state to report it (Besharov, 1990). Teachers, child care professionals, and others who report suspected child abuse or neglect in good faith are immune from legal action. Unfortunately, abuse and neglect come in several varieties and many degrees. Whether the crime is neglect, physical abuse, emotional abuse, or sexual abuse, schools are essential agencies in the reduction of the national child abuse crisis (Berger, 1995).

■ Physical Abuse

A physically abused child may show signs of injury—welts, cuts, bruises, burns, fractures, or lacerations—and these may be from newly inflicted injuries or from old, untreated ones. If an educator notices a suspicious injury on a student, he or she should document its placement and severity, look for evidence of multiple or repeated injuries, note any evidence that the injury was inflicted by an object, and record any explanation for the injury given by the student or his or her parent. The educator must then report the injury to the appropriate authority (Besharov, 1990).

In attempting to ascertain the extent of suspected physical abuse, a teacher should not remove any of a child's clothing. Only medical personnel, such as nurses or doctors who would undress a child as part of their professional responsibilities, should do so.

■ Emotional Abuse

Emotional abuse is defined as a "pattern of behavior that can seriously interfere with a child's positive emotional development" (American Humane Association, 1992b). Emotionally abusive patterns of behavior can include the following (American Humane Association, 1992a, 1992b):

- Terrorizing a child
- Continually rejecting a child
- Refusing to provide a child with needed nurturance
- Refusing to provide help for a child's psychological problems
- Neglecting to provide a child with needed mental or physical stimulation
- Forcing a child to become involved with drugs, criminal activities, or other corruptive forces

Unfortunately, teachers, as well as parents or other family members, are sometimes guilty of emotionally abusing children and adolescents.

■ Sexual Abuse

Sexual abuse occurs when any individual—adult or child—forces, coerces, or threatens a child to have any form of sexual contact or to engage in any type of sexual activity (Hagans & Case, 1988). It's important to the welfare of their students for teachers to have knowledge of the types of sexual abuse. Consequently, we provide the following brief descriptions of different types of sexual abuse (Kempe & Kempe, 1984):

- Incest: Physical sexual activity between family members
- Pedophilia: Sexual preference by an adult for prepubertal children
- Exhibitionism: Exposure of genitals by a male to boys, girls, and women
- Molestation: Fondling, touching, engaging in masturbation; kissing a child, especially in the breast and genital areas
- Statutory rape: penile-vaginal penetration, oral-genital contact, or anal-genital contact between children or between an adult and a child
- Rape: Sexual intercourse or attempted sexual intercourse
- Sexual sadism: Infliction of bodily harm
- Child pornography: Making photographs, videos, or films showing sexual acts including children
- Child prostitution: Having children perform sex acts for profit

■ Neglect

There are three types of neglect of children. **Physical neglect** refers to parents' failure to provide necessities such as adequate shelter, care and supervision, food, clothing, and protection. Physical neglect may also include medical neglect or abandonment. **Educational neglect** occurs when parents fail to make sure their children attend school, when they permit chronic truancy, or when they fail to attend to any special educational needs of their children. **Emotional neglect** includes refusing to provide children with psychological help they need, exposing children to abuse by someone else, and allowing children to use drugs or alcohol. Remember that neglect is lack of proper care, not a function of circumstance: "It is very important to distinguish between willful neglect and a parent's or caretaker's failure to provide necessities of life because of poverty or cultural norms" (U.S. Department of Health and Human Services, 1992, p. 2).

PARENT COMMUNICATIONS

Positive, frequent communication from schools to homes improves teacher-parent relationships (Ames, 1993; Chrispeels, 1996; Rosenthal & Sawyers, 1996; Thompson, 1996; Vickers, 1994; Zeldin, 1990). Teachers must make a commitment to keeping parents informed about special events, curricular goals, and specific ways parents can participate in their children's education.

Parent-teacher communication can be accomplished in many different ways, including through newsletters, parent letters, telephone calls, e-mail, a school Web page, open houses, parent meetings, individual conferences, class visits, and home visits. Whatever the format, parent-teacher communication should occur frequently—at least monthly. Particularly when parents or teachers have concerns or questions, sooner, rather than later, is the appropriate time to establish contact and voice those concerns or questions (Foster, 1994).

Parent meetings are a fairly typical way in which teachers communicate with parents. An often overlooked key to successful parent meetings is collaborative planning by teachers and parents. The more teachers seek parents' input and involve them in decision-making activities, the more likely parents are to take an active role in their children's education. Involving parents in planning meetings also establishes their sense of ownership in the process (Delgado-Gaitin, 1991). Inviting the children to parent meetings is another way to encourage parent participation.

PLANNING FOR PARENT PARTICIPATION

Schools also can work with parents to plan special activities designed to bring families to school under positive circumstances. Examples include Swim and Gym Night, a Fall Festival, a Pajama Party, a Mom and Me Night, a Dad and Me Night, a Family Book Fair, a Family Reading Night, or a Family Food Extravaganza. However, when planning such activities, remember that they must be responsive to the particular needs and interests of the families for whom they're designed.

GETTING FEEDBACK FROM PARENTS

Survey or interview parents early in the year to determine their needs and interests. This can be done using a simple written questionnaire, telephone surveys, on-site interviews, or informal discussions with parents. Sample survey questions include the following:

- What topics are you interested in learning more about?
- What time (include days and hours) is most convenient for you?
- Do you need child care?
- Do you need transportation?
- Would you be willing to serve on the Parent Planning Committee?

You can also compile a list of topics and have parents rank them from those they like most to those they like least. Then choose one of the most desired topics and begin the planning process.

WAYS TO COMMUNICATE WITH PARENTS

Parent communication is critical to student success. Begin thinking about how you will incorporate some of these ideas into your plans to build relationships and communicate with parents.

■ Newsletters and Parent Letters

Written formats for communicating with parents can be very effective. Your ability to write clear, concise, and well-organized letters and newsletter features is key. Frequent written communications support your goal of building successful relationships with parents.

A parent letter is an excellent vehicle for transmitting detailed information that parents need about their children, the school, or specific policies and procedures. Teachers often send a welcome letter to students and parents prior to the beginning of the school year. This beginning-of-the-year effort sends a clear message to parents, as well as to students, that you are interested in developing a positive, collaborative relationship with them.

Newsletters help keep parents up-to-date on classroom events and topics of study. Brief, targeted information can be included to educate parents. Other effective purposes for newsletters include sharing resource information, recruiting volunteers, featuring families, and acknowledging the efforts of a host of special people.

■ Open Houses and Parent Meetings

When planning open houses and parent meetings, you need to be extremely well organized and invite parent participation. Your list of "things to do" should include the following items:

- Find a meeting place.
- Set a date and time. Limit meetings to seventy-five minutes.
- Plan transportation.
- Arrange for child care, if necessary.
- Collaboratively plan activities with parents.
- Plan refreshments. Both parents and teachers appreciate food!

If the purpose of the parent meeting you are planning is primarily to provide information about a particular topic (such as a new reading program or substance abuse prevention), we suggest the following format:

1. Begin with a short introduction.
2. Include a short icebreaker, such as having parents introduce themselves by telling a humorous or memorable story about their children.
3. Present the topic—consider a variety of formats!
4. Provide opportunities for parents to respond or to participate actively in some way.
5. Allow time to reconvene for a short summary.
6. Close the formal portion of the program by asking parents to complete a written evaluation of the meeting.
7. Thank parents for coming, distribute handouts that suggest activities they can do at home with their children, and provide information about the next meeting.
8. Conclude with informal conversation, refreshments, or a fun family activity.

■ **Class Visits and Home Visits**

Traditionally, parents have been invited to visit their children's schools only on special occasions—to attend an open house, to meet with their child's teacher in a parent-teacher conference, or to participate in a school tour during National Education Week, for example. We would like to suggest that you consider breaking tradition! Instituting an open-door policy for parents and other special family members—that is, welcoming them in your classroom at any time—creates more fluid partnership opportunities. If you are really serious about making parents your partners in educating their children, then you will want to make their children's classroom accessible to them.

During most home visits, teachers take on the role of a resource person who is assisting parents in some way. For example, the teacher may be helping the parents fill out necessary forms for transportation or medical assistance. Though some situations may require this type of intervention, many innovative educational programs focus on home visits as a collaborative opportunity for both teachers and parents to interact with children. Parents can and should initiate home visits, plan an agenda for them, and share educational aspirations for their children. Through this type of collaborative home visiting, parents and teachers become equal partners in developing good educational programs for children. Successful home visiting programs depend on a teacher's ability to develop a trusting relationship with parents. If parents aren't comfortable with meeting in their homes, suggest meeting at a nearby park or restaurant.

■ **Communicating Through Technology: Telephone Calls, E-mail, and Web Pages**

Have you ever been fortunate enough to have a teacher telephone your parent about you? If so, did your teacher call to discuss your progress, or to report a concern or problem? Unfortunately, most who recall such a scenario probably won't remember it as a positive intervention. You, however, can be a teacher who uses the telephone to make positive contacts with parents. Parents are delighted to hear good things about their children. Establishing the practice of calling parents early in the year lets parents know that you are comfortable talking with them on the phone and that you welcome their phone calls. The telephone is a very powerful medium for keeping the communication lines open.

As more families and teachers go on-line, e-mail is becoming an attractive communication option. Though privacy issues certainly need to be considered (that is, will students see e-mail intended for their parents?), e-mail offers both teachers and parents the opportunity to make contact and respond when they have available time. Another great benefit of e-mail is that it lets you communicate a message to your entire class list or respond to a specific question from a parent or student.

Many schools now have their own Web pages that provide contact information and highlight special events, activities, curricula, and other information about the school. The Web provides another medium for disseminating written communications to families. Parents and students can access their school's Web page for a variety of purposes.

At this point you may be wondering how you ever will find time to communicate with parents, in addition to finding time to teach and plan. As more and more school districts come to value the involvement of families in their programs, more and more schools are hiring family support personnel, the individuals we discussed in the section on developing school-family partnerships, to support teachers and families. You do need to be realistic about the time that you have to accomplish your many professional tasks. Based on our professional experiences over many years of teaching, we can assure you that the time you invest in partnering and communicating with parents will reap rich rewards for you and your students.

As you begin to think about providing a welcoming atmosphere for families from a variety of cultures and family structures in your future classroom, the first step you can take is to develop an awareness of your own cultural and family values and recognize how they have shaped your attitudes and behaviors.

 In your teaching journal, write responses to the following questions, which will help you assess your cultural heritage.

1. What ethnic group, socioeconomic class, religion, age group, and community do you belong to?

2. What experiences have you had with people from other ethnic groups, socioeconomic classes, religions, age groups, or communities? How did you feel about these experiences at the time? Have your feelings changed?

3. When you were growing up, what did your parents and other significant adults in your life say about people who were different from your family?

4. What do you find embarrassing about your ethnic group, socioeconomic class, religion, age, or community? What would you like to change? Why?

5. What sociocultural factors in your background might contribute to your being rejected by members of other cultures?

6. What personal qualities do you have that will help you establish interpersonal relationships with persons from other cultures? What personal qualities may be detrimental? (Adapted from Randall-David, 1989)

PARENT-TEACHER CONFERENCES

Parent-teacher conferences have the potential to directly affect parent-teacher relations, and teachers are the main variable in determining whether their impact is positive or negative. Teachers' relationships with parents, their presentation style, and their preparation are key components of parent-teacher conferences.

THE PURPOSE OF CONFERENCES

Parent-teacher conferences serve a variety of purposes, both for parents and for teachers. Conferences provide a way for parents to gain a better understanding of the school and its programs, learn about activities they can get involved in to support their child's learning, observe their child's growth through evidence collected over a period of months, and share their perceptions and concerns with teachers to help them develop a more complete picture of their child.

For teachers, parent-teacher conferences are opportunities to

1. Learn about parents' expectations and impressions of the program and school

2. Describe students' progress and share suggestions with parents regarding how they can support their child's progress

3. Build a trusting relationship with parents

4. Communicate appropriate philosophies, explain classroom teaching practices, and promote positive parenting strategies (Markoff, 1992)

THE STRUCTURE AND CONTENT OF PARENT-TEACHER CONFERENCES

Typically, teachers should address the following three dimensions of a child's development at each conference:

Parent-teacher conferences should be structured in a way that allows parents and teachers to function as equals. (© David Young-Wolff/Photo Edit)

- Social and emotional behavior, such as relationships with adults, friendships with other children, and feelings
- Physical behavior, such as gross and fine motor skills, visual and auditory acuity, health and wellness, and nutrition
- Academic and intellectual behaviors, such as application of problem-solving strategies, research skills, scientific and mathematical thinking, and reading proficiency

Parent-teacher conferences should be structured in a way that allows parents and teachers to function as coequals who recognize each other's roles, respect those roles, and join together for the good of students (Losen & Diament, 1978). For example, to be a successful part of a reading program, parent-teacher conferences must be designed in such a way that both parties work together to establish priorities, develop common goals, and achieve concrete solutions focused on supporting a child's reading development (Fredericks & Rasinski, 1990).

DEFENSE MECHANISMS

If teachers become defensive or take an authoritarian rather than a collaborative stance during a parent-teacher conference, they are likely to compound rather than solve problems. The following defense mechanisms are typical of those that teachers sometimes resort to when conferencing with parents. What alternatives can you propose to lessen teachers' tendencies to rely on such mechanisms?

1. *Authoritarian dogmatism.* Teachers sometimes take the stance that they have answers because of their vast experience and, consequently, parents should be willing to accept those answers. What should you do if parents disagree with you? Always be prepared to clearly articulate the rationale for the instructional strategies you use and the rules and policies that guide your practice. Although parents won't necessarily agree with your practices, most will find them more palatable if there's a legitimate reason for them. In addition, find something that the parents and you can agree on!

2. *Not acknowledging limitations.* Some teachers find it difficult to admit their pedagogical limitations, but they would do well to state the obvious—they make mistakes, have shortcomings, and don't actually know everything there is to know. However, teachers also should assure parents that they are committed to ongoing professional development and are continually learning.

3. *Overuse of jargon.* Especially when they're nervous or uncomfortable, teachers sometimes use terms that may exclude parents from the conversation (such as *IEP, alternative assessment, curricular integration*). Teachers who want to conduct a reality check with regard to their reliance on educational jargon can make a list of terminology they frequently use that some people may consider jargon and then brainstorm alternate and easily understood terms to replace the jargon.

4. *Excessive interpretation.* Teachers should avoid overinterpreting a parent's question or comment. It's not necessary to have all the answers. Teachers can propose possibilities rather than answers and can encourage parents to reflect on their suggestions. They also can invite participation by framing open-ended suggestions such as "I'd be interested in knowing what you have found to be successful in this situation at home."

5. *Talking too much.* This defense mechanism goes hand in hand with excessive interpretation. Teachers are often inclined to dominate a conference by presenting a lot of information in a short period of time. Consequently, parents' participation is reduced to passive listening. Brief, focused notes can help prevent teacher domination of conferences. Teachers also can prepare open-ended questions or statements to elicit focused responses from parents, such as "I've noticed that Karen enjoys experimenting. Tell me about some of the experiments she's done at home."

6. *Labeling.* Teachers sometimes label students and share these labels with parents, and often these labels are based on teachers' subjective interpretations and judgments rather than on diagnostic tests. For example, a teacher might say, "Maurice is hyperactive and undisciplined" or "Chaka is a stubborn child." Such labels may confuse and upset parents. Rather than label students, teachers should describe learners' behaviors in specific terms. For example: "Maurice left his desk five times during a ten-minute mini-lesson" or "When I tried to talk with Chaka about her writing, she refused to listen and put her hands over her ears."

7. *Reverting to prejudicial opinions.* Teachers sometimes form opinions about children and their parents based on the observations and experiences of previous teachers, cumulative records, and experiences with siblings. We encourage you to take the time to form your own unique perceptions of students and to base your understandings on firsthand experience, contacts, and direct observations. If the teachers' lounge is a forum for uninformed gossip about children and their families, don't become part of the problem. If necessary, avoid spending time in the lounge.

8. *Making excuses.* Parents typically don't want to hear about teachers' occupational hazards and challenges—they want to hear about their children! Consequently, teachers should avoid using parents as sounding boards for their concerns. Conferences should remain focused on the student; if the discussion strays toward either the teacher's or the parent's problems, teachers should refocus the discussion (Losen & Diament, 1978).

SCHEDULING AND PREPARATION

Use of effective interpersonal skills during parent-teacher conferences, coupled with adequate planning and preparation, can help teachers avoid reliance on defense mechanisms. *Before the conference,* teachers should define specific goals they want to accomplish and write down questions and concerns for discussion. They also should arrange the environment in a manner that helps parents feel welcome and comfortable. For example, when teachers invite parents to join them at a table rather than talk at parents from the safety of the impenetrable fortress otherwise known as the "teacher's desk," parents are more likely to feel that they play an equal role in the parent-teacher conference.

During the conference, teachers should remember to do the following (Fouse, Biedleman, & Morrison, 1994):

1. Express their acceptance of parents' feelings and viewpoints
2. Avoid blaming, personal attacks, and name calling
3. Stick to the issues
4. Listen actively to what parents say
5. Avoid interrupting parents
6. Allow parents to fully express their points of view before responding
7. Recognize that parents may be acting out of lack of information rather than a lack of caring
8. Avoid attempting to force a particular point of view on parents
9. Recognize that both parents and school personnel are generally seeking what is best for the child

Even when parent-teacher conferences go well, they can be stressful for both parents and teachers. For many teachers, the first parent-teacher conference they ever attend is one they're responsible for conducting. That fact tends to make the experience even more stressful. Role-playing can serve as one means of preparing for parent-teacher conferences while still a preservice teacher. However, simulations cannot surpass the knowledge and experiences that the "real thing" provides.

Consequently, during the course of completing your clinical practice, student teaching, or internships, we encourage you to seek out opportunities to observe and participate in parent-teacher conferences. We have found that many cooperating teachers are willing to let their student teachers and interns take part in parent-teacher conferences. Often all parties involved—parents, cooperating teachers, and student teachers or interns—find the collaboration and interaction beneficial.

PARENTS AS VOLUNTEERS

The impetus to involve parents and the community in schools has come from the federal government. In fact, in 1968, the federal interagency requirements of the Department of Health, Education, and Welfare stated that all federally funded programs must document some form of parent and community involvement. These federal guidelines have had a significant influence on the emergence of volunteer programs in American schools. School volunteers are unpaid personnel who usually work on a temporary basis and perform tasks that supplement, but do not take the place of, the roles played by paid staff members.

INTERVIEWING, ORGANIZING, AND GUIDING VOLUNTEERS

Volunteers can support the school in a variety of capacities and should be drawn from all segments of the community. The majority of volunteers will be parents of the children that attend the school or program. Volunteers should be interviewed and placed in positions in which they can make significant contributions to the program. Desirable traits to identify in prospective volunteers include helpfulness, sincerity, creativity, dependability, reliability, confidentiality, and responsibility (Rasinski, 1995). The most important qualifications for volunteers include a commitment to sharing their time, energy, and expertise and an ability to show that they are dedicated to supporting and respecting students.

When organizing a volunteer program, it's important to plan and implement at least one formal orientation session that includes details regarding the goals and purposes of the school or program, the school's philosophy, specific duties and responsibilities of volunteers, the relationship of the volunteers to the staff, and an overview of dos and don'ts (Rockwell, Andre, & Hawley, 1996). This orientation should be followed by a series of opportunities that engage volunteers in learning how to successfully accomplish specific tasks and understand their roles. For example, when Therese prepared parent volunteers who facilitated a number of literacy activities in the writing center, she provided the parent volunteers with clear guidelines and expectations in an orientation session, asked the parents to observe writing activities in the classroom, conferenced with parent volunteers after they had an opportunity to see the students in action, and then created a schedule for the parents who were comfortable with the tasks and expectations involved.

TASKS FOR VOLUNTEERS

There are many potential volunteer opportunities in any school or program. Decisions about how to most effectively utilize volunteers need to be made collaboratively by teachers, parents, administrators, and community members. Volunteers who come to school eager to share their energies and talents are often frustrated with the limited direction and support they receive. Written role descriptions that detail volunteer tasks will help your school or classroom make your volunteer program a success. Volunteers can contribute as members of advisory councils, assistants in classrooms and resource centers, library and office helpers, clerical assistants, public relations advocates, and community and classroom educators. Following are some suggestions for activities that could be performed by classroom volunteers:

- Read and share stories with students (with the whole group, with small groups, and individually).
- Share information about their careers.

Volunteers can support the school in a variety of capacities and should be drawn from all segments of the community.
(© Joel Gordon)

- Share their musical talents with students
- Share multimedia resources with students
- Share their family culture with students
- Share a foreign language with students
- Photograph and videotape special classroom events
- Accompany students on field trips

We think you'll find that when you invest some time, thought, and energy in planning ways to involve parents positively in their children's education, your efforts generally will result in collaborative partnerships that benefit students, their families, and you as well. We guarantee that many of your students' parents will choose to be involved in their children's education. It's your job—and in your best interest, as well as your students' best interests—to make every reasonable effort to ensure that parent participation is positive.

SUMMARIZING WHAT YOU'VE LEARNED

- Avoidance, rather than collaboration, often characterizes teachers' approach to parents. To be empowered to interact with parents as educational partners, you must be knowledgeable regarding the importance of parent involvement and the essentiality of family communication.

- The first national education goal, that all children will start school ready to learn, requires both parent education and family involvement. Concerted efforts to connect families with schools and other human service agencies are necessary to promote parent education and family involvement.

- Parent involvement has emerged as a national priority in recent legislation.

- A number of family structures are representative of the American population today. These family structures include teen-parent families, single-parent families, blended families, adoptive families, divorced families, interethnic families, alternative lifestyle families, foster families, and families headed by grandparents.

- American children and their families are significantly affected by a number of societal factors including poverty, hunger, homelessness, unemployment, limited access to health care, substance abuse, violence, and child abuse and neglect. Mandatory reporting procedures require that teachers report suspected child abuse or neglect.

- Parent-teacher communication should occur at least once a month. Parent-teacher communication methods include parent letters, newsletters, open houses, parent meetings, class visits, home visits, telephone calls, e-mail messages, and Web pages.

- Teachers should address students' social and emotional behavior, physical behavior, and academic and intellectual behavior during parent-teacher conferences.

- Volunteers should be drawn from all segments of the community. A formal orientation should be provided for school volunteers. Volunteers should receive written role descriptions.

YOUR PROFESSIONAL TEACHING PORTFOLIO

- Develop a list of interview questions that focus on parent communication strategies. Using your questions, interview a primary teacher, a middle school teacher, and a secondary teacher. Compile a list of the strategies used by each teacher to communicate with parents. In writing about these strategies, compare and contrast the similarities and differences between them. Discuss which of these strategies you plan to incorporate in your future practice.

- Design a chart of support services and programs available to families. Include the following components in your chart: a brief description of the service or program, eligibility requirements, and contact information. Develop a written plan for disseminating this information to parents.

- Write a beginning-of-the-year parent letter or newsletter for your future classroom.

- During your field experiences, collect photographs that document your interactions with parents; include these in your Professional Teaching Portfolio.

Key Terms

Alternative lifestyle families (p. 135)

Authoritarian parenting style (p. 127)

Authoritative parenting style (p. 127)

Blended family (p. 131)

Culture (p. 134)

Educational neglect (p. 143)

Elementary and Secondary Education Act (ESEA) (p. 125)

Emotional neglect (p. 143)

Ethnicity (p. 134)

Family Educational Rights and Privacy Act (Buckley Amendment) (p. 137)

Foster care (p. 135)

Goals 2000: Educate America Act (p. 125)

Immigrant families (p. 134)

Intercultural marriages (p. 134)

Interethnic marriages (p. 134)

Laissez-faire parenting style (p. 127)

Legal guardians (p. 137)

Migrant families (p. 134)

Physical neglect (p. 143)

School-family compacts (p. 125)

Single-parent family (p. 129)

Transescence (p. 126)

Relevant Resources for Professionals

Books and Articles

• Boyer, E. (1992.) *Ready to learn. A mandate for the nation.* Princeton, NJ: Carnegie Foundation for the Advancement of Teaching.

• Children's Defense Fund. (1998). *The state of America's children yearbook.* Washington, DC: Children's Defense Fund.

• Coleman, M. (1997). Families and schools: In search of common ground. *Young Children, 52*(5), 14–21.

• DeFrancis, B. (1994). *The parents' resource almanac: Where to write, who to call, what to buy, and how to find out everything you need to know.* Holbrook, MA: Bob Adams.

Professional Journals in Education

• *Childhood Education*—Journal of the Association for Childhood Education International (ACEI). See Professional Organizations.

• *Young Children*—Journal of the National Association for the Education of Young Children (NAEYC). See Professional Organizations.

• *Reading Teacher*
International Reading Association
800 Barksdale Road

P.O. Box 8139
Newark, DE 19714

• *Family Relations*
National Council on Family Relations
1219 University Avenue SE
Minneapolis, MN 55414

Professional Organizations

• Association for Childhood Education International (ACEI).
ACEI is a professional organization for those involved in the education of children from infancy through early adolescence. This organization encourages professional growth of teachers and informs the public about the needs of children.
11501 Georgia Ave., Suite 315
Wheaton, MD 20902
301-942-2443 or 800-423-3563

• National Association for the Education of Young Children (NAEYC).
The National Association for the Education of Young Children is a nonprofit professional organization of more than eighty thousand members, dedicated to improving the quality of services provided to young children and their families. NAEYC

provides educational opportunities and resources that promote the professional development of teachers.

1509 16th Street., N.W.
Washington, DC 20036
800-424-2460

http://www.naeyc.org

Videos

A selection is available from the National Association for the Education of Young Children (see Professional Organization list for address, phone, and Web site).

- *Partnerships with Parents*
  This video emphasizes the importance of the parent-teacher relationships for children. The video also discusses how to establish and maintain positive communication and how to handle the most common problems teachers face when working with parents (28 minutes).
  Available from The Learning Seed
  330 Telser Road
  Lake Zurich, IL 60047
  800-634-4941
  LEARNSEED@AOL.COM

- *Understanding Our Differences: Mexicans and Americans*
  This video explores common misconceptions about Mexican culture, as well as stereotypes Mexicans have about their neighbors to the north (25 minutes).

Web Sites

- **Family Involvement Partnerships for Learning**
  http://www.ed.gov/PFIE/index.html

  Department of Education resources for parents, professionals, and the community.

- **National Coalition for Parent Involvement in Education**

  http://www.ncpie.org/

  The National Coalition for Parent Involvement in Education (NCPIE) is a coalition of education groups committed to building strong family/school relationships. This site includes conference, organization and resource information.

- **The National Parent Information Network (NPIN)**

  http://www.npin.org/

  The National Parent Information Network (NPIN) is a project sponsored by two ERIC clearinghouses: the ERIC Clearinghouse on Urban Education at Teachers College, Columbia University, New York City; and the ERIC Clearinghouse on Elementary and Early Childhood Education at the University of Illinois at Urbana-Champaign.

- **National Parent Teacher Association**

  http://www.pta.org/index.stm

  The National Parent Teacher Association (PTA) is a volunteer association that works exclusively on behalf of children and youth. This site includes links to program and convention information as well as information on legislative activity.

INSTRUCTION IN LEARNING COMMUNITIES

PART THREE

In Part Three we examine specific tasks teachers must perform for learning to take place, such as creating a culture that supports growth and learning, guiding students toward achievement, deciding what to teach, choosing the best method for teaching, planning an entire integrated unit of study, creating each day's instruction or lesson plan, and assessing student learning. Since it's important both for students and for teachers to have an indication of how students are doing, we discuss a variety of assessment approaches that go beyond multiple choice tests.

6

SCHOOLS AS CULTURES AND ORGANIZATIONS

— OR —

Even schools have culture!

SEEING THE BIG PICTURE: ORGANIZATIONAL CULTURE AND ENVIRONMENT

We begin this chapter by asking you to reflect on different uses of the word *culture* to remind you of what you already know about culture and to help you make meaningful connections between your existing knowledge and what you are about to learn. Put another way, we wanted to activate your existing **schema** for the concept of **culture** in preparation for adding to it by expanding your understanding of what *culture* can mean.

It's important to take the time to consider each school's culture and how it affects the teaching/learning process. This can lead to a better understanding of how to most effectively "get things done" within that school environment. For example, in another galaxy far, far away, Rita once was an itinerant teacher serving three different elementary schools in the same district. Because she was the first-ever coordinator of that district's new gifted education program, she spent much of her time in the role of a change agent attempting to address individuals' concerns and questions about the new program. Rita quickly discovered that "how we do things here" was very different for each of the three elementary schools, even though they were in the same district and were all located within a three-mile radius. The schools felt different, had different standard operating procedures, and were led by principals with disparate leadership styles. Consequently, Rita's attempts to get things done in those three different settings, coupled with the "culture shock" she occasionally experienced in moving from school to school, taught her to appreciate the value of studying and analyzing organizational environments and cultures in schools.

"The school cannot become a total learning organization until it becomes a 'community of learners.' Community is necessary because students need a supportive learning environment, one that is virtually risk-free, to pursue standards of high intellectual quality."

—Keefe & Jenkins, 1997, p. 7

Make a list of your experiences with culture. What does the term *culture* mean to you? Now, compare and contrast the following three uses of the word *culture:*

• Having lived in San Antonio his entire life, Nehemiah was familiar with many facets of Mexican culture.

• Louisa's knowledge of the classics and the extent of her travels caused her colleagues to conclude she was a highly cultured person.

• Beth found it challenging to adapt to the culture of her new school, since previously she had taught in more learner-centered environments.

In your teaching journal, create a three-ringed Venn diagram. Make a list in each section of the diagram that illustrates how these three meanings of *culture* are different, as well as the features they have in common.

Organizational environment and organizational culture are closely related concepts that are critical to understanding how an organization (including a school) functions. Each is an integral component of the other, and each affects the performance and productivity of the individuals within an organization. **Organizational environment** consists of the everyday social and physical surroundings in which people do most or all of their work (Amabile, Burnside, & Gryskiewicz, 1995). Working from that definition, organizational environment serves as the umbrella concept that encompasses organizational culture.

Organizational culture has been defined in a variety of ways, as even a cursory look at the literature on it reveals. One of the first definitions to catch on was Deal and Kennedy's: "the way we do things around here" (1982). But both before and since, a variety of other definitions have been suggested. Most of those share a common core, including shared values, beliefs, and expectations; common understandings; and a common system of symbols. We view **organizational culture** as the basic assumptions that operate within an organization (such as a school). These are revealed by the behavior of organizational members, as well as by certain value-led outward manifestations of those assumptions, such as the organizational structure, the management style of the organization's leaders, and the organization's physical setting (Jensen, 1988). Organizational culture also has an emotional dimension and reflects the importance of having a sense of identification and meaning, which often is derived from social groups. Culture acts as a kind of social glue that connects and holds together the organization's different parts. All of the members of an organization influence its culture and subcultures in one way or another (Carlson, 1996).

ELEMENTS OF ORGANIZATIONAL CULTURE

A prerequisite to understanding and managing organizational culture is the task of recognizing its outward manifestations when you see them. Consequently, in this section we identify key features of organizational culture and some of the observable behaviors that reflect cultural components. In doing so, we draw on the work of Deal and Kennedy (1982), who were predominant among those first to introduce the notion of corporate or organizational culture to the popular press. Because schools are examples of organizational environments, they possess their own unique cultures, just as other organizations do. Yes, even schools have culture.

■ Shared Values

Shared values are the bedrock upon which organizational cultures are built. They are the basic beliefs that provide a sense of common direction for organization members and provide guidelines for their day-to-day behavior. Values function as the heart of an organization's culture by establishing standards of achievement within the organization. The degree to which they are shared by all members of the organization determines the strength of its culture. In organizations that succeed, members identify, embrace, and act on their shared values.

Leaders of organizations with strong cultures talk openly and frequently about their organization's shared values and beliefs and don't tolerate deviation from the organization's standards. For example, a value that could serve as a core component of a school's culture is the notion that every student can learn or that every student has a contribution to make. In a school with a strong culture that subscribed to this value, school leaders would make it a point to communicate it frequently and consistently and to make it a visible component of the school's culture. Most importantly, they would model the enactment of that value—that is, they would not just "talk the talk" but also "walk the walk."

■ Rites and Rituals

Rites and rituals are activities that demonstrate for an organization's members its values, expectations, or accepted operating procedures. Some, such as meetings, are mundane and part of the daily routine of the organization. Others, such as awards ceremonies, are extravagant and provide powerful, visible examples of what the organization values. Unless organizational leaders tell people what they want them to do and how they want them to do it, they have no right to expect them to do it. Rituals and standards define acceptable decorum and call attention to the way procedures are expected to be carried out. Organizations with strong cultures have rites and rituals that have a visible and pervasive influence on "how we do things here."

Although rites and rituals can take many different forms (such as play, ceremony, or communication patterns), here we've chosen to focus on a ritual familiar to anyone who's spent much time at all in those organizations called schools—meetings! Although all organizations have meetings, their form varies widely with regard to several variables, including the following:

- *The number of meetings held.* Some organizations require many formal meetings; in others it's a major accomplishment to get everyone in the same place at the same time once a month.
- *The setting.* Business organizations most often favor formal conference rooms, but in schools meetings often are held in classrooms, auditoriums, or libraries. The size of the group dictates the setting to a large degree.
- *The table's shape.* No surprises here! Round tables facilitate good peer relations among meeting participants, whereas tables with distinct heads reinforce hierarchies.
- *Who sits where.* In some organizations, the seats are up for grabs; in others the acknowledged "boss" sits at the head of the table, with the next most important person seated beside him or her.
- *Number and composition of attendees.* In very formal organizational cultures, only peers attend meetings; junior people wait to be summoned. In less formal cultures, attendees represent a mixture of levels.
- *The conduct of the meeting.* Give-and-take characterizes the meetings in some organizations, whereas in others meetings are held in theater-like settings, with attendees mesmerized by dazzling multimedia presentations.

■ Social Standards

Social standards are another facet of an organization's rituals. For example, what is acceptable practice with regard to verbal communication? Do people refer to other organization members using formal titles? Are exchanges between administrators and the rank and file encouraged or discouraged? Is it acceptable for members to engage administrators other than their direct supervisors in conversation, or is it appropriate for them to respond but not to initiate conversation? Are side conversations tolerated at meetings? Is slang or occasional swearing tolerated at meetings? What about in the break room? Much of what goes on in organizations consists simply of people talking with one another. Consequently, setting standards for how they do this has a strong influence on culture. Variables such as public decorum, interpersonal behavior, presentation formats, reports, and procedures all have written or unwritten standards unique to particular organizational cultures.

■ Organizational Politics

If organizations have cultures—and they do—then organizational politics is inevitable. Etymologists trace the origin of the English word *politics* to the Greek word *polis*, which means an aggregate of many members. In other words, where two or more are gathered, there is politics. Aristotle believed politics provides an opportunity to create order from diversity while avoiding totalitarian rule, and he viewed human beings as political animals.

Politics is about power, competition, influence, and strategic negotiation. However, politics is also about culture, because within organizations politics involves the manipulation of metaphors, myths, symbols, and legends. Organizational politics focuses on the interpretation of facts rather than on the facts themselves (Carlson, 1996).

The adjective *dirty* has so often been used to describe politics and politicians that it has become an understood, and therefore unnecessary, descriptor. However, politics, both literally and figuratively, is not a four-letter word. In fact, political leadership and "good" politics are essential ingredients of effective, healthy organizations. Organizational leaders who possess a clear sense of themselves and a level of comfort with their organizations' political systems discover opportunities that they otherwise would not see.

Given the pervasive nature of organizational politics, we find it ironic when we so often hear teachers protest, "I just don't want to get involved in politics." We respond by pointing out to these teachers that they already are standing knee deep in politics, whether they wish to acknowledge it or not. Anyone working in the educational arena is "particularly vulnerable to external, macrolevel politics that soon get reflected in internal, microlevel politics" (Carlson, 1996, p. 65).

■ Cultural Networks

Cultural networks serve as an informal—but primary—means of communicating within organizations (including schools). Part of what cultural networks do is to transmit the organization's shared values and heroic mythology. All members of strong organizational cultures have, in addition to their designated jobs, other jobs—jobs that aren't printed on their business cards but are important nonetheless. Storytellers, spies, priests, whisperers, secretarial sources, gossips, and cabals make up a hidden power hierarchy within an organization, a hierarchy quite different from the official structure depicted on organizational flow charts. Cultural networks connect all parts of an organization, without respect for titles or positions. They not only transmit information but also interpret its significance for organization members. Especially in large organizations, making effective use of the cultural network is the only way to "get things done" and to understand what's really going on. Consequently, it's important to be familiar enough with the main players of this hidden hierarchy to recognize them and their roles when you see them. We profile five of those players here: heroes and heroines, storytellers, priests, whisperers, and gossips.

Heroes and Heroines An organization's *heroes and heroines* personify its values and set the standard in regard to performance, thereby providing tangible role models for others to follow. They are the motivators, the magicians, the "go-to" people others count on when things get tough—the symbolic figures whose deeds are out of the ordinary but not too far out. An organization's heroes and heroines possess unshakable style and character, which they use to demonstrate that the ideal of success is humanly possible. Managers run organizations, but heroes and heroines create them. In fact, they demonstrate many of the traits of creativity. They're intuitive and visionary and are willing to take calculated risks. Some are born heroes and heroines, such as Bill Gates, founder of Microsoft; Oprah Winfrey, the driving force behind Harpo Productions; John Dewey, the father of progressive education; and Maria Montessori, originator of the Montessori schools. Others are situational heroes and heroines—people anointed by their colleagues or supervisors in recognition of some aspect of their achievement or behavior, such as salesperson of the month or teacher of the year.

Mike was one of our heroes. By simply entering his school, he provided a living, breathing model of teacher leadership and raised the standards by which teacher productivity was appraised. The distance Mike raised the bar was most efficiently measured in feet rather than inches. Unquestioned competence, self-responsibility, and professionalism characterized Mike, his performance, and his interactions.

Lara was one of our heroines. She ached with caring for the early childhood special needs students she attempted to reach, and she willingly gave up planning periods to collaborate with an English as a Second Language (ESL) teacher to provide an inclusive environment for her students as well as her school's ESL students. On her own time, Lara planned ways to more effectively utilize the program assistants with whom she worked and to more effectively employ a comprehensive, integrated-services approach to meeting her students' special needs. You'll hear more about that approach in Chapter 13, in which we focus on collaboration and change.

Storytellers Why do people tell stories? First of all, they genuinely enjoy telling stories, but they also find the power and influence that come with the informal position of storyteller gratifying and even intoxicating. By simply interpreting what goes on within an organization to fit their own perceptions, storytellers can alter reality. Historians are a special type of storyteller who reinvent an organization's history by engaging in what we like to call selective remembering. In their retellings they leave out details that don't fit their purposes and embellish parts that they feel need a bit more pizzazz to sustain listeners' interest. *Storytellers* can preserve organizational values by imparting legends to new members—legends about visionary heroes, radical renegades, and an occasional organizational outlaw or two. We rather enjoy Deal and Kennedy's description of storytellers (1982) and find it insightful, on-target, and applicable to the storytellers we've met in school contexts, including various curmudgeonly custodians, seasoned secretaries, and loquacious librarians: "The best storytellers are typically found in positions that give them access to a great deal of information. They are usually in the epicenter of activity and free to be as eccentric as they choose. A storyteller needs imagination, insight, and a sense of details—a story can't be abstract. While the position of storyteller is a powerful one, it's not a leadership role. Many people fear storytellers because everything—and everyone—is grist for their story mills. Yet colleagues revere them and often protect them" (p. 88).

Lucille the elementary school librarian had lived in her community for decades. Her children all went to school in the district where she worked, her husband was a teacher in the district, and she spoke almost daily with the librarians at the other elementary schools. Consequently, Lucille had developed and nurtured cultural network contacts all over the district. In addition, the library where she worked served as her school's hub. Everyone passed through or by the library on their way to almost anywhere in the school.

Lucille was well situated, both physically and culturally, to receive and transmit information. And she loved telling stories, as was evidenced by the energy, animation, and inflection she invested in each story she told. Lucille could provide a blow-by-blow account of the closing of the Floyd Elementary School, complete with the accompanying histrionics and sordid political jockeying. She could replay the 1967 tornado that wiped out Roosevelt School and brought economic renewal and revitalization to the community. If you needed to know where the real power resided and whom to contact for a particular purpose, Lucille the librarian could deliver, and in the process of telling you a story or two save you precious time and countless steps.

Priests Organizations, like some churches, have priests. *Priests* are the designated worriers of an organization, as well as the guardians of its values. They worry about keeping the flock together, always find time to listen to confessions, and always have solutions to any dilemma—even moral ones. The job of priest carries the most responsibility of any other "job" in the cultural network. It should belong to CEOs or top administrators, but since they're not accessible to the masses on a daily basis, other, more accessible individuals must

The priests in a cultural network often are sought for advice.
(© Frank Siteman/PHOTO EDIT)

do the job. Priests are like storytellers who can't be bothered with details but instead rely on allegories to explain and comfort. They tend to be older than their colleagues, because being a priest requires maturity and seriousness. Priests recite the oral histories of their organizations, an ability that helps them fulfill their duty to communicate historical precedents for planned actions. Priests also console and aid people who recently have experienced defeat, disappointment, or frustration.

Helen excelled as a worrier; she worried on the collective behalf of her colleagues in the PreK–8 building where she taught first grade. Whether faced with dire circumstances or undifferentiated doldrums, many teachers sought out Helen to receive her advice, as well as her words of encouragement.

Everyone who knew Marjorie, a junior high English teacher, revered her as the school's high priestess. No, that wasn't her official title, and no one ever actually genuflected in her presence. However, like Helen, Marjorie definitely had earned the respect and admiration of colleagues, administrators, students, and their parents, and like Helen, she was a bit older than most of her colleagues. Even though their classrooms were not on anyone's way to anywhere in particular, people routinely ended up in Helen's and Marjorie's rooms. Their before and after school sessions did not result in world peace, but confessions were heard, coffee was consumed, and confidence was restored.

Whisperers *Whisperers* are the powers behind the throne—people who are movers and shakers despite having no formal position of power. Their power source is "the boss's ear." To be successful, whisperers must possess two critical skills. First, they have to be able to read the boss's mind quickly and accurately with benefit of few clues. Second, they must have a vast support system of organizational contacts and must work hard to stay current with anything and everything that's worth knowing within their organization. As one might predict, whisperers tend to be intensely loyal to the source of their power—the boss.

Leon and Doug were teachers who launched their administrative careers by whispering their perceptions of key events and school anecdotes in a superintendent's ear. Ruth was a school board secretary who also had access to a superintendent's ear and made herself an indispensable source of information. Both jobs—school board secretary and whisperer—were hers as long as she wanted them.

Gossips According to Deal and Kennedy (1982), *gossips* function as the troubadours of organizational culture. We find that depiction a bit too kind and generous. After all, some gossips simply delight in dishing the dirt. However, many organizational members appreciate the trivial day-to-day information communicated by gossips. They count on gossips to name names, along with dates, salaries, and current organizational events previously known only to a small and select group. If they fulfill no other purpose, gossips certainly do make organizational life more interesting. In other words, they're a good entertainment value!

Gossips: we've known a few—a few too many. Through expert use of innuendo and implication, gossips can alter the course of careers or at least color people's perceptions and shade their interpretations of events—both real and imagined. They also can serve as fairly innocuous conveyors of fairly accurate information regarding who's being interviewed for the middle school science position, who's seeing whom, and whether the kindergarten teacher is going to retire anytime soon.

Anyone who has opportunity to observe their organization's people and has ample access to the flow of information is well situated to serve as the organization's resident gossip. Secretaries, librarians, receptionists, and "lunch ladies" are likely candidates. Although we realize that women traditionally have held these positions and that traditional wisdom suggests that the role of gossip is typically filled by a woman, we caution you against concluding that most gossips are women or that most women are gossips.

As a matter of fact, that rumor probably was started by a man. And that man might have been Ray, a physical education teacher we knew who regularly collected information from a fifth grade teacher when she delivered her students to the gymnasium for class. Ray then would transmit that information to other teachers when he accompanied their students back to their classroom. Custodians, business managers, and other people whose schedules or positions allow them the freedom to roam around the building a bit also are likely candidates for the role of gossip.

BENEFITS OF STUDYING ORGANIZATIONAL CULTURE

If people are an organization's greatest resource, then it makes sense to find ways to use that resource as effectively as possible. A strong organizational culture can serve as a powerful lever for guiding people's behavior and enhancing their productivity. It provides a system of informal rules that spells out how people are to behave most of the time, and it encourages people to feel good about what they do, so they are likely to work harder. Leaders must clearly understand their organization's culture if they plan to use it to accomplish their goals (Deal & Kennedy, 1982).

Studying organizational culture also can help leaders learn how best to introduce and implement change. We'll explore this facet of **school culture** much more fully in Chapter 13, which focuses on change and the change process. Given the reform movement in education, schools don't have the luxury of ignoring their organizational cultures. If school culture can't be ignored, then it naturally follows that there is much to be gained from learning about it and about how to manage it.

"READING" AN ORGANIZATION'S CULTURE

Reading and understanding something as ambiguous and subtle as an organization's culture can be challenging. Organizational cultures aren't necessarily integrated, and different views of an organization may be held by members at its center and those at its periphery. Failing to accurately interpret organizational culture can lead to calamity and to the inability to accomplish organizational goals (Carlson, 1996).

If you want to get things done within your organizational environment, you'll find it helpful to acknowledge the existence and importance of the cultural network. In fact, you'll need to become a part of it, by cultivating contacts within the network yourself. Effective cultural networking involves treating all organization members with the deference and respect generally reserved for the head of the organization. All members of an organization play hidden, but potentially culturally important, roles—treat them accordingly. Effective cultural networking also means asking people to explain the meaning of the things you're seeing and experiencing. Ask them about the history of the organization and how certain policies and characteristics came to be.

However, don't rely solely on others' cultural readings. Use your own conceptual and observational skills to read the culture for yourself. You can learn a lot by listening, looking around, and deferring judgment. Particularly if you're new to the organization, it's helpful to study the physical setting, read what the organization says about its culture and itself, observe how people spend their time, and observe how the organization greets people—both visitors and members. Once you have become an integral part of the culture and have acquired an internal perspective, it's important to identify the career path progression within the organization and how long people stay with the organization. Other crucial facets of reading an organization's culture include analyzing what's discussed or written about in the organization and paying particular attention to anecdotes and stories that pass through the cultural network.

ORGANIZATIONAL CULTURE AND SCHOOLS

What, you may be wondering, does all of this business about organizational cultures and cultural networking have to do with you? Someday you'll teach in a classroom that has its own organizational environment, organizational culture, and cultural network—an environment, culture, and network that you create by virtue of the decisions you do and don't make. In addition, your classroom will be a microcosm within the larger context of the school that houses it, and that school will possess historically transmitted patterns of meaning—the norms, beliefs, traditions, and myths understood (maybe in varying degrees) by the members of the school community. The culture of that school will encompass daily rituals, important ceremonies, subcultures, underlying values, beliefs about the nature of learners and learning, assumptions about the purposes of schooling, and the school's basic organizational design (Stolp & Smith, 1995). It will be the setting in which you pursue your career.

SCHOOLS AS REFLECTIONS OF THEIR COMMUNITIES' CULTURES

Just as individual classrooms are microcosms of the schools that house them, schools are microcosms of the communities where they are located. As such, they reflect, to varying degrees, the values, beliefs, and behaviors of those communities. Continuing this outward journey to wider and wider concentric circles of influence, communities operate within the context of states, states within regions, regions within countries, and countries within the international arena. All of these contexts and organizations will have some type of effect on the school where you work. This may sound farfetched and only distantly related to the daily reality you'll experience as a teacher. However, regional, national, and international cultures do impose themselves on schools—in subtle as well as overt ways.

NATIONAL AND INTERNATIONAL CONTEXTS

For example, a study abroad course provided a group of preservice teachers an opportunity to observe some schools in Cheltenham, England. Early childhood, elementary, special education, and secondary education students all discovered a number of differences between the English schools they visited and the U.S. schools they were familiar with, and many of those differences reflected the two countries' different cultures and values. For instance, preservice teachers noted differences in word usage, inflection, and spelling and in the way students address teachers. Most notably, they noted that English headmasters typically lead students in daily worship sessions, including prayers, religious songs, and stories or lessons featuring biblical principles. Daily worship is a kind of vestigal organ—the appendix of the English educational system, if you will—a remnant of English education's origins in the Church of England. A parallel feature in the U.S. educational system is the nine-month school calendar—a structural leftover that originated in the agrarian age and reflects the nation's history.

SCHOOL CONTEXTS

Take a few moments to review the elements of organizational culture that we've discussed, and then begin to connect those elements to your prior school experiences—your schema. In that way, you can begin to construct your own understandings of school cultures, their major players, and their primary features. If you have difficulty doing this on the school level, try beginning with the classroom level. Every classroom has its own culture—its own version of "how we do things here"—and by now you've certainly experienced many of those cultures firsthand! For example, do you remember how the schools you attended felt? What smells, sights, and sounds permeated the hallways? Did those schools have an institutional feel that reminded you of a prison? A stiff and stilted feel that reminded you of a church? Or maybe the laid-back, informal feel of a perpetual party? Every school has its own unique atmosphere and climate—a tone that the school's leaders and cultural network players set and modify.

Remember the itinerant teacher who served the teachers and students of three different elementary schools belonging to the same district? Succeeding at "getting things done" at those three schools necessitated playing by three different versions of "how we do things here."

Just as individual classrooms are microcosms of the schools that house them, schools are microcosms of the communities where they're located.
(© Elizabeth Crews)

- At Lincoln School that meant operating within a benevolent autocracy. The Lincoln School principal cared about his teachers and students, loved to tell stories, and made most of the important decisions (as well as the coffee) without consulting teachers and staff. His office was the school's command post and the intercom his equivalent of Radio Free Europe.

- At Washington School that meant operating within a benevolent, laissez-faire state of chaos. This principal had formal authority but little functional authority. Teachers routinely staged coups, and no one moved, attended meetings, or made any final decisions without consulting one of two key teachers who possessed the functional authority in that school.

- At Jefferson School that meant operating within something resembling a democracy. This school's principal allowed teachers to make their own decisions as well as take responsibility for their own mistakes. Teachers had a voice in goal setting, and the principal was an advocate both for teachers and for students.

The itinerant teacher liked Jefferson School's version of "how we do things here" best of all and found it most conducive to her efforts to "get things done."

After reviewing the elements of organizational culture, connect those elements to your prior school experiences—your schema. As you make those connections, you'll begin to construct your own understandings of school cultures, their major players, and their primary features. Focus your reflections on one particular school or on one particular teacher's classroom in which you were a student.

In your teaching journal, characterize the organizational environment you've selected (perhaps with an analogy or metaphor). Then provide at least one example of each of these cultural elements of that environment: its shared values, its rites and rituals, and the players in its cultural network (that is, its heroes and heroines, storytellers, priests, whisperers, and gossips). Finally, describe how each one of your examples either facilitated or hindered the teaching/learning process.

DEFINING AND DESIGNING LEARNING ENVIRONMENTS

Now that you've used your conceptual skills to explore the organizational environments and cultures of schools—the larger context of the teaching/learning process—it's time to focus on the immediate context in which teaching and learning occur. Reflect on the contexts of some of your favorite and not-so-favorite recollections of school. What did you see? What did you hear? How did you feel? How would you describe what you saw, heard, and felt to someone else?

BEYOND CLASSROOM WALLS: THINKING OUTSIDE THE BOX

When considering the concept of **learning environments,** we encourage you to think "outside the box"—literally. Think beyond the classroom walls, which are much too limiting. Although the concept of a learning environment certainly includes the classroom, it's much broader than that. However, due to the fact that the concept of learning environments, like many other concepts, is culturally defined, you probably think of a classroom when you hear the term *learning environment.*

Many of the most important things people learn and teach, they learn and teach somewhere other than in classrooms. Both incidental and planned learning occur in places other than classrooms and at times other than the regularly scheduled school day. Playgrounds are part of the learning environment, as are hallways, basketball courts, recital halls, restaurants, buses, practice rooms, stages, and lunchrooms. For example, some teachers conduct classroom recess meetings as one way of helping children succeed socially (Thompson, Knudson, & Wilson, 1997).

As a former teacher of middle school students, Rita is a survivor of overnight retreats and field trips where the learning environment consisted of state parks, cabins, college campuses, and state capitol buildings. Although she has no medals to show for her perseverance and tenacity, she does have the satisfaction of knowing that the students who participated in those excursions often included them high on their lists of their most memorable and most worthwhile learning experiences. For Therese, the parent-child classes she taught provided her with special memories, as did the many outdoor educational activities she conducted with her four-year-olds. More recently, we both held undergraduate methods classes in the meeting rooms of London hotels and even in unused corners of hotel dining rooms and lobbies. What "out-of-classroom" educational experiences do you recall?

HOW TECHNOLOGY HAS CHANGED THE LEARNING ENVIRONMENT

Next, consider the effect that technology has had on the concept of learning environments. When students entered school even a few years ago, they had no prior experience with "surfing the Web," and their parents had no expectation that their children's schools and classrooms would or should provide students with access to the Internet. Today the story is much different. Advances in technology have ushered in the age of **asynchronous learning,** making it possible for learners to access information and their teachers at different times and from different places and greatly expanding the notion of learning communities and learning environments: "Technology places learners in touch with a universe of knowledge from which they can construct their own meanings. The learning environment is everywhere. Helping students make sense of expanding knowledge and conflicting values takes precedence over transmitting fixed bodies of information. The information highway is replete with opportunities for learning. Schools must prepare students to use them advantageously" (Keefe & Jenkins, 1997, p. 136).

When we entered school for the first time, computers were behemoths that filled entire rooms and were inaccessible to the general population, let alone kindergartners. Now, instead of writing letters to penpals, young learners can use the Internet to connect with children half a world away. Rather than copying the first paragraph about whales from the encyclopedia, they can visit Web sites published by marine museums and use software on CD-ROM to make multimedia presentations complete with sound, video, and graphics. Perhaps you have had the opportunity to take a college course that was offered on-line or that supplemented in-class activities with on-line support (such as syllabi, class notes, and chat rooms). What predictions do you make about the technological advances today's kindergartners will take for granted by the time they enroll in college?

TEACHERS' ROLES IN DEVELOPING CLASSROOM CULTURES

The quotation in the first Reflect & Respond in this chapter suggests that schools can't become total learning organizations until they become "communities of learners" (Keefe & Jenkins, 1997). How can teachers create such communities? Collective responsibility for student learning, academic emphasis, and high morale among students and teachers are key features of successful learning communities. In a study of three organizational characteristics of high schools—staff cooperation, teacher empowerment, and collective responsibility for learning—the first two characteristics showed no direct relationship with student achievement and engagement. However, collective responsibility for learning did demonstrate a positive correlation with student achievement gains, both early and late in high school (Lee, Groninger, & Smith, 1995). Teachers who emphasize collective responsibility for students' learning create learning communities characterized by the following attributes (Kruse & Seashore Louis, 1995):

- *Reflective dialogue between teachers.* Teachers engage in conversations about educational issues and student learning problems.
- *Deprivatization of teaching practice.* Teachers make a habit of examining their teaching behaviors, observing other teachers, and sharing strategies for improvement.
- *Collective focus on student learning.* Teachers are more concerned about outcomes and student performance than about teaching techniques and strategies.
- *Collaboration in professional development.* Teachers regularly work together to improve their professional skills and the organization of the learning environment.
- *Shared norms and values.* Teachers are committed to developing the school as a community.

Successful development of learning communities requires certain structural conditions—time to meet and talk, small size, physical proximity, team teaching, regular meetings, convenient communication structures, school autonomy, school-based management, and building-level selection and control of personnel. The successful development of learning communities also requires certain social and human conditions—staff openness to improvement and willingness to accept feedback, an atmosphere of trust and respect, an adequate knowledge and skill base for effective teaching and learning, supportive leadership, and an intensive socialization process.

■ Expect Students to Do Well

Business leaders who subscribe to the "Theory X" approach to human resource management assume that people can't be trusted and that they must be watched carefully if they are to produce anything at all. Leaders who subscribe to the "Theory Y" approach expect the best of people and assume that they can be trusted, possess the impulse to achieve, would rather create than destroy, and value meaningful work (McGregor, 1960). The "Theory Y" approach is not intrinsically good or good "because God said so"; it is good because it works—under certain conditions and with healthy, sophisticated, autonomous people (Maslow, 1965). Maslow stated that "it is well to treat working people as if they were high-type Theory Y human beings, not only because of the Golden Rule and not only because of the Bible or religious precepts or anything like that, but also because this is the path to success of any kind whatsoever, including financial success" (1965, p. 41).

Teachers' expectations often directly affect students' achievement and productivity. In other words, teachers often get just what they expect. Effective teachers "appreciate the truth in the statement: 'We are as we perceive other people perceive us' and recognize that self-fulfilling prophecy often plays a major role in performance and behavior" (Jensen, 1988, p. 71). Quite simply, there is a direct link between teacher expectations and student achievement: "If they anticipate that students will not perform well, they typically do not. If teachers expect—and require—that students perform in a quality manner, they typically do" (p. 64). Effective teachers expect the best of all of their students, while acknowledging that they will be disappointed at times.

■ Teach to the Top

Some teachers say that their solution to coping with the wide range of abilities they see among their students is to teach to the middle. However, if and when teachers actually succeed at locating this elusive "middle," they often find that nobody is really there! Like Utopia, it's a theoretical construct that exists in some people's minds but is not a part of people's day-to-day reality. Teachers who create cultures of productivity within their classrooms set and communicate high but reasonable expectations for *all* of their students and then provide a learning environment that enables their students to meet those expectations. As Carl Boyd, an award-winning teacher, once put it, "No one rises to low expectations."

SOME OPTIONS FOR "HOW WE DO THINGS HERE"

The attitudes, procedures, and routines teachers exhibit and follow speak volumes about their philosophies regarding the teaching/learning process, their values, and their views of the learning environment. For example, teachers who value collaboration in the teaching/learning process structure the learning environment to promote student interaction and to teach students how to work in groups. Teachers who believe schools should be learner-centered give students recognition, solicit their opinions, and act on their input (Dodd, 1997). Teachers who value intrinsic motivation provide opportunities for students to take responsibility for themselves and their own learning, such as by having students monitor and reflect on their own progress toward meeting self-selected goals (Jensen, 1988). Teachers who value extrinsic motivation use rewards, tokens, and stickers to reinforce student behavior and achievement. In Chapter 8, we'll revisit the concepts of intrinsic and extrinsic motivation and explore related issues, such as the use of rewards and punishment.

■ Help Students Help Themselves

Teachers who value learner independence do not do for students what they can or should do for themselves. Educators whose long-term goal is to develop self-directed, lifelong learners understand and appreciate the message contained in the statement "I only help you if you need me less after I've helped you." They recognize that a good education should enable students to leave school with the ability and confidence to function independently and successfully in the *real world*: "Because the future will certainly be characterized by change, teachers can prepare students by gradually making themselves unnecessary. That means they must work as hard to help students develop personal qualities such as commitment, self-control, critical and creative thinking, and a love of learning as they do to teach the content of the discipline" (Dodd, 1997, p. 12).

■ Procedures and Routines That Promote Independence

The procedures and routines of productive learning environments promote learner independence. Teachers who have created such environments do not hamstring students with written and unwritten rules that increase their dependence on teachers ("You must ask permission to sharpen your pencils") or unnecessarily restrict their independent decision making ("I'd like you to read one of the books from our classroom library rather than the one you brought from home"). We'll focus more on procedures, routines, and rules in Chapter 7.

Productive learning environments support individual differences while recognizing that some norms must be established. For example, class meetings

New teachers talk

How do you approach the task of creating a culture of productivity for your students and for yourself?

To create a culture of productivity, I clearly communicate my expectations to students. I also ask their expectations of me. I believe doing so adds to a feeling of mutual respect. For example, the first week of school we compiled a list of rules and consequences, as well as procedures for the classroom. The students were instrumental in this process, and it gave them a feeling of ownership in their learning environment. They clearly know what's expected of them in their classroom.

The students also did interviews of their classmates and participated in activities that provided them with opportunities to "practice" giving and receiving compliments. I let them know that it's okay to make mistakes, and hopefully it's an environment where they can feel comfortable doing

so. I think that helping students set realistic goals also makes a productive environment. Once they have achieved some success, then the ball starts rolling.

I make a conscious effort to watch the words I use with students. There is nothing quite like a sincerely given compliment to motivate a student or teacher. I also believe that variety is important to developing a culture of productivity. There are certain routines that help a classroom run smoothly; however, doing the same thing each day is boring for everybody. I use a variety of videos, music, slides, and transparencies, as well as activities that are student centered.

I also believe that understanding the world that kids live in is extremely important. I try to remain current on music, movies, language, and the social lives of my students. I feel that this helps me relate to them and that maybe they can then see I am a real person, too. I like to give my stu-

can help build learning communities in which students show respect for others, listen when others talk, do their fair share of the work, help peers learn, and collaboratively solve problems. Members of productive learning environments value cooperation and collaboration and place less emphasis on competition (Dodd, 1997).

CREATING CULTURES OF PRODUCTIVITY

If those in positions of leadership and authority—whether they be managers, supervisors, presidents, officers, mayors, teachers, coaches, or parents—could identify the environments preferred by organizational members and the cultures that enable them to be as productive as they possibly can be, leaders then could work to create those environments and cultures. In choosing to do so, they would be acting to maximize the quantity and quality of members' output, with the end result being increased productivity for organizations (Jensen, 1988). In Chapter 3, we underscored the importance of leaders' creating such cultures of productivity within their organizational environments. Effective teachers take on this leadership role and succeed in creating environments in which those around them can be productive. To create cultures of productivity

dents choices in their learning. I think this is a motivator to success. Lastly, I show an appreciation for students' work by displaying it in the classroom and having them share the things they're proud of.

I believe that all of these factors also create a culture of productivity for me. I try to meet students' expectations of me. I learn to understand my students and relate to their world, and I find their reactions stimulating. That's the really great thing about teaching—the uniqueness of the kids and their reactions.

—ROBIN, First-Year Middle School Teacher

Authors' Analysis

Because she was unable to relocate, Robin served as a substitute teacher for three years prior to securing her first full-time teaching position. Now that she's finally doing what she set out to do, she's excited about teaching middle school social studies in a large urban school district. Robin's also determined to do what she can to create a learning environment in which all of her students—a diverse population in her school—can succeed if they choose to do so. Consequently, she seeks to provide a variety of different learning opportunities that feature high levels of student engagement, and she actively involves students in making some of the decisions that affect them and their learning.

Now It's Your Turn

 How will you approach the task of creating a culture of productivity for your students and for yourself? In your teaching journal, describe at least five specific strategies you'll use to create a learning environment that facilitates—rather than hinders—the productivity and creativity of your students.

for themselves and for their students, teachers must (adapted from Akin & Hopelain, 1986):

1. Value productivity and results—not just activity
2. Facilitate an environment of trust and openness
3. Act with reliability so others will know how to act
4. Have high standards and expectations but achieve results without bossing
5. Communicate the mission
6. Learn from, as well as about, others by listening, observing, and asking questions

How can you apply these characteristics and behaviors to the teaching/learning process—specifically, to the challenge of creating learning communities and productive learning environments? Each one of these six points relates directly to the affective domain and involves developing a positive social-emotional environment that enables learners to succeed—to be as productive as they can be.

SETTING THE SOCIAL-EMOTIONAL TONE OF LEARNING ENVIRONMENTS

Organizational environment and culture affect the productivity of all of the members of a school, whether teachers or students (Cavanaugh & Dellar, 1997; Huang, Waxman, & Houston, 1993; Jensen, Kiley Shepston, Killmer, & Connor, 1994; Johnson, Ellett, & Licata, 1993; Kiley & Jensen, 1998; Templeton & Jensen, 1993). Just as different people perceive learning environments in different ways, school environments have different effects on different people. Some teachers and students are resilient enough to succeed in spite of unsupportive or dissonant learning environments, whereas others may wilt, whither away, whine, or engage in passive-aggressive behavior.

However, generally speaking, when organizational members are afraid to make mistakes for fear of being yelled at, embarrassed, or humiliated, they take few, if any, risks. They certainly don't ask questions. But when the school's mission statement supports the notion that every organizational member has a contribution to make and that all students can and will learn, teachers and administrators are then responsible for finding ways to enable all students to succeed (Keefe & Jenkins, 1997).

AFFECT HAS AN EFFECT: DEVELOPING A POSITIVE TONE

Can the affective tone of a learning environment really make that big of a difference? Consider the following scenario, extracted from Rita's school schema:

I loved school until my first day of kindergarten. However, it was downhill from there, as the rest of the year was filled with tears, nausea, and humiliation. The "Blue Cat Incident" (the title under which I've catalogued this particular trauma in my kindergarten schema) should serve as a representative example of the scenarios that characterized my first year of formal education.

Apparently Halloween was the upcoming holiday, for the instructions my young colleagues and I received were to draw and color a picture of a cat. Having by this time received more than adequate indoctrination to persuade me to become a card-carrying member of the teacher pleasers' club, I labored diligently at my assigned task. I was careful to include the appropriate body parts and the correct numbers of each (two eyes, four legs, one tail). However, drawing in perspective was not my strong suit, and I hadn't yet managed to achieve satisfactory results where the cat's legs were concerned when my teacher chose to engage in some formative—and public—evaluation of my artistic rendering.

What follows is my recollection of how I, as a five-year-old, recorded and responded to the teacher monologue prompted by my somewhat impressionistic representation of a cat. Stage directions are included in italics for those readers who would like to visualize the sad scene.

THE BLUE CAT INCIDENT

A One-Act, Pitiful Saga

SETTING:	MEAN OLD TEACHER'S KINDERGARTEN CLASSROOM
TIME:	ART CLASS—OR—TIME TO BE CREATIVE, AS LONG AS YOUR PICTURE LOOKS EXACTLY LIKE THE MEAN OLD TEACHER'S PICTURE
CHARACTERS:	MEAN OLD TEACHER, RITA, RITA'S TRAITOR COLLEAGUES

Mean Old Teacher (MOT): "Boys and girls, could I have your attention for a moment? I'd like you to look at Rita's picture with me."

MOT takes Rita's picture from her and holds it up for all to see.

MOT: "Rita's cat is blue. Are cats blue?"

The following line is spoken in unison, as the MOT leads the class in shaking their collective heads No:

MOT and Rita's traitor colleagues: "NO–O–O–O–O–O!"

MOT: "No-o-o-o, cats are not blue, and I asked you to color your cats black since it's Halloween."

Rita's bottom lip trembles as she sinks down in her chair.

Figure 6.1
Rita's Blue Cat

MOT: "And do cats' legs look like this?"

MOT points to Rita's feline depiction, which resembles Bambi on ice (that is, Bambi flat on stomach with all four legs going in different directions; see Figure 6.1). The following line is spoken in unison, as the MOT leads the class in shaking their collective heads No:

MOT and Rita's traitor colleagues: "NO–O–O–O–O–O!"

MOT: "No-o-o-o, cats' legs don't look like this, do they?"

At this juncture, the rest of Rita's body joins her bottom lip in trembling, she sinks down further in her chair, and she wishes desperately that she were at home, gagging into her mother's hanky as she did every morning before getting on the bus to go to school. Stage fades to black as Rita slowly loses consciousness.

Although I admit to adding the last line for dramatic effect, the rest of the pitiful saga is retold exactly as I remember it. The affective climate of my kindergarten learning environment had a profound effect on me and my productivity, but I'll spare you the sordid details. I'm sure it will suffice to say that, even today, the word *kindergarten* conjures up a huge selection of negative memories and stressful recollections for me.

Now contrast that sad scenario with the learning environment created by a junior high English teacher who never utters a negative statement about any student, never laughs at students' mistakes, and never allows students to laugh at other students' answers—no matter how off-base they are. Contrast it with a first-grade room where students cheer when they take out their math books and exhibit reverential awe as they take handfuls of magic from a "treasure box" in preparation for hearing someone share a favorite book while seated in a special reader's chair. We emphatically suggest to you that, yes, the affective tone of the learning environment can make that big of a difference!

ENSURING STUDENTS' EMOTIONAL AND SOCIAL SAFETY

As a teacher, your goal is to create for all learners what the best and wisest parents would want for their own children (Dodd, 1997). Productive learning environments begin with physical safety, which is a prerequisite to learning as well as to emotional and social safety. Maslow's physiological needs must be met first, and learning communities must first provide safe and secure environments for their students (Jacobson & Lombard, 1992).

The classroom social environment is one of the chief psychological determinants of academic learning: "Even when the instruction is intensive and the students' abilities considerable, these factors count for little if students see their classmates as uncooperative or their teachers as unfair" (Walberg & Greenberg, 1997, p. 45). A positive social climate allows students to share ideas through teams and cooperative groups, thereby promoting democratic decision making and fostering cohesiveness and satisfaction (Walberg & Greenberg, 1997). When learners enjoy themselves, they get more done. Students' feelings about their classes affect their interest and engagement in the subject matter and also help them acquire essential social skills.

MISTAKE MAKING AND RISK TAKING

Situational and environmental factors can be crucial variables in either hindering or facilitating creativity. In the absence of a supportive environment, creative performance may be hampered severely, particularly if an organization's members perceive that there is no tolerance for mistake making and risk taking (Amabile, Burnside, & Gryskiewicz, 1995; Crosby, 1968). However, as we mentioned earlier, different people perceive and respond to the same environment in different ways.

Interactions between individuals and their environment are complex and do not affect all people identically. Some who have studied the relationship between organizational environment and organization members' creative production speculate that people who are highly intrinsically motivated may be immune to environmental factors that others find destructive. They wonder aloud if there is a way to bolster people's internal motivation, to "immunize" them against the destructive effects of extrinsic rewards (Amabile, 1983; Kohn, 1987). For any given task, an individual's creative production depends on his or her intrinsic motivation to complete that task, the presence or absence of strong extrinsic constraints within the social environment, and the individual's ability to disregard whatever extrinsic constraints do exist (Amabile, 1983). In other words, teachers and parents can encourage creativity by reducing emphasis on extrinsic rewards and constraints.

CREATING RESPONSIVE LEARNING ENVIRONMENTS THAT ACCOMMODATE DIVERSITY

As Jensen (1988, p. 46) points out, "Research in the area of learning styles and hemisphericity definitely indicates that person-environment fit is a variable which can affect achievement and productivity." So what happens when "the way we do things here" doesn't match the individual needs or learning styles of some within the learning environment? In the classroom, the fit between individual students and the overall learning environment can be as important as individualized instruction. The results of one study indicate that higher individualization in instruction is associated with higher learning levels only in classes whose students prefer individualization. Such findings suggest that student achievement is likely to be greater in classrooms where there is a better fit between the actual learning environment and the environment preferred by students (Fraser & Fisher, 1983). Those results also suggest that teachers who wish to enhance student achievement should match their environmental individualization efforts with the preferences students demonstrate.

However, another study indicates that high achievers seem to have the ability to use an integrative style of information processing, using specialized cerebral functions of both the left and the right hemispheres, whereas low achievers seem to use only a right-hemisphere style of information processing (Okabayashi & Torrance, 1984). Those findings suggest that low-achieving students might benefit from learning how to integrate right- and left-hemisphere styles of information processing. And they might. However, a possibility that the authors of that study did not explore is that altering the learning environment of low-achieving students to match their preferred learning styles also might result in increased achievement.

Many researchers have studied learning styles and have provided a variety of viewpoints on how teachers can best make use of information about students' learning styles and learning environment preferences (for example, see Dunn & Dunn, 1978; Gardner, 1983; Gregorc, 1984). Research on learning styles and multiple intelligences can help you understand and value the perspectives of others and can help you identify and build on students' strengths. However, the central question remains: Should the learner be made to fit the environment, or should the environment be made to fit the learner? By now, we hope you recognize that the appropriate response to that question is, "It depends." It depends on the learner, the learner's developmental level, the teacher's instructional objectives, the teacher's long-term goals, and other variables related to the teaching/learning process.

EMBRACING DIVERSITY VERSUS TOLERATING DIVERSITY

Dodd (1997, p. 11) explains that "as students have become more diverse, establishing a comfortable and challenging classroom in which every student feels valued has become more difficult. Moreover, when teachers realize that they must also adapt their practices to accommodate a range of personal interests, abilities, and learning styles, the task may seem impossible." As we've acknowledged, there's no one magic answer to the challenge of creating learning communities that enable all students to succeed, but one suggestion is to make classrooms more like ideal homes. Instead of thinking only about the universal needs of many students, teachers also must begin to think of the particular needs of individual students, just as caring and committed parents do (Dodd, 1997). Teachers must simultaneously consider the needs, perceptions, and experiences of many learners, as well as the needs, perceptions, and experiences of individual learners.

GENDER DIFFERENCES

In its landmark 1992 book *The AAUW Report: How Schools Shortchange Girls,* the American Association of University Women points out that "whether one looks at preschool classrooms or university lecture halls, at female teachers or male teachers, research spanning the past twenty years consistently reveals that males receive more teacher attention than do females. In preschool classrooms boys receive more instructional time, more hugs, and more teacher attention. The pattern persists through elementary school and high school. One reason is that boys demand more attention" (AAUW Educational Foundation, 1992, p. 68). When boys call out answers, teachers typically listen to their comments. When girls call out answers, teachers typically respond by instructing them to raise their hands if they wish to speak. Even when boys don't volunteer, teachers are more likely to call on them.

Males also typically receive more of all four types of teacher comments—praise, acceptance, remediation, and criticism. However, the difference favoring boys is usually the greatest in the more specific instances of teachers' use of praise, criticism, and remediation. When teachers take the time and make the effort to specifically evaluate a student's performance, the student receiving the feedback is more likely to be male. These differences in teacher evaluations of male and female students have been cited by some researchers as a cause of "learned helplessness" in females (AAUW Educational Foundation, 1992).

Learned helplessness refers to a lack of academic perseverance and a debilitating loss of self-confidence. It's a theory used to explain why girls sometimes abandon academic challenges that boys persistently pursue. Males and females view academic failure very differently. Males attribute such failure to lack of trying and feel more effort is needed to be successful. Females are more likely to attribute their failures to a simple lack of ability (AAUW Educational Foundation, 1992).

Attempts to study relationships between gender and learning environment (such as Goh & Fraser, 1995; Townsend & Hicks, 1995) reveal that girls are more affected by the nature of classroom climate than are boys and that girls generally view classroom environments more favorably than do boys. In science learning environments, when teachers need assistance in carrying out demonstrations, 79 percent of the time they ask boys to carry out these demonstrations. Consequently, science classrooms tend to be dominated by boys, partially because they have more extensive out-of-school familiarity and experience with the subject matter (AAUW Educational Foundation, 1992).

Teacher attitudes reinforce differences in male and female student behavior. Teachers are more likely to give girls increased attention when they stay in physical proximity to them and to provide more detail when responding to boys' questions. Teachers also are likely to call on boys more often; more often accept boys' answers as correct, even though boys don't provide correct answers more often than girls do; and ask girls memory questions more often, whereas they tend to ask boys questions that require higher-level thinking. Even teachers of the gifted, both male and female, tend not to view gifted girls as logical thinkers and tend to judge gifted boys as better creative problem solvers and critical thinkers (Callahan, 1986).

Our own experience has revealed a number of gender differences among gifted students. For example, in a year of working with, interacting with, and observing fourth-grade gifted students, we found that the boys were much more verbal and assertive than the girls, much more likely to voluntarily respond to higher-level questions, and much more likely to be confident that their answers were "good" answers. This was true in spite of the fact that girls in general begin school with greater verbal ability than do boys and the fact that the girls in this particular group performed just as well academically as the boys did and had IQ scores in the same range as the boys in the group.

When we detect gender patterns in preservice teachers' behaviors and student interactions, we first document those patterns (for example, by tallying the number of times they call on boys versus the number of times they call on girls and then calculating the corresponding percentages). Then, during postobservation conferences, after asking the preservice teachers to reflect on their own performance, we ask, "Did you know that in a fifteen-minute instructional segment you called on boys to respond to all but three of the questions you posed?" or "Were you aware that whenever you asked students to help you distribute or collect materials you only asked boys for their assistance?" Almost always, the preservice teachers answer "No" to such questions. Although they may be attempting a politically correct response, in most cases we choose to believe that they truly aren't aware of the gender patterns they're exhibiting. You needn't wonder if you engage in similar gender patterns. Videotaping or even audiotaping can provide conclusive evidence, and no one has to see or hear the tapes but you! The classrooms of teachers who succeed at encouraging both girls and boys to participate have these characteristics in common: the classroom environment is respectful of all students, all students participate in class, and the classroom incorporates multiple modes of learning (Campbell & Storo, 1996).

SEXUAL HARASSMENT IN SCHOOLS

Sexual harassment begins early in life. Look at how students treat each other during school hours; it has significant negative implications for girls. Reports of student **sexual harassment**—unwelcome verbal or physical conduct of a sexual nature imposed by one individual on another—are increasing. Generally the harassment is initiated by males and directed toward females. Incidents of sexual harassment reveal as much about power and authority as they do about sexuality; the person being harassed usually is less powerful than the person doing the harassing. Although sexual harassment is prohibited under Title IX, sex-biased peer interactions appear to be permitted in some schools, if not always approved of. School authorities sometimes treat sexual harassment as a joke rather than as serious misconduct. It "occurs in the mundane, daily matters of school life: in the chemistry lab as well as in the carpentry shop, in the driver's ed. car, and on the practice fields of extra-curricular sports. Yet, despite its frequency, sexual harassment is rarely reported, tallied, investigated, or systematically documented" (AAUW Educational Foundation, 1992, p. 74).

When boys line up to "rate" girls as they enter a room, when boys treat girls so badly that girls are reluctant to enroll in courses where they may be the only female, when boys feel it is good fun to embarrass girls to the point of tears, it is no joke. Yet school personnel sometimes view these types of behaviors as harmless instances of "boys being boys." When teachers and administrators allow sexual harassment to continue, the clear message they send to both girls and boys is that girls are not worthy of respect and that appropriate behavior for boys includes exerting power over girls—or over other, weaker boys. In fact, being accused of being in any way like a woman is one of the worst insults a boy can receive (AAUW Educational Foundation, 1992).

When administrators choose not to confront students who use other students or teachers as convenient targets for sexual harassment, they tacitly give their permission and approval for the students to continue the harassment. We offer the following examples for your consideration:

■ Female students are afraid to walk through crowded hallways between classes because some male students see the crowded, unsupervised hallways as opportunities for groping.

■ The senior football star loudly offers an unsolicited and inappropriate comment about a female teacher's physique as she passes him in study hall. When the teacher reports the incident to the building principal, he instructs her to take it as a compliment.

■ A sixth-grade male would rather risk wetting himself than use the school restrooms, because older male students who consider him effeminate flush his head in the urinal when he goes to the restroom. His twin brother routinely calls him a woman because he likes to paint.

Physical safety is prerequisite to emotional safety. Emotional safety is prerequisite to learning. Both physical safety and emotional safety are foundations upon which productive learning environments must be built. Both must be "givens" of the learning environment for females as well as males, if in fact the mission of schools is to enable all students to learn and all students to succeed.

CULTURAL AND FAMILY DIFFERENCES

Culture is an important variable in the learning environment. It affects how students learn and what they learn. People from different cultures sometimes perceive and process information differently. Cultural contexts shape their responses. For example, some cultures reward competition, whereas others reward cooperation. Cultural diversity challenges teachers' competence. It requires them to take on multiple perspectives, engage in flexible thinking, and use more than one approach. However, teachers, whether experienced or novice, often don't think about culturally responsive pedagogy or reflect on how culture and teaching interact.

Many attempts have been made to study the relationships between culture and learning environments (such as Fisher & Waldrip, 1997; Huang & Waxman, 1996; Waxman & Ellet, 1992). Results indicate that the learning environments of predominantly minority classrooms are different from those of majority classrooms. African American and Hispanic learners view their learning environments less favorably than do Caucasian students in the same classrooms (Waxman & Ellet, 1992). Minority students generally perform less satisfactorily than do Caucasians, due to low teacher expectations, tracking practices, lack of a multicultural curriculum, school/home incongruences, and a substandard learning environment (Harris, 1997).

The kind of attention teachers give minority students tends to differ from the attention they give Caucasian students. At the elementary level, African American males tend to have fewer interactions overall with teachers than do other students, yet they receive four to ten times the amount of qualified praise ("That's good, but . . . ") than other students do. They also are viewed less favorably by their teachers and are seen as less able than other students (AAUW Educational Foundation, 1992).

The data are more complex for African American girls. Although they have less interaction with teachers than do Caucasian girls, they attempt to initiate such interaction more often than do Caucasian girls or boys of either race. African American girls also tend to receive less reinforcement from teachers than other students do, although their academic performance is often better than that of boys. When African American girls do as well as Caucasian boys in school, teachers attribute their success to hard work but assume that the Caucasian boys are not working up to their full potential. This, together with evidence suggesting that African Americans more often are reinforced for appropriate social behavior whereas Caucasians are reinforced for academic accomplishments, may contribute to low academic self-esteem in African American girls. In spite of their better performance, African American girls tend to value their academic achievements less than do African American boys. One study indicated that African American boys have a more positive perception of their own ability in science than do African American girls, although there were no differences in achievement between the two groups (AAUW Educational Foundation, 1992).

What systemic changes in schools and learning environments would support culturally diverse learners, some of whom live in poverty and urban centers? We offer the following suggestions for your consideration (National Center for Education Statistics, 1993). Many of these suggestions should sound familiar to you by now. We hope you'll recognize them as recommendations that could positively affect the development and long-term learning of all students.

■ *School-linked community services.* Schools must work with community and social agencies to provide collaborative social programs that serve multiple needs and entire families (that is, they should adopt a comprehensive, integrated model of services).

■ *Culturally compatible schools and classrooms.* School personnel must respect and assimilate the variety of cultural orientations and values learners bring with them.

■ *Teachers with high expectations who care and are culturally sensitive.* Teachers must accept and value differences and help students build on their strengths, prior knowledge, and prior experiences.

■ *Opportunities to learn.* For all students, schools must provide equitable access to content, quality instruction, and educational resources.

■ *School environments that foster resilience.* Resilience occupies the position at the positive end of the "at-risk" continuum. Schools and school personnel must protect and support students so resilience wins out over at-risk factors.

■ *Teacher engagement.* Teachers must collaborate with each other and take collective responsibility for student learning.

SPECIAL NEEDS DIFFERENCES

When integrating special needs students into "regular classroom" environments, the physical arrangement, as well as the social-emotional environment and the learning climate, must support those efforts (Reynolds, 1990). We realize that this probably seems like an obvious statement, but apparently sometimes it's so obvious that it's overlooked. The inclusion of special needs students often requires modifications in the learning environment and/or teachers' versions of "how we do things here" that are specific to one particular child or to one particular handicapping condition.

For example, the addition of hearing-impaired students to your class roster might mean that you will wear an electronic box that amplifies the sound of your voice or that you will get to learn some basic sign language. If the hearing impaired students' adaptive behavior includes lip reading, you'll learn to modify your movements around the classroom to ensure that they can see you when you speak. What changes would you need to make in the learning environment to accommodate students in wheelchairs or students who walk using crutches? Crowded classrooms with limited traffic routes restrict the independence of such learners, as do sinks and shelves that are out of reach. What special learning environment modifications might students with attention deficit disorder need? What if the new student who joins your class midyear comes with a Seeing Eye dog?

So many questions, so little time. As we said earlier, the inclusion of special needs learners means teachers must consider learning environment variables such as space, facilities, and furnishings, as well as the social environment and learning climate. Every member of the learning environment has a role to play in successful inclusion efforts. What students don't understand, they sometimes fear. Consequently, part of the teacher's job is to help students who are unaccustomed to interacting with people who are different from themselves become comfortable doing so.

WHAT STUDENTS NEED TO KNOW

Sometimes that job also includes helping students understand what special needs students are dealing with. Rita went to school with a boy who had muscular dystrophy. Neither she nor any of his classmates knew much about Gary's condition. They just noticed that from year to year he walked slower and fell down more frequently. In third grade, when Gary went to the hospital for some tests, his classmates made cards for him. Of course, when someone is in the hospital, what kind of cards do third graders think of sending him or her? Get well cards, of course. After the teacher looked through the stack of cards, which included predictable sentiments such as "Get well soon" and "We hope you're back soon, running around with us at recess," she spent some time explaining to a rather confused group of third graders that she couldn't send Gary their cards and that they'd need to make him different ones.

As fourth graders, Gary's classmates didn't understand his condition much better, but his wheelchair provided undeniable evidence that it wasn't improving. In fifth grade, when they attended his funeral together, they still didn't understand the disease that took Gary's life, even though they had watched the pattern repeated in his brothers. Rita has no recollection of any formal attempts on the part of school personnel to explain the situation that students had watched played out in Gary's family. In fact, she doesn't even remember hearing the words "muscular dystrophy" spoken out loud within the learning environment. If Gary were a student in your class, how would you help your students better understand his condition? How would you help Gary feel more comfortable in the learning environment?

A TEACHER'S VIEW

During Therese's preprimary teaching days, a number of special needs students were mainstreamed or included in her regular education classroom. She recalls the year Jamie, a cerebral palsied five-year-old, spent most of each afternoon in her classroom. He always arrived in his wheelchair, with walker and various adaptive devices in tow. Jamie's equipment, when lined up against the wall with the adaptive equipment of his fellow students, filled the corridor outside the classroom. However, in spite of all the hardware that accompanied him, what Therese remembers first and most about Jamie is his smile, his pleasant personality, and his willingness to share all his special adaptations (for example, scooter board, corner chair, "chubby" markers, communication board) with the other children in his class.

Therese always has been grateful for the opportunities she had to collaborate with special needs teachers and students. The children, whether regular education or special education, learned to accept and appreciate each other. These early inclusion experiences had a significant impact on the children and families involved, as well as their abilities to go beyond tolerating diversity to embracing and celebrating diversity.

WHAT TEACHERS NEED TO KNOW

As a teacher, it's not your job to know something about every childhood illness, disease, congenital disorder, learning disability, and special need. However, it is your job to find out about your students and their needs—special or otherwise. It's also your job to accommodate those needs, but there are people and resources available to help you do that. Get to know the social worker, psychologist, speech therapist, and other professionals whose job it is to help students—and to help teachers—accommodate students. And remember to get to know your students and their families; they're the ones with some of the most valuable information regarding how you can accommodate special needs within the learning environments you create.

EXPERIENTIAL AND SCHEMATIC DIFFERENCES

Just as you bring your own personal experiences and schema related to the educational process to this particular learning experience, your future students will bring with them experiential and schematic differences. Every student represents a unique composite of experiences and schematic configurations. Consequently, in addition to recognizing and responding to gender, cultural, family, and special needs differences, teachers must recognize and respond to experiential and schematic differences. Although students may look alike, sound alike, and behave in similar fashions, their learning needs often are dissimilar. These differences are attributable, in part, to students' unique prior experiences and to the schemata they've constructed based on those highly individualized experiences.

ARRANGING THE PHYSICAL LEARNING ENVIRONMENT

The physical setting in which instruction occurs affects learners' behavior, whether it's intended to or not (Weinstein, 1992). This occurs in two ways: directly, by the behavior the setting allows, and indirectly or symbolically, by the messages the setting communicates about what behaviors are permitted, how important learning is, and what the roles of the learners and teacher should be.

PHYSICAL SAFETY

As Maslow's hierarchy of needs illustrates, meeting physical needs is prerequisite to meeting learners' social, emotional, and instructional needs. In arranging the physical learning environment, students' safety must be a primary consideration. Common sense and thoughtful planning should guide teachers' decisions regarding furniture placement, the design of traffic patterns, storage of equipment and supplies, and other safety considerations.

PHYSICAL ARRANGEMENTS THAT SUPPORT INSTRUCTIONAL GOALS

In making decisions about the physical arrangement of classrooms, environmentally competent teachers consider what learners will be doing (reading or writing independently, viewing a videotape, working in cooperative learning groups, and so on) and design physical arrangements that support learners' activities. They consider the direct and indirect effects of spatial arrangements and determine which formations will maximize the effectiveness of the designed instruction. In other words, they make environmental design an integral part of their instructional design.

PHYSICAL ARRANGEMENTS THAT FACILITATE LEARNER INDEPENDENCE

A learner-centered environment supports students' desires to find out about things, facilitates the process of discovery, and, in general, meets learners' needs. A school whose mission involves working with learners has a climate very different from one in which educators are mostly thinking about how they can make students work harder or follow directions (Kohn, 1996b): "Put another way, in a 'doing to' classroom or school, the adults tend to focus on students' behavior in order to elicit compliance; the preferred methods are punishments and rewards. In a 'working with' environment, the focus is on students' underlying motives in order to help them develop positive values and a love of learning; the preferred methods include the creation of a caring community and a genuinely engaging curriculum" (Kohn, 1996b, p. 54).

LEARNER-CENTERED ENVIRONMENTS

It's one thing to talk about a learner-centered classroom, but it's another matter entirely to describe what such a place looks and sounds like. What might you expect to see in a learner-centered classroom? Consider the following variables and descriptors of learner-centered classrooms (Kohn, 1996):

- *Classroom organization.* The contents and organization of the classroom support and reflect a learner-centered philosophy. The arrangement promotes learner independence and facilitates a variety of instructional strategies and learning styles. The furniture can be rearranged quickly and easily to accommodate different instructional activities. Traffic patterns allow learners unrestricted access to centers, books, media, technology, computers, materials, and supplies without disrupting other students. Space is utilized fully, and lighting, temperature, and aesthetics contribute to a comfortable learning environment.

- *Furnishings.* Because learners come in different shapes and sizes, so do the furnishings provided for them. Chairs are arranged around tables to facilitate interaction among learners. Comfortable work areas accommodate a variety of learning styles.

- *Walls.* Walls are used to display information about, and products of, those who spend time together in the classroom (such as student work, signs, and visual displays). They show evidence of collaboration, as do the student-created bulletin boards.

- *Sounds.* Learner-centered classrooms are characterized by productive noise, on-task talk, and a hum of activity.

- *Location of teacher.* The teacher can be found working with, observing, and listening to students.

- *Teacher's voice.* The teacher's voice is warm, genuine, and respectful. Volume and inflection are appropriate to the situation. Yelling is not viewed as a motivational device!

- *Students' reaction to visitors.* Students welcome visitors and are eager to explain or demonstrate their projects or activities.

- *Class discussion.* Students talk directly to one another, rather than only to the teacher in response to specific questions. The emphasis is on thoughtful exploration of complex issues. Students ask questions as often as the teacher does.

- *Tasks.* Overlapping, simultaneous tasks characterize learner-centered classrooms.

- *School environment.* The entire school possesses an inviting atmosphere. Students' work is displayed in the hallways, and students often help out in the library or lunchroom. The office staff is friendly and welcoming toward visitors, students, and teachers, and the faculty lounge is warm and comfortable. The building itself is well maintained, and even the bathrooms are in good condition!

EVALUATING CLASSROOM LEARNING ENVIRONMENTS

Using simple questionnaires such as the *My Class Inventory,* teachers can measure their classrooms' psychosocial environments (see, for example, Fisher, Fraser, & Bassett, 1995; Wong & Fraser, 1996) and analyze how the learning environment is perceived by different students. For example, the results of one study indicate that, within each ethnic group represented in the class studied, the high-achieving students had significantly higher perceptions of their involvement, affiliation with one another, satisfaction, academic self-concept, and achievement motivation than did the low-achieving students

(Huang & Waxman, 1996). Even early childhood learners can provide information on their perceptions of their learning environments (Fisher, Fraser, & Bassett, 1995). Once teachers know students' perceptions of their actual learning environments and the learning environments they prefer, teachers can modify the classroom environment in the direction of learners' preferences, using input their students provide.

QUESTIONS AND CRITERIA TO GUIDE LEARNING ENVIRONMENT ANALYSES

In addition to standardized questionnaires, teachers can use checklists or selected questions to analyze and evaluate learning environments. Included within the following sections are questions that focus on different facets of the learning environment. Please note that although every question is not appropriate for every learning environment, questions such as these can guide your reflection on, and thinking about, classroom-level learning environments. Use them as starting points for developing your own learning environment assessment checklists. Then visit some classrooms to conduct on-site observations and analyses of different learning environments. You also can analyze and evaluate sketches of learning environments. However, remember that sketches offer limited information regarding the social-emotional dimensions of learning environments.

EVALUATING THE SOCIAL-EMOTIONAL ENVIRONMENT

Because providing a healthy and positive social-emotional learning environment is crucial to the teaching/learning process, here and throughout this chapter we have deliberately placed social-emotional features first in our discussions of learning environments. Firsthand observations that are guided by specific, predetermined criteria are the most accurate way to assess a classroom's social-emotional climate. The following questions provide examples of criteria appropriate for use in evaluating social-emotional environments:

1. Do learners seem happy to enter the environment?
2. Do learners actively participate in the instructional process?
3. Do learners interact with one another throughout the day?
4. Is there mutual respect between learners and adults and among learners themselves?
5. Do teachers support and encourage learners' work without interfering?
6. Are learners encouraged to cooperate with others in small and large groups?
7. Do teachers have and communicate goals for each learner that are appropriate for that learner's developmental level and that accommodate specific individual strengths and weaknesses?
8. Are learners aware of classroom procedures, routines, and rules?

9. Do learners have input regarding the creation of classroom rules?

10. Do the adults in the environment model appropriate behavior and language?

11. Does the environment promote learner independence?

12. Does the environment promote acceptance and accommodation of diverse family, ethnic, and cultural backgrounds?

EVALUATING THE PHYSICAL ENVIRONMENT

Safety is the first and most important criterion to consider when evaluating a classroom's physical environment. The degree to which the physical environment facilitates learner independence is another primary consideration. The questions in Figure 6.2 can guide you in assessing the physical environment of your classroom.

LEARNING ENVIRONMENTS AS REFLECTIONS OF TEACHING AND LEARNING PHILOSOPHIES

Classroom learning environments are reflections of the teaching and learning philosophies of the teachers that create them. In Figures 6.3 and 6.4, we've included some sketches of learning environments for your review and consideration. What predictions would you make about the educational philosophies and predominant teaching styles of the individuals who created these designs?

Using the questions from the preceding sections—or your own criteria—analyze and evaluate the classroom learning environment designs we've provided in Figures 6.3 and 6.4. Then share your evaluations with a small group of your peers. Use this collaborative opportunity to note differences and similarities among the different evaluations, ask clarifying questions, and share suggestions for modifications to the learning environment designs.

Then try designing your own learning environment. We think you'll find that it's much easier to critique someone else's design than it is to create your own and articulate the rationale for the decisions embedded in it. Or as a first-year teacher reflected, as Therese was helping her to arrange her classroom environment, "It was a lot easier to do this on paper than it is to do it for real!"

Your challenge is to design an environment that's appropriate to the developmental levels, special needs, prior experiences, and interests of the particular learners for whom you are creating it. How will you approach the task of creating a culture of productivity for your students and for yourself?

SUMMARIZING WHAT YOU'VE LEARNED

■ Organizational environment consists of the regular social and physical surroundings in which the people in an organization do their daily work (Amabile, Burnside, & Gryskiewicz, 1995). Organizational culture consists of the basic assumptions of an organization, which are reflected by the behavior of its people and various outward manifestations (structure, management style, physical

Figure 6.2 Factors in Assessing the Physical Environment

1. Is the classroom safe, clean, attractive, and well organized?

2. Are the classroom contents and arrangement appropriate for the learners?

3. Does the classroom reflect the curriculum, as well as the learners' interests and needs?

4. Is the work of all learners displayed?

5. Are the various centers and areas well defined and easily accessible to learners?

6. Are traffic patterns efficient and clear, and do they facilitate learners' mobility?

7. Can the teacher easily see all areas of the room?

8. Is there adequate space for activities and centers?

9. Can the room be rearranged easily and quickly to facilitate different instructional activities?

10. Does the room arrangement provide enough space for whole-class activities as well as individual activities?

11. Is the storage area efficient, convenient, attractive, and well organized for both learner and adult use?

12. Do the contents of each center change frequently enough to keep learners' interest?

13. Are there materials for both structured and open-ended activities, as well as materials that facilitate the development of a range of interests and skills?

14. Is the room comfortable in terms of furniture, heating, lighting, and ventilation?

15. Are the furnishings and equipment appropriate for the learners?

16. Does each learner have an individual storage space?

17. Is there a quiet space where learners can remove themselves from the group and the main flow of traffic? Are quieter and noisier areas separated?

18. Is the learning environment aesthetically pleasing?

19. Are all areas of the room used by all learners? Which areas are used the most and the least?

setting) of those unstated assumptions (Jensen, 1988). A school's culture is reflected in "the way we do things here."

■ Every organizational culture contains its own unique versions of the following features: a business environment, shared values, rites and rituals, organizational politics, and cultural networks.

■ A strong organizational culture can serve as a powerful lever for guiding behavior and can help individuals perform better in two ways: by providing a system of informal rules that spell out how people are to behave most of the time and

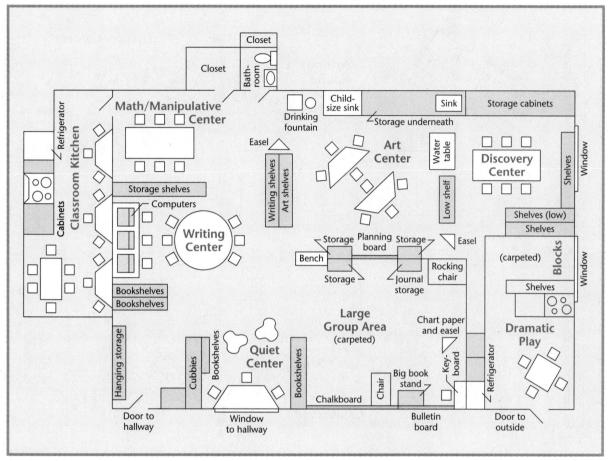

Figure 6.3
Primary Classroom Environmental Design

by making people feel better about what they do, so they are more likely to work hard.

■ Individual classrooms have their own organizational environments, organizational cultures, and cultural networks. These are created by teachers and are the products of their decisions. Classrooms are microcosms that exist within the larger context of the schools that house them.

■ Schools that function as effective learning environments have strong cultures that feature collaboration, freedom from risk, a focus on student learning, and a commitment to a systems approach to personal and organizational improvement (Kruse & Seashore Louis, 1995).

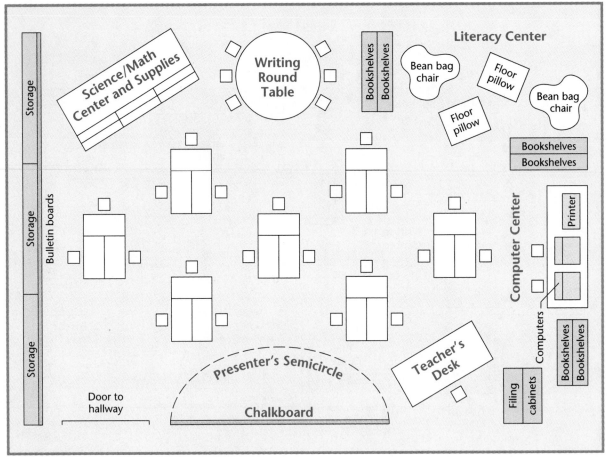

Figure 6.4
Middle-Level Classroom Environmental Design

■ The classroom social environment is one of the chief psychological determinants of academic learning. A positive social climate allows students to share ideas through teams and cooperative groups, thereby promoting democratic decision making and fostering cohesiveness and satisfaction (Walberg & Greenberg, 1997).

■ Although there's no one magic answer to the challenge of creating learning communities that enable all students to succeed, one approach is to make classrooms more like ideal homes. Instead of thinking only about the universal needs of many students, teachers also must begin to think of the particular needs of individual students, just as caring and committed parents do (Dodd, 1997).

■ The physical setting in which instruction occurs affects learners' behavior, whether it's intended to or not (Weinstein, 1992). These effects occur in two ways: directly, by the behavior the setting allows, and indirectly or symbolically, by the messages the setting communicates about what behaviors are permitted, how important learning is, and what the roles of the learners and teacher should be.

■ Using simple questionnaires, teachers can measure their classrooms' psychosocial environments and analyze how the learning environment is perceived by different students. Also, teachers can use checklists or selected questions to analyze and evaluate learning environments and focus on different facets of the learning environment. Firsthand observations guided by specific, predetermined criteria are the most accurate way to assess a classroom's social-emotional climate, as well as features of the physical classroom environment.

YOUR PROFESSIONAL TEACHING PORTFOLIO

■ Design a classroom learning environment. First, remind yourself of the philosophy and teaching/learning principles you want your teaching attitudes and behaviors to exhibit, and reflect on how the learning environment you design can best reflect those values. Then identify the students for whom you'd like to design an environment (preprimary, primary, middle, or secondary). Finally, compose a caption for your design that clearly articulates your rationale for the decisions you made in developing your environmental design. Your rationale should succinctly answer the question, Why am I doing what I'm doing? Before including your learning environment design in your professional teaching portfolio, solicit feedback from a variety of sources (preservice teachers, inservice teachers, professors, and students of the level for which your environment is designed). Be prepared to explain your design and the reasoning that led you to create it as you did.

Key Terms

Asynchronous learning (p. 171)
Culture (p. 158)
Cultural networks (p. 162)
Learning environments (p. 170)

Organizational environment (p. 159)
Organizational culture (p. 159)
Rites and rituals (p. 160)

Schema (p. 158)
School culture (p. 166)
Sexual harassment (p. 183)
Shared values (p. 160)

Relevant Resources for Professionals

Books and Articles

- Dodd, A. W. (1997). Creating a climate for learning: Making the classroom more like an ideal home. *The National Association of Secondary School Principals Bulletin, 81*(589), 10–16.

- Keefe, J. W., & Jenkins, M. (1997). *Instruction and the learning environment.* Larchmont, NY: Eye on Education.

- Kohn, A. (1996). "What to look for in a classroom." *Educational Leadership, 54*(1), 54, 55.

Professional Journals in Education

- *Learning Environments Research: An International Journal*
  Kluwer Academic Publishers
  P.O. Box 332   P.O. Box 358
  3300 AH Dordrecht   Accord Station
  The Netherlands   Hingham, MA 02018-0358

Professional Organizations

- Phi Delta Kappa.

  http://www.pdkintl.org/

  Phi Delta Kappa is an international professional fraternity for men and women in education. The membership is composed of recognized leaders in the profession and graduate students in education whose leadership potential has been identified.

- Study of Learning Environments.
  The Study of Learning Environments is a special interest group of the American Educational Research Association that provides a forum for the presentation and dissemination of research focused on issues and variables related to learning environments.

  Study of Learning Environments Special Interest Group
  American Educational Research Association
  1230 17th Street, N.W.
  Washington, DC 20036-3078

Web Sites

- **Education Index**

  http://www.educationindex.com/

  Education Index is an annotated guide to the best education-related sites on the Web. The sites are sorted by subject and developmental level and are annotated.

- **EdWeb**

  http://edweb.gsn.org/

  The purpose of EdWeb is to explore the worlds of educational reform and information technology. This site provides access to online resources around the world.

- **Internet Schoolhouse**

  http://www.onr.com/schoolhouse/

  The Internet Schoolhouse is a virtual school that promotes global friendship and twenty-first century learning. This site contains lists of links, classified by subject area, for educators and students.

INSTRUCTIONAL GUIDANCE: MOVING BEYOND CLASSROOM MANAGEMENT

— OR —

Control really is an illusion.

WHAT IS INSTRUCTIONAL GUIDANCE?

Whether you call it instructional guidance, classroom management, or discipline, entire books have been written on the subject of this chapter. Here, our goal is to provide you with an overview of the subject and to prompt you to reflect on what you think about instructional guidance. Please remember that we can't tell you everything you'll ever need to know about instructional guidance in this book. Even if you were to read every book ever written on the subject, you still wouldn't learn everything you'll ever need to know about instructional guidance. And there certainly are lots of books on the subject (for example, see Arends, 1997; Canter & Canter, 1993; Curwin & Mendler, 1988; Edwards, 1997; Emmer, Evertson, Clements, & Worsham, 1994; Faber, Maxlish, Nyberg, & Templeton, 1995; Hoover & Kindsvatter, 1997; Jones & Jones, 1995; Levin & Nolan, 1996).

Instructional guidance (more commonly referred to as classroom management or discipline) typically tops the list of issues that most concern new teachers. Even many experienced teachers continue to struggle with instructional guidance. For example, upon returning to teaching after a number of years in private business, a high school teacher reflected, "When I first started

"Let the wise listen and add to their learning, and let the discerning get guidance."

—Proverbs 1:5

Visualize yourself as a first-year teacher on your first day of teaching. How do you feel? Can you feel anything at all, or are you just numb with fear? Make a mental list of your fears and concerns (*"What if . . . "*). Which items on your "what-if" list give you the most distress, the most nervous perspiration, the severest heart palpitations? For many first-year teachers, "losing control" of their students and classrooms appears somewhere on their list of "what-ifs."

In your teaching journal, describe the scene the words "losing control" bring to mind for you. Then describe what you think most teachers mean and want when they talk about being in control. Finally, using best practice principles, explain how you could avoid the scene you've described and achieve the conditions teachers describe as being in control.

teaching, my biggest worry was about kids chewing gum. Now I worry about kids carrying guns." Because schools tend to mirror the violence of society, teaching is not without its occupational hazards. Some teachers long for the days when they worried more about stapling their thumbs than they do about the need to park in well-lit, heavily traveled areas.

GUIDANCE VERSUS DISCIPLINE

When teachers are insecure and lack confidence in their abilities, they tend to rely on teacher-centered approaches to instructional guidance that provide them with the illusion of control. However, there are many different ways to approach guidance. Before we consider some of the many different approaches, we begin by defining instructional guidance and differentiating it from discipline.

Discipline often implies punishment—such as standing in a corner—for inappropriate behavior. **Instructional guidance,** by contrast, reveals the teacher's belief in the positive potential of learners. Teachers who engage in instructional guidance think beyond conventional classroom discipline, which focuses on controlling learners or keeping them in line. Instructional guidance requires a positive learning environment that is developmentally appropriate and culturally responsive. It teaches learners the life skills they need as citizens of a democracy: "respecting others and one's self, working together in groups, solving problems using words, expressing strong emotions in acceptable ways, making decisions ethically and intelligently. Teachers who use guidance realize that it takes well into adulthood to master these skills and that, in learning them, children—like all of us—make mistakes. Therefore, because children are just beginning this personal development, teachers regard behaviors traditionally considered *mis*behaviors as *mistaken* behaviors" (Gartrell, 1997, p. 35).

Instructional guidance is not just reacting to problems or another term for permissive discipline. And it is not reducible to a commercial program. Guidance does not mean that chaos and permissiveness usurp structure, expectations, and organization. To the contrary, high expectations, structure, and organization are essential to, and compatible with, systems of responsive guidance.

Using instructional guidance means helping students learn from their mistakes rather than punishing them for their mistakes, empowering learners to solve problems rather than punishing them for having problems they can't solve, and helping learners accept consequences—but consequences that leave their self-esteem intact. "Guidance teaching is character education in its truest, least political sense—guiding children to develop the empathy, self-esteem, and self-control needed for autonomy" (Gartrell, 1997, p. 35).

Teachers who implement effective guidance systems make informed decisions according to the following principles: They realize that social skills are complicated and take years to acquire, reduce variables that contribute to students' mistaken behaviors, practice positive teacher-learner relations, use intervention methods that are solution oriented, build partnerships with parents, and use teamwork with adults (Gartrell, 1997).

CONTROL VERSUS POWER

In Chapter 3 we stated that when a student tells a teacher, "You can't make me!" the student is correct. First of all, we hope you won't want to have control over your students. Second, even if you do want it, you'll never really have it. Most students willingly choose to engage in socially acceptable behavior that allows teachers to teach and learners to learn. Those students who choose to use their considerable creative abilities to find multiple methods of distracting and disrupting generally succeed—at least initially.

Although teacher control is an illusion, teacher power is not. Teachers have the power to make learners feel miserable, stupid, and ridiculed, as well as the power to make learners feel self-confident, accomplished, and empowered. Where do teachers get this power? Teachers operate from four different power bases: referent power, expert power, legitimate power, and reward/coercive power. Students may view teachers as powerful because they are people whom students like (referent power), because teachers have special knowledge (expert power), because they see teachers as authorities (legitimate power), or because teachers have the power to reward and punish (reward/coercive power). Table 7.1 summarizes the characteristics and limitations of these four power bases.

YOU MAKE THE CALL

Given the fact that instructional guidance typically is a primary concern for new teachers, preservice teachers often like to pose "what-if" guidance scenarios and then seek foolproof answers for those situations. Perhaps you'll recall that our response to requests for clear-cut, black-and-white, no-risk solutions

Table 7.1
Teacher Power Bases

How does each power base work?	Referent	Expert	Legitimate	Reward/Coercive
Teacher provides motivation to behave because . . .	Students like the teacher as a person.	Teacher has special knowledge.	Teacher has legal authority.	Teacher can reward and punish.
What is the need for teacher control of student behavior?	Very low	Very low	Moderate	High
What are the requirements for using this power base?	Students must like the teacher as a person.	Teacher expertise must be perceived and valued.	Students must respect legal authority.	Rewards and punishments must be effective.
What are key teacher behaviors?	Communicates caring for students	Demonstrates mastery of content and teaching skills	Acts as a teacher is expected to act	Has and uses knowledge of students' likes and dislikes
What are the age limitations?	Useful at all levels	Less useful at primary level	Useful at all levels	Useful at all levels but less useful at senior high level
Are there any caveats?	Teacher is not the students' friend.	Heavily dependent on student values	Societal changes have lessened the usefulness of this power base.	Emphasizes extrinsic over intrinsic motivation

(Adapted from Levin & Nolan, 1996, p. 82)

to such problems is "It depends." The proper application of instructional guidance is always situation-specific. With that point in mind, what do you think you would do if confronted with the following situations?

Chaos at Recess

You're a student teacher taking your turn supervising recess, when a fight breaks out among some fifth and sixth graders. As fate would have it, an urgent parent phone call has delayed your cooperating teacher, and no certified teachers or paid school personnel are on the playground at that particular moment. Because you're student teaching in a third-grade classroom, you don't know any of the students involved. What do you do?

a. Tap the heels of your ruby slippers together and repeat quietly to yourself, "There's no place like home."

Students can learn conflict resolution strategies to help them solve their own problems.
(© Elizabeth Crews)

b. Form a committee to study the matter.

c. Use your cell phone to call your academic adviser and set up an appointment to discuss changing your major.

d. All of the above.

e. None of the above.

No One Is Listening

You're attempting to read the big book *A House Is a House for Me* to your first graders. It's the book you've selected to serve as the core book for your unit on houses and homes, and you've done your homework! Your lesson plans are both interesting and well organized, your procedures are complete, and your objectives and instructional activities are developmentally and culturally appropriate. However, no one is even listening to the book. Some students are chatting among themselves, others are pulling threads out of the carpet, and one student is incessantly tapping on the aquarium and talking to the fish. What do you do?

a. Give those students who aren't listening the patented "teacher look" you've been working diligently to perfect.

b. Send everyone out to recess fifteen minutes early.

c. Keep everyone—except yourself—in from recess.

d. Threaten to send those students who aren't listening back to kindergarten, since their behavior suggests to you that they apparently aren't ready for first grade yet.

   e. In a very loud, yet pitiful, voice, tell all the students how disappointed you are in their behavior.

   f. Consider all of the options provided in the Chaos at Recess scenario.

To the Principal's Office

In response to your request that he take his seat, a third grader engages in a tantrum—behavior consisting of yelling, turning red in the face, stomping his feet, and shaking his fists in your general direction. He announces in front of the entire class that he hates you, you always pick on him, you're not fair, and he's going to go tell the principal on you right now. (He's been to the principal's office before, so he definitely knows the way.) What do you do?

   a. Put your hand on your hip, glare defiantly at the student, and retort, "Go ahead. See if I care."

   b. Tell the student that if he leaves, he'll have detention for a week.

   c. Tell the student that if he cooperates for the rest of the day, he'll earn fifteen minutes of extra recess time.

   d. Tell the student that you think you hear his mother calling, but even if it isn't his mother calling, you'll be calling her soon if he doesn't sit down and be quiet.

   e. Retire to a nice quiet community on the outskirts of Saratoga.

   f. Consider all of the options provided in the Chaos at Recess scenario.

When I Was in School . . .

As the bus pulls away from the curb at the end of the day and you turn to go back into the school after completing your bus supervision assignment, your eye catches the cherubic face of one of your students, beaming at you from the bus window. You're about to smile and wave good-bye when your eye catches the student's extended middle finger, raised in a special salute intended just for you. What do you do?

   a. Yell, "Come back here, you little coward!"

   b. Stand there and suppress all of the inappropriate responses that come to your mind.

   c. Smile and marvel at your student's impeccable timing.

   d. Mutter to yourself, "When I was in school, we had respect for our teachers . . ."

   e. Devote your evening to brainstorming fitting responses to your student's salute.

   f. Consider all of the options provided in the Chaos at Recess scenario.

APPROPRIATE INSTRUCTIONAL GUIDANCE SOLUTIONS

Now perhaps you're consoling yourself with the delusion that these scenarios are too absurd or contrived to actually happen. If that's the case, then it's our duty to interrupt your delusion to assure you that each of the above situations did indeed transpire. Although the situations transpired, we're happy to report that no one expired as a result. Each scenario starred a student teacher or first-year teacher who survived—and no doubt learned from—the incident described.

Of course, part of the reason the starring teachers survived these situations is because they rejected most or all of the options listed here for responding to them. We hope the response options we provided seemed clearly inappropriate or ridiculous to you. Unfortunately, some of them also may sound familiar, because you've seen teachers resort to such measures when they didn't know what else to do. Fortunately, many unpleasant situations can be prevented through the consistent use of guidance approaches that feature on-target, developmentally appropriate instructional opportunities for students.

Reflect & Respond

 If you were to find yourself in the situations described in the scenarios, what would you do? Write down some possibilities for appropriate responses to these student behaviors. We'll revisit these scenarios at the end of the chapter and give you an opportunity to evaluate your initial responses and offer other possible responses.

GOALS OF INSTRUCTIONAL GUIDANCE

The whole point of guiding students' behavior is to help them become independent, lifelong learners and learn responsibility, self-discipline, self-monitoring, and self-control. These are the long-term goals of instructional guidance. **Self-monitoring** means consistently tracking, recording, and evaluating one's own behavior over time. **Self-control** goes a step further to encompass the management of one's own behavior based, in part, on information generated through self-monitoring (Walker, 1995).

Teachers must engage in behaviors and exhibit attitudes that will help move learners closer to achieving these long-term goals of instructional guidance. At the very least, teachers should not engage in behaviors and exhibit attitudes that get in the way of learners' making progress toward these goals. Consequently, we feel it's important to highlight some of the factors that facilitate the acquisition of independence, lifelong learning, responsibility, self-discipline, self-monitoring, and self-control.

GUIDING STUDENTS TOWARD THESE GOALS

■ Encourage Learners

Praise often involves flattery, rewards, and comparisons and sometimes is overblown. Praising students actually can lead to discouragement, by instilling the idea that work that isn't praised has no value. Praise tends to focus students' attention on winning a reward rather than on doing a task for the satisfaction that comes from learning. It can work against positive self-concept, lower students' confidence in their answers, and reduce the number of verbal responses they offer (Evans, 1996).

Encouragement, by contrast, is less judgmental and controlling than praise. It helps students appreciate their own behavior and accomplishments, while separating their work from their worth. Encouragement focuses on specific behavior ("Angela, I noticed how hard you've been working on your Power Point presentation"), as opposed to praise, which evaluates a finished product in general terms ("Angela, your presentation looks great").

The key to encouragement rests with avoiding discouragement. Teachers discourage when they set unreasonable and inappropriate standards for learners, focus on learners' mistakes in misguided attempts to motivate, make pessimistic interpretations about learners and their performance, compare learners, or dominate the learning process by being too helpful (Evans, 1996).

■ Promote Learner Independence

Although most everyone has the need to feel needed, effective teachers know that an important part of their job is to help their students need them less. They understand that there is such a thing as helping too much and that there are situations when helping actually hurts.

When helping hurts For example, did a well-intentioned adult ever redo something you'd truly worked hard on, because he or she wanted to make it "better"? Rita recalls the embarrassment she felt as a fifth-grade student when she discovered that a kind and caring teacher had "helped" her by performing some remedial repairs on a coffee can planter she'd made as a Mother's Day gift. Although there's no question that the planter benefited greatly from the teacher's intervention, Rita didn't really feel like giving it to her mother. The planter may have looked very nice, but it wasn't her work anymore.

When adults help too much, they send loud and clear messages to learners about their skills and competencies. Perhaps you can recall hearing a young child emphatically declare, "I can do it myself!" Perhaps you can recall being that child. "It" might have been pouring milk on your cereal, zipping your coat, tying your shoe, or getting yourself dressed. Later in life, "it" might have been making decisions regarding what electives to take, how to spend your free time, or who to spend your free time with. As parents of adolescents sometimes lament, "When kids are too young to help, they want to help. Then when they're old enough to help, they don't want to do anything." Might some of the adolescent attitude be attributable to learned helplessness?

When helping helps Teachers can promote learner independence by organizing the learning environment, including the physical layout of the classroom, in ways that reduce learners' dependence on the teacher or other adults. A well-designed learning environment reduces learners' need to ask, "What do I do next?" Effective teachers design and use guidance strategies and approaches that don't force learners to rely on them or other adults for materials, next steps, or permission to do what they need to do (such as sharpen their pencils or retrieve books and supplies from classroom shelves). Using multiple, overlapping tasks, these teachers empower learners to organize their own work and make some of the decisions regarding their work.

■ Provide Opportunities for Learner Choice and Decision Making

Kohn has much to say on the topic of choice and compliance. He equates compliance with punishment and concludes that "The more you punish someone, the more angry that person becomes, and the more 'need' there is to keep punishing" (1996a, p. 26). Compliance or punishment may work in the short term, but it also may have some unintended consequences. Consider the following hidden costs of compliance (Kohn, 1996a):

■ It teaches learners that when they don't like the way someone is acting, they can make something bad happen to that person until he or she gives in.

■ It warps the relationship between the punisher and the punished.

■ It impedes the process of ethical development by changing the focus from "What kind of person do I want to be?" to "What do they want me to do, and what happens to me if I don't do it?"

Students learn to make good choices by having the opportunity to choose—not by just following directions (Kohn, 1993a).

INSTRUCTIONAL GUIDANCE APPROACHES

We've already indicated that there are many books and viewpoints on the topic of instructional guidance. As Figure 7.1 illustrates, approaches to instructional guidance fall on a wide continuum, ranging from teacher-centered approaches that focus on discipline to learner-centered approaches that provide opportunities for student choice. The following paragraphs highlight these differing approaches, the theories they are based on, and their usefulness in the classroom.

TEACHER-CENTERED APPROACHES

Teacher-centered approaches to instructional guidance include the traditional model, the behavior modification model, the assertive discipline model, and the effective momentum model. As you read the following paragraphs, think about which approaches most closely match your developing views of learners and the teaching/learning process.

■ Traditional Model

In the **traditional model,** the teacher uses praise and rewards to correct student misbehavior.

Teacher-Centered

Traditional	Behavior Modification	Assertive Discipline	Effective Momentum Management	Reality Therapy
• Learners do not have active role • Uses rewards, tokens, and punishment • Teacher corrects student behavior	• Learners aren't expected to solve problems • Teachers evaluate environment and the effect on student behavior	• Learners must accept the consequences of their actions • Teachers treat all students alike	• Learners are responsive to environmental changes • Teachers use prevention strategies	• Learners have needs that must be met by home or school • Unmet needs cause student misbehavior • Teachers use natural and logical consequences to develop student responsibility

Figure 7.1
Instructional Guidance Continuum

Theory base The traditional model is based on a study of schooling in America conducted by John Goodlad, a prominent education reformer. It reflects a teacher-centered approach that is still widely used today (Baron, 1992).

View of learners Learners are not given an active role in monitoring their own behavior. They respond and react more than they act.

Teacher-student relationship This teacher-centered approach uses positive reinforcement, such as praise and token rewards. When positive reinforcement doesn't work, teachers employ intervention strategies, including punishment. The traditional model relies most frequently on the following strategies for controlling misbehavior (Baron, 1992):

- Avoiding or ignoring minor misbehavior
- Glancing or staring at offenders to communicate the teacher's annoyance
- Reminding students of appropriate behavior when misbehavior occurs
- Using commands and directives when students are out of order
- Issuing verbal threats
- Separating a student from the site of the misbehavior

Teacher's role The teacher's primary role is to correct students' misbehavior.

Limitations The traditional model's focus on misbehavior and its reliance on punishment constitute limitations. In addition to emphasizing negative behavior, the traditional model does not encourage students to take responsibility for their own actions.

Positive Discipline	**Teacher Effectiveness Training**	**Responsible Classroom Management**	**Community**
• Misbehavior is result of learners misjudging how to achieve their goals • Teacher helps students learn how to belong	• Every individual is unique, so learners must build their own confidence and solve their own problems • Teacher provides caring and open communication to help learners gain ability to solve own problems	• Learners are individuals to be treated fairly, not identically • Students encouraged to perform at high levels without using awards/bribery	• Learners are members of democratic society • Teachers and learners work together to solve problems

■ Behavior Modification Model

The **behavior modification** model doesn't expect learners to solve problems. Instead, the teacher observes student behavior and uses reinforcement to strengthen or diminish specific behaviors.

Theory base The work of Ivan Pavlov, Saul Axelrod, and B. F. Skinner provides the theoretical underpinnings for the behavior modification model. Skinner first tested his theories on pigeons and then applied the same techniques to humans. Stimulus-response theory, the foundation of the behavior modification model, asserts that the inner rational self is a myth and that environmental stimuli determine human behavior and can be modified to shape behavior to acceptable social standards. People work to avoid painful or unpleasant stimuli and seek those that are pleasant and rewarding (Skinner, 1968, 1982).

View of learners Behaviorists do not expect learners to solve problems based on their rational understanding of their inner selves.

Teacher-student relationship In this teacher-centered approach, positive and negative reinforcement are used to strengthen or diminish behaviors. Teachers can control the behavior management approach more precisely than they can control other approaches, because they can apply reinforcement based on precise readings of student behavior (Skinner, 1968, 1982).

Teacher's role The teacher's role is to evaluate the effect of variables in the learning environment on student behavior and alter those variables to produce acceptable behavior. First the teacher observes student behavior to establish a baseline; he or she then applies positive or negative reinforcement, measures the change in behavior, and reverses the procedure to double-check the effect of the positive or negative reinforcement (Skinner, 1968, 1982).

Limitations Behavior modification often is criticized as undemocratic and manipulative. Critics view its use of behavior control—without attempts to develop learners' rational capacities—as unacceptable in a society that professes to be based on democratic, humanistic principles. Behavior modification eliminates learner choice and problem solving and is highly teacher-centered (Queen, Blackwelder, & Mallen, 1997).

What behaviorists call reinforcement, others call bribery (for example, Kohn, 1993b). In response to this criticism, some (such as Walker, 1995) counter that reinforcement is used in a systematic fashion throughout all levels of society. For example, the government sets up incentives to encourage the public to behave in certain ways, and parents use reinforcement in the process of socializing children. Supporters of reinforcement and behavior management say it produces therapeutic benefits for children (Walker, 1995).

■ Assertive Discipline Model

In the **assertive discipline** model, the teacher applies the same standards and expectations to all students.

Theory base Lee and Marlene Canter (1976, 1985) developed the assertive discipline model. They based their model on assertion training, which postulates that people respond to conflict in one of three ways—passively, assertively, or with hostility.

View of learners When learners misbehave, they decide by choice to accept the negative consequences of their actions (Good & Brophy, 1994).

Teacher-student relationship In this teacher-centered approach, teachers treat all students alike. They apply the same standards to all students and have the same expectations for success for all students. Teachers adhere to their demands and never negotiate with noncomplying students. They use limit-setting consequences such as time outs, detention, and removal of privileges. Other strategies associated with assertive discipline include contracts, positive assertions, rewards, and the development of discipline plans (Canter & Canter, 1976, 1985, 1993).

Teacher's role Adherents of the assertive discipline model believe teachers possess the right to teach and meet basic student needs. Consequently, teachers also have the right to assert maximum control over student behavior within the classroom (Canter & Canter, 1976, 1985, 1993).

Limitations Critics contend that the assertive discipline approach produces an authoritarian environment in which students have virtually no rights and are mere followers of teachers' demands. Also, because this approach ignores individual differences, learners have no responsibility to develop self-control or the ability to build consensus.

Independent reviewers have concluded that Canter and Canter and associates have failed to conduct systematic research on the effectiveness of this approach, which they've been promoting for over two decades. The limited research available on the approach does not support Canter and Canter's claims for its effectiveness (Queen, Blackwelder, & Mallen, 1997).

■ Effective Momentum Management Model

The **effective momentum management** model emphasizes creating an environment that prevents disruptive behaviors.

Theory base After videotaping teachers in their classrooms and analyzing their behaviors, Jacob Kounin (1970) concluded that certain teacher behaviors resulted in higher student achievement and a lower incidence of discipline problems than did others and that the most effective teachers focused on prevention strategies rather than intervention strategies. Based on his findings, Kounin developed the effective momentum management model, which features intervention strategies.

View of learners Kounin views learners as being responsive to environmental changes and stimuli.

Teacher-student relationship This teacher-centered approach requires that teachers know their students and students' behaviors. Its array of prevention strategies includes the following (Baron, 1992; Kounin, 1970):

- "With-it-ness": awareness of all that's going on in the classroom (for example, monitoring the rest of the class while working with individual students)
- Overlapping: skill in handling two or more matters at the same time (for example, dealing with a misbehaving student while maintaining the flow of a lesson)
- Momentum: pacing instruction to address the lesson's objectives without digressions or distractions on the part of students
- Smoothness: skill in moving from one activity to another without being distracted by irrelevant matters (for example, switching from whole-group to small-group activities)

Teacher's role In the effective momentum management model, the teacher's role is to create a learning environment and conditions that prevent disruptive behaviors and misbehaviors.

Limitations Learners don't have much of a role in this approach, given its focus on prevention strategies, which are the teacher's responsibility to implement. In addition, Kounin doesn't address the question of what happens when prevention doesn't work, and there certainly will be times when prevention strategies don't work for every learner in every situation (Good & Brophy, 1994).

LEARNER-CENTERED APPROACHES

The reality therapy model serves as a bridge between the teacher-centered and learner-centered approaches. We include it here, under learner-centered approaches, because its emphasis on learner responsibility leads to the approaches at the learner-centered end of the continuum.

■ Reality Therapy Model

In the **reality therapy model,** teachers help students identify inappropriate behavior and plan more desirable behavior.

Theory base According to psychiatrist William Glasser, people must learn to acknowledge their irresponsible behavior and take the necessary steps to behave in more logical and productive manners. They must learn to accept the consequences of their actions and learn to live responsibly, without infringing on others' rights (Glasser, 1969, 1986).

View of learners Learners have certain needs that must be met either by the home or by the school. The cause of student misbehavior is unmet needs (Glasser, 1969, 1986).

Teacher-student relationship The focus is on the learners' misbehavior. Teachers help learners describe the inappropriate behavior and plan alternate and desirable behavior. Teachers use natural and logical consequences, rather than praise and punishment, to develop responsibility. Contracts and class meetings are strategies they use to define problems, propose solutions, and construct plans for change (Glasser, 1969, 1986; Good & Brophy, 1994).

Teacher's role The teacher's role is to help learners succeed at what they undertake, in their efforts to learn and in their pursuit of self-worth. If learners misbehave, the teacher's role is to help them meet their unmet needs. If learners can't adjust and make their behavior appropriate, the teacher finds ways to alter her or his own behavior or the learning environment (Glasser, 1969, 1986; Good & Brophy, 1994).

Limitations Some critics say the reality therapy model is not based on a realistic understanding of teaching or the amount of time teachers have to fulfill their instructional responsibilities. In addition, some students may have limited ability to develop effective plans for behavioral improvement (Queen, Blackwelder, & Mallen, 1997).

■ Positive Discipline Model

The **positive discipline** model emphasizes supporting students in reaching their goal of belonging and contributing.

Theory base Rudolf Dreikurs and Alfred Adler postulate that, within a social context, children strive to overcome a sense of inferiority by establishing a unique set of goals and a plan for achieving those goals (Dreikurs, Grunwald, & Pepper, 1982).

View of learners Misbehavior is the result of learners' errors in determining how to achieve their primary goals, the most important of which is belonging (Dreikurs, Grunwald, & Pepper, 1982).

Teacher-student relationship Positive discipline rejects the use of punishment, positive reinforcement, praise, and negative reinforcement. Encouragement, natural consequences, and logical consequences are among its fundamental components. Class meetings provide a format for discussing problems and policies and for modeling democratic processes (Dreikurs, Grunwald, & Pepper, 1982; Eaton, 1997; Nelson, 1987).

Teacher's role The teacher's role is to teach learners how to belong, to value equal rights and the dignity of all human beings, and to contribute to the communities in which they live (Dreikurs, Grunwald, & Pepper, 1982; Eaton, 1997; Nelson, 1987).

Limitations It can be difficult for teachers to determine the underlying goal of learners' behavior. Also, the difference between a logical consequence and punishment can be slight and potentially problematic. Finally, class meetings may add stress for students who don't possess the communication skills or emotional maturity to participate effectively in them (Queen, Blackwelder, & Mallen, 1997).

■ Teacher Effectiveness Training Model

The **teacher effectiveness training** model supports individuals in gaining confidence in their abilities by using open communication.

Theory base Thomas Gordon based his theory on the work of Abraham Maslow and Carl Rogers. According to this view, the cause of student misbehavior is teachers' forcing children to behave in a certain way, which interferes with their drive to achieve growth and to respond to their rational selves (Good & Brophy, 1994; Gordon, 1974).

View of learners The uniqueness of each individual makes it impossible for teachers to direct students appropriately. Learners must therefore develop confidence in their ability to listen actively, make decisions, take ownership of problems, and solve problems (Good & Brophy, 1994; Gordon, 1974).

Teacher-student relationship This learner-centered approach relies on open communication between students and teachers, with student-teacher relationships characterized by transparency or opennness, caring, interdependence, separateness, and mutual effort to meet each other's needs (Good & Brophy, 1994; Gordon, 1974).

Teacher's role The teacher's role is to use open communication to facilitate the development of learners' capacity for rational analysis and for solving life's problems. Teachers encourage learners to examine their feelings in a nonjudgmental manner to develop a rational understanding of their troublesome behavior (Good & Brophy, 1994; Gordon, 1974).

Limitations Differences in learners' growth and development make implementation difficult; some learners have difficulty with complex reasoning (Queen, Blackwelder, & Mallen, 1997).

■ Responsible Classroom Management Model

The **responsible classroom management** model considers learners as individuals to be treated fairly, but not necessarily identically.

Theory base The responsible classroom management model is based on the work of Abraham Maslow, Mortimer Adler, Erik Erikson, Richard Havighurst, Lawrence Kohlberg, and Jean Piaget. It postulates that all children move through several common developmental stages, which determine the behaviors, attitudes, cognitive capabilities, and physical characteristics that they exhibit at any particular time. These stages, in combination with children's interactions with others, influence the patterns of behavior that they adopt (Queen, Blackwelder, & Mallen, 1997).

View of learners This model assumes that most learners can be taught to behave responsibly in the classroom. Learners are considered individuals who must be treated fairly, but not necessarily identically (Queen, Blackwelder, & Mallen, 1997).

Teacher-student relationship In this learner-centered approach, teachers clearly state the objectives of all planned classroom activity. Precise and sensitive instructional guidance builds a foundation for responsible student behavior. Students are involved and encouraged to perform at higher levels. Teachers encourage and acknowledge exceptional performance and responsibility but don't use rewards or other forms of bribery to sustain responsible students. Use of external rewards is avoided. Teachers use natural and logical consequences to teach learners to self-correct their behavior (Queen, Blackwelder, & Mallen, 1997).

Teacher's role The teacher's role is to provide learners with unconditional acceptance, security, and the certainty of belonging. The teacher also helps learners develop problem-solving abilities; models values, attitudes, and behaviors that lead learners to behave responsibly; and develops responsible learners who can live productively in a democratic and multicultural society (Queen, Blackwelder, & Mallen, 1997).

Limitations Some criticize the model's use of logical consequences as thinly disguised punishment (Kohn, 1993b). If teachers are not sensitive to value conflicts, classroom interactions will remain shallow and unproductive (Queen, Blackwelder, & Mallen, 1997).

■ Community Model

The **community model** focuses on working together to solve problems.

Theory base Alfie Kohn builds on the work of John Dewey and Jean Piaget and on the notion that the goal of education is to prepare learners for participation in a democratic society (Kohn, 1991, 1993a, 1993b, 1996a).

View of learners Learners are members of a democratic society, are viewed positively, and are encouraged to become involved (Kohn, 1991, 1993a, 1993b, 1996a).

Teacher-student relationship This learner-centered approach focuses on developing relationships and caring communities and giving learners real choices. Teachers and learners work together to solve problems (Kohn, 1991, 1993a, 1993b, 1996a).

Teacher's role Kohn asserts that traditional classroom management consists of manipulating students' behavior, which is a convenient approach for the teacher because it assumes that the fault lies with the students (1993b). Kohn suggests that, instead, when there's a problem the teacher should focus on what students are being asked to do, not just on students who don't do what they're asked to do. When students are off-task, a teacher should ask himself or herself "What's the task?" rather than "How do I get students back on task?" When students behave inappropriately, the teacher needs to look at the classroom culture and climate she or he helped to create. The teacher's primary role is to build safe, caring learning communities (Kohn, 1993b).

Limitations Working with students to build safe, caring learning communities takes considerable time, patience, and skill. Consequently, quite often discipline programs revert to what's easy—punishments and rewards.

Kohn doesn't directly address violent and disruptive behavior. He also skirts the issue of alternatives to logical consequences, which he says are just another form of punishment. However, what he approvingly labels "making restitution" others would consider logical consequences (Eaton, 1997).

Kohn paints in broad strokes, which results in lack of specificity and tends to leave some important questions unanswered. For example, Kohn wonders aloud if rules are necessary; perhaps they are necessary for learners who like to know what the rules are before the game begins.

Your Model?

Which of the instructional guidance alternatives we've described best matches you and your beliefs? How does your view of learners mesh with the different models? What happens if you prefer a learner-centered approach to instructional guidance and the school where you're employed ascribes to the teacher-centered assertive discipline model? Keep these and similar questions in mind as we focus on some of the many facets of organizing the learning environment.

ORGANIZING THE LEARNING ENVIRONMENT

Among the many roles teachers play, one of the most important is providing organizational structures that increase the chances for learner success. This is what we mean when we say **organizational structures:** the way in which teachers organize people, time, space, resources, curricula, and materials. These things can directly affect learner success.

PURPOSE

There are three main purposes for imposing a system of organization on learning environments:

1. To set both learners and teachers up for success
2. To allow both learners and teachers to have more time for the business of learning
3. To facilitate the development of a culture of productivity, by valuing productivity and results, not just activity; by creating an environment of trust and openness; by acting with consistency so learners know how to act; by setting and communicating high standards and expectations; by communicating the organization's shared mission (that is, the long-term goals); and by learning from and about students by listening, observing, and asking questions (Akin & Hopelain, 1986).

CREATING LEARNING COMMUNITIES

In establishing cultures of productivity within their classrooms, teachers are actually going about the business that Kohn refers to as creating learning communities. Trust and openness serve as the foundation on which learners and teachers build such communities. That trust stems in part from a shared understanding of what is expected from all members of the community (such as high levels of productivity, consistency of expectations, and mutual respect). When teachers listen to, observe, and ask questions of learners, they model the interest and caring they want students to demonstrate as well.

ORGANIZING THE LEARNING ENVIRONMENT TO MATCH INSTRUCTIONAL OBJECTIVES

Keeping in mind that the purpose of organizing the learning environment is to set both learners and teachers up for success, to allow both learners and teachers to have more time for the business of learning, and to facilitate the development of a culture of productivity, it makes sense to match organizational structures to instructional objectives. Doing so increases the likelihood that learners will be able to achieve instructional objectives, because the organizational structures will complement and facilitate the instructional activity.

GROUPING STRATEGIES

Grouping strategies (that is, having students work as a class, in small groups, in pairs, or individually, depending on the instructional objective) are one type of organizational structure. They can either advance or impede learners' attainment of instructional objectives, depending on how well they're matched to the objectives and how well the teacher sets up the learning environment to accommodate them.

For example, prior to beginning a whole-group discussion, a teacher might have learners form a circle or semicircle. Since eye contact and nonverbal communication serve important roles in discussions, it's helpful if participants can see, as well as hear, one another. If the instructional objective requires collaborative responses, then the learning environment should enable learners to work effectively in small groups. Clustering desks or seating learners at tables are viable options for promoting collaborative efforts, as is asking groups to locate themselves at different points on the carpet. By contrast, individual work and conferencing require a quiet, more private place that is set apart from the high-traffic areas of the classroom.

In addition to rekindling learner interest, variety in group arrangements also can encourage students to try out different ways and styles of learning. Just because some students (Maybe you?) say they "hate group work," that doesn't mean teachers should never nudge them gently out of their individualized instruction mode and into the "real world" of collaboration. After all, most adults—and certainly teachers—must learn to interact effectively with other people to succeed in the workplace and in life. In the following sections, we describe whole-class, small-group, and individualized instruction.

■ Whole-Class Instruction

Large-group or whole-class arrangements are appropriate when the instructional objectives require presenting information to everyone in the class. Student presentations, unit overviews, video or multimedia presentations, guest speakers, readers' theaters, and literature sharing sessions are examples of activities that benefit from whole-class arrangements, which allow all students to see and be seen, to hear and be heard.

Although rows and columns may serve this purpose, if discussion is a part of the activity, physical arrangements that allow all participants to see and hear all other participants can facilitate discussion. Circles, semicircles, and U-shaped arrangements generally meet this criterion. However, certainly there are other possibilities. An eighth grader whose teacher often used circular arrangements to facilitate class discussion once asked her teacher, "Do we have to make a circle again?" The teacher replied, "No, you can sit in any arrangement you want, as long as everyone in the class can see everyone else."

■ Small-Group Instruction

Skills groups The small groups called **skills groups** consist of a heterogeneous mix of students who share a common instructional need. Once that need has been met, the group disbands. That need might consist of reaching a higher level of use with a particular skill, or learning a specialized skill that the rest of the class doesn't need to learn at that particular time. For example, a teacher might elect to use skills groups if some students need a clearer understanding of how to incorporate dialogue in their writing. Such a group could focus on the mechanics of including direct quotations within a story (that is, how to use commas, periods, and capitalization with quotations) and on finding alternatives to "he said," "she said," and "they said."

Teachers also might use skills groups to introduce a particular researching skill to a specific group of students. For example, if one group of students wants to use photographs and video clips to present the results of their research, a teacher can arrange a time to help those students learn the procedures for scanning photographs into a computer file or importing video clips into a multimedia presentation. Certain students also may need to acquire specific research skills to locate the information they need. These skills might include learning how to conduct computer-assisted searches, using microfiches, citing sources appropriately, or learning how to determine if Internet sources are valid and reliable.

Interest groups As their name implies, **interest groups** are small groups formed simply on the basis of students' interests. For example, for an interdisciplinary unit with the theme of "survival," one group of students might choose to read and discuss London's *Call of the Wild,* while others might select Paulson's *The Hatchet* or *Swiss Family Robinson* or *Robinson Crusoe.* Different small groups could then be formed to discuss each of these works.

Research interests also can lead to the formation of interest groups. An interest in "survival of the fittest" could lead a group of students to learn more about natural selection. An interest in space travel could lead another group to research what they would need to survive a trip to Mars and back, and an interest in medical advances could lead some students to research cancer survivors and the roles that attitude and humor played in their recovery processes.

Literature circles In **literature circles,** which are similar to adult book discussion groups, members choose their own books and discussion partners, establish a reading and meeting schedule, and determine how they will share their reading with one another. Students who are members of literature circles often use journaling or note-taking strategies to record their responses as they read and to guide discussions when they meet as a group (Daniels & Bizar, 1998).

Peer response and editing groups In the groups known as **peer response and editing groups,** three to five students meet regularly to offer one another feedback and advice on their writing. In some groups, students write their comments and edits directly on copies of their peers' drafts, whereas others limit feedback to oral comments.

■ Cooperative Learning Groups

One of the instructional strategies we profile in Chapter 9 is cooperative learning. Consequently, here we describe just two types of cooperative learning groups.

Jigsaw groups To use **jigsaw groups,** a teacher divides his or her class into a number of five- or six-member, heterogeneous study teams. Each member of each team is responsible for learning a portion of the material assigned to the team. After the teams have learned the material assigned to them, the teams split up, and members of different teams meet to discuss the information they were assigned to study. Students then return to their own teams and teach their group members what they learned from the other teams (Arends, 1998).

Group investigation In **group investigation,** five- or six-member heterogeneous groups select topics for study, and each member pursues an in-depth investigation of a chosen subtopic. Group members then synthesize the results of their investigations and collaboratively select an appropriate format for summarizing their results. Group members plan and execute a group presentation and then evaluate both the group's investigation process and its finished product (Arends, 1998).

■ Individualized Instruction

Sometimes a student's instructional needs necessitate the use of **individualized instruction.** Advanced study, specialized interests, and remediation, for example, all might require or benefit from individualized instruction. Tutors, mentors, parent volunteers, peer tutors—as well as teachers—may provide a student with individualized instruction.

Illnesses or physical conditions that prevent students from attending school for extended periods of time also may necessitate the use of individualized instruction. For example, as a freshman in high school, Rita had the dubious distinction of experiencing the formal curriculum via individualized instruction. A collision involving a tree and the toboggan on which she was a passenger resulted in a dislocated hip for Rita. Consequently, she was confined to a body cast and hospital bed for the following five weeks, and school came to her in the form of an itinerant teacher. We're pleased to report that both Rita and the teacher survived this ordeal, although the tree did not.

SCHEDULING

Schedules serve as an extension of teachers' philosophies and perspectives on the teaching/learning process. The schedule you establish and follow should reflect the beliefs you hold about learners, the learning process, and variables that impede or facilitate learning.

■ Daily Schedules

For example, if you subscribe to an integrated-curriculum approach to teaching and learning, your daily schedule should reflect that. Your schedule would consist of blocks of time for learning broad curriculum areas rather than distinct times for each identifiable curriculum component. Rather than stating that phonics is at 9:00, reading is at 9:30, and writing is at 10:00, your schedule might feature a daily language arts block from 9:00 to 11:00.

■ Unit Schedules

In addition, you likely would have unit schedules, because units are a useful technique for promoting and facilitating an integrated-curriculum approach.

Creating unit schedules might involve you in collaborative planning with other teachers. Sometimes teachers at the same grade level plan together and team-teach at least part of the day.

■ Collaborative Scheduling

Collaborative scheduling can facilitate combined class projects, as well as the scheduling of special classes, such as music, art, and physical education. At the middle school and high school levels, the implementation of an integrated-curriculum approach typically means that teachers from different content areas (history, sociology, mathematics, biology, chemistry, English) must meet on a regular basis to collaboratively plan and schedule instruction.

PROCEDURES AND ROUTINES

As indicated earlier, procedures and routines are legitimate features of organizational structures. They provide some of the reliability most learners need to feel comfortable and to be productive. Knowing what to expect with regard to "how we do things here" enables learners to act independently and reduce their reliance on the teacher.

■ Meet and Greet

Morning, or "meet and greet," routines tend to be particularly noticeable in early childhood and primary learning environments. However, middle school and secondary level classrooms also can benefit from some sort of established routines and procedures for entering the classroom and preparing for the day. Taking attendance and lunch count, organizing books and materials, and recording student work are among the more mundane but necessary details teachers must attend to.

However, attending to the affective domain is critical to creating a positive learning environment where students feel safe, comfortable, and welcome. Consequently, teachers need to acknowledge learners of all ages as they enter the learning environment and respond to them warmly and positively. Although doing so may interrupt other teacher tasks, such as assessing student work, recording grades, and completing last-minute preparations, meeting and greeting students is certainly as important—if not more important—as those teacher tasks it interrupts.

■ Distributing and Collecting Instructional Materials and Student Work

When learners know what the procedures and expectations are for their classroom arrival, teachers can focus more of their attention on meeting and greeting, as well as on listening to students and the things they've been waiting to share with a significant adult in their lives. The same is true regarding the distribution and collection of instructional materials and student work. When teachers establish procedures for these tasks and clearly communicate those procedures to students, students then have the independence to proceed without interrupting teachers to ask for directions. Learners are no longer frozen in time, waiting for an opportunity to ask teachers what to do next.

■ Transitions

Procedures and routines also make for smoother and more effective transitions. Because time on task and transitions affect academic achievement, and because there are so many transitions in a typical school day, it's critical for teachers to implement procedures that make transitions easier. Part of setting learners up for success is making sure they know what they are to do when they arrive at school in the morning; what happens in between classes or in between different instructional activities; what procedures they should follow regarding lunch, bathroom breaks, and other basic human needs; and what tasks need to be completed before they leave school each day.

Do you remember eating lunch on your first day of school? There was lots to learn! First of all, even before the day began your teacher already was asking you very pointed questions regarding your dietary decisions. Cold or hot lunch? White or chocolate milk? Peanut butter or plain? Did you bring your lunch money? When it was actually time to go to lunch, there was the whole business of lining up. The kids who brought their lunches had to be in the front of the line, right behind the line leader. Once you reached the lunch room, if you were having a hot lunch, you had to select a fork, spoon, and napkin (they didn't trust you with knives), slide your tray along the counter, smile at the "lunch ladies," pick up your milk, and then carefully negotiate the long and treacherous trip to your assigned table.

Hope you weren't too nervous to eat, because some teachers made an avocation out of "checking your tray." A clean tray is a happy tray, you know. You quickly learned that empty milk glasses are not useful receptacles for hiding unwanted green things such as creamed spinach (an example of incidental learning). Years later, milk cartons were introduced; they were much more useful for this purpose.

If you successfully passed tray inspection, you then had to return your tray to the kitchen, being sure to first place any paper products in the conveniently placed trash bin. Then it was outside for recess—no side trips to the restroom allowed. Recess had its own special set of procedures, but we'll spare you that particular group of organizational structures.

Our point is that, yes, procedures and routines can serve a purpose. However, they can effectively serve a purpose only when they're clearly communicated to learners, when teachers and learners collaboratively arrive at a shared understanding of what those procedures entail, and when learners understand exactly what the purpose of the procedures is. And once those conditions have been met, teachers cannot assume that learners will know how to follow the procedures or be able to follow them. For example, if teachers believe students should line up before being dismissed for lunch, they may need to teach students, especially very young students, what "lining up" means. For one kindergarten teacher we knew, lining up meant that the line leader stood on the floor tile with the star on it, and the other children lined up behind him or her on adjacent tiles, one child per tile. We wondered what purpose this precision served and if that purpose was ever communicated to the students. Because it takes time and effort to teach and learn procedures, it's important for teachers to implement procedures only if they serve necessary and legitimate purposes.

■ Contingency Plans

Establishing routines and procedures does not guarantee that instructional activities always will run smoothly and that every moment of every day learners will be productively engaged. Thus, in addition to establishing purposeful routines and procedures, effective teachers plan for interruptions and expect the unexpected.

They make use of if-then logic to respond to predictable interruptions, such as the inevitable fire drills, tornado drills, and picture days (for example, *if* the fire alarm sounds, *then* I grab the class roster, designated students make sure all windows are closed, students walk quietly and quickly to our designated place well away from the building, and the last student out of the room closes the door).

WHAT SHOULD YOU KNOW ABOUT RULES?

Rules function as effective components of organizational structures when they enable teachers to do their best at teaching and students to do their best at learning. However, some researchers question the need for rules, especially specific ones that come complete with predetermined consequences (Kohn 1996a). They wonder if they're necessary at all and say that specific rules make lawyers, always looking for loopholes, out of learners. Tell that to a young female teacher who, after working with middle school males for a week, felt the need to establish a new rule: "Don't touch the teacher."

THE PURPOSE OF RULES

What would happen if there were no rules? What would that do to learners? Are there students whose main recreational activity consists of finding ways to "beat the system," regardless of what particular system is in place? For example, when a group of high school students wore bedroom slippers to school, administrators told them they could not continue to do so without consequences. The students' response to the administrators was predictable: "There's nothing in the dress code that says it's against the rules to wear bedroom slippers to school." The next year, the school's dress code was amended to specifically prohibit the wearing of bedroom slippers. As an informed decision maker, what do you make of this situation? Was the school's response to the students' behavior appropriate?

THE GAME CALLED SCHOOL: NECESSARY AND UNNECESSARY RULES

Reflecting on her experience learning to play chess, Rita recalls the interesting teaching style her older cousin used to acquaint her with the rules of the game. During the course of playing a game of chess, this cousin would invoke a rule (for example, castling) and then explain to Rita what he had "done to her" and which rule he had applied in doing it. Rita would have much preferred knowing all the rules before the game began. Some learners (and teachers) feel the same way about the game called school. They want to know what the rules are before the game begins, and once the game has begun, they don't want the rules to change without their knowledge. For example, how comfortable would you be as a member of a learning environment in which the teacher didn't communicate her expectations, assessment procedures, and intended outcomes to you? How would you feel if when you asked a teacher about his expectations regarding what you'd be doing in the class and how your work would be assessed, he responded: "I'm not sure, but we'll figure all of that out as we go along"?

In most situations involving more than one person, rules of some sort can serve a useful purpose. With regard to instructional and organizational guidance, rules should be established only when they serve one or more of the following purposes (Cangelosi, 1990):

- They maximize on-task behaviors.
- They discourage disruptions to other classes or to people located in or near the school.
- They provide a safe, secure environment for students, school personnel, and visitors.
- They maintain acceptable standards of decorum among students, school personnel, and visitors to the school.

Rules that don't serve a legitimate purpose are not only unnecessary, they also can create problems in at least three different ways (Cangelosi, 1990):

- Students who follow unnecessary rules become conditioned to being regulated by an authority even when there's no rational basis for such regulation.
- Students who resist unnecessary rules generally "get into trouble," and as a result they may disengage from the learning process.
- Students tend to generalize that if some rules are unimportant, then other rules must also be unimportant.

GUIDELINES FOR DEVELOPING RULES

If and when you decide that a few carefully crafted rules could be helpful to your attempts to create a productive learning environment, ask yourself these questions: What kind of classroom culture and climate do I want to create? Would I want to be a student in this room? Whose classroom is this, anyway? What rules do students need to feel safe and to learn? What role should students play in developing rules?

AUTHORITARIAN VERSUS COLLABORATIVE RULE MAKING

Involving learners in developing rules that have the purpose of providing structure and guidance for the teaching/learning process can be an instructional activity in and of itself. **Collaborative rule making** can teach learners responsible citizenship skills and also can provide an appropriate middle ground between authoritarian administration and permissiveness (Schimmel, 1997). Authoritarian approaches to rule development violate effective teaching principles, encourage some students to subvert or ignore rules, and undermine students' self-discipline and citizenship education.

Such approaches to school code or student handbook development typically result in destructive rule making. Generally speaking, in authoritarian approaches, rules are negative, restrictive, and unexplained; students don't participate in rule development; rules are written and distributed in a formal, legalistic manner rather than in an educational manner; and rules lack standards or procedures.

Negative consequences tend to accompany authoritarian approaches to rules. For example, teachers become disciplinarians and policers of the student body rather than educators. Systems that depend on external control don't teach self-control. They make teachers responsible—not students. Consequently, it becomes teachers' responsibility to catch students "being bad" and punish them.

In contrast to authoritarian approaches to rule making, collaborative rule making features learner participation. Rules that result from collaborative processes tend to exhibit the following characteristics (Schimmel, 1997):

- *They're balanced, reasoned, and positive.* Rules identify expectations rather than describing what is unacceptable behavior.
- *They're educational.* Teachers teach rules in much the same way that they teach curriculum content.
- *They're fair.* Fair rules don't discriminate; are relevant to educational goals; are easy to understand; are clear, specific, and objective; are enforceable; and don't conflict with constitutional values.

GUIDELINES FOR EVALUATING EFFECTIVE RULES

Here are a few simple principles to guide the development and implementation of effective rules.

- *State rules positively.* That is, clearly state what is wanted, as opposed to what is not wanted (*"Listen to others,"* not *"Don't talk"*).
- *State rules in terms of behavior, when possible.* For example, what does "Work quietly" mean? Does it mean don't talk at all, talk quietly enough so that you don't disturb others who are working near you, or don't make so much noise that you disturb the class next door? When it is neither desirable nor possible to state rules in observable terms, then teachers and learners must collectively determine what the rules mean to them. *"Walk in the hallways"* is

an example of a rule stated in observable terms, whereas *"Be courteous"* is an example of one that is not.

■ *Make sure rules pass the "less is more" reality check.* Do the rules fit on the fingers of one hand? Or are there too many rules for students—and teachers—to remember? For example, the summer program we plan and implement has one overarching guideline: "Students who choose to behave in ways that interfere with other students' opportunities to learn and/or the instructor's opportunities to teach, in so doing choose to forfeit their own opportunities to participate in the Institute." That principle has served well as a criterion to guide our decisions regarding whether or not to allow students to continue their participation in the program.

■ *Communicate and collaboratively clarify what your rules mean.* Teachers and learners must arrive at a shared understanding of what their rules mean to them. In this case, failure to communicate can result in learners' and teachers' laboring under different assumptions about what rules mean and how they should be applied.

■ *Post the rules.* "Out of sight, out of mind" is a principle that sometimes applies to rules. However, it's difficult for members of a learning community to protest that they didn't know about a rule when it's posted in plain sight and printed in the students' own handwriting—or word processing.

■ *Apply the rules consistently.* If rules are truly necessary and serve a legitimate purpose, then they should be applied consistently. For example, if you and your students have a rule that states that, except in the case of emergencies or illness, work must be handed in on time, then you need to follow that rule—even if one of your favorite students calls you the night before a major project is due and wants to know if he really has to turn in his project the next morning.

INDIVIDUAL DIFFERENCES: IS THERE REALLY AN EXCEPTION TO EVERY RULE?

Having emphasized the importance of applying rules consistently, we now dare to ask, Is there really an exception to every rule? Might individual differences or special circumstances sometimes justify a rule exception? As you reflect on your school days, do you recall any situations when a rule exception was appropriate? Do you recall any teachers who made rule exceptions for what they considered to be legitimate reasons? If so, did you agree that the situations warranted the exceptions?

Given the fact that no one can predict every situation that might possibly transpire, it seems reasonable to conclude that there will be times when exceptions are made to rules to accommodate individual differences or to respond appropriately to special circumstances. For example, a school might have the policy that students must eat lunch in the cafeteria. However, if the cafeteria is not accessible to people with limited mobility, then some students may not be able to eat in the cafeteria.

Use what you know about the purposes of rules and the guidelines we've discussed for developing effective rules to evaluate the following rules, some of which were written by students. The first five rules (Prosise, 1996) are described as basic guidelines for successful interpersonal relations between teachers and students. In your estimation, how do they measure up to the guidelines for effective rules? **(1)** Listen when someone else is speaking. **(2)** Be respectful of people. **(3)** Use appropriate language. **(4)** Cooperate with others. **(5)** Raise your hand when you want to talk.

The following rules were developed by elementary students and their teacher. Do you think these guidelines would facilitate your attempts to create a culture of productivity for your students and yourself? What modifications, if any, would you make? **(1)** Listen to who is talking. **(2)** No fighting. **(3)** Be kind to classmates. **(4)** Raise your hand to talk. **(5)** Cooperate. **(6)** Don't disturb others when working.

Some teachers allow students to participate in proposing rules for teachers, as well as for themselves. The following rules resulted from one such collaborative effort at developing rules for teachers. How would you evaluate the effectiveness of these rules? Would they facilitate or inhibit your productivity as a teacher? What modifications, if any, would you make to them? Would you be willing to let your students propose rules for you? **(1)** No yelling. **(2)** Show kids what they need to learn. **(3)** Reward kids who do well. **(4)** Remove kids who inhibit learning. **(5)** Tell a few jokes. **(6)** Bring fun stuff to our room.

NATURAL AND LOGICAL CONSEQUENCES

The use of **natural consequences** is based on the principle that reality can influence students' behavior more than teachers can (Evans, 1996). For example, the natural consequence of pouring too much milk into a glass is that you get to clean up the spilled milk. Such situations serve as "teachable moments" that provide authentic and natural contexts for learning. "Children learn naturally if adults can resist the temptation to rescue them from every predicament in which they find themselves" (Eaton, 1997, p. 45).

Logical consequences are more complicated than natural consequences, but they still can be effective, says Eaton (1997). Kohn disagrees, calling logical consequences thinly veiled punishment (1996a). What are **logical consequences**? A student who is disruptive during shared reading is given the choice of listening quietly or returning to her seat. The purpose of the logical consequence is not to punish the student but to change the student's behavior. Consequently, a logical consequence must make clear the connection between a learner's behavior and the resulting action (Eaton, 1997).

Teachers may choose to use logical consequences when natural consequences interfere with other people's rights or negatively affect their well-being. For example, in the poem "Sarah Cynthia Sylvia Stout Would Not Take the Garbage Out" (from Shel Silverstein's *Where the Sidewalk Ends*), a natural consequence of Sarah Cynthia Sylvia Stout's refusing to take the garbage out is that the house begins to smell as the garbage piles up week after week. This is problematic if other people have to live among the mess. Sarah Cynthia Sylvia Stout's refusal to take the garbage out impinges on others' rights to clean air and hygienic living conditions. Therefore, in this situation, logical consequences are more appropriate than naturally occurring consequences. What would serve as a logical consequence for Sarah Cynthia Sylvia Stout's refusal to take the garbage out?

Now transport Sarah Cynthia Sylvia Stout to a classroom setting. What happens when her general untidiness impinges on the general ambience of the learning environment, as well as on the ability of others to breathe freely and concentrate on their work? What would serve as a logical consequence of Sarah's failure to tidy up her overflowing desk or properly dispose of the rotting banana peel buried among the mysteries crammed inside her cubby?

GUIDELINES FOR EFFECTIVE LOGICAL CONSEQUENCES

Should you choose to use logical consequences in response to students' actions, we offer the "four *R*" test (Evans, 1996) as a means of helping you determine if what you intend as a logical consequence is, in fact, logical and appropriate. Effective logical consequences

> *Relate* logically to the behavior.
>
> Are *reasonable*; that is, they focus on the immediate situation or event.
>
> *Respect* the student's dignity and do not judge the student as good or bad.
>
> Allow the student to be *responsible* or accountable for his or her actions.

With the four *R*'s of logical consequences in mind, how do the following consequences measure up?

- Repetitive sentence writing as a consequence of demonstrating disrespect to a teacher
- Copying pages from a dictionary as a consequence of failing to turn work in on time
- Running laps as a consequence of being tardy for gym class
- "Wearing" gum on your nose as a consequence of chewing gum in school
- Spanking as a consequence of talking back to a teacher
- Standing in a corner as a consequence of not listening in class

We hope you recognize all of the preceding punishments as obvious nonexamples of logical consequences. We remind you that just because an intervention appears to work—at least for the moment—that doesn't make it appropriate. Illogical consequences work for the wrong reasons! And it certainly is illogical to use intended learning outcomes as forms of punishment.

GOODNESS OF FIT

Teachers' instructional guidance approaches, educational philosophies, and leadership styles—along with their school's culture and organizational environment—are key variables that directly affect the teaching/learning process. In addition to affecting the teaching/learning process, these variables interact; that is, they affect one another. Consequently, teachers need to analyze these variables to determine their "goodness of fit." To what degree do these variables support one another and promote the same goals? To what degree do they create dissonance and represent conflicting goals? The greater their alignment or congruency, the more likely they are to contribute to the development of a positive learning environment where teachers can teach and all students can learn.

MATCHING YOUR INSTRUCTIONAL GUIDANCE APPROACH TO YOUR EDUCATIONAL PHILOSOPHY

Teachers often experience role conflict in their practice and also must deal with conflicting educational goals. However, teachers can reduce some of the

New teachers talk

During the course of an instructional activity, a seventh grader engages in off-task, disruptive behavior. You've already attempted to redirect her attention, but she has been nonresponsive. Therefore, you ask her to remove herself from the classroom. She clearly indicates to you that she's not going. The next voice you hear is one that vaguely resembles your own, except that it's higher pitched and louder than you remember your voice being. This voice intones, "You have a choice. You can leave, or I will help you leave." The student sits at her desk and does not move. What do you do now?

"Helping" the student leave the classroom implies to me some sort of physical assistance. I would never physically move a seventh grader who is sitting in her desk like a lump. Therefore, I wouldn't give her the choice of moving herself or having me help her. Instead, I would give her the choice of moving herself or receiving a consequence, such as a detention. In a seventh-grade classroom, I would have clearly stated rules and consequences that we would create as a class at the beginning of the year. These would be posted in the room. Therefore, the consequences should be no surprise when a rule is not followed. The rule that might be broken in this case is not following the teacher's directions.

—SHANNON, a Novice Teacher

Authors' Analysis:

Shannon's response acknowledges the danger inherent in making threats—even when those threats are

conflict in their professional lives by ensuring that there's no conflict between their approaches to instructional guidance and their beliefs about teaching and learning.

For example, if teachers ascribe to best-practice principles, then they view learning as a collaborative, social, democratic process. This implies that they would involve their students in making decisions regarding their own learning and learning environment—including establishing routines and procedures, organizing the learning environment, and making classroom rules.

If teachers believe that every learner possesses unique experiences and schemata, that every learner has different instructional needs, and that every learner has specific learning styles and preferences, what implications do those beliefs hold for their instructional guidance approach? What happens to notions of "group punishment" when teachers don't know exactly who the "perpetrator" was, when one consequence fits all, and when no special considerations are given when there are special circumstances?

Matching Your Instructional Guidance Approach to Your Leadership Style

In Chapter 3, we invited you to think of yourself as a leader and informed decision maker, and we presented three leadership skills and four leadership

framed as choices. However, when teachers react to students in anger, fail to predict student behavior, or neglect to think through consequences in advance, they sometimes find themselves in positions similar to the one described in this scenario. They may then feel the need to engage in face-saving behavior if they feel students are challenging their authority. As Shannon suggests, the preferred approach to this situation is for the teacher to avoid a public confrontation by clearly communicating expectations and consequences.

Now It's Your Turn

What would you do if you found yourself in this situation? Would you

a. Pray for guidance from above, even though it's a public school?

b. Announce a pop quiz?

c. Announce that you have a headache and you need to go to the nurse's office to lie down?

d. Direct the student to write the following sentence on the board one hundred times: "I will not frighten and intimidate the student teacher anymore"?

e. None of the above

 Confident that you have selected the last option from the choices provided, we now ask you to describe in your teaching journal how you would deal with the situation Shannon confronted.

roles. Now we invite you to consider how you will apply interpersonal, technical, and conceptual leadership skills in developing your approach to instructional guidance and how you will apply the leadership roles of organizing, planning, motivating, and ensuring quality in implementing that approach.

■ Instructional Guidance Approaches and School Culture

For example, how will your leadership style and interpersonal skills influence your instructional guidance approach in the context of your school's culture? If a school proclaims that it's learner-centered, then positive student-teacher relationships must be hallmarks of its instructional guidance system. Without positive student-teacher relationships, teachers often resort to what they know about "managing" student behavior and to what was "done to them" as students—attempts to control their behavior (Dollard, Christensen, Colucci, & Epanchin, 1996). However, sometimes students don't know how to form caring relationships with others, because a crucial prerequisite to learning to form relationships and caring for others is being cared for oneself. Consequently, taking the lead in developing relationships with students becomes an instructional guidance role for teachers (Noddings, 1992). What happens when teachers are uncertain about how to form caring relationships with their students?

■ Instructional Guidance Approaches and Diversity-Based Conflict

Teachers can begin to cope with diversity-based conflict by increasing their own cultural awareness and knowledge, recognizing their own biases, and reflecting on their own backgrounds and experiences. For example, a preservice teacher who recognized that she had limited experiences with minority students chose to focus her Professional Development Plan on expanding her experiences with minority students by visiting a variety of schools, observing at those schools, and interacting with teachers and students at those schools.

Teachers also need to help their students increase their cultural awareness, recognize their biases, and reflect on their background. Increased understanding of oneself generally leads to increased communication with others. Communication and collaboration are effective techniques for dealing with conflict. Cop-outs, cave-ins, confrontation, and compromise are less effective strategies (Scott, Gargan, & Zakierski, 1997).

FINDING YOUR LEADING AND TEACHING VOICE

Just as writers are encouraged to find their own unique style or voice, we encourage you to take the time and have the patience to discover and develop your own teaching voice. You might attempt to emulate some of your former teachers and apply some of the behaviors and attitudes you saw reflected in their teaching, but before you can succeed in that attempt you must first personalize the strategies and techniques those teachers used. You must make them your own; you must find your own voice.

INTERACTION STYLE

Although some teachers are quick to personalize their practice, others find the process of discovering their teaching voices more protracted and arduous. Your leadership style, organizational style, teaching philosophy, and approach to instructional guidance all will make major contributions to the development of your own unique teaching voice.

However, regardless of their individual style preferences, all teachers need to model appropriate behaviors for learners and exhibit characteristics and attitudes that exemplify effective interpersonal skills. Three basics of effective interpersonal interaction follow (Eaton, 1997):

1. Position yourself so you can comfortably look students in the eye. For young children, this means getting down to their level when speaking to them (by squatting or sitting in a chair). For adolescents, this may mean standing up if they are standing up.
2. Use students' names to help get and keep their attention.
3. Remain focused on learners when speaking to them and maintain eye contact, even though a group of twenty-five students offers many possibilities for distractions.

A group of experienced teachers suggested the following guidelines for building effective relations with students and modeling effective interpersonal skills for them (Prosise, 1996):

1. Be fair to all students.
2. Be consistent.
3. Listen.
4. Respect students.
5. Share feelings.
6. Don't take negative behavior personally.
7. Have a sense of humor.

APPROPRIATE USE OF HUMOR

Speaking of humor, every teacher could benefit from reflecting on Henry Ward Beecher's observation that "A person without a sense of humor is like a wagon without springs, jolted by every pebble in the road." The appropriate use of humor can function as a powerful and productive tool in the teaching/learning process (Dardick, 1990). It can reduce tension, increase motivation, and strengthen teacher-student relationships (Rareshide, 1993). Used appropriately, humor also can improve morale, alleviate stress, diffuse conflict, clarify a point, help students remember important information, encourage creativity, and present different points of view.

However, humor in the form of embarrassment, sarcasm, and ridicule is destructive and inappropriate (Wallinger, 1997). Remember—just because it works temporarily doesn't mean it's appropriate.

Remain focused on learners when speaking to them and position yourself so that you can maintain eye contact with them.
(© Joel Gordon)

YOU MAKE THE CALL—AGAIN

We're sure you remember those teachers whom you thought treated you fairly, as well as those teachers whom you thought treated you unfairly. We're just as sure that your students also will remember particular teachers for treating them fairly or unfairly. Consequently, we conclude this chapter by reminding you of some things you already know about effective instructional guidance and organizational stuctures. Remember: The affective dimension pervades all aspects of the teaching/learning process. Effective teachers establish cultures of productivity that enable all members of the learning community to succeed. Learning environments characterized by physical safety, a positive social-emotional climate, encouragement of intelligent risk taking, and the expectation that mistakes are a natural part of the learning process facilitate both the comfort and the achievement levels students experience.

Finally, we ask you to reflect on how you can use what you know about effective instructional guidance and organizational structures to inform the decisions you make. For example, how would you now respond to the scenarios presented at the beginning of this chapter? Before proceeding to the next item on your extended list of things to do, please take the time to revisit your original responses to those four scenarios, reevaluate your responses, and decide if you'd like to modify any of your original responses.

SUMMARIZING WHAT YOU'VE LEARNED

■ Instructional guidance involves teachers in creating positive learning environments that are developmentally appropriate and culturally responsive; helping students learn from their mistakes rather than punishing them for their mistakes; empowering learners to solve problems rather than punishing them for having problems they can't solve; and helping learners accept consequences, but consequences that leave learners' self-esteem intact.

■ Approaches to instructional guidance range along a continuum from teacher-centered approaches to learner-centered approaches. The traditional model, behavior modification model, assertive discipline model, and effective momentum management model are representative of teacher-centered approaches. The reality therapy model serves as a bridge between the teacher-centered and learner-centered approaches. Its emphasis on learner responsibility leads to more learner-centered approaches, which include positive discipline, teacher effectiveness training, responsible classroom management, and Kohn's theory of community.

■ Organizational structures—how teachers organize people, time, space, resources, curricula, and materials—directly affect learner success.

■ Grouping strategies (that is, having students work as a whole class, in small groups, in pairs, or individually) are one type of organizational structure. They can either advance or impede learners' attainment of instructional objectives, depending on how well they are matched to those objectives.

■ Schedules serve as an extension of teachers' philosophies and perspectives on the teaching/learning process.

■ Procedures and routines serve legitimate purposes as features of organizational structures. They provide some of the reliability most learners need to feel comfortable and to be productive.

■ Rules function as effective organizational structures when they enable teachers to do their best at teaching and students to do their best at learning (Cangelosi, 1990).

■ Teachers' instructional guidance approaches, educational philosophies, and leadership styles—along with their school's culture and organizational environment—are key variables that directly affect the teaching/learning process.

■ It's important to take the time to discover and develop your own teaching voice. Your leadership style, organizational style, teaching philosophy, and approach to instructional guidance all will make major contributions to the development of your own unique teaching voice.

■ The appropriate use of humor can contribute to the development of your teaching voice and can function as a powerful and productive tool in the teaching/learning process.

YOUR PROFESSIONAL TEACHING PORTFOLIO

■ Develop three to five rules that you believe are relevant and critical to any productive learning environment. Explain what contribution each of your rules makes to the teaching/learning process.

■ Describe your preferred instructional guidance approach, and explain how it complements your educational philosophy and leadership style and reflects your teaching voice.

Key Terms

Assertive discipline (p. 208)
Behavior modification (p. 207)
Collaborative rule making (p. 222)
Collaborative scheduling (p. 218)
Community model (p. 212)
Effective momentum management (p. 209)
Group investigation (p. 217)
Individualized instruction (p. 217)
Interest groups (p. 216)

Instructional guidance (p. 198)
Jigsaw groups (p. 216)
Literature circles (p. 216)
Logical consequences (p. 224)
Natural consequences (p. 224)
Organizational structures (p. 213)
Peer response and editing groups (p. 216)
Positive discipline (p. 210)
Reality therapy (p. 210)

Responsible classroom management (p. 212)
Self-monitoring (p. 203)
Self-control (p. 203)
Skills groups (p. 215)
Teacher effectiveness training (p. 211)
Traditional model (p. 205)

Relevant Resources for Professionals

Books and Articles

• Daniels, H., & Bizar, M. (1998). *Methods that matter: Six structures for best practice classrooms.* York, ME: Stenhouse Publishers.

• Eaton, M. (1997). Positive discipline: Fostering the self-esteem of young children. *Young Children, 52*(6), 43–46.

• Scott, C. C., Gargan, A. M., & Zakierski, M. M. (1997). *Managing diversity-based conflicts among children: Fastback 414.* Bloomington, IN: Phi Delta Kappa Educational Foundation.

• Wallinger, L. M. (1997). Don't smile before Christmas: The role of humor in education. *The National Association of Secondary School Principals Bulletin, 81*(589), 27–34.

Professional Journals in Education

• *Learning Environments Research*
Kluwer Academic Publishers, Spuiboulevard 50, P.O. Box 17, 3300 AA Dordrecht, The Netherlands
www.wkap.nl/journalhome.htm/1387-1579

Websites

• **Teachers Helping Teachers.** This website offers a format for teachers to exchange ideas and suggestions for instructional strategies, activities, and lesson plans.
www.pacificnet.net/~mandel/

• **Teachers.Net.** This Web site provides an on-line reference desk, an active chat board, and a lesson plan exchange.
www.teachers.net/

DEVELOPING CURRICULUM

— OR —

The textbooks and the curriculum are not one.

WHAT IS A CURRICULUM?

Synthesizing a definition of *curriculum* that encompasses all possible viewpoints is like coming up with a definition of *bread* that describes every possible variety of bread. All bread has certain key ingredients, but the recipe for one type of bread can differ significantly from the recipe for another type. For example, sticky buns and pizza dough are both considered a type of bread, but the ingredients, kneading process, baking time, and final product vary greatly. This chapter presents the key ingredients for developing curricula and discusses how the decisions made by key players—the "recipe" they follow—affect the development process and final product.

Curriculum theory—describing what curricula are and how they are developed—has been the work of researchers and theorists from many backgrounds. To give you a framework—the key ingredients of curriculum development—we share a few of these researchers' and theorists' ideas with you here. But remember that the learner is key to the curriculum and that there are many different curriculum varieties.

Some theorists define the **curriculum** as *all* the experiences a learner has in school. This means that your lunchroom experiences, playground feats, and time spent staying after school (whether to finish an assignment, write "I will not be late for school" fifty times on the blackboard, or help a favorite teacher clean the chalkboard) were all elements of your curriculum. Did you learn anything in the lunchroom, on the playground, or during after-school activities

"All too often we are giving our young people cut flowers when we should be teaching them to grow plants. We are stuffing their heads with products of earlier innovation rather than teaching them to innovate. We think of the mind as a storehouse to be filled when we should be thinking of it as an instrument to be used."

—J. W. Gordon

What do you think educators mean when they use the term *curriculum*? How would you describe the curricula for the courses in which you are currently enrolled?

In your teaching journal, write a two- to three-sentence description of the curriculum for this introduction to teaching course. What are you learning? What are the course objectives? Now, look back at the course description in the undergraduate catalog or on your syllabus, and note the similarities and differences between your brief description and the "official" version. Are there any differences? Why would there be? You, your classmates, and your professors play a critical role in the emerging curriculum for each of your courses. In fact, the course description you just wrote is probably quite different from the one written by the student sitting next to you and the one written by the student sitting in front of you. After you read this chapter, revisit your course description and decide if it effectively communicates the curriculum for this course.

(planned or unplanned)? Certainly you did. In fact, many of the things you remember about school you learned when you weren't in the classroom. However, how can you quantify, qualify, and measure these things?

CURRICULUM TYPES

A focused definition of *curriculum* has been offered by Eisner (1994), who suggested that "the curriculum of a school, or a course, or a classroom can be conceived of as a series of planned events that are intended to have educational consequences for one or more students" (p. 31). Although this definition sounds quite specific, a more in-depth look at Eisner's understanding of curricula reveals a great deal of ambiguity. According to Eisner (1994), "schools teach much more—and much less—than they intend to teach. Although much of what is taught is explicit and public, a great deal is not" (p. 87).

Eisner describes three distinct types of curricula. The first is the **explicit curriculum.** The explicit curriculum is the curriculum that is written down—the goals and objectives you find in a curriculum guide ("After reading a story, the students will identify the five literary elements—the setting, the characters, the plot, the theme, and the author's style"). The second one, the **implicit curriculum,** involves learning that takes place because students are part of the school culture. For example, Eisner suggests that one of the first things a student learns in school is to provide the teacher with what the teacher wants or expects. Although this is not an explicitly stated objective, the teacher's expectations are communicated to all members of the classroom.

The third curriculum Eisner identifies is the **null curriculum.** Although it may sound a bit paradoxical, the null curriculum is the curriculum that does not exist—what schools *do not* teach. Did the elementary school you attended have an art, music, and drama curriculum? What about athletics? When economic hardships befall schools, the fine arts curriculum is often cut. What implications does this have for students and the community? We could certainly provide many examples of the null and the implicit curricula. In fact, because we believe that the power of the **hidden curriculum** (the implicit and the null curriculum) is so critical, later in this chapter we include an entire section on the hidden curriculum. For the time being, begin to think of all the ways that Eisner's three curricula—explicit, implicit, and null—have influenced your life as a learner and will continue to influence your life as a teacher.

■ Five Concurrent Curricula

Another way of viewing the curriculum is Posner's Five Concurrent Curricula (1992), summarized in Figure 8.1. The curricula Posner identifies are the official, the operational, the hidden, the null, and the extra curricula. Several of Posner's terms and definitions seem to directly correlate with Eisner's: *official* and *explicit; hidden* and *implicit;* and *null* and *null.*

The **official curriculum,** according to Posner, is the written curriculum, documented in scope and sequence charts, syllabi, curriculum guides, course outlines, and lists of objectives. The purpose of the official curriculum is to give teachers a basis for planning lessons and evaluating students. In addition to prescribing specific goals, objectives, and outcomes for students, the official curriculum often serves as a basis for administrators to evaluate and supervise teachers.

The **operational curriculum** consists of what teachers actually teach and how teachers communicate to students the importance of what is taught. What teachers emphasize and what students are expected to know (that is, how students will be assessed) make up the operational curriculum. Although some suggest that students' knowledge can be accurately assessed only through

Figure 8.1
Posner's Five Concurrent Curricula

- *Official curriculum:* The curriculum described in formal documents
- *Operational curriculum:* The curriculum embodied in actual teaching practices and tests
- *Hidden curriculum:* Institutional norms and values not openly acknowledged by teachers or school officials
- *Null curriculum:* The subject matters **not** taught
- *Extra curriculum:* The planned experiences outside the formal curriculum

(Posner, 1992, p. 12)

testing, we believe that there are many ways to assess student performance. Consequently, we explore this concept further in Chapter 11, which focuses on assessment and evaluation.

The *hidden* curriculum involves values and norms that are infused into the curriculum but not openly acknowledged as part of it. Finally, the null curriculum, according to Posner, consists of all of the subject matter that is not taught, just as in Eisner's definition. For example, some schools have a character education program, a violence prevention program, or a substance abuse prevention program, but others do not. Why are certain curricular decisions made, and how do these decisions affect the overall education of the student? It comes down to the question of what is valued by the individuals within the school and community (most often the teachers, the principal, and the parents).

The *extra curriculum* includes all the planned experiences that take place within the context of the school but are not part of the official curriculum. The extra curriculum differs from the hidden curriculum and the null curriculum in that it is a planned, generally supported, and openly acknowledged part of the school experience. This dimension of the curriculum includes a number of peripheral, "extracurricular" activities such as athletics, Young Authors and Great Books clubs, the Odyssey of the Mind program, drama and musical productions, and regional competitions.

From this brief overview of curricular concepts, you can begin to appreciate the complexities of developing curriculum. Some elements of the curriculum can be concretely stated, but the most important concepts associated with curriculum development involve intangible concepts and abstractions. Put another way, "Curriculum development is the process of transforming images and aspirations about education into programs that will effectively realize the visions that initiated the process" (Eisner, 1994, p. 126). Based on your past experiences, what dimensions of the curriculum do you think receive the most attention in schools?

PURPOSES OF SCHOOLS AND SCHOOLING

The discussion of points around which curricular decisions are made—the nature of the subject matter, the nature of society, and the nature of the individual—brings us to a core question: What is the purpose of schools and schooling? As you might have guessed, there are a number of purposes we need to explore—purposes that emanate from different frames of reference. What purpose has been served by your thirteen plus years in school?

SORTING AND SELECTING

Most individuals have many memories of being compared to their peers during their school days. What was your class rank when you graduated from high school? What reading group were you in in first grade? Who was selected to participate in the districtwide spelling bee or the eighth-grade science fair?

Were you admitted to a certain college or program that some of your peers were not? Being sorted and selected (or *not* selected) for certain activities or programs is a purpose that schools have served for a number of years. As Stiggins (1997, p. 348) explains, "Sorting, society decided, would be an important social function of schools. By spreading students out along a continuum of achievement, schools could facilitate merging them into the various segments of the economic and social structure." In fact, this sorting function, which began around 1930 and has continued to the present day, prompted schools' reliance on standardized assessment methods that focus on comparing students against one another. Another term for comparing students in this way is **norm-referenced assessment.** Although norm-referenced assessment can be effective for some educational purposes, sorting and selecting students can also be problematic for many reasons. We explore many of these concerns in Chapter 11.

SOCIALIZING

Some believe that the major purpose of schools and schooling is socialization—teaching students to function effectively as members of society. For example, a professional development school that Therese partnered with developed an explicit curriculum on manners. It was the principal's belief that children need to learn manners to become effectively socialized; thus the school's teachers were given specific goals, objectives, and activities designed to teach manners. Parents also were involved in this program and were given responsibility for developing their children's manners at home.

PRODUCING LITERATE CITIZENS

Others believe that schools' main purpose is to teach students to read, write, and think. The assumption is that if students can do these things, they will function effectively as citizens and promote and uphold society. This purpose of schooling is often politically attractive, because students are seen as the next generation of voters and policy makers. Since the future state of the world is quite worrisome to some of society's mature citizens, its children often are saddled with the responsibility of making the world a better place than it was when they were born into it.

PROMOTING VALUES AND CARING

Some believe that schools and schooling exist to promote values and promulgate caring communities. Schools that define core values (such as tolerance, acceptance, trust, openness, and honesty) as essential to their vision and mission often focus on the development of values and values education as key to their educational purpose.

For example, at the Metcalf Laboratory School, one overriding school goal was that the school culture would promote, support, and be a caring community. To meet this goal, a plan was developed to enlist the school community—the students, teachers, parents, and community members—in developing a list of core values for the school. These core values were developed over a two-year period, using input from focus groups. Afterward, all the players—students, teachers, parents, and community members—collectively decided, after much discussion and debate, on ten core values, which have been infused into the school curriculum.

PROVIDING "SOCIALLY ACCEPTABLE INCARCERATION" OF CHILDREN

Although you may be surprised to see "socially acceptable incarceration" of children discussed as a purpose of schools and schooling, think of the uproar that would take place if tomorrow formal education were no longer compulsory. How would this change affect parents, the business community, and the economy of the region surrounding your school district?

One of our recent graduates teaches in a district that is dismally overcrowded. An innovation that was suggested to deal with the overcrowding problem there was to divide each school day into two shifts: one group of students and teachers would attend school from 6 A.M. to noon, and another group would attend from noon to 6 P.M. People in the community were extremely concerned about the possibility of students having so much free time—especially those who would have finished at noon. Even though all students would have attended school for the same number of hours as they always had, the challenges the community would have faced from changing the school's schedule proved daunting enough to enrage the business community, and the innovation was not adopted.

As you continue to explore the purposes of schools and schooling and to think about how these purposes affect curricular decisions, develop responses to the following four questions (Posner, 1992, p. 13):

1. What educational purposes should schools seek to attain?
2. What educational experiences can be provided that are likely to attain these purposes?
3. How can these experiences be effectively organized?
4. How can we determine whether these purposes are being attained?

Discussing the first two questions will help you think through a number of the issues investigated in this chapter. We deal with the third question in Chapter 10 and the fourth question in Chapter 11.

CURRICULUM CHALLENGES AND OPPORTUNITIES

In addition to pondering and preparing for some of the challenges of developing curricula, we invite you to think about the many exciting opportunities that await you as you begin to craft coherent and engaging curricula, both as a preservice teacher and as an inservice teacher. Relive some of your favorite learning activities; think about what you have learned; and, most important, envision how you will teach and lead in your future classroom.

CRITERIA FOR CURRICULAR DECISIONS

When engaged in curricular decision making, there are three basic points about curricula that decision makers should consider. Although the variations in how these points can be viewed are virtually endless, for sound, practical decisions about curricula, all three of the following points should be carefully considered (Marsh & Willis, 1995).

1. *The nature of the subject matter.* Does the subject matter being taught adequately represent to students the reality of the surrounding world? Later in this chapter, you'll read about how schema theory and constructivism connect. We included an example of a curriculum that provided authentic, real-life experiences designed to help middle school social studies students develop a frame of reference for understanding Reconstruction. This example challenges students to learn about the past by focusing on real-world solutions.

2. *The nature of society.* Does the curriculum sufficiently reflect a broad range of the cultural, political, and economic characteristics of the social context in which it exists, so that students can fit into society in the future and yet also be able to change it? Today in American society, knowledge increases at an exponential rate. Consequently, it is imperative that educators provide opportunities for students to problem-solve and develop the ability to use available resources and references to keep up with the ever-expanding knowledge explosion. A curriculum that focuses on the regurgitation of a select number of historical facts is inherently inadequate, considering the volume of information that will be available to today's elementary and secondary school students when they enter the work force in the twenty-first century.

3. *The nature of the individual.* Does the curriculum sufficiently account for the interests and developmental needs of individual students, so that each student can optimally benefit from it? No packaged curriculum can address the interests and needs of all students. For example, Therese's older daughter, Shauna, has strong mathematical and visual abilities and so chose to major in architecture. Therese's younger daughter, Megan, excels in the performing arts rather than the visual arts; she became a ballet major. Both were fortunate to be enrolled in a university laboratory school with a highly diverse curriculum that encouraged students to maximize their unique talents and strengths.

WHO DEVELOPS THE CURRICULUM?

Curriculum development, like many other facets of the teaching/learning process, is simultaneously affected by a wide range of variables. Often these variables compete and conflict with one another. Here we profile some of the major variables that affect curriculum development: teachers, state and federal governments, state and national goals, and textbook publishers.

TEACHERS

Among the variety of groups involved in curriculum development, teachers play a critical role. "Curriculum development in the context of education is, in this sense, a process that seeks the realization of certain ineffables.... One group continually engaged in this process is teachers.... Teachers inevitably have a range of options that they can exercise in the selection, emphasis, and timing of curricular events" (Eisner, 1994, p. 126).

STATE AND FEDERAL GOVERNMENTS

Other groups involved in planning curricula include school districts; state departments of education or committees working under the chief state school officer; research and development centers that create, assess, and market curricular materials; and commercial publishers. In addition to state departments of education, the federal government also strongly influences curriculum development. Chapter 12 discusses national standards, goals, and recommendations in detail. These play a major role in curricular reform and design. The federal government has access to two important resources for influencing curricula: money and publicity.

The Goals 2000 program (U.S. Department of Education, 1996) is a recent example of how the federal government influences curriculum development. As you may recall, one of the national education goals defined in Goals 2000 focuses on science and mathematics achievement for American students. When the president of the United States speaks to the nation and asserts that science and mathematics education is a national priority, conditions are created for bringing about a new emphasis in these areas across the entire country. Money is directed toward promoting the national goal. However, if science and mathematics education is emphasized, what happens to arts and music education, or language arts and social studies? The federal government plays an extremely important role in shaping school curricula.

Consider the dichotomy that exists between standards-driven reform and learner-centered reform. Standards-driven reform is concerned with what every student should know; learner-centered reform, by contrast, focuses on what students are ready to learn. How might this difference in focus affect the curricula each approach produces? What challenges and opportunities does each approach offer to teachers? Which focus is better—learners or standards?

TEXTBOOK PUBLISHERS

Another major influence on curriculum development is the educational publishing industry. How many textbooks would you estimate you have read since you started school? Do you remember textbooks that you enjoyed and those that you did not? Do you remember teachers who insisted on "covering" the curriculum by demanding that you consume the textbook from cover to cover? Many have suggested that the single most important factor influencing what students study in school, aside from teachers, is their textbooks. Because textbook authors and publishers play such a pivotal role in curriculum development, educators must be aware of their influence and impact. Educators must remind themselves that the textbook and the curriculum are not—and should not be—one and the same.

EXPANDING CURRICULUM DEVELOPMENT PERSPECTIVES

How does the diverse student population affect curricular goals and delivery, as well as assessment and accountability? Is it possible to design a curriculum that addresses the needs and interests of all learners?

ACKNOWLEDGING INDIVIDUAL DIFFERENCES

Eisner (1994, p. 5) asks, "Is a common standardized curriculum appropriate for a nation with 45 million students attending 110,000 schools in which $2^1/_2$ million teachers work? . . . We have 16,000 school districts in America and a tradition that puts a premium on community decision making regarding many, if not all, aspects of schooling. Is a one-size-fits-all curriculum desirable in a nation as diverse as ours?"

Much discussion of national curriculum and assessment initiatives has taken place over the past decade. Although the United States does have a national assessment program, participation is voluntary. Efforts to nationalize the curriculum have been daunting and are currently fraught with challenges. Key among these challenges is the issue of acknowledging individual differences and dealing with diversity. Can a teacher in Los Angeles teach the same curriculum in her bilingual kindergarten classroom as a teacher in Des Moines? Are resources provided in an equitable fashion so all students will have the same opportunities? Kozol (1991) reminds us that learners whose backgrounds are least congruent with the tasks that schools expect children to perform typically attend those schools most depleted in the resources teachers need to teach well and the resources students need to perform well:

> *If the New York City schools were funded, for example, at the level of the highest-spending suburbs of Long Island, a fourth grade class of 36 children . . . would have had* $200,000 more *invested in their education during 1987. Although a portion of this extra money would have gone to administrative costs, the remainder would have been enough to hire two extraordinary teachers at enticing salaries of $50,000 each, divide the class in two classes of some 18 children each, provide them with computers, carpets, air conditioning, new texts and reference books and learning games—indeed, with everything available today in the most affluent school districts—and also pay the costs of extra counseling to help those children cope with the dilemmas that they face at home. Even the most skeptical detractor of "the worth of spending further money in the public schools" would hesitate, I think, to face a grade-school principal in the South Bronx and try to tell her this "wouldn't make much difference." (Kozol, 1991, pp. 123, 124)*

During the 1920s and 1930s, it was popular to conceive of the United States as a great melting pot. America's post–World War I ethnic population was becoming increasingly diverse, with immigrants from the world's cultures arriving at all borders in huge numbers (Stiggins, 1997). The focus was on supporting and promoting a common language, culture, and heritage. Schools attempted to homogenize students. However, the melting pot image is problematic—it robs individuals of their uniqueness and their culture. According to Eisner (1994), "The old image of America as a melting pot that dissipates the distinctiveness of each group arriving on its shores will no longer do" (p. 23).

EXPANDING NOTIONS OF WHAT SCHOOLS SHOULD DO

As the old image of America as a melting pot gives way to a new image— "America as a patchwork quilt"—that celebrates diversity and the uniqueness of each family (represented by each square on the quilt), teachers and schools are being prepared to accept new roles. Teachers must commit to building strong relationships with students and their families, and schools must commit to meeting more of the interests and needs of students and their families. In the twenty-first century, schools will be seen as more than academic institutions and teachers as more than dispensers of knowledge. Schools and teachers will be expected to develop and implement curricula that enhance the physical, social, emotional, and cognitive development of students and their families while being ever mindful of the diversity of American society.

■ One School's Circle of Services

The Valeska Hinton Early Childhood Education Center, a school for three- to seven-year-olds and their families, has as its foundation this African proverb: "It takes a village to raise a child." The facility, designed specifically to reflect this philosophy, consists of four distinct "villages." In each village are five multiage classrooms housing preprimary students (three- and four-year-olds) and primary students (five- to seven-year-olds) as well as a kitchen, conference room, teacher planning office, and outdoor playground. Each classroom has a teacher and an associate teacher. A number of support staff, including a professional development coordinator, a lead teacher, a speech and language therapist, and a special education resource teacher, collaborate daily in the delivery of the year-round educational program. A total of approximately four hundred children and their families, 80 percent of whom qualify as low-income students and over half of whom are African American, are served by this center each year.

Under the visionary leadership of Mr. Ken Hinton, its first principal, the Valeska Hinton Early Childhood Education Center has dared to put children and families first, recognizing that parents are their children's first teachers. In developing a new paradigm for schools of the twenty-first century, the Valeska Hinton Early Childhood Education Center has adopted many innovations. The health care needs of the school's children and their families are monitored

The nutritional needs of children and their families are supported by a breakfast and family-style lunch program.
(© Susie Fitzhugh)

by a full team of health care professionals with offices in the school. Health screenings and medical interventions are performed daily. The nutritional needs of the children and their families are supported by a breakfast and family-style lunch program. The families' child care needs are supported by a sibling care program, which provides quality care for siblings while parents are involved in their children's classrooms or pursuing their own professional development (taking GED classes, participating in parent workshops, or volunteering in the school). In addition, an extended care program provides child care for children both before and after school. Finally, a family support coordinator and her staff focus specifically on the needs of parents through the school's family support program.

Parental involvement is not merely recommended at Valeska Hinton Early Childhood Education Center—it's required. Parents develop a portfolio to document their involvement as partners in their children's education. A record of parent participation activities is compiled by the Family Support Coordinator. Parents must be involved throughout one school year in at least thirty-six documented efforts to support their children. Parents read to their children, create games, facilitate workshops, volunteer in classrooms, attend parent-teacher conferences, participate in adopt-a-school events, and work on their parent portfolios. One team of parent volunteers presents a violence prevention program in each classroom, focusing on developing caring attitudes, dispositions, and behaviors.

As these examples make clear, the Valeska Hinton Early Childhood Education Center is actively involved in expanding the notion of what a school is and what it does. With such a wide-ranging and ambitious mission, curriculum development takes on a new dimension. Valeska Hinton Early Childhood Education Center is indeed an exciting and engaging place!

CREATING PEACEFUL SCHOOLS

A number of recent violent incidents in schools have resulted in student and teacher injuries and deaths. How can communities cope with violence in schools, and how can they begin to reverse the cycle of increased violence?

Even though television news reports and newspapers often depict American students as incorrigible and suggest that teachers are incapable of preparing a competent work force for the future, various surveys have documented that parents support their local schools and most believe that students are secure in the local school environment. Obviously, in some schools violence is a problem, but those schools appear to be more the exception than the rule. When learners express fears about school, those fears usually concern their ability to succeed academically and to interact positively with peers and teachers (Schulz, 1996).

When school violence does occur, where and how does it begin? Of the 3 million attempted or completed violent incidents that occurred in school buildings or on school property and that were documented by the Office of Juvenile Justice and Delinquency Prevention, all were perpetrated by individuals not enrolled at the school or by disturbed students who required special attention from professionals prepared to deal with disruptive or dangerous behavior (Schultz, 1996). Only 6 percent of all juveniles (and 18 percent of all delinquent youths) are responsible for 62 percent of all offenses (and 66 percent of all violent offenses) committed at schools (Miles & Simpson, 1994). It seems that only a small percentage of students is creating the image of an unsafe school environment. However, this small percentage of students cannot be ignored. The issue of violence prevention and education is one that must find its way into school curriculum development and reform efforts.

Experts in education suggest various methods to address problems associated with school violence. Many ideas, such as improving the degree of parent involvement and increasing the amount of quality time a teacher spends with students, can be implemented through dedicated effort from faculty members and school administrators. Other solutions, such as creating smaller schools and classrooms, might be possible but may prove a challenge, given a conservative fiscal climate. When one considers that the future of the world will be determined by the quality of each child's educational experiences, these solutions are worth attempting. Students deserve a chance to learn in positive environments that challenge them to achieve their personal academic goals and celebrate their peers' accomplishments (James, 1995).

THEORIES AND PRACTICES THAT PROVIDE A FOUNDATION FOR CURRICULUM DEVELOPMENT

Your ability to develop and share your curricular philosophy will provide you, and your future employer, with a clear understanding of your beliefs which, taken together, comprise a framework or scaffold—a teaching scaffold.

Have you ever painted a house or observed someone else creating a scaffold that would enable that individual to safely and efficiently ascend to the highest beam? The teaching scaffold that you create must enable you to connect your beliefs and philosophy so you can clearly chart your course through the curricular maze. In this section we present some guiding principles for your consideration. We are hopeful that you will weave these principles into your teaching scaffold.

DEVELOPMENTALLY AND CULTURALLY APPROPRIATE PRACTICE

The National Association for the Education of Young Children (NAEYC) has been the moving force behind the concept of developmentally appropriate practices (DAP). In 1987, NAEYC issued a set of guidelines for DAP that addressed settings for children from birth through age eight (Bredekamp, 1987). An updated version of these DAP guidelines was published in 1997 (Bredekamp & Copple). This long-awaited revision represents years of public and private discussion among professionals regarding the nature of best practice for young learners. The revised DAP guidelines address the programmatic areas of curriculum, as well as adult-child interaction, home-school relationships, and assessment and evaluation (Ketner, Smith, & Parnell, 1997).

More recently, **developmentally and culturally appropriate practice** (DCAP) has been presented as an extension of DAP. The main criticism of DAP is that it lacks multicultural sensitivity and therefore does not fully promote culturally appropriate practice (Bowman, 1992; Delpit, 1988, 1994; Jipson, 1991). To successfully implement DCAP, teachers need to be carefully educated within a well-organized, process-oriented teacher preparation program. In order to extend DAP to DCAP, the preparation of professionals must address, introduce, and structure certain existing notions and prevalent practices in education. DCAP-based preparation programs must both reflect and promote culturally congruent pedagogy.

The basic tenets of DCAP are age-appropriate instruction and instruction that is appropriate for each individual learner (Bredekamp & Copple, 1997). These goals are complementary. Age-appropriate instruction considers learners' cognitive, social, physical, and emotional status. Regardless of students' ages, good teaching must be personalized and must reflect teachers' attempts to meet learners' needs (Darling-Hammond, 1990; Isenberg, 1992). Individualized instruction focuses on meeting the personal needs and promoting the interests and capabilities of each learner. The framework is based on the constructivist approach. Central to the DCAP perspective is the notion that children should be in control of their own learning. This idea reflects the classroom application of the constructivist belief that children are active participants in, and contributors to, their own development as they mentally, physically, and socially explore objects, events, and people in their environment. Such rich interaction results in learners' constructing their own understanding rather than merely receiving knowledge from adults or adult-arranged experiences (Ketner, Smith, & Parnell, 1997). Teachers implementing DCAP focus on the process of change as learners progressively reorganize their understanding and move from one qualitatively different cognitive stage to the next (DeVries & Kohlberg, 1987; Fowell & Lawton, 1993).

Educators should make parents aware of the emotional costs of classrooms that are academically oriented and of the potential benefits of DCAP: "The emotional costs of academically oriented classrooms, particularly for minority children from low-socioeconomic families and especially boys, are real. Many children from all backgrounds exhibit more stress in didactic settings than in child-initiated environments" (Dunn & Kontos, 1997, p. 9).

■ What Is Culturally Congruent Critical Pedagogy?

Critical pedagogy refers to classroom teaching that proceeds from a consideration of students' everyday lives and experiences (Giroux & Simon, 1989). The notion of critical pedagogy is fundamental to multicultural education, since "Critical pedagogy is based on the experiences and viewpoints of students rather than on an imposed culture" (Nieto, 1992, p. 221).

Restructuring teacher preparation toward education that is truly multicultural is a challenging task. Some fundamental questions that preservice teachers must face head on include the following: How well do I know my own culture? In what way has my culture helped me become an educator committed to promoting an equal learning environment for all children? How well do I understand the goal of promoting multicultural education—that is, education that is culturally congruent and that provides appropriate learning experiences for all children?

MULTIPLE INTELLIGENCES THEORY

Multiple intelligences theory is a way of thinking about intelligence. In 1983, Howard Gardner defined intelligence as the ability to solve problems and create products valued in a particular cultural setting. According to Gardner, every individual possesses several different and independent capacities for solving problems and creating products. Gardner's theory of multiple intelligences includes the following four premises:

1. *There is more than one kind of intelligence.* Gardner originally named seven intelligences and recently has added an eighth. Each is discussed on the next two pages.

2. *Intelligence can be taught.* Intelligence develops in four stages, from novice to expert. First comes exposure, which activates the senses (for example, a child listens to Mozart twenty minutes a day from birth until he or she enters school). Second is the opportunity to explore and strengthen the intelligence (in preschool the child explores a variety of string instruments). Third is the formal "training" of the intelligence through the guidance of teachers and parents (the child is enrolled in formal violin lessons and takes a music theory class). Fourth is the "embrace," or mastery, of the intelligence (the child becomes a virtuoso violinist).

3. *A brain is as unique as a fingerprint.* Every individual is born with the poten-

tial to develop all eight intelligences and, throughout life's journey, develops unique strengths and deficits in various areas of intelligence.

4. *Intelligences are forever changing throughout life.* Ability and desire impact the development of the intelligences. Teachers must believe that every child can learn, and students must come to educational programs willing to learn (Gardner, 1983).

Carolyn Chapman's book *If the Shoe Fits . . . : How to Develop Multiple Intelligences in the Classroom* (1993) describes Gardner's eight intelligences as follows:

- *Verbal/linguistic intelligence.* Verbal/linguistic intelligence involves the ability to read, write, listen, speak, and link information. People with this intelligence are sensitive to the meanings of words and to their manipulation, formation, and selection. Poets, authors, reporters, speakers, teachers, attorneys, talk-show hosts, and politicians typically exhibit strengths in verbal/linguistic intelligence. This intelligence is emphasized in today's schools.

- *Musical/rhythmic intelligence.* All individuals have certain musical capabilities; the difference is that some people are more musically skilled or talented than others. Musical/rhythmic intelligence involves one's awareness, enjoyment, and use of the sounds of the world—both environmental and musical sounds. People with a more highly developed musical/rhythmic intelligence are singers, composers, instrumentalists, conductors, and those who enjoy, understand, or appreciate music.

- *Logical/mathematical intelligence.* Logical/mathematical intelligence incorporates both mathematical and scientific abilities. Mathematicians typically enjoy working with abstractions and exploring their possible ramifications. They enjoy working with problems that require a great deal of reasoning. Scientists, however, are characterized by a desire to explain physical reality. For scientists, mathematics serves as a tool for building models and theories. Mathematicians, engineers, physicists, astronomers, computer programmers, and researchers demonstrate a high degree of logical/mathematical intelligence.

- *Visual/spatial intelligence.* Visual/spatial intelligence involves the unique ability to accurately comprehend the visual world. Individuals with visual/spatial intelligence are able to represent spatial information graphically and have a keen gift for bringing forth and transforming mental images. Artists and designers have strong visual/spatial capabilities. Also included in this group are sailors, engineers, surgeons, sculptors, cartographers, and architects.

- *Bodily/kinesthetic intelligence.* Bodily/kinesthetic intelligence is based on the ability to control one's bodily motions and the talent to manipulate objects with deftness. Individuals with a strong bodily/kinesthetic intelligence interact with their environment through touch and movement and often have a highly developed sense of direction. People such as inventors and actors tend to have a great deal of bodily/kinesthetic intelligence; the role of their bodies is critical to their occupations. Others with substantial bodily/kinesthetic intelligence include dancers, acrobats, and athletes.

- *Intrapersonal intelligence.* Individuals with strong intrapersonal intelligence have an uncanny ability to understand their own feelings. They instinctively comprehend their own range of emotions, label them, and draw on them as a means of directing their behavior. In Gardner's words (1983), "the intrapersonal intelligence amounts to little more than the capacity to distinguish a feeling of pleasure from one of pain, and on the basis of such discrimination, to become more involved in or to withdraw from a situation" (p. 239). Examples of those with higher-than-average intrapersonal capabilities include the introspective novelist, wise elder, psychologist, or therapist—all of whom possess a deep understanding of their feelings.

- *Interpersonal intelligence.* Individuals with a high degree of interpersonal intelligence have a unique talent for understanding others. Those exhibiting this intelligence notice and understand the "moods, temperaments, motivations, and intentions" of others (Gardner, 1983, p. 239). People exhibiting this intelligence include religious and political leaders, parents, teachers, therapists, and counselors (Chapman, 1993).

- *Naturalist intelligence.* Individuals with naturalist intelligence have a highly developed ability to discriminate between different living things and to recognize and classify pertinent artifacts (Checkley, 1997). Some have suggested that students with naturalist intelligence have the ability to solve environmental problems (Meyer, 1997).

In addition to these eight intelligences, a ninth form—existential intelligence—is considered by some to be another distinct type of intelligence. **Existential intelligence** refers to the human inclination to ask very basic questions about existence, such as Who are we? Where did we come from? Why do we die? Gardner has not yet given existential intelligence his seal of approval, because he doesn't think there is compelling neurological evidence that it exists in the brain, which is one of his criteria for defining an intelligence (Checkley, 1997).

BRAIN-BASED LEARNING AND TEACHING

During the 1990s, an educational revolution occurred. This revolution involves the field of neuroscience—the study of brain development—which attracted unparalleled interest in the educational world and resulted in a theory often referred to as **brain-based teaching and learning.** Neurons, which make up about 10 percent of the brain's cells, are responsible for making the brain a thinking and learning organ. Humans have 100 billion neurons, and adults have about half the number of neurons found in the brain of a two-year-old (Jensen, 1998). These neurons are critical to the learning process. Learning changes the brain, because the brain rewires itself with each new experience. And this rewiring is critically important during the first few years of a child's life: "We now understand that the first 48 months of life are critical to the brain's development. While researchers have always known that infant development was important, they never knew just *how* important" (Jensen, 1998, p. 20).

One neurobiologist, Harry Chugani, has suggested that the experiences of the first year "can completely change the way a person turns out" (Kotulak, 1996, p. 46). Although heredity provides about 30 to 60 percent of the brain's wiring, environmental stimulation is responsible for the other 40 to 70 percent. "The brain can literally grow new connections with environmental stimulation" (Jensen, 1998, p. 30). Consequently, parents and educators possess enormous power to influence the development of the brain—especially during children's first four years—through educational enrichment.

How does brain-based learning and teaching connect with multiple intelligences theory? Actually, the two concepts connect very well, and both can be infused into a best-practice teaching and learning environment. Although our review of this topic is, of necessity, limited, we encourage you to learn more about brain-based teaching and learning. To get you started, we've included Figure 8.2, which lists the key principles of brain-based learning. Think about how you will incorporate these principles into the lessons, projects, and curriculum of your future classroom.

SCHEMA THEORY

What is schema theory? In its broadest sense, **schema theory** is a theory of knowledge (Rumelhart, 1980) that concerns the manner in which information is organized by the brain, encoded into memory, and retrieved from memory. The information that composes a schema can take a variety of forms. It can include concepts, qualities of an object, or sequences of operations. As a result, schema are networks of connected ideas (Slavin, 1998). An example of a schema is illustrated in the concept of "a dog." The features of a dog include four legs, hair, and nose. These features interrelate to construct the "dog" concept (Bigenho, 1992). If we were to ask you to draw a dog, we would tap into your schema or network of connected ideas about a dog. What experiences would influence your perceptions of a dog, as well as your abilities to holistically represent, in an artistic rendering, those perceptions?

You may remember the story of the "Blue Cat Incident" in Chapter 6. As a kindergartner, Rita's ability to draw a cat was not representative of her "cat" schema. However, because Rita's artistic rendering of the blue cat did not fit the teacher's perception of what a kindergartner's Halloween cat should look like, she was ridiculed by the teacher and her classmates. Connecting the schema of students and teachers is a continual curricular and assessment challenge.

In fact, different researchers seem to present opposing definitions, or constructs, of schema theory. One such dichotomy is illustrated in the fact that Rumelhart (1980) suggested that schemata represent knowledge rather than definitions, whereas Klatzky (1980) identified schema theory as "a set of rules for producing or describing a prototype" (p. 50). Since a description of a prototype

Figure 8.2
Key Principles of Brain-Based Learning

1. **Social brain**
   • The brain develops better in concert with others.
   • Intelligence is valued in the context of the society we live in.
2. **Memory and retrieval pathways**
   • Information and experiences are stored in a variety of interactive pathways.
3. **Uniqueness**
   • Every single brain is totally unique based on genetic history, chemistry, learning styles, personality, gender, personal history, and multiple intelligence.
4. **Impact of threat or high stress**
   • These alter and impair learning and even kill brain cells.
5. **The impact of chemistry**
   • Attention, rhythms of learning, and behavior are influenced by it.
6. **Developmental stages**
   • Some experiences are better done earlier than later.
7. **We're a pattern-forming, self-organizing system.**
   • Our behaviors are a result of spatiotemporal patterns of brain activity produced by cooperative interactions among neural clusters, governed by and predictable by nonlinear laws.
8. **Enrichment**
   • The brain can grow new connections at any age.
   • Complex, challenging experiences with feedback are best.
   • Cognitive skills develop better with music and motor skills.
9. **Mind-body**
   • Movement, posture, arts, and foods modulate our learning.
10. **Emotions are critical.**
    • Emotions and feelings drive our attention, meaning, and memory.
11. **Rich, non-conscious learning**
    • We process peripherals, and both parts and wholes simultaneously.
12. **The brain is meaning-driven.**
    • Meaning is more important to the brain than information.
13. **Models and programs drive our understanding.**
    • Intelligence is the ability to elicit and to construct useful patterns.
14. **Complex and adaptive**
    • Effective change involves the entire complex system.
    • Every brain adapts to its environment based on experience.

(Jensen, 1999)

(that is, a concept, such as a triangle) includes its ideal or characteristic features (for example, three sides), describing it is, in effect, the same as defining it.

Throughout this book we have invited you to construct a scaffold to enhance and expand your teaching schema, so by now this "teacher hanger" has become quite full—perhaps so full that you need to start adding more hangers to the main hanger to connect all your knowledge, skills, dispositions, memories, and experiences. Increasing the connections between the hangers that fit best together results in a more highly developed schema and a deeper understanding of the concept.

■ How Schema Theory and Constructivism Connect

Constructivism, one of the thirteen best-practice principles, was briefly introduced in Chapter 4. We revisit it here because the constructivist approach is related to the belief that humans, as they receive information, organize it around their previously developed schemata, or "networks of connected ideas" (Slavin, 1988). **Constructivism** is "based on the view that knowledge is actively constructed by individuals in interaction with the environment and with others" (Castle, 1997, p. 55). Constructivist teaching engages learners' interests, inspires active experimentation, and fosters cooperation (DeVries & Zan, 1994).

The theoretical underpinnings of constructivism go back to Piaget and Vygotsky. People's curiosity motivates them to construct representations in their minds about their experiences. Learners actively engage in the process of constructing their own knowledge from the information they acquire. Knowledge is constantly evolving and changing, as opposed to static; as learners have new experiences, they build on and modify their prior knowledge (Arends, 1998).

Vygotsky emphasized the social aspects of learning and believed that social interaction facilitated intellectual development and the construction of new ideas. In explaining what he termed the **zone of proximal development** (ZPD), Vygotsky suggested that learners have two different levels of development: actual development and potential development. Actual development refers to students' current intellectual functioning and ability to learn something on their own. Potential development refers to the level where learners can function or achieve with assistance from others, such as teachers, parents, or peers. The area between actual and potential development Vygotsky labeled the zone of proximal development (Arends, 1998). Teachers play a critical role in maximizing students' ZPD. To maximize the potential development of students, teachers must employ constructivist practices.

If active, engaging, authentic, and collaborative learning opportunities result in the construction of knowledge and understanding, then why are so many American classrooms led by teachers who dispense information for the purpose of information regurgitation? After you reflect on this question and discuss some responses to it, begin crafting a commitment statement that details how your teaching will differ qualitatively from merely dispensing knowledge and instead will provide daily opportunities for learning that are active, engaging, authentic, and collaborative.

What does constructivism look like in the classroom? Picture this scenario, which played out in a middle school social studies classroom (Duis, 1996, p. 145):

> *After being presented with the effects of the Civil War (e.g., statistics on the devastation in the South, casualties on both sides, the number of newly freed*

African-Americans, etc.), students (in groups of three or four) were asked to design a general plan to rebuild the nation and to make it whole again. Questions were posed to help the students get started, such as: What were the most pressing problems after the war? What groups of people needed the most help? What role could the government play in rebuilding the nation? After this activity, designed to help create schemata for the social policy of Reconstruction, the students were then ready to learn about the real Reconstruction.

How do constructivism and schema theory connect? Both concepts are based on the premise that learners create networks of ideas by scaffolding them into their prior knowledge and experiences. Therefore, it's imperative that constructivist teachers understand schema theory and empower students to create meaningful networks by acknowledging and assessing students' interests and prior experiences before implementing curricular components. Teachers must incorporate students' schemata when planning lessons, projects, and units of study.

We are hopeful that the insights and understanding you've developed regarding developmentally and culturally appropriate practices, multiple intelligences theory, schema theory, constructivism, and expanded roles for schools have you thinking about the types of curricula that we introduced at the beginning of the chapter. Which type of curricula is most significant? Which type of curricula is most tangible or intangible? The power of the hidden curriculum surfaces as a concept that begs for a more in-depth analysis.

Reflect & Respond

Now that you've reviewed Gardner's eight intelligences, consider whether you have witnessed them in any of your classmates, your family members, or yourself.

In your teaching journal, answer the following questions. Which of the eight intelligences have you developed to a high degree? How have these intelligences affected your learning? In addition to being aware of your own intelligences, how will you use your knowledge of multiple intelligences to support and enhance curricular development in your future classroom?

THE HIDDEN CURRICULUM: THE WHY, THE WHAT, AND THE HOW

Did you learn anything in elementary or high school that wasn't in any textbooks and wasn't reflected on any report cards? Take a moment to reflect on what you learned in school. Do you remember more about reading,

What hidden curricula do these two learning environments teach? What message do they send about the roles of learners and teachers?
(© Elizabeth Crews)

writing, math, science, and social studies or about who you liked to eat lunch with, what you did during recess, or how many Twinkies your best friend consumed on a certain day, at a specific time, during an oh-so-long-ago year? Do you think about favorite and not-so-favorite teachers and activities or about the day someone broke a school rule, and you were confined to quarters until the guilty party confessed? Much of what you learned in school cannot be located on any list of curricular goals and objectives; nevertheless, these "hidden lessons" have influenced you as a person and will continue to influence you as a teacher. Some no doubt had a positive influence on you; conversely, some may have had a negative influence on you.

The hidden curriculum is one of many intangibles that will affect you as a teacher. A number of researchers and scholars have studied these intangibles; however, all the research and scholarship in the world won't matter to you unless you take time to look at how your beliefs and attitudes affect your understanding of the hidden curriculum. That's why in this chapter we take time to explore the hidden curriculum in depth. As you probably know from taking photographs, zooming in on one particular point can cause the background to become unfocused. Be prepared to feel a little fuzzy as we engage your prior experiences and reflections throughout this chapter. Your willingness to learn about the intangibles of teaching as well as assess your own competencies will have long-lasting benefits for you and for the children and families you will soon touch.

Why Is It Important for Teachers to Reflect on the Hidden Curriculum?

The power of the hidden curriculum rests with teachers' understanding that everything they do and say, as well as everything they don't do and don't say, is reflected in the hidden curriculum. For example, will you meet and greet your students at the door each morning with a smile and "Good morning. It's good to see you!" or simply ignore them as you sit behind a stack of worksheets piled on your desk? If you take a moment to think about the short- and long-term impact of this "beginning of the day" ritual, you'll begin to understand the power of the hidden curriculum.

Here are a few more questions for your consideration:

- Will you encourage students to take responsibility for themselves by expecting them to come to class with the materials and work they need, or will you facilitate the development of learned helplessness by consistently allowing students to make excuses for their lack of preparedness?
- Will you nurture students' decision-making skills by allowing them to choose how their tasks are structured and sequenced, or will you routinely tell students exactly what to do, when to do it, and how to do it?

If you're worried that we could go on and on for days with this line of questioning, your worries are justified. Entire books have been written on the subject of the hidden curriculum. Our purpose here, however, is to make you aware of some of the components that contribute to the hidden curriculum so that you can use them to your advantage as you develop your own expectations, reflect on your own values, and, eventually, write your own questions.

What Is the Hidden Curriculum?

As suggested earlier, the term *hidden curriculum* refers to unofficial instructional influences that support or weaken goal attainment (McNeil, 1996). The tendency over time has been to view the hidden curriculum negatively, even though its power may indeed by very positive (Tanner & Tanner, 1995). Certainly, most of the factual information learned (or memorized) in school is quickly forgotten, but what is remembered and continuously regenerated is the **collateral learning** that takes place in school—the attitudes, values, feelings, and appreciation that accompany formal learning. Perhaps, then, the term *collateral learning* more appropriately describes this incidental and informal learning, which others label the hidden curriculum (Doll, 1996; Tanner & Tanner, 1995).

Eisner (1994) coined another term to describe the hidden curriculum—the *implicit curriculum*. He explained that the implicit curriculum is made up of values and expectations that are not included in the formal curriculum yet are absorbed by students during their school experience. One example Eisner gives of an implicit expectation students typically take in is the expectation that students will provide their teachers with whatever they want or expect. Did you, in fact, learn that your success in school was somewhat dependent on your willingness to go along with what your teachers expected? We certainly did! And although we're not suggesting that this is necessarily a negative thing, we are suggesting that the *appropriateness* of teacher expectations and value systems is, most definitely, critically important.

Think about how the implicit curriculum affected your precollege school days.

In your teaching journal, write down five teacher values and five teacher expectations you remember from your precollege school days. After developing your lists, answer the following questions:

- Do these same values and expectations affect you today, as a preservice teacher?

- Are they values and expectations that you would want to characterize yourself as a teacher?

- If so, how can you go about infusing these values and expectations into your professional life? If not, how can you go about amending them?

How Do You Deal with the Hidden Curriculum Once You Find It?

First of all, let us remind you of the warning that we shared at the beginning of this section. You may be feeling like all of this is a little fuzzy, difficult to pin down, and irritatingly intangible. If so, perhaps this bit of wisdom will reassure you: "[The] hidden curriculum can be viewed from various theoretical perspectives and has baffled experts for years" (King, 1986, p. 3).

Again, we remind you that what is important is that you, the preservice teacher, acknowledge the existence of the hidden curriculum in classrooms, accept that it is difficult to assess, and realize that it is a powerful force because of its impact on students' acquisition of values and norms (Weitz, 1988). To take a closer look at what this means in an actual classroom, bring your camera lens with you as you visit a first-grade classroom. The teacher in this particular classroom believes that children learn best in a nonthreatening atmosphere in which there is intellectual safety. From previous observations, we can tell you that this teacher often tells students that no one is perfect and that everyone makes mistakes, but it is important to try. As you walk into the room, you hear the teacher say, "Don't be afraid to talk to me, even though sometimes I may holler. If I holler, let me give you a hug as an apology. We all make mistakes. I do too."

What messages are conveyed in this communication? Do you sense a teacher who values honesty, encourages students to take risks, admits that she makes mistakes, and values hugging as a means of apologizing for making a mistake? Although we don't want to give the impression that we condone "hollering," we do appreciate the teacher's attempt to explain that she is not infallible and occasionally may be wrong. The apology alluded to in this scenario has nothing to do with her being wrong when discussing content but has everything to do with what is appropriate or inappropriate when focusing on process and affect.

Now walk into another first-grade classroom, across the hall. As you enter, once again with your introspective eye on the teacher, you hear the following statement loudly declared: "Why are some of you not saying the Pledge? Put your hand on your heart! Appreciate our freedoms . . . if not, put your name on the board." What messages are conveyed in this communication? What expectations and values seem to characterize this situation? How might these expectations and values influence this group of first graders? We'll let you make the call! Look at the two classrooms in the photos on page 253, and suggest what hidden curriculum might be portrayed in each.

The hidden curriculum is perceived in a variety of ways by a variety of individuals and groups. As this chapter continues to unfold, we intend to expand your awareness of how you are, and will be, influenced by unconscious and unplanned realities that affect your teaching life. Specifically, we share some myths and realities that affect the use of rewards and grading systems—two hidden curriculum components.

EXPLORING THE HIDDEN COSTS OF THE HIDDEN CURRICULUM: THE RISKS OF REWARDS AND GRADES

Do you remember teachers who displayed on the bulletin board only the 100 percent papers, decorated with stickers? Or perhaps you remember the number of free pizzas you were able to consume as a reward for reading a certain number of books? (Don't tell us you were one of those kids who had your parents or a friend sign your Book-It slips without reading the books!) Did you ever receive a grade you didn't earn or end up in a reading group that didn't challenge you? Our many school days have provided all of us with real-life, authentic experiences that have shaped our general impressions about which of these practices were effective and which were not effective.

Unfortunately, teachers often fail to take the time to reflect on the ramifications of their teaching decisions and choices and just incorporate practices that they think are effective because they've experienced them ("My favorite teacher always did it this way" or "I liked getting candy in school, so I think it's okay"). Since these choices are critically important, we explore in this section some specific hidden costs of the hidden curriculum—rewards and grading systems.

THE RISKS OF REWARDS

Many well-meaning teachers assume that the techniques they use to gain compliance from the family dog also are appropriate for "training" their students. The paradigm that characterizes their approach to student motivation is this: "Do this, and you'll get that." If the family dog returns to the back door, without running away, after going outdoors, it receives a prized biscuit. Likewise, when a student does what the teacher wants, the student receives a reward. When attempting to manipulate the behaviors of students, many teachers use gold stars, stickers, smiley faces, blue ribbons, trophies, certificates, candy, money (or tokens), extra recess time, and even praise—all of which qualify for our list of inappropriate rewards. All of these rewards are considered extrinsic and imply that learning for its own sake is not valued or valuable. Think of some of the ways you have seen this approach played out in your own experiences as a student: "If you're good for the substitute teacher, we'll have an extra half-hour of recess tomorrow" or "If your paper is the neatest one in the class, you'll get a gold sticker" or "The first row to finish their work gets to choose a piece of candy."

In an early childhood special education classroom Therese once visited, the children (only seven in number) received M&Ms if they didn't talk when they were waiting in line to get on the bus. Ironically, many of these children were in this program because of delayed expressive language development. Since the children were only at school for two and a half hours each day but were on the bus for approximately forty-five minutes each way, wouldn't it have been appropriate, Therese wondered, to instead provide some conversational modeling that the children could emulate on the bus?

Do rewards motivate students? Absolutely! But they motivate students to get rewarded, not to learn anything or to care about others. The use of extrinsic rewards can create a set of expectations on students' part that dampens their future interest in similar activities if extrinsic rewards are not provided. If a group of children is consistently led to believe that a reward will follow an activity, then they will be less likely to engage in that activity, even if it is inherently enjoyable, if they believe that a reward will not be provided (Lepper & Greene, 1978). As well as dampening students' interest in learning, extrinsic rewards fail to help children develop a commitment to being generous or respectful (Kohn, 1993b). When teachers engage in coercion, manipulation, and control, they teach students to be competitive and distrustful rather than to collaborate and take risks—two of the basic characteristics of a best-practice classroom.

In addition to undermining learning and caring, extrinsic motivators also undermine creativity (Sternberg & Kolligian, 1990). When teachers give extrinsic rewards for certain types of behavior that children choose because they are intrinsically worthwhile (reading, painting, sharing an empathetic response, helping a friend, and so on) they tend to reduce children's interest in performing those behaviors for their own sake.

Punishing and dangling rewards are teaching practices that educators cannot afford to follow if they value students' emotional and cognitive competence. Our discussion in Chapter 4 of emotional literacy provided you with many appropriate alternatives to replace these inappropriate teaching practices in your future classroom. We asked some new teachers how they have responded to the challenge of developing teaching practices that avoid punishment and rewards. To read their responses, see "New Teachers Talk" below.

THE RISKS OF GRADING SYSTEMS

Begin a class discussion about the meaning of a **community of learners.** Think back to the best-practice principles described in Chapter 4. Do the terms *democratic, collaborative,* and *cooperative*—which reflect three of the best-practice principles—emerge in your discussions surrounding the community-of-learners concept?

New teachers talk

Punishing and dangling rewards are teaching practices that educators cannot afford to promote if they value students' emotional and cognitive competence. What alternatives to these practices do you use to provide situations and experiences that students find intrinsically motivating?

When children are interested and excited about what they are learning, the research that they're involved in during their investigations is the motivation. When children direct, and are responsible for, their own learning, they feel empowered, and the need for a behavior reward system melts away. If children are given the opportunity to be problem solvers, they eventually develop the ability to monitor and regulate their own behavior.

—PAM, Fifth-Year Teacher

At the beginning of the year, we develop classroom agreements. Together, as a large group, the students decide which classroom rules we need in order to be effective learners. After developing the list of rules, I take the behavior expectations from the report card and ask the children to write, in their own words, what these mean. For example, one of the report card items is "Listen attentively." The children decided that "Listen attentively" means your eyes are forward, you're listening, you're not playing with items on your desk, and you're not making noises or talking, because that would distract the teacher and the other students. Both the classroom rules and the report card expectations are posted in the room to serve as constant reminders to the children.

In order to promote individual responsibility and self-assessment, the students complete a behavior accountability report once every week. The report includes a list of behaviors, with a blank preceding each item. The children assess their behavior using a 1, which means "I did a good job," or a 2, which means "I need to improve in this

After you've developed a fairly cohesive list of behaviors and descriptors that characterize a community of learners, ask your peers to think of the most effective ways to destroy such a community. What teaching practices would erode a community of learners? In discussing this exercise, Kohn says, "Don't be surprised if participants nominate competition as the number one community destroyer—not only awards assemblies but spelling bees, charts that rank students against each other, grading on a curve, and other things that teach each person to regard everyone else as obstacles to his or her own success" (1996a, p. 106).

Pitting students against one another to compete for high grades is a practice that is definitely alive, but inappropriate, in many classrooms today. Please realize that we are not saying that grading, as in evaluating performance, is not appropriate. Evaluation is critical to the teaching/learning process. Consequently, we provide an extensive review of evaluation and assessment in Chapter 11. However, we are saying that comparing students to one another (*norm-referenced assessment*), rather than collecting assessment data and interpreting them based on certain standards or criteria (**criterion-referenced**

area." After students complete the behavior accountability report, I conference with each student and ask, "Why did you assess your behavior this way?" I write down the child's comments on the report, which goes home with the student and must be returned the next day with a parent signature. Instead of my grading students' behavior, the students evaluate their behavior themselves and are held accountable for it. My goal is for students to set their own intrinsic expectations for excellence rather than to rely on rewards.

—BRAD, Third-Year Teacher

Authors' Analysis

Pam has observed, in her first few years of teaching, the impact of providing a learner-centered curriculum that is engaging and empowering for students. She has witnessed the importance of providing children with opportunities to investigate and solve problems. As a result of these opportunities, Pam's

students have developed the ability, for the most part, to be responsible and regulate their own behaviors. Though both Pam and Brad discussed the overall goal of student responsibility, Brad's response emphasizes a particular strategy that he employs as he interacts with intermediate-grade students. By investing time and attention at the beginning of the year, as well as each week throughout the year, Brad is communicating the high value that he places on appropriate behavior, student self-assessment, and parent involvement.

Now It's Your Turn

 What alternatives to punishment and rewards will you develop for your future classroom as you strive to provide situations and experiences that students will find intrinsically motivating? Record your responses in your teaching journal.

assessment), is a problematic practice. There are certainly valid reasons for normative reporting, but generally that is in the context of program evaluation.

Have you ever been in a course for which the professor announces, on the first day of classes, what percentage of students will fail this particular class? Does this announcement typically foster a sense of community among class members? Probably not! You are much more inclined to begin looking around the room to predict who will drop the course before the next class meeting. Conversely, have you had opportunities to collaborate with other students on written take-home exams, on course projects and presentations, on dialogue journals, or in cooperative learning groups? Think about the different attitudes, values, dispositions, and social skills that are promoted by each of the aforementioned approaches. Which classroom community would you rather be a part of?

A FINAL THOUGHT ON THE HIDDEN CURRICULUM

A school's hidden curriculum, along with its culture and the attitudes and values of its teachers, is one of its most pervasive and dominant features. As we conclude this section on the hidden curriculum, it's our hope that you'll continue to grapple with its impact as you explore the questions and scenarios that lie before you: "Many contradictions and paradoxes surround this issue, and it is up to educational experts, professionals in the field, scholars, and individual consumers to decide how to approach the hidden curriculum. Because of the pervasiveness of the hidden curriculum in our schools, education will be more effective when the hidden curriculum is better understood and the issues related to it are clearer" (King, 1986, p. 89).

CURRICULUM ARTICULATION

The fields of curriculum development and instruction are replete with a number of terms that may be unfamiliar to you. Since you will need to communicate effectively regarding curricular and instructional issues throughout your teaching career, it is necessary that you assimilate some new vocabulary. Consequently, we begin this section on **curriculum articulation**—communicating curricular goals and connecting them with instruction—with some key terms and definitions:

- **Program articulation** refers to the ways in which programs and curricula within or across grade levels connect with one another. A relevant program articulation question, for example, would be "How does the Reading Recovery Program connect with the first-grade language arts curriculum?"
- **Horizontal relevance** refers to the integration of curricular activities across a particular grade level (Kellough & Roberts, 1998). A relevant horizontal relevance question would be—"How do the key topics presented in fifth-grade science connect with the key concepts presented in fifth-grade math?"

- **Vertical articulation** refers to the overall learning continuum that begins in preK and extends through the twelfth-grade curriculum. A relevant vertical articulation question would be "Is the teacher's main responsibility to prepare students for the next grade?"
- *Curricular scope* refers to the continuum of curricula that will be presented for specific content areas. A relevant curricular scope question would be "What is the curricular scope of the third-grade social studies curriculum?"
- *Curricular sequence* refers to the relationship of a curriculum to preceding and subsequent curricula (Kellough & Roberts, 1998). A relevant curricular sequence question would be "What mathematics concepts do fourth-grade students need to master before they are introduced to long division?" (Curricular scope and sequence are often considered simultaneously; but remember that curricular scope refers to the content, whereas curricular sequence refers to the order in which the content is presented.)

CURRICULUM GUIDES

The twofold purpose of **curriculum guides** is to (1) communicate to teachers, parents, and the community the critical components of the curriculum and (2) provide a framework that guides curriculum development for students, teachers, and administrators.

■ What Should Curriculum Guides Include?

Curriculum guides may consist of a number of different components. Here we describe some items typically found in curriculum guides.

A curriculum philosophy statement This communicates the core beliefs and values that characterize the program. Questions that are key to the philosophy behind the curriculum should be answered in the philosophy statement. For example, a program or school district must wrestle with questions such as these:

- "Do we involve the parents and community members in delivering the curriculum?"
- "Do students participate in developing the curriculum?"

A curriculum vision statement This provides visionary guidelines that unify a school's dreams regarding the future. The following vision statement, taken from the Washington City Schools' Vision of Curriculum, articulates their dream of curricular excellence (Glatthorn, 1994, p. 26):

> *We, the educators of the Washington City School System, hold forth this vision of the curriculum of excellence we desire for all our students. We have a dream of a curriculum that is . . .*
>
> 1. *MEANINGFUL. The curriculum emphasizes the active construction of meaning, so that all students find purpose in their studies.*

Technology serves as one curriculum delivery system.
(© Elizabeth Crews)

2. *TECHNOLOGICAL. The curriculum uses technology as one delivery system, examines the influence of technology on students' lives, and gives students the skills they need to use the technology to accomplish their own purposes.*

3. *SOCIALLY RESPONSIBLE. The curriculum develops in students a sense of social responsibility, so that they become aware of their obligations and duties as citizens in a democracy and are especially sensitive to the needs of the poor and the aged.*

A curriculum mission statement This is a statement that reflects the core goals of the curriculum. The following mission statement reflects the school culture and commitment to curricular excellence of Bayview Elementary School, an alternative school located in an affluent northern California suburb. As an alternative school, Bayview enrolls students from throughout the entire district, rather than drawing its student population from the surrounding neighborhood as most schools do. Founded in 1971 in response to burgeoning interest in open education, Bayview remains an open school today and is characterized by, in the words of principal Alexander Ganz, "open doors, open policies, and open relationships" (Darling, 1994, p. 20). Ganz describes Bayview's mission in the school's 1993–1994 *Report to the Community* (quoted in Kass, 1993, p. 2):

> *We are committed to providing ongoing opportunities for all children to build strong self-concepts, develop positive and productive human relationships, and foster a lifelong love of learning. In order to meet the academic, emotional, physical, and social needs of our students, we continually strive to maintain a balance between the content and processes of learning, between intellectual and experiential education, and between the needs of the group and the needs of the individual. Because we believe equally in caring for each other and caring for our environment, teaching and learning at Bayview are characterized by activities that are developmentally-appropriate, child-centered, and designed—through*

collaboration and cooperation—to enhance children's perspectives and establish ties to the world in which we live.

Statement of the knowledge base for each content area The statement of the knowledge base for each area (language arts, mathematics, science, social studies, fine arts, health, and physical education) summarizes the research used in developing the curriculum and highlights exemplary practices in each content area. It guides the work of the curriculum developers and provides a framework for professional development of the staff. The knowledge base statement should summarize the following (Glatthorn, 1994):

- Research on effective teaching and on each specific content area that was referred to in developing the curriculum.
- Major national curriculum projects in each field.
- Recommendation of experts in each field.
- High-quality commercial materials to be included in the curriculum.

Hallmarks of excellence These are the desirable features of the curriculum for any given content area: "In one sense, they constitute a vision for that subject" (Glatthorn, 1994, p. 38).

The district's educational goals and content area mastery goals These usually emanate from state goals and the goals forwarded by professional organizations such as the National Council of Teachers of Mathematics and the National Science Teachers Association.

The curriculum framework This is a general description of the chief features of the educational environment and the curriculum to be developed. The framework should address certain key questions, such as these:

- For which students is the curriculum being developed? What grade levels and developmental levels are included?
- What time allocations are recommended for each content area? Is the proposed curriculum intended to occupy all the time allocated, or will it allow for school- or classroom-based enrichment?
- Has interdisciplinary integration been considered?
- Have the strands of the curriculum been identified?

The strands of the curriculum are the key components of each content area. They represent the recurring horizontal dimensions of the scope and sequence chart (see following section). Some examples include the following:

Content Area	Strand
English/Language Arts	Writing
Mathematics	Estimation
Social Studies	Citizenship

Scope and sequence charts These are usually developed concurrently with the curriculum guide to provide an outline of what content will be taught in what order. They are helpful in that they provide teachers with an overview of the explicit goals of the curriculum across and within grade levels and for each content area. One of the challenges of incorporating best-practice principles involves teaching without making the scope and sequence chart the lesson map. Instead, teachers use the information to guide their instructional decisions regarding the curriculum. It's also important for the scope and sequence charts to be developed by teachers rather than by textbook companies: "The intent is to develop a cadre of informed teachers who will make specific recommendations for the scope and sequence chart, doing so out of a sound and current knowledge of the field" (Glatthorn, 1994, p. 41).

Grade-level objectives These are delineated in each content area for each specific grade level. Often these objectives are developed by focusing on one strand (such as citizenship) and dissecting that strand into meaningful components that are then appropriately sequenced within each grade level. Consider this example, shared by Glatthorn (1994, p. 45). The citizenship strand is supported by the eighth-grade objective that students will effectively resolve group conflicts. The question then becomes, "What specific knowledge and skills are required for students at this grade level to resolve group conflicts?" The following grade-level objectives might be derived from this process:

> Listen attentively to the views of others.
>
> Express your own views clearly.
>
> Identify reasons for disagreement.
>
> Decide whether to compromise, continue to disagree, or seek additional information.

Recommended time allocations These are directly tied to a school's curricular philosophy and vision. Some schools develop charts that specify the number of minutes or time periods that must be allocated to each content area for each grade level by the week or month. It is important to recognize that time is a limited resource and that time allocations should reflect a school's educational priorities. Teachers, parents, students, and administrators should be involved in discussions that focus on the following questions:

> Is enough time being allocated to core content areas?
>
> Is enough time being allocated to learning and teaching opportunities that nurture the aesthetic and creative development of the learner?
>
> Is the program balanced and interdisciplinary?
>
> How does the allocation of time influence the infusion of best-practice principles into the teaching/learning paradigm?
>
> What role does the learner play in making decisions about time allocation?

Recommended teaching activities These also should be included in curriculum guides if they are to serve for teachers as relevant resources that identify authentic, concrete teaching activities teachers can actually use in developing lessons and curricula. Since much of the curriculum development process is abstract, it is difficult for teachers to develop a shared understanding without real-life examples. Another benefit of curriculum guides' including recommended teaching activities is that a number of teachers can share some of the suggested teaching activities in their classrooms and then compare and contrast the outcomes.

Recommended assessment/evaluation plans These are critical curriculum guide components, because curriculum and assessment go hand-in-hand. Assessment is discussed in detail in Chapter 11. For now, begin to think about ways that teachers can actually quantify and qualify what students know and can do. We believe that performance-based assessment is the best way to assess student learning. This involves a new way of thinking about assessment and evaluation. For example, is a multiple choice test the best way to measure students' creative thinking abilities? If not, what are some others ways to assess these competencies? How will you document students' creative thinking competencies? How will you explain this information to parents and administrators? Hopefully this line of questioning will begin to give you a feel for the complexity of assessment and evaluation. Assessment and evaluation must be viewed as multidimensional concepts that both balance and provide a foundation for the curriculum.

Lists of appropriate textbooks and resources Curriculum guides can also include lists of appropriate resources and textbooks. One of the major limitations in curriculum development often is the textbook. It is imperative that teachers do not see the textbook as the curriculum. Instead, the textbook must be viewed as a resource that supports curricular goals and objectives. There are many other resources, including electronic resources, that play a critical role in curriculum development. Often students are provided with only one view of complex issues through a textbook, and this is problematic. For example, many teachers validate the textbook view of Christopher Columbus as a famous explorer but neglect to discuss the negative impact of Columbus's voyage on the Native American population of North America (Brooks & Brooks, 1993).

Domains of Learning

A student-focused curriculum should focus on five areas of student development: cognitive, physical, psychological, social, and moral/ethical development. Physical development is connected to the psychomotor domain; psychological, social, and moral/ethical development are connected to the affective domain; and cognitive development is directly connected to the intellectual domain (Kellough & Roberts, 1998). Since you'll be planning curriculum for all of these domains, in this section we've included suggested categories or taxonomies for them. These categories can be very useful as you begin developing curricula.

SCOPE AND SEQUENCE OF PSYCHOMOTOR DEVELOPMENT

The **psychomotor domain** of learning involves functions ranging from the lowest level, simple manipulation of materials, to the higher level of communicating ideas and finally the highest level, creative performance.

Although researchers agree that these functions all belong to the psychomotor domain, there is less agreement on how to classify them within the domain. Curricular objectives are arranged in a hierarchy from those requiring simple gross locomotor control to the most creative and complex, requiring originality and fine locomotor control. Harrow (1977) developed the following **taxonomy** of the psychomotor domain. The levels are as follows:

1. *Movement.* This level involves gross motor coordination—carrying, grasping, jumping, walking, and so on.
2. *Manipulating.* This level involves fine motor coordination—building, connecting, calibrating, threading, and so on.
3. *Communicating.* This level involves the communication of ideas and feelings—describing, drawing, listening, analyzing, and so on.

SCOPE AND SEQUENCE OF AFFECTIVE DEVELOPMENT

The **affective domain** of learning involves feelings, attitudes, and values. At the lower levels it concerns mere acquisition of these components, whereas at the highest level it involves internalization and action. Krathwohl, Bloom, and Masia (1964) developed a useful taxonomy for the affective domain. The following are their major levels (or categories), from least internalized to most internalized (Kellough & Roberts, 1998, p. 215):

1. *Receiving.* The individual becomes aware of the affective stimulus and begins to have favorable feelings toward it.
2. *Responding.* The individual takes an interest in the stimulus and views it favorably.
3. *Valuing.* The individual shows a tentative belief in the value of the affective stimulus and becomes committed to it.
4. *Organizing.* Values become organized into a system of dominant and supporting values.
5. *Internalization of values.* Beliefs and behaviors are consistent and become a way of life.

SCOPE AND SEQUENCE OF COGNITIVE DEVELOPMENT

The **cognitive domain** is the domain of learning that involves mental operations (or thinking skills), ranging from the lowest level of simple recall of information to high-level, complex evaluative processes. One taxonomy that is arranged like a ladder—from simplest to most complex—has been developed by Bloom (1984). The six major categories in Bloom's taxonomy of cognitive objectives are as follows (Kellough & Roberts, 1998, p. 211):

1. *Knowledge.* Recognizing and recalling information
2. *Comprehension.* Understanding the meaning of information
3. *Application.* Using information
4. *Analysis.* Ability to dissect information into component parts and see relationships
5. *Synthesis.* Putting components together to form new ideas
6. *Evaluation.* Judging the worth of an idea, notion, theory, thesis, proposition, piece of information, or opinion

LEARNING-HOW-TO-LEARN STRATEGIES

"Learning how to learn" is an umbrella concept that includes topics such as metacognition, metacognitive strategies, study skills, research skills, and learning styles. Learning-how-to-learn strategies belong to the cognitive domain. In addition, learning-how-to-learn strategies are essential to the growth and development of lifelong learners. As such, they also are essential—although often neglected—curriculum components: "Learning to learn is an integrated, holistic, and systemic approach to enhancing one's efficiency and effectiveness as a learner. It moves people toward a critical consciousness of their learning processes. It encourages people to examine their judgments and actions that occur before, during and after learning experiences. This introspection and complementary action lead people to heightened insights concerning themselves as learners" (Roth, 1996, p. 3). Facilitating learning how to learn involves helping students become aware of their habits as learners. Learners can use reflection as one strategy for examining their learning processes. Journals and learning logs can serve as windows through which learners can view and monitor their own learning, discover idiosyncrasies, and think on paper about their own thinking.

PROBLEM SOLVING

Comparatively little class time is devoted to the development of learning strategies. Although gaining information is important, so is learning how to learn: "The major goal of teaching children should be to help them begin their role as lifelong learners" (Casey & Tucker, 1994, p. 140). U.S. business is demanding employees who enter the workplace equipped with the knowledge, skills, and dispositions to engage in collaborative problem solving (Collins, 1991). Children need to learn how to be effective learners, which includes being creative problem solvers with organizational and planning skills. Problem solving is a form of learning that involves recalling and combining relevant rules to form new, more complex rules. Effective problem solving also involves both cognitive and affective components. Consequently, teachers must use interventions and techniques that address the motivational and affective aspects, as well as the cognitive dimensions, of problem solving (Young, 1997).

Creative problem solvers are curious and inquisitive, enjoy figuring things out, seek out challenges, are persistent, are resourceful and flexible in the ways they approach tasks, are independent learners, feel confident about themselves as learners, and are risk takers. Effective planners think things through in advance, organize materials in a systematic way, gather what they need to complete projects, find appropriate work sites, and are systematic in the ways they approach different parts of a task. Effective learners also are willing to fail. Although they don't accept failure, they're comfortable with it and recognize that mistakes and failure are important components of learning and success (Casey & Tucker, 1994).

PLANNING

Teachers who emphasize problem solving incorporate both planning and organizational skills into the curriculum and make them as integral to their lesson plans as reading and mathematics. They encourage learners to think ahead before they begin projects. Learners in their classrooms come to expect them to ask, "What's your plan?" and they begin to view planning as an important part of their tasks as learners. In addition, they learn to evaluate their own plans and to revise them as necessary. Effective planning skills also can help students use their instructional time wisely, thereby increasing their time on task and achievement (Casey & Tucker, 1994).

REHEARSAL STRATEGIES

For learning to occur, learners must encode—or connect—new information to their prior knowledge and existing schemata. Strategies by which **encoding** occurs are called *rehearsal strategies*. They include rote and complex rehearsal. Simply repeating out loud or subvocalizing information learners wish to remember is called **rote rehearsal;** it's used to remember short lists, phone numbers, directions, and other simple information. Rote rehearsal doesn't provide much assistance in remembering complex information. This requires **complex rehearsal** strategies, which include underlining, highlighting, and making marginal notes. However, as you may have discovered on your own, underlining can prove ineffective as a rehearsal strategy if learners underline almost everything or if they underline information that is irrelevant while overlooking key points (Arends, 1998).

ELABORATION STRATEGIES

Elaboration strategies include a variety of skills that students can use to help them remember, assimilate, organize, and understand new knowledge and information. However, first students must know what elaboration strategies are, and then they must learn how to apply them.

■ Elaboration Strategies to Enhance Reading Comprehension

SQ3R and PQ4R are two strategies learners can use to enhance their reading comprehension and retention. SQ3R stands for Survey, Question, Read, Review, Recite, whereas the steps of PQ4R include Preview, Question, Read, Reflect, Recite, Review. Both strategies guide learners through the following processes. First of all, learners preview or survey what they are about to read. Then they formulate questions to guide their reading, and read the selection. Next, depending on whether the strategy being used is SQ3R or PQ4R, learners either review what they've read and then recite or describe what they've read, or they reflect or think about what they've read, recite or describe what they've read, and then review the main points of what they've read. SQ3R and PQ4R can be particularly helpful when applied to content-area reading, such as social studies and science texts.

■ Note Taking

Note taking is one of those things that almost every student does but few students do well. For some students, taking notes means copying all of the text printed in boldface type. For others, taking notes means desperately attempting to scribble down every word of an overhead transparency or slide before the instructor moves on. Do you remember learning how to take notes? Or did you learn to take notes through trial and error?

Unfortunately, few teachers ever make a formal attempt to help their students learn to take notes. It's as though everyone assumes students automatically know how to take effective notes that will help them learn, remember, and organize information. However, somewhere within the formal curriculum, teachers must help students acquire effective note-taking skills, if note taking is an elaboration strategy students will be expected to use. Identifying main ideas and supporting details are important components of note taking.

■ Analogies

Analogies are comparisons that point out similar features of things or ideas that are otherwise different (for example, a heart and a pump, fuel and food, telegraph lines and the nervous system). When used as elaboration strategies, analogies can help students draw comparisons between familiar concepts and new concepts they're learning. Successfully drawing such comparisons can result in increased understanding of new and unfamiliar concepts.

ORGANIZATION STRATEGIES

Organization strategies include identifying key ideas or facts from a larger array of information, regrouping or clustering them, and dividing them into smaller subsets. Outlining is an organization strategy that you likely have used many times. Webbing or mapping is a visual organization strategy used to show how main ideas and subcomponents of topics or concepts are related to one another.

Mnemonics are organization strategies that assist memory by helping the learner form associations that don't naturally exist. Applications of the principles of mnemonics include acronyms, chunking, and the link-word method. As you probably know, acronyms consist of the first letters of words people want to remember. For example, HOMES is an acronym designed to help people remember the names of the five Great Lakes—Huron, Ontario, Michigan, Erie, and Superior.

Chunking involves attributing personal meaning to letters and numbers to make them more memorable (vanity license plates are an example). People often use chunking to remember number strings, such as phone numbers and social security numbers. Finally, in the link-word strategy, learners create a mental image that links a familiar English word to an unfamiliar foreign language word. That mental image serves as a link that helps them remember the foreign word and its meaning.

METACOGNITIVE STRATEGIES

Metacognitive strategies help learners understand their own thinking processes. These provide learners with knowledge about various learning strategies and when to use them. One such strategy is *cognitive monitoring,* which consists of learners' selecting, using, and monitoring learning strategies appropriate to their learning styles and the situation at hand. For example, visual learners might use concept mapping, whereas all learners could use think-alouds to increase their understanding and awareness of their own thought processes.

RESEARCH STRATEGIES

Research strategies are potentially powerful tools students can use to increase their independence and autonomy as learners. However, before students can apply research skills, they first must learn how to find out things for themselves. Attempts to facilitate students' acquisition of research skills benefit from a systematic, developmental approach. Just as students don't learn other skills and concepts all at once, for them to reach the point where they can effectively and independently apply research skills takes time, planning, sequential instruction, and guidance.

■ Helping Students Learn How to Find Things Out for Themselves

Attempts to teach students research strategies, or how to find things out for themselves, need to begin by describing what research is. For example, if you ask a third grader what research is, he or she might simply shrug or else offer a vague explanation. However, if you ask what a report is, the third grader likely will be able to provide a fairly specific and descriptive response. Many third graders' schema for *reports* includes something along the lines of finding the "W" encyclopedia and copying the first paragraph under the heading "Whales." Updating that schema could result in a modified paradigm that includes such things as computers, CD-ROM encyclopedias, and the Internet.

■ Whole-Class and Small-Group Research

Clearly, teachers must describe what they do and do not mean by research and must acquaint students with the many different steps research involves (selecting and narrowing a topic, developing research questions, conducting surveys and interviews, locating resources, using the library, outlining, note taking).

With instruction and guidance, even very young learners can acquire and apply research skills. Their initial research attempts can be organized as whole-class or small-group efforts and can focus on topics that are of interest to them and emerge from questions that they ask. For example, a small group of first graders chose to research the North Pole. Their questions led them to several discoveries, but the discovery these young researchers were most impressed by was the fact that there are actually two North Poles—one magnetic and one geographic.

■ Formulating Research Questions

Webbing can serve as an effective tool for helping students explore their questions and ideas and narrow their research focus or topic. For instance, if a group of students announces they're going to research the topic "dogs," you could help them use webbing to map out the questions they'd like their research to answer. Once they've added all of their questions to the web, with your guidance they can identify one or two particular subtopics to explore or the five or six questions they want most to answer.

■ Using the Library

Think about the libraries you entered as a first grader. Now visualize the libraries you use today. Computer-assisted searches, on-line catalogs and databases, CD-ROM resources, information on microfiche, the Internet, Web sites, and interlibrary loan programs are features that have transformed libraries into multimedia centers. Although knowing how to alphabetize and how to use indexes still are relevant library skills, effectively using libraries today requires computer literacy and a willingness to approach and use technology that may be unfamiliar, whether you are a student or a teacher.

■ Using the Internet

The Internet can serve as a valuable learning and instruction tool. Web sites, Internet searches, chat rooms, and e-mail all are potential sources of information and interaction for learners. However, teachers have an obligation to address safety and ethical issues related to Internet use. These include high-tech plagiarism in the form of copying and pasting without citing sources and "downloadable" research papers, evaluation of the credibility of information and information sources, access to Web sites that feature pornography and other material that's inappropriate for young learners, and careful use of chat rooms.

■ Organizing Information

Given the fact that the quantity of information in the world doubles every year, the ability to manage and organize information has become increasingly important. Collecting data is only one small piece of the research puzzle. Knowing what to do with all of the data is a necessary prerequisite to finding usable answers to research questions. Consequently, analyzing, synthesizing, and evaluating information all are critical research skills.

■ Presenting Research Results

Finally, once students have addressed and answered their research questions, they must decide how to present the results of their research. Multimedia presentations provide one vehicle for showcasing research results and can be quite effective as long as they complement the particular research project. Effective research presentations combine clarity and creativity and actively engage listeners through a variety of approaches, including the use of visuals to emphasize and help listeners remember key points. Students need guidance and suggestions regarding different and creative ways to "show what they know."

SUMMARIZING WHAT YOU'VE LEARNED

- Although the curriculum has been defined as all of the experiences a learner has in school, a more focused definition, proposed by Eisner (1994), suggests that curricula are series of planned events intended to have educational consequences.

- We suggested five specific purposes of schools and schooling that have evolved over time: sorting and selecting, socializing, producing literate citizens, promoting values and caring, and providing "socially acceptable incarceration" of children.

- As a teacher, you will be responsible both for developing curriculum content and for applying a number of curricular processes. As you make curricular decisions, you'll need to consider the subject matter (content area); the cultural, political, and economic characteristics of society; and your individual students.

- Teachers play a critical role in the curriculum development process. Other groups involved in planning curriculum include school districts, the national and state governments, research and development centers, and commercial publishers.

- Curricular challenges for teachers include articulating state and national goals, keeping the curriculum learner-centered, accommodating individual differences, and expanding notions of what schools can do.

- To expand your understanding of many of the underlying principles and philosophies that provide a foundation for curriculum development, we included information on developmentally and culturally appropriate practices, multiple intelligences theory, brain-based learning and teaching, schema theory, and constructivism.

- Viewed as an "intangible" of teaching, the hidden curriculum refers to instructional influences that support or weaken goal attainment.

- Curriculum articulation provides educators with an authentic context for reviewing and analyzing curricula. The analytical process of developing curriculum guides provides teachers with the knowledge and ability to synthesize appropriate curricula for their own classrooms.

- The three domains of learning are the cognitive domain, the affective domain, and the psychomotor domain. The scope and sequence structure for each of these domains correlates with key curricular components: intellectual development is connected to the cognitive domain; physical development is connected to the psychomotor domain; and psychological, social, and moral/ethical development are connected to the affective domain.

■ "Learning how to learn" is an umbrella concept that includes topics such as metacognition, metacognitive strategies, study skills, research skills, and learning styles. Learning-how-to-learn strategies are essential to the growth and development of lifelong learners.

YOUR PROFESSIONAL TEACHING PORTFOLIO

■ Review at least two different curriculum guides that have been provided by your professor. Based on your review, develop written responses to the following questions: (1) What information did you find contained within the curriculum guides? (2) As a beginning teacher, of what use is each type of information to you? (3) What did you find helpful and "user friendly" about the curriculum guides? (4) What did you find confusing or difficult to understand about the curriculum guides?

■ After responding to each of these questions, develop a written plan that articulates how you will use curriculum guides to inform your curriculum planning.

■ Observe a classroom for at least one hundred minutes over a two-week period, and cite specific examples you see of each of Eisner's curricula: the explicit curriculum, the implicit curriculum, and the null curriculum. Discuss, in writing, how you will use your knowledge of these three types of curricula to make curricular decisions in your future classroom.

Key Terms

Affective domain (p. 266)
Analogies (p. 269)
Brain-based teaching and learning (p. 248)
Cognitive domain (p. 266)
Collateral learning (p. 254)
Community of learners (p. 258)
Constructivism (p. 251)
Criterion-referenced assessment (p. 259)
Critical pedagogy (p. 246)
Curriculum (p. 233)
Curriculum articulation (p. 260)

Curriculum guide (p. 261)
Developmentally and culturally appropriate practice (p. 245)
Encoding (p. 268)
Existential intelligence (p. 248)
Explicit curriculum (p. 234)
Hidden curriculum (p. 235)
Horizontal relevance (p. 260)
Implicit curriculum (p. 234)
Multiple intelligences theory (p. 246)
Norm-referenced assessment (p. 237)

Null curriculum (p. 235)
Official curriculum (p. 235)
Operational curriculum (p. 235)
Program articulation (p. 260)
Psychomotor domain (p. 266)
Rote rehearsal (p. 266)
Schema theory (p. 249)
Taxonomy (p. 266)
Vertical articulation (p. 261)
Zone of proximal development (p. 251)

Relevant Resources for Professionals

Books and Articles

- Department of Education. (1996). *Introducing Goals 2000: A world-class education for every child.* Washington, DC: U.S. Department of Education.

- Eisner, E. W. (1994). *The educational imagination: On the design and evaluation of school programs* (3rd ed.). New York: Macmillan.

- Gardner, H. (1983). *Frames of mind: The theory of multiple intelligences.* New York: Basic Books.

- Glatthorn, A. (1994). *Developing a quality curriculum.* Alexandria, VA: Association for Supervision and Curriculum Development.

- Jensen, E. (1998). *Teaching with the brain in mind.* Alexandria, VA: Association for Supervision and Curriculum Development.

- Kohn, A. (1996). *Beyond discipline: From compliance to community.* Alexandria, VA: Association for Supervision and Curriculum Development.

Professional Journals in Education

- *From Now On*
  An on-line journal published by Jamie McKenzie with articles on topics such as assessment, curriculum, grants, research, staff development, and technology planning.

  http://fromnowon.org/.www.html

Professional Organizations

- Association for Supervision and Curriculum Development.
  An international, nonprofit, nonpartisan education association committed to the mission of forging covenants in teaching and learning for the success of all learners. ASCD provides professional development in curriculum and supervision, initiates and supports activities to provide educational equity for all students, and serves as a world-class leader in education information services.

  http://www.ascd.org/

Websites

- **CCCnet**
  An award-winning Internet product developed by educators at Computer Curriculum Corporation. CCCnet provides K–8 curriculum extensions in math, science, reading, and social studies that enhance classroom learning. All content is correlated to national and state standards and offers on-line and off-line assessment opportunities.

  http://www.cccnet.com/

- **NSTA's Scope, Sequence & Coordination Project**
  The National Science Teachers Association and its Scope, Sequence & Coordination Web site offer ninth- and tenth-grade science teachers hundreds of curricular resources derived from *A Framework for High School Science Education,* an NSTA publication. The micro units, composed of labs, readings, and assessments for teachers and students, were developed and tested for the purpose of meeting the National Science Education standards.

  http://www.gsh.org/NSTA_SSandC/

Videos

- *The Brain and Learning:* This four-video set and facilitator's guide explain how the brain functions and show examples of brain-friendly learning experiences. Available from the Association for Supervision and Curriculum Development.

  http://www.ascd.org

- *Constructivism:* This two-video set and facilitator's guide feature innovative educational settings and teaching strategies. Available from the Association for Supervision and Curriculum Development.

  http://www.ascd.org

INSTRUCTIONAL STRATEGIES AND APPROACHES

9

— OR —

If the only tool you have is a hammer, you see everything as a nail.

WHY USE A VARIETY OF INSTRUCTIONAL APPROACHES?

Imagine what would happen if as a teacher you only had one instructional strategy—one tool—to help learners acquire new skills or content. No matter what the situation was, who your students were, or what your students needed, your response would be the same. What would happen if your students failed to learn via the one tool you had to use? What would you do then? For your "Plan B" would you resort to the MOTS approach (more of the same) or perhaps the LAS approach (louder and slower)? Would those be your only two choices? If you allowed your current knowledge and skill base to limit your options, then yes, these would be your only choices. However, we're hopeful that you would assume the role of educational leader, informed decision maker, and lifelong learner and make it your goal to find other options and learn how to use them. That is, you would learn a variety of instructional approaches and acquire the knowledge and skills needed to effectively apply them in appropriate situations. We're also hopeful that you would never find yourself in this situation because you recognize the importance of responding

"There are many different ways of understanding . . . and, correspondingly, many different ways of teaching to understand."

—Passmore, 1982, p. 210

Reflect on the various teachers you've had and the different strategies and approaches they've used to help you learn. Which approaches did you most enjoy? What strategies seemed most effective at helping you learn and remember information, concepts, and skills? What do you think made those strategies effective for you?

In your teaching journal, describe two or three different instructional strategies that benefited you as a learner. Then speculate about why those particular teaching approaches worked for you.

to a variety of learners, learner needs, and learning situations with a variety of instructional approaches and strategies.

Abraham Maslow, whose name you likely know in connection with his hierarchy of needs, is credited with the notion that if the only tool people have is a hammer, they tend to see and respond to everything as if it were a nail. Such a limited view leads to what we refer to as "high-impact maintenance," which can prove effective in certain situations (hammering down a loose nail on a deck) but disastrous in others (hammering on the television set in an attempt to adjust the horizontal hold). But what does Maslow's severely limited tool supply have to do with instructional strategies and approaches?

As a learner, what instructional strategies and approaches did you most enjoy?
(© Joel Gordon)

DIFFERENT STRATEGIES FOR DIFFERENT LEARNERS

In Chapter 5, you read about the importance of family involvement and how it begins with teachers' acknowledging and responding to the diversity of learners and their families. As you know, diversity comes in a variety of forms, including racial, ethnic, religious, linguistic, social, and economic diversity as well as diversity resulting from disabilities and special learning needs. In Chapter 8, you read about a number of variables that affect curricular development and decision making. In addition to learner diversity, those variables include learners' prior knowledge and schemata, multiple intelligences, developmentally and culturally appropriate practice, and different learning styles. Just as these variables affect curricular development and decision making, they also affect decisions regarding instructional strategies and approaches. Teachers must inform their decisions about which teaching tools and techniques to use with knowledge related to individual learners and diverse learning needs. They also must consider learners' prior knowledge and experiences so they can effectively connect what learners already know and can do with the new knowledge and skills they are learning.

DIFFERENT STRATEGIES FOR DIFFERENT TYPES OF LEARNING

In deciding what instructional strategies and approaches to implement, teachers also must consider the kind of knowledge they are attempting to help students learn, because people learn different types of knowledge in different ways. Consequently, attempts to acquire different types of knowledge benefit from different types of teaching strategies, just as different carpentry tasks require different tools.

■ Declarative, Procedural, and Conditional Knowledge

Declarative knowledge is knowledge about something, and **procedural knowledge** is knowledge about how to do something. **Conditional knowledge** is knowledge about when and why to use particular examples of declarative or procedural knowledge, that is, knowing when to apply knowledge appropriately. Identifying and describing five different instructional strategies is an example of declarative knowledge, appropriately implementing a particular teaching approach is an example of procedural knowledge, and knowing when and why to apply a particular instructional strategy in a particular teaching/learning situation is an example of conditional knowledge. By the way, these examples also describe the learning outcomes we have in mind as we write this chapter. Table 9.1 provides more examples of the three different kinds of knowledge.

ROLE OF METACOGNITION

Simply defined, **metacognition** is thinking about thinking. Learners engage in metacognition when they think about their own thinking processes and choose learning strategies that are appropriate for specific tasks. Metacognition has two main components. The first component is knowledge about cogni-

Table 9.1
Kinds of Knowledge

Declarative Knowledge	Procedural Knowledge	Conditional Knowledge
Knowing about something	*Knowing how to do something*	*Knowing when and why to use particular knowledge*
The parts of a bike	How to ride a bike	When to pedal, coast, or brake
Addition and subtraction are inverse operations	How to add and subtract	When to use which mathematical operation
Music expresses emotions	How to use different objects to create music	What types of objects create sounds that express particular emotions
Many people speak Spanish	How to speak Spanish	When to use knowledge of Spanish
The Internet provides access to a wealth of information	How to use the Internet	What types of information to access and which uses of that information are ethical

tion—the information and understanding learners have of their own thinking processes and their knowledge of various learning strategies to use in particular learning situations. Perhaps you recognize this as declarative knowledge, or knowledge about something. The second component of metacognition is cognitive monitoring—learners' ability to select, use, and monitor learning strategies that complement their learning styles and the specific situation. Perhaps you recognize this as a combination of procedural and conditional knowledge, inasmuch as learners must know how to use learning strategies and then know when and why to use particular strategies (Arends, 1998).

What is the significance of metacognition? It enables learners to monitor their own learning, analyze their own miscues, and make their own predictions. Learners who can effectively do these things can take more responsibility for their own learning. Once they're aware of their cognitive style and the different ways they approach different tasks, they can use that information to make decisions about how to structure and organize future learning situations.

Teachers can use think-alouds to model metacognitive strategies. In Chapter 2, we used think-alouds to walk you through the process of creating a professional development plan. Use that experience as an example of how to apply the think-aloud concept to a specific process consisting of a number of discrete steps. As their name implies, think-alouds consist of learners' thinking out loud about the thinking they're doing at the time. If you wanted to model for students how to approach a complex task or problem, you could use the think-aloud method to provide a running monologue that described the different thinking strategies you used to address the problem and the sequence in which you implemented those strategies. (It also would be important to explain why you used those particular strategies and why you sequenced them as you did.)

In addition, you could help your students learn to use think-alouds as a way to monitor their own thinking. This also would provide you with a window into students' thinking processes, allowing you to do the following: assess their ability to appropriately apply various thinking strategies, analyze their miscues, identify faulty information, and detect erroneous connections in their thinking.

THINKING STRATEGIES

B esides metacognition, there are other types of thinking, including critical thinking, creative thinking, and productive thinking. Teachers who facilitate their students' thinking create learning environments that encourage thoughtfulness by facilitating debate and discussion of different viewpoints. They provide learners with opportunities to plan and witness the consequences of their activities, design learning opportunities that require experimentation, ask learners to reflect on their work in written logs or journals, and encourage learners to think aloud while demonstrating their understanding. Teachers who facilitate their students' thinking also use cooperative learning strategies that require learners to exchange information and viewpoints (Duis, 1995). (Later in this chapter we'll focus on the application of cooperative learning as an instructional strategy.)

There are two main phases in the development of most new ideas: the germinal phase and the practical phase. During the **germinal phase,** ideas are generated and manipulated—they sprout. This type of soft, divergent thinking is known as **creative thinking.** During the **practical phase** ideas are evaluated and implemented—they are harvested. This type of hard, convergent thinking is known as **critical thinking** (von Oech, 1983). Both creative and critical thinking play crucial roles in cognition—one is not better or more worthwhile than the other. When used appropriately, each has an important contribution to make to the teaching/learning process and to the development of new ideas.

CREATIVE THINKING

Emile Chartier, a prominent philosopher, once reflected that "Nothing is more dangerous than an idea when it is the only one you have" (quoted in von Oech, 1986, p. 78). Unfortunately, we've all had ample opportunity to witness the truth in this statement. People who believe they have no other viable options sometimes resort to violence or substance abuse to "solve" their problems. People who don't take the time or make the effort to consider alternative perspectives and viewpoints only see one way to do things.

Some people have suggested that the degree to which individuals use their creativity and imagination is inversely proportional to the amount of punishment they believe they'll receive for using them (von Oech, 1983). What applications does this notion have to schools? Why is it that, historically, schools and those who have peopled them often have placed great emphasis and value on finding "the one right answer" and conformity? Although it's true that many questions do have just one right answer (such as "What's the capital of Illinois?" or "What's two plus two?"), many other questions have a variety of possible answers and require innovation and different ways of thinking. In fact, most of life's important questions don't have just one right answer ("How can we break the cycle of child abuse?" and "How can we feed the hungry?"). Attempts to address such questions benefit from multiple perspectives and multiple approaches. Picasso observed that "Every child is an artist. The problem is how to remain an artist after he grows up" (von Oech, 1986, p. 78). That is a challenge that faces schools and that would benefit from creative thinking that incorporates multiple perspectives and multiple approaches.

Multiple perspectives certainly exist when it comes to defining creative thinking. As stated above, creative thinking may be described as the germinal, divergent phase of thinking. **Divergent thinking** is the process of generating ideas, making new connections, perceiving gaps, and identifying paradoxes. It's looking at the same things many other people have looked at before but seeing those things in different ways. Divergent or creative thinking also is imagining many new and unusual possibilities, thinking and experiencing in varied ways, considering different viewpoints, and elaborating on alternatives (Isaksen, Dorval, & Treffinger, 1994). In the following sections, we highlight two creative thinking strategies.

■ Scamper

Rudolph Flesch suggested that "Creative thinking may simply mean the realization that there's no particular virtue in doing things the way they have always been done" (quoted in von Oech, 1986, p. 78). So much for the creativity-killing excuse "But we've always done it this way." One strategy for attempting to climb out of such mental ruts is known by the acronym SCAMPER (Eberle, 1971). As Figure 9.1 indicates, the letters of the acronym stand for *Substitute; Combine; Adapt; Modify, magnify, minify; Put to other uses; Eliminate;* and *Reverse and rearrange*. The SCAMPER technique can be put to many uses. Consider the many ways that people have found to *reverse* the process of "going to the store" and instead have the store "go to the customer" (such as mail order, Web pages, and telemarketing). Think about the many inventions that are the product of *combining* two or more items (clock radio, telephones with built-in answering machines). List some of the innovations that *minifying* existing products has generated (transistors and smaller televisions and radios, microchips and microcomputers, optic fibers and communication technology, medical technology and arthroscopic surgery). We're confident you can add to this very brief list of the many innovations SCAMPERing has produced.

■ Brainstorming

Brainstorming is a creative thinking strategy that you probably have used, even if you didn't call it brainstorming. Utilized appropriately, it can facilitate the idea generation process. Since people often are familiar with brainstorming, they have many different notions of what it is and how to do it. For that reason, when we use brainstorming with learners—whether adults or younger

Figure 9.1 **Scamper**	**S**	**SUBSTITUTE** What could you substitute? What might you do instead? What would do as well or better?
	C	**COMBINE** What could you combine? What might work well together? What could be brought together?
	A	**ADAPT** What could be adjusted to suit a particular purpose or condition? How could you make it fit?
	M	**MODIFY, MAGNIFY, MINIFY** What would happen if you changed the form, composition, or quality? Could you make it larger, greater, or stronger? Could you make it smaller, lighter, or slower?
	P	**PUT TO OTHER USES** How could you use it for a different purpose? What are some new ways to apply it? What does it suggest?
	E	**ELIMINATE** What could you subtract or take away? What could you do without?
	R	**REVERSE, REARRANGE** What would you have if you reversed it or turned it around? Could you change the parts, order, layout, or sequence?

(Eberle, 1971)

learners—we take the time to review the guidelines for brainstorming. That way we're assured that everyone has some level of shared understanding regarding the purpose and process of brainstorming. Here are the brainstorming guidelines we use:

1. *Produce many ideas.* This is the principal idea behind brainstorming. The purpose of brainstorming is to think of as many ideas as you can relating to a particular topic. Even if you don't think an idea is very creative, say it anyway. We sometimes refer to the process of getting past your first twenty to twenty-five ideas, which often are quite common, as "draining your brain of purple monkeys." If someone tells you *not* to think about purple monkeys, the first thing you have to do is think about purple monkeys. By the same token, if you tell yourself not to think of a common idea that comes to mind first, you'll likely find yourself thinking it. Instead, get rid of it by saying it or writing it down.

2. *Produce unusual ideas.* Once you've gotten past your "purple monkeys," you can begin to generate ideas that are a bit more original, unique, and

novel. Remember that different and weird ideas are good. Humor and playfulness often facilitate the creation of unusual ideas.

3. *Hitch a ride on other ideas.* We're not advocating academic dishonesty, as in stealing other people's work. However, we are encouraging you to build on existing ideas, whether yours or someone else's. With younger students, we typically explain that hitching a ride or piggybacking on other people's ideas is not copying or cheating but an effective way of thinking of more ideas.

4. *Defer judgment.* Brainstorming is definitely not the time to form a "yeah-but committee." Judging and evaluating the worth of ideas at this stage interferes with the purpose of brainstorming, which is the production of many ideas—regardless of their quality. Wait until later to tell other group members why their ideas won't work or why your idea is the greatest discovery since electricity. And even if you want to tell people how great you think their ideas are, wait until later. Deferring judgment means you wait until later to judge both the merits and the "demerits" of ideas.

5. *Stay on task.* This guideline tends to be more difficult for adults to follow than for younger learners. Off-task talk gets in the way of producing relevant ideas. Brainstorming is not the appropriate time for analyzing the economy, examining the pros and cons of daylight savings time, discussing what you did last night or your plans for tonight, or engaging in other conversation unrelated to the brainstorming topic.

As with any other procedure, teachers must take the time to teach students the proper process for brainstorming. Protesting that students "just can't handle working in groups" is an unconvincing excuse for choosing not to make use of brainstorming. We have found brainstorming to be an effective and efficient way of administering a friendly form of preassessment and of determining learners' interests when selecting themes for future integrated units. Of course, students also can use brainstorming to generate possible topics for research and writing, solutions to self-selected problems, and ideas for presenting the results of their research and problem solving. Brainstorming applications are limited only by your imagination.

Creative thinking thrives in an environment that rewards risk taking, curiosity, and imagination. Brainstorming also can serve to bolster the self-confidence of learners, once they believe that there truly is no one right answer during brainstorming sessions and that, in fact, all responses are accepted.

CRITICAL THINKING

Critical thinking is a form of convergent thinking that seeks a single response or the most acceptable solution (Lyman, Foyle, & Azwell, 1993). Whereas creative thinking is the germinal phase of idea generation, critical thinking is the practical phase, when ideas are "harvested" (that is, evaluated and implemented). It includes the processes of analyzing, categorizing, comparing, contrasting, refining, developing, and selecting ideas. Critical thinking also involves examining arguments and assumptions, reaching and evaluating inferences and deductions, setting priorities, and making decisions (Isaksen, Doral, & Treffinger, 1994).

■ Bloom's Taxonomy

Many different taxonomies have been developed for critical thinking. Arguably, the most well known of these classification systems is Bloom's Taxonomy (Bloom, 1956), which consists of six categories or levels: knowledge, comprehension, application, analysis, synthesis, and evaluation (see Table 9.2). Because Bloom's Taxonomy is a hierarchy, the implication is that when learners engage in a thinking strategy that appears at the top of the hierarchy, they are able to do so because they also are using all of the thinking strategies below or preceding it. Therefore, all levels of the taxonomy are important and essential components of critical thinking. However, analyses of curriculum guides, instructional plans, and the actual teaching that occurs in classrooms often reveal that as much as 80 percent of instructional time is spent at the knowledge and comprehension levels, which are the two lowest levels of Bloom's Taxonomy.

Although knowing and understanding information is an essential starting point, it's not where learning should end. Learners also must have opportunities to apply what they know, to analyze and synthesize information, and to evaluate their own work and that of others. With that clarification in mind, consider the definitions and examples of the six levels of Bloom's Taxonomy that appear in Table 9.2. The examples we provide relate to the book *A House Is a House for Me* (Hoberman, 1978), which we have used with a variety of learners, ranging from primary students to adults. We often use this book to illustrate how Bloom's Taxonomy can serve as a tool by which teachers can provide curricular adaptations to accommodate a wide variety of learners' diverse schemata and prior experiences.

PRODUCTIVE THINKING

Productive thinking is a combination of creative and critical thinking; therefore it includes both divergent and convergent, soft and hard, germinal and practical thinking. To take ideas from germination to fruition requires engaging in the following four main roles (von Oech, 1986, p. 16):

1. When you're searching for new information, be an Explorer.
2. When you're turning your resources into new ideas, be an Artist.
3. When you're evaluating the merits of an idea, be a Judge.
4. When you're carrying your idea into action, be a Warrior.

The Explorer and Artist roles primarily involve creative or divergent thinking, whereas the Judge and Warrior roles require critical or convergent thinking.

Productive thinking consists of five different components—**fluency, flexibility, originality, elaboration,** and **evaluation**—which you can find

Table 9.2
Bloom's Taxonomy: Levels, Definitions, and Examples

Level and Definition	Example
KNOWLEDGE: Remembering previously learned materials; recognition and recall.	*Identify three types of traditional Native American dwellings.*
COMPREHENSION: Grasping the meaning of the knowledge being learned; translating information into your own words.	*How are animals' homes an example of adaptation?*
APPLICATION: Using learned materials in new situations and real-life circumstances.	*In what ways could mathematical concepts and skills help you build a house?*
ANALYSIS: Breaking down information or material into its elements or parts so that its organizational structure may be understood.	*Compare and contrast the housing and shelter needs of Bedouin nomads and Eskimos.*
SYNTHESIS: Putting separate parts together to form a new whole; taking information from various sources and creating a new whole.	*Design a house that is friendly to the environment.*
EVALUATION: Judging the value of material or information for a given purpose, with judgments based on predetermined criteria or standards.	*When considering the issue of endangered species, whose housing rights are more important to consider—animals or humans? Provide a rationale to support your answer.*

(Bloom, 1956)

embedded in the Explorer, Artist, Judge, and Warrior roles. Definitions and examples of these five components, again based on *A House Is a House for Me,* appear in Table 9.3. Young and old learners alike can learn the different components of productive thinking and how to use them. Teachers who make it a point to label the kind of thinking being used for a particular task facilitate students' attempts to learn the components, their definitions, and their appropriate applications.

Reflect & Respond

Under what situations are you the most creative? What variables or conditions increase your creativity? What variables or conditions inhibit it?

In your teaching journal, make two lists. In one list, record variables, factors, or conditions that get in the way of your creativity. In the other list, record variables, factors, or conditions that tend to increase your creativity. Then, using your knowledge of creativity inhibitors and facilitators, describe strategies you might employ to create a learning environment that will support your future students' attempts at creative idea production.

Table 9.3
Components of Productive Thinking

Component and Definition	Example
FLUENCY: Generating many possibilities or producing lots of ideas. Quantity is valued over quality.	*Name all the things that come to mind when you think about houses.*
FLEXIBILITY: Seeing things from a different point of view or breaking away from habitual patterns of thought.	*Illustrate or describe your house. Then do it again, only this time from an ant's perspective.*
ORIGINALITY: Seeing in a unique way or thinking in a new or novel pattern.	*Name all the things you can think of that are houses for other things.*
ELABORATION: Augmenting or modifying an idea with more information in order to improve it.	*Using the pattern Hoberman employs in her book A House Is a House for Me, write your own "house" book. Or, design the house or habitat that would be ideal for you.*
EVALUATION: Judging the worth of an idea, based on predetermined criteria or standards.	*Select the two best ideas from your group's list of things that can be houses for other things. Before you do this, determine the criteria the group will use to decide which ideas are the best ones.*

CHOOSING INSTRUCTIONAL STRATEGIES AND APPROACHES

Different types of learners and learning require the use of an array of instructional strategies. A number of studies and researchers have underscored the need for a variety of approaches (such as Clark, 1993; Dunn, 1996; Ragan & Smith, 1994).

USING A VARIETY OF APPROACHES AND STRATEGIES

In making decisions regarding the selection of instructional approaches, teachers must remember that models of teaching aren't fixed, inflexible, immutable formulas for teaching. Neither do learners have fixed learning styles that don't change or grow. Teaching models and methods thus possess significant flexibility, just as students possess great learning capacities and adaptability. It's okay to take learners outside of their comfort zones sometimes for the purpose of introducing them to different styles and different ways of knowing. Just remind yourself to "stretch but not break" (Joyce, Weil, & Calhoun, 2000).

Having said that, we must hasten to add that "goodness of fit" is a critical criterion to consider in choosing instructional strategies and approaches. In addition to being developmentally and culturally appropriate for the learners they're designed to help, instructional approaches must be appropriate for the kinds of knowing (such as declarative, procedural, conditional) that the instructional objectives involve. Teachers also must use assessment strategies that are appropriate for both the instructional objectives and the instructional strategies used. Finally, teachers must select and employ organizational structures (such as appropriate learning environments, room arrangements, procedures) that complement and facilitate the instructional approaches they choose to apply.

DESIGNING LEARNING ACTIVITIES THAT ARE BOTH FUN AND FUNCTIONAL

Fun is relative and situational. What one person finds funny and humorous, someone else may not, and what's funny today might not be funny tomorrow. Fun also is a voluntary experience. To experience fun and find something humorous, individuals must consciously or unconsciously perceive a situation as enjoyable. Fun can serve as an intrinsic motivator, inasmuch as people tend to seek pleasure and avoid pain. It can allow learners to try new things without fear of making mistakes, looking silly, or feeling awkward (Bisson & Luckner, 1996).

Consequently, fun should be a part of the natural learning process. When playing and having fun, learners tend to lose social inhibitions. Fun and play can eliminate factors that inhibit socialization. Fun can set free the inner self, allowing learners to try new things, trust others, keep trying, be more creative, and take emotional risks. It also can reduce stress and help learners relax. Fun produces positive effects on the teaching/learning process and serves as a powerful tool for enhancing a motivating and safe learning environment (Bisson & Luckner, 1996).

Humor and laughter help relieve tension, make learning more human, reduce learners' fears and anxieties, increase student interaction and participation, make the learning environment more enjoyable, and are essential for emotional health and well-being. Humor also can serve as a powerful tool for productive classroom communication and can help capture and keep students' attention. People tend to remember humorous incidents better than others, which suggests that humor can maximize students' recall in instructional situations, particularly when the humor is spontaneous and is relevant to the topic being taught (Carlson & Peterson, 1995; Dickmeyer, 1993).

Teachers are crucial to the presence of humor in the classroom and are key to creating learning environments in which it can flourish. Teachers must model constructive, appropriate uses of humor and acknowledge students for appropriate uses of humor (Bergen, 1992; Carlson & Peterson, 1995). Teachers who model and value appropriate uses of humor use a variety of strategies to foster enjoyable and humorous approaches to the teaching/learning process. For example, they display playfulness, take risks, try out new behaviors, acknowledge and laugh at their own mistakes, are open to learners' ideas, and communicate the message that learning can be fun, even though it requires hard work and persistence. Teachers can use the following strategies to link humor and learning (Bergen, 1992):

- The *performance strategy* involves modeling humor in the direct instructional role to help hold learners' interest and to contribute to a warm, comfortable learning environment. For example, teachers can read books or poems that include incongruous language, settings, characters, or actions. They also can share humorous anecdotes that relate to the topic or task they're presenting.

- The *indirect facilitation strategy* involves teachers encouraging humor by selecting instructional materials that provide opportunities for learners to express humor and then ensuring that learners have time to use those materials. Books of limericks, poems, or puns can serve this purpose, as can stories that encourage sound and word play (such as Delacorte and Witte's *The Book of Terns,* 1978; Fleischman's *Joyful Noise,* 1988; Parish's *Amelia Bedelia,* 1963). In fact, the use of humor in literature contributes to three categories of reading skills: discerning the author's purpose, making inferences, and evaluating content (Carlson & Peterson, 1995). Kids love books that incorporate humor. Consider, for example, the popularity of Dr. Seuss's many books, including his classic *The Cat in the Hat* (1957); Silverstein's poetry books, such as *Where the Sidewalk Ends* (1974) and *A Light in the Attic* (1981); and Scieszka's *The Stinky Cheese Man and Other Fairly Stupid Tales* (1992) and *Math Curse* (1995).

- The *eliciting strategy* involves teachers explicitly eliciting learners' humor. They can do this by asking learners to share riddles or jokes (socially appropriate ones, of course) or to describe funny things that have happened to them. Teachers also can ask learners questions that cause them to reflect on why they laugh at the things they do. Such focused reflection can help students learn more about the cognitive processes that underlie humor. This strategy, of asking learners to reflect on and think about their responses to and uses of humor, is actually a variation on metacognition.

- The *respondent strategy* involves teachers simply being appreciative of and responsive to learners' attempts to use humor appropriately. Teachers can encourage students to elaborate on their humorous ideas or creative stories; convey the message that they value humor, by listening attentively and appreciatively when students share humorous anecdotes; and respond playfully when students play a good-natured joke on them.

DESIGNING AND DISGUISING PRACTICE THAT'S BOTH FUN AND FUNCTIONAL

Although not every minute of school (or life) can be fun, that doesn't mean teachers don't have an obligation to try to make it as fun as possible. Just as teachers can use what they know about humor and learners' responses to it in designing and implementing instructional strategies, they also can incorporate humor in activities designed to provide practice in particular skills. One of the easiest, yet most important, things teachers can do to make practicing skills more fun is to just say no to "seatwork." Even the term itself sounds boring and painful. What it typically implies is that students sit at their tables or desks and complete worksheets (purple dittos or, more often today, blackline masters) to provide reinforcement and practice of particular concepts and skills.

However, there are better ways of providing and disguising opportunities for such practice—ways that are characterized by best-practice principles such as experiential learning, collaboration, student choice, and reflection. Of course, making practice better also means making it fun, whenever possible. Just because repetition is an inherent part of skills practice and is generally necessary to achieve *automaticity* (the point at which a skill becomes automatic and the learner doesn't have to consciously think about performing it) doesn't mean such repetition can't be embedded in a context that learners find enjoyable, or at least not painful. For example, games, books on tape, and computer software are formats that many learners find enjoyable. Since students are more likely to engage in pleasurable skills practice than in painful skills practice, disguising such practice and making it fun can increase their achievement.

Whatever the format used, certain principles should guide teachers' attempts to provide learners with skills practice. First of all, teachers should assign short, meaningful amounts of practice. Perhaps you've heard the axiom "You can never get enough practice." Yes, you can. In fact, you can get too much practice. If you've ever practiced making free throws or worked on your backhand for an extended period of time, you've experienced what too much practice can do to your concentration and what fatigue—mental or physical—can do to attempts to improve performance, form, and technique. Thus, although it's important for students to practice enough to reach the point of automaticity, it's also important to know when students have practiced enough and to distinguish between massed and distributed practice. *Massed* (or *continuous*) *practice* generally is used to learn new skills and can lead to boredom and fatigue if overused. *Distributed practice*—practice divided into segments—is most effective for refining already familiar skills (Arends, 1998).

Whatever kind of practice is being used, teachers must design practice opportunities that are relevant to the contexts in which students will be expected to use the skills they're practicing. In other words, teachers must facilitate the transfer of learning. Practice that is real and meaningful to students—that takes place in an authentic context—is more likely to facilitate learners' attempts to actually apply the skills they are practicing. For example, if the only practice students get in identifying and using dictionary guide words (the two words that appear at the top of each page, signifying the first and last words on the page) is to circle on a worksheet the words that would appear on a particular page, then the probability that they'll actually make use of guide words when attempting to locate entries in dictionaries, encyclopedias, or telephone books is quite low. However, if students' practice includes use of authentic materials and authentic tasks (such as locating particular services in the Yellow Pages or finding key social studies concept words in the dictionary), the probability that they'll learn the skill well enough to use guide words proficiently is much higher.

When assigning independent practice (that is, out-of-class work), then, teachers should ensure that students can perform the work successfully. If students are to complete the work at home, teachers also should communicate clearly to parents the level of involvement expected of them. Finally, teachers should provide timely feedback on independent practice. The following guidelines (Arends, 1998) contain important points to remember and apply as you check students' understanding and provide feedback on their skills practice, whether it is guided or independent:

1. Provide students with feedback as soon as possible after they practice.
2. Make feedback specific—both positive and negative.
3. Concentrate on behaviors rather than intent.
4. Provide developmentally appropriate feedback.
5. Emphasize praise and feedback for correct performance.
6. When giving corrective feedback, demonstrate how to perform the task correctly.
7. Help learners focus on processes rather than outcomes.
8. Teach students how to assess their own performance and provide feedback to themselves.

CHARACTERISTICS OF EFFECTIVE INSTRUCTIONAL APPROACHES

The most succinct way to summarize the characteristics of effective instructional models, strategies, and approaches is simply to say that effective instructional approaches demonstrate best-practice principles. In Chapter 4 we introduced you to thirteen best-practice principles (Figure 4.2) and urged you to use them in making decisions regarding the teaching/learning process. Here we urge you to use those same principles as criteria to guide your reflections about the strengths and limitations of various instructional approaches.

■ Authentic Instruction That Builds on Learner Interest

As several of the best-practice principles (such as student-centered, authentic, and holistic) imply, relevance is an important variable in the teaching/learning process. If something is important or relevant to students, they're more likely to actively participate and experience long-term learning. Authentic methods of instruction require learners to produce (rather than just reproduce) knowledge that is relevant to their own lives and to achieve in ways that are of value to themselves and to society (Duis, 1995; Hoover & Achilles, 1996).

However, authentic instruction and learning require time. Teachers can reprioritize their curricula and methods to find more time for authentic learning. Sometimes less is more. "Studying a few topics in depth yields greater student interest and understanding than studying many topics superficially. Teachers must practice 'selective abandonment' in pruning their curricula" (Duis, 1995, p. 3). This sometimes is referred to as the post-hole approach to teaching (Zemelman, Daniels, & Hyde, 1998), because the idea is to provide opportunities for learners to dig deeply into a few key topics and then to help them draw connections between the "post holes" they create in the process. Deep learning is more likely to be long-term learning, as opposed to superficial learning, which barely scratches the surface.

■ Choice, Active Engagement, and Problem Solving

In today's work environment, the only constant is change. Information expands exponentially and job requirements shift capriciously, demanding flexible thinking and action on the part of workers. Employees must be able to operate effectively and productively in collegial, collaborative problem-solving teams that function independently (Short & Greer, 1993). Consequently, teachers and the learning environments they create must empower students to become independent, lifelong learners. Empowerment implies that learners have opportunities for choice, decision making, autonomy, participation, and responsibility.

In learning environments designed to facilitate learners' construction of their own knowledge, both teachers and learners have and make choices, take risks, and enjoy figuring out new things by themselves. Learners in such classrooms begin to construct important lifetime dispositions, including a sense of their own responsibility as well as concern and respect for others. They also learn that making choices means they will many times be wrong and that they can learn from their mistakes. As Piaget emphasized, learners construct the intellect by thinking through many levels of being wrong. The more responsibility for intellectual and social problem solving that teachers shift to learners, the more likely it becomes that learners will construct interpersonal and intellectual understanding (Wakefield, 1994).

The spirited give-and-take of active learning can't occur when teachers reserve all of the decision making for themselves. An appropriate role for teachers, then, rather than making choices for learners, is to encourage the exchange of viewpoints and to foster learning climates where being wrong begins, rather than ends, class discussions. Allowing learners to make choices also reveals what they're curious about, and encouraging a sense of wonder contributes to learners' intellectual stretching more than making choices for them ever could. "The opportunity to construct meaning is enhanced as the child actively seeks to resolve the intellectual tension related to his own curiosity" (Wakefield, 1994, p. 14). Piaget called this intellectual tension **disequilibrium.**

■ A Variety of Learner Response Formats

Multisensory learning gives students opportunities to create their own knowledge and is the foundation for creating conceptual understanding. Consequently, teachers must design learning environments that stimulate and facilitate learners' discovery, exploration, and understanding through a number of sensory gates. Students learn through direct experiences with real people and objects and by exploring their environment with all of their senses. They then combine all of their sensory experiences to achieve more complex and complete schemata (Staley, 1997).

For example, if you were teaching an interdisciplinary unit on the integrating theme of houses and homes, then you would want to create opportunities for students to use all of their senses to learn concepts and skills related to that theme. If a salt marsh were the particular "home" you were focusing on, how could you help your students see, smell, taste, touch, and hear that environment?

■ Well-Integrated Curricular Components

For interdisciplinary units, a particular theme is used to integrate various curricular subjects. Successfully combining curricular components and helping learners create connections between different subjects, concepts, and issues characterize effective teaching—regardless of the particular approaches or models employed. Consequently, as you select and use instructional models, remember that combining curricular components and creating connections are goals to aim at and hit—consistently and repeatedly.

■ Culturally Responsive Strategies

Effective instructional approaches are culturally responsive and culturally relevant. That is, they include strategies designed to improve the academic performance and enhance the self-esteem of all learners, including those whose racial, ethnic, or linguistic heritage differs from those of the Anglo-European population. Culturally inclusive approaches promote harmony between different ethnic groups and increase all students' knowledge of their cultural heritage. In addition, culturally responsive instructional strategies create connections between different curricular components, are authentic, are learner centered, and are relevant to learners' real lives. Such relevance and connections can be achieved in part by using materials from learners' cultures and history to illustrate specific principles and concepts. Culturally responsive approaches also help develop critical thinking skills, encourage cooperative learning, teach whole-language principles, build self-esteem, and recognize multiple intelligences and diverse learning styles (Abdal-Haqq, 1994).

Many resources exist to assist teachers in implementing culturally responsive instructional strategies. For example, there are checklists that help teachers assess curricular materials for cultural relevance. Several of these checklists identify biases, both subtle and blatant, that teachers should look for in books and other instructional materials. These biases include invisibility, stereotyping, unreality, language bias, selectivity and imbalance, and fragmentation and isolation. Other resources include *AskERIC*, an Internet-based question-answering service designed specifically for educators. Within 48 hours following requests, *AskERIC* staff members respond to teachers' requests with information from the ERIC database and from other Internet resources. The *AskERIC* electronic library provides lesson plans; resource guides; reference tools, including electronic searches; and full-text ERIC digests. Teachers can access it directly via the Internet at <http://www.genome.ou.edu/eric.html> (Abdal-Haqq, 1994).

■ Appropriate Use of Technology

Speaking of technology, effective instructional approaches use it appropriately. As long as a school is equipped with a few essential technological tools, such as Internet access, appropriate software, and adequate computers, the possibilities for using technology as part of the teaching/learning process are limited only by educators' ideas and creativity. For example, students can use e-mail to connect with mentors ("telementoring") and electronic "pen pals," and teachers and students can use e-mail to continue discussions beyond the regular school day or year.

The Internet serves as a gigantic virtual library, containing an ever-expanding repository of information that both students and teachers can use. Electronic mailing lists, virtual classrooms, Web sites, and Internet search engines are among the many Internet-based instructional tools teachers can utilize. In addition, there is a whole universe of educational software packages and interactive CD-ROMs that can be used for computer-based instruction, including programs that allow learners of almost any age to create multimedia presentations or their own home page on the World Wide Web (Dede, 1998).

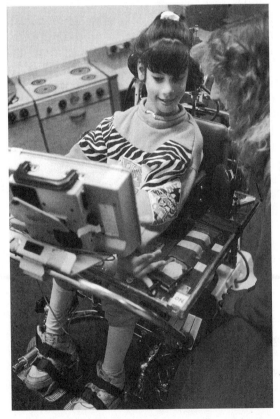

Assistive technology increases, maintains, or improves the functional capabilities of individuals with disabilities.
(© Susie Fitzhugh)

Assistive technology   Assistive technology (AT) is another way technology can be used to improve teaching and learning. AT is a product of the Technology Related Assistance Act (TRAA) of 1988, which provided funds to the states for the purpose of supplying assistive technology to all citizens, with no distinction made between adults and children. TRAA defines **assistive technology** as "any item, piece of equipment, or product, whether acquired commercially, off the shelf, modified, or customized, that is used to increase, maintain, or improve the functional capabilities of individuals with disabilities" (quoted in Behrmann, 1998, p. 75).

AT tools include computers, electronic equipment, software, pencil grips, mouth sticks, mechanical hoists, and a wide array of other assistive devices. AT vision tools include computer screen enhancement and speech output mechanisms, such as talking books. AT hearing tools include special telecommunication and translation devices, amplification devices, and environmental indicators, such as lights substituted for fire alarms, doorbells, and telephone rings. AT communication tools include sign language, lip reading, communication boards, touch screens, and digitally recorded voice output. Finally, AT orthopedic tools include mobility devices, pointing devices, and computer access devices, such as voice recognition, adapted keyboards, and touch-sensitive computer monitors (Behrmann, 1998).

Several Web sites contain information pertinent to assistive technology and the legislation that created it, including the Council for Exceptional Children (CEC) site, the National Center for the Improvement of Practice (NCIP) site, and the Trace Center site (see Relevant Resources for Professionals at the end of this chapter).

BUILDING AN INSTRUCTIONAL STRATEGIES REPERTOIRE

O nce again, we find ourselves in the position of attempting to summarize in a relatively brief overview a topic to which entire books have been devoted. Therefore, we remind you that our purpose here is to provide you with an *introduction* to teaching models and strategies. Please view it as a point from which to begin your further exploration and study of teaching models. Use the References section at the end of this book to continue learning about teaching models and strategies.

In preparing this overview we selected a range of approaches appropriate for different teaching/learning situations and occupying different positions on the learner-centered/teacher-centered continuum, including direct instruction, presentation, concept teaching, inquiry learning, creative problem solving, cooperative learning, simulation, and discussion. As you read about these different models and strategies, we encourage you to reflect on their potential for emulating best-practice principles.

DIRECT INSTRUCTION

Teachers often use some form of **direct instruction** to teach basic skills, facts, and knowledge. Direct instruction is an appropriate approach for teaching both procedural and declarative knowledge. Typically it includes the following steps (Gunter, Estes, & Schwab, 1995):

1. *Review previously learned material.* Students must understand how their existing knowledge and skills relate to their new learning. Therefore, direct instruction begins by reminding students of what they already know, so that they can connect new learning to that knowledge.

2. *State objectives for the lesson.* Teachers then communicate the instructional objectives to students, in terms they can understand. It's also important for teachers to clearly articulate why they're doing what they're doing. That way, students will know the intended purpose and relevance of the instruction.

3. *Present an advance organizer for the new material.* An **advance organizer** is simply a statement or concept a teacher makes or presents to help students

understand how previous information relates to new learning and connect what they already know with what they're about to learn. An effective advance organizer sets the stage for learning and serves as a point of reference throughout the lesson. The concept that's selected to serve as the advance organizer should be an idea that's more general than the new material and that provides learners with a context for the new learning. For example, *land forms* would be an appropriate advance organizer for a lesson on geographical terminology associated with mountainous regions (such as *plateaus, peaks, valleys, buttes, crevices, cliffs*). In presenting new information, teachers also must help students make connections between what they already know and what they're being asked to learn. In other words, teachers need to apply the principles of schema theory.

4. *Guide practice and provide corrective feedback.*

5. *Assign independent practice and provide corrective feedback.*

6. *Review periodically and provide corrective feedback if necessary.*

Previously we discussed the importance of teachers' providing immediate feedback as learners practice new skills and concepts. Guided practice plays a feature role in direct instruction. As learners move on to independent practice and maintenance, teachers still need to monitor student performance to ensure skills and concepts are being practiced and reviewed accurately and appropriately (Gunter, Estes, & Schwab, 1995).

Kathryn Blok, who several years ago served as a reading methods instructor

New teachers talk

Describe the decision-making process you use in selecting instructional strategies that are appropriate for particular teaching/learning situations. What variables do you consider in making decisions regarding your choice of instructional strategies, and what criteria guide your decisions?

I try to involve my students in two in-depth projects a year. When we aren't involved in a project, I use units that have been successful in previous years. I truly believe that when learners are involved in an in-depth investigation, when they're actively engaged in an activity, when they're excited about what they're learning, and when they're directing the project, that's when the most brain growth occurs.

—JANA, Third-Year Teacher

I use a variety of instructional strategies in my classroom. I believe teachers must have a large repertoire of strategies and must be willing to use any one at any given time. That depends on several things. First, I have to take into consideration what the students were doing before the activity. I like to provide a change of pace by interspersing cooperative group work with individual tasks. I believe I know my students best, and that's why I choose the best strategies for them. What works

at Calvin College, summarizes direct instruction as follows: "I'll tell you. I'll show you. I'll lead you. Now you show me."

"I'll tell you" includes stating objectives and presenting new information. "I'll show you" involves teachers modeling or demonstrating skills and procedures for students. "I'll lead you" is the stage that provides learners with opportunities for guided practice, and "Now you show me" provides learners with opportunities to demonstrate that they have met the instructional objectives. Those opportunities can take a variety of forms, as you'll see in Chapter 11, on assessment and evaluation.

PRESENTATION

Teachers often use—and sometimes overuse—the **presentation model** to help students learn and retain declarative knowledge. When used effectively, this model also can help learners acquire effective ways of thinking about, assimilating, and processing information. Typically the presentation model includes the following steps (Arends, 1998):

1. *Present objectives and establish set.* Teachers begin by communicating the instructional objectives to students in terms they can understand. Once again, it's also important for teachers to clearly articulate why they're doing what they're doing. That way, students will know the intended purpose and relevance of the instruction.

2. *Present an advance organizer.* As noted previously, an advance organizer sets

one year might not work the next. I plan lessons by looking at our county's Quality Core Curriculum. Then I decide what approach would be best for my students to learn and retain certain information. If time permits, I do more hands-on activities where the students can work in small groups. Projects, discussions, and authentic assessment take place throughout that time.

—JESSE, Second-Year Teacher

Authors' Analysis:

Themes that run through both of these teachers' responses are student involvement and active engagement in the learning process. Jana also emphasizes the importance of learners' directing their own learning.

Now It's Your Turn

How will you decide which instructional strategies you'll use in different situations? In your teaching journal, describe the decision-making process you'll use in selecting instructional strategies. What variables will you consider and what criteria will guide your decisions?

the stage for learning and serves as a frame of reference throughout the lesson, a focal point around which learners can organize and store information logically so that they'll be able to retrieve it easily later.

3. *Present learning materials.* As with direct instruction, teachers using the presentation model must organize the content in a logical manner beforehand. In addition to presenting the content in a logical sequence, teachers should attempt to view the content from their students' perspectives so they can present the material in ways that will be meaningful for learners.

4. *Check for understanding and strengthen learner thinking.* In the fourth and final phase of the presentation model, teachers ask questions that provide opportunities for learners to reflect on the lesson's content. These questions also encourage students to apply critical thinking strategies as they use the information and concepts they've learned. Their responses allow teachers to assess students' understanding of the concepts presented and to extend and strengthen students' understanding of these concepts.

CONCEPT TEACHING

Concept teaching strategies are designed to facilitate learners' acquisition of declarative knowledge. One particular concept teaching strategy is the *concept attainment model.* It includes the following steps (Gunter, Estes, & Schwab, 1995):

1. *Select a concept and determine its type.* The concept attainment model is appropriate for teaching concepts that have clear criterial attributes and distinguishing features (such as classification systems in biology, parts of speech, geometric shapes, types of sentences). Complex concepts that are abstract and subject to personal interpretation (such as freedom, ethics, cooperation) are more difficult to address effectively via the concept attainment model.

   There are three types of concepts. **Conjunctive concepts** are constant and do not change. For example, the land form known as an island always is a body of land completely surrounded by water, and the geometric shape known as a square always is a closed figure consisting of four equal sides and four equal angles. In contrast to conjunctive concepts, **disjunctive concepts** can take alternative forms. For example, the concept of *noun* can have a variety of forms, including pronoun, proper noun, collective noun, and common noun. Finally, **relational concepts** describe relationships between two or more other concepts. For example, the concept *time* describes relationships between the concepts *seconds, minutes, hours, days, weeks, months, years, decades,* and *centuries.* It's important for teachers to be able to distinguish between the different types of concepts, because the variable of concept type affects the ways in which concepts are learned. Consequently, it also should affect how teachers organize instruction and which instructional strategies they select and implement.

2. *Identify the concept's critical attributes.* During the instructional planning stage, teachers identify qualities that are essential to the concept. These often are referred to as **critical attributes.** For example, having three sides

is a critical or essential attribute of a triangle, whereas being blue is a non-critical attribute.

You may be tempted to think that identifying a concept's critical attributes is an easy task, but our experience indicates that preservice teachers sometimes struggle with this task. For example, what are the critical attributes of the concept *bird*? Without giving the matter much thought, you might say that "Birds fly, of course, so that's a critical attribute." But after reflecting a bit you might remember that some birds don't fly, such as emus, ostriches, and penquins. You also might reflect that not everything that flies is a bird (for example, flies, moths, butterflies, jets, and helicopters all fly). But then again, all birds have wings, don't they? Yes, they do—but is everything that has wings a bird? Ladybugs, bats, and an assortment of other animals have wings, as do planes and some Roman and Greek gods and goddesses. That fact leads you to the conclusion that you must add other critical attributes to *wings* to exclude all other concepts except *birds*. You can no doubt appreciate that this seemingly simple task requires careful analysis on teachers' part to ensure that they provide students with accurate, specific, complete introductions to concepts and their critical attributes.

What are the critical attributes of the concept *bird*?
(© Larry West/FPG INTERNATIONAL)

3. *Develop positive and negative examples of the concept.* During the instructional planning stage, teachers also develop positive and negative examples of the selected concept. Sometimes these are called examples and nonexamples. Initially, teachers should provide very straightforward, clear-cut examples and nonexamples. Eventually they can present concept examples and nonexamples that require higher degrees of discrimination and analysis. For example, for the concept *noun,* teachers could begin with examples such as *animal* and *day* and nonexamples such as *always* and *of.* However, they would not begin with words that sometimes function as nouns but also can function as other parts of speech (such as *run* or *can*).

4. *Introduce the process to the students.* As with any other strategy, students must have opportunities to learn how to use the concept attainment model. Teachers could incorporate a think-aloud into their instruction as they model the process and guide learners through the different steps of the model.

5. *Present the positive and negative examples and list the critical attributes of the concept.* After presenting the examples and nonexamples they have identified, teachers then present the critical attributes of the concept.

6. *Develop a concept definition.* Once the concept's critical attributes have been identified, teachers can facilitate students' attempts to define it. If all of the critical attributes have been correctly identified, the concept definition typically becomes quite obvious. For example, a triangle's critical attributes are three sides, three angles, and a closed figure; a concept definition for *triangle*, then, could be "A triangle is a closed figure that has three sides and three angles."

7. *Give additional examples of the concept.* Once students develop a concept definition, teachers can provide additional examples. However, more important, they can invite learners to provide their own examples.

8. *Discuss the process with the class.* During this step, teachers facilitate discussion of the process, focusing on learners' reactions to the concept attainment model—how difficult or easy they found it and what they liked or disliked about it. Teachers also can use this step to incorporate a review of the concept attainment model.

9. *Evaluate students' understanding.* Having discussed the process, it is then time to focus on student performance. Can they recall and apply the concept definition and produce original examples that demonstrate their understanding of the concept?

■ Concept Relationships

When implementing the concept attainment model, it's important to teach the relationships between various concepts. Relationships between concepts can be described as either superordinate, coordinate, or subordinate. For example, *triangle, square,* and *circle* all occupy a subordinate position in relation to *shapes* but have a coordinate relationship with one another. By contrast, *triangle* occupies a superordinate position in relation to *right, isosceles,* and *equilateral.* Although all triangles are shapes, not all shapes are triangles, and a right triangle is both a type of triangle and a shape (Gunter, Estes, & Schwab, 1995).

INQUIRY LEARNING

The **Suchman inquiry model** is an approach for teaching problem solving through discovery and questioning. It's based on the belief that the strategies scientists use to solve problems and explore the unknown can be taught and learned and that people learn best those things that puzzle and intrigue them. Generally, any problem-solving attempt begins with the recognition that a problem exists and a willingness to accept the challenge of finding solutions. The next steps typically involve gathering information through questioning and research, forming hypotheses, and testing possible solutions in a variety of contexts. A combination of individual and cooperative efforts often benefits problem-solving processes. Problem solving, in turn, offers benefits to learners and to the teaching/learning process. Those potential benefits include the following (Gunter, Estes, & Schwab, 1995): an increase in intellectual potency, a shift from extrinsic to intrinsic rewards, learning the heuristics of discovery, and improved memory processing.

The Suchman inquiry model is an appropriate approach when problems have more than one acceptable response. Consequently, it would be appropriate to use it to postulate reasonable hypotheses explaining why changes of the Earth's tides seem to be related to the Earth's position relative to the moon. However, it would not be appropriate to use it in response to a question asking who was president of the United States during the Civil War.

The Suchman inquiry model typically includes the following steps (Gunter, Estes, & Schwab, 1995, p. 159):

1. Select a problem and conduct research.
2. Introduce the process and present the problem.
3. Gather data.
4. Develop a theory and verify or disprove it.
5. State the rules and explain the theory.
6. Analyze the process.
7. Evaluate the process and results.

CREATIVE PROBLEM SOLVING

Creative problem solving (CPS), as its name signifies, is another approach to problem solving. CPS is a systematic process for approaching a problem in an imaginative way that will result in effective action. As Isaksen, Dorval, and Treffinger (1994, p. 33) explain, "Problem solving and creative thinking are closely related. Creative thinking produces new outcomes, and problem solving involves producing novel responses and outcomes to new situations. Problem solving often has creative aspects, but creativity is not always problem solving."

CPS can be analyzed at several different levels. The most general level includes three components: understanding the problem, generating ideas, and planning for action. Although earlier versions of CPS were more linear (for example, Parnes, 1981), the CPS components don't necessarily happen in any particular order. Because CPS is situational, the sequence of components and the time spent on each component depend on the situation and the problem being addressed. Once again, "It depends." Each CPS component includes specific stages, and each of those stages, in turn, has two phases: divergent and convergent thinking. As we discussed earlier, the goal of divergent, or soft, thinking is the production and generation of many unusual options, whereas the goal of convergent, or hard, thinking is the analysis, evaluation, development, and refinement of the ideas generated from divergent thinking (Isaksen, Dorval, & Treffinger, 1994). Following are the three components of CPS:

1. *Understanding the problem.* This component includes the three stages of mess finding, data finding, and problem finding. Before a problem can be solved, someone must first recognize that it exists. Someone has to notice that there's a problem in need of attention; this is what "mess finding"

refers to. Then they must locate as much information as they can that relates to that particular "mess" (data finding). This information may come in a variety of forms, including facts, opinions, observations, testimonials, and artifacts. Next, they must formulate a problem statement that does not preclude possible solutions; this is the problem-finding stage. For example, asking "How can I unlock my car, now that I've locked my keys in it?" does not allow solutions that involve other ways of getting where you need to go, such as taking a cab or bus or asking a friend for a ride. If the most immediate problem is to get to a specific place in a timely manner, then the problem statement should be modified to something like: "How can I get to my appointment on time, in spite of the fact that I've locked my keys in my car?"

2. *Generating ideas.* This is the CPS component that features idea finding. Having already developed a clear and precise problem statement, here the focus changes to producing many ideas for consideration as possible solutions. Although brainstorming and divergent thinking play key roles in all stages of CPS, during the idea-finding stage they take center stage. Here, the admonition to defer judgment definitely should be heeded, as the purpose of idea generation is to produce as many ideas as possible and, in the process, avoid mental ruts and tunnel vision.

3. *Planning for action.* This component includes solution finding and acceptance finding. First, assuming the role of Judge (von Oech, 1986), problem solvers evaluate the ideas they've generated, using the predetermined criteria they've developed for that purpose. However, having a workable or even a great idea is insufficient. Many great ideas never see the light of day. That's why problem solvers must next assume the Warrior role (von Oech, 1986), as they move on to the acceptance-finding stage. Acceptance finding involves marketing the agreed-upon solution—"selling it" to the "consumers," or the people whose approval and cooperation are needed for implementation (Isaksen, Dorval, & Treffinger, 1994).

COOPERATIVE LEARNING

People's environments affect their behaviors. Deming, who introduced the concept of Total Quality Management, estimated that 85 percent of people's behavior is attributable to the environment in which they operate, which implies that changing the environments in which people operate will change their behavior as well. The interaction patterns utilized within organizations play dominant roles in shaping those environments, and, consequently, the behavior of the people within those environments. When individuals must compete for limited resources, competitive interaction patterns result. In competitive environments there are typically few winners and many losers. When people act on their own behalf with little or no regard for what others are doing, individualistic interaction patterns result. In individualistic environments, members have little motivation to collaborate. By contrast, when the success of one individual is tied to that of other organization members, cooperative interaction patterns result. In cooperative environments, members collaborate for the purpose of achieving mutual goals (Daniels & Gatto, 1996).

James Watson, codiscoverer of the double helix and a Nobel Prize winner, once said, "Nothing new that is really interesting comes without collaboration." Vygotsky, an eminent Russian psychologist, reflected, "What children can do together today, they can do alone tomorrow" (Johnson & Johnson, 1994, p. 86). Cooperative learning is an instructional approach that both Watson and Vygotsky could advocate. Its purpose is to make group members stronger as individuals.

■ Traditional Learning Groups Versus Cooperative Learning Groups

Cooperative learning is many things: positive interdependence, individual accountability, collaboration skills, and heterogeneous grouping. There are also some things cooperative learning is not: it's not new, it's not magic, it cannot be used entirely by itself, it cannot be learned all at once, and it cannot be used all of the time (Jacobs, 1997). Teachers who overlook some of the "nots" associated with cooperative learning may also overlook some potential problems and challenges, including students' or teachers' inexperience with cooperative learning, cultural differences, students' unfamiliarity with one another, group size or physical proximity, an uninteresting or artificial cooperative task, satiation with a task, lack of task completion, or need for increased motivation in the direction of the task (Putnam, 1997).

■ Elements of Cooperative Learning

Cooperative learning can be used effectively at all grade levels, in every subject area, and with any task. It is a generic human endeavor that affects many different instructional outcomes simultaneously. As Johnson and Johnson (1994, p. 76) put it, "The truly committed cooperative learning group is probably the most productive instructional tool educators have." Five elements are essential to cooperative learning:

- *Face-to-face promotive interaction* is the term used to describe cooperative learning's emphasis on students' helping, assisting, supporting, encouraging, and praising one another's efforts to learn. This element includes orally explaining how to solve problems, discussing concepts being learned, teaching knowledge to group members, and connecting past and present learning.

- *Individual accountability* implies that each individual's performance is evaluated and the results are given to the individual as well as to the group. Consequently, members of cooperative learning groups know who needs more assistance, support, and encouragement and that they can't glide by on the work of others.

- *Interpersonal and small-group skills,* both in the form of task work and teamwork, are essential elements of cooperative learning. Students must engage in both simultaneously. Therefore, teachers must facilitate learners' acquisition of social skills for high-quality cooperation, as well as their leadership, decision-making, trust-building, communicating, and conflict-management skills.

■ *Group processing* is another essential element of cooperative learning. Group members discuss the degree to which they're achieving their goals and maintaining effective working relationships. They also describe what actions are helpful and unhelpful and make decisions about what behaviors to continue or change.

■ *Positive interdependence* is the most important element and the heart of cooperative learning. When engaged in cooperative learning tasks, students must understand that they sink or swim together; one cannot succeed unless everyone succeeds. There are three steps to fostering positive interdependence:

1. Assign the group a clear, measurable task.

2. Create positive goal interdependence. That is, make it clear that individual members can attain their goals only if the group attains its goals. This ensures that the group is united around a common goal.

3. Supplement positive goal interdependence with other kinds of positive interdependence, such as **role interdependence,** which is created when group members have complementary, interconnected roles (such as reader, recorder, reporter); **resource interdependence,** sometimes referred to as a "jigsaw," in which group members might need to share one set of materials and subdivide them so each member is responsible for a certain part; **task interdependence,** where a division of labor is created and the actions of one group member must be completed if the next group member is to complete his or her responsibilities; and **reward interdependence,** where group members learn new material together, are assessed individually, and then are rewarded on the basis of a performance ratio, such as 50 percent credit for every problem they solve correctly and 50 percent of the group members' average performance (Johnson & Johnson, 1994; Putnam, 1997).

■ The Structural Approach to Cooperative Learning

Cooperative learning takes many different forms. The structural approach to cooperative learning emphasizes the use of particular structures to influence learners' interaction patterns.

Think-Pair-Share One example of the structural approach is Think-Pair-Share, a simple, efficient, effective cooperative learning strategy. As its name implies, it includes three steps (Arends, 1998, Lyman, Foyle, & Azwell, 1993; Putnam, 1997):

1. *Thinking.* Teachers ask a question or introduce an issue, and students think alone about the answer or issue for a minute or so.

2. *Pairing.* Students pair off and for four or five minutes discuss what they've been thinking about.

3. *Sharing.* Pairs share their answers and ideas with the whole class.

Numbered Heads Together For this approach, rather than directing questions to the whole class, teachers use the following four-step structure with small groups of students (Arends, 1998; Putnam, 1997):

1. *Numbering.* Teachers divide the class into teams of three to five students. Students in each team number off, so each member on a team has his or her own number between 1 and 5.

2. *Questioning.* Teachers ask students a question.

3. *Heads Together.* Team members put their heads together to figure out the answer and to make sure all team members know the answer.

4. *Answering.* Teachers call out a number, and students from each team with that number raise their hands and provide answers to the whole class.

Team Word-Webbing For this approach, team members write simultaneously on a piece of chart paper. They draw main concepts, supporting elements, and bridges representing relationships between ideas and concepts (Putnam, 1997).

■ Modifying Cooperative Learning for Learners with Special Needs

With some modifications, cooperative learning also can be used effectively with special needs learners. For example, teachers can modify the instructional objectives to better suit this group of learners. Or they can use the same objective but a different method for student response, the same objective but a modified presentation of material, the same objective but a reduced workload, or the same objective but a lower level of expectations. Teachers also can use personalized objectives, similar to those that appear in individualized educational plans (IEPs). In addition, teachers can modify instructional materials or the learning environment and provide tutorials, study skills, and individualized support. Finally, to accommodate special needs, teachers can use a jigsaw method of cooperative learning to address differing ability levels. With a jigsaw method, the learning task is divided into pieces, with each piece requiring different skills or a different level of ability (Putnam, 1997).

SIMULATION

If you're ever tempted to doubt the significance of simulations as an instructional strategy, consider the flight simulator or a simulated automobile. Better to crash virtually rather than really! Simulations offer learners the advantage of beginning with simple tasks and then progressing safely to more complex tasks. The **simulation model** allows students to learn from self-generated feedback, by playing out specific situations within a controlled environment and then modifying their behavior based on their reactions and performances. Carefully planned, well-organized simulations can be used successfully with learners of almost any age. Of course, teachers must design simulations that are appropriate for their students' learning needs and developmental levels.

Younger learners typically need more structure and simpler simulations than older learners do.

For example, secondary students could participate in a collective bargaining simulation to apply concepts they've learned about, as well as their communication and negotiation skills. To connect simulations with specific content students are learning, teachers can place them within a particular context. For example, a teacher could connect the collective bargaining simulation with history content by telling students to imagine their negotiations are taking place during the period when the transcontinental railroad was built. Students could then speculate how history might have been different had laborers who worked on the transcontinental railroad engaged in collective bargaining to improve their salary, benefits, and working conditions.

The simulation model typically includes the following steps (Joyce, Weil, & Calhoun, 2000):

1. *Orientation.* Teachers begin by presenting the simulation's topic and the concepts it incorporates. They then explain the simulation process and provide an overview of it.

2. *Participant briefing.* In the second phase, teachers describe the scenario for the simulation. They also explain the rules and procedures of the simulation and discuss the roles and goals of simulation participants and the types of decisions they will make. Finally, they assign roles and hold a brief practice session.

3. *Simulation operations.* Teachers are now ready to conduct and administer the simulation activity. This phase includes making observations, collecting feedback, evaluating performance, assessing the effects of participants' decisions, and clarifying misconceptions as the simulation progresses.

4. *Participant debriefing.* Without this fourth and final phase, the simulation model offers only an activity or a source of entertainment and falls short of serving as an instructional strategy. The debriefing stage provides a forum for participants to summarize what happened and to share their perceptions of those events. It also permits teachers and students to summarize challenges they encountered in participating in the simulation and insights it gave them, to analyze the processes the simulation involved, to compare the simulation to the real world, to connect the activity to course content, and to evaluate and modify the simulation.

Teachers who use simulations as an instructional approach play four different roles (Joyce, Weil, & Calhoun, 2000):

1. First, teachers must clearly explain the simulation's rules and procedures.

2. Second, teachers function as referees. They must ensure that students follow the rules and procedures that have been established and communicated for a particular simulation.

3. Third, teachers serve as coaches. As necessary, they offer simulation participants advice designed to help them play better.

4. Fourth, teachers play the role of discussants. As indicated previously, simulations are incomplete if they don't include a debriefing component.

DISCUSSION

The first step of the discussion model is one that teachers sometimes overlook. Teachers who effectively implement the **discussion model** first read any material they've asked their students to read and prepare questions designed to focus the discussion. Once they've developed the questions, they then cluster and sequence the questions in a logical way. Only then do they introduce the model to their students and conduct the discussion (Gunter, Estes, & Schwab, 1995).

However, perhaps more often than most teachers would care to admit, these initial steps are glossed over, and the teacher instead relies heavily on "in-flight planning" (commonly referred to as "flying by the seat of your pants"). Fortunately, some teachers excel in this area, but the quality of almost all instruction, discussions, and questions improves significantly with planning. For example, one of the most memorable negative examples of discussion planning and preparation we've ever seen was a preservice teacher's lesson plan that stated simply, "Discuss the Civil War." Needless to say, among the feedback we offered to that preservice teacher was the suggestion to narrow the discussion through the use of preplanned questions designed to focus learners' attention on particular, specific facets of the Civil War (such as economic effects, family conflicts, slavery as a moral issue, abolitionists and the role they played, secession). As suggested by the following description of the discussion model (Arends, 1998, p. 378), a lesson's objectives should guide teachers' selection of questions and provide the focus for the discussion.

1. *Provide objectives.* Teachers tell students the objectives for the discussion and gets students ready to participate.

2. *Focus the discussion.* Teachers provide a focus for discussion by describing ground rules, asking an initial question, presenting a puzzling situation, or describing a discussion issue.

3. *Hold the discussion.* Teachers monitor students' interactions, ask questions, listen to ideas, respond to ideas, enforce the ground rules, keep records of the discussion, and express their own ideas.

4. *End the discussion.* Teachers help bring the discussion to a close by summarizing or expressing the meaning the discussion has had for them.

5. *Debrief the discussion.* Teachers ask students to examine their discussion and thinking processes.

The discussion model relies heavily on questions. Questions and teachers' use of effective questioning techniques constitute yet another instructional strategy. Because novice teachers often struggle with the art and science of question asking, we've chosen to devote some time and attention in the next section to a discussion of questioning techniques and considerations.

WHAT ROLE CAN QUESTIONS PLAY IN THE TEACHING/LEARNING PROCESS?

In "real life," people ask questions for practical reasons—to obtain information, to help them make more informed decisions, to compare their thoughts and beliefs to someone else's, or to understand a perspective different from their own (Chuska, 1995). How do these reasons compare to the reasons classroom questions are asked? Typically, questions asked in classrooms are not based on the actual needs or interests of teachers or their students. Because teachers generally know the answers to the questions they ask, they don't learn anything new from the responses. However, students' responses can provide teachers with windows into students' thinking, logic, misconceptions, and error patterns.

Almost all of the questions students ask, both in and out of the classroom, have practical purposes. Learners ask questions to request permission, to get directions, to learn something new, to clarify, to make plans, to become better acquainted with someone, to resolve discrepancies, to make decisions, and to learn about others' experiences. The challenge for teachers is to transfer "real-life" reasons that learners ask questions to the classroom and the teaching/learning process.

All learning begins with questions. Questions generate interactions, such as conversation and debate. Skillful questioning leads to increases in active student involvement, interaction among students, student-initiated questions, higher-level thinking, and achievement of educational goals. Good questions help teachers and students alike to focus on generalizations, laws, concepts, and principles rather than on low-level objectives and outcomes. "Questions are fundamental to teaching because they encompass the three central components of effective teaching: They provide information; they help students connect that knowledge to previous and subsequent learning; and they take students to the highest levels of learning, in which they apply knowledge in various situations in their lives" (Chuska, 1995, p. 7).

WHAT KINDS OF QUESTIONS PROMOTE HIGHER-LEVEL THINKING?

Questions that promote higher-level thinking typically meet four conditions:

1. *They give learners something to think about.* There's a problem to solve; a decision to make; a dilemma, uncertainty, or paradox that requires further analysis.
2. *They allow students to draw on their past experiences, providing a reference point from which to think.* They also help students detect, analyze, and understand the filters through which they view reality and the biases and prejudices that affect their learning.

3. *They include a reason to think about the material.* Knowledge that stops with facts, rather than utilizing information, is of limited utility. Teachers can use the phrase "in order to" to help develop questions that give students a reason to think. For example, "I'm going to teach research skills in order to . . ." or "I'm going to teach fractions in order to . . ." If teachers complete such sentences with real-life reasons, they can encourage students to think and to apply the facts and skills they learn (Chuska, 1995).

4. *They promote different ways of thinking.* Teachers can plan for teaching ways of thinking by using the following steps (Chuska, 1995, p. 25):

- Introduce the thinking skill.
- Assign a task using that thinking skill.
- Debrief the results of the task.
- Reteach as necessary to improve the thinking skill.
- Apply the thinking skill to a new task.
- Compare the results with the previous effort.

Thinking skills should be integrated and infused into the curriculum rather than taught in isolation. A comprehensive thinking skills scope and sequence plan identifies the thinking skills and strategies to be learned throughout the curriculum, locates them in the subject areas where they are to be taught, and arranges them in the sequence in which they're to be introduced and applied (Beyer & Backes, 1990).

WHAT STRATEGIES CAN TEACHERS USE TO INCORPORATE MORE DIVERGENT AND LESS CONVERGENT QUESTIONS?

Many research studies indicate that teachers ask questions at the lowest cognitive levels 60 to 80 percent of the time (Otto, 1991). Others suggest that only about 5 percent of teacher questions can be categorized as divergent, or high-level, whereas 85 percent or more of teacher questions are at the recall level (Downing & Gifford, 1996). This is true in spite of the fact that teachers typically are encouraged to ask at least twice as many higher-order questions as lower-order questions.

■ Use Bloom's Taxonomy to Guide Questioning

Categorizing questions can prove helpful in developing interesting and challenging questions. Bloom's Taxonomy (see Table 9.2) is perhaps the guide most commonly used to analyze and categorize questions (Bloom, 1956). Teachers tend to rely on intuition-based questions if they are not familiar with specific questioning strategies, don't know how to use questioning strategies, and are unaware that evidence suggests that incorporating questioning strategies can lead to increased student achievement and knowledge retention. Teachers sometimes have little confidence that what they do can affect student learning. Unfortunately, when that's the case, it follows that they see little connection between their teaching and student accomplishments (Otto, 1991).

Three basic types of questions can help focus learners' thinking on specific concepts, skills, procedures, or content. These include preinstruction questions, during-instruction questions, and postinstruction questions.

FOCUSING LEARNERS' THINKING

■ Preinstruction Questions

Questions that precede instruction are designed to serve a variety of purposes, including creating an anticipatory set; motivating students in the direction of the learning objective; helping students set goals; determining learners' readiness for a specific task, skill, or concept; stimulating learner thinking; conveying a purpose; and creating a positive learning atmosphere. Preinstruction questions also can serve to activate students' prior knowledge and existing schemata. Four questions can help teachers determine where to begin instruction and how far to take it (Chuska, 1995, p. 31): What do learners already know about the new topic? What do learners think they know? What do learners want to know? What do learners feel or believe about an issue or problem?

These four questions share some similarities with the **KWL strategy,** which features the questions "What do you *know*?" "What do you *want* to know?" and "What did you *learn*?" The first two questions are used prior to instruction to determine learners' knowledge base and schemata for the lesson topic and to determine what they're interested in learning about it. The third question is designed to follow instruction and to determine new knowledge learners have acquired as a result of instruction.

■ During-Instruction Questions

Questions teachers ask during the course of instruction typically are designed to inspire students' thinking and reflection as learning occurs, allow students to review material, involve students in evaluating their understanding of implicit and explicit learning, and encourage students to think ahead—to predict, anticipate, and identify trends and patterns. Students can do all of these things by analyzing and critiquing, anticipating outcomes, summarizing, detecting biases, and examining alternative viewpoints (Chuska, 1995).

■ Postinstruction Questions

Questions teachers ask following instruction are designed to determine the consequences of actions, ideas, and situations; summarize; identify examples or analogies; reflect on what was learned; draw conclusions; synthesize information and use it, along with past learning, in new ways; and extend students' learning (Chuska, 1995). However, one of the most important purposes of postinstruction questions is often overlooked. Since time is almost always a limiting factor in the teaching/learning process, teachers sometimes don't provide any true closure to lessons or activities. Instead they may find themselves simply directing their students to move on to the next item on the agenda, whether it be recess, lunch, music, or physical education. When teachers neglect to ask postinstruction questions, they miss out on an opportunity to connect the concepts and skills that serve as the focus of the current lesson to past and future learning. This oversight ignores the critical role that connections and transference play in learners' schema development.

PURPOSES AND TYPES OF QUESTIONS RELATED TO READING

With regard to reading, there are three types of questions: textually explicit, textually implicit, and scriptally implicit. *Textually explicit questions* can be answered by information printed in the text; sometimes they're called recall or factual recall questions. *Textually implicit questions* can be answered using information contained in the text, but the information may not all be located in one place and the answer may require synthesis of information and the use of inference. *Schema-based questions* can be answered only by the use of external or nontextual information, or scripts, or schema; such questions typically require synthesis and evaluation (LeNoir, 1993).

QUESTION-AND-ANSWER RELATIONSHIPS

Another way of thinking about questions with regard to reading is **question-and-answer relationships** (QARs), which include "Right There," "Think and Search," "Author and You," and "On Your Own." In this classification, "Right There" equates to textually explicit questions and "Think and Search" to textually implicit questions, whereas "Author and You" and "On Your Own" are two variations of schema-based questions. Figure 9.2 illustrates the relationships

Figure 9.2
Question-and-Answer Relationships

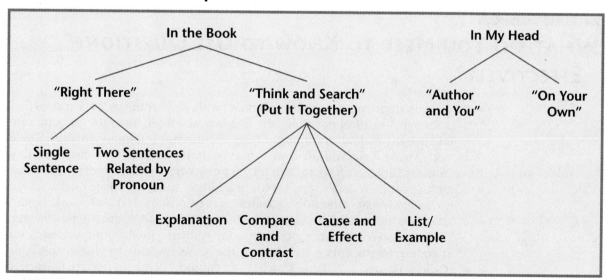

(Raphael, 1986)

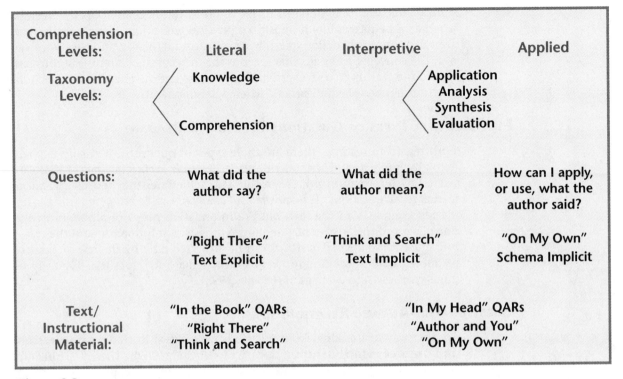

Figure 9.3
Question-and-Answer Relationships: Levels of Understanding

among the four types of QARs, and Figure 9.3 illustrates the different levels of thinking (Vacca & Vacca, 1996).

WHAT DO YOU NEED TO KNOW TO USE QUESTIONS EFFECTIVELY?

If questions are to provide learners with opportunities to express their thoughts and feelings about the instructional topic, then they require careful thought and advance preparation. Off-the-cuff questions often are irrelevant, vague, or confusing and can even hinder rather than help learning. Students shouldn't have to "fish for" or guess what teachers have in mind (Karmos, Greathouse, & Presley, 1990). In addition to asking vague questions and giving inadequate attention to planning questions, other question-asking idiosyncrasies often exhibited by teachers include repeating questions, repeating student answers, answering questions for students, interrupting students, not attending to students, and selecting the same students to answer questions (Orlich, Harder, Callahan, Kauchak, & Gibson, 1998). By contrast, teachers who make effective instructional use of questions do the following (Orlich, Harder, Callahan, Kauchak, & Gibson, 1998):

- Ask questions that are clear, brief, and specific.
- Use systematic questioning techniques and a variety of questions.
- Adapt questions to learners' cognitive levels and affective needs.
- Encourage participation of all students.
- Encourage students to ask questions.

REASONS STUDENTS ARE RELUCTANT TO RESPOND TO QUESTIONS

There are a number of reasons students commonly cite for not responding to questions. As a teacher, how could you address the following student concerns (Chuska, 1995)?

- They're afraid to fail.
- They're afraid of ridicule.
- They lack confidence because of past failures.
- They're unsure of the expected response.
- They're afraid to speak in class.
- They're uninterested in the topic or are apathetic.
- They're unwilling to be labeled a "brain" by other students.
- The question is too complex or unclear.
- The question is above their experiential level or is intimidating to them.
- A response is expected too quickly.
- They don't know the answer.
- They find the answer difficult to express.

How might you structure the learning environment—both the physical environment and the affective environment—to promote and encourage more active learner participation and more student responses to your questions?

HOW TO ENCOURAGE STUDENT RESPONSES

Teachers can increase the probability of providing circumstances that motivate and interest students by ensuring they incorporate activities that provide relevance, ownership, connections, authenticity, responsibility, active participation, and learner choice. Basically, teachers need to apply best-practice principles (Zemelman, Daniels, & Hyde, 1998) to the question-asking process. Teachers who wish to encourage students to respond to questions also can ask fewer questions, provide time for answers, pay attention to students who are answering questions, and talk less (Chuska, 1995).

HOW TO CALL ON STUDENTS

For students who are reluctant to talk in front of the class, teachers can structure small-group activities that provide a format in which they may be more likely to participate. By experimenting with a variety of different response formats, both written and oral, teachers eventually will succeed at identifying formats that accommodate different learners and their concerns about participating in class discussions.

Teachers who know their students well also know how to set students up for success by asking hesitant or shy "nonvolunteers" open-ended questions to which they can respond appropriately. Brainstorming activities serve as one vehicle that allows all students to participate successfully in class activities and to provide "right answers" to teacher questions. Questions that ask students for their opinions, their preferences, or their evaluations and judgments also allow all students opportunities to respond successfully. Examples of such questions include:

- What's your favorite color?
- What do you like to do when there's nothing you have to do?
- What do you think of the school lunch menus?
- What are some alternative uses for a drinking glass?
- If you could be rich or famous, but not both rich and famous, which would you choose to be, and why?

How to Frame Questions

How teachers ask questions is as important as the questions they ask. Their facial expression, inflection, tone, gestures, physical position in relation to students, and other affective dimensions are critical variables, as is the manner in which they frame questions. We encourage you to use the following frame for questions that require learners to engage in higher-level thinking:

1. Ask a question.
2. Pause for ten to fifteen seconds.
3. Call on a student to respond.

■ Wait Time and Its Benefits

The above sequence encourages all students to attend to the question, as opposed to the sequence that begins with calling on a student and then asking a question. Although the results of some studies indicate that teachers wait only a fraction of a second between asking students a question and then answering it before the student does or calling on another student, there are some very compelling reasons for pausing between posing a question and asking students to respond to it (Orlich, Harder, Callahan, Kauchak, & Gibson, 1994).

■ Why Wait? Student Payoffs

Although wait time doesn't typically have any effect on student responses to lower-level questions, it can produce positive effects on their responses to higher-level questions. An obvious benefit of wait time is that it gives students time to think—first of all about teachers' questions and then about their responses to those questions. Other wait-time payoffs for students include increases in student participation, student talk, student confidence, student-initiated questions, student-to-student interaction, and academic achievement, and decreases in the number of students who don't respond, student confusion, and peer interruptions.

■ Why Wait? Teacher Payoffs

Initially, teachers may experience increased anxiety as they learn to implement wait-time strategies. However, those who acquire the patience to be comfortable with a bit of classroom silence discover that wait time produces payoffs for teachers as well as for students. Wait-time teacher benefits include less teacher talk, less repeating of questions by teachers, and less repeating of student responses by teachers; fewer questions per class period and fewer lower-level questions; and more divergent questions, more application questions, more multiple-response questions, and more probing (Orlich et al., 1994).

STUDENT RESPONSE PATTERNS

Student responses to teachers' questions tend to fall into one of the following four categories:

1. *Correct and firm.* Teachers should follow this type of student response with a new question designed to keep the pace of the lesson moving and to avoid overemphasis on success.

2. *Correct, but hesitant.* Teachers should provide some encouragement to this type of response, which usually occurs during the initial stages of learning.

3. *Incorrect and careless.* Teachers should correct and move on in cases where students know the process necessary to provide a correct response but instead make careless mistakes.

4. *Incorrect and lacking knowledge of facts or process.* Teachers should follow this type of student response by prompting, asking a simpler question, or reteaching in a different way (Gunter, Estes, & Schwab, 1995).

HOW TO RESPOND TO STUDENTS' RESPONSES

Just as learning styles and instruction must be tailored to individual needs, so does the way teachers respond to individual students' responses. Teachers who know their students well and are adept at reading their nonverbal behavior can apply that knowledge and skill to the task of providing appropriate feedback to student responses. They also can incorporate humor appropriately and judiciously in their feedback to student responses.

■ Prompting

Prompting consists of reinforcing students positively while encouraging them to expand or elaborate on their answers (such as "Your prediction was right. When we boiled the water in the pan, it eventually disappeared, but where do you think it went?" or "But what word do we use to describe water's disappearing act?"). Teachers' attempts to prompt student responses often benefit from observing students' nonverbal cues and restating questions at lower levels of thinking. However, in their attempts to prompt student responses, teachers should not resort to sarcasm (Orlich et al., 1994).

■ Probing

Probing questions help students think systematically and encourage them to reflect before they respond rather than impulsively blurting out the first response that occurs to them. Questions that ask for more specificity, greater elaboration, or the rationale and reasoning underlying students' responses are probing questions (Karmos, Greathouse, & Presley, 1990). For example, "Why do you think that?" "How did you come to that conclusion?" "What do you base that assumption on?" "What effects might such a change have on the environment?" "What specifics can you provide?" are all probing questions.

■ Redirecting

When teachers accept several students' responses to the same question prior to offering any feedback, they're implementing a strategy known as *redirecting*. That is, they pose the same question to different students. Teachers ask the question, wait for responses from several students, listen carefully to what each student has to contribute, and then respond in a way that communicates to participating students that they have contributed positively to the discussion (Karmos, Greathouse, & Presley, 1990).

EFFECTIVE QUESTION ASKING: PLANNING AND IMPLEMENTATION

One of the characteristics that typically distinguishes novice teachers from veteran teachers is the ability to apply the art and science of asking the right questions at the right times in just the right ways. However, there is much that all teachers—both beginning and experienced—can do to improve their instructional questioning strategies. We offer the following recommendations for your consideration. Many of them will probably sound familiar to you, as they represent a synopsis of this chapter's discussion of question-asking strategies.

■ Plan some questions as you prepare your lesson plans. Consider your instructional goals, and emphasize questions that reinforce them. The questions you ask will help students see what topics you consider important.

■ Ask clear, specific questions that require more than a yes or no answer. Avoid ambiguous or vague questions such as "What did you think of the story?" If students do respond with a yes, no, or too-short answer, ask a follow-up question that will encourage them to expand, clarify, or justify their answers.

■ Use vocabulary that students can understand. Students cannot respond well to questions that contain unfamiliar terms.

- Ask questions in an evenly paced, easily identifiable order. Students might be confused by random, rapid-fire questions. Use questions to signal a change of topic or direction.

- Ask questions from all levels of Bloom's Taxonomy (knowledge, comprehension, application, analysis, synthesis, evaluation). Mixing more difficult questions that require synthesis and evaluation with lower-level questions can keep students actively switching gears, making connections between concepts, integrating new information and experiences with their existing schemata, and applying the knowledge and skills they're learning.

- Use questions to help students connect important concepts (such as "Now that you've learned about conservation of energy, how does this information help you relate the kinetic and potential energy of an object?").

- Use questions to give you feedback on whether students have understood the material ("Which part of the activity was the most difficult for you, and why?").

- Allow sufficient time for students to answer your questions (ten to fifteen seconds). Students need time to think about your questions and organize their answers before responding. Learn to wait until you get a student response. The resulting silence may be uncomfortable sometimes, but it's necessary in order for students to understand that you're serious about wanting answers to your questions. You can ask students to write down their responses to a question, then call on several students (multiple-response format) to share their answers. This technique requires all students to become actively involved in thinking about the questions you pose.

- Rephrase questions when students don't respond in the manner you anticipate. Admit that your original question may have been confusing.

STUDENT QUESTIONS

In addition to encouraging students to respond to questions, teachers need to encourage students to ask questions. Student-generated questions indicate that students are actively involved and participating in the teaching/learning process and also provide observant teachers with information regarding learners' individual interests, schemata, misconceptions, and information processing. Use the following guidelines to encourage your students to ask questions:

- *Make it easy for students to ask, as well as answer, questions.* Learning environments should be risk-free for asking questions. Banish the notion of "a stupid question" from your classroom. Communicate to students from their first day with you that you expect and want them to ask questions. "You don't have any questions about that, do you?" serves as a deterrent to student questions rather than an invitation. Replace that question with questions such as "What questions do you have?" "What parts are unclear?" "Would you like another example to help you better understand this idea?" "Who can add another example to help make this idea even clearer?"

- *Make time for and expect student questions throughout your class.* Rather than leaving only two or three minutes for questions at the end of class or the end of the day, encourage students to ask questions at any time. Consistently waiting until the end of a lesson or the end of the day to ask, "What questions do you have?" becomes a signal for class to end, as opposed to an opportunity for students to ask thoughtful questions.

- *Pause to allow students to formulate questions.* This is another important and appropriate use of wait time. Asking students to write down questions they have actively engages all students, rather than just a few. After providing students with time to formulate and write their questions, you may then ask several students to share their questions.

- *Ask other students to answer student questions.* This strategy tends to encourage discussion and direct interaction between students, without unnecessary teacher direction.

- *Have students formulate questions prior to class.* This can serve as a variation on the KWL strategy. Students come to class with questions about the chapter they read or questions left unanswered by their reading or previous class discussion.

Remember, this chapter serves only as an introduction to instructional strategies and approaches and the many issues and variables associated with them. As you continue to grow and develop as a teacher, you'll add to your repertoire of instructional strategies—both in terms of quality and quantity. Doing so will increase the probability that you'll have the appropriate tools to use in specific teaching/learning situations.

SUMMARIZING WHAT YOU'VE LEARNED

- Teachers must respond to different learners, learner needs, and learning situations with a variety of instructional approaches and strategies. In deciding what instructional strategies and approaches to implement, teachers also must consider the kind of knowledge they are attempting to help students learn, because people learn different types of knowledge in different ways.

- Students' use of think-alouds also provide teachers with a window into learners' thinking processes, thereby allowing teachers to assess learners' abilities to appropriately apply various thinking strategies as well as analyze students' miscues, identify faulty information, and detect erroneous connections in their thinking.

- There are two main phases in the development of most new ideas: the germinal phase and the practical phase. During the germinal phase, ideas are generated and manipulated. This type of soft, divergent thinking is known as creative thinking. During the practical phase, ideas are evaluated and implemented. This type of hard, convergent thinking is known as critical thinking (von Oech, 1983).

- Productive thinking is a combination of creative and critical thinking. Therefore, it includes both divergent and convergent, soft and hard, germinal and practical thinking. To take ideas from germination to fruition and on to implementation requires engagement in the following four main roles: the Explorer and Artist roles, which primarily involve creative or divergent thinking; and the Judge and Warrior roles, which require critical or convergent thinking.

■ Effective instructional strategies and approaches adhere to best-practice principles. They also make fun a natural part of the learning process. Fun produces positive effects on the teaching/learning process and serves as a powerful tool for enhancing a motivating and safe learning environment.

■ The instructional approaches featured in this chapter include direct instruction, presentation, concept teaching, inquiry learning, creative problem solving, cooperative learning, simulation, and discussion.

■ Almost all questions students ask, both in and out of the classroom, have practical purposes. The challenge for teachers is to transfer the "real-life" reasons that learners ask questions to the classroom and the teaching/learning process.

■ All learning begins with questions. Skillful questioning leads to increases in active student involvement, interaction among students, student-initiated questions, higher-level thinking, and achievement of educational goals.

■ Three basic types of questions can help focus learners' thinking on specific concepts, skills, procedures, or content: preinstruction questions, during-instruction questions, and postinstruction questions.

■ How teachers ask questions is as important as the questions they ask. Their facial expression, inflection, tone, gestures, and physical position in relation to students are critical variables, as is the manner in which they frame questions.

YOUR PROFESSIONAL TEACHING PORTFOLIO

■ Design a chart or matrix that summarizes the phases, purposes, and appropriate applications of different instructional strategies (such as direct instruction, the presentation model, concept teaching, the Suchman inquiry model, creative problem solving, cooperative learning, the simulation model, the discussion model, and literature-based instruction).

■ Develop an instructional plan that showcases your ability to effectively incorporate questioning strategies in the teaching/learning process. Later in your preservice teacher preparation, videotape yourself teaching such a lesson and then write a self-assessment piece in which you analyze your teaching performance, cite strengths, and describe how you would modify your instructional plan.

Key Terms

Advance organizer (p. 293)
Assistive technology (p. 292)
Brainstorming (p. 280)
Concept teaching (p. 296)
Conditional knowledge (p. 277)
Conjunctive concepts (p. 296)
Creative problem solving (p. 299)
Creative thinking (p. 279)
Critical attributes (p. 296)
Critical thinking (p. 279)
Declarative knowledge (p. 277)
Direct instruction (p. 293)
Discussion model (p. 305)

Disequilibrium (p. 290)
Disjunctive concepts (p. 296)
Divergent thinking (p. 280)
Elaboration (p. 283)
Evaluation (p. 283)
Flexibility (p. 283)
Fluency (p. 283)
Germinal phase (p. 279)
KWL strategy (p. 308)
Metacognition (p. 277)
Originality (p. 283)
Practical phase (p. 279)
Presentation model (p. 295)

Procedural knowledge (p. 277)
Productive thinking (p. 283)
Question-and-answer relation-
    ships (p. 309)
Relational concepts (p. 296)
Resource interdependence (p. 302)
Reward interdependence (p. 302)
Role interdependence (p. 302)
Simulation model (p. 303)
Suchman inquiry model (p. 298)
Task interdependence (p. 302)

Relevant Resources for Professionals

Books and Articles

- Delacorte, P., & Witte, M. C. (1978). *The book of terns*. Middlesex, England: Penguin Books.

- Dunn, R. (1996). 19 easy-to-try ways to turn on students. *Teaching K-8, 27*(3), 50, 51.

- Fleischman, P. (1988). *Joyful noise: Poems for two voices*. New York: The Trumpet Club.

- Hoberman, M. A. (1978). *A house is a house for me*. New York: Viking.

- Isaksen, S. G., Dorval, K. B., & Treffinger, D. J. (1994). *Creative approaches to problem solving*. Dubuque, IA: Kendall/Hunt.

- Parish, P. (1963). *Amelia Bedelia*. HarperCollins Publishers.

- Putnam, J. (1997). *Cooperative learning in diverse classrooms*. Upper Saddle River, NJ: Prentice-Hall.

- Scieszka, J. (1992). *The stinky cheese man and other fairly stupid tales*. New York: Scholastic.

- Scieszka, J. (1995). *Math curse*. New York: Viking.

- Seuss, Dr. (1957). *The cat in the hat*. Boston: Houghton Mifflin.

- Silverstein, S. (1974). *Where the sidewalk ends*. New York: Harper & Row.

- Silverstein, S. (1981). *A light in the attic*. New York: Harper & Row.

- Staley, L. (1997). Teaching strategies: "What does purple smell like?" *Childhood Education, 73*(4), 240-242.

- von Oech, R. (1983). *A whack on the side of the head*. New York: Warner Books.

- von Oech, R. (1986). *A kick in the seat of the pants*. New York: Harper & Row.

Professional Organizations

- Best Practices in Education.
  A not-for-profit organization dedicated to working with American teachers to find effective educational practices from other countries to adapt and apply in U.S. schools. This organization sponsors innovative projects and facilitates their delivery to U.S. classrooms in pre-kindergarten through twelfth grade.

  http://www.bestpraceduc.org/

- The North Central Regional Educational Laboratory (NCREL).
  A not-for-profit organization dedicated to helping schools—and the students they serve—reach their full potential.

  http://www.ncrel.org/

Professional Journals in Education

- *Instructor*
  P.O. Box 53896
  Boulder, CO 80322-3896
  1-800-544-2917

  http://www.scholastic.com/instructor

- *Language Arts*
  Published by the National Council of Teachers of English
  1111 W. Kenyon Road
  Urbana, IL 61801-1096
  1-800-369-6283

  http://www.ncte.org

- *Technology & Learning Online*

  http://www.techlearning.com/

- *Young Children*
  NAEYC
  1509 16th St., NW
  Washington, DC 20036-1426
  1-800-424-2460

  http://www.naeyc.org

Web Sites

- **Council for Exceptional Children**
  Information on special education and links to other organizations.

  http://www.cec.sped.org/ericec/links.htm

- **ERIC**
  ERIC provides lesson plans, resource guides, and other valuable resources for teachers.

  http://www. genome.ou.edu/eric.html

- **National Center for the Improvement of Practice**
  Information on technology access in early childhood special education.

  http://www.edc.org/FSC/NCIP

- **Teaching Strategies**
  Teaching Strategies enhances the quality of early childhood programs by offering practical, developmentally appropriate curriculum materials, professional development programs, parenting resources, and staff development services.

  http://www.teachingstrategies.com

- **Trace Center**
  Information on resources for assistive technology and computer access.

  http://www.trace.wisc.edu

- **INSTRUCT**
  INSTRUCT is intended to provide on-line teacher professional development for planning, instruction, and assessment of mathematics classes.

  http://instruct.cms.uncwil.edu/

- **The Thinking Page**
  The Thinking Page is dedicated to providing information about ways for individuals and organizations to improve their thinking.

  http://www.thinking.net/

- **Just Think**
  Just Think's goal is to collaborate with educational organizations and the entertainment industry in teaching young people critical-thinking skills for evaluating today's media and providing them with production tools to create their own media projects.

  http://www.justthink.org/

- **The Science Learning Network**
  The Science Learning Network explores how telecomputing can support inquiry-based science education.

  http://www.sln.org/

10

INSTRUCTIONAL PLANNING

— OR —

Lesson plans that don't fit in a box

THE CONTEXT AND COMPONENTS OF UNIT PLANNING

A **unit** is a collection of lessons, activities, and resources that are connected by a unifying concept or topic. In a primary classroom, a unit might be built around the topic of plants, "creepy crawlies," or grandparents. For example, students might read about grandparents, interview their own grandparents, create a time line of one or more grandparents' lives, and connect research on immigration and Ellis Island to their investigations of their grandparents' life experiences.

In the intermediate classroom, teachers might integrate history and literature by having students read novels set during major historical events (such as having the students read *Johnny Tremain* when they study the Revolutionary War). Interdisciplinary instruction is a hallmark of the middle school movement and is facilitated by block scheduling and team teaching. Middle school students involved in interdisciplinary instruction explore topics that are grounded in real-life problems and experiences such as survival or relationships. Later in this chapter we provide more information about interdisciplinary instruction.

Daniels and Bizar (1998) developed a model for establishing curriculum units at the secondary level. Students identify questions and concerns about themselves and about the world, and these questions and concerns eventually lead to topics that are investigated throughout the year in all content areas. For example, one high school we know of selected tolerance as a unit topic, and it was explored and studied by all ninth-grade students throughout the year.

"If telling were the same as teaching, we'd all be so smart we could hardly stand it."

—Mager, 1984a, p. 7

We find Mager's conclusion intriguing. What do you think brought him to it? What makes telling and teaching so different? Picture yourself as a student five, ten, or fifteen years ago. Think about learning experiences that you found engaging at different times in your prekindergarten through high school days. What set those experiences apart from ones you found less engaging or mundane?

In your teaching journal, speculate about the reasoning behind Mager's quotation. Then, based on your prior learning experiences, describe what you believe distinguishes teaching from telling. Share your reflections with a peer, and discuss the similarities and differences in your experiences and responses.

TYPES OF UNITS

Three types of instructional units have been described by Feldhusen (1994): the resource unit, the content-oriented unit, and the conceptually oriented unit. The **resource unit** is described as a group of learning centers that are organized to promote independent, small group, or self-directed study. The **content-oriented unit** originates within a particular content area, such as science or social studies, but involves topics that can be investigated across all content areas, such as small animals or neighborhoods. Finally, the **conceptually oriented unit** involves the investigation of more broad-based topics. The broad foundation of conceptually oriented units provides learners with many opportunities to discover relationships between different ideas. Some examples of conceptually oriented unit topics include communication, conflict, patterns, power, and traditions. In Chapter 8 we presented schema theory as a structure for integrating curricula. As students discover relationships between ideas in a conceptually oriented unit, they are expanding their schemata by scaffolding these ideas.

GLOBAL UNITS: PASSPORTS TO LEARNING

Units that are open-ended enough to be part of an entire school's curriculum are known as *global units*. For example, a unit on endangered species could be a global unit. Each class in a school could choose to study different animals or issues related to endangered species, based on the students' interests and level of understanding. Students within and across grade levels could then share their learning experiences, and the unit could culminate in a schoolwide Family Night, with each class presenting a display or production to showcase their learning. This is an excellent way for parents and community members to participate in integrative teaching and experience the powerful learning opportunities that take place in dynamic school cultures.

■ Choosing an Appropriate Topic: Questions to Get You Started

In addition to *topic* and *concept*, you will also encounter the terms *theme* and *thematic teaching* in the context of instructional planning. A theme is similar to a topic in that it provides a unifying instructional focus. For clarity, we have decided to use the term *topic* to signify topics, concepts, and themes when referencing integrative units.

After reviewing a variety of sources that focus on topic selection (Dearden, 1984; Katz & Chard, 1997; Peterson, 1988; Robison & Spodek, 1965; Spodek, 1988), the following questions were suggested. It's important to consider every topic in light of these questions. Some topics are much too limiting, whereas others may be so obtuse that they don't provide enough focus.

1. *Is the topic appropriate for the grade level and developmental level of your students?* What expectations do you have for your students in math, science, social studies, language arts, fine arts, health, and physical development? Where can you go to get some help if you're not sure? One of the challenges that faces preservice teachers, and sometimes inservice teachers, is to develop an understanding of realistic, appropriate expectations for students within and across various grade and developmental levels. Curriculum guides, state and district learning goals, and scope and sequence charts are great places to start. Also, do some kid watching and observe the kinds of behaviors, attitudes, skills, and concepts that evolve as you spend time in classrooms with real students.

2. *Are students interested in the topic?* What's the best way to find out if students are interested in feathers, fish, or fossils? Ask them! Unit topics must evolve from real, live learners. Creating a KWL chart (What do you *know*? What do you *want* to know? What have you *learned*?), brainstorming ideas in cooperative learning groups, and interviewing groups of individual students are just a few ways that you can begin the process of preassessment. This process answers a few very important questions for you, the teacher (such as "What topics are interesting for the students in this class?" "What do they already know about this topic?" and "What would they like to know?"). Student interest in the topic is key to student success and motivation.

3. *Does the topic relate to the students' lives?* One suggestion shared by Lilian Katz, coauthor of *Engaging Children's Minds: The Project Approach*, for answering this question is to take a ten-minute walk around the area where your school is located. While taking this walk, make a list of all the things that are available, in your school neighborhood, for students to observe and study. Perhaps your school is located near a pond, a construction site, a wooded area, or a factory. What opportunities for study does your school's location provide? Because most students live in the school neigh-

borhood, the realities of the geographic area in which they live and go to school are topics that directly affect them on a daily basis. Think of your school community, and the area around it, as a real-life laboratory that is available for investigation.

Let's say that your fifth-grade curriculum guide states that "Students will demonstrate an understanding of the processes involved in a presidential election." If your students are not interested in the topic of elections and there are no real-life applications of it in their lives (such as mock elections in school), it is your job to create and sustain student interest in the topic. How will you do that? How about setting up an election in your classroom or working collaboratively with other teachers to conduct a schoolwide election? Students can design voting machines, create ballots and ballot boxes, make campaign buttons and posters, debate the qualifications of the candidates, and judge the credibility of the sources used by the campaign managers in developing their platforms. This approach will both peak student interest in the topic and provide a real-life application of it, because you will have designed an integrative unit, with student cooperation, to achieve these essential outcomes.

4. *Does the topic support the values and culture of the community and society?* This question has far-reaching implications that directly affect the multicultural health of your curriculum. Let's suggest that you develop an integrative unit on the topic of American heroes. Are the heroes you select representative of different ethnicities, races, genders, ages, and time periods? How are these demographics balanced in your curricular design? How will you help students develop an appreciation for, and acceptance of, American heroes who may represent cultures or values different from their own?

To answer the question of whether a topic supports the values and culture of the community and society, it is necessary to take some time to reflect on those values and that culture. We would like to suggest three goals that should be infused into your curriculum to encourage antibiased and multifocused exploration of these topics. First of all, it is necessary to develop students' awareness of various values and cultures by exposing them to a wide array of cultures and values. Secondly, curricula must be designed to promote appreciation of various cultures and values that exist within a community and society. And, finally, acceptance of the cultures and values of different groups and individuals is the long-term goal of a multicultural curriculum. One of the most appropriate ways that we have found to incorporate these three goals into the curriculum is to use quality multicultural children's literature.

5. *Does the topic have the potential for in-depth and long-term learning across all content areas?* One of the questions preservice and inservice teachers commonly ask when discussing integrative unit planning is, "How long should my integrative unit be?" Since an integrative unit involves in-depth investigation and learning opportunities in all content areas, most integrative units should last at least one month. In a later section we'll suggest some

scheduling formats that will help you think through the elements involved in planning for in-depth learning.

6. *Is the topic worth knowing about?* It is said that the amount of information in the world currently doubles every twelve to eighteen months. Against this background, the question of topic worthiness becomes a key consideration in integrative unit and project planning. Should students spend an entire month of the school year studying apples? Or should this topic be expanded to fruits and vegetables, or perhaps trees?

7. *Does the topic support the learning goals and objectives outlined in your curriculum guide?* Remember the curriculum guide we discussed in Chapter 8? You probably will be presented with a district curriculum guide when you accept your first teaching position. How will you ensure that the integrative units you develop will satisfy the learning goals and objectives for the grade level you will teach? Your ability to plan and mediate the curriculum with your students becomes a challenging, but necessary, task.

WHAT ARE THE COMPONENTS OF AN INTEGRATIVE UNIT?

We began this chapter by giving a definition of a unit. We continue by focusing on the components of a particular kind of unit—an integrative unit. An **integrative unit** is a collection of lessons, activities, and resources connected by a unifying concept or topic that is contextualized in a real-life framework, and promotes active learning as learners acquire knowledge, performances (skills), and dispositions.

DEFINITION OF AN INTEGRATED CURRICULUM

An **integrated curriculum** incorporates the interrelationships or connections between different developmental domains and content areas. These are the glue that bonds together the many pieces of the curriculum. In addition to having interrelated and connected developmental domains and content areas, integrated curricula have the following characteristics (Wortham, 1996):

■ *They are contextualized.* For learning to be relevant and purposeful, it must be grounded in a context (framework) that is meaningful to learners and related to their prior experiences.

■ *They promote active learning.* Learners construct meaning as they engage in hands-on experiences involving materials and other people. Integrative units promote these kinds of learning activities.

■ *They are designed to interrelate development with knowledge, performances (skills), and dispositions.* In contrast to the academic approach to instruction, in which cognitive development is seen as most important, an integrated curriculum promotes both cognitive and affective development while connecting knowledge, performances (skills), and dispositions with the learners' social, emotional, physical, and cognitive development. Later in this chapter you will read more about an integrated curriculum.

INTEGRATIVE UNIT OUTLINE

You can use the outline in Figure 10.1 to help you develop your first integrative unit. Although the list may seem fairly extensive, you'll notice that many of the items on it are resources that your students and you will develop collaboratively to support the unit. These resources will expand as you present the unit over a number of years. In fact, every time you teach the unit, the learners, the resources, and the activities will change, keeping your teaching fresh and keeping you engaged in your teaching. Have you ever known a teacher who has repeated his or her first year of teaching for the last thirty years? Using integrative units will ensure that this never happens to you!

DEVELOPING EACH COMPONENT OF YOUR INTEGRATIVE UNIT

Review Figure 10.1 and begin to think about what you already know about each section. A short description of each component of the integrative unit plan follows.

- *Overview.* This includes information about the students' age or the grade-level focus of the unit, a brief synopsis of the intended classroom population (number of students, gender breakdown, cultural backgrounds, and anticipated special needs), and the unit topic, theme, or concept.

- *Rationale.* Develop a one- or two-paragraph rationale statement that concisely articulates the reasons why you have selected this topic/theme/concept for your integrative unit.

- *Goals and major concepts.* Develop a curriculum web that includes key concepts and topic subcategories, as well as a list of goals for your unit. We will review sample curriculum webs later in this chapter.

- *Daily lesson plans.* Detailed explanations for developing each of the five lesson plan components are included later in this chapter.

- *Learning environment design.* Later in this chapter you will explore the benefits of learning centers and read about many different kinds of learning centers. Use these ideas, as well as the sample classroom designs, to develop an ideal classroom to support your integrative unit.

- *Overall schedule.* The overall schedule, which takes the place of your lesson plan guide, provides an annotated schedule for each school day. Your daily schedule is determined by your overall schedule, which includes a brief sentence or phrase to indicate what is planned for each section of the day during the duration of the integrative unit. We've included a sample overall schedule in Figure 10.2 to provide you with an example of one way an overall schedule could be designed.

Figure 10.1
Outline for an Integrative Unit

Overview

Rationale

Goals and major concepts

Daily lesson plans
   Objectives: What do you plan to teach?
   Rationale: Why do you plan to teach it?
   Materials: What resources do you need?
   Procedures: How will you teach this lesson?
   Assessment/evaluation: How will you assess/evaluate students, as well as
     document their learning?

Learning environment design

Overall schedule

Daily schedule

Family involvement plans

Resources
   Visual aids
   Interactive bulletin boards
   Documentation/display areas
   Children's literature
     Big books
     Core books
     Literature sets
     Poetry
     Narrative text
     Expository (informational) text
     Children's literature software
   Curriculum guides
   Textbooks
   Appropriate computer software
     CD-ROM encyclopedias and databases
     Simulation software
     Information processing software
     Internet access/Web sites
   Audiovisual resources
     Videotapes
     Laser disks
     Slides
     Maps
     Artifacts
   Field trip and resource visitor list

Figure 10.2 Overall Schedule

		Integrative Unit Weekly Schedule				
Week _____						Topic _____

Learning Centers	Daily Schedule	Monday	Tuesday	Wednesday	Thursday	Friday	
	(Add before copying)						Assessment Evidence Collected This Week:
Family Contacts							
Research Groups							
	Notes	Notes	Notes	Notes	Notes	Notes	

(Enlarge as desired)

■ *Daily schedule.* Base your daily schedule on a six- or six-and-a-half-hour day. Be sure to allow enough time during your classroom workshop blocks for students to become engaged in a variety of large-group, small-group, and individual activities, including activities in learning centers. We've included a sample daily schedule for a primary classroom (first through third grade) in Figure 10.3.

■ *Family involvement plans.* Involve families—parents, siblings, and, when appropriate and possible, extended family members—in your integrative unit planning. You might begin or end the unit with a family activity. Invite family members to share a special talent, favorite book, or family artifacts with the class. Students might develop family time lines, interview selected family members, complete surveys at home with other family members, or prepare a favorite family recipe. For example, during an integrative unit on wheels, Therese's children were asked to list all the things that they could find at

Figure 10.3 **Primary Classroom Daily Schedule**		
	8:30–8:45 A.M.	Journal-writing and record-keeping activities
	8:45–9:10 A.M.	Opening class meeting: warm-up activities—poetry, songs, etc.; calendar; news of the day; discussion of day's activities
	9:10–9:30 A.M.	Shared reading: one previously read book, child-selected, and one core book selected by teacher to complement integrative unit
	9:30–11:00 A.M.	Reading/writing workshop: possible options include minilessons for modeling/discussing a new reading/writing strategy or concept; peer and teacher conferencing; literature circles; shared and independent writing activities; guided reading; buddy reading; integrative unit learning center options
	11:00–11:30 A.M.	Special areas: physical education, music, art, drama, foreign language
	11:30–12:00 P.M.	Lunch
	12:00–12:30 P.M.	Outdoor activities
	12:30–1:00 P.M.	Read-aloud
	1:00–2:30 P.M.	Math/science/social studies workshop: possible options include minilessons for modeling/discussing a new math, science, or social studies concept or strategy; math tubs; science experiments and data collection; problem solving; journaling; peer and teacher conferencing; integrative unit learning center options
	2:30–2:45 P.M.	Drop everything and read (DEAR)
	2:45–3:00 P.M.	Closing class meeting: review of the day's activities and goal setting for tomorrow

home, in their kitchens, that had wheels. Remember, parents are your partners—involve them!

- *Resources.* Resource development is a very important component of an integrative unit. It is not necessary to have a full complement of resources during the planning stages, but it is important to begin thinking about resource cost, availability, balance, and variety at this stage. This section of your integrative unit will be full of lists, diagrams, ideas, and contact information.

CREATING CROSS-CURRICULAR CONNECTIONS

In the American educational system, knowledge is generated and assessed within certain long-established discipline areas, such as mathematics, science, social studies, fine arts, language arts, and physical education. However, the separate-subject approach often leaves students with a disconnected view of knowledge, and it fails to reflect the way people attack problems in the real world. This compartmentalization of knowledge creates an educational delivery system that is unrealistic and, often, not engaging for learners or teachers. Curricula should be based on problems, issues, and conflicts that are a part of people's real lives. What's the sense of separating mathematics from science when one provides a powerful set of tools and knowledge that informs the decisions and thinking of the other? As Daniels and Bizar (1998, p. 20) note, "Real living requires us to draw on many domains of knowledge, multiple strategies of thinking, and diverse ways of knowing."

MAJOR PURPOSES FOR AN INTEGRATED CURRICULUM

For students to experience and participate in a well-designed and organized integrated curriculum, it's helpful to set priorities and purposes for learning. The following major purposes (Roberts & Kellough, 1996) provide a focus for your development of an integrated curriculum. You'll recognize that each purpose is built on best-practice principles and knowledge about how children and adolescents learn. Integrated curricula are designed to:

1. Teach students to be independent problem solvers
2. Involve students in direct, purposeful, meaningful, and authentic learning
3. Help students recognize that what they learn in different subject areas is interrelated
4. Help students follow their individual interests and take responsibility for their own learning through personalized learning opportunities
5. Design situations in which students learn what they want and need to know rather than what a particular curriculum dictates
6. Encourage students to work with others in cooperative learning situations, such as partnerships and small groups, that focus on the social value of learning

7. Emphasize the process of learning as whole and connected rather than as a series of specific subjects and disparate skills

In addition to these goals, integrated curriculum units should be designed to encourage students to do the following (Pigdon & Woolley, 1993, p. 16):

- Develop understandings through sustained interaction, conversation, or discussion about concepts, ideas, values, and modes of presenting information
- Develop an understanding of the variety of ways in which we can present, represent, and transform ideas about the world
- Build on and extend their personal, out-of-school experiences and knowledge
- Understand the difference between real-world, factual experiences, and exploration of knowledge and fictional, imagined worlds
- Develop a sense of reflection about their world and their environment that leads to action, control, and conservation

WHY IS AN INTEGRATED CURRICULUM IMPORTANT?

A strong theoretical and philosophical foundation for curricular integration has been developed by a number of researchers who have studied a variety of curriculum-related topics. Studies on student inquiry (Beyer, 1985; Costa, 1985), class management in an atmosphere of active inquiry (Harmin, 1994), schema theory (Bruner, 1986; Vygotsky, 1978; Wells, 1986), and the whole-language (or literature-based) approach (Goodman, 1986) all lend support to the assertion that curricular integration is a valuable, reflective, and effective way for teachers to teach and students to learn (Roberts & Kellough, 1996). We explored many of these constructs in Chapter 8 and will continue to discuss many different ways of integrating curricula later in this chapter.

As Pigdon and Woolley (1993, p. 6) explain, "An integrated approach allows learners to explore, gather, process, refine, and present information about topics they want to investigate without the constraints imposed by traditional subject barriers." Integrating the curriculum means including both content and process in the curricular equation. Content subjects (social studies, science) are essentially concerned with ideas about how the world works, whereas process subjects (language, mathematics, art, music) provide a continuum of options for representing how learners make sense of the world. In an integrated framework, product and process are balanced, and learners incorporate both curricular components when learning about a specific topic such as spiders or the Olympics.

Consider the isolated bits of information that were presented to you about a host of different topics throughout your years as a student in elementary and secondary school. Perhaps this anecdote, which recaptures how students in one school were taught about the nation of Japan over an eight-year period, will sound familiar to you and help you recollect how these experiences have affected your own learning.

In the first grade, where children often study concepts of the family, their teacher read them stories about families from several cultures around the world; one story was about a Japanese family. A music teacher taught the children a Japanese folk song in the second grade and a traditional Japanese dance in the third grade. In the fourth grade, an art teacher helped the children experiment with origami. The children also studied geographical regions of the world in their fourth grade year; there was some discussion of islands and island nations in that study. Finally, in middle school, the children studied aspects of Asian cultures, including Japanese culture. (Wood, 1997, p. 4)

Although this may seem like a familiar story, it's not one that you want to repeat when you become a teacher. Why? Many of the theoretical constructs that will help you answer this question were presented in Chapter 8. Every teacher is concerned about students' academic skills and about providing sufficient practice for students in a variety of skill areas. Unfortunately, many of the skills that students learn are practiced in a decontextualized fashion—on a worksheet or in a workbook—that has nothing to do with solving a real-life problem or developing an educational goal. Integrated curricula provide for the application of meaningful skills in meaningful contexts. "Almost any subject . . . is best taught when it is needed to accomplish something else" (Wakefield, 1993, p. 137).

INTERDISCIPLINARY INSTRUCTION

Interdisciplinary instruction is synonymous with an integrated curriculum. Rather than being subject- or discipline-focused, interdisciplinary or integrative instruction focuses on a central topic. Integrative units of study can be designed for all horizontal levels—preprimary, primary, intermediate, middle school, and secondary school. Since it is important that the topics connect with curricular goals and objectives, the selected focus for different horizontal levels is a major curricular decision. "Me and My Family," "My Neighborhood," or "Small Animals" would be appropriate themes for a preprimary or primary integrative unit, whereas "Communication," "Transportation Through the Ages," "Immigration," or "Mysteries" would be appropriate for an intermediate or middle school integrative unit. Integrative units at the secondary level seem to be most effectively connected across disciplines when they are conceptually focused. For example, secondary students might study equity and diversity as integrative themes connecting American literature, geometry, American history, consumer economics, and wellness.

SOME BASIC STRUCTURES FOR CURRICULAR INTEGRATION

Educators have created a number of terms and structures that can be applied when designing integrated curricula. In this section we present a variety of structures to help you organize interdisciplinary instruction for your future classroom. We've decided to highlight the Project Approach, the Reggio Emilia

Approach, literature-based instruction, curriculum webbing, and learning centers as key structures that you can become familiar with and apply as you design your integrative units.

THE PROJECT APPROACH

A **project,** Katz (1994, p. 1) explains, "is an in-depth investigation of a topic worth learning more about. The investigation is usually undertaken by a small

---

Figure 10.4

An Example of the Project Approach

The Supermarket

To provide you with an example of the different phases of the Project Approach, we'll focus on kindergarten-aged students. When planning a project that features the supermarket, the three phases would develop in the following ways.

Getting Started

The children and teachers begin by brainstorming a list of all the things they can think of that are found in a supermarket. From this list, they then develop a **curriculum web,** which is a visual diagram of key concepts and activities that they generated in the brainstorming session. It is important to note that the web is an "in-process tool" that can be amended at any time. After creating the web, the teachers ask the children to share what they already know about the supermarket to bridge the learners' prior experiences with the emerging topic. Next, a list of questions, generated by the children and documented in a language chart by the teachers, is created. These questions help to frame the selection of activities, field experiences, resources, and investigations. Teachers plan field experiences, contact experts, and invite parents to participate in the project, as they begin making preparations to move into the second phase of the project.

Field Work

During the second phase of the project, the investigation of the supermarket is in full swing. Teachers and children sketch a visual design for their classroom supermarket. Parents and businesses that have been contacted begin sending empty food containers and sacks. Shelves are organized around categories determined by the children (such as *drinks, cereal, bread, supper,* and *Don't eat*). As additional food containers trickle in, additional categories are suggested. The children create labels, signs, posters, newspaper ads, and money. They also cut, paint, and connect boxes to create the "Kiley Corner Grocery Store." Each day, as the children review the day's activities, teachers record their new questions and listen to their new ideas and suggestions for the next day's investigations.

A few days before the planned trip to the supermarket, several experts visit the classroom. Family members who work in supermarkets, a produce manager, a butcher, a cashier, and a delivery worker might be invited to visit the classroom to share their supermarket experiences. In small groups, children interview the "experts" to find answers to their questions.

Teachers and the children set up a literacy area, which includes children's books about supermarkets and related topics, flyers from supermarkets, posters, ads, videos, and other related resources. During group time, the children explore the materials and discuss their findings.

group of children within a class, sometimes by a whole class, and occasionally by an individual child. The key feature of a project is that it is a research effort deliberately focused on finding answers to questions about a topic posed either by the children, the teacher, or the teacher working with the children. The goal of a project is to learn more about the topic rather than to seek right answers to questions posed by the teacher." Figure 10.4 provides an example of a project.

Finally, it's time to visit a real supermarket. The children board the school bus, armed with their clipboards for sketching their notes and observations. Many parents join the children as they board the bus. Children are in groups of five, with each group chaperoned by a parent, teacher, or other interested adult. The children enter the supermarket with an assignment chosen from the list of questions generated in the classroom. One group interviews the store manager, another visits the frozen food section with their thermometers in hand, and a third group measures the length of the supermarket aisle using a large roll of adding machine tape.

After the exciting supermarket experience, the children work on their representations and dictate their experiences to their teachers and parent volunteers. Early sketches emerge as works of art. Class books, sequenced photograph books, thank-you letters, and supermarket word lists abound in the writing center. The adding machine tape that was used to measure the supermarket aisle is measured again and again using unifix cubes, paper clips, rulers, and string. Teachers and children work collaboratively to take photographs and develop graphs to illustrate the relationships among all the data collected.

For several days, students are actively engaged in acting out their experiences in the "Kiley Corner Grocery Store." Now that the children have accumulated many new experiences and answers to a number of their questions, the store transforms to a new level. New categories are created for the shelves—a bakery, a meat department, a dairy case, a frozen foods aisle, a produce section, a cereals aisle, and a household items section. New price lists are generated, balance scales to weigh fruit and vegetables are requested, and calculators become a necessary tool for creating receipts.

Culminating and Debriefing Activities

After several weeks, the children's interest in the supermarket seems to lose its spark. This is the teachers' cue that it's time to celebrate the project and move on to another exciting topic. The parents, expert visitors, other teachers, and other children in the school are invited to a "Supermarket Celebration." The children create invitations, put finishing touches on their displays, and plan an agenda for the celebration, complete with refreshments. On the evening of the event, children act as hosts for the visitors to their classroom. They gleam with excitement and pride as they show and tell about what they have learned. And the teachers involved enjoy the moment as they begin to think about the next project topic. Although tired, they realize how grateful they are that they decided to become teachers.

(Adapted from Borgia, 1996)

The following theoretical underpinnings serve as the rationale for and foundation of the **Project Approach:**

1. Learners need to make sense of their world.

2. Horizontal relevance is more important than vertical articulation. Perhaps you recall from Chapter 8 that *horizontal relevance* refers to how concepts and topics relate to each other within the same grade level, and *vertical articulation* refers to how concepts and topics at one grade level relate to concepts and topics at different grade levels. Focusing on what students are learning is more important than "getting students ready for the next grade." An overemphasis on vertical articulation may result in "pedagogical paranoia" (Katz, personal communication, 1994).

3. Learners need to develop a disposition for in-depth study.

4. An extended period of time is needed to enable learners to wrap their minds around a topic.

5. Play is a natural way for children to learn, because children are natural-born anthropologists.

6. Learners need opportunities to experience *real* environments.

7. Learners need opportunities to apply skills in meaningful ways.

8. Learners need a continuity of experiences to develop social competence. "If a child doesn't achieve social competence by the age of six, he/she is at risk for the rest of his/her life" (Katz, 1994, personal communication).

WHAT KEY EXPECTATIONS SHOULD A PROJECT MEET?

An effective project meets the following criteria:

1. It involves group discussion.

2. It includes a field experience component.

3. It provides a variety of ways of representing knowledge and comprehension, such as dictation, measurement, sculptures, writing, drawing, and dramatic play.

4. It requires investigation—interviewing; surveying; collecting information by researching books, brochures, databases, pictures, photographs, newspapers, cereal boxes, travel brochures, and other authentic sources.

5. It must include documentation of the processes and products used to complete it. This is an important communication tool for learners, parents, other school staff, administrators, and the community. Documentation can include poster displays, project webs, photographs, labels, videotapes, class books, sequencing activities, portfolios, and language charts.

HOW DOES PROJECT WORK SUPPORT AN INTEGRATED CURRICULUM?

Advocates of the Project Approach do not suggest that project work should constitute the whole curriculum. Rather, they suggest that it is best seen as complementary to the more formal, systematic parts of the curriculum. Project work is not a separate subject, like mathematics; it provides a context for applying mathematical concepts and skills. Nor is project work an "add on" to the basics; it should be treated as integral to all the other work included in the curriculum. Project work does the following: provides learners with opportunities to apply specific skills, features learners' proficiencies and strengths, stresses intrinsic motivation, and encourages learners to determine what to work on (and accepts them as experts about their own needs; Katz, 1994).

THE PHASES OF A PROJECT

In Phase 1 of a project (referred to as the Getting Started phase in the Project Approach; Katz & Chard, 1989), the learners and teacher devote several discussion periods to selecting and refining the topic to be investigated. The topic may be proposed by a learner or by the teacher. Once the topic has been selected, teachers usually begin by making a web or concept map, based on a brainstorming session with students. These webs are displayed in the classroom throughout the project and provide a framework for designing the project investigation and selecting specific activities and documentation efforts.

Phase 2, Field Work, consists of direct investigation, which often includes field trips to investigate sites, objects, or events. In Phase 2, which is the heart of project work, learners are investigating, drawing from observation, constructing models, observing closely, recording findings, exploring, predicting, discussing, and dramatizing their new understandings (Chard, 1992).

Phase 3, Culminating and Debriefing Events, includes students preparing and presenting reports on their results, in the form of displays of findings and artifacts, talks, dramatic presentations, or guided tours of their constructions (Katz, 1994). This phase emphasizes the development of documentation, which we discussed in the previous section on key expectations of a project.

SELECTING APPROPRIATE TOPICS

Katz and Chard (1989) discuss the differences between decontextualized teaching and project work. In project work, the course of the project is negotiated by the learners and the teacher. Activities are focused on investigation and are directed by a research question or narrative. Katz and Chard warned that limited topics that do not relate to learners' daily life experiences often result in learners studying unrelated and unfamiliar material. Take, for example, a letter-of-the-week curriculum. "If the theme is 'The Letter M,' the children could . . . draw pictures, read, create, or act out stories about a market, a mouse, the moon, a motor, and so on. Logical, sequential, or cause-effect relationships among the four items cannot be uncovered through active investigation, discussion, interviews of experts, looking things up, and other typical project activities" (Katz & Chard, 1993, p. 210).

Selecting topics definitely is an important dimension of integrating curricula. A number of considerations come into play. Topics should relate to learners' own everyday, firsthand, personal experiences; allow for the integration of a range of subjects or disciplines; provide for the study of objects or phenomena that are real, that will be useful in later life experiences, and that are worth spending time to investigate; incorporate opportunities for problem solving, investigation, collection, cooperation, construction, creation, and dramatic play; and include parents who might be available for direct observation, consultation, and, possibly, field trips (Katz & Chard, 1993).

It's important for project topics to emanate from learners' experiences. It's *critically* important that project topics designed specifically for preprimary- and primary-aged students emanate from the students' direct experiences with the world around them. For that reason, we suggest that you begin by thinking about topics that meet the following criteria: nature, water, community resources, vehicles, buildings, and objects and materials. Avoid topics related to things that are not real (fantasy television or movie characters, stuffed animals, amusement park attractions), the past (dinosaurs, historical events and people), things that are not part of the students' experiential base (outer space, foreign countries), and places or objects not in the children's surroundings (the bottom of the ocean, the rain forest; Borgia 1996).

THE REGGIO EMILIA APPROACH

Another interdisciplinary structure, the Reggio Emilia Approach, incorporates the Project approach and offers additional vision and depth to the concept of integrated curricula. Because the Reggio Emilia Approach grew out of a parent cooperative movement, it explicitly recognizes the partnership between parents, educators, and children. With the **Reggio Emilia Approach,** children learn through cooperating with other children and their teachers in long-term projects based on children's interests and centered around the creative arts. Topics flow from the children's interests, curiosity, and understandings. Projects and activities are not fragmented. Rather, they build on one another over time, as the children revisit their original work and ideas and refine them using new experiences, activities, and forms of expression. Time is also important in building and sustaining collaborative relationships. Through conscious use of space, color, natural light, attractive and appropriate learning materials, and displays of children's work, the environment serves as another teacher and is inviting to learners, teachers, families, and visitors.

A number of trends in contemporary U.S. education suggest an affinity for the Reggio Emilia Approach (New, 1994). As educators advocate building a professional culture in schools (Lieberman, 1988) that acknowledges the importance of teachers who are empowered as thinkers (Murray, 1986), research on teacher collaboration points to the usefulness of the Reggio Emilia Approach as a strategy for bringing about educational improvement and reform (Ellis, 1990). American educators have much to learn from the Reggio Emilia construct.

LITERATURE-BASED INSTRUCTION

Literature-based instruction involves using trade books—that is, literature not specifically developed for the education market—as opposed to textbooks (often called basals) in the teaching of language arts and other related areas

Literature-based instruction involves using trade books—literature not specifically developed for the education market. (© Michael Weisbrot)

(Hancock & Hill, 1987; Hiebert & Colt, 1989; Tunnell & Jacobs, 1989; Zarrillo, 1989). Such literature must be the primary, if not the only, reading material used in instruction.

■ Who Promotes Literature-Based Instruction?

Literature-based reading instruction has been promoted by educators with a whole-language perspective toward literacy development (Altwerger, Edelsky, & Flores, 1987; Goodman, 1986; Newman, 1985; Smith, 1971). The **whole-language** philosophy proposes that instruction should keep language whole and involve children in using it purposefully and functionally. Goodman (1986), a leading advocate of this philosophy, states that teachers should put aside carefully sequenced basal readers and encourage students to read books for information, for enjoyment, and to cope with the world around them. Literature-based instruction is supported by a strong theoretical base and extensive research (Giddings, 1991).

The National Association for the Education of Young Children (NAEYC) Guidelines for Developmentally Appropriate Practice are highly compatible with the recommendations of many authorities in the field of whole-language instruction and early literacy (Cambourne, 1988; Galda, Cullinan, & Strickland, 1993; Goodman, 1986; Holdaway, 1979; Routman, 1991; Weaver, 1994). Both sources—the NAEYC guidelines and whole-language advocates—indicate that young children learn to read best in an environment in which they are immersed in language, when they are allowed sufficient time and opportunity to explore a wide variety of written materials and literacy activities, and when instruction reflects their current knowledge level and their attempts to construct new knowledge. Others (Field & Spangler, 1995; Fisher, 1991; Kamii, Manning, & Manning, 1991) also stress the value of children's play as a crucial foundation for literacy.

■ Does Research Support Literature-Based Instruction?

Children who learn to read before going to school, and those who rapidly learn to read once they begin school, have been read to from their very early years. These children have developed a sense of story, and they read for information and enjoyment (Durkin, 1961; Goodman, 1986; Hoskisson, 1979; Newman, 1985). Good readers read for meaning and correct themselves when they make a mistake that doesn't make sense. Also, good readers reread favorite books and thereby develop fluency (Lamme, 1987). Interest, purpose, and choice are important in the behavior of good readers (Bondy, 1985; Hickman, 1977; Rasinski, 1988).

Children who are taught reading primarily with basal reading programs tend to develop behaviors and notions that are not consistent with the behaviors of good readers. Studies have consistently concluded that children in basal reading programs focus on materials and procedures rather than on meaning. These children place emphasis on decoding, vocabulary, and accuracy (Cairney, 1988; Hiebert, 1983; Johns & Ellis, 1976; Unsworth, 1984).

■ How Does Instruction Differ in a Literature-Based Program?

Instead of beginning with fragments of language, such as letters and sounds, teachers should use complete forms of written language, such as stories, poems, and signs, to develop students' reading, writing, talking, listening, and thinking skills. Teachers should encourage children to determine for themselves whether or not what they read makes sense (Giddings, 1991). Picture a five-year-old beginning reader walking down a familiar street and spotting a small sign hanging on the door of a barbershop that says "Back Soon." If this child is in a kindergarten class in which each letter of the alphabet is presented as an isolated concept and sound, the child might decide that he can't read the sign because he hasn't learned the last letter of the first word yet. Although he will recognize *A, B,* and *C,* he will not attempt to make sense of the sign, because he is limited by his isolated understanding of letters and sounds. But if this child's teacher uses literature-based instruction, in which written language is presented in context and making sense of print is valued, the child will allow the barbershop pole and time of day to guide the invitation that has been presented to him—the invitation to make sense of the sign based on the situation and his vast exposure to letters, sounds, words, and signs. The child in the literature-based classroom has developed the disposition to use his background knowledge while he searches for meaning.

A number of instructional strategies and approaches—including many that you read about in Chapter 9—are implemented in a literature-based reading program. As a teacher, you will need to develop your interests as well as those of your students, be aware of many curricular strategies and options, and ultimately make appropriate choices regarding your literature-based instruction. To get started in implementing a literature-based reading program, consider developing three key dimensions of your reading program: individualized reading with self-selection of reading material and self-pacing, integrative literature units, and core books. We've only scratched the surface of the topic of implementing literature-based instruction. However, there are many excellent resources that will help you begin thinking about creating a vibrant curriculum using literature.

■ What Is a Core Book?

Teachers face many challenges as they make the transition from basal-driven to literature-based instruction (McGee & Tompkins, 1995). One such challenge is determining which pieces of literature will be featured as core books in their curricula. A **core book** is a literature selection that takes on a central and unifying role in a literature-based curriculum. In your classroom library, you will have multiple copies of your core books, generally six to eight copies of each selection, which will be used in both shared reading and guided reading activities. Jonathan, a middle school teacher, selected *Stone Fox* as a core piece of literature for his classroom. The following brief summary describes the story's theme: "In this story a 10-year-old boy, Willy, must care for his ill grandfather and run their potato farm. Willy manages to harvest the potato crop by himself but learns that the government will take the farm unless he finds a way to pay for 10 years of back taxes. Willy wins the needed money in a dog sled race with the sacrifice of his faithful dog, Searchlight, and with the help of *Stone Fox*, a Shoshone Indian" (McGee & Tompkins, 1995, p. 405).

Jonathan uses a core literature approach (Zarrillo, 1989), selecting literature that is closely tied to his social studies program. He includes *Stone Fox* in an integrative unit in which his students read a variety of poetry, information books, and folklore related to several American Indian tribes (McGee & Tompkins, 1995). Since the theme of Jonathan's integrative unit is American Indians, he selects core literature that integrates and develops that theme across the curriculum.

■ Selecting Literature

Using trade books in instruction enhances both literacy development and learners' interest in reading (Hoffman, Roser, & Farest, 1988; Morrow, 1992; Morrow, O'Connor, & Smith, 1990). There is much value in exposing students to the natural language used by writers of children's and adolescents' books (Giddings, 1991). Moreover, the illustrations provide aesthetic, creative, and original perspectives on a myriad of topics and concepts that are meaningful to students.

So where do you begin your quest for exciting and appropriate literature? You may have been fortunate enough to have taken a dynamic children's or adolescents' literature course during your teacher preparation program. But whether or not you have taken such a course, you need to discover your personal connection to literature written for children, adolescents, and young adults. What types of books do you enjoy? Who are your favorite children's authors and illustrators? What books make you laugh? What books make you cry? We know many teachers who are passionate about children's literature—including us! Once you catch the children's literature bug, you will find yourself wandering through bookstores and libraries at all hours of the day and night.

The following literature selection guidelines are just a starting point for thinking about beginning your literature resource development. Since we have taught children's literature courses for a number of years, we have discovered that preservice teachers who begin choosing appropriate literature to support their units and projects generally have a fairly extensive collection of resources, and an even more extensive wish list, by the time they complete their teacher preparation program. Many of our students share lists of their favorite literature requests with their families and friends and put children's and adolescents' books at the top of their birthday and holiday wish lists.

Literature Selection Guidelines

■ Choose literature from every genre—folk tales, fables, and myths; poetry; fantasy and science fiction; modern fiction; historical fiction; biographies; and informational books—and check to see that your collection is balanced.

■ Choose picture books that represent a variety of artistic media and techniques: watercolor, charcoal, oil paint, collage, photographs, sketches, and so on.

■ Choose books that represent a variety of authors and illustrators.

■ Choose books that represent all cultures, genders, and age groups, and once again, check to see that your collection is balanced.

■ Choose big books, when appropriate, to support your literature-based shared reading program.

■ Choose books that support and extend your integrative unit goals and objectives.

■ Choose books that are appropriate for reading aloud, shared reading, guided reading, and independent reading.

■ Choose some books that can be extended in the technology center through audiotapes, videotapes, and computer software.

In addition to the guidelines listed here, in the Relevant Resources for Professionals section of this chapter we've included some of our favorite resources for choosing quality literature. Please understand that this is a very brief representation of the resources that are available to you, but this list provides you with a good starting point for researching literature written for children, adolescents, and young adults.

■ Be Aware of Your Cultural Perspectives and Biases

Since one of the most visible changes occurring in literacy instruction today is the expanded use of literature, it's likely that this focus will continue to expand into the next millennium. Unfortunately, literature-based literacy programs are disturbingly alike in one significant respect—lack of cultural understanding on the part of teachers. This "cultural gap," a void in teachers' knowledge base about culture as it relates to literacy and literature, is a profound problem.

The need for educators to understand and deal with the cultural dimensions of learning and teaching is a growing concern for American education (Giroux & McLaren, 1986; Trueba, Jacobs, & Kirton, 1990; Willinsky, 1990). Equitable and effective literature-based instruction cannot grow magically from teachers' good intentions or incidentally from their extant professional knowledge (Barrera, 1992). The key to developing cultural understanding is to accept the idea that "it is culture, not biology, that shapes human life and the human mind" (Bruner, 1990, p. 34). Human beings are cultural beings, shaped or constituted by culture—but also involved in shaping and generating culture (Geertz, 1973). People are not born *with* culture but are born *into* a culture, and their entry into meaning is through that culture. Culture is not the solitary invention of the individual; it is learned and social (Bruner, 1990; Peacock, 1986).

From a multicultural perspective, we can identify a number of potential curricular and instructional problems. First, the core literature is often dominated by topics and characters that do not reflect the faces, experiences, and histories of children from a variety of cultures. There is a marked homogeneity that renders some children's lives and experiences invisible. Second, even when "multicultural" literature *is* featured, the authors and illustrators are often mostly English-speaking European Americans, with little of the core literature written or illustrated by individuals from other linguistic or cultural backgrounds (Barrera, 1992). We offer the suggestions in Figure 10.5 to assist you in selecting literature that is diverse and appropriate for your future classroom.

CURRICULUM WEBS

To design and implement an integrative unit, teachers need much more than a topic. Decisions must be made about the focus of topics, instructional goals, and strategies (Lipson, Valencia, Wixson, & Peters, 1993). Achieving a balance between concepts and processes, as well as between learner-initiated and teacher-initiated activities, is no small task. In addition, teachers must be concerned about including a variety of grouping structures—small-group, large-group, and individual learning experiences (Goetz, 1985).

Webbing helps learners gain insights into relationships between ideas and concepts. Through this process, students can begin to apply critical and creative thinking skills and strategies.

■ Getting Started with Curriculum Webbing

The following four-step process, adapted from Barclay, Benelli, Campbell, and Kleine (1995), will help both novice and experienced teachers develop engaging and productive topic cycles.

1. *Identification of a topic and related subtopics*

   - Is this a topic that learners are naturally curious about?
   - Do learners already have some understanding of, and experience with, this topic?
   - Will learners gain new knowledge and understanding about their world and its people from participating in this unit?
   - Does the topic lend itself to incorporating learning experiences from most, if not all, curricular areas?
   - Does the topic lend itself to the exploration of a variety of related subtopics?
   - Will there be ample resources available for this topic?

2. *"Topicstorming"*

   - Are most, if not all, curricular areas represented?

Figure 10.5
Promoting Diversity Through Your Literature Selection

Check the illustrations.

Look for stereotypes. Are females always depicted in domestic roles, or are Native Americans depicted as savages?

Look for tokenism. Do all minority faces look alike, or are they individuals depicted genuinely, with distinctive features?

Check the story line.

Standard for success. Is "making it" in the dominant white society projected as the only ideal?

Resolution of problems. How are problems presented, conceived of, and resolved in the story?

Role of women. Are the achievements of girls and women based on their own initiative and intelligence, or are they attributed to their good looks or their relationships with male characters?

Look at the lifestyles.

If the illustrations and text attempt to depict another culture, do they go beyond oversimplifications and offer genuine insights into other lifestyles?

Weigh the relationships between people.

Are relationships between individuals of differing cultures, as well as relationships between family members, depicted appropriately?

Note the heroes and heroines.

Are all cultures, genders, and age groups represented in your children's literature collection?

Consider the effects on a child's self-image.

Are norms established that could limit any child's aspirations and self-concept?

Consider the author's or illustrator's background and perspective.

What qualifies the author or illustrator to deal with a particular topic?

Watch for loaded words.

Examples of loaded words, words that have insulting overtones, include *savage*, *primitive*, *conniving*, *lazy*, *superstitious*, *treacherous*, and *crafty*.

Check the copyright date.

Do the text and illustrations accurately depict a current and balanced perspective on the topic?

(Adapted from Hendrick, 1992, pp. 605–607)

- Is there a balance of experiences: inquiry activities, shared reading and writing, independent reading and writing, oral sharing, and reading aloud?
- Is there a balance of small-group, large-group, and independent learning experiences?
- Are there both indoor and outdoor experiences?
- What additions can be made to the present learning centers to enhance the unit?

- What new centers or learning stations need to be created?
- What long-range projects might the students pursue?
- Are there outside visitors, field experiences, or computer resources that might enhance this unit?
- How will learners' families be involved in the unit?

3. *Identification of desired learning outcomes*

- What specific knowledge might learners acquire during this unit?
- What process knowledge or skills might learners gain through their participation in this unit?
- What habits and attitudes might learners develop as a result of their participation in this unit?

4. *Preparation for teaching*

- What initiating and culminating activities might be used?
- How might the classroom be arranged to facilitate learner interaction during this unit?
- Have I collected the necessary literature, poems, manipulatives, technology, and other resources?
- How will I assess student learning throughout the unit?
- How will I evaluate the effectiveness of the learning experiences within the unit?
- What collaborative learning or other grouping arrangements will students need to use? What can I do to facilitate this?

■ Including Learners in the Webbing Process

Incorporating learners' interests, background knowledge, experiences, and questions is key to the development of a theme/topic/concept web. You might consider beginning the year with a web about your classroom to help students understand how they will be encouraged to learn:

1. Brainstorm a list of rules, ideas, questions about, and equipment related to, for example, "Our Fourth-Grade Classroom."
2. Write the words *Our Fourth-Grade Classroom* in the center of a large chart.
3. Ask students to add related information to the web, connecting it to the center box. This information is typically taken from the brainstorming list, which learners can refer to during the webbing session.
4. Ask the students to add more supporting details to expand the web. See Figure 10.6 for an example of a class web.

This example can be used as a model for making individual webs or other small- or large-group webs. Once students feel comfortable with the webbing process, they can help in developing curricular webs during the initiation phase of each new integrative unit.

Figure 10.6
Sample Class Web

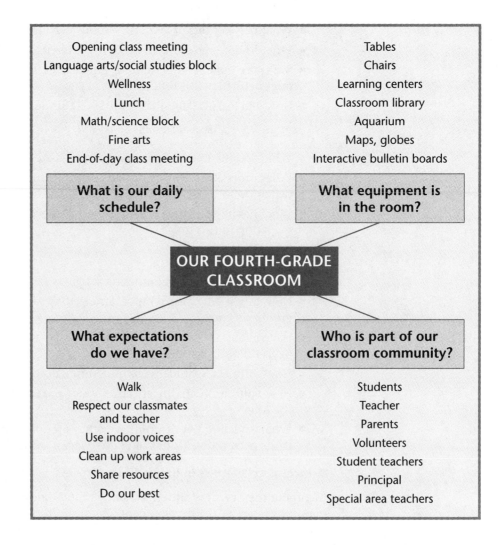

OUR FOURTH-GRADE CLASSROOM

What is our daily schedule?

- Opening class meeting
- Language arts/social studies block
- Wellness
- Lunch
- Math/science block
- Fine arts
- End-of-day class meeting

What equipment is in the room?

- Tables
- Chairs
- Learning centers
- Classroom library
- Aquarium
- Maps, globes
- Interactive bulletin boards

What expectations do we have?

- Walk
- Respect our classmates and teacher
- Use indoor voices
- Clean up work areas
- Share resources
- Do our best

Who is part of our classroom community?

- Students
- Teacher
- Parents
- Volunteers
- Student teachers
- Principal
- Special area teachers

There are many ways to develop curriculum webs. The more comfortable you are with webbing, the more you will use this organizational method in your classroom. Figure 10.7 offers some examples.

LEARNING CENTERS

Walk into Debra Kunze's second- and third-grade classroom in the middle of March, and you might observe the following learning center design (Daniels & Bizar, 1998, p. 90):

- A writing center, where students pursue their own writing projects
- A math center in the form of a store with priced items, play money, cash registers, sacks, and receipts

Figure 10.7 Project Webs and School Bus Webs

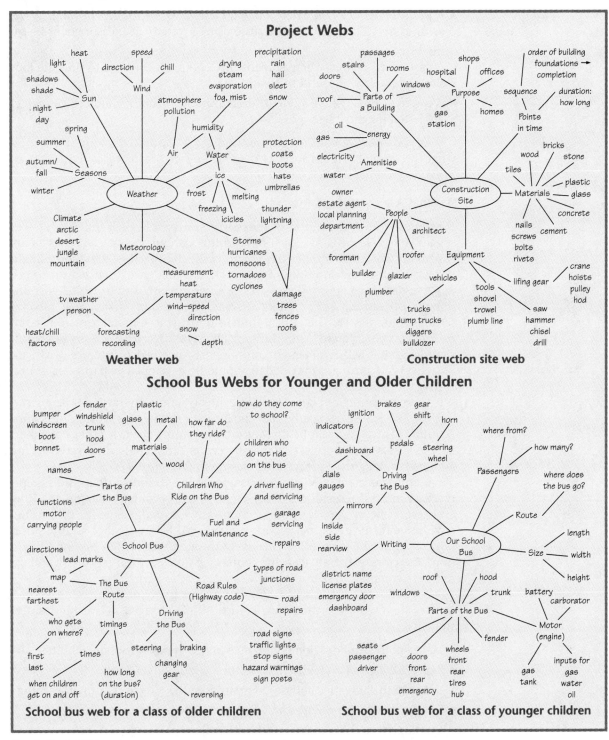

(Katz & Chard, 1989)

- A measurement center, where students test various attributes of water as well as measure volume and temperature using a variety of measurement instruments

- A "geosafari" center, where students use computer software to find the locations of countries around the world

- A physics center, where students design simple machines and bridges, which are tested for strength

As you visualize your journey around this exciting classroom, think about what the students are learning as they are engaged in center activities for approximately an hour each day.

■ What Are Learning Centers?

For a more formal definition of **learning centers,** Daniels and Bizar (1998) suggest the following: "Centers or learning stations are special spots in the classroom where the teacher has set up curriculum-related activities that students can pursue autonomously" (p. 91). In Chapter 6 we discussed the importance of designing appropriate learning environments and provided you with samples of learning environment designs. A classroom design that incorporates learning centers is a critical dimension of your curricular plan. For that reason, we invite you to begin thinking about how learning centers in your future classrooms will complement and support your curricular topics, goals, and objectives. A learning center design should be developed as part of each integrative unit you create.

There are several types of learning centers. Simple interactive learning centers can be created using a bulletin board with pockets for written directions. Learning centers also can be displayed on an empty shelf or other flat surface in the classroom. In more elaborate centers, materials and activities are arranged in designated areas in the classroom (Wood, 1997).

Learning centers often are key components of minds-on/hands-on preprimary, primary, intermediate, middle school, and secondary classrooms. However, we believe that learning centers are *essential* elements of learning environments for preprimary- and primary-aged learners, since children from birth to age eight learn most effectively through sensory and motor stimulation. Therefore, elaborate learning centers are necessary in preprimary and primary classrooms.

The following list (Isbell, 1995) emphasizes many of the reasons learning centers are essential for these age groups. While engaged in learning centers, students:

- Make choices and develop confidence in their problem-solving abilities
- Expand their oral and written communication skills
- Enhance their creative abilities, determining the direction of their learning
- Select a variety of resources based on their interests
- Develop social skills as they work with others
- Experience a variety of roles and learning perspectives

- Develop responsibility
- Set goals, develop plans, and perform a task to completion
- Develop longer attention spans and the ability to focus while engaged in active learning pursuits
- Enhance their self-image as they learn that they can influence their world by participating in a variety of learning centers

Because developing learning centers is an important and time-consuming task, we have provided you with some details about a variety of learning centers. It's our hope that you'll be able to picture these centers in your mind and develop a lot of ideas and positive energy that will motivate you to design stimulating and engaging classrooms. Although the learning centers you select should support your curricular goals and objectives as well as reflect the interests of your students, it is important to include some of the following centers in a classroom for preprimary- or primary-aged learners, regardless of the curriculum or students.

■ A Family Living Center

The family living center is an essential component of any preprimary or early primary classroom. This area provides the perfect transition from home to school. Young children are familiar with the roles and materials they will discover and develop in the family living center. In this safe environment, children can play out their ideas, role-play their experiences, and experiment with a variety of authentic props (Isbell, 1995). Some materials to include in a family living center are kitchen appliances, a small table with chairs, cooking utensils, empty containers that promote the discovery of environmental print, and a collection of dress-up clothes that represent a variety of cultures.

■ Math/Block Center

For over 150 years, blocks have been essential in classrooms for young children (Isbell, 1995). Block play enhances all areas of children's development, including physical, motor, social, and cognitive domains. The block center is designed to facilitate active construction, the discovery of mathematical and spatial relationships, the connection of print to actual objects and actions, and the development of positive social relationships. Many props can be added to the block center, including math manipulatives, to give children an opportunity to connect blocks with other materials to promote mathematical, logical, and spatial development. Some materials to include in a block/math center are a set of unit blocks, miniature multicultural people, miniature animals, miniature transportation vehicles, a variety of math manipulatives, and a large piece of carpet to cover the flooring (for sound absorption).

■ Art Center

As children paint, sculpt, and draw in the art center, they experiment with a variety of different media and begin to understand their world as they develop a number of skills and act on many creative ideas. The process of creating is more important than the products the children develop (Isbell, 1995). The art center should be a place for exploration and discovery, risk taking, and dream making. Some materials to include in an art center are an easel; a water source; a variety of painting and drawing tools such as paintbrushes, sponge brushes, paint rollers, Q-tips, and popsicle sticks; scissors; glue; and paste.

■ Sensory Center

Exploration and experimentation with a variety of natural materials—sand, water, rice, corn—take place in the sensory center. As children interact with the sensory materials, they refine their coordination and develop new approaches for successful use of a myriad of tools (Isbell, 1995). Children's interest in this center makes it an effective place to increase their attention spans while they are involved in a number of skill-based thinking and social activities. Some materials to include in a sensory center are a sensory table (many different varieties are available); shower curtain liners (place on the table tops and on the floor under the sensory table); a small broom and dust pan; sterilized play sand; colored water; rocks, pebbles, pieces of wood, and shells; and funnels, a strainer, sponges, and straws.

■ Library Center

The library center should be designed to hook children into books and capture their interest in a variety of related resources. It should include a listening area with audiotapes, a flannelboard area with storytelling media, and a relaxed reading area. Books should be displayed so children can see the covers and easily select books that appeal to them. Soft pillows, stuffed toys, quiet music, and cozy quarters enhance the library center environment.

Some materials to include in a library center are a well-balanced, culturally diverse collection of appropriate children's literature, children's magazines, a cassette tape player or CD player, headphones, and books with tapes.

■ Writing Center

The writing center provides a special place in the classroom that is reserved to promote the writing of young children. An interest in writing and communication is critically important for young children. In this center children write lists and letters; create books, recipes, phone books, invitations, and signs; copy text from children's literature or displayed language charts; create new words and patterns; and experiment with a variety of writing media. Some materials to include in a writing center are a typewriter, word processor, or computer; magic slates, chalkboards, or wipe-off cards; a variety of writing tools; glue; scissors; classroom post office with mailboxes for each child; a variety of types of paper; construction paper; newsprint; and tagboard.

■ Music/Movement Center

A music/movement center is an area where children can experiment with a variety of media that create rhythmic and musical tones and sounds and inspire a wide range of movement. In this center, children become musicians and dancers who compose their own music, create their own movements, and joyfully share their musicality with their peers and teachers. Some materials to include in a music/movement center are rhythm instruments (rhythm sticks, sand blocks, wood blocks, drums, triangles), bells, shakers, a cassette or CD player, and music from different cultures, with appropriate instruments.

■ Science/Discovery Center

Young children are curious about the things in their world. Encourage their inquiry into the natural world with a science/discovery center, where children become scientists who observe, examine, compare and contrast, collect and analyze data, and draw scientific conclusions. The science/discovery center invites children to engage in wondering and questioning, thinking and imagining. Some materials to include in a science/discovery center are magnifying glasses, plastic gloves, an aquarium (for fish or plants), class pets (hamster, guinea pig, hermit crabs, bunny), and clear plastic jars with lids.

■ Social Studies/Museum Center

In a museum center, social studies concepts are developed and displayed. Family timelines, favorite foods from around the world, famous Americans, the Statue of Liberty, and train travel are all topics that could be developed in a museum center. The major focus of this center is to provide opportunities for learners to connect with their community and develop an appreciation of how history and geography affect their world. Some materials to include in a social studies/museum center are photographs, artifacts, reproductions, timelines, displays, and maps.

■ Technology Center

In a technology center, learners engage in activities that are both intriguing and accessible. A variety of appropriate software, as well as peripheral tools that support the needs of diverse learners and learning styles, are essential features of such a center. One of the powerful services teachers can provide by means of computers and technology support materials is to give students a "microworld." A microworld is a software program that lets children play and discover concepts and cause-effect relationships in a virtual environment constructed specifically for this purpose. It serves as a bridge between hands-on experience and abstract learning, letting children learn about a topic through exploration and experimentation that they could not perform in the real world (Papert, 1980; 1993). Microworlds are harder to find than drill-and-practice programs, but the simulations they provide—as long as they are developmentally appropriate for the learners using them—are much more valuable than drill software (Davis & Shade, 1994). One example of a microworld program is EZ Logo, which is often used to introduce young children to geometric concepts.

A number of assistive devices may be necessary to make the technology center accessible to all students. A TouchWindow screen, special switches, an

A variety of appropriate software, as well as peripheral tools that support the needs of diverse learners and learning styles, is an essential feature of a technology center.
(© Michael Zide)

IntelliKeys keyboard, and a variety of other adaptive equipment and software are available from a number of vendors. Some materials to include in the technology center are a computer with a color monitor, color printer, microphone, mouse, joystick, and CD-ROM player, CU-See Me cameras, digital cameras, headsets, software, and instructions for accessing the Internet.

■ Other Learning Center Options

We've discussed in detail a number of typical learning centers for preprimary and primary classrooms to get you thinking about the purpose of each type of center, but the lists and rationales we've provided are only starting points. We're confident that you can add many more ideas and infuse your own creativity into designing a myriad of appropriate learning centers for your future classroom. In addition to the centers we've suggested, a number of other options exist, depending on your interests, the interests of your students, and your curriculum.

For example, if you are engaged in an integrative unit on construction, you might want to develop a woodworking center for your classroom, or if food is the featured topic, you might want to set up a separate cooking or restaurant center. Many fast-food restaurants will provide teachers with environmental print and props to enhance classroom learning centers. Certain unit topics lend themselves to the development of sociodramatic centers in which students learn about a topic by engaging in a variety of social role-playing activities. Suggestions for sociodramatic centers include a grocery store, hospital, bakery, shoe store, gas station, train or bus station, garden shop, pet shop—the options are endless. If you're preparing to teach in a middle level or secondary classroom, you can take many of the learning center options that we've provided to create your own connections, designs, and materials lists.

The Role of Collaboration in Integrative Unit Planning

If you've wondered whether thinking up unit topics and creating curriculum webs might be more fun and productive if you teamed with other teachers, we'd like to say yes, go for it! Teaming with other teachers to brainstorm concepts and categories, come up with activity and assessment ideas, and share resources is one of the most productive and enjoyable ways to develop integrative units. By encouraging colleagues to engage in creative thinking and to exhibit their flexibility, fluency, creativity, and originality, you are providing opportunities to think and plan collaboratively with them. James Watson emphasized the benefits of collaboration with his observation that "Nothing new that is really interesting comes without collaboration."

One of the biggest problems teachers have in planning an integrated curriculum is lack of time. You must be committed to finding opportunities to team with colleagues as you plan integrated units. Special subject area or resource teachers (for example, art, music, drama, computer, foreign language, library/media, physical education/health, gifted, and special education teachers) must be involved in the planning process and must be encouraged to buy in to the importance of integrated units.

How can schools develop and support teaming opportunities for busy teachers? Weekly horizontal team meetings are a great way to begin. All teachers (special area, special education, and regular education), assistant teachers, and an administrative liaison (such as principal, assistant principal, lead/mentor teacher) meet every week for one hour to discuss curricular integration across grade levels. The meetings are held at the same time each week, and teachers are paid to meet and plan. For example, the primary horizontal meeting includes all staff involved with students from prekindergarten through second grade; the intermediate horizontal meeting includes all staff involved with students in the third and fourth grades; the middle school horizontal meeting includes all staff involved with students from fifth through eighth grade; and the secondary horizontal meeting includes all staff involved with high school students. This structure may be altered depending on the size of the district, the curriculum and assessment design, and the district grade-level divisions.

However, the focus of these weekly meetings is not up for negotiation. The driving force behind the weekly meetings is the goal of developing an integrated curriculum and assessment program that involves and challenges each and every staff person, as well as each and every student in the building. It is imperative that a written report be submitted to the principal and district curriculum coordinator or curriculum committee chair each week. This report serves to keep the lines of communication open and fluid—conditions that are necessary to support and enhance change and curricular growth.

ISSUES SURROUNDING INTEGRATIVE UNITS

In Chapters 8 and 9 you explored some important concepts and heard some compelling teacher stories dealing with designing curricula. We also discussed a number of instructional strategies and approaches for delivering and developing curricula in the context of the classroom.

Our experience, and that of many other teachers, has made it clear that one of the most important abilities you must develop before you can plan integrative units and create connections for students is to be able to explain why you teach in this way. From your very first job interview, you will be asked to articulate your philosophy of teaching. Embedded within that philosophy must be a passion for creating connections for your students. The words, expressions, attitudes, and knowledge you share with parents, colleagues, administrators, and your students will make or break your opportunities as a teacher to create curricular connections through the development of integrative units.

"YEAH BUTS" AND INTEGRATIVE UNITS

If integrative units are so important for both teachers and students, then why don't more teachers implement them? Perhaps the "yeah-but" that is most often recited for not implementing an instructional innovation is the lamentation, "Yeah, but my principal won't let me!" Although this "yeah-but" sometimes appears in slightly altered form ("Yeah, but our school district won't let us"; "Yeah, but our curriculum guides aren't set up that way"; "Yeah, but other teachers in my building don't teach that way"), the message is still the same. These "yeah-but" teachers, when asked how they know their principals won't let them, often don't have a definitive answer. In fact, in most cases they have not asked their principals about the possibility of implementing the practice in question.

For example, in Rita's first year of teaching, she didn't like using the spelling book she'd inherited from the previous fifth-grade teacher. However, since the books had been ordered and district funds had been sacrificed to pay for them, Rita felt compelled to use them. She reached that conclusion in spite of what she knew about the importance of offering contextualized instruction, providing authentic experiences, and integrating and connecting the different components of the language arts. She also reached that conclusion in spite of the spelling series' decontextualized "sneaky phonics" approach, which featured graphemic patterns (for example, *weigh, sleigh, way,* and *slay*) to the exclusion of meaningful connections. Eventually Rita summoned her courage and timidly inquired of her colleagues, "Why do we use these spelling books?" Her well-intentioned colleagues replied, "Because the principal says we have to."

Since she had been teaching for only a few months and consequently had not been completely inculcated into the politically correct mode of operation, rather than dropping the matter, Rita took it to the principal. Perhaps being young and naive has its virtues. Rita simply asked, "Do I have to use the spelling books?" The principal simply replied, "No." (He was a man of few words.) Being young and naive also has its drawbacks. In retrospect, Rita should have asked a second question: "May I use the money that would have been spent on spelling books to purchase trade books instead?" With that experience, Rita's schema for "live and learn"—otherwise known as "don't give up something without getting something in exchange"—was created.

Other "yeah-buts" you may encounter on the subject of creating and implementing integrative units include, "Yeah, but it takes a lot of time to design units, and we don't have enough time to eat lunch, let alone collaborate on units"; "Yeah, but you need lots of money to do that right, and we don't have lots of money"; "Yeah, but to do it right I'd need to collaborate with the other teachers in my building, and they aren't interested"; "Yeah, but parents won't understand or support curricular integration since they turned out fine without it"; and "Yeah, but I've taught thirty years without units, and I can teach another two years without them and then retire." Although we promise not to provide a story to go with each of these "yeah-buts," we list them here to demonstrate that change produces resistance to change. If you go looking for reasons not to implement an innovation, then that's what you'll find. However, it's also true that if you go looking for reasons why you *should* implement an innovation, then you're sure to find those, as well.

BENEFITS OF INTEGRATIVE UNITS

Concentrate for a moment on positive memories you have about learning new concepts, ideas, or processes in school. What do you remember most about being a kindergartner, a third grader, a sixth grader, or a junior in high school? Are the facts about photosynthesis paramount in your memory bank, or is it easier for you to remember the field trip to the botanical gardens that was organized as a culminating activity? Do you recall which day you learned what letter of the alphabet in kindergarten, or do you remember the day you created an erupting volcano at the science center (to help you remember the letter *V*, of course)?

To help you support your decision to use integrative units when speaking with colleagues, administrators, and parents, we now discuss some of the reasons why designing and implementing such units is important. Integrative units that are developed using themes or topics

1. Facilitate and stimulate natural and authentic learning experiences for students and teachers

2. Build on student interest
3. Provide a meaningful context for the development of curricular objectives across all grade and developmental levels
4. Facilitate curricular integration

For example, an integrative unit on money could provide many real-life applications. Do you remember a time when Grandma gave you a dime but gave your sibling two nickels? You threw a fit, right there in the middle of the candy aisle, because you thought Grandma had given your beloved sister or brother "more" money than you. Certainly a scenario such as this constitutes a real-life application of the concept of money and a situation students can relate to. That makes it real—authentic (Reason #1). Because it's real, it carries with it a naturally occurring, built-in motivation for learning. The situation gets your attention and holds your interest (Reason #2). Obviously, you'd rather not believe that Grandma loves your sibling more than she loves you. Surely, there must be another explanation for why she gave that brother or sister more money than she gave you. If you could comprehend the fact that one dime equals two nickels, you could then place it in a meaningful context (Reason #3) and apply it to that context. Of course, that would provide an acceptable explanation. Grandma loves you the same, because one dime is the same as two nickels. Armed with the awareness that the concept of money holds real-life significance for you, a clever and informed teacher could have used that hook as a launching pad for an instructional unit that integrated the curriculum via the concept of money (Reason #4).

A kindergarten teacher might decide to do an integrative unit on "neighborhood restaurants" (such as Pizza Hut, Burger King, or McDonald's). Why is it important for kindergartners to learn about the concept of money? Certainly, they should be exposed to how the market economy works and the way people use money to purchase things they need and want. A unit on neighborhood restaurants could provide authentic exposure to the concept of money right in the classroom, which could include a center designed as a Pizza Hut, complete with student-made menus, cash registers, money, pizzas, pitchers of soda, and red-checkered tablecloths. This would give students an opportunity to engage in social studies (dramatizing the role of the consumer and of restaurant workers), math (adding check totals, making change, and creating checkered tablecloths), language arts (writing and reading the menu, taking orders), and science (designing the cardboard box that serves as an entryway and the crate that functions as an oven).

A fourth-grade teacher might develop an integrative unit on community businesses and support students in their analyses of the supply-and-demand contrasts that exist among area businesses. For example, drought impacts the price of produce, and a work stoppage affects the supply of available new cars. Certainly, these analyses would involve an understanding and application of the concept of money. A middle-school or secondary teacher might ask students to create their own businesses and outline a one-year projection of income and expenses. Once again, a well-developed understanding of the concept of money, as well as economic forces, is critical to the classroom application of this unit.

PLANNING: PROCESS AND PRODUCT

We devoted the first half of this chapter to a fairly extensive discussion of the multifaceted task of connecting different parts of the curriculum and developing integrative units. However, we intentionally kept our focus on the goal or product of planning (the what) and the instructional benefits of creating connections between curricular components (the why). In the second half of this chapter we turn our attention to the different levels and processes of instructional planning (the how).

LEVELS OF INSTRUCTIONAL PLANNING

As you may recall from Chapter 3, planning is one of the four roles of leadership. Teachers engage in planning on a daily basis, and instructional planning constitutes a major portion of the planning teachers do. Although teachers tend to focus primarily on day-to-day instructional planning, there are actually three types of planning teachers need to address: long-range planning, mid-range planning, and short-range planning.

■ Long-Range Planning

Long-range planning is the most comprehensive type of instructional planning, as well as the type of planning that teachers are most likely to neglect. Long-range or yearly planning identifies the general curriculum content and its sequence, which typically are framed by district curriculum objectives. Teachers who engage in long-range planning generally include ordering and reserving instructional materials as part of the planning process, in addition to identifying the instructional scope, sequence, and annual learning goals (Glatthorn, 1993).

■ Mid-Range Planning

Mid-range planning includes term and unit planning. As you already know from the first half of this chapter, unit planning results in well-organized, sequenced, integrated learning experiences based on student interests, prior experiences, and instructional needs, as well as on established curricular goals. Term planning involves outlining the content and skills to be included in the next three months and creating a weekly schedule that supports the term's goals and priorities (Glatthorn, 1993).

■ Short-Range Planning

Short-range planning consists of weekly and daily lesson planning. Weekly planning includes developing and organizing the week's lesson plans within the framework of the established weekly schedule, whereas daily lesson planning involves organizing the learning environment and materials for the next day, making last-minute decisions, and adjusting the schedule to fit last-minute changes or special events such as picture day and assemblies (Glatthorn, 1993). For better or worse, teachers tend to focus the majority of the energy, attention, and time they devote to instructional planning on short-range planning.

THE INSTRUCTIONAL PLANNING PROCESS

Planning typically improves results for any activity. Instructional planning provides a sense of direction for both teachers and learners and lets students know about the learning tasks they're performing and become aware of the goals embedded within those tasks. For purposes of analyzing the instructional planning process, we'll discuss four key components of planning: purpose, structure, assessment, and alternatives.

■ Planning the Purpose of Instruction

Goals, objectives, or intended accomplishments constitute the purpose of instructional plans, and "the most effective plans begin with some conceptualization of intended learning outcomes" (Pellicer & Anderson, 1995, p. 79). However, we need to acknowledge that achieving certain educational goals or objectives is not always the impetus behind instructional planning. Teachers sometimes develop "survival plans," with the primary purpose of keeping students busy or in their seats and quiet. Some teachers also engage in activity-oriented instructional planning. Activity-oriented plans have no identified desired outcome. Nonetheless, teachers plan and implement activity-oriented instruction in the hope that students will learn something from it, recognizing that different students may learn different things from the same activity (Pellicer & Anderson, 1995).

■ Planning the Structure of Instruction

Planning the structure of instruction refers to selecting specific instructional activities and resources for a particular plan, as well as determining how the instruction will be sequenced. Examples of instructional activities include discussions, use of learning centers, simulations, and problem solving activities. Instructional resources include items such as computers, videos, overhead projectors, books, rulers, calculators, glue, and paper.

As you know, sequencing of instruction implies that certain concepts, skills, or activities must precede other concepts, skills, or activities. There are several approaches to sequencing. One is task analysis, which "requires identifying the prerequisite knowledge and skills that are needed by students to achieve a particular goal. Once these prerequisites have been identified, they are sequenced accordingly. The major assumption underlying task analysis is that knowledge and skills exist in some type of hierarchy and that learning occurs as students move from lower positions on the hierarchy to upper ones.

Thus, task analysis is based on a somewhat bottom-up approach to learning" (Pellicer & Anderson, 1995, p. 79).

Advance organizers are another sequencing tool. Because they provide context for the instruction that follows, they're particularly appropriate for instruction that focuses on concepts. Advance organizers are more general, abstract, and inclusive than the instructional concepts they precede. As such, they represent a top-down approach to sequencing. For example, you might choose to use the concept *land forms* as an advance organizer to introduce the concept of *plateaus*. *Land forms* is an appropriate choice as an advance organizer for *plateaus* because it is a more general concept that encompasses the narrower concept of *plateaus*.

Now, take a moment to consider how the principle of advance organizers relates to schema theory. Recall that schema theory holds that the way people learn and remember is directly affected by their prior experiences and that learning can be positively affected by creating connections between new learning and prior learning and experiences. Advance organizers are an attempt to help learners connect what they know to what they're about to learn. They help learners know what mental "file" to put the new information in, how to store it, and what prior experiences and previous learning to connect to it so they'll be better able to retrieve it when they need it.

Other approaches to sequencing emerge from the subject matter. For instance, chronological sequencing involves presenting material in an order that corresponds to the order in which certain events (such as historical events) occurred. Conceptual sequencing involves ordering based on relationships among a subject matter's concepts. For example, in mathematics, addition typically is taught before multiplication, since multiplication builds on the concept of addition and basically is a fancy form of addition. Science also uses conceptual sequencing (for example, classification), as does social studies (for example, neighborhood, city, state, country); (Pellicer & Anderson, 1995).

■ Planning Assessment and Evaluation

Assessment and evaluation make up another critical planning component. Process evaluation measures the degree to which instructional plans have been implemented successfully. Product evaluation measures the degree to which the purpose of those plans has been achieved. It requires data or evidence about or from students (Pellicer & Anderson, 1995). As you'll discover in Chapter 11, there are several assessment alternatives and formats teachers can implement to provide learners opportunities to show what they know and what they can do.

THREE PHASES OF INSTRUCTIONAL PLANNING AND DECISION MAKING

Teachers engage in instructional planning and decision making almost continually. They plan prior to instruction, while implementing instruction, and following instruction. These planning times sometimes are referred to as the preinstructional phase, the interactive phase, and the postinstructional phase. They entail the following (Arends, 1998):

- The **preinstructional planning phase** includes choosing content, choosing an instructional approach, allocating time and space, determining structures, and determining motivation.
- The **interactive planning phase** consists of presenting, questioning, assisting, providing for skills practice, making transitions, and guiding learners.
- The **postinstructional planning phase** involves checking for understanding, providing feedback, assessing and evaluating student performance, and communicating the learning outcomes to students and parents.

INSTRUCTIONAL TIME

If teachers are to plan effectively, they need to understand some important variables related to time and appreciate their implications for the planning process. For example, although the total amount of time learners typically spend in school is 180 days per year and six or seven hours per day, the amount of time learners actually attend school—called *attended time*—is less than this total time. Illness, snow days, dental appointments, truancy, and power failures reduce students' attendance time from the total time required by law. In addition to total time and attended time, the following types of time also have implications for teachers' instructional planning (Weinstein & Mignano, 1996):

- *Available time* refers to the time during the school day that is available for academic purposes. Attended time—when reduced by lunch, recess, fire drills, extracurricular activities, and other noninstructional events—constitutes available time.
- *Planned academic time* refers to the time set aside for different subjects and activities. For example, a third-grade teacher might schedule a ninety-minute language arts block, sixty minutes for learning centers, and fifteen minutes for free reading.
- *Actual academic time* consists of the time teachers actually spend on academic tasks or activities; it's also known as allocated time or opportunity to learn. A teacher may plan a thirty-minute skills lesson, but due to her students' late return from music she may be left with only twenty-five minutes for instruction.
- *Engaged time*, sometimes referred to as time on task, is the time learners actually spend on academic activities or tasks. Just because teachers are teaching doesn't guarantee that students are listening, participating, and engaging actively in the planned instructional activities.
- *Academic learning time* is the time learners spend engaged in academic tasks at which they're successful. Even when students are on task, that engaged time converts to academic learning time only when students' efforts result

in actual learning. Perhaps you can recall times when, as a learner, you worked very hard but had very little to show for your efforts. For example, you may have spent a great deal of time attempting to prove an algebraic theorem or write a convincing appeal for recycling without ever reaching your intended goal.

Academic learning time is the type of time that is most closely related to student learning and achievement. For that reason, it's the type of time teachers must have in mind as they engage in instructional planning.

AN INSTRUCTIONAL ASIDE: THE LESSON PLAN BOOK

By now you've no doubt noticed that we make a habit of revisiting previous concepts you've read about and connecting them to other concepts. Our attempts to help you make connections between what you know and what we're asking you to learn is an application of schema theory. Schema theory encourages teachers to build on learners' prior experiences and also reminds educators that the way learners store concepts affects their ability to retrieve those concepts.

For example, when engaged in the process of showing us what they know (while responding to essay questions), preservice teachers have on occasion approached us with their essay exams in hand, pointed a weary finger at a particular question, and demanded to know, "What list do you want here?" Such a question tells us more than we want to know about the way the askers have prepared—or not prepared—for the opportunity to show us what they know! Our experiences suggest that "crammers," in their panic to "learn" material for a test, resort to simply memorizing lists, without understanding the significance of the concepts contained in those lists (and almost certainly without seeing any connections between them). Because you're an aspiring teacher, we'd like very much for you to actually remember and apply what you learn from this book, as well as from the courses you take. Consequently, we'll persevere in our quest to highlight connections between what we hope you know and understand at this point and the new concepts we're inviting you to learn.

In Chapter 1 we asked you to resurrect recollections of your own school experiences. Those prior experiences, besides influencing your general views of the teaching/learning process, also color your ideas of what instructional planning means. Whether as an elementary or secondary student or as a preservice teacher observing in preK–12 classrooms, you likely have at least caught glimpses of "the lesson plan book." Do you remember what it looked like? Was it a collection of boxes with designated places for the teacher to identify the subjects the boxes relate to and/or specific days of the week? What was in those boxes? Page numbers? Activity descriptions? Although those lesson plan books you caught glimpses of may have been artifacts of the instructional planning process, they certainly are not synonymous with instructional planning. As the subtitle of this chapter, "Lesson Plans That Don't Fit in a Box," suggests, there is much more to effective instructional planning than identifying page numbers or math problems for students to complete.

FIVE QUESTIONS TO GUIDE INSTRUCTIONAL PLANNING

In Chapter 2 we introduced you to the notion of professional development plans (PDPs). In addition to encouraging you to use PDPs throughout your professional lives, we suggested five simple questions to use in formulating them. We think so highly of those five questions and their simplicity that we use slightly altered versions of them to guide our instructional planning. When preservice teachers ask us what particular lesson plan format we want them to use, our response is that we don't care what format they use, as long as their lesson plans answer these questions, which we have outlined here.

WHAT AM I GOING TO DO?

Instructional goals, objectives, performance statements, and other expressions of intended student outcomes all are responses to the question, "What am I going to do?" Whereas Chapter 8, with its focus on developing and designing curricula, focused on goals, here the focus is on objectives. What's the difference between goals and objectives? What's the similarity? What's the connection or the relationship between the two? Which is the larger concept? The following paragraphs address these questions.

■ Goals

Goals are the "big ideas" of education. When educators discuss the purpose of schools, they are talking about the goals of education, such as "To produce contributing members of society" or "To develop each student's full potential." When teachers describe long-term learning outcomes ("I want my students to be lifelong learners" or "I want my students to read for enjoyment"), they are likewise referring to goals. General instructional goals describe intended outcomes for specific disciplines or domains, such as literature appreciation or mathematical proficiency; they identify the desired ultimate student performance. By contrast, when teachers identify more immediate desired learning outcomes and state them in terms of measurable student behaviors, they are formulating objectives.

■ Instructional Objectives

Instructional objectives are statements that describe teachers' intentions for students' growth and change. Like road maps, they help teachers and learners know where they're going and when they've arrived at their destination. And like road maps, some instructional objectives are simple, whereas others are complex.

Teachers clarify their instructional goals by defining specific learning outcomes, or objectives, related to them. These outcomes describe the skills or performance learners exhibit once they've achieved the goals. Consequently, instructional objectives should be relevant to the goals they support and representative of the tasks and performances related to them.

A student performance is any measurable student response that is a result of learning (Gronlund, 1995). Instructional objectives describe particular student performances (for example, composing a business letter that includes a heading, an inside address, a greeting, a body, a closing, and a signature). However, there is a striking lack of consensus regarding exactly what components instructional objectives should include beyond such performances. Different theorists advocate different standards regarding the development of instructional objectives. For example, Mager (1984b) would include conditions and criterion levels (see following discussion) as well as observable learner behaviors, whereas Gronlund (1995) would identify only expected performances.

Instructional goals and objectives provide both direction for instruction and guidelines for assessment. They also communicate the instructional intent and focus to learners, parents, other teachers, and administrators. Instructional objectives assist instructional planning efforts by guiding the selection of methods, materials, and appropriate assessment procedures. Well-written, specific objectives can play a key role in assessment by clearly describing the types of student performance that are anticipated (Gronlund, 1995). In portfolio assessment, instructional objectives guide learners' decisions concerning what to include in their portfolios. Objectives also help teachers determine what items to include on observational instruments, rating scales, checklists, and matrices.

■ Mager's Theory of Instructional Objectives

According to Mager, an "objective is a description of a performance you want learners to be able to exhibit before you consider them competent. An objective describes an intended result of instruction, rather than the process of instruction itself" (1984b, p. 3). For Mager, usefully stated objectives successfully communicate intended instructional results to the readers and include the following three components:

- *Performance, or students' observable behavior.* What are learners expected to be able to do? Some performances are directly observable (overt), whereas others cannot be observed directly (covert). When performance is covert, Mager suggests adding an indicator behavior to the objective. For example, "identify" is a covert performance. Perhaps learners are to identify correct responses by underlining or circling them. Those are the indicator behaviors.

- *Conditions, or testing situation.* Under what conditions should learners be able to perform the intended outcome or result?

- *Criteria for acceptable performance.* How well must learners perform the intended outcome or result? Mager (1984b, p. 96) asserts that for a performance criterion to be useful, it should "(1) [say] something about the quality of performance you desire, (2) [say] something about the quality of the individual performance rather than the group performance, and (3) [say] something about a real, rather than an imaginary, standard."

Mager combined these three components into an instructional objective regarding teachers' understanding and application of objectives: "Given any objective in a subject area with which you are familiar, in all instances be able to identify (label) correctly the PERFORMANCE, the CONDITIONS, and the CRITERION of acceptable performance when any or all those characteristics are present" (1984b, p. 3).

■ Gronlund's Theory of Instructional Objectives

Mager's critics argue that his format, when used exclusively, leads to overemphasis on the prespecification of learner outcomes, reductionism, and neglect of many of the most important goals of education. They contend that both learners and teachers must see the big picture rather than just isolated specific objectives. Critics also suggest that many of the more complex cognitive processes aren't readily observable, so they might be neglected because they are not easy to measure (Gronlund, 1995; Wiley, 1990–1991). Other theorists favor writing objectives in more general terms and then adding specifics later (Gronlund, 1995).

Gronlund (1995) cautions against developing objectives that are too narrow or too broad and suggests that conditions and standards shouldn't be included in objectives for purposes of regular classroom instruction, although they may be helpful for programmed instruction and mastery testing. Gronlund contends that including conditions and standards results in long, cumbersome lists that restrict teachers' freedom. He recommends that teachers consider conditions and standards at the time student performance is assessed. Gronlund also points out that the standard may change from the beginning of a unit of study to the end. Consequently, he is among those who advocate a two-step process of stating the general instructional objectives and then further defining them with specific learning outcomes.

■ Domains and Objectives

Psychomotor (physical) objectives often are the easiest to write, because learners' performance is easily observed in this area (for example, word processing, handwriting, performing sit-ups). Objectives that feature the lower levels of the cognitive domain (information recall) are also fairly easy to write. In fact, because low-level cognitive objectives typically are the easiest to write, they tend to be overemphasized. However, complex cognitive objectives (such as problem solving) shouldn't be omitted just because they're not directly observable and consequently are difficult to define in terms of specific outcomes.

Most teachers find affective objectives (attitudes, feelings, dispositions) the most difficult to write, because of the vagueness of the terminology, the numerous ways affective outcomes can be classified, the need to account for covert behavior, and the fact that more complex affective outcomes are closely integrated with other behaviors and therefore are difficult to isolate and state in specific terms (Gronlund, 1995). When attempting to write affective objectives in terms of overt behaviors, teachers must be careful not to neglect inner, unobservable feelings. Although teachers should use precise terminology when defining affective objectives, they shouldn't ignore important outcomes because they're difficult to define in precise terms.

■ Objectives and Constructivism

By stating that lesson plans should answer the question "What am I going to do?" we're proposing that you need to have a clear idea of where you're going before you begin. You also need to be able to articulate to students, parents, principals, and other stakeholders in the teaching/learning process where you're going. Why do we think that's so important? After all, some might suggest that identifying a desired student outcome runs counter to the constructivist notion of allowing students to construct or build their own learning in their own ways.

Regarding the juxtaposition of objectives and constructivism, quite simply, we don't see a conflict. Both teachers and students can benefit from moderate doses of guidance and structure in the teaching/learning process. Both can benefit from knowing and understanding where they're headed. In fact, specific, intentional, identified outcomes are often desirable. Just as when playing a game it's helpful for the participants to know and understand the "aim of the game," in structuring learning experiences, it's helpful for the participants to know and understand that there is a point to what they're doing.

Letting students in on such secrets also helps them see the big picture, as they learn to put the different pieces of learning together to create an integrated whole. Perhaps you've noticed that in formal education, particularly at the secondary level, educators do a very good job of dividing the curriculum into subject chunks (for example, twentieth century American literature, world history, chemistry), but they're not nearly so devoted to helping students put those isolated chunks back together in ways that are meaningful to them. Recall from our discussion of integrative curricula that this issue serves as a compelling rationale for theme-based instructional units designed to integrate curricular areas.

One final point with regard to constructivism and objectives: just because teachers identify learning outcomes doesn't mean that they will prescribe how each and every student must arrive at those outcomes. In fact, acknowledging and providing for differences in students' learning styles, prior experiences, and learning needs constitutes yet another reason to clearly communicate intended learning outcomes to students. In effect, teachers are saying to students, "Here's the direction we're headed, and here's where we all need to end up, but there are lots of different ways you can get there." Yes, learning can simultaneously be constructivist and goal-directed.

■ Developing Objectives: A Think-Aloud

Well-written objectives also can make assessing student learning less difficult. Here's where our friendly acronym SAM can be of assistance. When developing and critiquing objectives, we focus on three main attributes: *specificity, attainability,* and *measurability.* Specific objectives identify observable student behaviors and make it possible for teachers to assess whether students have, in fact, met those objectives. They also describe what learners *will* do, as opposed to what they *won't* do ("Listen" as opposed to "Don't talk"). Attainable objectives set students up for success, by identifying learning outcomes that are logical next steps in the learning process. They're also appropriate to the developmental levels of students. Measurable objectives identify criterion levels or acceptable levels of performance. They tell both teachers and students what constitutes a "good" performance.

To find perfect nonexamples of specific, attainable, and measurable objectives, you need look no further than the New Year's resolutions people make and break on an annual basis. Consider these classics: exercise more, study more, spend less money, watch less television.

Besides the fact that they often feature the words *less* and *more,* what do you notice about these resolutions? Comparing them against the SAM standards, how do they fare? Are they specific? Of course not! If they were, somebody might try to hold you to them. Are they attainable? We can't really tell, because they're so vague. Are they measurable? No, because they don't identify acceptable levels of performance. For example, with the resolution "Eat less," if you're accustomed to consuming eight pizzas a day, and you cut back to seven, have you met your objective? Is a reduction of one pizza good enough?

You'll note that many of the resolutions identify what you're *not* going to do, as opposed to what you're going to do, in contrast to effective objectives, which are positively stated. Objectives also focus on and build on learners' strengths. Instead of operating from a deficit model of education (that is, habitually identifying learners' weaknesses), teachers need to identify what learners can do—what they do know—and use those as starting points. Teachers can't add to or build on something that doesn't exist, and neither can learners.

Looking back at the New Year's resolutions, how could you transform them from weak, ambiguous, ill-defined objectives to specific, attainable, measurable objectives? Let's begin with the ever-popular "Exercise more." At least it's positively stated. It also identifies only one task or concept, which is important. Including more than one task or concept per objective can cause confusion when it comes to assessing outcomes. For example, if in one objective you state that students will divide words into syllables and circle syllables that contain long vowel sounds, you're asking for two completely different behaviors that involve two completely different concepts. It's entirely possible that students may be able to divide words into syllables but be unable to identify those syllables that have long vowel sounds. What you actually have are two objectives, so it's best to write them as such.

So you've decided that "Exercise more" is positively stated and identifies only one behavior or concept. Those are two points in its favor, but that's all the points it earns. Obviously it's not specific and it's not measurable, and because it's so vague, you have no way of determining if it's attainable. So how do you improve it? First of all, you decide what you mean by "exercise." Do you mean some form of aerobic or cardiovascular exercise? Sit-ups, maybe? Golfing? What? Since research strongly supports the benefits of aerobic exercise, we'll identify that as the type of exercise.

Now, what about a performance criterion? That is, how will you know you've met your objective? If you simply state that you will engage in aerobic exercise, how will you know you've accomplished your objective? (For example, if you jog around the block once a month, will you have met the objective?) Making the statement more specific helps define the performance criterion: "Three times a week, for at least thirty minutes each time, I will engage in aerobic exercise." Now, how can you make the term *aerobic exercise* more specific? You can do that by adding conditions, such as "Three times a week, for at least thirty minutes each time, I will engage in aerobic exercise that is compatible with my spaghetti knee." Now you know that the aerobic exercise might include swimming, biking, or walking, but it definitely will not include running, racquetball, or tennis.

You've now developed an objective that meets the SAM criteria—that is, it's specific, it's attainable, and it's measurable. It's specific because it identifies the conditions (compatible with my spaghetti knee) under which the behavior can be performed. It's attainable because the criterion level (three times a week for at least thirty minutes each time) identified is reasonable. It's measurable because the specific behavior (aerobic exercise) identified is observable, and in order to measure something you must first be able to see or hear evidence of it.

■ Selecting Verbs Appropriate for Objectives

If that seemed like a lot of work, it's only because it *is* a lot of work. In our opinion, writing effective objectives is one of the most challenging parts of instructional planning, just as identifying observable behaviors is one of the most challenging parts of writing objectives. In fact, the key to writing specific objectives is verb selection. Although people often think that adjectives are the most descriptive parts of speech, it's verbs that either propel writing forward or drag it into a passive state. So the next time you're writing poetry, concentrate on verbs that agitate, emote, and paint pictures. And the next time you're writing objectives, concentrate on verbs that describe, specify, and lead to documentation of learners' performance.

■ Selecting Verbs Appropriate for Expressing Performance Outcomes

Finally, objectives that clearly specify observable behaviors, criterion levels, and conditions give teachers a huge head start in their attempts to answer the question "How did I get the job done?" This is true because their responses to that question involve identifying procedures for assessing the degree to which students met the stated objective and are therefore directly connected to their responses to the question "What am I going to do?" Figure 10.8 lists verbs that are appropriate for expressing a variety of different performance outcomes. Later in this chapter you'll read more about responding to the question "How did I get the job done?"

WHY AM I GOING TO DO IT?

As many of our former students will testify, we repeatedly and emphatically remind all our students to always know why they're doing what they're doing. Then we go on to emphasize the importance of being able to clearly articulate the rationales for one's instructional decisions to students, parents, and administrators. However, the second question of instructional planning—"Why am I going to do it?"— often goes unanswered, even by teachers who dutifully

Figure 10.8 Verbs Appropriate for Various Performance Outcomes

Creative Behavior				
STUDENTS WILL	generalize	rearrange	restate	simplify	reorder
	rewrite	rename	modify	reconstruct	retell
	synthesize	predict	revise		

Complex Logical/Judgmental				
STUDENTS WILL	analyze	contrast	substitute	structure	discover
	define	assess	criticize	evaluate	suggest
	conclude	induce	combine	reduce	generate
	plan	compare			

General Discriminative Behavior				
STUDENTS WILL	choose	detect	distinguish	pick	omit
	separate	select	differentiate	identify	isolate
	order	point	describe	discriminate	indicate
	list	match	place		

Mathematical Behavior				
STUDENTS WILL	add	count	compute	reduce	circumscribe
	check	calculate	tabulate	verify	solve
	derive	subtract	divide		

Lab Science Behavior				
STUDENTS WILL	estimate	infer	observe	manipulate	organize
	react	graph	calibrate	demonstrate	operate
	report	record	extrapolate	conduct	formulate
	classify	weigh	measure	balance	increase
	itemize	predict			

construct SAM objectives that include observable student behaviors, criterion levels, and conditions. Unfortunately, neglecting to respond to the question "Why am I going to do it?" can result in specific, attainable, measurable, but meaningless objectives.

For example, consider this objective: "Following a unit of study on Iowa history, students will write the names of all ninety-nine counties in Iowa, with correct spellings."

What's the observable behavior?—Writing the names of Iowa counties.

What's the criterion level?—All ninety-nine counties correctly spelled.

What's the condition?—Following a unit of study on Iowa history.

What's the point?—We don't know!

Reflecting on possible, defensible rationales, the best we can do is to speculate that knowing the names and spellings of all ninety-nine Iowa counties is

Figure 10.8 Verbs Appropriate for Various Performance Outcomes *(cont.)*

Social Behavior STUDENTS WILL	*accept* *allow* *answer* *argue*	*discuss* *disagree* *cooperate* *compliment*	*participate* *laugh* *join* *invite*	*volunteer* *permit* *praise* *reply*	*interact* *contribute* *communicate*
Language Behavior STUDENTS WILL	*abbreviate* *alphabetize* *articulate* *capitalize*	*indent* *outline* *print* *pronounce*	*punctuate* *read* *recite* *speak*	*spell* *state* *summarize* *syllabicate*	*translate* *verbalize* *write*
Study Behavior STUDENTS WILL	*arrange* *itemize* *underline*	*compile* *categorize* *note*	*label* *diagram* *record*	*locate* *cite* *search*	*classify* *organize*
Physical Behavior STUDENTS WILL	*march* *knock* *skate* *float*	*catch* *chase* *lift*	*hit* *swing* *pitch*	*climb* *toss* *swim*	*jump* *throw* *stretch*
Arts Behavior STUDENTS WILL	*assemble* *brush* *build* *form*	*handle* *heat* *construct* *paint*	*color* *melt* *illustrate* *carve*	*stir* *trace* *varnish*	*saw* *polish* *trim*

(Reprinted with permission of Calvin K. Claus)

part of that canon of what "every culturally literate Iowan should know." However, because we don't buy that as a defensible answer to the question "Why am I going to do it?" we might propose this as an alternative objective: "Following a unit of study on Iowa history, students will identify that Iowa has ninety-nine counties and will state three implications that fact has for the structure and organization of county government in the state of Iowa." With that alteration, rather than just listing isolated facts, students will be encouraged to take one fact (that Iowa has ninety-nine counties) and relate it to the whole picture of Iowa's governmental structure. In other words, the modified objective asks students to place the single fact in a larger context.

So, it's necessary to have a defensible rationale. It's also imperative for teachers to clearly articulate their rationale to students, parents, principals, colleagues, and other constituencies who have the right to demand a reasoned response to the question "Why am I going to do it?" If teachers find they can't clearly articulate their reasons for a particular objective, student activity, or unit of study, then they need to revisit the simple, but important, question "Why am I doing this?" If honest answers to this question result in responses such as "Because I don't know what else to do," "Because I've always done it this way," or "Because this is what the textbook says to do next," then teachers have abdicated their role as decision makers for that of "assistants to materials" (Durkin, 1989).

Sometimes in their attempts to respond to the question "Why am I going to do it?" teachers say enthusiastically, "Because it's fun!" Even though *fun* is one of our favorite words, in terms of instructional planning, it needs to be paired with the word *functional*. Instructional time is a limited resource. Consequently, teachers need to ensure that the instructional activities they plan serve dual purposes. Whether learners are cooking, dissecting, going on field trips, or creating string art, there must first and foremost be a defensible, instructional purpose behind it. Or as Bruner stated it, "The first object of any act of learning . . . is that it should serve us in the future" (1960, p. 17).

WHAT DO I NEED TO DO IT?

Materials that support instruction take many forms. Technology has added breadth and choice to the array of possibilities available for supporting and enhancing the teaching/learning process. So, what do you need to do it? If your plans call for estimating and then measuring the amount of snow it takes to equal one inch of rainfall, what materials will your students and you need to do this? If you want your students to plan a trip from New York City to Los Angeles, what resources are available to help them succeed at this task? In fact, doesn't this task involve many subtasks?

Who can help you locate and provide the resources your students and you will need? What role can your school's librarian or media specialist play in helping you locate appropriate materials to support your instruction? Can you identify parents or students who possess expertise or resources that will enhance the teaching/learning process? How can you connect with other teachers and students who are involved in similar projects or activities (for example, via the World Wide Web, computer programs, peer tutoring, collaborative or team planning, mentors, resource teachers, or reading buddies)? What related children's literature, both expository and narrative, is available to use for curricular integration?

Taking the time to answer these questions, as well as the question "What do I need to do it?" can account for the difference between haphazard, fly-by-the-seat-of-your-pants teaching and teaching that is characterized by efficiency and organization. Spontaneity is great when used in moderation, but as a rule it is always preferable to have a plan.

HOW AM I GOING TO DO IT?

The first words that came out of the student teacher's mouth immediately after being observed by her university supervisor were, "I know, I know—I should have given them the pencils *after* I explained the directions!" Yes, sequencing is important in relation to teachers' answers to the question "How am I going to do it?" Sometimes teachers make the mistake of assuming that their students can read their minds. Other times they forget that, even though they've been doing something or thinking about a concept for many years, for their students it's the very first time. Consequently, it's imperative that teachers have in mind a clearly defined procedure or task analysis before initiating an activity.

■ Procedures, Sequencing, and Task Analysis

After a few attempts at planning instruction, you'll likely conclude that different types of instructional activities and different subject areas require you to think about instructional procedures in different ways. Whereas learning certain types of content generally does not require one particular sequence of instruction, learning other types (especially procedural knowledge) generally does require an identifiable sequence of instruction. For example, it's fairly inconsequential whether students learn states and capitals in fourth grade or fifth grade. However, there is a preferred sequence in teaching certain mathematical skills and concepts, such as understanding addition before turning to multiplication.

Speaking of skills, try taking a simple skill or task and analyzing it. Tying shoes is simple, right? In ten steps or less, identify the procedures for tying shoes. First of all, what's the operational starting point? Does the task begin with finding your shoes? Does the task begin with putting your shoes on the right feet? Does the task begin with lacing your shoes? Or is it simpler to avoid the issue and buy shoes with Velcro fasteners? For the sake of discussion, let's say you begin with your left shoe on your left foot and your right shoe on your right foot—laces intact. Now that you've identified the operational starting point, what do you do? Do you make an X and then make one bunny ear? Or do you cross one lace over the other lace and make two bunny ears? What if you're left-handed? What if you're a visual learner instead of an auditory or kinesthetic learner? Does that change the sequence at all? Obviously, it's easier to wear sandals or go barefoot rather than complete a task analysis for tying your shoes, but approaching life that way isn't going to get you through the big interview!

Hopefully you're getting the idea that analyzing learning tasks and planning instructional sequences require careful thought and preparation. As we emphasized earlier in this book, alternatives or contingency plans are an essential component of instructional planning. Teachers need to constantly ask "What if?" Engaging in if-then thinking enables them to anticipate potential problems and provide plausible alternatives. Failing to prepare Plan B, Plan C, and Plan D for that inevitable time when Plan A doesn't work results in teachers' resorting to the "louder and slower" approach. Just because students don't "get it" doesn't mean they've failed. Perhaps, instead, when students don't "get it," teachers have failed to accommodate the many learning styles represented in their classroom.

We're not saying that teachers need to script every line they are going to utter throughout the day. In fact, for the most part we find that procedures written in paragraph format are difficult to follow. However, we are saying that careful preparation can lead to increases in teachers' self-confidence and clarity of thought, and this in turn can lead to students acquiring the concepts and skills articulated in instructional objectives.

■ Planning for Closure

Time constraints may cause teachers to neglect an essential instructional task—summarizing the lesson. This step, known as providing closure, provides teachers with an opportunity to connect current learning to past learning and to prepare students for future learning (Pellicer & Anderson, 1995). Due to the importance of creating connections between what students know and what they're being asked to learn, when some part of instruction must be omitted due to time constraints or other reasons, teachers should omit content or practice but never delete closure.

HOW WILL I KNOW I'VE DONE IT?

As stated earlier, objectives that specify observable student behaviors, criterion levels, and conditions make it easier for teachers to formulate appropriate responses to the question "How will I know I've done it?" Teachers who succeed at designing and implementing effective learning opportunities understand the important link between specific objectives and assessment procedures. Consequently, they create assessment opportunities that emerge from clearly stated objectives.

■ Specific Objectives and Assessment

For example, for the objective "Using a Venn diagram, students will identify five similarities and five differences between their own housing needs and the housing needs of Australian Aborigines," assessment of student outcomes would simply involve determining whether students had included five similarities and five differences on their diagrams. If their diagrams meet these criteria, then students have met the stated objective, and you as a teacher have succeeded at "getting the job done." If some students identify only one similarity or difference, then they have only partially met the objective, and you as a teacher have had only limited success "getting the job done." Consequently, many times assessment is a matter of ascertaining to what degree students have met stated objectives.

■ Assessment Criteria

Clearly defining performance objectives makes assessment procedures more obvious, clearer, and easier to develop. Teachers can convert lists of specific learning outcomes to checklists or rating scales. When objectives focus on a product, teachers can identify the predetermined characteristics that define a satisfactory product. For example, if the task is to write a business letter, a teacher might specify the following performance criteria:

■ Letter contains standard business letter elements, including heading, inside address, greeting, body, closing, and signature.

- Letter follows standard business letter format, including alignment of all elements on left margin, colon following greeting, and appropriate spacing and margins.

- The student expresses ideas clearly; writes well-structured, relevant paragraphs; employs standard English usage and spelling; and uses correct punctuation and capitalization.

■ Matching Assessment Procedures to Objectives

Certainly there are many ways to assess student learning, but teachers need to search for the most appropriate matches between assessment strategies and the stated instructional objectives. For example, if the instructional objectives describe originality and creativity as desired outcomes for students' writing, then the assessment strategies teachers use must complement those objectives. That may sound obvious, but what sometimes happens is that teachers assess what is easy to assess (such as spelling, handwriting, and subject-verb agreement) rather than variables that are "fuzzier" (such as character development, plot structures, compelling descriptions). Assessment, like listening, is something all teachers do but few do well. In Chapter 11 we focus on assessment and evaluation as processes critical to informing instructional decision making.

SELF-ASSESSMENT AND REFLECTION

A second important facet of responding to the question "How will I know I've done it?" involves self-assessment and reflection on the teacher's part. Here, appropriate follow-up questions include "What went well? What do I need to do differently next time? What, if anything, do I need to reteach?" and "What, if anything, do I hope never to do again?" Other questions teachers can use to guide their assessments of their instructional plans include the following (Pellicer & Anderson, 1995, p. 84):

1. Is the purpose or goal of the lesson or unit made clear?
2. Are the activities likely to engage students in the process of learning? (That is, are they likely to be excited about the activities or bored to tears by them?)
3. Are the activities likely to lead students to attain the lesson or unit purpose or goals?
4. Are the needed materials and other instructional resources (such as computer software and videotapes) available and accessible?
5. Is an amount of time to be devoted to the lesson or unit specified? If so, does it seem reasonable?
6. Does the plan specify a way to gauge and/or monitor purpose/goal attainment?
7. Does the plan include provisions for providing students who are initially not attaining the purpose or goal opportunities to do so? If so, do these provisions seem reasonable?

Self-assessment and reflection are activities in which students can engage as well. If teachers wish students to assume responsibility for their own learning, then teachers need to build in opportunities for students to learn to evaluate their own work and identify logical next steps in their individual learning processes.

YEAH, BUT REAL TEACHERS DON'T PLAN THAT WAY!

Because we teach preservice teachers, we know you're probably developing your list of "yeah-buts." Chief among those "yeah-buts" is the often-heard lamentation of the novice teacher, "Yeah, but real teachers don't plan that way!" We offer as a more accurate statement, "Yeah, but *experienced* teachers don't plan that way!" Here again, we refer to what we know about schema theory to explain the differences that exist between the way novice teachers plan and the way experienced teachers plan. If you've never helped third graders develop Venn diagrams, then you have no prior experience from which to draw in providing that particular support to those particular learners. Consequently, we would advocate that you rely on a higher degree of structure and planning for that process than would a veteran teacher who has successfully helped fifteen years' worth of third graders create Venn diagrams.

DIFFERENT APPROACHES TO THE INSTRUCTIONAL PLANNING PROCESS

If you fail to find this reasoning concerning instructional planning compelling, then we refer you to research that indicates that experienced teachers use a cyclical or nonlinear approach to planning, whereas novice teachers utilize a linear approach (Arends, 1998; Glatthorn, 1993).

THE RATIONAL-LINEAR INSTRUCTIONAL PLANNING MODEL

The **rational-linear instructional planning model** is the dominant perspective on instructional planning. It emphasizes defining goals and objectives as the first step in a sequential planning process. Once teachers have identified instructional goals and formulated specific objectives relating to those goals, they then plan actions (instructional activities) to satisfy those objectives. Lastly, they specify the learning outcomes that will result from the actions they've planned. Consequently, the rational-linear instructional planning model can be represented as follows:

$$\text{Goals} \rightarrow \text{Actions} \rightarrow \text{Outcomes}$$

THE NONLINEAR INSTRUCTIONAL PLANNING MODEL

Teachers who use the **nonlinear instructional planning model** begin the planning process by developing instructional activities. Then they connect those activities to the outcomes they will produce. Finally, they identify the goals to which the outcomes relate. The nonlinear approach has been described as the "ready-fire-aim" approach, in contrast to the more traditional (linear) "ready-aim-fire" approach (Fullan, 1991). Consequently, the nonlinear instructional planning model can be represented as follows:

$$\text{Actions} \rightarrow \text{Outcomes} \rightarrow \text{Goals}$$

COMPARING NOVICE TEACHERS' AND EXPERIENCED TEACHERS' PLANNING

Experienced teachers, in their planning processes, tend to focus on content and specific instructional activities rather than on objectives. Novice teachers often find it difficult to learn planning skills from experienced teachers, because of the following reasons: experienced teachers think differently about planning than novice teachers do, much of the planning process is not directly observable, experienced teachers can't accurately describe their thinking and instructional decision making in ways that novice teachers can understand, and experienced teachers approach planning and instructional decision making from a vantage point informed by years of prior experience.

PRESERVICE TEACHERS' REFLECTIONS ON INSTRUCTIONAL PLANNING

We asked two preservice teachers to reflect on the process of planning integrative units. Both created units for intermediate-level students. However, Emily collaborated with another preservice teacher to develop an integrative unit early in her preservice preparation, whereas Tina developed and taught her unit as part of her novice teaching experience. The particular lessons they focused their reflections on (see the New Teachers Talk feature that begins on page 380) both contain a preassessment component. However, Emily's lesson features preassessment of learners' content knowledge, whereas Tina's lesson features preassessment of learners' skill levels. Figure 10.9 profiles Emily's lesson plan, and Figure 10.10 profiles Tina's lesson plan.

TEACHER PLANNING RECOMMENDATIONS

By way of summarizing our discussion of instructional planning and the processes it entails, we share the following recommendations:

1. *All teachers should plan.* Unless teachers can visualize instructional possibilities, they're unlikely to achieve meaningful goals. Also, instructional planning transforms curricula into instruction. This notion is particularly important when curricula are new—or new to the teachers who must implement them. In the process of planning, teachers learn the subject matter better themselves; prepare or acquire necessary instructional materials; and make decisions regarding the content, pace, sequence, clarity, and completeness of the curricular materials they are expected to use (Pellicer & Anderson, 1995).

    Yes, planning takes time. When teachers feel that they're too busy to plan and that they're paid only to teach, they typically spend most of their

Figure 10.9
Emily's Lesson Plan

A Walk Through the Rain Forest

Objectives

1. After researching one feature of rain forests, student pairs will synthesize the results of their research in a format that includes both print and visuals and that allows them to share their findings with other class members.

2. After completing their research projects, student pairs will share their findings with their classmates in a five-minute presentation that convincingly explains to their audience why the feature they profiled is an important component of rain forests.

Rationale

This lesson provides an opportunity for students to learn in-depth about particular rain forest species and resources and the importance of those species and resources. The lesson also creates the need for students to learn and apply research skills.

Materials

- KWL Chart (Form #1)
- Book: *A Walk Through the Rainforest;* other books and reference materials related to the rain forest
- Paper
- Supplies for creating visuals (markers, poster board, computer hardware and software, digital camera, video camera and recorder)

Procedures

We will begin the lesson with a KWL chart, which will be used throughout the duration of the unit. Ask the students what they *know* about rain forests and what they *want* to know about rain forests. The last column will be saved for what students *learned* from the unit study [see Form #1 on page 376]. At the beginning of each class period, the teacher will conduct a review of what has been learned so far, using questions to elicit this information from the students. At the end of each class, we will summarize what we learned that day.

Day 1

1:00–1:15: Begin KWL chart. Using their own individual KWL charts, students list what they already *know* about rain forests and what they *want* to know about rain forests. On large group KWL chart, teacher summarizes what the class as a whole already *knows* about rain forests and what they *want* to know about rain forests.

1:15–1:40: Invite students to the carpet area, where they sit in a semicircle on the floor. Introduce the book *A Walk Through the Rainforest.* Ask the students to make predictions about the book's contents. Record their predictions on chart paper for future reference. Then provide students with a purpose for listening: "Listen carefully as I read the book to see how many of our predictions are accurate." The teacher then reads the book aloud, pausing to emphasize main points and invite students' reflections and responses. After reading the book, the teacher asks students to review their predictions and compare them against the book's actual contents.

Figure 10.9
Emily's Lesson Plan *(cont.)*

1:40–2:00: Teacher distributes handouts, which describe the rain forest research activity [see Form #2 on page 376]. Together the class discusses the activity and clarifies the expectations, both regarding the process and the product. After student pairs are determined by random assignment, the pairs brainstorm possible research topics. They consult the resource materials provided as needed. After brainstorming possibilities, student pairs then narrow their possibilities to three or four research topics.

Day 2

1:00–1:10: The teacher leads a discussion regarding what students learned from the book they read together the day before (*A Walk Through the Rainforest*). This information is added to the *learned* column of their KWL charts.

1:10–1:20: Student pairs share with the class their short lists of possible research topics. With the teacher's guidance, the class as a whole collaboratively determines which topic each student pair will research. The main criterion that guides this selection process is diversity of choices.

1:20–1:50: After reviewing the project and process expectations and clarifying any questions, students go to the library to research their topics, using microfiche, consulting journals, checking out reference materials, and so on.

1:50–2:00: After students return to the room, they again add new information to the *learned* column of their KWL charts.

Day 3

1:00–1:15: Begin by conducting a review of what students have learned so far about rain forests. Ask students to share brief updates of their research progress and to identify next steps.

1:15–1:50: Student pairs continue their research, using reference materials and the Internet. The teacher floats from pair to pair to check progress and answer questions.

1:50–2:00: Review what students learned through their research and add main points to KWL charts.

Day 4 and Day 5

Similar to Day 3. By Day 5, all student pairs should be finished with their research and should be working on the format of their presentations.

Day 6

Final in-class opportunity to work on rain forest presentations. Outline with students expectations for their research presentations.

Day 7 and Day 8

Student pairs share research findings.

Day 9

Final review of research findings. Students make final additions to KWL charts, which the teacher collects.

Figure 10.9
Emily's Lesson Plan *(cont.)*

Assessment and Evaluation

Assessment will be based on the lesson's objectives. The KWL charts will serve as a primary assessment tool. The charts will be used for preassessment, formative assessment, and summative assessment. The teacher and students will compare what the students already knew and wanted to know to what they actually learned. The research presentations also will be evaluated. They should focus on the selected rain forest features, clearly describe and illustrate those features, and explain the contributions those features make to the rain forest.

Revision

The teacher will make anecdotal notes about students' progress, in order to modify instructional plans appropriately and revise the time line if necessary. In addition, at the end of each day, journal writing will relate to rain forest topics. The students' writing also may provide information regarding what instructional modifications need to be made.

**FORM #1
RAIN FOREST KWL CHART**

WHAT I **KNOW**	WHAT I **WANT** TO KNOW	WHAT I **LEARNED**

**FORM #2
PROJECT RAIN FOREST**

After brainstorming possible rain forest topics, your partner and you will offer three or four possible topics to the class for their input. Collaboratively, one rain forest topic for every student pair will be selected. Working together, your partner and you will research your rain forest feature and develop an appropriate format in which to present your research findings. Your presentation should meet the following criteria:

1. Clearly identify, describe, and illustrate your rain forest feature.

2. Identify the layer of the rain forest where your feature can be found.

3. Persuasively explain why your feature is an important part of the rain forest. What contribution does it make?

4. Explain why you included this feature on your short list of rain forest features you wanted to know more about.

5. Combine print and visuals to create a five-minute presentation of your research findings.

6. Use a variety of sources in your research and at least five different sources.

**Figure 10.10
Tina's Lesson
Plan**

Preassessment: Ability to Work Successfully in Small Groups

Objective
Working in groups of five or six, students will construct ID badges following a specific set of directions.

Rationale
This lesson will give me the opportunity to identify any potential difficulties students may have when working together in groups and/or following a specific set of instructions.

Materials
Yarn
Index cards
Markers
Overhead transparencies: "Rules for Working in Groups," "Group Roles"
Envelopes
Paper
Pencil
Sample ID badge
Directions for making name badge

Procedures
1. Explain that the class will be participating in a cooperative group project.
2. Review and discuss expectations for working in groups.
3. Present the overhead transparency "Rules for Working in Groups."
4. Have a student volunteer read each rule.
5. Ask for student volunteers to role play following the rules and breaking the rules.
6. Check for students' understanding of the rules.
7. Work with students to agree on a method of getting their attention while they're working in groups (for example, turning off the lights, catchword or catchphrase, hand in the air).
8. Explain to the students that they will be working in their groups to create a travel brochure or folder that should convince people to visit the location featured.
9. Explain that, to complete the project, the students also will be going to the library to do research. Library expectations will be discussed later (Wednesday).
10. Tell the students that the actual project will begin on Wednesday.
11. Students' first task as a group will be to make ID badges.
12. Show the students a sample ID badge.
13. Discuss group roles and responsibilities, using the overhead transparency entitled "Group Roles."

14. Explain that each student has been assigned to a group, and group coordinators already have been chosen.

15. Designate areas of the room for each group.

16. Once students are in their groups, they have five minutes to decide who will be in what role.

17. When the groups have designated their roles, group coordinators should raise their hands.

18. Group coordinators will get from the teacher the directions for making ID badges.

19. Emphasize that group coordinators should read all of the directions before beginning the project.

20. Once all groups have finished making their ID badges, ask students for feedback. How did they like working together? What could they do better?

21. Explain that the students will be looking at travel brochures on Wednesday to get ideas on how they might want to design their own travel brochures.

22. Explain that the students will have the choice of designing a travel brochure that features a foreign country or a state.

Assessment

Assessment will consist of teacher observation and a checklist. The directions given to the students for making the ID badges can serve as the basis for the checklist. Through observation, the teacher can determine whether the students had specific problems working in their groups. The presentation portion of the lesson should indicate whether the groups completed the lesson successfully as well.

DIRECTIONS FOR MAKING ID BADGES

The coordinator should read ALL of the directions before beginning the project.

1. Materials Handler/Timekeeper

This person should go to the table and get enough index cards and yarn for each person in the group. One envelope is needed, as well as one marker for the group to use. This person also should make sure that the ID badges are finished in ten minutes.

2. Recorder

The recorder should write the group members' names and roles on the index cards. The group name should be written on the front of the envelope and on the back of each card. Use a marker for all of the writing.

3. Illustrator

The illustrator should make a symbol to represent the group and should draw the symbol on each index card.

4. Coordinator

It's up to the coordinator to make sure that everyone does his or her job and contributes to the project. Without being too bossy, the coordinator keeps the group on task. It's also the coordinator's job to let the teacher know when his/her group has finished its ID badges.

Figure 10.10
Tina's Lesson
Plan *(cont.)*

5. Presenter

Once all the groups have finished, the presenter will stand and tell the class the name of the group, the names of the group members, and their corresponding roles.

Note: It is the whole group's responsibility to come up with a group name. Remember that everyone's opinion counts! If you don't understand something, try to work it out as a group FIRST; then ask the teacher. Each member can attach the yarn to his/her own ID badge.

Once all of the presentations have been made, the materials handler should collect all of his/her group members' ID badges and place them in the envelope. Then the envelope should be given to the teacher.

time teaching. Instructional planning happens either "in-flight" or during out-of-school time. Teachers should make a concerted effort to engage in instructional planning before the school year begins and during the first few weeks of school. Such planning has long-term effects and establishes a framework of procedures, routines, expectations, and schedules.

Sometimes teachers use constructivism as an excuse not to plan. However, all kinds of effective teaching require careful attention to planning. In fact, effective teaching, effective planning, and effective organization are all strongly related variables in teaching. Teachers who employ "fluid constructivist" planning engage in a plan-act-observe-evaluate cycle of instruction, which helps them make decisions (Henderson, 1996).

2. *Teachers need to use instructional plans as guides rather than scripts.* Even the most well thought out instructional plans sometimes cannot be enacted as envisioned. Interruptions, unavailability of materials, equipment breakdowns, and interruptions all can contribute to aborted plans. Overly scripted teachers often find it difficult to deal with unanticipated problems, whereas flexible teachers can adapt to the ever-changing demands of instruction (Pellicer & Anderson, 1995). The degree to which teachers are able to anticipate and adapt to unexpected wrinkles ranges from planned flexibility to flexible planning. However, the fact that plans often must be modified is not an excuse for not planning.

3. *Teachers must know when and how to modify their instructional plans.* Random adaptation serves no useful purpose. Effective teachers "read" their students and respond appropriately. Through observation, adept use of questions, and attention to students' nonverbal signals, teachers can discern who's "getting it" and who's not, identify misinformation students have picked up, and determine when they've totally overshot or undershot their students. This is where the art and science of teaching meet (Pellicer & Anderson, 1995).

It's essential for teachers to plan and prepare for adaptation. It's also imperative for teachers to provide learners with a variety of ways to show what they know and what they can do. Consequently, assessment and evaluation serve as the focus of Chapter 11.

SUMMARIZING WHAT YOU'VE LEARNED

■ There are three types of instructional units—resource units, content-oriented units, and conceptually oriented units. Global units feature topics that are open-ended enough to be developed across a variety of grade levels.

New teachers talk

Reflecting on a lesson plan that you developed as a part of an instructional unit in your preservice teacher preparation, share your responses to the following questions regarding the instructional planning process.

What contribution did this particular lesson make to the goals of the unit you created?

This particular lesson plan contributed to the goals of the unit by helping the students become familiar with different features of the rain forest. I feel this is of prime importance, because learning about the features of the rain forest is an essential element in comprehending why the rain forest is an important part of our ecosystem. Students need to be able to make connections, and if they haven't had the opportunity to learn about what's in the rain forest, then they won't be able to make the connection of why the rain forest is essential for human existence.

What was the most difficult aspect of planning the lesson?

As with any lesson, the most difficult part of planning this lesson was trying to think about how the lesson would be implemented in an actual classroom. On paper, the lesson may look great and may seem beneficial for the goals of the unit. However, in the classroom, it can be completely ineffective. It's not always possible to predict students' responses. Therefore, the teacher must be flexible, accommodating, knowledgeable, and creative.

What was the least difficult part of creating this lesson plan?

The easiest part of planning the lesson was the introduction. As we designed the lesson, an important goal of ours was to incorporate the KWL chart at the beginning of the unit. We felt this would give us a "steppingstone" for the rest of the unit. Using a KWL chart as a preassessment tool is beneficial, because it's a strategy that provides the opportunity for students to individually express what they know about the rain forest in a stress-free environment. There are no right or wrong answers when the KWL strategy is used as a preassessment tool. Rather, the chart simply indicates where the students stand and where they want to go. Furthermore, the chart can spark new teaching ideas. A teacher cannot know everything, and a KWL chart can lead a teacher in the right direction to capture and maintain learner interest.

What are the strengths of the lesson?

I think the strongest aspect of this lesson plan is that it provides all learners the opportunity to excel in some area. The lesson plan includes a wide variety of skills for students to demonstrate their knowledge of and apply. These include research skills, artistic skills, writing skills, public speaking skills, interpersonal skills, computer skills, and listening skills. Students can learn and excel in dif-

■ The key difference between a unit and an integrative unit is curricular integration. An integrative unit must be contextualized in a real-life framework and must promote active learning, as students acquire the knowledge, performances (skills), and dispositions intended. An integrated curriculum incorporates connections between developmental domains and content areas.

■ An integrative unit should include an overview, a rationale, goals and major concepts, daily lesson plans, a learning environment design, an overall schedule, a daily classroom schedule, family involvement plans, and resources.

ferent ways, and by including a wide variety of skills in the lesson, the students will have several opportunities to increase their learning.

Another strength of the lesson is that it incorporates large-group, small-group, and independent learning. A teacher must incorporate a wide variety of teaching strategies in order to reach as many students as possible. Some students like to work with little teacher guidance; some like to work with their peers; some like to work with complete teacher direction.

A third strength is that the end of the lesson makes a direct connection to the beginning of the lesson. At the bottom of the Project Rain Forest handout, we indicated that students will collaborate to create their own Walk Through the Rain Forest book. I think this culminating activity will encourage the students to learn, because they can see a goal, a purpose for the goal, and a connection to the goal at the end.

Given what you now know that you didn't know when you first developed this lesson plan, how would you revise it?

After completing my student teaching, I now look back at this lesson plan and realize there are several aspects I would change. First, I think I would put more thought into how this lesson contributes to my goals for the unit and my goals as a teacher. Did I put too much focus on this one project, instead of broadening the learning process? I now think the project may be too time-consum-

ing, a factor that easily could result in lack of sustained student interest and diminished learning outcomes.

Furthermore, I think the questions I included in the Project Rain Forest handout would limit the students. Instead of specifically laying out questions, I should have made simple suggestions. My goal was to encourage creativity, and I honestly feel the questions may stifle creativity.

Third, in a real-life application, I would not give an assignment at the introduction of a unit. An early assignment such as research might discourage student enthusiasm, interest, and participation. I think a more intriguing and real-world application would have been more appropriate for an introduction to the unit. Plus, if this is the first day I am introducing the rain forest to the students, how would they know what animals and plants live in the rain forest? How would they know what to brainstorm if the rain forest is a foreign concept to them?

Fourth, I think the time schedule may be too rigid. Teaching isn't about following an exact schedule; it's not an exact science. I know there are time constraints in teaching, but planning can't be based solely on time. That isn't beneficial for the students or for the teacher.

Fifth, do I want to carry this lesson out over several days? What if the lesson bombs on the first day? I think if I'm going to plan a lesson out over several days, I definitely should be convinced it's exciting and interesting. More important, I need to consider if the students have a large enough knowledge base to complete the project.

Finally, I would change the evaluation process. I failed to include strategies to assess the students' abilities to work in small groups and their ability to work independently with little teacher guidance. The evaluation process also neglects student participation. These all are important factors that need to be included. I'm sure as I continue to learn and develop professionally, I'll make even more changes in the evaluation process. However, these are the changes I recognize at this point in time.

—EMILY, Preservice Teacher

Authors' Analysis

Emily's reflections regarding her first attempt to develop an integrative unit remind us of conversations we've had with other preservice teachers. They might stop us in the hall a few semesters after they completed their first units to assure us that their instructional planning has greatly improved. Or we might catch up with them in our role as university supervisors of their student teaching or internship experiences. At that point they confess that they reviewed their first attempts at constructing integrative units and were dismayed by their "poor quality." Those conversations serve as teachable moments that allow us to discuss the value of encouraging *approximations* of desired behavior, rather than rigid requirements, and emphasize that different evaluation criteria are appropriate for different levels of development—whether learners are seven, fifteen, twenty-two, or forty.

The passage of time, coupled with Emily's increasing knowledge base, allowed her to see some unintended limitations and unnecessary restrictions in the lesson plan that she and her collaborator had developed two years earlier. However, Emily also succeeded at identifying strengths in her first instructional planning attempt.

What contribution did this particular lesson make to the goals of the unit you created?

This lesson was the first lesson in a unit that featured researching and designing travel brochures or folders. Although it's not flashy or ultra creative, it served an important purpose. I implemented this unit while novice teaching with three classes of fifth graders. Two of the classes had over thirty students, and the third class had twenty-four students. The unit provided an opportunity for the students to use many of the skills they'd acquired in social studies, language arts, art, and mathematics.

Students were to work in small groups to create travel brochures or folders that would convince people to visit their particular country or state. For most of the students, this was their first experience working in groups of more than two or three, as well as the first time many of them used the library for obtaining information about a specific topic.

My cooperating teacher cautioned me about letting these classes work in groups. It was the beginning of the year, and the classes weren't exactly "whipped into shape" yet with regard to following expectations for engaging in socially appropriate classroom behavior. But, being brave (or extremely naive), I chose to go ahead and teach the unit the way I had planned to teach it. However, I used this lesson as a preassessment tool to determine how the students would work together. Their task was relatively simple, and if they could handle this, I was fairly confident that they would be able to handle working together to research and design travel brochures or folders.

What was the most difficult aspect of planning the lesson?

I found that there were two things that were difficult in planning the lesson. First, I had to make sure that I had a job for each group member. The job had to be meaningful and keep the students actively engaged throughout the activity. Second, I was worried about time. I didn't want to go over my time limit, because the students switched classrooms each period, and I had one day to teach and complete the lesson. I also didn't want the students to complete the task in fifteen minutes.

What was the least difficult part of creating this lesson plan?

Because I had a clear and concise objective in mind, the actual writing of the lesson plan was the least difficult aspect. I knew exactly what I wanted to get out of the lesson (an idea of how the students would work in groups and follow directions). Having a specific format for writing the lesson plan was important. It was extremely easy to follow, because I was very specific and orderly when I wrote out the lesson.

What are the strengths of the lesson?

One of the strengths of the lesson is that it's simple and easy to follow. I believe that lessons don't have to be the huge, extravagant presentations that some preservice teachers may think they have to be. My lesson, though simple, was an extremely important part of the unit as a whole. It prompted any changes that I made in the rest of the unit, because I was able to see if certain students had problems working with others, staying on task, fulfilling assigned job roles, et cetera. I also liked this lesson, because it gave students opportunities to work together and make choices.

Given what you know now that you didn't know when you first developed this lesson plan, how would you revise it?

There are a few things I would change to make this lesson more effective. Due to the large class sizes and time constraints, I should have had the desks prearranged into groups of five or six. I soon realized it takes 35 fifth graders quite a while to rearrange their desks. I should have placed name tags on the desks so students knew what groups they were in.

I also would rethink the decisions I allowed the students to make. For example, as a class, I wanted to determine a system that would allow me to get the students' attention quickly and easily. My efforts to be democratic turned into a fiasco. I had decided to take suggestions from the class and then vote on them. Well, I had a few comedians who came up with inappropriate suggestions that got the entire class "worked up." I realized I should have had something in mind to use as a signal. If I were their full-time teacher, I think things would have worked out differently.

Finally, I would have shortened the lesson for the larger classes and lengthened the lesson

for the smaller class. I didn't realize how long it would take a large group of fifth graders to make ID badges. Although I could have taken two days to complete the lesson for the two larger classes, the smaller class completed their ID badges in twenty minutes! I learned that time is an essential part of planning lessons, because it really flies when you're in front of a classroom.

I have to say that this lesson was fun for the students. I could tell they enjoyed the opportunity to work together and do something other than fill out worksheets or listen to a teacher lecture. Although things got chaotic at times, it was well worth the effort to get the students to interact with each other. I believe that, with practice, students can learn to work together in an effective manner.

—TINA, Preservice Teacher

Authors' Analysis

Tina's honest and realistic appraisal of her lesson plan indicates that she possesses and effectively applies self-assessment and reflection skills. We concur that her lesson plan serves a specific purpose that relates directly to her unit as a whole. Given her cooperating teacher's words of caution regarding her students' lack of prior experience working collaboratively in small groups, Tina chose to acknowledge that advice by designing a lesson intended to assess students' abilities in this area. What are some tasks other than making ID badges that Tina could have used to assess students' ability to work in small groups?

Now It's Your Turn

 Perhaps you noticed that Emily wrote her lesson plan procedures in a narrative format, whereas Tina used a numbered list to organize her procedures. Which format did you find easier to follow?

In your teaching journal, identify the advantages and disadvantages of each format—narrative and list. Then explain which format you think you'll use more often as you develop your own lesson plans. Explain the reasoning behind your preference.

■ Many constructs for integrating curricula have been explored in previous chapters. Student inquiry, active inquiry, schema theory, and whole-language approaches all support curricular integration. In addition to supporting these approaches, curriculum integration needs to be a major emphasis in your future classroom, because students need opportunities to develop their multiple intelligences, to interact socially, and to be able to apply their academic skills to the real world in which they live. Many special needs learners function most effectively in regular classrooms that feature an integrated curriculum.

■ There are a variety of structures that promote curricular integration. The Project Approach involves an in-depth investigation of a topic.

■ The Reggio Emilia Approach incorporates the Project Approach. Children learn cooperatively as they engage in long-term projects.

■ Literature-based instruction involves using a variety of children's literature in the teaching of language arts and other related content areas. In a literature-based classroom, students learn to read, write, talk, listen, and think through being exposed to whole pieces of written language, such as stories, poems, and signs, rather than isolated fragments, such as letters and sounds.

■ Curriculum webbing involves a four-step process: identifying a topic and related subtopics, "topicstorming," identifying desired learning outcomes, and preparing for teaching. It's important to include students in the webbing process. Webbing will help you and your students gain insights into the many connections and relationships that emerge from a topic.

■ Learning centers are areas in the classroom that have been designed to promote activities related to specific curricular areas or subjects. Learning centers should be incorporated into your classroom design and feature hands-on activities related to particular integrative units.

■ Teaming with other teachers is one of the most productive ways to develop integrative units. Schools can support collaboration by providing opportunities for you to meet with colleagues to discuss curricula. Meet at least one hour per week with other teachers, including special area and resource teachers, to discuss curriculum integration and assessment programs and to share resources.

■ Long-range or yearly planning identifies the general curriculum content and its sequence, which generally are framed by district curriculum objectives. Mid-range planning includes term and unit planning. Short-range planning consists of weekly and daily lesson planning.

■ Instructional planning provides a sense of direction for both teachers and learners and makes students aware of the goals behind the learning tasks they're performing.

■ Teachers engage in instructional planning and decision making almost continually. They plan prior to instruction, while implementing instruction, and following instruction. These planning times sometimes are referred to as the preinstructional phase, the interactive phase, and the postinstructional phase.

■ Lesson plans need to answer the following questions: What am I going to do? Why am I going to do it? What do I need to do it? How am I going to do it? How will I know I've done it?

■ Research indicates that experienced teachers use a cyclical, or nonlinear, approach to planning, whereas novice teachers use a linear approach (Arends, 1998; Glatthorn, 1993). The nonlinear approach has been described as the "ready-fire-aim" approach, in contrast to the more traditional (linear) "ready-aim-fire" approach (Fullan, 1991).

■ All teachers should plan. Teachers need to use instructional plans as guides rather than scripts. Teachers must know when and how to modify their instructional plans.

YOUR PROFESSIONAL TEACHING PORTFOLIO

■ The topic of this chapter presents many opportunities for you to show what you know and document your progress. As you develop the components of your first integrative unit, be sure to save them for your Professional Teaching Portfolio. You may want to use your initial efforts as artifacts or showcase these products in your "Best Works" collection. Items you should definitely save include curriculum webs, lesson plans, learning environment designs, overall schedules, daily classroom schedules, family involvement plans, and resource lists.

Key Terms

Content-oriented unit (p. 321)
Conceptually oriented unit (p. 321)
Core book (p. 339)
Curriculum webs (p. 332)
Goals (p. 360)
Instructional objectives (p. 360)
Integrated curriculum (p. 324)
Integrative unit (p. 324)
Interactive planning phase (p. 358)

Interdisciplinary instruction (p. 331)
Learning center (p. 346)
Literature-based instruction (p. 336)
Long-range planning (p. 355)
Mid-range planning (p. 355)
Nonlinear instructional planning model (p. 372)
Preinstructional planning phase (p. 358)

Postinstructional planning phase (p. 358)
Project (p. 332)
Project Approach (p. 334)
Rational-linear instructional planning model (p. 372)
Reggio Emilia Approach (p. 336)
Resource unit (p. 321)
Short-range planning (p. 355)
Unit (p. 320)
Whole language (p. 337)

Relevant Resources for Professionals

Books and Articles

- Daniels, H., & Bizar, M. (1998). *Methods that matter: Six structures for best practice classrooms.* York, ME: Stenhouse.

- Katz, L., & Chard, S. (1997). *Engaging children's minds: The Project Approach.* Norwood, NJ: Ablex.

- Roberts, P., & Kellough, R. (1996). *A guide for developing an interdisciplinary thematic unit.* Englewood Cliffs, NJ: Prentice-Hall.

Professional Journals in Education

- *ALAN Review*

  http://scholar.kib.vt.edu/ejournals/ALAN/alan-review.html

  Regularly updated electronic version of the quarterly journal of the Assembly on Literature for Adolescents, with full texts of scholarly articles and back issues.

Professional Organizations

- Council for Pre-Service Technology.
  The Council for Pre-Service Technology (CPT) is a professional organization with both institutional and individual members. The purpose of the CPT is to promote the use of instructional technology in the education of preservice teachers through sharing information, study, experimentation, and demonstration and to provide leadership in pre-service technology education. Links to member institutions of the council and activities of the CPT are found at this site.

  http://www.macomb.k12.mi.us/cpt/cpt.htm

- International Reading Association.
  Publishes *The Reading Teacher,* the *Journal of Adolescent & Adult Literacy,* the *Reading Research Quarterly, Lectura y vida,* and *Reading Online.* Visit *Reading Online* at

  http://www.readingonline.org.

  800 Barksday Road, PO Box 8139
  Newark, DE 19714-8139

Videos

- *Block Scheduling: Time to Learn*
  This three-video series provides a guide for making the transition from the traditional high school schedule to block scheduling.
  Available from
  Phi Delta Kappa International
  Center for Professional Development & Services
  PO Box 789
  Bloomington, IN 47402-0789

  http://www.pdkintl.org

- *For Our Student, For Ourselves: Learner-Centered Principles in Practice*
  This multimedia package contains two videos and a facilitator's manual. Three high schools are featured: a small rural school, a school in a suburban setting, and an urban school. Viewers visit these three high schools and observe students, teachers, and administrators using learner-centered principles to guide their educational reform efforts.
  Available from
  Phi Delta Kappa International
  Center for Professional Development & Services
  PO Box 789
  Bloomington, IN 47402-0789

  http://www.pdkintl.org

Web Sites

- **Cyberbee**
  An Internet guide for K–12 teachers. Topics at this site include citing resources, copyright, curriculum ideas, safe kids on-line, Web construction, and Web evaluation.

  http://www.cyberbee.com/

- **Educator's Rest Stop**
  The Educator's Rest Stop contains tips for finding and becoming involved with Internet-based projects along with lists of the most successful projects on the Internet. This site also includes links to Web sites full of Internet projects and other educational sites.

  http://forum.swarthmore.edu/~carol/website.html

- **Kidopedia**
  An on-line encyclopedia written entirely by children from around the world, with instructions for posting entries and for creating local "kidopedias."

  http://rdz.stjohns.edu/kidopedia/

- **Kids' Web**
A Web guide specifically for children, with links to a variety of sites relating to literature, the arts, science, social studies, games, and sports.

http://www.npac.syr.edu/textbook/kidsweb/

- **Science Web Sites**
This San Francisco–based museum provides a site filled with interactive explorations pertaining to science, art, and human perception.

http://www.exploratorium.com

A site dedicated to exploring the science of bugs and worms.

http://www.yucky.com

A great site to visit for information and activities related to the happenings of our solar system and the universe.

http://www.spaceday.com

- **Teacher Resource Page**
Small site with user-friendly organization; especially helpful for elementary teachers beginning to use World Wide Web resources in the classroom.

http://grove.ufl.edu:80/~klesyk/

Literature Resources

- Association for Library Service to Children. (1995). *The Newbery and Caldecott Awards: A guide to the medal and honor books*. Chicago: American Library Association. This regularly updated resource provides short annotations for the winners and runners-up of these prestigious ALA-sponsored awards.

- *Children's books: Award and prizes*. (1993). New York: The Children's Book Council. This publication lists award-winning titles, as well as state "Children's Choice" awards for exemplary trade books.

- **Children's Literature Gopher**

This Web site provides information on authors, book awards, conferences and events, on-line texts and journals, other Internet resources, college course syllabi, and more.

gopher://lib.nmsu.edu:70/11/.subjects/Education/.childlit

- Helbig, A., & Perkins, A. (1994). *This land is your land: A guide to multicultural literature for children and adults*. Westport, CT: Greenwood. An extensive critical listing of titles featuring African Americans, Asian Americans, Hispanic Americans, and Native Americans.

- International Reading Association. "Children's Choices." A list of exemplary, "reader friendly" children's literature, published every October in *The Reading Teacher*.

- International Reading Association. "Teachers' Choices." A list of exemplary "teacher-selected" children's literature, published every November in *The Reading Teacher*.

- **Children's Literature Web Guide**

This Web site provides links to children's publishers and booksellers, conferences and book events, children's writing, children's literature discussion groups, journals, book reviews, and resources for storytellers, parents, teachers, writers, and illustrators.

http//www.ucalgary.ca/~dkbrown/index.html

11

ASSESSMENT AND EVALUATION

— OR —

Authentic opportunities for learners to show what they know

WHAT ARE ASSESSMENT AND EVALUATION?

The terms *assessment* and *evaluation* are often used interchangeably. For our purposes, we will refer to **assessment** as the process of collecting performance data and to **evaluation** as the process of bringing meaning to that data. However, other authors may use the term *assessment* in a broader context, and this term may mean different things to different people—parents, educators, and administrators. For example, the definition of assessment offered by Evans and Evans (1992, pp. 69, 70) combines the process of collecting data with the process of bringing meaning to it: "Assessment is a process in which information is systematically gathered concerning a student's qualities, characteristics, behaviors, and the environment to aid in teaching. Assessment consists of more than the simple administration of tests. Rather, it is an ongoing problem-solving process that seeks to understand fully the student's unique skills and abilities and the manner in which he or she interacts with the environment. Information gleaned from assessment can be used to determine educational placements, develop instructional programs that are most appropriate and fully meet the needs of the student, and monitor these programs on a frequent basis."

"Those who believe in our ability do more than stimulate us. . . . They create for us an atmosphere in which it becomes easier for us to succeed."

John Lancaster Spaulding

Since you have been a student for many years, no doubt you've had many personal experiences with assessment and evaluation, and you may still feel the effects of some of those experiences, both positive and negative. For example, although she is now a few decades beyond fourth grade, Therese still bristles when she thinks about the grade she received in reading at the end of that year in school. On a happier note, she often revels in the memory of her senior year culminating piano recital.

In your teaching journal, share one personal assessment experience from elementary school, either positive or negative, that continues to affect you. After sharing your experience, discuss the feelings that surround this school memory.

ASSESSMENT AND EVALUATION: INTERRELATED CONCEPTS

Assessment and evaluation are best thought of as interrelated concepts. Assessment refers to data collection and the gathering of evidence (Routman, 1991). Assessment also can be thought of as the ongoing act of collecting various types of information about individuals or groups of individuals in order to understand them better. After the data are collected, evaluation is necessary. Evaluation implies bringing meaning to data through interpretation, analysis, and reflection (Routman, 1991). Evaluation involves the development of a judgment regarding the quality, value, or worth of assessment data, based upon established criteria. Both assessment and evaluation are necessary components of the process that often is referred to as assessment.

LOOKING BACK, LOOKING FORWARD—JOINING AN ASSESSMENT REVOLUTION IN PROGRESS

The topic of assessment and evaluation is at center stage in many educational circles today. These processes are undergoing such tumultuous change that many educators have suggested that we are experiencing an assessment revolution. This chapter will help you become aware of key issues in assessment and evaluation and deal effectively with them throughout your teaching life.

You've learned a lot about instructional strategies, developing integrative units, and writing lesson plans. Now, begin to think about how you will assess and evaluate students' performance on the lessons, activities, and integrative units you've been planning. Also, ponder how you will assess and evaluate students' responses to the dynamic, higher-level questions you've crafted. Will you assign a grade? Use a checklist or rubric? What assessment and evaluation options will you have? Will you have to administer achievement tests? And how will you report the information you gather to parents?

Before you plan where to go next, it's helpful to know where you've been—especially when you're in the midst of a revolution! After a brief historical review of assessment and evaluation, we'll discuss the differences between alternative assessment and traditional assessment and examine best practices in assessment and evaluation. We'll also highlight significant issues surrounding assessment and evaluation today—understanding cultural and language differences, as well as assessing and evaluating special needs and at-risk students. Finally, we'll share a number of alternative assessment strategies and provide examples and explanations to get you started designing an alternative assessment program. Because you are probably most familiar with traditional rather than alternative assessment practices, you should be prepared to entertain some new ideas. Remember, minds are like parachutes—they function best when open!

ASSESSMENT AND EVALUATION: A HISTORICAL PERSPECTIVE

The primary purpose of early assessment was to exclude certain individuals—from society, from schools, and from the military (Stewart, Choate, & Poteet, 1995). Remember our discussion in Chapter 8 of the purposes of schools and schooling? One of the purposes we discussed was sorting and selecting students, a function that schools began performing in the 1930s and still actively perform today. Teachers sort students into high, middle, and low ability groups; decide who should and should not be included in gifted or remedial programs; and recommend students for resource services (such as reading recovery, assistance with their speech, or intervention to help students deal with learning disabilities).

The testing movement began to flourish in the United States in the early twentieth century, prompted by the work of Alfred Binet and his colleagues. Their efforts culminated in the 1905 Binet-Simon Scale, considered the first modern intelligence test. Lewis Terman standardized the Binet-Simon Scale in 1916 and developed the Stanford-Binet Intelligence Test (Tindal & Marston, 1990).

During the 1920s and 1930s (following World War I), America's population became increasingly diverse. At the time it was popular to think of the United States as a "great melting pot," and so U.S. schools provided a homogenizing experience, with the goal of making everyone the same rather than celebrating differences. In the midst of this focus on sameness, increasing numbers of students entered American schools, as immigrants continued to arrive in huge numbers. This influx led to the "assembly line school" concept, which was further supported by the introduction of standardized achievement tests (Stiggins, 1997).

In 1939, David Wechsler introduced the Wechsler Intelligence Scale, which focused on what was regarded as the global nature of intelligence. Testing became a common practice in U.S. schools. Many new tests were developed, and norm-referenced testing continued to evolve from the 1930s to the 1950s (Stewart, Choate, & Poteet, 1995). Thereafter, standardized testing continued to grow, becoming a twentieth-century educational phenomenon. A 1950 high school graduate might have taken three standardized tests during his or her K–12 education, whereas a student finishing school in 1989 would have taken as many as twenty-one standardized tests. Add the time required just to take all these tests to the time spent preparing for them, and you can easily appreciate the effect that the growth in standardized testing has had on instructional time over the years (Perrone, 1990). Increased emphasis on testing and test results has resulted in test-driven curricula in many districts. Think back to your school days. How many standardized tests did you take between kindergarten and twelfth grade? How did they affect the education you received?

After World War II, criterion-referenced tests (generally, teacher-made tests or textbook chapter tests), designed to measure academic achievement, began to play a critical role in education (Stewart, Choate, & Poteet, 1995). In addition to the growth in testing, services for students with disabilities also grew tremendously following World War II (McLoughlin & Lewis, 1994). Many abuses and criticisms of assessment accompanied this growth. In 1957, much attention was focused on the overall quality of American education after the Soviet Union successfully launched the first Earth-orbiting satellite, Sputnik. Since then, testing has been used both to laud and to decry the status of American education (Poteet, Choate, & Stewart, 1993). In 1975, Public Law 94-142, the Education for All Handicapped Children Act, significantly improved the assessment of students with disabilities. This legislation called for fair, appropriate, multifaceted assessment implemented by a multidisciplinary team.

In 1983, following the publication of *A Nation at Risk*, a report that severely criticized the quality of American education, many states developed statewide testing programs as part of their reform efforts (Stewart, Choate, & Poteet, 1995). An update on state assessments is provided at the end of this chapter, and a discussion of the impact that *A Nation at Risk* had on education reform is included in Chapter 12.

Assessment is big business today in American schools. More than 20 million standardized tests are administered annually to 44 million students in elementary and secondary schools (Ysseldyke, Algozzine, & Thurlow, 1992). And as the assessment field has continued to evolve, both purposes and procedures have changed dramatically. These changes have been wholeheartedly endorsed by some educators and bitterly rejected by others. Assessment is, indeed, a controversial topic!

Measuring intelligence is another very controversial issue today—one that deserves your attention. The debate over intelligence testing centers on two concerns: whether intelligence is one entity or is made up of a set of factors, and whether intelligence is changeable (McLoughlin & Lewis, 1994).

Because we have discussed multiple intelligence theory and the eight ways of knowing, you can begin to understand the complexity of assessing intelligence. It's important to be aware of the dangers in regarding IQ scores as the only window on students' abilities.

How Do Teachers Deal with the Assessment Dilemma?

How is the assessment revolution affecting real kids and real teachers? The conflicting demands of reform efforts and standardized tests can confuse the teaching/learning process. "Amid the hubbub of school reform, teachers are actually receiving a schizophrenic message: teach in creative, innovative, constructive ways, but tell your students that they will be tested differently" (Daniels & Bizar, 1998, p. 205). Teaching methods that are effective at raising scores on tests that focus on lower-level thinking tasks—knowledge and comprehension—are the opposite of strategies that promote complex cognitive thinking, problem solving, and creativity. Unfortunately, "the people running our country's 'official' education reform, that is, politicians, state legislators, governors, and blue-ribbon panels of businessmen, don't know or care much about the structures of Best Practice education. . . . But they do care a lot—a whole lot—about test scores" (Daniels & Bizar, 1998, p. 204).

How does a teacher deal with these contradictions in the classroom? First of all, realize that standardized tests are here to stay, and accept that reality. Historically, American society has placed great value on test results. It's your responsibility as a teacher to understand the purposes and value of a variety of different assessment tools and to advocate for *appropriate* assessment. This means understanding what information is gleaned from specific tests and how this information should be shared with students, parents, and the community. Take, for example, the achievement test scores in your own school records. Do you understand how many ways your scores have been reported—in terms of raw scores, stanines, percentiles, percentages, and grade equivalents? Can you interpret the meaning of each score in each subtest and how it compares to the composite score? If you're not confident of your ability to interpret assessment information, set some learning goals for your upcoming coursework in assessment. For the time being, remember that standardized tests are designed to provide a broad indication of student achievement rather than a high-resolution portrait of it. They provide little information of value for day-to-day instruction (Stiggins, 1997).

■ Traditional Assessment and Alternative Assessment: What's the Difference?

Assessment reform initiatives are plentiful. They're reflected in the rise of alternative assessments, changing curricula, and the expectation that teachers and learners will embrace new teaching and learning paradigms. These include literature-based instruction; whole-language instruction; interdisciplinary, integrated teaching; collaborative teaching; cooperative learning;

inclusion; authentic curricula and assessment; and an emphasis on developing higher-order thinking, problem solving, and performance. By now, we're confident that these approaches are familiar to you. These best-practice approaches will serve as the warp upon which you weave your teaching and your assessment program.

Habgood (1993, p. 81) describes the difference between traditional and alternative assessment this way:

> *The essential difference between traditional assessment (teacher-made tests) and alternative assessment seems to be learner self-regulation. Typically, in a multiple choice testing format, the student is given his or her grade with a rationale explaining why a particular answer is correct. By comparison, alternative assessment makes available the scoring criterion or rubric in the beginning, and the student constantly applies the criterion during the assessment task. The student grades the final work and perhaps compares its merits to other works produced. This has exciting possibilities for the world of work. . . . By giving students practice in self-assessment measured against specific criteria, we are preparing them for employment.*

Many labels are used to describe alternatives to traditional, standardized assessment, including *direct assessment, performance assessment, authentic assessment,* and *portfolio assessment.* Although each type of assessment emphasizes subtle differences, "all exhibit two central features: first, all are viewed as alternatives to traditional multiple choice, standardized achievement tests; and, second, all refer to direct examination of student performance on significant tasks that are relevant to life outside of school" (Worthen, 1993, p. 445).

WHAT PURPOSES DO ASSESSMENT AND EVALUATION SERVE?

Assessment and evaluation systems serve multiple purposes:

Determining students' prior knowledge. This type of evaluation can be performed dynamically, in the context of teaching, or more formally, based on specially designed tests that identify students' strengths and weaknesses in specific areas. Determinations of students' prior knowledge provide a basis for curricular planning and change. We've discussed brainstorming and curriculum webbing as initial steps in designing integrative units. These are forms of preassessment that measure students' prior knowledge.

Providing data for curricular revisions. Evaluation is a feedback mechanism for educational improvement. When student performance is viewed as an indicator of program effectiveness, the likelihood of curriculum improvement increases, and a major contribution is made to improving the quality of education. Curricula are informally revised by the teacher on a moment-by-moment basis, as the lesson or activity emerges in the classroom context. It's also important that curricula be officially revised, based on program evaluation data.

Offering constructive feedback to students. Students learn most effectively when they receive feedback that facilitates and motivates their learning. This feedback may come from their teachers, from other support professionals, or from their peers. It's a continual challenge to stretch students without breaking them.

Allowing learners to show what they know. As you know, students bring with them to the teaching/learning process a variety of strengths and types of intelligences. Consequently, it's the teacher's responsibility to promote students' ability to perform and share their abilities in a variety of contexts.

Anticipating learners' educational needs. Educational needs are the products of judgments about what counts in educational matters. It's important to remember that your values—both cultural and educational—will influence the decisions you'll make regarding the future educational needs of your students.

Determining if curricular objectives have been achieved. Educational programs should be driven by clearly formulated objectives. Objectives are the criteria for determining whether the program has been effective (Eisner, 1994).

The public has come to expect grades, because that is what education has provided. Alternatives in assessment and evaluation are necessary in order to move beyond grades as the only tool that educators use to communicate assessment and evaluation information.

MEASURING ASSESSMENT QUALITY

Consider the following three questions:

1. How accurate is the information gathered?
2. How confident are you in drawing conclusions about a student's performance from the assessment score?
3. Is the assessment fair to all students?

Each of these questions corresponds with one of the three fundamental psychometric concepts used in assessment research: reliability, validity, and fairness.

RELIABILITY, VALIDITY, AND FAIRNESS

When reviewing assessments, it's important to evaluate the reliability, validity, and fairness of each assessment tool you have used. **Reliability** refers to the accuracy of students' scores or outcomes. It refers to the degree to which similar scores are likely to be produced in subsequent administrations of a given test or alternative assessment. A test or alternative assessment is highly reliable if it minimizes chance factors that can lead to inaccurate scores or outcomes.

Validity concerns how closely the test or alternative assessment measures what it is intended to measure. Does the test or alternative assessment allow accurate conclusions to be made about the knowledge, skills, or dispositions being assessed? How closely related or analogous are the knowledge, skills, or dispositions being assessed and the test or alternative assessment?

Fairness measures the likelihood that all students of equivalent ability will achieve similar scores or outcomes. If earning a good score or outcome depends partly on demographic factors (such as students' gender, race, ethnicity, or socioeconomic status), the assessment is considered low in fairness (Rahn, Stecher, Goodman & Alt, 1997).

ASSESSING THE QUALITY OF YOUR ASSESSMENT PROGRAM

The National Forum on Assessment, a coalition of education and civil rights organizations, views high-quality assessment as essential to high-quality education. The forum asserts that powerful, fair assessment methods used by skilled educators are necessary for educating *all* children to high standards (National Center for Fair and Open Testing, 1995).

The following principles are intended to facilitate the transformation of assessment practices. They can guide changes in curriculum and instruction that are designed to improve student learning.

Improve and support student learning. Assessment practices and methods should be consistent with teacher and district learning goals, the curriculum instruction, and current knowledge regarding how students learn. In-class assessment (assessment that is integrated with the curriculum and instruction) is the primary means of assessment. Information for accountability and improvement comes from regular, continuing work of students in schools and from large-scale (statewide or national) assessment. Rigorous technical standards for assessment must be developed and used to ensure high-quality assessments and to monitor the actual educational consequences of assessment.

Assess and evaluate performance fairly. Assessment systems must ensure that all students receive fair treatment, so as not to limit students' present and future opportunities. Assessments allow for multiple methods to assess student progress and are created or adapted appropriately to meet the specific needs of particular populations, such as English as a second language learners and students with disabilities.

Draw on professional collaboration and development. Effective assessment systems depend on teachers and other educators who understand the full range of assessment purposes, use a variety of suitable methods, work collaboratively, and participate in ongoing professional development to improve their capability as assessors. Schools of education prepare teachers and other educators well for assessing a diverse student population. Educators determine and participate in professional development related to assessment and work together to improve their assessment programs.

Encourage community participation and communication. Parents, students, and members of the community should join a variety of experts, teachers, and other educators in shaping the assessment system. Discussion of assessment purposes and methods should involve a wide range of people interested in education. Educators, schools, districts, and states should clearly and regularly discuss assessment system practices and student and program progress with students, families, and the community. Examples of assessments and student work should be made available to parents and the community.

Allow for regular reviews. Assessment systems should be regularly reviewed and improved to ensure that they are beneficial to all students. Reviewers should include stakeholders in the education system and independent experts.

What Is Best Practice in Assessment and Evaluation?

Zemelman, Daniels, and Hyde (1998) provide the following list of best-practice indicators as another way of focusing on high-quality assessment and evaluation:

- The purpose of most assessment is formative, not summative.
- Most evaluation is descriptive or narrative.
- Students are involved in record keeping and in judging their own work.
- Teachers triangulate their assessment.
- Evaluation activities are part of instruction.
- Teachers spend a moderate amount of time on evaluation.
- Where possible, competitive grading systems are abolished or deemphasized.
- Parent education programs help community members understand the value of new approaches to evaluation.

Reflect & Respond

Think about instructional changes that would have resulted in your preK–12 education if the criteria suggested by Zemelman, Daniels, and Hyde had been appropriately followed.

In your teaching journal, write about three evaluation experiences you have had, and indicate whether those experiences supported or did not support best practice.

THE CHALLENGE OF DESIGNING EQUITABLE ASSESSMENT AND EVALUATION SYSTEMS

Ensuring equity in assessment involves examining deep attitudes and values regarding the social purposes of assessment. As discussed previously, a historic and central purpose of assessment has been to sort or rank students according to presumed inherent abilities—in effect, to create winners and losers. The current assessment reform movement represents a major shift in values, toward using assessment to ensure that all students have equitable opportunities to learn and achieve at the highest possible level (Gordon, 1993).

■ Alternative Assessment of Nondominant Language and Cultural Groups

Alternative assessment of nondominant language and cultural groups is of enormous interest and concern because there is hope that alternative assessments will reveal what these students know and can do, and there is fear that the same inequities that are associated with traditional norm-referenced tests will recur (Estrin, 1993).

Unlike norm-referenced assessments, alternative assessments have the potential to inform instructional planning by linking directly to students' learning experiences and to the contexts of those experiences, including the cultural contexts of a pluralistic student population. Other desired outcomes of using alternative assessments with nondominant language and cultural groups include the following (Estrin, 1993):

■ Students will be more intensely engaged as participants in their own learning.

■ Student growth and achievement will be communicated more effectively to parents and the community.

■ Teachers will be stimulated to improve their teaching.

■ At-Risk Students and Alternative Assessment

Teachers would like to believe that they do what they do to help students learn. However, in reality they often do what they do to help students learn to take tests. The purposes of the writing, grammar, and spelling tests students take are to compare learners with one another, to place students at different developmental levels, and to diagnose students' learning problems, often for the purpose of removing at-risk students from regular classrooms. The result can be harmful, particularly to low-achieving students. "Students at risk of failure in our public schools face a daily barrage of low grades and evaluations that continually confirm their secret suspicions that they are not able to learn" (Townsend, Fu, & Lamme, 1997, p. 71).

It's no fun to be constantly reminded that you are failing or not doing as well as the student who sits in front of you. It's especially stressful for students who deal with daily family conflicts, hunger, physical or emotional abuse, or low self-concept to carry home a bookbag full of red marks, negative comments, and low grades. By contrast, learners flourish when parents and teachers take an interest in students' development, focus on their strengths, and set realistic instructional goals.

The use of IQ scores to place students in special education programs is a significant concern, given the limitations of intelligence testing, discussed earlier. Assessment bias in special education is part of a larger debate that touches on equity and the role that race, perceptions of intelligence, income, and gender play in assessment. The diversity needs of America's youth are not being addressed by many assessment and evaluation programs throughout the country. Is litigation the only answer to this pressing dilemma? How are learners' needs to be served? As Lindfors (1987, p. 412) argues, "There has been and continues to be in our society a deep and pervasive confusion of 'cognitive ability'

New teachers talk

What do you find to be the most challenging about providing learners with a variety of authentic opportunities to show what they know and can do? Describe an alternative assessment strategy that you have found to be particularly effective.

In today's classrooms, learners come from many diverse backgrounds. Learners speak different languages, live in a variety of family structures, experience both wealth and poverty, practice different religions, and represent many ethnicities. Additionally, learners have varied learning styles and perform at different levels. They have a variety of interests and excel in different areas. When a teacher decides to provide learners with authentic opportunities, it is best to connect that learning to the students' interests and previous knowledge. Because learners' backgrounds are so diverse, it is challenging for teachers to find links that best meet the needs of all learners. It is necessary for teachers to teach learners in ways that engage them in learning and make learning meaningful.

An assessment strategy that I have found to be successful is to provide learners with opportunities to apply their knowledge to "real-life" situations and their own personal experiences. Clearly explaining your expectations will help learners produce quality work. For example, learners could write a letter to a character in a story, providing advice or a possible solution to a problem, rather than writing a book report. Or, students could take on the role of a travel agent who must investigate a state or country (of their choice) and design a travel brochure and poster to advertise and promote travel to that area. This scenario would be more meaningful than having the students write a research paper.

Although it is challenging to provide learners with a variety of authentic assessment opportunities, it is critically important. Students who are engaged in hands-on, real activities will be able to show what they know and can do in a variety of ways.

—SHANA, Preservice Teacher

I use the Work Sampling Assessment System and love sharing the students' portfolios with their families during parent-teacher conferences. When the students are involved in choosing the work samples that go into the portfolios, they are en-

with 'school success.'" This confusion impinges on the lives of at-risk and special needs students, creating disappointment and despair.

■ Recommendations for Moving Toward Equitable Alternatives in Assessment and Evaluation

How can you prepare now for designing equitable assessment and evaluation systems once you begin your practice? Review this list of recommendations, and begin thinking about your professional development goals that relate to assessment and evaluation issues (Estrin, 1993):

1. Set clear student assessment targets or performance goals.
2. Be flexible.

couraged to think about what they did and why—to actually think about their own learning. I believe this metacognitive process is very important. Both the Work Sampling Assessment and the Project approach, which are implemented in my classroom, encourage students to think!

—VICTORIA, Third-Year Teacher

I have found it to be quite challenging to assess students according to their own individual abilities and skills. I constantly need to reflect upon what I have taught to ensure that I am assessing based on my objectives.

Portfolios have been an excellent form of assessment in my classroom. The students save their projects, interviews, and portraits in a file throughout the semester. At the end of the semester, the students and I conference about what they should put into their permanent portfolios. These portfolios follow them throughout elementary school.

During the portfolio conferences, we discuss each learner's accomplishments and growth throughout the semester. We also target some areas that need improvement. I feel this makes the students accountable and responsible for their learn-

ing. It also helps them develop goals for the next semester.

—SHAUNA, First-Year Teacher

Authors' Analysis

These three teachers all struggle with the challenges of authentic assessment. However, because they've experienced the power of authentic assessment in their classrooms, they're committed to providing many opportunities for students to show what they know and are able to do. We were extremely impressed with their learner-focused responses! And we applaud these teachers for their willingness to move beyond traditional assessment.

Now It's Your Turn

 It might be most meaningful for you to respond to this question based on your own experiences as a learner.

In your teaching journal, discuss at least three challenges you have faced when communicating what you know and can do in a classroom situation. Describe an alternative assessment strategy that might have enhanced your ability to communicate and demonstrate your competencies.

3. Collaborate with members of your local community to learn what is valued, and incorporate community resources and values into your classroom.

4. Use multiple sources of performance data when evaluating students.

5. Be aware of the powerful influence of student motivation and interest on assessment programs.

6. Adapt assessment instruments to meet the personalized needs and interests of your students.

7. Enhance your assessment knowledge base by incorporating culturally responsive content and goals in your professional development program.

WHAT DO TEACHERS NEED TO KNOW AND BE ABLE TO DO TO ASSESS AND EVALUATE STUDENTS?

What do teachers need to know and be able to do to assess and evaluate students? Here are some points to keep in mind, taken from the Washington State Classroom Assessment Competencies for Teachers (Stiggins, 1997, p. 107):

1. Teachers must be competent masters of each of the achievement expectations they hold as important for their students. That mastery must be at a sufficient level of understanding for teachers to be able to translate those expectations into quality assessments.

2. Teachers must understand all the various purposes of assessment in schools and know how each level of assessment use (from classroom to building to district to state and beyond) impacts the quality of a student's schooling experience.

3. Teachers must understand and be able to apply standards of assessment quality.

4. Teachers must be able to identify an appropriate assessment method from among several available options, and they must be able either to select previously developed assessments, or develop new assessments that fit the contexts.

5. Teachers must be able to store, retrieve, and communicate assessment results to users of that information in a timely manner that assures complete and accurate understanding of those results on the part of all relevant users.

6. Teachers must know and be able to meet standards of professional (fair, legal, and ethical) practice in conducting classroom assessment practices.

7. Teachers must understand and remain sensitive to the personal consequences of their assessments for their students and the families of those students.

As you develop these competencies, it is essential for you to experience alternative assessment as a learner yourself. Perhaps your professors are utilizing performance-based assessment in your teacher education courses. As we move into the twenty-first century, many university programs are incorporating alternative assessments, such as portfolios and competency-based rubrics, into their professional preparation programs. Emphasis on the reciprocal relationship between assessment and curriculum requires changes in teacher preparation programs—changes that will dramatically influence the ways teachers teach (Poteet, Choate, & Stewart, 1993).

Use the information in the remainder of this chapter to begin moving toward achieving your goals. With that recommendation in mind, we now move to a section on integrating assessment and evaluation into day-to-day teaching. In this section we share many assessment strategies that will become a part of your teaching life. Your preparation to provide leadership during the ongoing assessment revolution begins now!

BALANCING YOUR ASSESSMENT PROGRAM: A QUADRANT APPROACH

We recommend that you divide your assessment program into the four areas (quadrants) outlined in Figure 11.1 and determine what kinds of data you will collect. You'll be able to determine your collection strategies after you decide

Figure 11.1 **Balancing Your Assessment Program: The Quadrant Approach**	**Observation of Process**	**Observation of Product**
	anecdotal records	literature response logs
	interviews	reflection logs
	retellings	student-created questions/tests
	shared reading/writing experiences	writing samples (plays, poems)
	audiotapes	projects
	videotapes	graphs/charts/illustrations
	oral presentations	research reports
	learning centers	portfolios
	Contextualized Measures	**Decontextualized Measures**
	inventories, checklists	standardized achievement tests
	teacher-made tests	state competency tests
	informal reading inventories	criterion-referenced tests
	interest/attitude surveys	norm-referenced tests
	dictations	diagnostic tests
	holistic writing assessment	readiness tests

(Adapted from Anthony, Johnson, Mickelson, & Preece, 1988)

on the purpose of your assessment. For example, if you're assessing students, the focus will be on the process as well as on student products; if you're assessing the effectiveness of your program, the focus will be on a number of contextualized and decontextualized measures.

SEQUENCING THE ASSESSMENT AND EVALUATION PROCESS

It's helpful to have a sequence in mind when you begin designing your assessment and evaluation system. You'll begin by observing. Then you'll collect data, record the observations and data, interpret and analyze the observations and data, report the information, and apply your findings to the teaching/learning process (see Figure 11.2). If you think of this process as circular, you'll be able to move forward and backward through the cycle, based on each student's particular situation. Take this scenario, for example:

> Jody, a new student, joins your fourth-grade classroom late in November. Your observations, the data you've collected, and the information you've recorded lead you to refer Jody for diagnostic testing by early January. After

Figure 11.2
The Cycle of Assessment and Evaluation

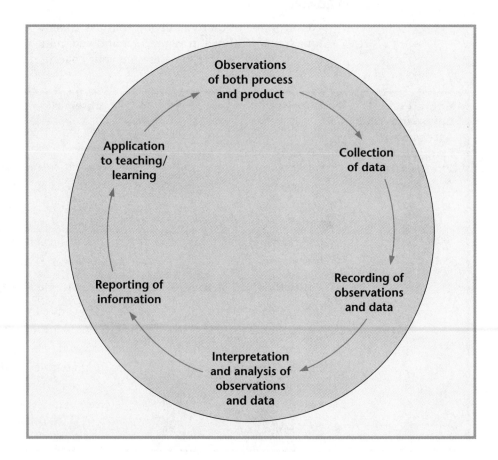

meeting with her parents and receiving their written permission for this testing, the process, in essence, begins again. The special services staff observe Jody in a variety of contexts, record data based on their observations and your referral comments, interpret and analyze the information, and report their conclusions in a conference. They recommend special education services, so an individualized education plan (IEP) will be developed by special services staff and then signed by Jody's parents. After the special services team completes their assessment and evaluation, they meet with the parents for an IEP conference. As the regular education teacher, you work collaboratively with the special services team to develop an inclusionary plan that meets Jody's needs.

The next few sections provide examples of real-life alternative assessments that you can consider for your own use. **Alternative assessment** refers to any type of assessment in which students *create* responses, as opposed to choosing them from a given list. Many resources are available to help you develop alternative assessments for your lesson plans and integrative units. It is our hope that this overview will get you to first base. From there, you'll continue to add to your knowledge and experiential base—and, we hope, hit many home runs before you end your teaching career!

Throughout your teacher preparation program, you'll develop knowledge, performances, and dispositions that will enhance your ability to meaningfully and appropriately assess and evaluate your future students. Take a few moments to assess your professional development at this time. After reading the following statements, rate your competency with regard to assessment and evaluation on a scale of 1 to 10, with 1 being low and 10 being high (Routman, 1991):

- I have a thorough knowledge of developmental learning processes and curricula.
- I can clearly articulate my beliefs about assessment and evaluation.
- I have knowledge and experience in collecting, recording, interpreting, and analyzing multiple sources of data.
- I am flexible and willing to try out and value multiple evaluation procedures to gain a complete picture of the learner.
- I have made a strong commitment to implementing meaningful assessment and evaluation systems in my future classrooms.

In your teaching journal, set some new goals, or focus the goals that you may have developed after contemplating the section on equitable assessment (see page 397). Make a list of the strengths you will bring to the assessment process, as well as the challenges you may encounter.

PERFORMANCE ASSESSMENT AND AUTHENTIC ASSESSMENT

For a **performance assessment,** students demonstrate their competencies or knowledge by creating an answer or developing a product (Feuer & Fulton, 1993). Performance assessments are the norm in many countries and have been preferred by vocational education for a number of years (Stewart, Choate, & Poteet, 1995). Many of the assessments we'll be suggesting here, and many of the instructional strategies and structures we suggested in previous chapters, qualify as performance assessments (such as projects, interviews, oral presentations, constructed-response questions in which students create their own answers, essays, experiments, demonstrations, and portfolios).

Authentic assessment is actually a subset of performance assessment that requires realistic expectations set in real-life contexts. Wiggins (1989) describes four basic characteristics of authentic assessment:

1. It is designed to represent performance in the field.

2. The criteria for attaining stated objectives are given far greater attention during the teaching and learning process than the attention given to criteria in traditional assessment approaches.

3. Student self-assessment plays an integral role.

4. Students are expected to present and defend their work to ensure genuine mastery.

Authentic assessments provide opportunities for students to show what they know and are able to do within and across a number of disciplines. Some examples of authentic assessment items include an audiotape of a student reading to a peer; a log of books read, with critiques; a debate on a current issue; an article for the school paper; a design for a room or bulletin board; a performance in a play; an original recipe; an original investigation and report; a map of the community; and an advertising campaign for a political candidate (Stewart, Choate, & Poteet, 1995).

PERFORMANCE ASSESSMENT FOR SPECIAL NEEDS STUDENTS

Although performance assessment is gaining popularity in general education, its uptake in special education has been slower paced (Poteet, Choate, & Stewart, 1993). Even though most states include one or more performance components in their statewide assessment programs, provisions for students with disabilities vary (Roeber, Bond, & van der Ploeg, 1993). This is somewhat concerning, given the fact that the principles that underpin performance assessment—such as behavioral, curriculum-based, direct, ecological, and functional assessment—have historically prevailed in special education (Coutinho & Malouf, 1993). And as Meisels (1987, p. 71) points out, "Tests that exclude children from public education services or that delay their access to the educational mainstream . . . are antithetical to legal and constitutional rights to free education and equal protection."

Previously we presented some assessment issues that affect nondominant language and cultural groups, as well as at-risk and special needs students. Although performance assessment is more widely accepted in regular education than in special needs education, it's extremely important that you prepare performance-based assessments appropriate for the students with special needs who will be members of your future classrooms. Teaming with special educators and resource staff in your schools will be critical as you design your alternative assessment and evaluation system. Remember that you have been invited to lead—not follow.

PORTFOLIOS

Portfolio assessment refers to assessment based on "a collection of selected student work—products of performance assessment that serve as the basis for ongoing evaluation but may or may not reflect authentic tasks" (Stewart, Choate, & Poteet, 1995, p. 22). Portfolio assessment provides "records of a student's work over time and in a variety of modes to show the depth, breadth, and development of the student's abilities; it is the purposeful and systematic collection of student work that reflects accomplishment relative to specific instructional goals" (Pierce & O'Malley, 1992, p. 2). Examples of items that students may choose to add to their portfolios include an audiotape of a story retelling; a journal of writing ideas; a student-written book; descriptions and diagrams of problem-solving processes; journal notes recording mathematical investigations; a computer-generated map of a student's neighborhood; sketches, paintings, sculptures, and photographs; journal entries that include self-evaluations; representative work samples (all discipline areas); case studies; awards and honors; photographs; and reflections (Stewart, Choate, & Poteet, 1995).

Portfolios offer opportunities for the entire educational community—students, parents, district personnel, and other interested parties—to view the intersection between instruction and assessment (Paulson, Paulson, & Meyer, 1991). Portfolios should be constructed with five elements in mind: collaboration, an expanded view of learning and knowledge, a place to view processes, exploration of multiple perspectives, and reflection and self-assessment (Seely, 1994).

It's also important that you and your students determine the purposes of classroom portfolios, as the first step in the portfolio assessment process. We have suggested a number of examples of items that students could include in their portfolios. The following questions will help you talk with your students about why they are constructing portfolios and will facilitate the goal-setting process:

- Why will you be designing a portfolio?
- What purpose will the portfolio serve? How will it help you learn?

- What data will you collect for it?
- How much data will you collect, and how often will you collect them?
- How will the portfolio be evaluated?

TYPES OF PORTFOLIOS

There are four main types of portfolios—showcase portfolios, documentation portfolios, evaluation portfolios, and process portfolios. The type of portfolio to use in a given situation depends on the purpose of the assessment.

■ Showcase Portfolios

Showcase portfolios are the type of portfolio most commonly used in classrooms today. A **showcase portfolio** is a collection of work that both a student and his or her teacher believe represents that student's best efforts (Seely, 1994). "Because the student selects most of the entries, a showcase portfolio paints a unique portrait of the individual over time" (Valencia & Calfee, 1991).

■ Documentation Portfolios

Documentation portfolios are the second most commonly used type of student portfolio. A **documentation portfolio** is a collection of work that provides evidence of student learning and growth. Virtually any piece of evidence that the teacher and student believe to be pertinent to documenting the student's learning can be included in a documentation portfolio. Included in the collection are rough drafts, notes from brainstorming activities, various math tasks, rubrics, checklists, rating scales, anecdotal records, photographs, peer evaluations, self-evaluations, and a variety of projects (Seely, 1994).

■ Evaluation Portfolios

The purpose of the **evaluation portfolio** is to evaluate students on preselected tasks, using predetermined criteria. Examples of evaluation portfolios include Vermont's Literacy Assessment Project and California's Literacy Assessment Project (Seely, 1994). These evaluation portfolios have been designed as alternative state assessments.

■ Process Portfolios

A fourth type of portfolio assessment is the process portfolio. A **process portfolio** is a collection of items and artifacts demonstrating work that typically is a part of a larger project. The learning process and self-reflection are highly valued in this portfolio. What makes a process portfolio different from a documentation portfolio, which has similar purposes, is the collection of materials. Items in a process portfolio include drafts, notes, and lots of evidence of reflection that supports the learning process (Seely, 1994).

Figure 11.3
Electronic Portfolios

ADVANTAGES

Teachers can
- Import large quantities of information and data
- Attach endless work samples
- Increase authentic communication between home and school
- Prepare students for the school-to-work transition
- Tie student work to district standards
- Easily locate student work
- Cross-reference student work
- Provide students with electronic feedback
- Assess a wide range of skills
- Collect student work over a number of years

Students can
- Engage in self-reflection
- Use multimedia tools to connect work (school) and real life
- Store and retrieve their work
- Make their work accessible to others
- Review their performance
- Make decisions regarding their performance
- Direct and produce their own learning

CHALLENGES

- Electronic portfolios can be expensive.
- Electronic portfolios require a great deal of time.
- Schools/programs may have limited electronic resources.
- Teachers, students, parents, and administrators may lack technical proficiency.
- Teachers may lack professional development.
- Technology may be unevenly distributed for access to all audiences.

■ Electronic Portfolios

Many exciting developments are on the horizon with respect to storing student portfolios. **Electronic portfolios** are simply portfolios that are stored electronically—either on a disk, on a CD-ROM, or on the Web. A number of computer software programs have been designed to help students and teachers develop portfolios. Many peripherals, such as optical scanners and rewritable CD-ROMs, make storing student products electronically a real possibility. Storage is often a critical problem for schools, but electronic portfolios make long-term storage and easy retrieval of student work possible.

After extensively reviewing the literature on electronic portfolios, we've developed a fairly lengthy list of advantages of using them and a much shorter list of challenges (see Figure 11.3). Since the advantages far outweigh the disadvantages, we recommend that you invest some time and energy in contemplating how you will use electronic portfolios.

A number of computer
software programs have
been designed to help
students and teachers
develop portfolios.
(© José L. Pelaez/THE
STOCK MARKET)

CHECKLISTS AND RUBRICS

Checklists are prepared lists of competencies or behaviors that anchor a
teacher's observations of a particular student or group of students. Many
teachers or teams of teachers design their own checklists to match their curricular goals and objectives. The education literature offers many checklists, from
every content area, for your consideration.

RUBRICS

■ What Is a Rubric?

A **rubric** is a scoring guide that helps to establish uniformity in evaluation of a
student product or performance. A rubric allows for differentiation, using an
articulated scale, between various student responses to the same prompt or
assigned task. It also defines a range of responses, from excellent to inappropriate.

■ How Many Kinds of Rubrics Are There?

There are two basic types of rubrics: holistic and analytic. A **holistic rubric**
results in one score that represents an evaluation of the total performance or

product. An **analytic rubric,** by contrast, separates the total performance or product into several elements or criteria.

■ What Are Some Hints for Developing a Rubric?

Following are some suggestions for developing rubrics:

- Use a project or activity that you have already introduced in the classroom, so you will be familiar with the full range of performances.
- Decide on the expectations and criteria that are important, and select an appropriate type of rubric—analytic or holistic—for them.
- Decide on the range of point scores. An even number, 4 or 6, is usually best, because it reduces the temptation to give the "middle" score.
- Limit the number of criteria you evaluate in one assessment to no more than five or six.
- Begin by describing your acceptable standard. Then describe performance that would qualify as "exceptional," performance that would qualify as "developing" or "in progress," and performance that is clearly unacceptable. Use clear, objective—not subjective—language. Remember our discussion about writing objectives? Clearly written objectives with conditions, observable behaviors, and criterion levels are great allies when it comes to developing rubrics!
- Try out your rubric. See if it works with actual student products or performances. Don't be afraid to revise your rubric.
- Let your students see the rubric *before* they perform the task or create the product. It will help to make the assignment clearer—and your students will know what the expectation is!

TEACHER OBSERVATION

Good teachers always have been kid watchers. The concept of kid watching is not new. It grew out of the child study movement, which reached a peak in the 1930s and provided a great deal of knowledge about human growth and development. Teachers can translate child study into its most universal form: learning about children by watching how they learn (Goodman, 1986). Being a good kid watcher is a necessary skill in an integrated classroom where multimodal assessment is valued. What will you need to know and be able to do to qualify as a "good kid watcher"? We suggest an in-depth understanding of, and experience with, human growth and development. In addition, you will need the following abilities: to apply your knowledge of child development on a continual basis; to listen; to focus on relevant information; to be unbiased; to know what to look for, to describe what you see, and to record and categorize your observations; to separate your observational descriptions and your evaluative judgments; to design learning environments and activities that promote hands-on learning and collaboration; and to effectively report your observations, in both written and oral form, to parents, colleagues, and administrators.

Does that sound like a tall order? We think so! Being an effective observer requires lots of motivation, as well as lots of practice. Throughout your teacher preparation program, you will have many opportunities to develop your observation skills. The reason we highlight observation in this section is because it is the foundation for teachers' assessments and evaluations. In other words, your assessment and evaluation program will be only as good as your observation skills. Consider this scenario, written in two different ways by two teachers:

TEACHER A

Two second-grade children, Angel and Elisa, are playing catch with a large red ball on the playground. After approximately three minutes of playing catch, Angel catches the ball, puts it on the ground, and runs off to join Joy and Juan, who are jumping rope. Elisa sits down in the space where she was standing and starts crying quietly. Two other children, Jenny and Jeremy, notice Elisa crying and walk over to her, sit on the ground with her, and ask, "Why are you crying?" Elisa doesn't respond.

TEACHER B

Angel and Elisa were playing catch, when Angel got bored and decided to do something else. Because Elisa is a big crybaby, she just sat on the ground and whined. Jenny and Jeremy tried to help her, but Elisa is just too stubborn.

As you can imagine, this scenario could continue on and on—in fact, it might be interesting for you to finish the scenario based on what you know about second graders. However, the important questions are these: "How are these two scenarios qualitatively different?" and "Which teacher is the better kid watcher?" Teacher A focuses on relevant information, describes what she is seeing, and appears to be unbiased. Teacher B, by contrast, interjects a number of negative, evaluative words, makes judgments about children's intentions, and seems biased. How might the children in this scenario be evaluated differently by Teacher A and Teacher B on a checklist, rating scale, or rubric? Have you ever been in a situation where you were evaluated unfairly by a teacher who had biased or limited information? Use those experiences to remind yourself how important it is to be a "good kid watcher"!

One way that you can begin to fine-tune your observation skills is to try writing anecdotal records as you observe students and teachers during your clinical experiences. Think of an **anecdotal record** as a written snapshot of an event. Describe the event in detail, including what the students say as well as what they do. Always include key information: the student's name, the date and time, the setting, and the activity. Figure 11.4 provides a sample anecdotal record for you to review.

Figure 11.4
Sample of an Anecdotal Record

Child's name: Sam	**Date:** Oct. 5, 1999	**Time:** 11:00 a.m.
Setting: Classroom	**Activity:** Journal Writing	

Sam slowly picked his journal out of the box and plopped it down on the table. His fists were clenched at his side, and his eyes were downcast. Jamie, one of the other children, asked Sam, "What are you going to write about in your journal?" Sam shouted, "I do not know and I do not care!" Sam stared at the journal cover for fifty seconds, then got up quickly and moved to a corner of the classroom. Sam then began writing and did not stop for ten minutes. After he completed his journal, he walked to the journal storage box calmly, smiled, and put his journal back in the box.

(Adapted from Charbonneau & Reider, 1994, p. 114)

Since you will record and collect a number of anecdotal records, you'll look for patterns in a collection of evidence before making judgments. Let's suppose that Sam consistently gets annoyed at the beginning of journal writing time. After collecting a number of anecdotal records, you might share your observations with Sam, Sam's parents, or the principal to determine an appropriate course of action.

SURVEYS, INTERVIEWS, AND STUDENT-TEACHER CONFERENCES

SURVEYS

For a **survey,** students must respond to particular questions or rate items. For example, a mathematics survey might be designed to be completed at the beginning of the year by sixth-grade students, with a threefold purpose: to get to know something about the students' attitudes toward math, to determine the students' histories with math, and to communicate to the students that their ideas will have an important place in the classroom.

INTERVIEWS

For an interview, students respond to questions or rate items orally. Interviews can be conducted by peers, classroom volunteers, or teachers. It's important that copious notes be taken documenting the interviewee's responses to the questions. The interviewer should attempt to keep the student engaged in the conversation but shouldn't encourage particular responses. It's critical that interviews be open-ended. Here are some examples of prompts for a reading attitudes and interests interview:

- If you could read anything, what would you read?
- Tell me about one of your favorite authors or illustrators.
- What is one of your favorite magazines? Why do you like it?
- What part of the newspaper do you like best? Why?
- What would you like to learn more about?

STUDENT-TEACHER CONFERENCES

In a **student-teacher conference,** the teacher talks with a student to help the student reflect on her or his work. Student-teacher conferences are one of the most underutilized assessment strategies. Even conferences as short as three minutes and spaced as far apart as two weeks can have a surprisingly strong impact on students' learning (Graves, 1983, 1994). Here are some guidelines for conducting student-teacher conferences:

Preparing for Conferences

- Begin by explaining how conferences will work, so students will know what to expect and will come to conferences prepared. You may need to role-play with a few students to get the ball rolling at the beginning of the year.
- Set up a conferencing area in the classroom, with a round table and an appropriate number of chairs for individual, as well as small-group, conferences. The conferencing area should be away from very active areas but fairly centrally located, so you can see what's going on with the other students. To signal collaboration, sit next to the student rather than across the table from him or her. Avoid conferencing over the teacher's desk—if you have one. Both the teacher and the student should be prepared to take notes during the conference; be sure there are appropriate supplies at the conferencing table.
- Set up a workable plan for scheduling conferences. You might schedule conferences with literature study groups, project groups, or research groups on a weekly basis. It's also important to schedule individual conferences with students and to allow them the opportunity to request a conference. Have a clipboard with a sign-up sheet for open conference time each week. Don't let a few students monopolize the conference time, and make it clear that you may request students to conference with you at any time.

Beginning Conferences

- Begin with open-ended statements or questions to get the conference started: "Anna, tell me about your 'insectlopedia.' What part are you working on right now? How do you plan to add the illustrations?" Choose questions that students can answer, and ask questions that will lead students to discover appropriate next steps. If students want to read a short section of their journal, story, or letter, be a good listener—and take this opportunity to jot down some anecdotal notes.

Student-teacher conferences as short as three minutes and spaced as far apart as two weeks can have a surprisingly strong impact on students' learning.
(© Robert Llewellyn)

Ending Conferences

■ Keep conferences short—three to five minutes. Ask students to finish each conference by telling you what they will do next, and ask them to write down any further questions for a future conference.

■ Types of Conferences

A number of different conference types have been suggested by Daniels and Bizar (1998). Which of these types of conferences could you incorporate into your novice or student teaching?

> *Process conference.* During this conference, the teacher asks three questions:
>> What are you working on?
>>
>> How is it coming?
>>
>> What will you do next?
>
> *Status-of-the-class conference.* This is a whole-group conference held at the beginning of a workshop session, during which each student shares what, and with whom, she or he will be working that day.
>
> *Read-aloud conference.* This type of conference is used when students are working on a writing product (such as a story, letter, or report); they read a section of the piece aloud to a teacher to receive oral feedback.

Summarizing conference. Teachers ask students to tell about their work instead of sharing samples of it.

Content conference. In this type of conference, teachers offer information, suggest authors, or share "mini lessons" for the purpose of developing the meaning and content of a project or report.

Dialogue journal conference. In this format, the teacher and students exchange notes—a written version of a conference.

Editing-publication conference. The purpose of this type of conference is to engage collaboratively in the final proofreading of a draft for publication or display.

Small-group conference. For this type of conference, the teacher meets with a group of three or four students who are working collaboratively in a research study group or on a project. The teacher functions as the thinking coach and promotes collaborative problem solving.

Peer conference. Once students are comfortable with genuine give-and-take conferencing, they can engage in their own conferences—any of the many types highlighted—without the teacher, as long as the conferences are productive, develop student responsibility, and foster educational growth.

PEER ASSESSMENT

In **peer assessment,** either an individual student or a small group of three or four students is called on to evaluate the work of one or more peers. Peer evaluation is a powerful strategy, both for the student who is being evaluated and for the student or students who are completing the evaluation.

SELF-ASSESSMENT

Self-assessment and self-evaluation also are extremely effective strategies for promoting in-depth learning with a focus on continual growth and improvement. You've had many opportunities throughout this book to reflect on your previous and current educational experiences and apply what you're learning. A writing self-assessment might list the student's name, the title or type of writing, and the following open-ended sentences:

I chose this writing for my portfolio because . . .

This writing shows that I have learned . . .

My future goals . . .

TRIANGULATED ASSESSMENT

A **triangulated assessment** simply refers to an assessment tool that gives you three windows or modes for evaluating students' competencies. An example of a triangulated assessment is the Work Sampling Assessment (Meisels,

1995), which is triangulated into three parts: checklists in each domain, a portfolio, and a narrative summary.

TEACHER RECOMMENDATIONS FOR IMPLEMENTING AN ALTERNATIVE ASSESSMENT PROGRAM

Teachers who were members of an alternative assessment study group (Hange & Rolfe, 1994) made recommendations after six months of developing and implementing alternative assessments in their classrooms. Some of their recommendations were to start small, to develop clear rubrics, to expect to use more time at first, to adapt existing curricula, to have a partner, and to communicate to students and parents that the alternative assessment is highly valued.

GETTING STARTED WITH ALTERNATIVE ASSESSMENTS: NINE TECHNIQUES TO TRY

Educators who have been actively involved in developing alternative assessment systems suggest starting with these activities and items when designing assessment and evaluation programs: group activities; logs and journals; creative and critical problem solving activities; open-ended questions; student-generated questions; authentic performance tasks, concerning real-life problems; portfolios; oral presentations; and research projects (Hange & Rolfe, 1994).

GRADING AND REPORT CARDS

SCREENING, TESTS, AND GRADING

Screening, often used to determine students' readiness for school or specific programs, provides an opportunity to look at the developmental skills of a large number of students in a limited amount of time (IASCD Early Childhood Committee, 1989). Because screening provides only a snapshot of students' development and competencies, screening results should not be used to determine individualized learning goals or to design programs for learners. Many types of screening measures are available and, if used appropriately, provide preliminary information that can be extremely helpful in identifying students who may benefit from further diagnostic testing.

The term *test* has many varied interpretations. A test is an instrument used to assess knowledge or skills. We're confident that you've had many experiences with testing during your school days. These experiences have provided you with a beginning understanding of the many types of tests, some formal and some informal, used to assess knowledge and skills. Although a detailed description of testing is beyond the scope of this book, consider the impact that the different types of tests you've taken—achievement tests, college entrance exams, chapter tests, spelling tests, teacher-made tests—have had on your educational development. Have the tests you've taken provided you with opportunities to show what you know and can do? How have these tests been interpreted? In most cases, tests are graded, and the grade becomes the ultimate focus of the test.

So, what's in a grade? According to Stiggins (1997, p. 409), *grading* is "the process of abstracting a great deal of information into a single symbol for ease of communication." Obviously, the relevance of the symbol that is communicated—the grade—is directly correlated with the quality of the test and the individual interpreting the test. The next section invites you to think about the roles grades have played in your life and how the grades your future students will earn can be effectively communicated to promote student learning and success rather than engender despair and failure. Although alternative assessments provide some options beyond grading, at some time during your teaching career you most likely will be called on to assess students using grades.

ARE YOU MAKING THE GRADE?

The majority of parents and communities still expect students to be graded in school, especially in middle school and high school. The fact is, grades play a significant role in many educational programs—including in higher education. Take a moment to reflect on the role grades have played in your life. Many of your most positive (or perhaps most bitter) experiences in school have centered around a grade. Because such significance has traditionally been assigned to the symbols A, B, C, D, and F, many students have received grades that they have not earned. And conversely, many teachers have not assigned grades in an equitable fashion. In fact, grades are one of the realities of higher education that often, in our view, get in the way of professional teacher preparation. Students who are motivated only by grades often lose sight of course objectives and the many opportunities they have to show what they know through well-designed assessment programs.

For this reason, some teacher preparation programs use alternative, nongraded assessment for clinical experiences courses like novice teaching and student teaching—the preprofessional internships—and others are moving in that direction. Rather than receiving a grade, students develop a collection of their performances that show what they know and can do, while their cooperating teachers and university mentors provide evidence in the form of anecdotal records, checklists, rating scales, rubrics, and narrative summaries to document students' performance. Which type of evaluation do you think would be more valuable to you and to future employers?

Grading is often a major concern for new teachers. Begin planning for it now, so you will be effective at assigning grades if they are a required component of your evaluation program when you begin teaching. Remember, the purpose of grades is to communicate student proficiency. Any other purposes are inappropriate.

■ Avoiding Common Grading Problems

The following list provides you with some grading guidelines to help you recognize some typical grading challenges. If you're aware of potential problems, you'll have the opportunity to make decisions regarding how to avoid these common pitfalls (adapted from Stiggins, 1997, p. 434):

■ Grade on achievement of prespecified targets only, not on intelligence, effort, attitude, or personality.

■ Always rely on the most current information available about student achievement.

■ Devise grades that reflect achievement status with respect to preset targets, rather than improvement.

■ Decide borderline cases with additional information on achievement.

■ Keep grading separate from punishing and rewarding.

■ Change all policies that lead to miscommunication about achievement.

■ Advise students of grading practices in advance.

■ Add further detail (narrative comments) to grade reports when needed.

■ Expect individual accountability for learning, even in cooperative environments.

■ Give credit for evidence of extra learning—not just for doing extra work.

REDESIGNING REPORT CARDS

As assessment and evaluation programs change to match changing curricula, many schools and districts are redesigning their reporting systems as well as their report cards. Report cards don't necessarily contain grades, but they might incorporate some type of scale to indicate student performance. However, as many teachers and school districts begin the movement away from grades, Glazer (1995, p. 98) cautions them to be honest about their intentions. "It is important to be honest with yourself and with your children. The alternative tools that you choose must be honest alternatives—not merely camouflaged labels for A, B and C." If grades are required in your school district, you will need to work diligently to develop a fair, equitable, and reasonable system for assigning them. And if you have the opportunity to design a more appropriate, alternative assessment and evaluation system, you will need to provide direction and support and take on a leadership role.

The Metcalf Laboratory School, a preK–8 public school where Therese taught for a number of years, is continuously involved in assessment reform. Working collaboratively, Metcalf teachers have proposed many alternatives to the traditional report card. Although many different formats and prototypes have been drafted over the years, we share with you the First Grade Language Report in Figure 11.5 as one example of a revised report card. Notice that the marking code is, in essence, a rating scale. This format focuses on reporting a student's competencies (rather than grades), as well as his or her continual progress over 4 nine-week periods.

Figure 11.5
First-Grade
Language
Report

READING	WRITING
Reading Attitudes	**Focus**
• Enjoys books	• Adheres to instructions
• Chooses to read	• Develops appropriate ideas
• Self-selects appropriate books	• Considers audience and purpose
Shared Book Experience	**Writing Strategies/Organization**
• Listens attentively	• Generates ideas to write about
• Responds to questions, text, and pictures	• Presents ideas in clear, logical order
• Joins in when able	• Edits/Revises
Reading Strategies	**Style**
• Understands/Uses 1 to 1 matching	• Chooses appropriate words
• Reads for meaning	• Uses descriptive language
• Uses graphophonic cues	• Exhibits variety of sentence patterns
—initial/final consonants	**Mechanics**
—digraphs	• Spells known words correctly
—consonant blends	• Attempts to spell unknown words
—vowels/vowel combinations	• Uses inventive spelling
• Makes predictions about text	• Uses correct punctuation
• Self-corrects errors	• Uses correct capitalization
• Helps self when in difficulty	• Uses standard language
• Recognizes high frequency words	
• Reads fluently	

Figure 11.5
First-Grade Language Report *(cont.)*

Comprehension	MARKING CODE
• Retells story in own words	• **B = Beginning**
• Uses context to identify new words	• **D = Developing**
• Understands main ideas	• **I = Independent**
• Makes inferences	• **(blank) = not yet evaluated**
• Identifies problem/conflict in a story	

COMMENTS	
Period 1 Date:	Period 2 Date:
Period 3 Date:	Period 4 Date:

(Adapted from Gehrenbeck, 1994)

WHAT'S HAPPENING CURRENTLY AT THE STATE AND NATIONAL LEVELS?

Here we provide you with an overview of assessment initiatives and programs being implemented at the state and national levels. Ideas and efforts currently under way include the following (Anderson & Ellis, 1992): creating a national assessment system, developing performance assessments in a variety of content areas, increasing understanding of commonalities and differences among content areas, clarifying the consequences of using national assessments, and investigating the impact of national assessment efforts on fundamental teaching and learning.

There are many national and state programs that may affect you in the future or perhaps already have affected your educational development. Since this information changes often, it's important to keep current with the many reform initiatives.

The *National Assessment of Educational Progress (NAEP)* is a national assessment program, currently coordinated by the U.S. Department of Education and contracted out to the Educational Testing Service (ETS). NAEP provides the only longitudinal assessment of student learning nationwide. NAEP assessments are administered every other year to a nationally representative sample of students in grades four, eight, and twelve (Anderson & Ellis, 1992).

The *National Assessment Governing Board (NAGB)* is an advisory board responsible for recommending the direction of NAEP policies and practices.

The *Council of Chief State School Officers Student Assessment Consortium (CCSSO SAC)* established the *State Assessment Consortium (SAC)*, which is exploring strategies that link state, national, and international assessments in an effort to help states network to develop useful tests (Anderson & Ellis, 1992).

In addition, most states operate some type of statewide assessment program, using instruments developed by the state or commercially available tests. The trend in some state-level programs is toward performance-based, portfolio, and "enhanced multiple choice" assessments. However, the level of development and distribution across the curriculum and across grade levels varies considerably from state to state.

Public Law 100-297 (also known as the **Stafford-Hawkins Act**), passed in 1988, established the National Assessment Governing Board and set provisions for developing a national examination, without prescribing a specific model for such a test. Nearly any of the various alternatives described in this chapter might address the need, identified in this legislation, for a nationwide appraisal of student learning (Anderson & Ellis, 1992).

General Educational Development (GED) tests were designed in 1942 by the American Council on Education to enable persons who have not graduated from high school to demonstrate the level of mastery normally acquired from four years of secondary school study. Each of the five tests (writing skills, social studies, science, interpreting literature and the arts, and mathematics) uses a multiple choice question format, and the writing skills test includes an essay.

The *Scholastic Aptitude Test (SAT)*, published by the College Entrance Examination Board, and the *American Council on Testing (ACT)* exam, published by American College Testing Programs, are two tests commonly used by universities and colleges to help them make decisions about potential students' likelihood of succeeding in college. The tests measure verbal and quantitative abilities, using multiple choice questions, and are administered several times a year in all states.

The *Secretary's Commission on Achieving Necessary Skills* (SCANS) was asked to examine the demands of the workplace and determine whether students are capable of meeting those demands. Their investigations resulted in identification of essential competencies and "foundation" skills for twelfth graders, which should be an integral part of every student's school experience.

A FINAL WORD ON ASSESSMENT AND EVALUATION: NO CRYSTAL BALL

Although we have set our sights on promoting alternative assessment and evaluation systems, we have no crystal ball to help us predict how the assessment revolution will end. Coping with reform can be somewhat disconcerting at times, but it's important to keep your eye on the goal of developing and implementing effective assessment and evaluation systems for your future students. Two of the scarcest resources in the American educational system are money and time, both of which contribute to many of the decisions that schools make. In general, alternatives to multiple choice assessment are more expensive and time-consuming to develop, administer, and score (Hoover & Bray, 1995; Stecher, 1995). For example, it has been suggested that science performance tests cost about thirty times as much to score as do multiple choice tests (Stecher, 1995). Thus, schools will need to commit considerable professional time and expertise to producing and scoring alternative assessments—or allocate funds to purchase them.

The ultimate outcome of the assessment revolution depends on how several critical issues are resolved. Chief among these issues are appropriate assessment and evaluation standards, cost, reasonable standards for at-risk students, technical adequacy, and the professional development of educators (McLaughlin & Warren, 1994). Resolving these issues will demand professionals who are willing to cope with change, collaboration, and culture—topics explored in Chapter 13.

SUMMARIZING WHAT YOU'VE LEARNED

■ Assessment and evaluation are interrelated concepts. Assessment refers to data collection and can be thought of as the ongoing act of collecting various types of information about individuals or groups of individuals in order to understand them better. Evaluation implies bringing meaning to data through interpretation, analysis, and reflection and involves developing a judgment regarding the quality, value, or worth of assessment data, based on established criteria.

■ Assessment is rapidly assuming its rightful role as the centerpiece of instruction (Elliott, 1994).

■ The primary purpose of early assessment was to exclude individuals from society, school, and the military (Steward, Choate, & Poteet, 1995). Sorting and selecting students are practices that still are alive and actively pursued in schools today.

■ How does a teacher deal with assessment contradictions in the classroom? First of all, realize that standardized tests are here to stay. Historically, American society has placed great value on test results. It's your responsibility as a teacher to understand the purposes and value of a variety of different assessment tools and to advocate for appropriate assessment.

■ Assessment and evaluation systems serve multiple purposes, including assessing prior knowledge, providing data for revising curricula, offering constructive feedback to students, allowing learners to show what they know, anticipating students' educational needs, and determining if learning objectives have been achieved.

■ Measuring the quality of assessment involves three factors: reliability, validity, and fairness. Use the following principles as guides in developing high-quality assessment: employ assessment practices and methods that are consistent with your learning goals, the curriculum, and current knowledge regarding how students learn; ensure that all students receive fair treatment; understand the full range of assessment purposes; invite parents, students, and members of the community to join a variety of experts, teachers, and other educators in shaping the assessment system; regularly discuss assessment practices and student progress with students, families, and the community; and regularly review and improve assessment systems to ensure that they are beneficial to all students.

■ Alternative assessment includes any type of assessment in which students do not choose a response from a given list. In performance assessment, students demonstrate their competencies by creating an answer or developing a product (Feuer & Fulton, 1993). Authentic assessment is a subset of performance assessment that requires realistic expectations set in real-life contexts.

YOUR PROFESSIONAL TEACHING PORTFOLIO

- Begin saving your portfolio entries electronically.
- Develop some alternative assessments—checklists, rating scales, rubrics, interviews, surveys— for the lesson plans you developed in Chapter 10.
- During your clinical experiences, record some anecdotal notes you can share in your portfolio. Compare and contrast your anecdotal records for different grade levels.
- Photograph student work samples and portfolio entries.
- During your clinical experiences, videotape conferences that you lead with both parents and students. With the participants' permission, include these videotaped conferences in your portfolio.

Key Terms

Aternative assessment (p. 403)
Analytic rubric (p. 409)
Anecdotal record (p. 410)
Assessment (p. 388)
Authentic assessment (p. 404)
Checklists (p. 408)
Documentation portfolio (p. 406)
Electronic portfolio (p. 407)
Evaluation (p. 388)

Evaluation portfolio (p. 406)
Holistic rubric (p. 408)
Peer assessment (p. 414)
Performance assessment (p. 404)
Portfolio assessment (p. 405)
Process portfolio (p. 406)
Public Law 100-297 (p. 420)
Reliability (p. 394)
Rubric (p. 408
Screening (p. 415)

Self-assessment (p. 414)
Showcase portfolio (p. 406)
Stafford-Hawkins Act (p. 420)
Student-teacher conference (p. 412)
Survey (p. 411)
Triangulated assessment (p. 414)
Validity (p. 395)

Relevant Resources for Professionals

Books and Articles

- National Center for Fair and Open Testing. (1995). *Principles and indicators for student assessment systems.* (ERIC Reproduction Document No. ED 400 334)
- Putnam, J. (1997). *Cooperative learning in diverse classrooms.* Upper Saddle River, NJ: Prentice-Hall.

Professional Organizations

- The American Educational Research Association (AERA).
  The AERA is concerned with improving the educational process by encouraging scholarly inquiry related to education and by promoting the dissemination and practical application of research results.
  http://aera.net/

• The American Evaluation Association (AEA).
The AEA is an international professional association of evaluators devoted to the application and exploration of program evaluation, personnel evaluation, technology, and many other forms of evaluation.

http://www.eval.org/

Videos

• *Redesigning Assessment Series*
Travel to classrooms where assessment approaches turn students from passive test takers into active, independent learners. View numerous examples of performance-based assessments. Three 24- to 40-minute videotapes and three 50-page facilitator's guides.

Association for Supervision and Curriculum
  Development
1703 North Beauregard Street
Alexandria, VA 22311-1714
800-933-2723

http://www.ascd.org

Web Sites

• **The Consortium for Equity in Standards and Testing (CTEST)**
CTEST focuses attention on how educational standards, assessments, and tests can be used more fairly.

http://www.csteep.bc.edu/ctest

• **ERIC Clearinghouse on Assessment and Evaluation**
The ERIC Clearinghouse on Assessment and Evaluation seeks to provide balanced information concerning educational assessment and resources to encourage responsible test use.

http://ericae.net/

• **The National Center for Research on Evaluation, Standards, and Student Testing (CRESST)**
Funded by the U.S. Department of Education, CRESST conducts research on important topics related to K–12 educational testing.

http://cresst96.cse.ucla.edu/

TEACHERS AS PROFESSIONALS: CHANGE AND GROWTH

In Part Four we investigate what it means to continue to develop your professional skills as a teacher. Part of the excitement that comes with being a teacher is that of remaining a lifelong learner. There are professional standards and policies to learn and uphold. Continued collaboration with peers will provide support and insight. The culture of the school is continually changing and requires periodic reassessments. Finally, with all these skills in place, the professional teacher works creatively toward positive change.

12

PROFESSIONAL STANDARDS FOR TEACHING, LEARNING, AND CURRICULA

— OR —

Policy, practice, and other puzzles

NATIONAL STANDARDS, GOALS, AND RECOMMENDATIONS: THE ORIGINS OF EDUCATION REFORM

December 7, 1941, said Franklin D. Roosevelt, was "a day that will live in infamy." Most people who were living at that time can recall exactly where they were and what they were doing when they first heard that Pearl Harbor had been bombed. The same can be said of the assassination of John F. Kennedy; John Glenn's historic first orbit around the Earth; Neil Armstrong's walk on the moon; Martin Luther King, Jr.'s "I have a dream" speech; the explosion of the *Challenger* space shuttle with Christa McAuliffe on board; and the bombing of the federal building in Oklahoma City. All were national events that substantially altered the United States' course in some way or another.

Although people are not likely to remember exactly where they were and what they were doing when *A Nation at Risk* was published, this event likewise altered the United States' course. At the time of its publication in 1983, few predicted the impact that *A Nation at Risk* would have. In 1983, while Rita was

"One need not assume school failure to propose school reform."

—Bracey, 1994, p. 9

Teachers—especially first-year teachers—sometimes are so preoccupied with survival that they don't want to be bothered with talk of standards and research. They tend to view standards as the realm of bureaucrats and research as the realm of "ivory tower" professors. They just don't see how these things connect with their day-to-day teaching lives. However, even factors teachers don't recognize or acknowledge can have a direct impact on them.

In your teaching journal, make at least three predictions regarding how standards will be relevant to you as a beginning teacher. Next, record three predictions concerning how research results will affect you and the instructional decisions you make. After you finish this chapter, revisit your predictions, assess their accuracy, and modify them as you see fit.

surviving her first year in a new teaching position after completing her master's degree and Therese was in her second year as a preprimary teacher at Metcalf Laboratory School, the battle over the merits of *A Nation at Risk* was just heating up. It continues today. Here we attempt to summarize that debate, because *A Nation at Risk* and the discussion it has provoked provide the context for much of the education reform efforts—including the current emphasis on standards-based reform—that have occurred since its release. Our summary includes the perspectives of ardent defenders, dissidents, and detractors. Anyone with an opinion—informed or otherwise—has waded into what the authors of *A Nation at Risk* described as a "rising tide of mediocrity" to enter this great education debate!

THREE NEW TYPES OF STANDARDS

Education reform initiatives typically center around one of three different types of standards: **content standards,** which focus on curricula; **performance standards,** which focus on student work and assessment; and **school delivery standards,** which focus on resources and support for schools, teachers, and children. Each of these types of standards has three primary objectives: increase student achievement to a level that is competitive with that of other industrialized nations, restore public confidence in education, and maximize the potential for success of all learners. Teacher involvement in standards-based reform efforts has taken many different forms. In addition to authoring standards, teachers have participated in field tests of new standards, helped translate new standards into teachable lessons, initiated standards-setting projects, and served as critics of national standards-setting efforts (Abdal-Haqq, 1995).

NEW STANDARDS FOR TEACHERS

The National Commission on Teaching and America's Future (NCTAF) describes teacher education program accreditation (NCATE), initial teacher licensure (INTASC), and advanced professional teacher certification (NBPTS) as the three-legged stool of teacher quality. For them, this three-legged stool of quality assurance becomes sturdier as standards become more clearly developed and articulated to guide teacher learning across the career span. The commission recommends that this triangulated framework continue to guide education policy across the nation, so that "every teacher prepares at an NCATE-accredited institution, demonstrates teaching competence as defined by INTASC standards for initial licensing, and pursues accomplished practice as defined by the [NBPTS]" (National Commission on Teaching and America's Future, 1996, p. 29).

WHAT DO NATIONAL STANDARDS HAVE TO DO WITH YOU?

Schooling in the United States can be improved by strengthening the professional status of teachers and other educators, the crucial players needed to reform the schools. No lasting positive change will occur in schools unless the professionals who run those schools make it happen (Berliner & Biddle, 1995). That's what all of this has to do with you! "Something must be done to change the perceptions that educators lack any special expertise. Such perceptions negatively affect how students, administrators, and the public at large interact with educators. These negative perceptions also influence how educators feel about themselves, about one another, and about their profession. If we are going to attract and retain truly competent teachers, these perceptions must change. We must take steps to demonstrate that effective teachers possess (and apply) a unique body of specialized knowledge. The way to accomplish this goal is to help display teachers as the experts that they are" (Tauber, 1992, p. 98).

NEW STANDARDS FOR LEARNERS

In the past, schools and teachers often had different expectations for different students. This approach to setting educational goals—tracking—was supported by various organizational practices and structures, including ability grouping, reading groups, retention, acceleration, college preparatory programs, vocational programs, and advanced placement programs. Because of the significant ramifications for this practice suggested by the creation of national standards and goals, later we compare the research on tracking to what actually happens in practice relative to tracking.

WELCOME TO THE REVOLUTION OF EDUCATION REFORM!

In the United States, an education revolution is under way, and those who are preparing and inducting new teachers are at the very center of it. American society is attempting to reshape the mission of education. The evolving expectation is that schools will ensure learning and that teachers will no longer just "cover the curriculum" but also will create bridges between the needs and interests of each learner and the attainment of challenging learning goals. All students, rather than only a few, will be prepared to think critically, solve problems, produce, and create. To achieve this outcome, teachers must possess as deep a knowledge base about learners and learning as they do about subject matter and teaching strategies (Darling-Hammond, 1995).

THE DEBATE OVER SETTING STANDARDS

During the Reagan administration, *A Nation at Risk* was published (in 1983) and the National Board for Professional Teaching Standards was created (in 1987). President Bush, "the education president," gave the country America 2000 (in 1990) and six national goals for education, along with other initiatives. The Clinton administration added two national education goals and launched Goals 2000 (in 1994). The political rhetoric that emerged from each of these administrations implied that setting educational standards would be a "bottom-up" approach to reform. However, since programs such as Goals 2000 are federally funded, securing funding requires developing local standards that match or complement (ostensibly voluntary) national standards (Clinchy, 1995). This fact has led some critics to question the value of such initiatives and even to suggest that the very idea of standards may be suspect:

> It is this "ideology of control" that many critics of the standards-driven agenda believe has, over the years, kept the principals and teachers in our public schools from becoming truly professional educators. These opponents believe that teachers cannot exercise their own intelligence, their own creativity and ingenuity, and their own sense of what the students entrusted to their care need to know and might respond to if they are told at every turn exactly what they must teach and what their students are going to be tested on by the "authorities." . . . For Noddings, Darling-Hammond, and a growing number of others, the continued and continuing attempt to specify on a national level "what every student should know and be able to do" and thus what all teachers and schools must teach are a part of a misguided agenda. (Clinchy, 1995, p. 9)

Noddings (1992) has referred to standards-driven reform as a "hapless drive for academic adequacy." Darling-Hammond (1993a) has recommended that, rather than focusing on externally mandated standards, teachers should construct learning experiences that permit students to confront powerful ideas, think critically, invent, produce, and solve problems. Mandated standards, some fear, may actually work against independent and creative thought.

There is great potential for conflict in attempts to set standards for "what every student should know." For example, the National Council of Teachers of English, the International Reading Association, and the Center for the Study of Reading at the University of Illinois received funding from the Department of Education (DOE) to draft curriculum standards in English. However, the DOE rejected the standards this group proposed and terminated their funding. Kenneth

Goodman, a professor of language, reading, and culture at the University of Arizona who helped draft those standards, reports that the DOE rejected the standards because it concluded they were excessively concerned with process and insufficiently concerned with products or outcomes (Goodman, 1994).

This unsuccessful attempt at establishing standards—and others like it—certainly send cautionary signals about continuing such efforts. Some critics already have tolled a death knell for such efforts and have suggested relegating all existing draft standards to the circular file. Clinchy (1995, p. 11) provides one of the more colorful predictions of the future of the standards movement: "The attempt on the part of scholarly organizations and government bodies to decide 'what all students should know' and then to pass those decisions down to states and local school districts is an enterprise fraught with great intellectual and social dangers and burdened with the prospect of inevitable and endless controversy. Indeed, it is altogether possible—and perhaps it is all too likely—that this part of the standards-driven agenda will self-destruct, that it will simply sink into a morass of name-calling and an orgy of ideological charge and countercharge."

A NATION AT RISK

A Nation at Risk spawned much of the reform (and rhetoric) that followed its publication in 1983. Its impact on American educational policy has been profound. "Not since the Soviet launching of Sputnik in 1957 has the topic of educational reform figured so prominently in American public discourse. This blue ribbon report was followed by lively public discourse, the emergence of numerous additional reform reports and educational policy documents, the publication of essays and studies in the scholarly educational literature, legislative action and gubernatorial attention in many states across the country, and widespread corporate involvement" (Hunt & Staton, 1996, p. 271).

The National Commission on Excellence in Education (NCEE), wrote *A Nation at Risk* to summarize the work its members completed in response to the following mandate given to them by Secretary of Education Terrence Bell (Hunt & Staton, 1996):

1. Assess the quality of U.S. schools and colleges.
2. Compare and contrast secondary education in the United States with the educational systems in several other advanced industrial countries.
3. Study how college and university admission requirements have affected the high school curriculum and how the latter has influenced the former.
4. Identify and study schools and education programs that are successful and those that aren't.
5. Assess how major changes in the last quarter century have affected student achievement and the schools.
6. Make practical recommendations for action intended to improve the qual-

ity of schooling in America, with a special emphasis on the education of teenage youth.

The NCEE made recommendations in five areas: content, standards and expectations, time, teaching, and leadership and fiscal support. *A Nation at Risk* called for higher standards for learning and teaching, increased funding, more leadership from both government and school officials, longer school days, a longer school year, stricter attendance policies, stricter conduct policies, more homework, and requirements that students pass courses to be eligible to participate in extracurricular activities (also known as "pass to play"). The report also identified five "new basics" for high school students: four years of English, three years of mathematics, three years of science, three years of social studies, and one-half year of computer science. In addition, the report strongly recommended two years of a foreign language for college-bound students.

A Nation at Risk's authors discussed connections between the country's education and economy, concluding that the quality of U.S. education and the quality of U.S. life were inextricably linked—and both were in jeopardy. For example, the report stated that "For the first time in the history of our country, the educational skills of one generation will not surpass, will not equal, will not even approach those of their parents" (National Commission on Excellence in Education, 1983, p. 11). Of course, criticism of the U.S. educational system isn't new. As early as 1883, J. M. Rice contended that U.S. public schools lacked adequate supervision, were controlled by politically corrupt boards, and were deluged with incompetent teachers (Bracey, 1994).

CRITICAL RESPONSE TO *A NATION AT RISK*

Ten years after *A Nation at Risk* was first published, a number of reviews attempted to summarize and assess what progress had been made since its release. Some assessments were more dismal and damning than others. For example, Crosby (1993) proclaimed that U.S. students were still at risk and that the report's language, though startling, was on target. Referring to the report's assertion that "If an unfriendly foreign power had attempted to impose on America the mediocre educational performance that exists today, we might well have viewed it as an act of war" he stated, "this nation has proved time and again that it is its own worst enemy. We do not need foreign enemies as long as we continue to self-destruct. Our children might be better off if they declared sovereignty and then asked for foreign aid" (Crosby, 1993, p. 599). Crosby went on to say that a gap existed between the rhetoric and the reality of equal opportunity in U.S. schools and that at-risk students often do not ceive the same opportunities as well-off children do.

Those who suggested that little had changed from 1983 to 1993 (i tion to Crosby, see Edwards & Allred, 1993) also suggested a number ble reasons for the report's lack of influence on educational reform:

- Educators, teachers, administrators, and government officials that the reforms proposed in *A Nation at Risk* would produce provements the schools needed.

- Leadership was lacking.
- Financial resources were inadequate.
- Schools tend to resist change, and implementing the report's recommendations may have been too difficult and complex a task for them.
- The suggested changes were too great.
- More time was needed.
- Local educators didn't feel any ownership of the recommended reforms and were more comfortable pursuing their own efforts to improve education in their districts.

Four prominent education reformers—John Goodlad, Henry Levin, Phillip Schlechty, and Ted Sizer—saw both the report and the following ten years a bit differently. They concluded that *A Nation at Risk* had "put educators on the defensive, generated regulations and mandates imposed from above, created rigidity and stifled creativity, and led to an atmosphere of political polarization susceptible to facile and dangerous solutions" (Asayesh, 1993, p. 9). They also emphasized the role that communities need to play in school improvement and that reform efforts must go beyond the schools to embrace the communities of which they are a part.

Some continue to criticize *A Nation at Risk* for what they see as its inaccuracies and misinterpretations. Berliner and Biddle (1995, p. 3), for example, contend that the report "made many claims about the 'failures' of American education, how those 'failures' were confirmed by 'evidence,' and how this would inevitably damage the nation," but the "evidence" did not appear in the report, and the report did not even indicate where it might be found. Furthermore, they continue, although the U.S. media touts Japanese schools as a system to emulate, Japanese education has had its own problems, including violence, crime, suicides, bullying, and excessive dropout rates.

With regard to the report's claim that U.S. students' achievement has declined, Berliner and Biddle (1995, pp. 34, 35) counter with the following alternative perspective:

> *Standardized tests provide no evidence whatever that supports the myth of a recent decline in the school achievement of the average American student. Achievement in mathematics has not declined—nor has that for science, English-language competency, or any other academic subject that we know of. Moreover, support for the myth of achievement decline has always been weak. Indeed, the two of us know of only one test, the SAT, that ever suggested such a decline—and, as readers know by now, the SAT is a voluntary test and each year is taken by differing types of students, which means that its aggregate results are not valid for judging the performance of American schools. Instead, the evidence suggests that average school achievement has either been stable or has increased modestly for a generation or more. And, although top-ranked students and those from "advantaged" homes have tended to hold their ground, those from "less advantaged" homes have recently shown achievement gains. . . .*
>
> *Endless repetition of a myth does not make it true. On the contrary, the evidence makes it clear that student achievement in America has actually been*

growing in specific, if modest, ways. Remarkably, this growth has occurred when many measures—particularly those for poverty, violence, TV viewing, overworked and absent parents, and the like—indicate that more of our children are leading difficult lives. (1995, pp. 34, 35)

The quotation accompanying the first Reflect and Respond feature in this chapter suggests that the impetus for many reform efforts is a perception of failure on the part of the schools. As Bracey commented in relation to the effects of *A Nation at Risk:* "Much of the attempted educational reform that followed this 'paper Sputnik' also mistakenly coupled an appropriate desire to improve education with an inappropriate assumption that the system had failed" (1994, p. 11). Bracey pointed out that children spend only 9 percent of their lives between birth and age eighteen in school, yet the thinking persists that the schools should lead the nation forward. How much can the schools accomplish alone, without the assistance or support of families, their communities, and other social institutions?

Not only the report's conclusions but also the data on which they were based were questioned by some. Indeed, there is some consensus that the report was intended more as a political treatise than as a useful tool for educational reform. There also is general agreement that the report didn't address certain key issues, including the broader purpose of education, the needs of at-risk students, the financial cost of reform, and various wider, systemic problems affecting schools.

THE OTHER SIDE

Was *A Nation at Risk*'s call to arms heeded? Goldberg and Renton (1993, p. 16) say the answer "must be an emphatic yes." According to them, the report served as a powerful catalyst that roused people to action and launched an unprecedented reform movement. They conclude that "enormous strides" have been made in leadership, standards, and content, and they support that conclusion by pointing to governors becoming involved in education reform, states raising graduation standards, and more students meeting those standards. In fact, the data reported for the ten years following the report's release indicate that the greatest change occurred in the areas of attendance, pass-to-play, and student conduct requirements, whereas modest change occurred with regard to longer school days, a longer school year, and increased homework.

Goldberg and Renton (1993) also credit *A Nation at Risk* for the establishment in 1987 of the **National Board for Professional Teaching Standards (NBPTS)**. The NBPTS is a private organization created to develop a voluntary, nationwide system of board certification for experienced teachers (you'll read more about it later in this chapter). In addition, they credit *A Nation at Risk* with increasing people's interest in alternative routes to teacher certification, which they call "another popular means of boosting teacher quality." "Through alternative certification, talented individuals interested in teaching were allowed into the classroom, under close supervision, without first having to complete traditional teacher education programs" (Goldberg & Renton, 1993, p. 21).

Although alternative certification sounds reasonable in theory and likely has put some talented individuals in the classroom, we must question Goldberg and Renton's assertion that it is popular, boosts teacher quality, and provides for close supervision of those individuals who receive it. There is ample evidence that alternative certification has placed some unqualified individuals in teaching positions where they received little guidance. At least some alternative certification programs seem to be built on the premise that all "talented individuals" can be successful, effective teachers with little or no preparation. Having seen many examples to the contrary, we must take exception to that view.

BELL'S POINT OF VIEW

Terrence Bell—the former secretary of education who created the National Commission on Excellence in Education (NCEE), appointed commission members, and gave them their mandate—refers to the ten years following the publication of *A Nation at Risk* as a "splendid misery for American education" (1993, p. 597). Bell believes that school leaders must turn to parents and community members to address today's challenges, because many of the negative influences children face come from outside the school. As stressed in Chapter 5, parent involvement in schools is key to children's learning success.

Bell stresses that because the human brain attains much of its physical size and weight during the first five years of life, young children should live intellectually active lives, filled with stimulation from print and spoken language, math concepts, colors, and geometric shapes, for their brains to attain their

Parents need to take advantage of "teachable moments" that occur at the breakfast table, in the car, or during the course of typical and special family activities.
(© Michael Zide)

full developmental potential (Bell, 1993). It is particularly important, he says, for parents and child care workers to take advantage of opportunities for "incidental teaching"—that is, to seize informal "teachable moments" that occur at the breakfast table, in the car, or while children are getting ready for bed. Early learning and incidental teaching in homes and child care centers also are prerequisites to successful school reform initiatives.

CURRENT EDUCATIONAL GOALS

Richard W. Riley, one of Bell's successors as secretary of education, believes the United States is "no longer a nation at risk, but a nation on the move—a nation turning the corner, raising its standards and reaching for excellence for the 21st century" (1995, p. 3). He contends that the educational reform efforts under way in many states are beginning to make a difference and that the collective efforts of reformers "are starting to overcome the greatest barrier to the future of American education: the tyranny of low expectations" (p. 4).

GOALS 2000

The **Goals 2000: Educate America Act** was passed in 1994 to bring U.S. educational reform efforts into the twenty-first century. The initiative has met with mixed reactions. One observer predicted that "No matter how well intentioned [the act] may be, it is doomed to failure" (Seidman, 1995, p. 1). However, another touted the act as the driving force behind ongoing efforts to raise standards, to get technology into classrooms, and to ensure that high expectations are set for students, teachers, and parents (Riley, 1995). Goals 2000 was based on America 2000, a 1990 version of a set of national educational goals encompassing school readiness; school completion; student achievement and citizenship; science and mathematics achievement; adult literacy and lifelong learning; and safe, disciplined, and drug-free schools (National Education Association, 1991). The 1994 version (Goals 2000) added a goal for teacher education and professional development and one for parent participation.

According to a U.S. Department of Education pamphlet (1996), Goals 2000 was designed to

- Help develop and implement higher academic standards
- Provide schools and communities with the tools and flexibility they need to do the job, and hold them accountable for results
- Create partnerships between educators, parents, businesspeople, and other community members for the purpose of providing every child with a world-class education
- Encourage parents and family members to become more involved in children's education
- Strengthen and improve teacher preparation, textbooks, instructional materials, technologies, and overall school services so teachers and students will have the tools they need to improve teaching and learning

- Produce better ways of assessing student performance
- Develop rigorous occupational skill standards that will define the knowledge and skills needed for complex, high-wage jobs
- Provide seed capital to help schools, school districts, and states develop reform and improvement plans

Annual reviews that assess U.S. schools' performance with respect to the eight goals identified by Goals 2000 are published and widely distributed (for example, *Ready Schools,* 1998; *The National Education Goals Report Summary: Mathematics and Science Achievement for the 21st Century,* 1997; *The National Education Goals Report: Building a Nation of Learners,* 1995). Interested individuals also can access reports on national education goals on-line. We encourage you to browse the National Education Goals Panel Web site at <http://www.negp.gov>.

In addition to setting specific education goals, Goals 2000 established the National Education Standards and Improvement Council (NESIC). One of NESIC's duties is to identify areas for which specific educational standards ought to be developed. However, this mandate raises many questions, such as how assessment and content are to be aligned; which subjects should be included; the role of the affective realm in education; and the need to address issues such as accommodation of diversity, individualization, multiple performance standards, definition of standards, the voluntary nature of the standards, and standards as a de facto national curriculum (Mulcahy, 1994).

STATEWIDE LEARNING GOALS

In many states, the national education goals put forth in America 2000 and Goals 2000 inspired the creation or revision of state learning goals. For example, in July 1997 the Illinois State Board of Education adopted its revised *Illinois Learning Standards.* Those learning standards include thirty different goals in seven different areas: English/language arts, mathematics, science, social science, physical development and health, fine arts, and foreign languages. Each of those thirty goals includes two to six learning standards, and there are five different benchmarks for assessing progress in each goal: early elementary, late elementary, middle/junior high school, early high school, and late high school. (Table 12.1 details Goal 1 from the Illinois standards and illustrates how the goals and standards are benchmarked for late elementary, middle/junior high school, and late high school.) What do educators do with such goals? They use them as a basis for developing curricula, instruction, and assessment tools.

NATIONAL PROFESSIONAL ORGANIZATIONS

Teaching is at the core of education reform. Consequently, the single most important action the United States can take to improve its schools is to strengthen the teaching that takes place within their walls. Unlike medicine, law, or architecture, the teaching profession has not historically had a codified body of knowledge, skills, and dispositions defined as essential to accom-

Table 12.1
Goals and Standards Benchmarking for English/Language Arts, State of Illinois

STATE GOAL 1: Read with understanding and fluency

As a result of their schooling, students will be able to:

Learning Standard	Late Elementary	Middle/Junior High School	Late High School
A. Apply word analysis and vocabulary skills to comprehend selections	**1.A.2a** Read and comprehend unfamiliar words using root words, synonyms, antonyms, word origins, and derivations **1.A.2b** Clarify word meaning using context clues and a variety of resources, including glossaries, dictionaries, and thesauruses	**1.A.3a** Apply knowledge of word origins and derivations to comprehend words used in specific content areas (scientific, political, literary, mathematical) **1.A.3b** Analyze the meaning of words and phrases in their context	**1.A.5a** Identify and analyze new terminology, applying knowledge of word origins and derivations in a variety of practical settings **1.A.5b** Analyze the meaning of abstract concepts and the effects of particular word and phrase choices
B. Apply reading strategies to improve understanding and fluency	**1.B.2a** Establish purposes for reading, survey materials; ask questions; make predictions; connect, clarify, and extend ideas **1.B.2b** Identify structure (description, compare/contrast, cause and effect, sequence) of nonfiction texts to improve comprehension **1.B.2c** Continuously check and clarify for understanding (*in addition to previous skills,* clarify terminology, seek additional information) **1.B.2d** Read age-appropriate material aloud with fluency and accuracy	**1.B.3a** Preview reading materials, make predictions, and relate reading to information from other sources **1.B.3b** Identify text structure and create a visual representation (graphic organizer, outline, drawing) to use while reading **1.B.3c** Continuously check and clarify for understanding (*in addition to previous skills,* draw comparisons to other readings) **1.B.3d** Read age-appropriate material with fluency and accuracy	**1.B.5a** Relate reading to prior knowledge and experience and make connections to related information **1.B.5b** Analyze the defining characteristics and structures of a variety of complex literary genres and describe how genre affects the meaning and function of the texts **1.B.5c** Evaluate a variety of compositions for purpose, structure, content, and details for use in school or at work **1.B.5d** Read age-appropriate material with fluency and accuracy
C. Comprehend a broad range of reading materials	**1.C.2a** Use information to form and refine questions and predictions **1.C.2b** Make and support inferences and form interpretations about math themes and topics **1.C.2c** Compare and contrast the content and organization of selections **1.C.2d** Summarize and make generalizations from content and relate them to purpose of material **1.C.2e** Explain how authors and illustrators use text and art to express their ideas (point of view, design hues, metaphor) **1.C.2f** Connect information presented in tables, maps, and charts to printed or electronic text	**1.C.3a** Use information to form, explain, and support questions and predictions **1.C.3b** Interpret and analyze entire narrative text using story elements, point of view, and theme **1.C.3c** Compare, contrast, and evaluate ideas and information from various sources and genres **1.C.3d** Summarize and make generalizations from content and relate them to the purpose of the material **1.C.3e** Compare how authors and illustrators use text and art across materials to express their ideas (foreshadowing, flashbacks, color, strong verbs, language that inspires) **1.C.3f** Interpret tables that display textual information and data in visual formats	**1.C.5a** Use questions and predictions to guide reading across complex materials **1.C.5b** Analyze and defend an interpretation of text **1.C.5c** Critically evaluate information from multiple sources **1.C.5d** Summarize and make generalizations from content and relate them to the purpose of the material **1.C.5e** Evaluate how authors and illustrators use text and art across materials to express their ideas (complex dialogue, persuasive techniques) **1.C.5f** Use tables, graphs, and maps to challenge arguments, defend conclusions, and persuade others

(Adapted from Illinois State Board of Education, 1997)

plished practice. Misconceptions and lack of consensus regarding what constitutes effective teaching have persisted (Baratz-Snowden, 1993). Therefore, several national organizations have attempted to respond to the need to professionalize teaching. These organizations are described in the following paragraphs.

THE NATIONAL BOARD FOR PROFESSIONAL TEACHING STANDARDS

In 1987, the National Board for Professional Teaching Standards (NBPTS) was established to develop rigorous standards and assessments for certifying highly experienced and accomplished teachers. Education reformer Adam Urbanski said of the NBPTS's creation, "What you are watching here is nothing less than the birth of a profession" (Lathlaen, 1990, p. 50).

The NBPTS consists of sixty-three members, including outstanding teachers, teacher educators, school board members, governors, legislators, and administrators. The majority of its members are teachers, because if meaningful change in education is to occur, teachers must play a central role (Laws, 1991). By including a majority of educators on the NBPTS, the board acknowledges that outstanding teachers are the most important element in education (Cascio, 1995).

The NBPTS certification system includes three components (Koprowicz, 1994):

1. *Standards.* Professional consensus regarding what teachers should know and be able to do

2. *Assessment.* Valid and accessible means of evaluating teachers against standards

3. *Professional development.* Opportunities for teachers to strengthen their practice through self-examination

NBPTS certification provides an alternative for teachers who wish to advance in their profession without leaving the classroom. Historically, teaching has been a very flat, or horizontal, career that offered few avenues for "on-the-job" advancement. NBPTS certification is designed to serve as a fair and legitimate means of recognizing teaching excellence, with the hope that excellent teachers will remain in the classroom and that excellent teaching will lead to improved student learning (Koprowicz, 1994).

Reformers also hope that NBPTS policies will encourage minority college graduates to consider careers in teaching. Strengthening the profession may result in an improved and larger candidate pool. In addition, the NBPTS proposed that teachers employed in schools where at least 75 percent of the students are economically disadvantaged receive bonuses once they earn NBPTS certification (Koprowicz, 1994).

The NBPTS standards and assessments are based on five major propositions that many teachers and researchers agree are essential to accomplished teaching (Baratz-Snowden, 1993; Darling-Hammond, 1995; Buday & Kelly, 1996; Baratz-Snowden, Shapiro, & Streeter, 1993; Barringer, 1993; Ordovensky, 1990):

1. Teachers must be committed to students and their learning.

2. Teachers must know the subjects they teach and know how to teach those subjects to students.

3. Teachers must take responsibility for managing and monitoring student learning.

4. Teachers must think systematically about their practice and learn from experience.

5. Teachers must be members of learning communities.

■ National Board Certificates

As of 1998, the NBPTS awarded six different teaching certificates, each recognizing excellence in teaching a specific developmental level (see Figure 12.1). In structuring its certificates and assessment processes, the NBPTS's work was guided by four understandings (Laws, 1991, p. 38):

■ All teachers should possess a core of professional knowledge and skills, regardless of whom they teach or what they teach.

■ Teachers should have knowledge and skills specific to the developmental stages of the children under their care.

■ Teachers in each subject area should command a core of subject- and discipline-specific knowledge.

■ Teachers should demonstrate depth as well as breadth of knowledge in the disciplines they teach, as well as skill in conveying that knowledge to their students.

■ Opposition to the NBPTS Standards

To date, the strongest opposition to the NBPTS standards has come from the American Association of Colleges for Teacher Education (AACTE). Although it supports the concept of a national certification process, the AACTE objects to the NBPTS's failure to include graduation from a school of education as a prerequisite for NBPTS certification. The board explained that it rejected an education degree as a prerequisite because "it would exclude candidates who have not graduated from teacher education programs" and yield some control of the process to other groups such as the National Council for Accreditation of Teacher Education. The board ruled out state licensing, it said, because "there is almost as much variety among state standards as there is among states" (Ordovensky, 1990, p. 19).

The NBPTS's rationale for its decision failed to impress some critics, among them John Goodlad, who at that time was president of the AACTE. Goodlad responded to the board's decision not to include an education degree and state licensure as prerequisites for national certification with the following question: "They say the reason for eliminating all of those things is that you'll be eliminating people who haven't met standards. . . . Isn't that what it's all about?" (Ordovensky, 1990, p. 19).

Figure 12.1
Framework of National Board Certificates

Early Childhood (Ages 3–8)

Generalist

Middle Childhood (Ages 7–12)

Generalist
English/Language Arts
Mathematics
Science
Social Studies/History

Early and Middle Childhood (Ages 3–12)

Art
Foreign Language
Guidance Counseling
Library/Media
Music
Physical Education/Health

Early Adolescence (Ages 11–15)

Generalist
English/Language Arts
Mathematics
Science
Social Studies/History

Adolescence and Young Adulthood (Ages 14–18+)

English/Language Arts
Mathematics
Science
Social Studies/History

Early Adolescence through Young Adulthood (Ages 11–18+)

Art
Foreign Language
Guidance Counseling
Library/Media
Music
Physical Education
Agriculture, Business, Health Occupations, Home Economics, and Industry

For teachers of special needs students, the National Board will develop assessments for teaching practice specialties to be added as a third dimension to these certification fields.

(Koprowicz, 1994)

INTERSTATE NEW TEACHER ASSESSMENT AND SUPPORT CONSORTIUM

The **Interstate New Teacher Assessment and Support Consortium (INTASC)** operates under the auspices of the Council of Chief State School Officers, a consortium of more than thirty states and professional organizations. The council created a set of performance standards for beginning teacher licensure and an assessment process for measuring beginning teachers' performance against the INTASC standards.

■ Standards for Beginning Teachers' Licensure and Development

The Council of Chief State School Officers designed the INTASC standards to dovetail with the NBPTS standards and to assess teaching in terms of "how well teachers can plan and teach for understanding, connect their lessons to students' prior knowledge and experiences, help students who are not initially successful, analyze the results of their practice on student learning, and adjust it accordingly" (National Commission on Teaching and America's Future, 1996, p. 29). The ten INTASC standards appeared in Figure 2.7 on page 52 as part of the discussion of how you can use the standards to guide your professional development.

A portfolio is one way you can document and demonstrate your competencies for potential employers.
(© Michael Zide)

NATIONAL COUNCIL FOR ACCREDITATION OF TEACHER EDUCATION

In 1997, the **National Council for Accreditation of Teacher Education (NCATE)** printed its revised—and more rigorous—standards for teacher preparation programs. These standards are linked to those of the NBPTS and INTASC and are designed to hold schools of education and their programs accountable. Approximately 500 of the 1,200 U.S. teacher education programs have earned NCATE accreditation.

NCATE accreditation is one of the principal ways the teaching profession ensures high-quality teacher preparation. NCATE is a collaborative, nongovernmental, nonprofit enterprise composed of thirty national professional organizations, including the Council for Exceptional Children (CEC), the National Science Teachers Association (NSTA), the American Association of Colleges for Teacher Education (AACTE), the Association of Teacher Educators (ATE), the

American Federation of Teachers (AFT), the National Education Association (NEA), the National Board for Professional Teaching Standards (NBPTS), and the Association for Childhood Education International (ACEI); five hundred accredited institutions; policy-making, subject-specific, child-centered, technology, specialist, and administrator organizations; and two thousand volunteer professionals and members of the public. There are forty-one state-NCATE partnerships designed to align state and NCATE teacher preparation program approval. These members and partners collaborate with NCATE in many ways, including providing curriculum guidelines, serving on the NCATE board of examiners and executive board, and coordinating joint annual data collection efforts (National Council for Accreditation of Teacher Education, 1997).

The NCATE stamp of approval assures the public of the following (Cody, 1998, p. 5):

- The school of education has undergone rigorous external review by professionals in the field and members of the public.

- Candidate performance is assessed throughout the program and before the candidate is recommended for licensure.

- The program meets the standards set by the field at large, including practitioners—the process is not an ivory tower one but is a working partnership among higher education, PreK–12 schools, and policy makers.

New teachers talk

Select one of the INTASC standards and describe how you could document your competencies in that area for a potential employer.

I would choose Standard #3, Adapting Instruction for Individual Needs: "The teacher understands how students differ in their approaches to learning and creates instructional opportunities that are adapted to diverse learners." I could document my competencies by developing a portfolio in which I included items that portray my ability to create instructional opportunities for diverse learners.

In this portfolio I could include lesson plans that describe a variety of instructional techniques and adaptations to the activities. I also could include documentation of the effectiveness of the lessons when used with a variety of learners. A record of observations, anecdotal notes, photographs, and personal reflections could describe the students' engagement, interest, motivation, and success.

A professional teaching portfolio could document my abilities to adapt instruction for students who learn best in small groups, large groups, or on an individual basis; students who learn through different learning styles; students who have special needs; students who are gifted or talented;

■ NCATE Curriculum Guidelines

NCATE-accredited institutions must demonstrate how they prepare teachers to meet new licensing standards regarding knowledge, performance, and dispositions in curriculum planning, assessment, instructional guidance, instructional strategies for diverse learners, and parent and colleague collaboration. To receive and continue their NCATE accreditation, institutions also must demonstrate how they prepare teachers to successfully enable their students to meet the standards developed by professional associations such as the National Association for the Education of Young Children (NAEYC), the National Council of Teachers of Mathematics (NCTM), and the International Reading Association (IRA).

Recent NCATE initiatives include the creation of professional development school standards and evaluation of teacher candidate performance by on-site examining teams (Levine, 1998; Wise, 1998). Historically, NCATE on-site examining teams evaluated curricula and looked for evidence that NCATE standards had been met. However, in the fall of 1997, NCATE's executive board voted unanimously to design and implement a performance-based system of teacher education accreditation. That means future NCATE site-based visits will include evaluation of the knowledge, performances, and dispositions of teacher candidates—preservice teachers such as yourself. This change was motivated by the fact that teachers' capabilities are the number one variable in

and students whose first language is not English. My competencies would be demonstrated by how students grow and learn with respect to adaptations made. In addition, a videotape would allow a potential employer to observe my competencies with regard to adapting instruction to meet individual needs.

—SHANA, Preservice Teacher

Authors' Analysis

Shana's response reflects her knowledge of and experience with portfolios. As a preservice teacher, she used a product portfolio to document that she had

met or exceeded the requirements of her teacher preparation program. Because Shana is comfortable with using professional teaching portfolios, it's natural for her to consider using one to document her competencies with regard to INTASC Standard #3.

Now It's Your Turn

 Select one of the INTASC standards in Figure 2.7 (page 52), and in your teaching journal make a list of different ways you could document and demonstrate your competencies with regard to that standard. How will you show your future employer what you know and can do?

enhancing student learning. To review NCATE's standards—both for teacher education institutions and for professional development schools—see its Web site at <http://www.ncate.org>.

THE ROLE OF RESEARCH AND PROGRAM EVALUATION IN EDUCATION STANDARDS

Given the many attempts that have been made to reform, renew, or restructure American education, one would hope that reformers and policy makers would have learned something from past attempts—both failed and successful. For example, reform proposals are more likely to succeed if they follow the guidelines in Figure 12.2.

Although the list in Figure 12.2 may sound impressive, Berliner and Biddle suggest that it skirts a crucial criterion. They emphasize that attempts "to improve education are more likely to succeed if they are associated with research suggesting that they actually work" (1995, p. 345).

RESEARCH AND THEORY ARE RELEVANT TO PreK–12 TEACHERS

Education reform initiatives are more likely to succeed if research suggests that they actually will work. What a novel idea! Each school day, the United States spends $1.5 billion on its schools. Its fifteen thousand school districts employ more than 2.5 million teachers, who teach more than 44 million students in eighty-four thousand schools (Mosteller, Light, & Sachs, 1996). With that level of investment, it makes sense to figure out what works and what doesn't, before beginning a new reform effort. "Thus, plans for improving education should solve the problems they were supposed to solve or generate other lasting benefits that educators, students, parents, or others concerned with education can detect. Unfortunately, only a few improvement efforts actually

Figure 12.2 **Education** **Reform Proposals**	**Education reform proposals are more likely to succeed if they** • Reflect genuine (rather than fictitious) problems faced by schools • Are based on attainable goals that are shared by the people concerned • Are planned with an understanding of structural forces in the society and the education system that will affect the proposed changes • Encourage, and respond to, debates about alternatives between educators, students, parents, and others affected by those proposals • Involve plans for both starting and maintaining the program • Enlarge (rather than restrict) the lives of affected people • Are adequately funded (Berliner & Biddle, 1995, p. 345)

generate benefits—positive and detectable outcomes; and this is surely a major reason why most reform efforts are abandoned. Despite good intentions, a lot of effort, and no little expense, a great many programs designed to improve our schools fail simply because they don't work" (Berliner & Biddle, 1995, p. 345).

WHEN RESEARCH AND PRACTICE DON'T MATCH

Research and program evaluation can play important roles in planning and assessing education reform. However, these activities must themselves be carefully planned and implemented by people who have nothing to lose or gain by their outcomes. Once multiple measures and several valid research studies indicate the outcomes, benefits, and risks of particular innovations, programs, or instructional strategies, then those results must be communicated clearly and directly to the practitioners implementing them. And the task of education reform does not end there. The next step, which often is a challenging one, involves practitioners' making instructional and implementation decisions based on the results of research and program evaluation.

■ Example: Round Robin Reading

Round robin reading is the practice of having one student read aloud while other students follow along in their books. Teachers typically call on students to read small sections of text, or students take turns reading based on where they are seated.

You may recall some of your own experiences with round robin reading. Maybe you counted ahead in the book to find the paragraph you would be reading aloud, so you could practice it quietly until your turn came. Then once you had had your turn, you either followed along with the reader, even if the reading was halting, slow, and painful—for the reader as well as the listeners—or perhaps you quietly attended to your own agenda once you knew you were not likely to be called on to read again, since you already had done so.

Round robin reading is counterproductive to learning to read, especially when used with children who are not effective readers. This is not breaking news. For a century now, educators have had access to information that indicates that round robin reading does not contribute to reading achievement and, in fact, gets in the way of helping children learn to read. As long ago as 1908, the use of round robin reading was criticized and questioned (Durkin, 1989). It is a source of—rather than a cure for—discipline problems. Quite simply, "the data are unmistakable in condemning the routine practice of requiring silent readers to follow the oral reading of poor and mediocre readers" (Gilbert, 1940, p. 621). However, many teachers still use round robin reading on a regular basis. Consequently, we use it as a striking example of an area in which educational practice does not match what the research has to say about an instructional strategy. That is, the research clearly indicates that round robin reading not only doesn't help learning but actually gets in the way, yet some teachers continue to use it. Read-along audiotapes, CD-ROM literature, and something as simple as silent reading or paired reading provide appropriate alternatives to round robin reading.

■ Example: Active Learning Versus "Dittomania"

The dichotomy between active learning and "dittomania" offers another example of a mismatch between research and practice. Throughout this book we've stressed the importance of active learning opportunities that offer students authenticity, engagement, choice, and relevancy. Although Dewey and others long ago documented the merits of experiential learning, or learning by doing (Zemelman, Daniels, & Hyde, 1998), many teachers still fall under the spell of "dittomania." Just what is the appeal of instruction that depends primarily on worksheets? Convenience, security, time savings, and laziness are factors that can lead teachers to rely on decontextualized, fill-in-the-blank, short-answer exercises—the type of activities commonly seen on dittos, worksheets, and blackline masters. Chapter 9 offers many alternatives to "dittomania."

MAKING INFORMED DECISIONS ON INCLUSION AND INDIVIDUAL DIFFERENCES: TRACKING, RETENTION, AND ACCELERATION

If practice doesn't follow research even when researchers' conclusions are compelling and clear, imagine what happens when the message is somewhat mixed. That's the case with tracking, a topic that almost everyone—not just educators—has opinions about. Sometimes those opinions are informed by research and sometimes they're influenced by hearsay, but most often they're brought about by people's personal experiences. We summarize the research on tracking here because it's such a volatile topic and, more importantly, because the whole notion of standards directly affects tracking and the related topics of retention, acceleration, and ability grouping.

INCLUSION

We begin this discussion by describing an alternative to tracking: inclusion. **Inclusion** is the practice of providing for learners' special needs within a regular classroom environment. As you'll discover in Chapter 13, successful inclusion relies heavily on collaboration between many different people, including learners, parents, regular classroom teachers, special educators, speech therapists, physical therapists, nurses, occupational therapists, vision specialists, psychologists, English as a second language teachers, adaptive physical education teachers, and administrators. Without professional development opportunities for the personnel involved, regular structured time for collaborative planning, and a willingness on the part of everyone involved to extend themselves and to make a long-term commitment to inclusionary practices, inclusion initiatives simply will not succeed.

TRACKING

The United States has a history of providing comprehensive, common schooling for all students, as opposed to the two-tiered educational systems seen in some European countries. In the United States, it's difficult to find schools that offer only a college-preparatory curriculum or only vocational courses, whereas England has its grammar (college preparatory) schools and its secondary modern (vocational) high schools. In many European countries, students must select which path they will take—college prep or vocational—at a relatively young age. By mid-adolescence this "selecting and sorting" has already occurred, and students not attending college preparatory schools may enroll in "academic" high schools only if they pass state-administered examinations. "In contrast, Americans have long embraced the common-school ideal and have supported comprehensive high schools because they presumably offer more opportunities and bring students from all walks of life together. But does this mean that 'student sorting' is avoided in American education? Not at all. American schools also sort students, but the sorting procedures are different because they are based on academic tracks associated with different curricula that are offered in a common school building" (Berliner & Biddle, 1995, p. 247). In fact, **tracking** has been used throughout the history of education in the United States (Evans, 1996). There are only two primary types of tracking: curricular tracking, which refers to steering students toward specific course sequences, such as vocational or college preparatory courses, and ability tracking. However, tracking can take many formats, including retention, acceleration, ability grouping, educational sorting, and the use of reading groups (Alexander, Entwisle, & Dauber, 1994).

At the primary level, teachers who use reading groups often do so mainly as a form of "classroom management." Usually there are three or four reading groups, regardless of the children's ability levels. Consequently, sometimes children with satisfactory or even above-average performance find themselves in low-skill reading groups. At the high school level, there's little movement between curriculum tracks once initial assignments have been made; when movement does occur, it usually is from a higher to a lower track (Alexander, Entwisle, & Dauber, 1994).

Typically, discussions of tracking center on one or more of the following four themes (Lockwood, 1996, p. 8):

1. Tracking, considered in isolation from instruction and curriculum as a purely structural practice, is not the real issue facing schools. Instead, more complex and difficult questions related to curriculum and instruction are the more substantive and difficult problems with which schools must contend.

2. Arguments about whether or not to track instruction further polarize districts and communities and can lead to a climate in which nothing productive related to better curriculum and instruction will be achieved.

3. Heterogeneous instruction does not mean that students with poor academic backgrounds are left to flounder; it also does not mean that the bright-

est students carry the burden of learning for the others. . . . When heterogeneous instruction "works," it does not hold back advanced students—nor should it.

4. Heterogeneous instruction does not mean everyone should be treated the same, nor does it mean everyone is the same.

■ To Track or Not to Track?

Most educators and policy makers agree on the need to provide equitable opportunities for all students to learn challenging curricula. Most even agree that simply willing higher expectations without giving attention to effective teaching practices will not produce higher student achievement. However, the agreement ends when it comes to the question of how to provide these equitable opportunities. Although historically tracking has frequently been implemented in an attempt to match educational delivery to students' presumed needs (Alexander, Entwisle, & Dauber, 1994), many view it as a device for constructing failure (for example, Cochren, 1996; Kozol, 1991; McDermott, 1995; Oakes, 1992; Partridge, 1996; Sapon-Shevin, 1994; Weinstein, 1996; Welner & Oakes, 1996). Certainly that can be the case when tracking practices limit students' mobility and when placement decisions are made on the basis of single test scores and single point differences (Weinstein, 1996). Critics of tracking call for the dismantling of stratifying practices and the implementation of more inclusive and challenging schooling that features high expectations for a diverse student population. They also point out that tracking runs counter to American ideals and that detracking is more in keeping with the democratic way of life and therefore should be implemented if the best interests and needs of all children are to be met (Partridge, 1996).

■ Tracking and Diversity

When access to particular tracks is restricted and movement between tracks is limited, tracking can constitute a form of in-school segregation and can perpetuate unequal opportunities and unequal socialization within classrooms (Cochren, 1996). Some tracking practices have, in effect, resegregated schools along racial lines (Sapon-Shevin, 1994). Consider, for example, that nationwide African American students are three times more likely than Caucasian students to be placed in classes for the mentally disabled and only half as likely to be placed in classes for the gifted (Kozol, 1991). In fact, Hispanic students and low socioeconomic status students, along with African American students, are more likely than Caucasian students to be enrolled in lower-track classes and less likely to be enrolled in upper-track classes (Rees, Argys, & Brewer, 1996).

Compelling data reveal that tracking decisions may create or reinforce prejudices and may prompt discriminatory treatment that favors students in high-ability groups and tracks. For instance, studies have revealed all of the following (Berliner & Biddle, 1995, p. 322):

■ Less able teachers are more often required to teach students in low-ability tracks.

- Teachers prepare less for low-ability-track classes.

- Teachers often form the same number of ability groups within their classrooms, regardless of whether their students are relatively homogeneous or heterogeneous in ability.

- Students in lower-status groups frequently pick higher-status students to socialize with, but higher-status students don't reciprocate.

- Students judged to be more capable tend to be given tasks with more complexity and more meaning, and they have more chances to perform publicly. Students judged less capable are assigned more drill and practice and have fewer chances to assess their own capabilities.

- Students judged to be more capable are given more new content to learn, are afforded more choices about tasks to do, are assigned tasks that require more challenge, and get to work more often with other students who are high in motivation and achievement.

Evaluations of tracking programs often have exposed them as ineffective and discriminatory pedagogical practice. Not only has tracking been recognized as poor policy; its legality has been questioned and contested in court (Welner & Oakes, 1996). However, tracking is not only about race. Consider this statement:

> *Whereas African American and Latino children disproportionately wind up in the lower-track classes, most of the children who are disadvantaged by tracking are poor and working-class Whites. The segregative mechanism of tracking, at least ostensibly, is ability. However, like racial segregation, tracking builds inequalities into school that both devalue and materially disadvantage those groups that are least able to defend themselves. Ability, like race, is a social construction that leads schools to define and treat children from powerless groups— Black, Brown, and White—as expendable. Thus, like racial segregation, tracking carries with it class-based damage that can neither be avoided nor compensated for.* (Oakes, 1992, p. 91)

■ Tracking, School Culture, and Politics

Tracking is an entrenched part of school culture and thus is difficult to remove. Various defenses of tracking are heard:

- It's more democratic for students to compete with others of comparable abilities.
- Tracking helps develop better student attitudes.
- Studies have indicated that teachers favor grouping.
- Grouping is a fact of life.

In fact, tracking is associated with many serious problems. Although it is supposed to benefit all students, increase learning, and enhance learners' attitudes about themselves and about schooling, the evidence suggests it doesn't accomplish these goals. Lower-track students generally learn more when offered opportunities that are typically reserved for high-track students (Oakes, 1992).

■ Tracking and Gifted Learners

When tracking systems do produce positive effects, they tend to benefit only students in the higher tracks. However, some opponents of tracking say high-ability students learn just as well in mixed-ability groups (Oakes, 1992). Others (Evans, 1996) contend that grouping gifted students for part of the school day can stimulate and motivate them, and they caution that all students need opportunities to achieve at their maximum level of potential. Still others argue that although abolishing tracking would have a significant positive impact on students in the lower tracks, those improvements would come at the expense of students in upper-track classes (Argys, Rees, & Brewer, 1996). One of those who asks, "Detracking at what cost?" concludes that "If excellence is what is important, evidence does not support the use of heterogeneous grouping for all students all of the time. Options must be included for grouping and re-grouping based upon interest, need, and ability. Furthermore, all students must have an equal opportunity to achieve at their fullest potential. . . . Excellence requires some element of equality; moreover, more equality of opportunity encourages more excellence" (Evans, 1996, p. 12).

■ Of Equality, Equity, and Excellence

A somewhat lengthy review of the literature on tracking reveals a need to clarify the difference between *equity* and *equality*—two terms often evoked in the name of excellence. We often hear these terms used interchangeably to mean "identical treatment." We agree that **equality** refers to same or identical treatment. However, with regard to educational policy and practice, at least, **equity** refers to fairness, which is not necessarily the same thing as identical treatment. We believe all students possess the right to have equal educational opportunities and equal access to educational programs. That is, all students deserve competent and caring teachers, well-stocked libraries, computers in every classroom, and adequate school funding.

However, because we believe no two learners are exactly the same, we cannot advocate that all learners be treated identically with regard to instructional approaches and strategies. If individual and cultural differences are to be acknowledged and accommodated, then educators cannot provide identical instruction for all students. For example, in spite of the fact that students at the same grade level possess reading proficiencies that range from well below grade level to well above grade level, all students in the same class routinely are provided with identical copies of the same social studies book, which they are expected to read. That constitutes equality (sameness), but as an instructional practice it certainly is not equitable (fair).

The call for excellence implies providing challenges and having high expectations for all learners. Excellence must go far beyond basic skills—whether they be the new basics or the old—and must include creativity and higher-order thinking. What occurs in the classroom is the critical variable. Regardless of the organizational structure employed, the ultimate goal is an appropriate education for all students, which includes *equal* opportunities for all learners to meet high but reasonable expectations and the use of *equitable* instructional practices that are responsive to individual and cultural differences.

A fifth grader who missed three days of school due to illness dutifully completed her makeup work when she returned to school. That work consisted, in part, of completing three pages in her language arts workbook. After the student completed those pages and checked her own work against the key her teacher provided, the teacher opened her grade book to record the student's three perfect scores. Upon doing so, she discovered that she already had recorded three A's for the student, because "I knew you'd get them all right even before you did them."

The student beamed at this admission and returned to her seat, feeling validated and affirmed. However, ten years later, as a preservice teacher, she awoke to this question: "If that teacher knew I was going to get them all right even before I did them, then why did I have to do them?" This anecdote serves as an example of equal (identical) treatment that wasn't equitable (fair).

Can you recall times from your PreK–12 experiences when you were treated equally but not equitably? In your teaching journal, describe at least one such incident, either from your own experiences or from the experiences of someone you know. Then compare your example to those of other preservice teachers.

■ So, Is Tracking Useful?

Only a handful of well-designed studies have explored the academic benefits of tracking, and of those, none had unequivocal results. Consequently, sustained inquiry on the practice of tracking is still needed (Mosteller, Light, & Sachs, 1996). Other studies indicate that teaching in detracked classes fosters a richer use of language and a larger variety of teaching methods than what is found in tracked classes. Students and teachers in detracked classes reported a preference for cooperative learning, but no significant achievement differences existed between students in tracked and detracked classes. Also, research results provide no evidence to support the notion that instructional practices in tracked classes are more effective or efficient than those in detracked classes. Such results suggest that teachers should adapt instruction to accommodate a wider range of student achievement and interests within a single classroom (McDermott, 1995).

Although the water is somewhat murky regarding the effectiveness of tracking for high-ability students, the data clearly indicate that tracking brings more liabilities than assets for students in lower tracks (Cochren, 1996; Kozol, 1991; McDermott, 1995; Oakes, 1992; Partridge, 1996; Sapon-Shevin, 1994; Weinstein, 1996; Welner & Oakes, 1996). Certainly there is room for improvement in the ways schools manage heterogeneity, such as identifying alternatives for ability groups and tracks and acknowledging and accommodating different learning styles (Berliner & Biddle, 1995).

Some have suggested that tracking persists because it benefits teachers rather than students. For example, some teachers view tracking as a means of reducing the range of student needs and abilities within one classroom, and consequently the need to differentiate instruction. However, teachers also can serve as the vehicles by which tracking can be eliminated (Cochren, 1996). Educators who wish to eliminate tracking will find that a clear mission statement, school-based leadership, professional development and support, a thoughtful change process, changes in school routines, and changes in state and district policies are all essential to the attempt (Wheelock, 1992).

■ Is It Time for an Overhaul?

Does the U.S. educational system need a basic overhaul if the nation's schools are to be places where all children can learn? Certainly, systemic change is needed to link social service programs to the education system, improve children's readiness to enter school, and create and implement accountability systems that the public understands and accepts. However, if the goal is to replace ability grouping and tracking with flexible educational strategies that meet learners' needs, several challenges must be met (Brown & Goren, 1993, pp. 4–6):

1. Educators need to rethink the school day, and perhaps the school calendar, so that students who need more time to learn can get it.

2. Curricula at all levels must be enriched and perhaps integrated, and students need more experience with activities that stress analysis, critical thinking, and problem solving.

3. Teachers need to learn and use multiple instructional strategies that appeal to different learning styles and to deploy resources in the classroom more strategically.

4. Flexible school organization and decentralized decision making would enable schools to make their own decisions on curricula, instruction, and assessment.

5. Schools need to look at alternative assessment strategies that will reflect student learning more accurately.

6. Schools must explore alternative ways to integrate the instruction of learning disabled, physically challenged, and gifted students into the regular classroom.

7. States and districts must enhance the capacity of schools and school practitioners to direct and implement change and address any financial inequities that may exist.

8. Students need incentives to work hard and must understand what the stakes are if they do not.

What do you think of these recommendations? Do you agree that students need incentives to work hard? What kind of incentives? Should those incentives respond to external or internal motivation?

RETENTION

Educators need to look at the whole picture—the broader system of tracking—to understand and accurately portray the situation. However, when students have experienced low ability groups, special education, and retention, retention is typically held accountable for their troubles (Alexander, Entwisle, & Dauber, 1994). "This piecemeal approach to studying educational sorting is a drawback, and potentially a serious mistake. By examining each kind of sorting separately, the consequences of retention could be over- or under-estimated, misconstrued, or missed altogether, depending on how these other practices intersect with retention and affect students" (Alexander, Entwisle, & Dauber, 1994).

■ What Is Retention?

Retention is the practice of having students repeat a grade (or as a kindergarten teacher once put it, "spend two fun years in kindergarten"). On occasion, retention has been used to keep a student in the same grade for three years. You may have heard retention referred to as repeating, failing, or flunking a grade, but have you ever heard it referred to as *academic red shirting*? That's a term that has its origins in collegiate sports.

As you probably know, if an athlete is "red shirted," that means he or she is kept out of competition, usually for one year, but still is eligible to compete for the same number of years as other athletes. Red shirting is a strategy used to buy time: time for injuries to heal, time for football players to get bigger, or time for athletes to improve their skills. Academic red shirting also buys time, and it typically is used prior to a child's enrollment in kindergarten, with the idea that the child, who may have a "late birthday," will have the benefit of another calendar year to grow, mature, and develop more self-reliance.

At the PreK–12 level, educators generally work to keep retention rates low, but at the college level personnel work to keep retention rates high (that is, to keep students returning to complete their degrees). However, the research and practices you'll read about here focus on retention as a form of tracking in which students repeat a grade.

■ To Retain or Not to Retain?

Discussions of retention tend to evoke very personal recollections: "My parents made me repeat first grade, and I still haven't forgiven them for it" or "I spent two years in kindergarten, and I turned out okay." Every time retention becomes the focus of class discussions among our students, people share their personal experiences with retention, either from a parent's perspective or a student's. Although personal experience with a given practice certainly can have a powerful influence on one's opinions about that practice, it is not a valid basis for assessing if the practice is viable, because no one ever knows how things would have turned out if a different route had been taken.

Retention is one of those hot-button topics that people are prone to making into an either/or, black/white, this/that, yes/no issue. That is, the debates surrounding retention seem to imply that educators have only two choices, with no in-between positions possible: they must practice retention or they must practice social promotion. However, there are alternatives to social promotion that don't include retention, just as there are alternatives to retention that don't include social promotion.

■ What Does the Research Say About Retention?

Although some studies indicate that retention can have positive effects (for example, Alexander, Entwisle, & Dauber, 1994; Kundert, May, & Brent, 1995; Pianta, Tietbohl, & Bennet, 1997), most suggest that retention is more problematic than beneficial. For example, a 1995 study compared students whose school entrance had been delayed a year (remember academic red shirting?) with students who had been retained in later elementary grades. The study revealed significant differences in IQ between the two groups, with the delayed-entry group having the higher scores, but no significant differences in achievement test scores for either group or gender (Kundert, May, & Brent, 1995). In a 1997 study, retained kindergartners showed decreased conduct problems and decreased shy or anxious behavior compared with a matched set of first-year kindergartners of the same age. Although the retainees didn't differ from their age mates on problem behaviors, they did demonstrate lower tolerance for frustration and poorer work habits at the end of first grade. However, compared to themselves over a period of two and a half years, retained children showed reductions in behavior problems, whereas their tolerance for frustration and their peer relations remained unchanged (Pianta, Tietbohl, & Bennet, 1997).

A 1994 study focused on the use of retention in a large, urban, lower-income, predominantly minority school system. The authors concluded that for that particular population, retention had mainly positive effects and led to improvements in some students' attitudes about themselves and school. However, not all repeaters benefited from retention. Positive effects were "found mainly for youngsters held back only once, and for youngsters held back after first grade. Despite the preponderance of positive effects, retention does not cure children's problems. The distinction between 'solution' and 'some help' is critical, and glossing it over has created much of the confusion surrounding retention. The boost children get from repeating a grade, though real, is limited: most one-time repeaters realize some benefits, but remain far behind their age-mates" (Alexander, Entwisle, & Dauber, 1994, p. 214).

It is noteworthy that even though Alexander, Entwisle, and Dauber (1994) find in favor of retention when it's narrowly defined and confined to the one particular population they studied, they also caution that "if the goal is to have children who are not well prepared succeed in school, retention is not a solution. . . . Retention supplies the additional time needed by some students, but a lasting solution requires more than simply going over the same material twice" (p. 233).

Are there problems and pitfalls associated with retention? Consider the following indictment of retention as a form of tracking:

> *School districts throughout the nation regularly retain students as a way of dealing with diversity in ability. Well over a million American students are retained in grade each year, and the overwhelming majority of them are poorly served by that practice. Making students repeat a grade stigmatizes those students and suggests to the world that they are incompetent. Retention in grade is also a very good predictor of drop-out rates. And students who are retained learn less than if they had remained with their agemates. All considered, there is remarkably little to recommend retention in grade as a strategy for handling diversity.* (Berliner & Biddle, 1995, p. 327)

Other researchers (for example, Roderick, 1995; Tanner & Combs, 1993) also draw attention to the strong association between retention and dropping out of school. Students who have been retained are older than their classmates, and during adolescence this may increase their frustration and disengagement, making them more likely to drop out. The conclusion these researchers have reached is that retention doesn't appear to improve school performance but does send a strong message that teachers and the school don't consider the student capable.

■ Who Is Retained?

Children considered for retention often have poor academic skills, are small in stature or young for their grade, have moved or been absent frequently, do poorly on prescreening assessments, or have limited English-language skills. They also are likely to be male, to be minority, to exhibit high activity levels, to be members of families of low socioeconomic status, and to have parents who are unwilling or unable to intercede for them (Robertson, 1997). Like other forms of tracking, retention tends to result in discriminatory practices that work against those who may have begun life with a number of disadvantages. Consequently, retention should be used rarely (such as in cases of extended absences where the situation causing the absences no longer exists) and certainly should not be used more than once with the same student. In fact, retaining students more than once increases the probability that they will drop out of school to a near certainty.

■ Retention and Teachers

In a 1993 study, a randomly selected national sample of 880 first- and fifth-grade teachers reported their perceptions of student retention. The study revealed that most teachers see retention as beneficial. Teachers advocate retention to improve students' academic performance and believe in it as a way to facilitate student growth and maturity and to increase students' success in learning (Tanner & Combs, 1993). In a 1996 study, researchers presented six hundred kindergarten teachers with the case studies of eight hypothetical children.

The teachers were not significantly more likely to recommend retention for boys or for August birthday children, although the trend was toward retaining younger children. However, the teachers were more likely to recommend retention for children described as dependent and somewhat immature—even though all eight children were presented to the teachers as having successfully completed the academic requirements of kindergarten. Older teachers were more likely than younger teachers to recommend retention. Those teachers who recommended retention most often gave low independence and immaturity as reasons for their recommendation (Bergin, Osburn, & Cryan, 1996).

Obviously, such opinions run counter to most of the research on retention. Like round robin reading, teachers—and administrators—often continue to implement retention even though the research base suggests that in most cases the drawbacks outweigh the benefits. Here, again, a serious gap exists between research and practice.

■ Alternatives to Retention

Given the questionable benefits of retention and the many problems associated with it, finding alternatives to it should be part of all academic improvement efforts (Robertson, 1997). For Berliner and Biddle (1995), the solution—and alternative—to retention is time. They say all but a small number of students can master the curricula, given the time to do so. For them, time—not ability—is the determining factor in achievement.

Berliner and Biddle (1995) say the key to maximizing schools' effectiveness lies in creating lessons that bring together students whose knowledge of the subject being taught is about equal—regardless of whether they acquired that knowledge quickly or slowly. This model proposes that learners be moved upward through the curriculum as fast as their achievements warrant. Rather than an age-grade organizational pattern, it follows a rate-of-learning organizational pattern. Consequently, classes would include students who varied greatly in age. One individual could be at a variety of levels, given a variety of achievement in different subject areas. In a rate-of-learning model, all lessons taught, from kindergarten to high school graduation, would be designed to help students move through the curriculum at their own rate.

According to Berliner and Biddle, a rate-of-learning organizational pattern would guarantee that all students would be challenged in the most beneficial ways throughout their schooling. Therefore, they advocate their rate-of-learning model as an alternative to both retention and acceleration, which would eliminate the need not only for tracking but also for magnet schools, gifted programs, and remedial programs. They also contend that a rate-of-learning organizational pattern could avoid many problems associated with special education programs, since they believe that many students labeled "learning disabled" are merely slow learners in one or more crucial subjects (Berliner & Biddle, 1995).

What do you think about Berliner and Biddle's proposal? Does it possess the potential to benefit students? What questions would need to be addressed to successfully implement a rate-of-learning organizational structure? What changes would need to be made in the current organizational structure and design of schools? What questions would you like to ask Berliner and Biddle about their recommendation? What "yeah, buts" do you have for them?

ACCELERATION

■ What Is Acceleration?

One researcher suggests that the term *acceleration* rightfully should be used to refer to the rapid rate of a child's cognitive development, not the educational interventions provided (Van Tassel-Baska, 1992). However, **acceleration** typically is used to refer to instructional practices that enable students to move more rapidly through the curriculum. Consequently, accelerated students master curricular skills, content, and objectives ahead of their agemates.

■ What Forms Can Acceleration Take?

Acceleration can take a variety of forms (Robinson & Noble, 1992; Rogers & Kimpston, 1992):

Early entrance. Children who demonstrate readiness and advanced development enter kindergarten or first grade one to two years earlier than the usual beginning age.

Grade skipping. Learners are double-promoted to bypass one or more grades.

Nongraded classrooms. Learners are placed in classrooms that bear no particular grade level and progress through the curriculum at paces appropriate to their individual abilities.

Curriculum compacting. Learners test out of previously mastered skills and content and focus only on mastery of other areas, thereby moving more rapidly through the curriculum.

Grade telescoping. Learners' progress through the middle school or high school grades is reorganized to shorten the time by one year.

Concurrent enrollment. Learners attend classes in more than one building level during the same year. (For example, a student might attend literature classes at a middle school and trigonometry classes at a secondary school.)

Subject acceleration. Learners bypass the usual progression of skills and content in one subject and progress at the regular instructional pace in the remaining subject areas.

Advanced placement. Learners take courses with advanced or accelerated content for the purpose of testing out of or receiving credit for completion of college-level coursework.

Mentorship. Learners are matched with subject matter experts or professionals to further explore an interest or area in which they're particularly strong and which can't be accommodated within the regular educational setting.

Credit by examination. By successfully completing examinations, learners are awarded a specified number of college credits upon entrance to college.

Early admission to college. Learners enter college as full-time students without completing high school.

■ To Accelerate or Not to Accelerate?

If one finds international data on student achievement, dropout rates, and delinquency valid, then one must concede that they suggest that a disproportionately high percentage of the United States' most capable learners aren't maximizing their abilities (Van Tassel-Baska, 1992). Restricting academically talented students "to a rigid instructional pace and a 'grade-appropriate' curriculum may place them at risk for declines in motivation and achievement" (Mills, Ablard, & Gustin, 1994, p. 495). At the very least, U.S. schools may be asking too little of their brightest students. Worse, they may be preventing them from learning what they're capable of learning.

Some researchers contend that the brightest students have suffered the most dramatic setbacks over the past two decades and are at risk. They conclude that "By encouraging students to learn as much as they are capable of learning and allowing them to learn at whatever pace is truly compatible with their level of ability and motivation, we can only improve the educational environment for all students" (Mills, Ablard, & Gustin, 1994, p. 508). Doesn't that sound a bit like Berliner and Biddle's rate-of-learning organizational structure (1995)?

■ What Does the Research Say About Acceleration?

Reviews of acceleration outcomes have been markedly positive (Lynch, 1994; Rimm & Lovance, 1992; Rogers & Kimpston, 1992). The research base suggests that bright students benefit academically from more challenging learning environments and are not harmed socially or psychologically from the practice of acceleration. Some researchers view acceleration as one means of providing appropriate curricula and services at a level commensurate with a gifted student's demonstrated readiness and need. They argue that without some form of grouping, a differentiated curriculum is difficult if not impossible. They also contend that ability grouping in and of itself is not a problem. However, problems may result when flexibility and imagination are lacking in the application of educational principles (Van Tassel-Baska, 1992).

A case study that profiles one mother's experiences with acceleration (Merlin, 1995) provides a parent's perspective on acceleration. Although this mother encountered resistance to acceleration from the educational establishment on the grounds that it may be detrimental to children socially, emotionally, or even academically, she continued to advocate for challenging and appropriate instruction. Her efforts resulted in her daughter's experiencing a number of forms of acceleration, which included summer school, concurrent enrollment, grade skipping, course skipping, accelerated courses, and summer camp. Due to a combination of various acceleration strategies, this student finished the eleventh grade at age fifteen. Her mother reports that her daughter, who looks forward to going to school each day, finally is having her social, emotional, and academic needs met.

Others who are considering acceleration as a possible method of providing for students' individual differences may find some of the following questions helpful in guiding their thinking and decision-making processes (Tomlinson, 1994):

1. Is the student feeling happy, productive, and challenged in school?
2. Is there a less radical mechanism than acceleration for providing the student with academic challenge and satisfaction?
3. Does the student feel acceleration is the right thing to do?
4. Are school personnel and parents supportive of the idea?
5. Is acceleration seen as an "open" rather than a "closed" option? That is, can the decision to accelerate be reversed or modified if developing situations warrant a change?
6. If more radical acceleration (such as grade skipping) appears to be the best option, have parents, students, and administrators discussed the implications for receiving academic credit for advanced classes prior to high school, the advanced learning options that are available in later grades, the implications for athletic eligibility at the secondary level, the potential impact of the child's physical size on his or her later adjustment if the child is physically small, social adjustment with older peers, the potential impact on college admission, and the child's emotional readiness for change?

■ Who Is Accelerated?

The primary challenge associated with acceleration comes in identifying gifted students and in ensuring that students of lower socioeconomic status, minority students, and female students are considered for acceleration on an equal basis with other students. However, given the educational establishment's history of resistance to acceleration, the most accurate response to the question "Who is accelerated?" is "Hardly anyone." The results of a 1994 study on acceleration and grade skipping in 105 districts' middle and secondary schools revealed that only 15 percent of the districts who responded to the survey had formal policies about grade skipping. However, 57 percent indicated that, although there was no formal policy, there was an unwritten policy that students should never be allowed to skip a grade. Twenty-seven percent of the responding districts had policies that allowed content acceleration, but 73 percent had no written policies concerning it. Those districts that reported using content acceleration said its use was arbitrary and haphazard (Reis & Westberg, 1994).

Referring to the educational establishment's resistance to acceleration, one highly gifted eighth grader commented, "Their attitude seems to be that if God had wanted me to be in 9th grade, He would have had me born a year earlier" (Gross, 1994, p. 27). Exceptionally gifted students are aware that they differ radically from their peers, both academically and emotionally. In Gross's 1994 study, students who had been accelerated indicated that they greatly preferred it to remaining at their former grade level and that they benefited academically, socially, and emotionally. The major challenge in acceleration comes in convincing educators of the benefits of radical acceleration—placing students several years beyond their typical grade level.

■ Acceleration and Teachers

As we already have indicated, historically there has been a "deliberate shunning" of acceleration by the educational establishment. One study even revealed that the majority of gifted program coordinators were philosophically opposed to acceleration (Van Tassel-Baska, 1992). However, a 1993 study suggests that, contrary to common belief, the fear that acceleration usually leads to academic, social, or emotional maladjustment is not supported (Sayler & Brookshire, 1993). In fact, most students who entered school early or skipped elementary grades did not report unusual social isolation or experience profound emotional difficulties. In addition, they exhibited serious behavioral problems less frequently than did other students.

Although the reviews of acceleration have been markedly positive, perceptions of it among teachers and administrators are markedly negative (Lynch, 1994; Rimm & Lovance, 1992; Rogers & Kimpston, 1992). Why? Acceleration goes against the current organizational and philosophical structure of American schools; it challenges the democratic purposes of schools, by allowing some to get ahead; and it usually takes the form of grade skipping, leaving the possibility that skill gaps will develop. People's preconceived opinions, rather than facts, form the basis for most of their objections to acceleration. Those attitudes improve dramatically and fears decrease when school officials or parents have personal or family experiences with acceleration (Sayler & Brookshire, 1993).

■ Alternatives to Acceleration

Although there is obvious disagreement regarding how to meet the wide-ranging needs of a diverse student population, there certainly is agreement that students are diverse. Reflecting on that diversity, Theodore Sizer observed, "That students differ may be inconvenient, but it is inescapable. Adjusting to those differences is the inevitable price of productivity, high standards, and fairness to students" (quoted in Tomlinson, 1994, p. 42). It is also the road to providing an appropriate and challenging education for all students.

Those who find acceleration objectionable must identify alternative strategies for providing an appropriate and challenging education for all students. As already noted, Berliner and Biddle (1995) propose a rate-of-learning model as one such alternative. Increased flexibility within classrooms and more chal-

Figure 12.3 **Suggestions for Reducing Tracking**	1. Provide a rich core curriculum that is complex and challenging.
	2. Take informal knowledge seriously.
	3. Allow multiple right answers to many kinds of problems.
	4. Promote the social construction of some types of knowledge.
	5. Engage students in long-term, self-selected projects.
	6. Develop authentic assessment alternatives that don't pit students against one another.
	7. Utilize cooperative learning activities, peer tutoring, and cross-age tutoring.
	8. Collaborate with specialists, program assistants, parent coordinators, and parents to help learners and meet their needs.
	(Berliner & Biddle, 1995)

lenging, on-target instruction within an inclusive setting are some additional possibilities.

FINAL THOUGHTS ABOUT TRACKING, RETENTION, AND ACCELERATION

If all teaching embodied best-practice principles, there would be no need—or perceived need—for tracking, retention, acceleration, or ability grouping, because all students would be actively engaged in appropriate, challenging, authentic, and relevant learning opportunities. Consequently, we consider best-practice principles an appropriate alternative approach to tracking. Figure 12.3 contains additional recommendations for reducing reliance on tracking. We hope you'll detect some similarities between them and the best-practice principles we introduced you to earlier. We include them here to remind you that, as an educator, you have viable alternatives to tracking and social promotion.

We conclude our discussion of tracking, retention, and acceleration with the following perspective on individual differences:

Segregation by age and presumed ability are not good solutions for the problem of heterogeneity. The proper solution is to treat heterogeneity as an asset, as a part of life, and to design school experiences to accommodate it and take advantage of it. To do this properly would maximize student achievement and create a better climate in schools. And it would mean that we are conducting education in ways that are far closer to our democratic ideals. Multi-age classes and ungraded schools are designed to accommodate differences in children's rates of learning and may even save money when compared with traditional forms of instruction that require extra expenses for special education. It is surely in the interests of the nation to experiment more with such flexible structures for schools. (Berliner & Biddle, 1995, p. 328)

Try replacing *heterogeneity* with *diversity* in this quote from Berliner and Biddle. What do you think would happen if all educators viewed diversity as an asset—a positive variable that enhances and enriches every learner's education? And when educators value diversity as an asset, how does that affect the myriad instructional decisions they make?

SUMMARIZING WHAT YOU'VE LEARNED

- Education reform initiatives typically center around one of three different types of standards: content standards, which focus on curricula; performance standards, which focus on student work and assessment; and school delivery standards, which focus on resources and support for schools, teachers, and children. These standards have three primary objectives: to increase student achievement to a level that is competitive with that of other industrialized nations, to restore public confidence in education, and to maximize the potential of all learners to succeed.

- In the United States, an education revolution is under way, and those who are preparing new teachers are at the very center of it. American society is attempting to reshape the mission of education. The evolving expectation is that schools will no longer only "cover the curriculum" but will ensure student learning and address the needs and interests of each learner. All students, rather than only a few, will be prepared to think critically, solve problems, produce, and create. To accomplish this, teachers must possess as deep a knowledge base on learners and learning as they do on subjects and teaching strategies (Darling-Hammond, 1995).

- *A Nation at Risk,* a report written by the National Commission on Excellence in Education (NCEE), spawned much of the reform that has followed its 1983 publication. The NCEE made recommendations in five areas: content, standards and expectations, time, teaching, and leadership and fiscal support.

- The Goals 2000: Educate America Act (1994) was passed to carry educational reform efforts into the next century. Goals 2000 includes six goals: improve students' readiness for school; improve school completion rates; improve student achievement and citizenship; improve student performance in science and mathematics; improve rates of adult literacy and lifelong learning; and provide safe, disciplined, and drug-free schools.

- The National Board for Professional Teaching Standards (NBPTS) developed rigorous standards and assessments for certifying experienced and accomplished teachers. The NBPTS certification system includes three components: standards, assessment, and professional development.

- The National Council for Accreditation of Teacher Education is one of the primary means by which the teaching profession helps ensure high-quality teacher preparation. NCATE is a collaborative, nongovernmental, nonprofit enterprise composed of thirty national professional organizations, five hundred accredited institutions, two thousand volunteer professionals and members of the public, and forty-one state/NCATE partnerships. NCATE standards are linked to those of the NBPTS and INTASC and are designed to hold schools of education and their programs accountable.

■ Research and program evaluation play important roles in planning and assessing education reform. However, they themselves require careful planning and implementation by people with nothing to lose or gain from their outcomes.

■ If practice doesn't follow research, even when the results are compellingly clear, imagine what happens when the messages research sends are somewhat mixed. That's the case with tracking, a topic that almost everyone has opinions about. Sometimes those opinions are informed by research; sometimes they're influenced by hearsay; most often they're determined by personal experience with the system. The whole notion of standards directly affects tracking and the related topics of retention, acceleration, and ability grouping.

YOUR PROFESSIONAL TEACHING PORTFOLIO

■ At some point in your teaching career, you likely will be asked to provide evidence of your teaching competencies with regard to specific criteria, such as those outlined in the INTASC standards. Begin to think about how you can use a portfolio to document your teaching knowledge base, performances, and dispositions.

■ Carefully review the INTASC standards and brainstorm artifacts, attestations, productions, and reproductions you can begin collecting and organizing to help demonstrate your competencies in those areas. Then make a list of items you want to be sure to include in your professional teaching portfolio. Remember that one item, such as an integrated unit, might serve to document your competencies for a number of different standards. The captions and reflections you include in your portfolio will be crucial components that explain your rationale for selecting the items you have included.

Key Terms

Acceleration (p. 457)
Content standards (p. 427)
Equality (p. 450)
Equity (p. 450)
Goals 2000: Educate America Act (p. 435)
Inclusion (p. 446)

Interstate New Teacher Assessment and Support Consortium (INTASC) (p. 441)
A Nation at Risk (p. 430)
National Board for Professional Teaching Standards (NBPTS) (p. 438)

National Council for Accreditation of Teacher Education (NCATE) (p. 441)
Performance standards (p. 427)
Retention (p. 453)
Round robin reading (p. 445)
School delivery standards (p. 427)
Tracking (p. 447)

Relevant Resources for Professionals

Books and Articles

- Kozol, J. (1991). *Savage inequalities: Children in America's schools*. New York: Crown.

- National Commission on Excellence in Education. (1983). *A nation at risk: The imperative for educational reform*. Washington, DC: U.S. Government Printing Office.

- National Commission on Teaching and America's Future. (1996). *What matters most: Teaching for America's Future*. New York: Teachers College.

Professional Organizations

- The Interstate New Teacher Assessment and Support Consortium (INTASC).
  INTASC, which operates under the auspices of the Council of Chief State School Officers, created performance standards for beginning teacher licensure and a corresponding assessment process designed to measure beginning teachers' performance against the INTASC standards. INTASC believes effective teachers integrate content knowledge with pedagogical understanding to ensure that all students learn and perform at high levels.
  http://www.ccsso.org/corestan.html

- The National Board for Professional Teaching Standards (NBPTS).
  The NBPTS works to strengthen the teaching profession and to improve student learning in America's schools.
  http://www.nbpts.org/

- The National Commission on Teaching and America's Future.
  The mission of this commission is to provide an action agenda for meeting America's educational challenges, by connecting higher student achievement with the need for competent teachers who are committed to meeting the needs of all students.
  http://www.tc.columbia.edu/~teachcomm

- The National Council for the Accreditation of Teacher Education (NCATE).
  NCATE's primary mission focuses on ensuring that institutions that prepare teachers meet or exceed specific standards and criteria.
  http://www.ncate.org/

Web Sites

- **National Education Goals Panel**
  Eight national education goals have been established for the nation as a framework for education reform. As part of this effort, the National Education Goals Panel (NEGP) was created in 1990 to measure the nation's progress toward reaching these goals. The NEGP Web site offers a variety of resources to help you find out about the goals, the nation's and each state's progress toward achieving them, and key issues in the area of education reform. The site displays tables and charts showing changes in a variety of indicators since the goals were adopted.
  http://www.negp.gov/

- **Teachers and Goals 2000**
  This Web site is designed to provide teachers with information related to Goals 2000. Topics addressed include education partnerships, professional development, sample standards, and the origin of Goals 2000.
  http://www.ed.gov/G2K/teachers/index.html

- **Developing Educational Standards**
  Developing Educational Standards is a list of annotated links to sites at the international, national, state, and local levels that contain information on educational standards. There are also links to clearinghouses, labs, and other organizations that include standards information, as well as newspapers and magazines. This page is maintained by Charles Hill of the Putnam Valley, New York, schools.
  http://putwest.boces.org/Standards.html

COLLABORATION, CULTURE, AND CHANGE

13

— OR —

Working creatively within the system

CREATING A CULTURE OF COLLABORATION

In effective schools, collaboration, culture, and change are inseparable: each affects and acts on the others. Organizational culture has featured prominently in several chapters of this book (most notably Chapter 6), and collaboration and change are recurring themes we've woven into several different discussions (for example, discussions of professional development, teachers as leaders, interdisciplinary planning, and instructional guidance). Recall from Chapter 6 that we defined organizational culture as the basic assumptions that operate within an organization, and we discussed how it is reflected by the behavior of organization members and by various outward manifestations of the organization's values, including its structure, management style, and physical setting (Jensen, 1988).

Viewing schools as organizations, it follows that a school's culture consists of the basic assumptions that operate within it as reflected by the behavior of its teachers, students, and other members and the outward manifestations of its values, such as how communication flows within the school, the principal's leadership style, the frequency and structure of meetings, and learning environment designs. If we accept the premise that school culture, or "how we do things here" (Deal & Kennedy, 1982), permeates every dimension of schools and affects every interaction that takes place in them, then we must conclude that it also has a significant effect on collaboration initiatives and change efforts in schools.

Collaboration is more than mere cooperation (which sometimes can be reduced to begrudging compliance). Instead, collaboration refers to two or more individuals' or organizations' working together toward a common goal.

THIS CHAPTER

▸Defines and provides examples of collaboration, culture, and change in education

▸Discusses change as a process, levels of change, and the stages of concern that typically accompany change

▸Describes the roles collaboration, culture, and change play in professional development

▸Describes the purpose of and philosophical premise behind the comprehensive, integrated-services approach to addressing the special needs of learners and their families

▸Identifies organizational features that facilitate the comprehensive, integrated-services approach to addressing the special needs of learners and their families

▸Identifies the major variables school leaders must address as they plan and implement programs to help new teachers

▸Identifies typical survival concerns of new teachers, as well as practices and interventions that often help them cope with those concerns

"Collaboration holds great promise for addressing many of educators' and the public's demands for fundamental change in the schools, as well as creating a climate in which all students can become successful learners."

(Gable & Manning, 1997, p. 222)

Referring to the exponential growth of knowledge and rapid rate of change that have occurred in this century, futurist Alvin Toffler predicted that "The illiterates of the 21st century will not be those who cannot read and write, but those who cannot learn, unlearn, and relearn." What implications does Toffler's prediction hold for you as you enter the teaching profession?

In your teaching journal, brainstorm a list of all the ways you can think of that change may affect the teaching/learning process throughout your lifetime. Next, select from your list the three change factors you believe will have the most significant impact on schools and schooling. Then, describe possible ways that schools, school leaders, and teachers (yourself included) can respond to those three factors. Finally, discuss your predictions and suggestions with other preservice teachers.

"Working together" includes implementing change, as well as participating in ongoing planning to identify problems and systematic analysis to evaluate progress toward meeting stated goals (that is, formative and summative evaluation).

As for change—it's time someone acknowledged simply and honestly that change is almost always messy and is often arduous and time-consuming. After all, **organizational change** involves disrupting the status quo and introducing an innovation that those leading the change effort believe will lead to enhanced performance or improvements of some sort. Such disruptions are not always invited or welcomed, and they always produce an affective response in those who are asked to change. Throughout this chapter you'll read much more about change as a developmental process.

EXAMPLES OF COLLABORATION AND COPING WITH CHANGE

Many of the initiatives undertaken in PreK–12 settings during the past twenty years have involved organizational and cultural change efforts that benefit from collaborative approaches. Such initiatives include site-based management, teacher induction, mentoring, peer coaching, action research, inclusion, professional development schools, year-round schools, multiage grouping, the middle school concept, and a host of other innovations that require changes in practice, attitudes, and "how we do things here." Add to this already overwhelming list the restructuring of initial and continuing teacher preparation, and the combination may be enough to produce panic attacks in even the most long-suffering and persevering of teachers!

Because our goal here is to inform rather than to overwhelm, we have chosen to apply the posthole theory (Zemelman, Daniels, & Hyde, 1998) to our discussion of collaboration, culture, and change. Therefore, rather than grazing the surface of numerous different initiatives, we focus here in-depth on three initiatives that require collaboration and changes in school culture: professional development schools (PDSs); the comprehensive, integrated-services approach to addressing the special needs of learners and their families; and teacher induction. However, first we provide an overview of the change process and the ways individuals typically respond to change.

THE ONLY CONSTANT IS CHANGE

In spite of the fact that, historically, change in education has been slow and arduous, we can promise you that change definitely will be a real and tangible component of your teaching career. First, effective teachers engage in an ongoing process of self-renewal and professional development, which involves change. Whether teachers retire after a forty-year career or resign to pursue another profession after five years, hopefully when they exit the teaching arena they are not the same teachers they were when they first entered the field. Second, as the needs of society and political agendas change, eventually schools also change.

Although change can be a positive and productive process, many people would rather it didn't involve or affect them—thus the expression "The only one who appreciates change is a wet baby." However, just as change is an undeniable part of life, it also is an undeniable part of teaching, learning, and their many associated variables. Consequently, it makes sense for educators to attempt to understand how change occurs, how to facilitate change, and how individuals respond to change.

UNDERSTANDING THE CHANGE PROCESS: ASSUMPTIONS OF THE CONCERNS-BASED ADOPTION MODEL

Although some school reform initiatives ignore the research on change, many educators do plan and implement change initiatives with an understanding and appreciation of change as a developmental process that every individual responds to differently. For example, the West Virginia Early Childhood Transition Initiative (1995), an interagency change effort designed to develop a seamless system of services for young children (birth to age 5), was monitored using a multiyear program evaluation plan based on the Concerns-Based Adoption Model (C-BAM). School improvement initiatives (Griswold, 1993;

Light, 1996), assessment initiatives (Francis & Hord, 1995), and technology initiatives (Hope, 1995) also have made use of C-BAM principles.

C-BAM rests on the following key assumptions regarding change and change initiatives (Hall, 1974):

- Change is a process—not a one-time event.
- Change is accomplished by individuals first—then institutions.
- Change is a highly personal experience.
- Consequently, change efforts must focus on people first and the innovations second.
- Change entails developmental growth in feelings and skills.

How do decision makers use these assumptions as they plan change initiatives? Unfortunately, many times they do not. Often, designs for implementing change in schools involve "one-shot" inservice programs rather than ongoing professional development geared to the specific needs and concerns of the people responsible for implementing a new program, approach, or strategy. There is much to be gained by identifying individuals' concerns about innovations, as well as the degree to which they are implementing them. C-BAM can facilitate this process. Consider the C-BAM stages of concern and levels of use (Hall, 1974), which are profiled in Table 13.1 and Table 13.2.

BEGINNING TEACHERS' CONCERNS

Compare the following stages of beginning teachers' concerns to the stages of concern outlined in C-BAM (Theis-Sprinthall & Gerler, 1990):

Table 13.1 **Stages of Concern: Typical Expressions of Concern About an Innovation**	**Stages of Concern**	**Expressions of Concern**
	REFOCUSING	I have some ideas about something that would work even better.
	COLLABORATION	I am concerned about relating what I am doing with what other instructors are doing.
	CONSEQUENCES	How is my use affecting learners?
	MANAGEMENT	I seem to be spending all my time getting materials ready.
	PERSONAL	How will using it affect me?
	INFORMATIONAL	I would like to know more about it.
	AWARENESS	I'm not concerned about it.

The awareness, informational, and personal stages focus on the SELF; the management stage focuses on the TASK; and the consequences, collaboration, and refocusing stages focus on the IMPACT of the innovation.

(Hall, 1974)

Table 13.2 **Levels of Use of an Innovation: Typical Behaviors**	**Level of Use**	**Behavioral Indices of Level**
	RENEWAL	The user is seeking more effective alternatives to the established use of the innovation.
	INTEGRATION	The user is making deliberate efforts to coordinate with others in using the innovation.
	REFINEMENT	The user is making changes to increase outcomes.
	ROUTINE	The user is making few or no changes and has an established pattern of use.
	MECHANICAL USE	The user is making changes to better organize use of the innovation.
	PREPARATION	The user is preparing to use the innovation.
	ORIENTATION	The user is seeking out information about the innovation.
	NONUSE	No action is being taken with respect to the innovation.

NONUSERS of the innovation operate at the nonuse, orientation, and preparation levels, whereas USERS operate at the mechanical use, routine, refinement, integration, and renewal levels.

(Hall, 1974)

1. Concerns about factual and informational matters
2. Concerns about self
3. Concerns about management
4. Concerns about student learning and professional collaboration

You'll note that both begin with informational and awareness issues and then progress to concerns about self, concerns about management, and finally concerns about how teachers' behaviors affect others, including students and colleagues. Acknowledging that change is a developmental process—both in terms of the stages of concern those experiencing it pass through and in terms of their ability and willingness to implement it—is the first step in understanding how best to facilitate change initiatives. Acknowledging change as a developmental process also can help individuals who are being asked to implement an initiative better understand the feelings they experience as they respond to and engage in the change process.

Change and Organizational Culture

Studying organizational culture can help educators decide how best to introduce and implement change. Schools have an obligation to provide organized, systemic professional development for teachers to help them adapt to change (Patterson, 1993). After all, change cannot be mandated; it's the result of individuals' changing. Teachers influence change because they're at the center of the learning process and play a major role in establishing "how we do things here." Consequently, schools only improve when individual teachers change their behaviors, attitudes, and beliefs to take on leadership roles (Fullan, 1993).

PROFESSIONAL DEVELOPMENT SCHOOLS

Professional development schools (PDSs) are an educational innovation designed to simultaneously restructure and renew PreK–12 schooling and teacher preparation. As we suggested in Chapter 12, the term *professional development school* is used in a variety of ways. What one person labels a PDS,

New teachers talk

If the only constant in the teaching/learning process is change, then what implications does that hold for teachers?

This implies that, as educators, we must be lifelong learners who are open to new ideas. Teaching methods, teaching strategies, technology, and curricula are constantly expanding, and as educators learn about these changes, they will be better prepared to meet the needs of all learners. It's important for us to read new research, join professional organizations, communicate with parents and students, be involved in the community, collaborate with colleagues, and reflect on our own actions. With so many changes, we cannot be the type of teachers who teach the same thing, the same way, year after year.

—SHANA, Preservice Teacher

Teachers must be reflective practitioners who are willing to embrace change. They must realize that, even though doing so may cause discomfort, embracing change can produce positive results. Every student brings change, every class is change, and every year is change. Teachers must be flexible and do what is best for each and every child they come in contact with.

—MARNI, First-Year Teacher

Teaching is a lifelong learning process. No one can ever know everything. Since teachers always should be learning, they also always should be changing. As a first-year prekindergarten teacher, I find myself learning new things every day and adapting the things I learn to my teaching style and classroom. There are many ways for me, as a new teacher, to learn things. I learn from the children in my class. When a child yells out, "We've done this before. This is dumb," I know it's time to reevaluate that lesson. In addition, I learn from my coworkers. It's common to find us in each other's rooms asking what lessons and activities worked and didn't work and changing our plans accordingly.

I'm in graduate school. Consequently, that provides me with professional development opportunities that have helped me learn additional effective methods of teaching children.

I also find myself sitting through many district-provided workshops on the latest research and ways of teaching. Some workshops I find more valuable than others, but no matter what, I always learn something. Often I leave a workshop and immediately change a piece of my classroom curriculum.

A final and very important way I learn is from the parents of the children I teach. I encourage

others might view simply as a school in which a college-based teacher preparation program places many of its students for field experiences. Such discrepancies helped fuel the movement to create standards for PDSs.

Although definitions of PDSs vary, most PDSs "can be characterized as collaborations between schools and colleges or universities (and sometimes community agencies) that focus on: (1) the preparation of preservice teachers; (2) the continued professional development of experienced educators at school and college; (3) high quality education for diverse students; and (4) continuous inquiry into improving practice. . . . As they strive to achieve these objectives, PDSs inevitably transform the roles, the relationships, and the responsibilities of teachers and administrators at the school and at the university" (Teitel,

parents to come talk to me about anything at any time. They take me up on that offer and give me many suggestions for lessons.

Whether teachers know it or not, they are learning. Because of my journaling and reflecting on each day, I find myself learning from the little things in life. I hope every teacher recognizes and takes advantages of the many ways of learning that ultimately result in change.

—ANN, First-Year Teacher

Because change is the only constant in the teaching/learning process, educators must realize that they always will continue to be learners. Expanding knowledge and advancements in technology mean that educators will have new information to teach and new ways to do so. From educational research come new ideas on how to teach most effectively. Teachers will be faced with the task of deciding which ideas they will accept or reject. Flexibility and an openness to new ideas are critical.

Continuing professional development is so important, because it helps those in the educational field keep up with the changes that may affect them. More important, however, is the fact that, because they are leaders in their classrooms and schools, educators should realize that change

does not have to be something that only happens *to* them. They are in the position to make change happen. The only way to make the most effective changes is to be knowledgeable about the field, so decisions will be informed ones.

—ANGIE, First-Year Teacher

Authors' Analysis

We're impressed by the insight and depth these teachers' responses reflect. They realistically acknowledge change as a permanent and ongoing part of their professional lives. In addition, they indicate a willingness to take responsibility for planning and participating in professional development opportunities that will help update and expand their knowledge base and enhance their teaching effectiveness.

Now It's Your Turn

 Now that you've considered other novice teachers' responses to the preceding question, what's your prediction regarding how you'll respond to the challenge of change as a constant that directly affects the teaching/learning process? In your teaching journal, "think out loud" about steps you might take to remain current and to update your skills and knowledge base once you begin teaching.

1997, p. 9). When PDSs emerge from true collaborative efforts between PreK–12 schools and universities, they can play key roles in education reform, by creating new frameworks for teaching and learning. Successful PDSs become living laboratories, providing environments that facilitate student and faculty inquiry as well as collaboration across disciplines (Sattler & Jensen, 1998).

THE PDS INITIATIVE

Since the mid-1980s, policy makers and educators have devoted significant time and attention to PreK–12 school reform, the redesign of teacher preparation programs, and the establishment of PDSs (Abdal-Haqq, 1995; Carnegie Corporation of New York, 1986; Holmes Group, 1986; Metcalf-Turner & Fischetti, 1996; Sattler & Jensen, 1998). The role of PDSs in teacher preparation is comparable to the role teaching hospitals play in the preparation of health care professionals. Schools are used to provide field experiences for preservice teachers as well as ongoing professional development for veteran teachers. The overall goal is to refine professional practice and to provide a built-in, ongoing system for reform that is informed by applied research (Sattler & Jensen, 1998).

PRACTITIONER PARTICIPATION IN PRESERVICE TEACHER PREPARATION AND INDUCTION

Some envision a paradigm for professional development that features collegial work settings, team teaching, school improvement networks, and school-university collaboration (Darling-Hammond, 1992). Expanding on this paradigm, others (Lieberman & Miller, 1992) focus on developing a culture of inquiry within each school and providing professional growth activities that are in synch with the school culture. This approach recognizes specific dilemmas and problems experienced by beginning teachers, while still maintaining and supporting their professional development.

Shifting attention to the role of the university, others (Aaronsohn, 1996) have concluded that when novice teachers have direct, continuing access to teacher educators for support as these new teachers work at letting go of traditional assumptions, they can gradually realize that goal. In light of this conclusion, it seems critical to ask which professional development models are most effective for fostering the university connection in teacher induction. Dunifon (1985) presents such a model, which features teams of colleagues from PreK–12 schools and the university. Team members are selected on the basis of the individual and collective strengths required to facilitate the personal and professional development of beginning teachers. This team works with teacher inductees in assessing learning strategies, designing classroom environments, and creating an awareness of the school culture. Furthermore, the team takes active responsibility for helping inductees and the school system solve the problems and address the opportunities that emerge over time.

In addition to collaborating as team members, university faculty teach in

PreK–12 classrooms while PreK–12 teachers reciprocate by teaching on the university campus. This arrangement facilitates the engagement of both university faculty and PreK–12 teachers in their own professional growth and development, as a consequence of their involvement with the induction process (Kiley Shepston, Jensen, Alm, & Beaver, 1997).

A PROFESSIONAL DEVELOPMENT SCHOOL CASE STUDY

The university where we teach has formed PDS collaborative partnerships. We'll refer to these partnerships to give you a sense of how one PDS collaborative works. The mission of Bradley University's College of Education and Health Sciences focuses on preparing students to serve as leaders within the human service professions, which include nursing, physical therapy, dietetics, counseling, and administration as well as teaching. The college has established PDS relationships with four schools, which collectively provide an early childhood setting, a K-8 setting, a middle school setting, and a secondary setting. College student involvement in these PDS sites consists of completing field-based coursework, action research projects, observations, practica, and internships. Students majoring in nursing, counseling, administration, early childhood education, elementary education, special education, and secondary education fulfill some of their program requirements at the different PDS sites (Sattler & Jensen, 1998).

In addition to supervising college majors at the PDS sites, Bradley faculty collaborate with PDS faculty and staff in several other ways. For example, Bradley faculty members serve as PDS coordinators at each site, helping identify the needs of PDS faculty and students and working with PDS personnel and other faculty to address those needs via inservice programs, workshops, and research projects. Family education activities, individual consultations, assessment of individual students, classroom visits, and teacher observations are additional examples of how Bradley faculty are involved at PDS sites. PDS and Bradley faculty also collaborate on action research projects and professional development plans (Sattler & Jensen, 1998).

Bradley students benefit from the PDS partnerships by gaining public school experience and learning how different human service professionals collaborate to meet the needs of learners and their families. In addition, Bradley students also become mentors for one another, and PDS students benefit from the personal attention and services offered by Bradley students and faculty. The college students serve as role models for the PreK–12 students at the PDS sites. Interacting with college students helps younger students realize that they can go to college, too (Ridgeway, 1996). One PDS principal commented, "To a certain extent, some of the children have emotional concerns. When they have a need to interact on a one-to-one basis, and a Bradley student provides a listening ear, it does a lot for that child" (Ridgeway, 1996, p. 18).

The primary mission of schools is to increase the probability that students will be successful and will develop as whole learners—socially, intellectually, physically, and emotionally. A PDS principal observed that Bradley's role in addressing that mission is an integral part of the school's success: "Our partnership with Bradley has provided a dimension of professionalism that most public schools don't have the luxury of providing. People get so involved with the rush of daily life that they forget education is not only a science, it's also an art. With this relationship, you have theory and practice put together" (Ridgeway, 1996, p. 18).

THE COMPREHENSIVE, INTEGRATED-SERVICES APPROACH

Although some education and health care service-provision models include integrated school- and community-linked services, most emphasize prevention in their approach to families and local needs (Dryfoos, 1994; 1996). Professionals who subscribe to a **comprehensive, integrated-services approach** to the provision of education and health care acknowledge that all aspects of individuals' lives affect their success as students, patients, family members, and community residents. For example, untreated ear infections may delay language skills, and poor nutrition often results in poor performance or learning (Sattler & Jensen, 1998). At-risk students are of particular concern for schools, health care agencies, and social service agencies. However, all students can benefit when human service professionals implement an **integrated therapy team (ITT)** approach to providing services. Working collaboratively, these practitioners can address the social, physical, and psychological issues that affect children, families, and communities, without duplicating services and getting in one another's way (Sattler & Jensen, 1998).

APPLYING THE COMPREHENSIVE, INTEGRATED-SERVICES APPROACH IN SCHOOLS

Inclusionary practices in schools sometimes are based on the belief that students' special needs are best met by providing integrated services. Although many factors affect the effectiveness of comprehensive, integrated-service delivery systems, the team that delivers the services is the most crucial component. Critical—but often over looked—dimensions that provide a framework for team approaches to meeting learners' special needs include schools as organizational cultures, teachers as leaders, the creation of cultures of leadership, and collaboration (Jensen & Kiley, 1998).

We hope those dimensions sound very familiar to you by now! We have devoted entire chapters of this book to discussing schools as organizational cultures and teachers as leaders, emphasizing that schools can facilitate teachers' development as leaders by establishing cultures of leadership. Rather than repeat ourselves here, we simply refer you to Chapter 3 and Chapter 6 for a review of organizational cultures, teachers as leaders, and the creation of cultures of leadership. Each of those concepts has a major role to play in providing a framework for ITT approaches to meeting learners' special needs. Collaboration also makes a significant contribution to such approaches. In addition, it serves as a unifying theme throughout this book—a theme we highlight here because of its key role in team approaches to providing for learners' special needs.

■ Collaboration

Collaboration features prominently in efforts to provide integrated education and health care services to students and their families (Hanson & Lynch, 1995; Jensen & Kiley, 1997b; Kaufman & Brooks, 1996; Northfield & Mitchell, 1995). Collaborators must have time to meet and plan and the ability to accept and even value the tensions that are part of collaboration (Johnston & Thomas, 1997; Rainforth & England, 1997).

Dealing with students with serious medical conditions, as well as other at-risk students, brings additional challenges and tensions to collaboration. It's imperative that partnerships exist within and among school communities and community social services and health care agencies. These partners must collaboratively plan, develop, implement, and evaluate comprehensive programs that support the ongoing inclusion of each child (Bartlett, 1994). However, because social service agencies and schools inhabit different worlds, there often are culture clashes between them, and integrating school and agency personnel can create obstacles to the delivery of integrated services (Batenburg, 1995).

To help minimize the conflicts that are an inevitable part of collaborating with others, a number of researchers have provided guidance for developing effective collaborative teams (for example, Friend & Cook, 1996; Gable & Manning, 1997; Hewit & Whittier, 1997). Creating successful teams involves establishing trust, developing common beliefs and attitudes, empowering team members, effectively managing meetings, and providing feedback about teaming (Dukewits & Gowin, 1996). Inclusion creates opportunities for teachers to function as leaders and decision makers and requires a different way of thinking about learning—it involves change. Consequently, teachers need to be actively involved in the change process if their behaviors, attitudes, and beliefs regarding inclusion are expected to change.

School leadership is also a key variable in successful collaboration, as well as in successful inclusion initiatives. Principals must create conditions that ensure professional development is a part of the school culture, remembering to create consensus, promote shared values, and ensure systematic collaboration (DuFour & Berkey, 1995).

CHARACTERISTICS OF INCLUSIVE SCHOOLS

Schools that support and facilitate the inclusion of special needs students share the following seven characteristics (Burnette, 1996). As you review them, you'll note that these characteristics involve some form of collaboration, culture, or leadership.

> *A sense of community.* Inclusive schools embrace the philosophy that all students belong in and can learn in the mainstream of school and community life. They value diversity and accept and support all learners by helping them develop feelings of self-worth, pride in their accomplishments, and mutual respect.

Inclusive schools encourage their students and staffs to support one another through collaborative arrangements, such as buddy reading, peer tutoring, team teaching, and teacher-student assistance teams.
(© Susie Fitzhugh)

Leadership. Principals of inclusive schools involve their staffs in strategic planning and implementation of change initiatives.

High standards. Inclusive schools provide students with opportunities for high achievement. The content and delivery of instruction reflects both students' needs and an emphasis on high standards.

Collaboration and cooperation. Inclusive schools encourage their students and staffs to support one another through collaborative arrangements such as buddy reading, peer tutoring, team teaching, cooperative learning, and teacher-student assistance teams.

Changing roles and responsibilities. Inclusive schools modify staff and teachers' traditional roles. For example, teachers do less direct teaching and assist more, and school psychologists work more closely with teachers in their classrooms.

An array of services. Inclusive schools offer their students access to an array of coordinated education, physical health, mental health, and social services.

Partnerships with parents. Inclusive schools welcome parents as equal and essential partners in their children's education.

ORGANIZATIONAL FEATURES THAT FACILITATE THE COMPREHENSIVE, INTEGRATED-SERVICES APPROACH

In a succinct and interesting statement, Kohn (1996a) suggests that "To meet needs, we need to meet" (p. 87). That is, to meet students' needs, teachers, support staff, and family members need to get together, to become involved in

Figure 13.1 **Integrated** **Therapy Team** **Programs:** **Key Assertions**	**ASSERTION 1** Children and families that participate in successful ITT programs benefit from the collaboration and shared expertise of the human service professionals involved. **ASSERTION 2** Human service professionals must demonstrate effective interpersonal skills and informed, collaborative decision making to function successfully as members of ITTs. **ASSERTION 3** Successful implementation of the ITT approach requires school environments and cultures that support the collaborative efforts of ITT members. **ASSERTION 4** Change initiatives, such as the ITT approach, must include professional development opportunities, expectations, and commitments for all who participate. (Jensen & Kiley, 1998)

programs that focus on collaboration and the importance of effective, integrated learning environments and that emphasize the critical nature of affective behaviors. Figure 13.1 profiles four key assertions regarding successful attempts to respond to learners' special needs via an ITT approach.

However, when attempts to provide comprehensive, integrated services using a team approach make no provision for collaborative planning, schedule limited time for team members to meet, and offer no guidance or clear direction, they illustrate the worst form of empowerment. Such attempts expect ITT members to implement an organizational value (such as collaboratively providing for special needs) without the preparation necessary to succeed. Ill-conceived attempts to plan and deliver integrated services can also create tension between team members. As one might anticipate, this tension carries over into the learning environment, where it affects students, canceling out many of the potential benefits a collaborative approach has to offer (Jensen & Kiley, 1998).

■ A Collaborative Culture

Failed or aborted attempts to implement comprehensive, integrated services attest to the critical need for school cultures that support collaboration. In the absence of the dimensions crucial to successful collaboration (leadership, staff development, planning time, a shared mission, clear communication, staff empowerment, consistent expectations, and collegiality), ITT members' time, energy, and attention will be consumed by mere survival. Without these dimensions the team's efforts will lack a clear sense of direction, causing the team to waste a considerable amount of time (Jensen & Kiley, 1998).

■ Program Evaluation

Sometimes, even when a written program description indicates that ITT members will engage, both individually and collectively, in self-assessment, this doesn't happen formally. Other times, no provisions for formal program evaluation—internal or external—are even planned. Those involved in ITT initiatives must take the time to plan and implement formal evaluations, if program strengths are to be acknowledged and program weaknesses addressed.

■ Collaborative Skills

The long-term success of school improvement efforts depends on the ability of participants to function productively together (Donaldson & Sanderson, 1996). Effective interpersonal and professional relationships are critical to the creation and maintenance of successful integrated therapy teams: "Today's human service professionals must demonstrate effective interpersonal skills and informed, collaborative decision making in order to function successfully as members of these teams. It is no longer enough—and in fact it was never enough—for them to master the knowledge bases appropriate to their disciplines (e.g., physical therapy, learning disabilities, counseling, pediatric nursing). Any health care consumer who has heard the conflicting opinions of different health care providers as they talked about—but not to—the consumer understands and appreciates the need for human service professionals who operate successfully as members of an integrated team" (Sattler & Jensen, 1998, pp. 97, 98).

■ Leadership

All of those responsible for creating school environments and cultures conducive to the success and productivity of principals, special education administrators, lead teachers, and other education and human services professionals in the schools must identify and respond appropriately to organizational variables that facilitate or impede attempts to provide comprehensive, integrated services to special needs learners. They also must enable teachers and other human service professionals to serve in leadership roles.

■ Professional Development

School districts must provide ITT members with appropriate, ongoing professional development opportunities and expect that they will routinely take advantage of them. In addition, ITT members must take responsibility for and plan their own professional development. When change initiatives such as the ITT approach include opportunities and expectations for professional development for those delivering the services, students and their families benefit directly (Jensen & Kiley, 1998).

HELPING NEW TEACHERS

Teachers seem to receive and endure more unsolicited and uninformed criticism than most other professionals do. However, those who have observed or experienced the teaching profession firsthand generally conclude that teaching—when done well—is one of the most difficult and challenging occupations one can pursue. How is it then, that until relatively recently, few formal efforts have been undertaken to help novice teachers acclimate to the challenges of teaching (Bey & Holmes, 1990; Caccia, 1996; Chester & Beaudin, 1996)?

Glasser (1992) asserts that being an effective teacher is society's most difficult job. He points out that most managers in business manage workers who are fairly cooperative, find their jobs somewhat satisfying, and want to be there. However, in schools, "teachers and administrators [are] trying to manage huge numbers of students who actively and passively resist what they are asked to do. From the superintendent down, all school managing is difficult, but teaching—the daily face-to-face managing of many resistant students—is not only the hardest job in the school, it is the hardest job there is" (p. 17).

HELPING OR HINDERING?

Launching then from the premise that effective teaching is a difficult—if not the most difficult—task, it is at the least curious and at the most disturbing to note that, historically, little attention has been given to the enculturation process which new teachers experience as they begin their careers. In the absence of teacher induction programs, novice teachers have been left to fend for themselves and to discover for themselves the answers to the question of "how we do things here." However, in many instances, not only has the system done nothing to assist new teachers with the transition process, it has routinely set up road blocks for them as well. These road blocks have taken a variety of forms, such as being invited to serve as the cheerleading sponsor, having the least user-friendly teaching schedule, and being given the honor of teaching the classes no other teachers want. (Jensen & Kiley, 1997b, p. 37)

As Glasser argues, "Teaching is a very hard job that needs ample compensation and considerable on-the-job training for the lifetime of the teacher. Less than this will not suffice" (1992, p. 24). Unfortunately, mentoring programs are absent in many districts. Certainly there is a need for what Glaser refers to as "on-the-job training." However, formal and informal mentoring can support teacher collaboration at both the preservice and inservice levels, and both preservice and inservice mentoring relationships have the potential to enhance the professional development of teachers.

THE VALUE AND SKILLS OF COLLABORATION

If, in fact, mentoring can enhance the professional development of both preservice and inservice teachers, what can be done to facilitate it? We offer three simple, but essential, recommendations for individuals and organizations that wish to increase the probability that teachers will seek mentoring relationships (Jensen & Kiley, 1997b, p. 42):

1. Teach the value and skills of collaboration.
2. Model and encourage the practice of helping new teachers and experienced teachers make meaningful connections.
3. Establish organizational cultures that support mentoring.

Mentoring is a type of collaboration. Therefore, if teachers do not value collaboration or are hesitant to work cooperatively with other teachers, they typically will not seek mentoring relationships. Historically, even teachers in adjacent classrooms often have worked in isolation from each other, knowing little about how the other teaches (that is, his or her instructional approach, philosophy, and guidance style).

Sometimes teachers view collaboration as a threat to their autonomy. Experienced teachers who are a bit insecure about the quality of their work also may feel threatened by the enthusiasm and current knowledge base many novices bring with them to their first teaching positions. For example, one veteran teacher, after visiting a first-year teacher's classroom that was filled with learning centers and was attractively arranged, commented, "You may be enthusiastic now, but you'll get over it in a couple of years." So much for a welcoming atmosphere and a spirit of collegiality!

Ideally, teachers need to learn the value and skills of collaboration at the preservice level. If collaboration is part of many of their preservice professional development activities, it will be more natural for them to initiate or engage in collaborative relationships at the inservice level. Activities such as collaborative reflections, group research projects, paired instructional planning, team teaching, and even small-group discussions provide avenues for education majors to begin to value collaboration and to acquire the skills of collaboration. Some of those skills include the following (Jensen & Kiley, 1997b, pp. 42, 43):

1. Identifying and clearly articulating a shared purpose

2. Knowing and clearly articulating the rationale behind the decisions one makes

3. Listening with the intent to understand the messages colleagues are attempting to communicate

4. Engaging in reflection and self-assessment

5. Accurately identifying one's own strengths and areas requiring growth

ORGANIZATIONAL FACTORS THAT CONTRIBUTE TO TEACHER ATTRITION

Although the challenges and pitfalls of the first few years of teaching are fairly well acknowledged, significant assistance with the enculturation process has been slow in coming. Also commonly acknowledged is the high attrition rate for new teachers (Glasser, 1992; Gordon, 1991; Holden, 1995). Nationally, estimates of beginning teacher attrition range from 30 percent within the first two years to more than 50 percent within the first four years. Ignoring the induction needs of novice teachers also negatively affects their teaching quality and leads to their adopting a survival approach to teaching, which includes strategies that actually prove counterproductive to effective teaching (Holden, 1995). In spite of what is known, this fall how many first-year teachers still will face their first day of class and their first year of teaching with only the most minimal guidance ("Lunch is at 11:20; You have hall duty every Wednesday")?

What causes high attrition rates during the first few years of teaching? Some point to a supposed declining quality of new teachers; others blame teacher education programs. However, research has revealed that many of the challenges new teachers encounter are organizational or environmental in nature, emerging from the conditions of schools as workplaces and the culture of the teaching profession. The following paragraphs describe environmental difficulties that await many novice teachers (Gordon, 1991).

■ Difficult Work Assignments and Unclear Expectations

Whereas in other professions novices gradually take on increasing levels of responsibility, beginning teachers often start out with as many, or even more, responsibilities than veteran teachers have and are expected to possess similar expertise. Also, new teachers sometimes inherit the most time-consuming and least rewarding assignments, are given larger classes, and are saddled with more duties than experienced teachers (Gordon, 1991).

Schools have a plethora of procedures and policies—both written and unwritten. Different and conflicting expectations make it difficult for novice teachers to read and understand school cultures well enough to know exactly what is expected of them (Gordon, 1991).

■ Inadequate Resources

First-year teachers sometimes enter classrooms that over the summer have been raided by other teachers. When a teacher resigns, other teachers sometimes view the resignation as an opportunity to "trade in" their own classroom equipment and furniture for newer or better models, which they scavenge from the classroom of the teacher who resigned. Such raids, although not intended to harm first-year teachers, can leave new teachers, who are most in need of high-quality instructional resources and materials, with some of the oldest and worst materials found in the school (Gordon, 1991).

■ Isolation

Sometimes experienced teachers are reluctant to offer assistance to beginning teachers, even when it's obvious that a novice is in serious need of some help. This reluctance reflects the traditional cultural norm of teaching, which portrays first-year struggles as a right of passage and offers of assistance as interference. In addition, beginning teachers sometimes view asking for help as an admission of failure and a sign of incompetence (Gordon, 1991).

■ Role Conflict

For many first-year teachers, their entry into the profession parallels their entry into the "real world," which may include a host of changes in their personal lives, such as moving to communities where they know no one, finding affordable housing, buying and paying for a car for the first time, or adjusting to married life. The conflicting roles of teacher and young adult can contribute to new teachers' perceptions that they're not playing either role well (Gordon,

1991). Once feelings of incompetence and plummeting self-confidence enter the picture, guilt and unhappiness generally follow close behind.

■ Reality Shock

Facing the sometimes harsh realities of the teaching profession can serve as a rude awakening for novice teachers. Those who've eagerly anticipated the opportunity to function as creative, autonomous professionals may discover that their teaching philosophies conflict with their district's prescribed curricula, textbooks, and instructional programs. Failure to cope with the resulting "reality shock" sometimes reduces beginning teachers' ability to cope with other environmental difficulties (Gordon, 1991). A reduced coping capacity also can reduce teachers ability to transfer the knowledge, performances, and dispositions they learned during their teacher preparation to the stark realities of the classroom.

COMBATING ATTRITION THROUGH TEACHER LEADERSHIP

If administrators want to keep excellent teachers in education, they need to develop new roles for them that extend beyond the classroom. As we noted previously, 50 percent of new teachers remain in the profession for less than five years. Teacher isolation, absence of career ladders, low salaries, and lack of leadership responsibilities contribute to this situation. For high-ability teachers, teacher leadership is generally appealing if it influences student learning.

Teachers who view themselves as leaders also can help overcome resistance to change. When teacher leaders participate in shaping and leading change, there's less resistance. Creating teacher ownership in the change process allows teachers to participate actively in decision making, thereby decreasing resistance to change. After all, it's more difficult to criticize something when you're a part of it.

Teacher leadership provides a form of career enhancement and professional development by offering opportunities for teachers to expand their areas of influence. In leading others, teachers remain actively involved and learn about their own practice. Taking on leadership roles can encourage them to engage in reflection, thereby helping them improve their own performance. Influencing other teachers is another potential benefit of teacher leadership. When their colleagues respect teacher leaders, they are influenced by them. Teacher leaders can then serve as mentors to other teachers and help them improve their performance (Katzenmeyer & Moller, 1996).

TEACHER INDUCTION

The professional development process that novice teachers experience in their first few years of teaching, often called **teacher induction,** is best understood as a rite of passage into the culture of teaching (Berman, 1994). One researcher (Vonk, 1995) describes three dimensions of novice teachers' professional development, beginning with preservice teacher education and extending into the induction period:

- The personal dimension, which comprises issues relating to teachers' development as people (such as maturation, emotions, developing knowledge about oneself, and using oneself as an instrument)

- The knowledge and skills dimension, which comprises issues relating to teachers' development as professionals (such as the development of academic and pedagogical content knowledge and the development of instructional guidance skills)

- The ecological dimension, which comprises issues relating to the environment in which teachers are developing (that is, all of the issues related to the socialization of teachers in a certain school context, such as adapting to a certain school culture and meeting the demands of colleagues, school administrators, and parents)

SCHOOL CULTURE AND BEGINNING TEACHER ASSISTANCE EFFORTS

A significant element of all successful teacher induction programs is a supportive relationship between novice teachers and mentors. In fact, it has been suggested that effective pairing of novice teachers and support teachers is probably the most powerful and cost-effective element of induction programs (Huling-Austin, Putnam, & Glavez-Hjornevik, 1986). Well-designed and well-implemented teacher induction programs facilitate the development of positive attitudes toward teaching; contribute to the retention of teachers; and, when focused on enhancing professional skills, can improve teachers' performance (Feiman-Nemser & Parker, 1992; Huling-Austin, 1990a; 1990b; Klug & Salzman, 1991; Yosha, 1991).

MENTORING

Many definitions of mentoring have been offered, analyzed, and discussed (for example, see Bey, 1990; Bova & Phillips, 1984; Huling-Austin, 1990a, 1990b; Little, 1990; Stoddart, 1990; Theis-Sprinthall & Sprinthall, 1987). However, we favor the following definition of mentoring, because it encompasses both the preservice and the inservice setting. Anderson and Shannon (1988, p. 40) describe **mentoring** as "a nurturing process in which a more skilled or more experienced person, serving as a role model, teaches, sponsors, encourages, counsels, and befriends a less skilled or less experienced person for the purpose of promoting the latter's professional and/or personal development. Mentoring functions are carried out within the context of an ongoing, caring relationship between mentor and protege."

SCHOOL CULTURES THAT FACILITATE TEACHER INDUCTION AND MENTORING

Although no one can guarantee the success of every beginning teacher, instructional leaders, administrators, and teacher educators do have opportunities to create cultures that support novice teachers' professional development. Given the critical role mentoring plays in teacher induction, an obvious—and imperative—first step in establishing organizational environments that facilitate the development of effective teacher induction programs is for leaders (administrators, lead teachers, and teacher educators) to model the process by serving as mentors themselves. Leaders can also actively help establish mentoring relationships by bringing together people with complementary personalities, similar interests, and shared missions. To succeed in this intermediary role, leaders must learn from, as well as about, novice teachers and master teachers by listening to them, observing them, and asking them questions (Akin & Hopelain, 1986).

Another prerequisite step is for leaders to create an atmosphere of openness and trust within their organizations. Collaboration initiatives such as mentoring cannot thrive in the absence of clear communication, a shared mission, teacher empowerment, and consistent expectations (Jensen & Kiley, 1997b).

TWO TEACHER INDUCTION CASE STUDIES

Occasionally teacher educators have the good fortune and joy to participate in the preservice preparation of remarkable individuals. Such was the case when our paths crossed with those of one extraordinary early childhood education major and one exceptional elementary education major. These preservice teachers both graduated with honors and with their department's acknowledgment that they were the top students in their respective majors. They were not at all typical preservice teachers; they were typical only in terms of their age.

Given their accomplishments and the positive and comfortable mentoring relationships we had developed with them, it seemed logical to continue working with them once they began teaching. Teacher induction provided a logical focus of study. After all, if the best and the brightest experience painful transitions into the field of teaching, how are those with minimal competencies expected to survive?

Sensing that such an opportunity would not soon come our way again, we initiated a study of these two exemplary individuals' teacher induction experiences. (One of them would be involved in a formal teacher induction program; the other would not.) After several informal discussions about the teacher induction process and the two very different school environments these two new teachers would be entering, we collectively determined a course of action. The following paragraphs summarize the findings reported in a paper published on the study (Kiley Shepston, Jensen, Alm, & Beaver, 1997).

We asked the novice teachers to record in journals their experiences, observations, and reflections throughout their first year of teaching. We also made site visits to the schools where the novice teachers worked, had them visit our campus and present to preservice teachers, and engaged in a great deal of informal, free-flowing discussion with them.

By the time our study was nearing completion, the two teachers were finishing their third year of teaching. Both were still at the schools where they had begun their teaching career. Sophie, the early childhood special educator, had

Figure 13.2
Survival Concerns

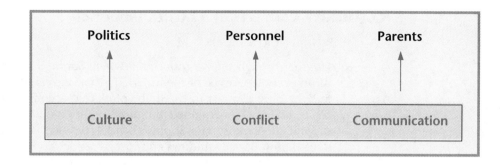

grown accustomed to (although not comfortable with) the sound of bullets ricocheting near her urban school's playground as she invited her young students, many of whom spoke only Spanish, to join her on the carpet—away from the windows. Cliff, the elementary educator, taught fourth grade in an affluent suburb. He joked that he spent his time dodging BMWs rather than bullets.

That comment characterizes the different experiences of these two teachers who confronted many of the same problems and challenges, but did so within two widely disparate school cultures residing at opposite ends of a socioeconomic continuum. Although both beginning teachers dealt with curriculum dilemmas and often worried they weren't doing enough to meet their student's needs, their journal entries, observations, and comments on their experiences focused primarily on three themes: *politics*, *personnel*, and *parents*. The three components of *culture*, *conflict*, and *communication* created a context for those emerging themes (see Figure 13.2), and subsumed under those three headings were a variety of expectations specific to the communities and clientele the teachers served.

For example, the early childhood teacher encountered the challenge of getting parents to attend conferences and staffings (meeting designed to discuss a students individualized education plan [IEP] and progress, normally attended by the parents, the child's teacher, and specialists providing services to the child). When they did attend, she struggled to communicate clearly with them, since most of them spoke little or no English, and her Spanish was limited. By contrast, the fourth-grade teacher had very involved parents. However, some of that involvement took the form of uninformed criticism, unrealistic expectations, and unwarranted fears (such as the fear that a low score on a fourth-grade math assignment would prevent a student from getting into the Ivy League college of his or her choice).

The cognitive and affective dissonance experienced by the two novice teachers resulted from the difference between what their hearts wanted to do and their heads knew they could do and revealed pressure points that sometimes accompany teacher induction. That dissonance also revealed the high—and sometimes unrealistic—expectations they had of themselves. It highlighted their need to find a balance between what their hearts wanted to do and what their heads knew they could do.

COMMUNITY CONTEXTS OF TEACHER INDUCTION

■ Inner-City Context

Driving through the neighborhood where Sophie's school is located brings to mind every stereotype of the inner city that one can imagine. Gang graffiti offers the only contrast to the drab colors that accompany poverty and the absence of hope. Abandoned buildings, burned-out cars, and scattered litter provide the backdrop for Sophie's school, the only safe haven many of its students know. Barred windows and locked school doors greet visitors, who must ring a buzzer and identify themselves prior to being allowed to enter.

Once inside, the harshness is softened somewhat by colorful displays of student work and friendly greetings. However, the institutional feel is perpetuated by the fact that the building holds many more students than it was designed to accommodate. This overcrowding is due, in large part, to an influx of Hispanic students. Many of these students and their parents speak little English, and some are illegal aliens. Both teachers and materials are in short supply, because funding has failed to keep pace with student enrollment.

■ Suburban Context

The neighborhood where Cliff's school is located brings to mind every stereotype of wealthy suburbia that one can imagine. Its families are housed in comparative opulence, and Cliff's students are chauffeured to and from their various after-school activities in a variety of luxury vehicles, from Toyota Land-Cruisers to Cadillacs and, yes, BMWs.

Gang graffiti offers the only contrast to the drab colors that accompany poverty and the absence of hope.
(© Ann Chwatsley/JEROBOAM)

The school itself is remarkably plain and not as "well-heeled" as the neighborhood that surrounds it. In fact, many of the textbooks in use have exceeded the typical "shelf life." However, security concerns do not overtly intrude on the physical environment, and both inside and outside there is room to breathe.

THE FIRST THREE YEARS

YEAR ONE: SURVIVAL OF THE FITTEST

Although Sophie had to fend for herself until she was adopted by an experienced teacher, Cliff was matched with a mentor teacher close to his own age. However, once his principal had set up this mentoring relationship, little else was done in the way of formal teacher induction.

■ Politics, Personnel, and Parents

As is true for many first-year teachers, mere survival became Sophie and Cliff's primary objective. In fact, when asked to identify the best thing she did during her first year of teaching, Sophie responded, "I didn't give up." The journals Cliff and Sophie kept throughout their first year of teaching revealed that most of their joys and celebrations resulted from student interactions, whereas most of their frustrations and challenges resulted from politics, personnel, and parents. However, the manner in which politics, personnel, and parents affected the teaching/learning process differed for the two teachers, because their school cultures were different. Inasmuch as communication styles and strategies for coping with conflict are subcomponents of organizational culture, these things also differed at the two schools.

Sophie's survival concerns centered on her program assistants. As a young teacher working in a supervisory position over two women more than twice her age, Sophie quickly discovered that most of the decisions she made would be questioned. In addition, her program assistants chose not to implement some of Sophie's decisions. Their constant questioning caused Sophie to question her own decisions, along with her ability and her sanity. After hearing her own supervisor's conclusion regarding one program assistant, Sophie noted in her journal that "I got another confirmation that I am not crazy; she is a difficult person to deal with."

Meanwhile, Cliff's version of school politics juxtaposed parents and his fellow fourth-grade teacher in an uncomfortable situation in which they were compared and contrasted rather than encouraged to work together. Although a five-year teaching veteran, Cliff's colleague had spent each of those five years at a different school, a fact that apparently was common knowledge among the fourth graders' parents. Consequently, even though parents questioned many of Cliff's decisions and strategies, they also were endlessly comparing Cliff and the other fourth grade teacher. These comparisons generally favored Cliff and left him in the unenviable position of being caught in the middle of a conflict that eventually led to his colleague's dismissal.

During his first year, Cliff also discovered the heavy influence of competition and parental pressure on his school's culture. The conflict that parents' unreasonable expectations can create is aptly illustrated in one of Cliff's journal entries, which describes an encounter he had with a parent after a student performed poorly on a social studies assignment and subsequently dissolved into an ocean of tears and fears.

> *B is the perfect child. Handsome, smart, etc. Mom is a very prominent PTO mom, so I had her come in to talk about what happened. She told me that B has several aunts and uncles who went to Yale and Harvard and that her husband went to Northwestern. The family members have told B that they would love to take him to these colleges. B wants to be a doctor, of course. But—here's the sad thing— Mom and Dad have told B that he can go to any college he wants, but if he wants to go to Harvard or Yale, he has to get all As. Yes, this is fourth grade I teach. . . . Her kid is going to get ulcers. . . . I tried to tell her how I want B to enjoy what he is doing and not freak out about the grades. He was sure that an 87 he received a couple of weeks ago was the worst grade anyone could get. It's sad, but the competition is fierce up here. It's all a game, whose kid does what. Not in my room.*

YEAR ONE REFLECTIONS: SURVIVAL

When asked to reflect on her first year of teaching, Sophie offered the following insights:

> *It's been a week since I said good-bye to my first group of students. I felt more relief than grief to be ending the year. There were many challenges I had to overcome—many of them outside the four walls of the classroom. My initial fears of the neighborhood were put to the background, while problems with my program assistants came to the forefront. Of all the issues that sprang up, that one seems to stand out above the rest. After months of trying various professional approaches to tactfully inform and inspire them, with the intention of having them become more productive and appropriate in the classroom, I resorted to an unprofessional solution that worked.*

Sophie then went on to describe a rather loud conversation she had with one of her program assistants. Her message was received, and Sophie did see evidence of positive change in the manner in which her program assistants interacted with students. The entire experience of dealing with program assistants motivated her to devote a great deal of the summer between her first and second years of teaching to writing a program assistants' manual. That manual provided a clear job description for program assistants and outlined Sophie's expectations for them. In addition, the manual articulated her philosophy of working with special needs children and, with resounding clarity, answered the question of why she implemented particular instructional strategies.

In recollecting positive first-year events, Sophie described her experience of serving on the school improvement committee. Although parts of that process were frustrating ("people who don't listen and who must always talk";

"reinventing the wheel"), other parts brought feelings of satisfaction ("being an integral part of the group with new/fresh ideas to offer"). Sophie also stated there was "satisfaction in getting to know the movers and shakers in the district" and that the process was "helpful in understanding political climate and in developing my decision making, as well as offering good networking with an involved staff."

In reflecting on their first year of teaching, both Sophie and Cliff identified victories, which often took the form of invaluable growth opportunities they never would have asked for. Sophie recollected obstacles she overcame, such as "standing up to my program assistants, gaining respect from my principal, becoming confident in my abilities to complete paperwork efficiently and accurately, and overcoming my fear of the neighborhood and transportation problems."

Cliff's summary of his first year of teaching featured his affective response to his experiences. Rather than attempt to paraphrase it, and in so doing alter the intent and the message, we present his summary in its entirety.

> *I will never forget my first week. I had dark circles around my eyes. I felt like I had no clue. Not much has really changed. The circles are lighter. I still have no clue. I've learned so much it is unreal. I have so much to learn it is even more unreal. College prepped me well—as well as it could, probably. But the majority you cannot learn until you struggle with it. You cannot begin to call yourself an educator until you are so tired because you are working twelve-plus hours a day. You cannot call yourself an educator until you sit awake worrying that you aren't doing enough. You cannot call yourself an educator until you are depended upon by twenty-plus young people to be there each and every day. You cannot call yourself an educator until you have sat at home feeling like crud because you didn't accomplish a thing that day. You cannot call yourself an educator until you see students smile because you helped them. You cannot call yourself an educator until you have to scrap your best-laid plans because they just won't work. You can't call yourself an educator until you are convinced you are insane for wanting to become one.*
>
> *I've said this before. From 9:05 to 3:35, I am the happiest person there is. Dealing with the students makes it worthwhile. The outside pressure, politics, and administrative crud make me hate what I do. Fortunately, in the yin-yang of things, the students have the upper hand and make me enjoy what I do more than I hate it. When the day comes that the other half of my world gains the momentum, I will need to find something else to do. It may be twenty years from now. It may be two years from now. I don't know. I do know that I will never learn more about teaching than I have learned in this first year. I will learn each and every day I step in the classroom, but I will never learn more in a year's period than I have this year.*
>
> *If I were to tell prospective teachers anything about their first year, it would be this:*
>
> *You will hate what you do.*
>
> *You will be exhausted physically and mentally.*
>
> *You will think there is no way out.*

You will have no idea what you are doing or why, at times.

You will wonder how anyone does this for an entire career, year after year.

You will think you are the worst teacher ever, some days.

You will see demise directly resulting from your actions.

And things will change, slowly:

You will begin to predict problems and correct them before they occur.

You will think and make more decisions in a single day than most people do in a week.

You will see success that is a direct result of your actions.

You will become strong as a result of your responsibilities.

You will learn how to fail in order to succeed.

You will learn how to ask questions and who to ask them of.

You will understand what you are doing and why.

You will learn to adapt.

You will be proud to be a young professional educator.

You will love what you do.

There is one catch. You will not realize any of the above until you have lived it. You cannot give up or pass judgment after one month or two. You have to survive the worst year of your career—your first year. It will probably not be the most enjoyable year of your career. But it will undoubtedly be one of the most beneficial.

I could talk for quite some time about what I have learned and observed. I hope this journal has given a glimpse of the changes I have undergone. The metamorphosis of a first-year teacher is pretty much like that of a butterfly, if all goes right. You start out ugly. You end up pretty decent looking. You can also fly if you want to.

YEAR TWO: CONFIDENT? YES. COMFORTABLE? MAYBE. COMPLACENT? NEVER!

Sophie and Cliff reacted similarly at the conclusion of their first year of teaching. Sophie talked of feeling "more relief than grief" when reflecting on saying good-bye to her first group of students, whereas Cliff stated that his reaction to the end of his first year was "an anxious sigh." However, both began year two with heightened confidence and increased comfort.

■ Parents and Politics

Sophie's concerns over her program assistants were remedied by the hiring of two new program assistants and by the program assistant manual she developed over the summer. With her students, as well as with her program assistants, Sophie established high expectations, defined roles, and set limits. However, frustrations over politics and parents replaced her first-year frustrations over personnel.

Although Sophie was pleased with the progress her children had made in reading and with the fact that she had helped open the eyes of some staff and parents regarding the potential of the special needs children she taught, in her second year of teaching she became disenchanted with prevailing parental attitudes and school politics. Sophie's journal also reflects her frustration with the absence of a structured and well-planned response to the need for parent education.

■ Balancing and Building

In Cliff's second year of teaching he continued building on the experiential base he acquired in his first year and attempting to balance many competing interests. Cliff explained that his first year "was a constant reorganization of my professional perception as I struggled to find the balance between theory and practicality. In my second year, I was able to finally build off a base of practical experience." Cliff's reflections also indicate that in his second year of teaching he came to value the role that experience can play.

YEAR THREE: CIRCLE OF CONCERN VERSUS CIRCLE OF INFLUENCE

Passionate, perseverant, and *perplexed* are three descriptors that characterized Cliff and Sophie as they concluded their third year of teaching. Having moved from the inward-looking stance of the survival years to the outward-looking stance they now employed, they had developed a broader vantage point and a different perspective. Their "circle of concern," as Covey (1989) would say, had expanded significantly, leaving them with the onerous task of determining how far-reaching their circle of influence actually was—or was not.

■ The Big Picture

The challenges Sophie and Cliff saw confronting children, families, and society were daunting. Even a cursory look at the big picture revealed issues that required, as Cliff put it, more than a quick fix. During the course of an informal review of their third year of teaching, Sophie and Cliff identified several such issues, including parent education, the impact illegal aliens have on school systems, unions that protect incompetent teachers, the correlation between tenure and complacency, obsession with test scores in the name of accountability and standards, matching assessment with instruction, curriculum coverage versus depth, and not being able to give students much-needed hugs due to fear of wrongful accusations of inappropriate touching.

Cliff and Sophie exhibited a need to talk about the larger issues and challenges confronting education and a desire to listen to others' perspectives. They also acknowledged their need to identify issues to focus on and to address those they believed they could do something about. In terms of coping with the dissonance such issues evoke, Cliff and Sophie indicated that, when possible, they worked creatively within the system. However, sometimes their attempts to cope with ever-present negative variables such as child abuse and homelessness involved emotional distancing. As Sophie said, "Sometimes I sleep better when I'm numb to it all." Although Sophie and Cliff continued to struggle with ongoing issues involving politics and parents, they also struggled to achieve a balance between what they knew needed to be done and what they knew they could deliver.

■ Plateaus

Fear of complacency and of becoming too comfortable motivated Cliff and Sophie to push themselves. Both identified comfort as a problem and spoke of

New teachers talk

Sophie: Parents and Politics

As much as I have grown to love the children I teach, I've also become frustrated with what seems to be a cultural tendency for parents not to acknowledge the role they can play in their children's education. As a whole, the parents I work with respect educators—probably more so than most Americans [do]—but they do not assist educators or recognize themselves as educators of their own children. They say: "You are the maestra; you teach my child. I love and feed and protect my child." . . .

Most of us feel we do our best with the children when they are in our classes, and we leave the rest to the powers that be. What happens to them as young adults when their neighborhoods tempt them with gangs, drugs, and guns? Have we prepared them to think with their futures in mind, or are they focused solely on the present? Are they confident? Do they set goals and work to achieve them? Do their parents know where they are and what they are doing? Do the children feel their parents care? These are all things parents need to do to carry on what a teacher works on in the classroom. How do we teach the parents who don't know this—that their role is vital? The needs are many, and I am only one. Although I believe I will find my niche in this business, and I will find the team to help me lead the children, I

will not be satisfied until I see the family become an active part. . . .

We do have a handful of dreamers, but they are disjointed. Perhaps we need better leadership within the groups of concerned teachers who realize the importance of parent involvement. Perhaps we need risk takers who will act first on some issues and ask later about which rule they broke for the sake of educating. We need more support. It won't be found financially, so we'll need to find it another way.

Cliff: Balancing and Building

I never used to give experience the credit it deserved. I was, in many ways, bitter toward those in the profession who had many years of experience. I thought that experience didn't make a good teacher (and it doesn't automatically). There was a part of me that wanted to be an instructor because I had horrible experiences as a student. I saw instructors who did the same things, year after year—instructors that paid no attention to their actions and didn't listen to their students. During my own teacher preparation, I saw some of the same. I still see the same today. But I also have seen many individuals who do pay attention and do listen. I have seen individuals who have not repeated their first year of experience for the

the need for someone to challenge them. Only halfway through their third year of teaching, Cliff and Sophie talked about plateaus and the fact that they generally did not recognize until later when they had hit one. That lack of self-awareness seemed to disturb them the most. They felt a sense of responsibility, which they occasionally wished they could abandon ("Leave me alone; I don't want to think"). However, their consciences constantly goaded them: "Don't become what you've despised"; "Laziness isn't an excuse"; "I was taught better than this"; "If there's no fire, I'm out of here."

last twenty years. I have seen and worked with individuals who have experiences that I crave. They are wise, if that doesn't sound flippant. The knowledge they hold as a result of their experiences is invaluable. It is gold.

But their experiences aren't what made them good teachers—reflecting upon and using their experiences for future decisions has. And it took me a while to really understand the role my experiences played on a daily basis—how vital it was to look, listen, and reflect. It took me my first year to realize that I needed to do myself what I asked my students to do. Although I may hold the title of teacher, I am just as much a student as the ten-year-olds I teach.

What I was then able to do in my second year fascinated me. I now was able to begin to recall and apply. I was able to predict and "preact" instead of react. I had gained experience. More important, I had learned to utilize the experience I had gained. . . .

On the other hand, I realized that teaching was a part of my life and not my whole life. I found that I had to say "no" to working some nights. I had to have fun during the week, too. So I experimented until I found a level and balance I was comfortable with. Yes, undoubtedly, I was not the uptight, do-your-job-twenty-four-hours-a-day-or-you-will-get-fired guy I was the first year.

Authors' Analysis

Although Sophie was pleased with the progress her children had made in reading and with the fact that she had helped open the eyes of some staff and parents regarding the potential of the special needs children she taught, in her second year of teaching she became disenchanted with prevailing parental attitudes and school politics. Sophie's journal also reflects her frustration with the absence of a structured and well-planned response to the need for parent education.

Cliff's first year helped him learn to cope with the "red tape" of teaching and find a "comfortable and consistent way" to deal with pressure. For him, the solution lay in keeping his sense of humor and his ability to question. He relaxed, laughed with his students, remembered to enjoy teaching, and became more comfortable interacting with staff and parents as well as his students. As Cliff's comfort level increased, his interpersonal skills improved, thereby compounding his self-confidence. Of course, as his confidence increased, his anxiety decreased. Cliff made a conscious decision to focus on things he had some control over (his classroom, his instructional decisions) and to devote less mental energy to things over which he had little or no control (the school administration, parents, school politics). As he began to relax and enjoy himself at work, he began to relax more at home as well.

■ **Personal Lives**

For both Sophie and Cliff, significant others helped them accept the difference between what their hearts wanted to do and what their heads knew they could do. Cliff volunteered that having the sounding board and emotional support of a significant other made a big difference between his second and third years of teaching. Sophie and he both elaborated on the important role that people in their personal lives played in helping them deal with job stress and helping them achieve balance between their personal and professional lives. They described the importance of having someone assure them that they "were not nuts," someone who knew them well enough to recognize when they could not handle any more than they already were carrying, someone who was willing to carry some of the load. For Cliff and Sophie, their significant others positively affected their ability to cope successfully with stress.

WHAT LIES AHEAD?

Their first year of teaching found Sophie and Cliff operating in survival mode most of the time. However, while Sophie characterized year two as "make or break," Cliff described his second year of teaching as a time to catch his breath and look forward, confident that year two had to be better than year one. When we concluded our teacher induction study, Sophie and Cliff were well into their third year of teaching. Sophie had experienced a great deal of success and liked what she was doing. She had hit her stride and seemed to be in the process of defining her personal mission in life, a mission that likely will involve serving as a bridge between the culture of her school and that of the Hispanic children she teaches. Cliff had made plans for the next formal phase of his professional development, which he thought would involve completing both a master's program and a doctoral program. Although he still was passionate about teaching, Cliff saw himself continuing in the teaching role within the context of higher education.

■ **University-School Connections**

Cliff and Sophie's experiences seem to support the conclusion that novice teachers who have direct and continuing access to teacher educators for support while they work with their students to let go of traditional assumptions can gradually begin to realize their visions (Aaronsohn, 1996). Sophie and Cliff's comments throughout their first three years showed that they valued their ongoing connection with their university and found that it challenged them to continue their professional development.

For example, on-site visits from university mentors produced in Cliff and Sophie a mixed reaction of excitement and panic. They were anxious to have these people who had participated in their preservice development see the environments in which they were working, and simultaneously they were nervous about having them observe their teaching. Reflecting on this combination of euphoria and nausea, Sophie commented, "You were the first people to walk in my room whose opinion of my teaching I valued and cared about. I didn't want to screw up." Over two years later, Cliff was still apologizing for what he perceived as a lack of quality and depth in the lesson he was teaching during our visit to his classroom.

Teacher induction programs that feature university partnerships can make significant contributions to the professional development of all involved: novice teachers, experienced teachers, administrators, and university personnel. Professional development schools are one vehicle for implementing such programs.

■ Teacher Induction Conclusions

The challenges Sophie and Cliff faced as beginning teachers often related to the question of "how we do things here." The ability to understand one's school as an organization, how to effect change within that organization, and how people in that organization relate to one another is essential. Consequently, both at the preservice stage and at the teacher induction stage, the subject of school culture must be addressed.

By attending to the variable of school culture, teachers can learn both how to accommodate change and how to serve as change agents. Teachers also can broaden their understanding of school culture by learning about the cultures of the students and families they serve. An ongoing commitment to creating school cultures that facilitate professional development and systemic change is a necessary precondition for the creation of teacher induction programs that succeed in assisting novice teachers in their efforts to construct answers to the question of "how we do things here."

■ Continual Change and Collaboration

If the only constant in the teaching/learning process is change, what implications does that premise hold for those who enter and remain in the education profession? One implication is clear: if you plan on becoming a teacher, you definitely should plan on remaining a learner for life. Teachers must continue to anticipate, adapt, and act to change and participate in collaborative change efforts throughout their careers. For these reasons, exemplary educators view teaching as lifelong learning and systematically pursue professional development and renewal.

SUMMARIZING WHAT YOU'VE LEARNED

- ■ In effective schools, collaboration, culture, and change are inseparable. A school's culture consists of the basic assumptions that operate within it, as reflected by the behavior of its members and the outward manifestations of its values. School culture significantly affects collaboration initiatives and change efforts.

- ■ Collaboration consists of two or more individuals or organizations working together toward a common goal. This includes implementation and evaluation as well as planning. Organizational change involves disrupting the status quo to produce enhanced performance or improvements of some sort.

■ Effective teachers engage in ongoing professional development and self-renewal. Schools also change as the needs of society and political agendas change. Just as change is an undeniable part of life, it also is an undeniable part of teaching and learning. Consequently, it makes sense for educators to learn how change occurs, how to facilitate it, and how individuals respond to it.

■ Professional development schools (PDSs) simultaneously restructure and renew PreK–12 schooling and teacher preparation. PDSs can play key roles in the movement to restructure education by creating new frameworks for teaching and learning. Successful PDSs become living laboratories that facilitate student and faculty inquiry, as well as collaboration across disciplines (Sattler & Jensen, 1998).

■ All students can benefit when human service professionals implement a team approach to providing services. Working collaboratively, these practitioners can address the social, physical, and psychological issues that affect children, families, and communities, without duplicating services and getting in one another's way.

■ There is a need for what Glaser refers to as "on-the-job training" for teachers. However, formal and informal mentoring can support teacher collaboration at both the preservice and inservice levels, and both preservice and inservice mentoring relationships possess the potential to enhance the professional development of teachers.

■ The professional development process that novice teachers experience in their first few years of teaching, often called teacher induction, is best understood as a rite of passage into the culture of teaching (Berman, 1994). Vonk (1995) describes three dimensions of novice teachers' professional development: the personal dimension, the knowledge and skills dimension, and the ecological dimension.

YOUR PROFESSIONAL TEACHING PORTFOLIO

■ If you've been involved in implementing change or have served as a change agent, use those experiences to demonstrate your receptivity to change, as well as your understanding of the change process and how to effectively plan, introduce, and implement organizational change initiatives.

■ As you approach the completion of your preservice teacher preparation, begin to think about how you will continue your professional development as an inservice teacher. Consider including in your professional teaching portfolio some sort of plan for your ongoing growth. For example, some people broadly outline five- or ten-year plans; others articulate detailed plans for the next step in their professional development.

Key Terms

Collaboration (p. 465)
Comprehensive, integrated-
  services approach (p. 474)
Integrated therapy team (ITT)
  (p. 474)

Mentoring (p. 483)
Organizational change (p. 466)
Professional development
  schools (PDSs) (p. 470)

Teacher induction (p. 482)

Relevant Resources for Professionals

Books and Articles

- Gable, R. A., & Manning, M. L. (1997). The role of teacher collaboration in school reform. *Childhood Education: Infancy Through Early Adolescence, 73*(4), 219–223.

- Rainforth, B., & England, J. (1997). Collaborations for inclusion. *Education and Treatment of Children, 20*(1), 85–104.

- Teitel, L. (1997). Professional development schools and the transformation of teacher leadership. *Teacher Education Quarterly, 24*(1), 9–22.

Professional Journals in Education

- *From Now On*
  From Now On (FNO) is an on-line journal published by Jamie McKenzie. Articles on topics such as assessment, curricula, grants, research, staff development, and technology planning are included.

  www.fno.org/

Web Sites

- **The Circle of Inclusion**
  Designed for early childhood service providers and families of young children. Offers demonstrations of, and information about, the effective practices of inclusive educational programs for children from birth through age eight.

  www.circleofinclusion.org/

- **Laboratory for Student Success**
  Laboratory for Student Success (LSS) seeks to achieve high academic standards in urban schools in the mid-Atlantic region and nationally through a comprehensive program of urban education enhancement. Topics include research and development, comprehensive school reform, communities for learning, and resources. This Web site's specialty area is urban education.

  www.temple.edu/departments/LSS/

- **Middleweb**
  Middleweb contains middle school reform resources for educators and parents, links to curricula, and other middle school resources.

  www.middleweb.com/

- **Pathways**
  Designed to assist with school improvement efforts, Pathways applies research to school and classroom practice in the areas of assessment, technology, math, science, literacy, parent involvement, school-to-work, leadership, and professional development. Pathways is a product of the North Central Regional Educational Laboratory in cooperation with the Regional Educational Laboratory network.

  www.ncrel.org/sdrs/pathwayg.htm

TEACHERS AS LIFELONG LEARNERS

— OR —

Don't blame your college for what you don't know ten years from now.

THE ART AND SCIENCE OF THE JOB SEARCH

Teaching will challenge you with overlapping goals right from the start, even before you have completed your teacher preparation program. Thus, with regard to your job search, we encourage you to heed Covey's admonition (1989, p. 53) to "Begin with the end in mind."

BEGIN WITH THE END IN MIND

Although you haven't yet finished your teacher preparation program, it's time to begin thinking about where you'd like to teach. In particular, consider in which state you'd like to teach. If you want to teach in a state other than the one where your teacher preparation program is located, make sure your academic adviser and teacher certification officer know that! They—and you—can then consult the certification or licensure guidelines for the particular state or states where you think you might seek employment.

For example, two students enrolled in an Illinois teacher preparation program told Rita that they were going to get married and move to Wisconsin, where they hoped to find teaching positions. After congratulating them on

"If you are lucky enough to find a way of life you love, you have to find the courage to live it."

—John Irving, *A Prayer for Owen Meany*

Reflect on the relevance and significance of Irving's conclusion for you as you prepare to enter the teaching profession.

In your teaching journal, speculate about the challenges you may face as a novice teacher. Describe at least three situations you may find yourself in that will call for the courage to engage in principled leadership and remain true to your convictions. Then predict how you think you will respond when confronted with those challenges and situations.

their engagement and inquiring about their wedding plans, the next question Rita asked was, "Did you know that the state of Wisconsin requires eighteen weeks of student teaching for certification?" They didn't. Shortly after that conversation, they met with their teacher certification officer and director of clinical experiences, who arranged for them to begin their student teaching before the sixteen-week semester actually began. Doing so enabled the students to complete Wisconsin's eighteen-week student teaching requirement.

When advisers and certification officers know in advance that a preservice teacher plans to seek work in another state after graduating, they can generally build into his or her program of study the necessary coursework and student teaching experience to satisfy the particular certification requirements of that state. However, it's your responsibility to make your adviser and certification officer aware of your plans!

HELPFUL TERMS TO KNOW WHEN BEGINNING YOUR JOB SEARCH

Every profession has its own distinctive nomenclature or jargon. Teaching is no exception. To familiarize you with some of the terminology you're likely to encounter as you begin your job search, we highlight the following terms:

- An **interstate certification contract** is a program that enables teachers and other education professionals to have their credentials recognized in other states. Currently thirty-two states are participating members of such contracts. To find out if your state is one of them, contact your state certification Web site.

- **Reciprocity** is an agreement by which teaching credentials from one state are honored by other states' credentialing agencies. This agreement may be regional or among several states.

- A **collective bargaining agreement** is a written record of an agreement between a bargaining agent such as a National Education Association (NEA) or American Federation of Teachers (AFT) local affiliate and a school board.

Such agreements typically specify working conditions, salaries, and evaluation procedures for local employees.

- A **contract** is a legal document that specifies a teacher's duties, responsibilities, teaching assignment (grade, subject), and salary for a specific time frame (such as August 2000 to June 2001). A teacher employed by a given board of education is legally bound to perform specific duties for a specific salary only when a written contract is signed by both the teacher and board chair.

FROM DIPLOMA TO CONTRACT: WALK IN THE PARK OR HIMALAYAN TREK?

When we meet with prospective college students interested in becoming teachers, they often ask us if it's difficult to get a teaching job. Our response typically is, "It depends." For example, it depends on the type of teaching position an applicant is looking for. It also depends on the applicant's mobility and on how open he or she is to considering a wide range of possibilities. We encourage you to cast your net as wide as you can, get your foot in the door, and "work the Web" to find out about the communities you're considering. Don't decide that you only want to teach fourth grade in the elementary school you attended as a child. If you draw your circle of possibilities that small, someone will literally have to die or retire before you can get the teaching position you want.

■ Teacher Gluts and Shortages

Based on estimates of future school enrollment and teacher retirement rates, the U.S. secretary of education predicts that by 2004 the United States will need 2 million new teachers. This estimate may overstate the true need, since in some states many teacher candidates have been waiting in the wings. Still, other states find themselves facing record teacher shortages at the turn of the century. For example, California is already in desperate need of teachers—not just in crowded urban areas but in rural communities as well.

The biggest areas of need continue to be bilingual education, special education, math, and science. However, the need for industrial arts teachers also is growing, because of an increase in industrial arts programs that feature computer education. In addition, home economics—now often called home ecology, family and consumer sciences, or family life—is making a strong comeback. For example, Illinois is experiencing a severe shortage of family and consumer sciences teachers, coupled with a marked reduction in the numbers of family and consumer sciences teacher preparation programs.

■ Positioning and Marketing Yourself

Unfortunately, being an outstanding candidate will not necessarily guarantee you a teaching position. Several other variables, including supply and demand, informal networking, and school politics, can confound the job-seeking process. Although some factors are beyond your control, many are not. It makes sense to spend your time, attention, and energy on what you can affect rather than waste time fretting about what you cannot.

For instance, you can participate in mock interviews with principals at your field experience sites to improve your ability to clearly articulate your strengths, teaching philosophy, experience, and preparation. That's one area where you can take control. However, if you're a woman looking for a primary teaching position, you can't change the fact that if both you and an equally qualified man interview for such a position, the male candidate will more likely be offered the job, due to the small number of male teachers at the primary level.

PROFESSIONAL TEACHING PORTFOLIOS

Chapter 2 provided a detailed discussion of professional development plans and professional teaching portfolios. As you prepare for your job search, we encourage you to create a product portfolio that will showcase your teaching expertise and experiences. See Chapter 2 for a list of items to include in your professional teaching portfolio.

■ Electronic Portfolios

In Chapter 2 we also mentioned that you can use technology to enhance your professional teaching portfolio. In addition to being visually appealing, an electronic portfolio will demonstrate your technological literacy to prospective employers. You might choose to format your portfolio on a CD, which you can then leave with prospective employers to supplement your face-to-face presentation of your qualifications. You also could create your own home page on the Web to house your portfolio. Posting your portfolio on the Web allows prospective employers to access it easily no matter what type of computer they use, avoiding the hardware compatibility problems CDs can sometimes present.

■ Résumés

A résumé describing your education; range of teaching experience; other, related work experience; honors; and accomplishments typically will be part of your professional teaching portfolio. Technology can play a role here as well. Software programs such as *Résumé Expert* can help you format your résumé attractively. In addition, you might post your résumé on the Web or fax it to prospective employers. Check your college's career center for more ideas.

INTERVIEWING

Finally, when you present yourself to prospective employers, focus on the fact that you are a competent teacher, not on the fact that you "love kids" (National Education Association, 1998). As we often have said, if loving kids were sufficient to be an effective teacher, then most everyone's grandparents would be great teachers, but they're just not.

Figure 14.1
Tips That Will Set You Apart from Other Candidates

- Compile a well-organized, well-designed professional teaching portfolio that includes your philosophy of education, photographs of your teaching, samples of your projects and teaching materials, student work samples, and video documentation of your teaching.
- Make local contacts by visiting schools and talking to principals and teachers.
- Don't rule out substitute teaching. Many first-year teachers landed their positions because they made a positive impression as a substitute.
- Invest time and energy in finding out about the community in which you would like to teach and its children. Take a good look at surrounding schools as well.
- Use the Internet to job search. There are many Web sites that feature education job listings, and school districts are beginning to post positions on their home pages, as well as in electronic job search listings. See state certification Web sites to find contact information.
- Build leadership experiences for your résumé and professional teaching portfolio by joining and volunteering to serve as a leader in student professional organizations. Attend conferences and area meetings as a student member.
- Use job interviews as opportunities to talk about how you would teach and collaborate within a specific school culture. Don't forget to include your volunteer education activities as examples of your strengths.
- Always follow each interview with a letter of appreciation to the interviewing official. Not following through may cost you a future opportunity to work with this school.
- Always visit the school before signing a contract.
- Never sign contracts with more than one school system at a time—breaking a contract is a violation of professional ethics.

(Adapted from National Education Association, 1998, p. 19)

■ Setting Yourself Apart from Other Candidates

Remember that your goal and challenge is to distinguish yourself—in a positive and effective way—from the other hopefuls swimming beside you in the applicant pool. Before each interview, ask yourself why this search committee or principal should hire you and not the other hundred candidates, and be prepared to answer that question out loud, because some interviewers are partial to asking it. To help you create a lasting—and favorable—impression, we offer several recommendations in Figure 14.1.

■ State Certification Web Addresses

As mentioned previously, if you're not familiar with the initial certification or licensure requirements for the particular state or states where you think you'd like to teach, you should discuss these requirements with your academic adviser and teacher certification officer as soon as possible. However, we also encourage you to take the initiative to seek out this information for yourself. Responsibility for oneself is a hallmark of a competent teacher. Both preservice teachers and inservice teachers benefit when they assume responsibility for planning and implementing their own professional development. If you've not yet taken on this responsibility, then it's time you did so, and a simple first step you can take in this direction is to obtain information on the certification or licensure requirements of the states where you're interested in teaching. You may wish to make initial contacts with state teacher certification or licensure offices via the Internet. Consult a Web directory or your teacher certification officer for the addresses of the sites you'd like to access.

Entering the "Real World"

I n this final chapter, we'd like to review some of the things we hope you know about the teaching/learning process and teaching as a profession. We'd also like to help you make some connections between where you are now and where you ultimately hope to be in your first teaching position. Consequently, we begin by exploring the transition from preservice to inservice teaching and then discuss first-year induction issues. Before providing a bit of closure, we offer some thoughts regarding planning for your ongoing professional development.

Comparing Student Teaching or Internships to the First Year of Teaching

■ Research on Student Teachers

Providing effective instructional and classroom guidance continues to be a major concern for student teachers. Student teachers most frequently report problems with excessive student talking, uncooperative behavior, instructional issues (such as predicting how long particular lessons or activities will take to complete), students not doing their work, and insolent or rude student behavior (Reed, 1989). Another common theme in the research on student teachers is a move from unrealistic optimism or idealism at the start of a student teacher's preparation program to realism by the end of it. Some researchers speculate that the vast majority of student teachers have a tendency to believe that problems that plague others will not happen to them (Weinstein, 1989). As noted previously, novice teachers tend to get into difficulty if they deviate from their scripted lesson plans, because they haven't yet developed appropriate alternative instructional strategies to draw on in various teaching situations, as expert teachers have (Livingston & Borko, 1989).

■ Research on First-Year Teachers: "Self as Teacher"

Researchers often have characterized the transition between student teaching and the first year of teaching as one involving some degree of "reframing" (Russell & Munby, 1991). The first year of teaching also involves the development of new perspectives concerning what the role of teacher is about and what the profession entails. First-year teachers in Canada identified these common themes (Olson & Osborne, 1991):

Initial orientation to the job	Finding security
Feeling a sense of responsibility	Balancing process and content needs
Concern about ability to meet their expectations	Self-evaluation and goal achievement
Anxiety about control	Search for understanding
Need for affiliation with colleagues	Change in role orientation

Support for first-year teachers often assumes that the tension between theory and practice that commonly is experienced by student teachers is no longer a problem. However, making the connection between theory and practice can be somewhat daunting for first-year teachers as well as for interns and student teachers. Examining the relationship between theory and practice also can make a major contribution to the development of beginning teachers (Russell, 1988). Understanding and exploring connections between theory and practice gets new teachers into the habit of reflecting on their practice. So do school cultures that encourage teachers to assume leadership and decision-making roles. In fact, those teachers who exhibit more mature reflection when encountering challenges usually work in schools that value teacher decision making and give teachers more autonomy to experiment with their instructional strategies (Kilgore, Ross, & Abikowski, 1990).

DEVELOPING EXPERTISE

The end of your teacher preparation program is the start of your continuing professional development (Kyriacou, 1993). Some observers have noted a need for further research on the development of expertise during teachers' first year of teaching (Kyriacou, 1993).

Key areas for research include the following:

1. What knowledge, understanding, and skills concerning effective teaching do student teachers develop during their teacher preparation programs? What should they develop?

2. How can teacher preparation programs best monitor and develop such expertise?

3. How does such expertise develop further during the first year of teaching? How should it?

4. How can such further development best be monitored and fostered?

5. To what extent do different methods of teacher preparation and recruitment foster the development of effective teachers? How might these methods be improved?

A recent national survey demonstrated that the first year of teaching is a sobering experience for most new teachers and that during that year new teachers' belief in their own efficacy and in the learning potential of their students declines (Harris & Associates, 1991). Nearly every study of retention in the teaching profession identifies the early years as the riskiest on the job, the years in which teachers are most likely to leave the profession (Charters, 1970; Grissmer & Kirby, 1987; Mark & Anderson, 1985; Murnane, Singer, & Willet, 1988, 1989; Willet & Singer, 1991). Even among those who remain, the early years are more difficult than they ought to be and fail to allow careful, thoughtful development of teaching expertise (Bullough, 1990; Darling-Hammond, 1988; Huling-Austin, 1987).

MAKING THE TRANSITION FROM PRESERVICE TEACHER TO FIRST-YEAR TEACHER

Well-designed, intensive induction support improves teacher retention, performance, and career satisfaction. It also fosters teacher reflection and collegiality. Thus, formal induction programs should be an integral part of all new teachers' professional development. During the induction period, new teachers should be supported and formatively assessed in ways that recognize the complexity of teaching and the variety of approaches that contribute to teaching success (Bartell, 1995). An induction period should be structured to provide for a gradual introduction to the responsibilities of teaching; afford each new teacher access to experienced colleagues for information, advice, and assistance as needed; and require each beginning teacher to demonstrate competence in the profession.

The induction phase cannot be viewed in isolation. Teacher induction builds on teacher preparation programs, leading to continued growth and development. Policies designed to facilitate entry into the profession need to be developed in tandem with policies that guide the initial preparation and ongoing development of teachers (Bartell, 1995).

INDUCTION AND DIVERSITY

California is only one of an increasing number of states that have begun to institute formal teacher induction policies (Interstate New Teacher Assessment and Support Consortium, 1992). California educates the most culturally diverse student population in the world. More than 4.9 million students attend public schools in California. One-third of California's students come from homes where a language other than English is spoken; multiple languages are spoken in most of California's classrooms (Bartell, 1995). This diversity can present challenges for the new teacher: "No matter what initial professional preparation teachers receive, teachers are never fully prepared for classroom realities and for the responsibilities associated with meeting the needs of a rapidly growing, increasingly diverse student population" (Bartell, 1995, p. 29).

The California New Teacher Project (CNTP) was initiated in 1988 to study alternative methods of supporting and assessing new teachers. From 1988 to 1992, thirty-seven local and regional pilot projects explored innovative ways of supporting and assessing over 3,000 first- and second-year teachers. The long-range purpose of the project was to develop a comprehensive statewide strategy for the certification and professional induction of new teachers. Senate Bill 148—the Bergeson Act—required state education agencies to evaluate how different support and assessment approaches could lead to state policies that might help

- Retain capable teachers
- Improve the teaching abilities of beginning teachers
- Improve teaching of a diverse student population
- Identify beginning teachers who need additional assistance and those who would be more successful in another profession

An extensive program evaluation using many different data collection methods—including questionnaires, interviews, classroom observations, and rating scales—revealed that well-developed induction programs could increase the retention rates of beginning teachers and improve their performance (Ward, 1992; Ward & Dianda, 1990).

INDUCTION AND TECHNOLOGY: INTERNET-BASED TEACHER HELP LINES

Many universities are setting up teacher help lines to help their preservice teachers bridge the gap between their teacher preparation programs and their first year of teaching. The University of Northern Iowa (UNI) is one example of a university that has recently set up a teacher help line. The Internet-based service provides new teachers, or teachers who have changed positions, an easy way to contact UNI faculty with teaching-related questions (Purdy, 1998). Amy, a recent graduate of UNI, shared her enthusiasm about the teacher help line: "I think it will be very beneficial to me, just to have contact with the UNI faculty to get advice on problems I'm having or things I'm looking for. And the Internet and e-mail is a great way to deliver the service, especially since I'm looking for a teaching job out of state" (quoted in Purdy, 1998, p. 7).

Faculty are also excited about the teacher help line, because it provides education professors with an avenue for keeping in touch with their graduates and supporting them through their first years of teaching. William Waack, emeritus director of teacher education at UNI, shared the following endorsement of the new teacher help line: "The Teacher Helpline will help those beginning teachers who so many times tend to feel isolated and have no one to turn to when classroom crises occur. It also confirms our philosophy that our graduates should never feel that they have graduated from the university; rather they should feel that they are graduating into it" (p. 7).

How do teacher help lines work? After accessing the site through the World Wide Web (UNI's teacher help line's address is <www.uni.edu/coe/teach. helpline>), teachers can submit an on-line form with their questions. Questions are then forwarded to an appropriate faculty member, who sends an e-mail response directly back to the new teacher. While you are still enrolled in your teacher preparation program, develop a list of contact information, including Web sites, that will help you link with your university and peers when you move into your first teaching position.

Your First Year of Teaching: Survival of the Fittest

As you enter the teaching profession, it will be easy for you to view your inexperience and naivete as liabilities. Certainly some others may choose to view them that way, and in some respects they are, but being new to a situation also can be an asset. As Garfield the cat reflected while seated next to Odie the dog—who was perched nonchalantly on a tree branch—"It's amazing what one can accomplish when one doesn't know what one can't do." As a new teacher, you hopefully won't already have placed artificial, self-imposed limits on yourself and the strategies you're willing to try. You only have one year to be blissfully oblivious to the organizational politics that have preceded your arrival, so make the most of it.

The most important thing you can do as a new teacher is listen—and most people make better listeners when they have their own mouths closed. Yes, you'll have much to offer, but it's difficult to learn about your new organizational culture without listening attentively and observing carefully. Remember the importance of discovering "how we do things here." Also remember and apply the following first-year teacher survival guidelines:

- Carefully plan your first teaching day.
- Develop positive relationships with your students.
- Develop positive relationships with your students' parents and seek their support.
- Develop positive, collaborative relationships with your colleagues, administrators, and support staff.
- Communicate clearly and regularly with your administrators.
- Listen and observe carefully and attentively to read, interpret, and understand the school culture.
- Set monthly and annual goals and engage in long-term planning.
- Create a positive learning environment.
- Identify community resources.
- Apply the skills and roles of leadership.
- Set high but reasonable goals and expectations for yourself.
- Seek guidance from your fellow teachers.
- Take advantage of teacher induction programs.
- Find an informal mentor if your school has no formal induction program.
- Maintain university connections.
- Keep in touch with college professors who served as mentors to you.
- Admit what you don't know, and then find the answers you need.

Find an informal mentor if your school has no formal induction program. (© José L. Pelaez/THE STOCK MARKET)

- Remind yourself of what you do know:

  The answer to most questions in the teaching/learning process is "It depends." Situation-specific decision making is a critical component of effective teaching.

  The affective dimension pervades all others.

  The only constant is change.

FRAMEWORK FOR BEGINNING TEACHERS: WHAT DO TEACHERS NEED TO KNOW AND BE ABLE TO DO?

The Farwest Laboratory for Educational Research and Development's *Draft Framework of Knowledge, Skills and Abilities for Beginning Teachers* (1995) defines a vision of effective teaching in the initial years of service. This framework describes six domains of knowledge and skills. For your convenience, the following list identifies the chapters in which we've addressed each of these different domains:

- **Domain 1: Create and maintain an effective environment for student learning.**

  Chapter 3: Teachers as Leaders and Decision Makers

  Chapter 6: Schools as Cultures and Organizations

  Chapter 7: Instructional Guidance: Moving Beyond Classroom Management

- **Domain 2: Understand and organize content knowledge for student learning.**

TEACHERS AND CONTINUING EDUCATION: IT'S GOOD TO HAVE A PLAN!

Teaching is a complex activity that develops over time (Bartell, 1995). As noted previously, teachers' concerns change during the course of their careers (Veenmam, 1984; Zeichner, 1983). Therefore, expert teachers tend to view teaching differently than novices do (Berliner, 1986; Borko & Livingston, 1989). However, when teachers, regardless of their level of experience, successfully collaborate as colleagues, their teaching expertise is most effectively fostered and developed (Ackland, 1991; Hargreaves & Dawe, 1990; Zimpher & Rieger, 1988).

CHARTING YOUR COURSE FOR LIFELONG LEARNING

No teacher can learn everything he or she will ever need to know about teaching during a preservice preparation program (Carter, Sabers, Cushing, Pinnegar, & Berliner, 1988; Feiman-Nemser, 1983; Little, 1989; Shulman, 1986, 1987). Consequently, all teachers must become "managers of their own inquiry" (Darling-Hammond, 1994) and lifelong students of the profession. Now that your professional development has begun, will it ever end? We certainly hope not! As you frame your professional future, consider the professional development principles in Figure 14.2.

EFFECTIVE PROFESSIONAL DEVELOPMENT

In some states, for many years all that's been required for teachers to renew their teaching certificate or license is to pay an annual fee. If they chose to, teachers could complete their entire career without taking even one additional course or credit beyond their undergraduate degree. However, when it comes to teachers' ongoing professional development and continuing education, business as usual will not suffice. "As we approach the 21st century and face increasing pressures on schools, we can no longer afford to ignore the development of personal and professional effectiveness skills along with content and pedagogy in the development of educators" (Malone & Tulbert, 1996, p. 47). Teachers who remain actively involved in their own professional development and take a planned approach to their continuing education exhibit the ability to develop a personal mission and participate in the overall school mission; evaluate—and when necessary and appropriate, shift—paradigms to see the world through the eyes of others; develop and use effective interpersonal skills; use action research to evaluate their own activities and solve problems; resolve conflict in ways that everyone benefits; and continually renew the body, mind, and spirit (Malone & Tulbert, 1996).

Schools and administrators that overtly support and demonstrate a strong commitment to the professional development of teachers provide four necessary and essential conditions for effective professional development: leadership, resource and policy support, norms of collegiality and experimentation, and adequate time (Bull, 1994). Leaders who seek to create school cultures that support the professional development of teachers also are guided by the following principles: that effective professional development is school-based; incorporates coaching and other follow-up procedures; is collaborative; is embedded in the daily lives of teachers, providing for continuous growth; and focuses on student learning and is evaluated, at least in part, on that basis (Bull, 1994). (See Figure 14.3.)

SETTING YOUR ASPIRATIONS HIGH: WILL YOU BE ONE OF AMERICA'S BEST AND BRIGHTEST TEACHERS?

Teachers who serve as effective educational leaders and informed decision makers take an active role in their professional development and remain lifelong learners. Consequently, we encourage you to take a planned approach to your continuing education. For example, rather than accumulating a motley collection of courses, inservice enrichments, workshops, and continuing education credits, consider pursuing a graduate program. Teachers who find themselves with a B.A. or B.S. plus thirty credit hours of extra coursework often wonder how they arrived at that point. The benefit of hindsight causes them to ask, "What if I'd invested my time and energy in a graduate program instead

**Figure 14.2
Professional
Development
Principles**

Principle 1
Teacher learning is a lifelong process that begins at the preservice level and continues throughout a teacher's career. The uncertain context of teachers' work makes learning a lifelong corollary to teaching.

Principle 2
Reflection and inquiry are the methods by which teachers learn. These processes engage teachers in examining their practice and constructing new knowledge that will guide their future work.

Principle 3
Teachers reflect about their past, present, and future experiences in school. Learning to view experience as the content of teacher reflection is an important part of professional development.

Principle 4
When teachers reflect, they reflect about something. Because this something is the "matters of school life," these matters or experiences of teachers must be captured in some form so that teachers can reflect about them.

Principle 5
Not only do teachers need the time and opportunities to reflect on their work; they need to do so in the company of others with whom they can construct meaning.

Principle 6
To construct meaning (or to learn) within a collaborative context, teachers need the opportunity to speak and be heard as well as to listen and respond to the thoughts and beliefs of others.

Principle 7
Teachers' collaborative learning groups should be structured to incorporate multiple perspectives, because these differences will stretch teachers' opportunity to learn and better reflect the complex world.

Principle 8
Conflict is a necessary outcome of a collaborative structure in which teachers come together to discuss issues of importance to them. Rather than inhibiting learning, conflict can enhance it by causing people to stretch in their understandings and create alliances across differences, ultimately benefiting everyone.

Principle 9
Given that they focus on different "matters at hand," collaborative learning groups need to accommodate changing leadership configurations according to the problem under consideration, the group's current membership, and what outcomes are needed.

(Lambert, Kent, Richert, Collay, & Dietz, 1997)

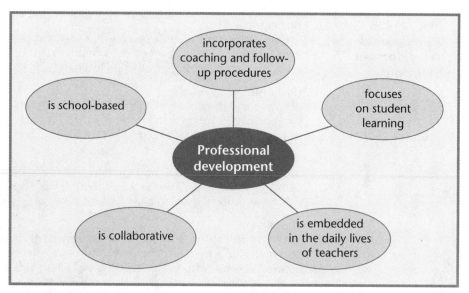

Figure 14.3
Principles Guiding Effective Professional Development

of taking the workshops and continuing education courses that presented the least inconvenience or the least challenge?"

We also encourage you to take responsibility for your own professional development by engaging in long-term planning, setting professional and personal goals, and developing strategies for achieving your goals. Keep your knowledge base current by attending professional conferences, participating in

Rather than accumulating a motley collection of courses, workshops, and continuing education credits, consider pursuing a graduate program. (© Leslye Borden/Photo Edit)

action research projects, keeping current with the education literature, and collaborating with colleagues. Of course, professional development plans can help focus your efforts and guide your goal setting. So can participating in the National Board for Professional Teaching Standards (NBPTS) certification process, which we described in Chapter 12.

REMINDERS, RECOLLECTIONS, REFLECTIONS, AND RESPONSES

We'd like to take a moment to remind you of some things we hope you already know, resurrect some teaching/learning recollections, ask you to engage in some reflection regarding those recollections, and invite a personal response from you related to your recollections and reflections. For instance, perhaps you recall that Rita loved school until her first day of kindergarten. The unfortunate "Blue Cat Incident" accurately captures the affective tone of her kindergarten schema. Fortunately, Rita's "school daze" schema also includes several positive recollections, as well as teachers who made a significant and positive difference for her.

What do you want your students to remember about you and your teaching?
(© Susie Fitzhugh)

MAKING MAGIC, MAKING MISTAKES, OR MAKING MISERY

As described in Chapter 1, our school experiences from the student perspective include a variety of recollections, ranging from the negative, humiliating, and horrifying to the positive, edifying, and enlightening. Perhaps the same is true for you. All teachers have the potential to make misery, make mistakes, or make magic for their students. What distinguishes teachers who provided positive learning experiences—made magic for you—from those who created negative learning environments—made misery for you?

■ Planning for Magic

As a teacher, how can you increase the probability that you'll make magic more often than mistakes and misery? We propose that you can plan for magic to happen rather than wait for serendipity to create a magical moment here and there. In fact, magical moments seldom result from serendipity; rather, they come from effective teaching. Teachers who blend the science and art of effective teaching with experience and reflection on their practice are more apt to make magic than are teachers who have some or all of the puzzle pieces but haven't managed to put them all together yet to form the whole picture. The following story illustrates this point:

> *I just couldn't stop it. "The thingamabob that does the job is bibbidibobbidi-boo." That refrain from Walt Disney's* Cinderella *kept running through my mind as I sat in the back of the classroom, wearing my supervisor's hat and observing a student teacher trying her wings for the first time. She was nervous, and her frequent glances in my direction told me that she was also worried about what I might say. I smiled reassuringly, but at that moment I wished I could be more like Cinderella's fairy godmother and simply speak some magic words that would make everything fall into place for my young colleague. She was trying so hard and had such high expectations. But there was no magic—not for her, not for me, and not for her students.*

New teachers talk

What do you want your students to remember about you and your teaching? How do you want them to describe you to others?

A s a special education teacher, I want my students to remember that I challenged them and gave them opportunities to accomplish things they never thought they could. I would like my students to describe me to others as fair, nonjudgmental, flexible, and challenging.

—TYLER, Preservice Teacher

I want to be remembered as a believer in discovery. Anyone can spout facts in front of a classroom. I want to teach. I want to challenge. I believe that it's by experimenting, formulating ideas, testing those ideas and evaluating the process, discovering the work of others, and figuring out a way to creatively convey knowledge to others that the learning really happens. I want my students to remember my obvious enthusiasm for learning new ideas, as well as their own enthusiasm. I want them to remember their active role in the learning process and their feelings and ideas about their learning, and I want them to grow from that knowledge. I want to be described as excitable and exciting. I probably wouldn't mind being called a little wacky. I would like to be known for high expectations and for the fun that can be had in the process of learning.

—GAIL, Preservice Teacher

I want my students to remember me as a fun, flexible, and fair teacher. I never want them to be bored with the curriculum. I want them to remember how I never put them on the spot in front of the class. I want my students to tell others that I was the best teacher they've ever had. I

After 20 years as a teacher, I had forgotten how difficult it is to pull together all the lessons learned in education courses and somehow weave them into the act we call "teaching." The student teacher was doing a competent job, but there was no life, no energy, no—I keep coming back to that word—magic. Perhaps it was simply that she was new at this task. But I had seen this same type of competent yet lifeless presentation from teachers (including myself) who had much more experience. There was more to the lack of magic than simply inexperience. (DeFelice, 1989, p. 639)

Can you build magic into the teaching/learning process? Absolutely! Can you guarantee that every teaching and learning scenario you create will make magic for every learner, as well as for you? Absolutely not! For example, Rita loved teaching until the first day of her first year of teaching. (Notice any pattern here?) This in spite of the fact that she experienced many magical moments during her student teaching, successfully completed her teacher preparation program, and experienced a few epiphanies that caused her to conclude beyond a shadow of a doubt and past a shade of a maybe that "Teaching is what I was born to do!" Bold words from someone who during her first year

want them to tell others that I handled touchy situations with respect and professionalism. I want them to say that their parents thought I was a genuinely caring and concerned person who truly believed in all the children in my classroom.

—ANDRIANA, First-Year Teacher

I want students to remember that I was always honest with them and valued them. I would like students to recall my teaching as animated and unorthodox. I try to have fun with what I'm doing. Hard work can be fun and rewarding in itself. I want my students to describe me as humorous, well-spoken, caring, and honest. I always hope to be described as competent and responsible. I want people to be able to count on me when I'm given responsibility.

—MITCH, Third-Year Teacher

Authors' Analysis

Reviewing these teachers' responses reminds us once again that the affective dimension pervades every facet of the teaching/learning process. Each of the four teachers emphasized affective qualities and characteristics, such as honesty, enthusiasm, responsibility, humor, caring, and fairness. In addition to the affective dimension, their responses featured teaching and learning as processes that should provide appropriate challenges, as well as flexibility and fun.

Now It's Your Turn

 In your teaching journal, record your own responses to the above questions. At this point in your preservice preparation, what do you think you'll want your students to remember about you and your teaching, and how do you think you'll want them to describe you to others?

of teaching often looked longingly out her classroom window at her car and pondered, "I have the keys right here in my desk. I could just leave and never come back."

PERSON-ENVIRONMENT FIT

A combination of organizational-environment and discipline concerns over-shadowed much of Rita's first year of teaching, as did culture conflict. She soon discovered that what she had learned about effective teaching did not mesh well with what her principal believed effective teaching should look like. For example, she began the year by introducing her fifth- and sixth-grade language arts students to centers and small-group activities. However, following her principal's first observation and evaluation, that all changed, due to his suggestion that whole-group teaching results in higher student achievement than small-group instructional strategies. Shell-shocked and unable to clearly articulate her rationale for why she was doing what she was doing, Rita "folded" rather than attempt to be a change agent. She also disengaged from the organizational environment as much as possible. Her initial experiences with the school's culture made her reluctant to collaborate with other teachers or to ask for their assistance in coping with first-year challenges, which included attempting to establish credibility with some fairly challenging students. And she definitely wasn't comfortable with the notion of taking her questions to the principal.

In short, the magic had disappeared, and she didn't know how to get it back. Year two and year three brought some improvement, but Rita was neither as happy nor as effective a teacher as she wanted to be. Her solution was to return to college full-time to complete the master's program she had begun. Following that year, she began a new teaching position in a new school and was relieved to find that her experiences there were quite different from her first three years of teaching. Rita found herself in an environment in which she was encouraged to think for herself and to make her own decisions—an environment in which the principal played both a supportive and a supporting role. His actions demonstrated that he viewed Rita as a credible professional whose judgment, leadership, and teaching he respected.

The magic had reappeared. Rita considers her years in that position as some of the most productive of her professional life. She enjoyed what she was doing, believed in what she was doing, and never had worked harder in her life. Was she a different person than the first-year teacher just described? In some respects, yes. She had learned a few things from the bumps and bruises she accumulated in her first teaching position, as well as from the graduate work she'd completed. Education does change people, whether they're aware of and acknowledge those changes or not. So do the organizational environments in which they work.

Person-environment fit can facilitate people's productivity and creativity, and the lack of it can impede their productivity and creativity. Different people require different things from their work environment and from their supervisors' leadership styles to be as productive as they're capable of being. That's what we mean when we talk about person-environment fit. For example, some teachers flourished in Rita's first school environment, but she did not. That doesn't mean it was a horrible organizational environment or that Rita was a horrible teacher—even though she certainly felt horrible. Many new teachers find both their teaching voice and a suitable person-environment fit on their first try. Therese did, and we certainly hope you do. However, if on your first try you don't find exactly what you're looking for in a school culture and organizational environment, please don't jump to the conclusion that you're a horrible teacher, you chose the wrong major, or you should retire from teaching.

OUR BEGINNING AND ENDING PREMISE: GREAT LEADERS TEACH AND GREAT TEACHERS LEAD

Although we cannot—and, in fact, no one can—guarantee you magical moments every time you engage in the teaching/learning process, we can recommend some fundamentals that increase the probability of your creating magical moments. Many times, small modifications in what teachers build into the teaching/learning process yield very different results. Although you—like all teachers—will make mistakes along the way, your consistent application of the following principles will help you make more magic than misery for your students and yourself.

■ LISTEN: To Your Students, and Also to Your Heart

We remind you that "What happens in the classroom between people is more important than any assignment, curriculum, procedure, or content. If the people relate to each other in an environment of acceptance and trust, content and competence will grow." It's easy for first-year teachers to lose sight of this point when they're sinking in a sea of survival concerns. We hope the following "card trick" will serve as a reminder of the magic that genuine listening holds.

Sometimes in your attempts to successfully play the teaching role, you may wish your hand held a spade, so you could dig a hole, crawl in it, and bury yourself. Other times you may—for only a fleeting moment—ponder that a club might be the card of choice, serving as a better motivational tool than the more restrained motivational techniques you learned in college. Then there may be times when you look at every card you hold as a diamond in the rough, in need of fine-tuning and precision crafting. However, we encourage you to lead with your heart, although sometimes it may pain you a bit.

Learners of every age can distinguish between genuine and disingenuous words, actions, and attitudes. That is, they know phoniness when they encounter it. Consequently, we invite you to lead and listen with your heart. Listening with your heart, leading with your heart, and listening to your heart when making decisions that affect the lives, learning, and self-concepts of your students are critical to making magic in the classroom.

■ EFFORT: Work Hard, but Also Work Smart

Thomas Jefferson once observed, "I'm a great believer in luck, and I find the harder I work the more I have of it." Occasionally people drone on about how hard they work, seeking a bit of sympathy from those around them or just seeking to make certain everyone knows how hard they work. However, sometimes those who talk the most about working hard don't have much time left over, after all their talking about it, for working. To the best of our knowledge, employers don't hand out awards or salary increases to the employees who are the first ones in the building or the last ones to leave each day. In fact, rather than signaling productivity, that behavior might signal inefficiency and ineffective use of time, too many trips to the water cooler, or too much time spent fulfilling the role of the organization's resident storyteller or gossip.

We encourage you to work hard but also to work smart. In other words, don't *tell* people how hard you work, *show* them what you accomplish. In addition, help your students learn the skills, strategies, and attitudes that will enable them to work both hard and smart.

■ ALWAYS BELIEVE: First in Yourself, and Then in Your Students' Abilities to Succeed

Moorfield Stacy offered this bit of encouragement: "Have confidence that if you have done a little thing well, you can do a bigger thing well, too." You can build on small successes to succeed at larger tasks. The same is true for your students. Set them up for success by creating learning opportunities at which they can succeed. Then provide them with increasingly challenging tasks.

Sometimes teachers see little growth in particular students, even though they patiently attempt to help these students learn. Teachers must become accustomed to accepting deferred gratification, because with some students they won't get to see the results of their best efforts and conscientious caring. For these students, the "light might not dawn" until a year or more later, when they begin to make connections between what previous teachers were attempting to teach them and what they're currently learning.

Resist the temptation to seal a student's fate by assuming that she or he will never "get it," will never learn, or will never succeed. The minute you quit believing in a student and his or her ability to succeed, you become an ineffective teacher for that student, as well as an impediment and road block to that student's learning.

■ DEMAND THE BEST: First of Yourself, and Then You Have the Right to Demand Your Students' Best Efforts

Teaching is somewhat like listening. Many people do it, but few people do it extremely well. Perhaps that's because in both endeavors it's easy to slide by with minimal effort. Consequently, some teachers choose the easy way out and adopt a "I don't get paid to think" mentality. Where do people get the idea that teaching is an easy job, designed for those who don't quite have what it takes to do something else? Where do college students get the idea that an education major is for students who can't deliver high ACT or SAT scores or who "wash out of" engineering, premed, business, or other "more challenging" majors? Although part of the answer may emanate from the familiarity with schools that most people have, part may also stem from ineffective teachers who choose to invest only the minimal effort required to retain their positions. Unfortunately, some teachers quit teaching several years prior to their retirement. We encourage you to retire from teaching before you quit and before you reach the point where you're not willing or able to demand the best of yourself.

We also encourage you to demand the best of your students. Well-intentioned teachers sometimes think they're helping students by asking less of them. Teachers may figuratively or literally pat students on the head and console them with "Don't worry, honey. Maybe you'll get it next year." Expecting less of students and demanding less than their best work and best efforts certainly are not helpful practices. As Carl Boyd, an award-winning teacher, stated, "No one rises to low expectations." As Rita says, "Doing only what you have to do is choosing to be less than a success."

■ ESTABLISH CULTURES OF PRODUCTIVITY: First for Yourself, and Then Set Your Students Up for Success by Providing a Learning Environment That Allows Them to Succeed

We remind you that effective leaders create cultures of productivity for themselves and for those around them. Earlier we shared with you Akin and Hopelain's characteristics of leaders who create cultures of productivity (1986). Adapt those characteristics to fit yourself, as an educational leader whose responsibility and goal is to create a culture of productivity for your students. For example:

1. Value productivity and results, rather than activity, for both your students and yourself.
2. Encourage an environment of trust and openness.
3. Act with reliability and dependability so your students will know how to act.
4. Have high standards and expectations for your students, but achieve results without bossing or nagging or whining.
5. Communicate your mission (for example, tell students what you want them to leave with that they don't have when they first enter your classroom).
6. Learn from—as well as about—your students, their parents, and your colleagues by listening, observing, and asking questions.

■ REMAIN A LEARNER: The Most Effective Teachers Value Lifelong Learning and Remain Learners Throughout Their Lives

Chester Bernard offered the opinion that "To try and fail is at least to learn; to fail to try is to suffer the inestimable loss of what might have been." We invite you to keep this observation in mind as you map out your professional development plans. We also remind you to retire before you quit teaching. Although it's possible to "coast" through several years of a teaching career, we're hopeful that you'll make the choice and commitment to remain personally engaged in the learning process throughout your career. Students who have the opportunity to learn with teachers who are themselves still learning have the added benefit of seeing their teachers model the skills and dispositions of a lifelong learner. In the area of lifelong learning, as in most other areas, teachers who lead by example generally are recognized by their students and colleagues as the most trusted, respected, and credible leaders. Teachers who remain learners throughout life also tend to be more receptive to change and more likely to serve as change agents and facilitators.

■ Identify and Build on Your Strengths and Those of Your Students

Charles Garfield (as opposed to Garfield the cat) devoted several years to the study of individuals he calls "peak performers." For Garfield, peak performers are people who consistently distinguish themselves from others by their exemplary performance in their chosen field (1986). His conclusion, following extensive study of such people and their development, is that "The difference between peak performers and 'everybody else' is much smaller than 'everybody else' thinks. The peak performers know that it's a small difference, but other people erroneously believe that the gap is much wider than it really is" (Trubo, 1983, p. 56). The good news in Garfield's conclusion is that if you choose to, you can be a peak performer. The bad news is that Garfield has robbed you of any and all excuses you might offer to explain away your achieving anything less.

One of the characteristics peak performers typically exhibit is the ability to build on their strengths. Prerequisite to building on one's strengths is the ability to identify them. What are your strengths? To what degree can you comfortably and confidently describe them to others? How can you leverage your strengths to become an even more effective and productive teacher? Many times people find it easier to identify their weaknesses than to name their strengths. Perhaps that's true for you as well. However, you can't build on something you haven't yet found, so we encourage you to figure out what you're good at and to use those strengths to acquire others.

We also encourage you to apply this same strategy to your students. Look for their strengths, and help them to do the same. Resist the temptation to operate from the deficit mode of teaching, in which teachers spend a great deal of time and energy focusing on what students can't do and what they're not good at, rather than on emphasizing what students can do and what they are good at. We recall the experience of one mother, a student in one of our classes, who described two different conferences she had concerning her son with two different special service providers. She walked away from the first conference wondering just what her son could do, because for half an hour she had listened to a recitation of what he *couldn't* do. However, she walked away from the second conference on an emotional high, because for half an hour she had listened to a description of what her son *could* do. She pointed out that both providers presented the same test scores and assessment information, but one emphasized what the data said her son *couldn't* do, whereas the other emphasized what the data said her son *could* do. One focused on weaknesses, the other on strengths. It's a difference in approach that can make a difference for your students, their parents, your colleagues, and yourself.

THE WHOLE IS GREATER THAN THE SUM OF ITS PARTS

When you successfully combine all these variables—that is, when you

> **L**isten to your students—and also to your heart; use the right amount of
>
> **E**ffort (work hard, but also work smart);
>
> **A**lways believe in your and your students' ability to succeed;
>
> **D**emand the best of yourself as well as your students;
>
> **E**stablish a culture of productivity for yourself and your students;
>
> **R**emain a learner throughout your life; and identify and build on your
>
> **S**trengths and those of your students, LEADERS "magically" appear.

Teachers must serve as educational leaders and informed decision makers. We can guarantee few things in life, but we do guarantee that if you don't function as the leader in your classroom, someone else will.

PRESERVICE PREDICTIONS

Although we can't guarantee what kind of teacher you'll be, our years of experience working with preservice teachers have yielded the ability to make fairly accurate predictions regarding the kind of teachers the undergraduates we work with and observe throughout their teacher preparation program are likely to become. For example, we can identify preservice teachers who are likely to adopt an "I don't get paid to think" mentality; those who are likely to adopt best-practice approaches; those who are likely to become change agents, change advocates, and change facilitators; those who are likely to be "folders"; and those who are likely to become "shakers."

■ Who Are Folders?

Folders are new teachers who choose to perpetuate the status quo, bow to peer pressure, and take the easy way out. The teaching profession historically has had a surplus of folders.

■ Who Are Shakers?

Shakers are new teachers who create pockets of excellence, have a vision and articulate it clearly, and seek out and find colleagues to collaborate with who share their vision. The teaching profession currently is actively recruiting shakers.

FINAL REMINDERS AND RESPONSES

We close in the same way we began—by reminding you that the world already has more than enough mediocre teachers. William Ward observed, "The mediocre teacher tells. The good teacher explains. The superior teacher demonstrates. The great teacher inspires." We certainly agree that great teachers often do inspire. They also make mistakes along the way, but they definitely create more magic than misery. Remember to allow yourself and your students to learn from mistakes and to view them as a natural and appropriate part of the teaching/learning process.

Reflect & Respond

Remember our earlier invitation to contact some—at least one—of your former teachers who had a significant impact on your life to tell them what you appreciated about them? If you've not yet done so, we encourage you to make the time to follow through on your good intentions. What do you remember most about teachers who made positive and significant differences in your life? Once you become a teacher yourself, we're confident that you'll quickly discover how important, powerful, and meaningful words of genuine appreciation from both former and current students can be.

In your teaching journal, draft a letter of thanks to a former teacher who made a significant and positive difference in your life. Provide that teacher with specific examples of how she or he made learning meaningful, memorable, fun, and functional for you. After fine-tuning your letter, deliver it to your teacher of choice—in person, if possible.

THE PROFESSIONALIZATION OF TEACHING

Finally, if you're an individual who understands the caring, commitment, and competence that exemplary teaching requires and are willing to invest the necessary time and energy to develop the knowledge, performances, and dispositions that characterize effective teachers, we invite and warmly welcome you to the teaching profession. We also invite you to use what you know about making magic to incrementally move along the continuum of teaching effectiveness from being a good teacher who explains to becoming a superior teacher who demonstrates and then a great teacher who inspires. What will your students remember most about you and your teaching?

SUMMARIZING WHAT YOU'VE LEARNED

■ Examining the relationship between theory and practice can make a major contribution to the development of beginning teachers.

■ A professional teaching portfolio profiles your strengths, experiences, and qualifications for prospective employers and can be used to distinguish yourself from other applicants.

■ Effective teacher induction programs build on initial teacher preparation and facilitate continued growth and professional development.

■ Teachers who serve as effective educational leaders and informed decision makers take an active role in their professional development and remain lifelong learners.

■ Great leaders teach and great teachers lead.

YOUR PROFESSIONAL TEACHING PORTFOLIO

■ The primary purpose of your professional teaching portfolio is to profile your strengths, experiences, and qualifications and to distinguish yourself from other teaching applicants. Review everything in your portfolio with this purpose in mind.

■ Consider including in your portfolio a response to common interview questions such as "Why should I hire you instead of the other one hundred applicants?" You might head this production "What do I have to offer your school and district?" or "What knowledge, performances, and dispositions would I bring to my first teaching position?"

Key Terms

Collective bargaining agreement (p. 499)

Contract (p. 500)

Interstate certification contract (p. 499)

Reciprocity (p. 499)

Relevant Resources for Professionals

Books and Articles

• Covey, S. R. (1989). *The seven habits of highly effective people.* New York: Simon & Schuster.

• Darling-Hammond, L. (1994). *The current status of teaching and teacher development in the United States.* Washington, DC: National Commission on Teaching and America's Future.

• Shapiro, B. (1994). Assessing America's best and brightest teachers: The National Board for Professional Teaching Standards. *The Professional Educator, 17*(1), 41–48.

Organizations

- National Board for Professional Teaching Standards (NBPTS)

  http://www.nbpts.org

- NBPTS
  26555 Evergreen Road
  Suite 400
  Southfield, MI 48076
  800-228-3224

  info@nbpts.org

Web Sites

All of the following Web sites list employment opportunities for educators.

- **Academic Employment Network**

  www.academploy.com/

- **Education Jobs Page**

  www.nationjob.com/education

- **Education Jobsite**
  A national source for K–12 teaching and administrative opportunities

  www.edjobsite.com/

- **Educational Placement Service**

  www.educatorjobs.com/

- **Education World's Education Employment Center**

  www.education-world.com/jobs/

- **National Educators Employment Review**

  www.teacherjobs.com/

- **National Association of Teachers' Agencies**
  The mission of NATA is to serve administrators in their search for talented educators to meet their staffing needs. Qualified educators are guided toward appropriate opportunities that meet their career goals.

  www.tiac.com/users/incinc/nata/nata_home.html

GLOSSARY

Acceleration: Moving students through the curriculum more rapidly than the regular or normal pace.

Advance organizer: A statement or concept a teacher makes or presents to help students understand how previous information relates to new learning and connect what they already know with what they're about to learn.

Affective domain: The domain of learning that involves feelings, attitudes, and values.

Alternative assessment: Any type of assessment in which students create responses, as opposed to choosing them from a given list.

Alternative lifestyle families: Families headed by gay parents.

Amygdalae: Two almond-shaped organs inside the brain that research indicates receive and send all emotional messages.

Analogies: Comparisons that point out similar features of things or ideas that are otherwise different; used as elaboration strategies to help students draw comparisons between familiar concepts and new concepts they're learning.

Analytic rubric: A *rubric* that separates the total performance or product into several elements or criteria.

Anecdotal record: A written "snapshot" of a learning event that describes the event in detail, including the student's name, the date and time, the setting, the activity, and what the student says as well as what he or she does.

Assertive discipline: A teacher-centered approach to classroom management in which the teacher applies the same standards and expectations to all students; based on assertion training.

Assessment: The process of collecting performance data; compare with *evaluation*.

Assistive technology: Equipment or methods used to maintain or improve the functioning of individuals with disabilities.

Asynchronous learning: Instruction in which learners and teachers can access information at different times and from different places, greatly expanding the notion of learning communities and learning environments.

Authentic assessment: A subset of performance assessment that requires realistic expectations set in real-life contexts.

Authentic learning experiences: Learning opportunities that are real to students and have meaning that extends beyond the school context (for example, exploring real ecological problems in their community instead of completing a worksheet on ecosystems).

Authoritarian dogmatism: A stance teachers sometimes adopt as a defense mechanism, in which they present themselves to parents as all-knowing experts whose methods are beyond question.

Authoritarian parenting style: A parenting style characterized by a demanding parent, absolute rules, a restrictive environment, punitive control, and inappropriate expectations.

Authoritative parenting style: A parenting style that stresses democratic decision making, guidelines and parameters, effective communication, problem solving, and self-discipline and responsibility.

Behavior modification: A teacher-centered approach to classroom management in which the teacher doesn't expect learners to solve problems but instead observes student behavior and uses reinforcement to strengthen or diminish specific behaviors.

Blended family: A family in which one or both parents bring with them children from a previous marriage.

Bodily/kinesthetic intelligence: The ability to control one's bodily motions and the talent to manipulate objects with deftness; one of the multiple intelligences described by Howard Gardner.

Brain-based teaching and learning: A theory of learning, derived from recent research on the brain, that describes how learning changes the brain physically.

Brainstorming: A creative thinking strategy used to generate ideas.

Checklists: Prepared lists of competencies or behaviors that anchor a teacher's observations of a particular student or group of students.

Cognitive dissonance: A condition in which one person's understanding of a situation or event conflicts with new and different information and perspectives.

Cognitive domain: The domain of learning that involves mental operations (or thinking skills), ranging from the lowest level of simple recall of information to high-level, complex evaluative processes.

Collaboration: Two or more individuals or organizations working together toward a common goal; more than mere cooperation.

Collaborative learning experiences: Learning activities that students work on together, in groups.

Collaborative reflection: An intervention in which education students "recruit" inservice teachers to discuss with them the concepts and topics they are exploring in their teacher preparation program.

Collaborative rule making: An approach to classroom rule making that can provide an appropriate middle ground between authoritarian administration and permissiveness; can teach learners responsible citizenship skills.

Collaborative scheduling: Constructing schedules to facilitate combined class projects and special classes such as music, art, and physical education; typically used by middle and high school teachers from different content areas, to coordinate instruction.

Collateral learning: Incidental, informal learning; the attitudes, values, feelings, and appreciation that accompany formal learning in schools; the hidden curriculum.

Collective bargaining agreement: A written record of an agreement between a bargaining agent such as a National Education Association (NEA) or American Federation of Teachers (AFT) local affiliate and a school board; typically specifies working conditions, salaries, and evaluation procedures for local employees.

Community model: A learner-centered approach to *instructional guidance* that focuses on students working together to solve problems.

Community of learners: A class that reflects the best-practice principles of democratic decision making, collaboration, and cooperative learning.

Comprehensive, integrated-services approach: An approach to the provision of education and health care that acknowledges that all aspects of individuals' lives affect their success as students, patients, family members, and community residents.

Concept teaching: A strategy for facilitating learners' acquisition of declarative knowledge.

Conceptually oriented unit: A unit of instruction that involves the investigation of more broad-based topics, providing learners with many opportunities to discover relationships between different ideas.

Conceptual skills: Leaders' abilities to understand the complexities of the organization where they work (such as a school) and where and how they and their actions fit into that organization.

Conditional knowledge: Knowledge about when and why to use particular examples of *declarative knowledge* or *procedural knowledge*.

Conjunctive concepts: Concepts that are constant and do not change; compare with *disjunctive concepts* and *relational concepts*.

Constructivism: A best-practice principle, based on the belief that learners organize new information around previously developed schemata.

Content-oriented unit: A unit of instruction that originates within a particular content area, such as science or social studies, but involves topics that can be investigated across all content areas, such as small animals or neighborhoods.

Content standards: One of three types of standards that education reform initiatives typically center around; focus on curricula; compare with *performance standards* and *school delivery standards*.

Contract: A legal document that specifies a teacher's duties, responsibilities, teaching assignment (grade, subject), and salary for a specific time frame.

Core book: A literature selection that takes on a central and unifying role in a literature-based curriculum.

Creative problem solving: A systematic process for approaching a problem in an imaginative way that will result in effective action.

Creative thinking: Soft, divergent thinking; occurs during the *germinal phase* of new idea development.

Criterion-referenced assessment: An assessment technique in which a teacher collects assessment data and interprets them based on certain standards or criteria; compare with *norm-referenced assessment*.

Critical attributes: Qualities of a given concept that are essential to that concept.

Critical pedagogy: Classroom teaching that proceeds from a consideration of students' everyday lives and experiences.

Critical thinking: Hard, convergent thinking; occurs during the *practical phase* of new idea development.

Cultural networks: An informal but important means of communicating an organization's shared values and heroic mythology within the organization.

Culture: The traditions, beliefs, art and literature, philosophies, social structures, language, history, accomplishments, and so on of a distinct group of people, such as an ethnic group, a country, or an organization (including a school).

Curriculum: The materials a learner studies; defined by some theorists as *all* the experiences a learner has in school.

Curriculum articulation: Communicating curricular goals and connecting them with instruction.

Curriculum guide: An overview that communicates to teachers, parents, and the community the critical components of the curriculum and provides a framework that guides curriculum development for students, teachers, and administrators.

Curriculum processes: How the contents of curricula are taught.

Curriculum webs: A planning tool in which a curriculum is represented visually as a web; helps teachers achieve a balance between concepts and processes and between learner-initiated and teacher-initiated activities.

Decision making: A part of or corollary to leadership that involves influencing others to pursue goals that represent their values and motivations as well as one's own; also see *leadership.*

Declarative knowledge: Knowledge about something; compare with *procedural knowledge* and *conditional knowledge.*

Developmentally and culturally appropriate practice (DCAP): An extension of developmentally appropriate practice (DAP) that compensates for DAP's lack of multicultural sensitivity by promoting culturally congruent pedagogy.

Direct instruction: An instructional strategy often used to teach basic skills, facts, and knowledge; appropriate for teaching both procedural and declarative knowledge.

Discussion model: An instructional strategy in which the teacher reads material assigned to students and prepares questions to focus classroom discussion.

Disequilibrium: The intellectual tension related to a child's curiosity, according to Piaget.

Disjunctive concepts: Concepts that can take alternative forms; compare with *conjunctive concepts* and *relational concepts.*

Dispositions: Habits of mind or tendencies to respond to certain situations in certain ways; curiosity, friendliness or unfriendliness, bossiness, and creativity are all examples of dispositions that parents and teachers can strengthen or diminish by setting learning goals for children.

Divergent thinking: The process of generating ideas, making new connections, perceiving gaps, and identifying paradoxes; looking at the same things many other people have looked at before but seeing those things in different ways; creative thinking.

Documentation portfolio: A collection of work that provides evidence of student learning and growth.

Educational neglect: When parents fail to make sure their children attend school, permit chronic truancy, or fail to attend to any special educational needs of their children.

Effective momentum management model: A teacher-centered approach to classroom management that emphasizes creating an environment that prevents disruptive behaviors.

Elaboration: Augmenting or modifying an idea with more information in order to improve it; one of the five components of productive thinking.

Electronic portfolio: A professional teaching portfolio stored and distributed in electronic form, such as on the Web or on CD-ROM.

Elementary and Secondary Education Act (ESEA): Recent major legislation that has made it a national priority to involve parents in their children's education.

Emotional brain: The part of the brain that regulates emotions; the limbic brain; see also *amygdalae.*

Emotional intelligence: Emotional well-being; the ability to identify and manage one's feelings, control impulses, handle stress, read social and emotional cues, listen to others, resist negative influences, understand the perspective of others, and understand what behavior is acceptable in a certain situation.

Emotional literacy: For teachers, the ability to create a classroom community that consistently supports and nurtures appropriate norms, values, and behaviors.

Emotional neglect: Neglecting a child's emotional needs; includes refusing to provide needed psychological help, exposing a child to abuse by someone else, and allowing a child to use drugs or alcohol.

Encoding: Learners connecting new information to their prior knowledge and existing schemata.

Equality: Identical treatment for different individuals; not necessarily the same thing as fairness; compare with *equity.*

Equity: Fairness; not necessarily the same thing as identical treatment; compare with *equality.*

Ethnicity: The general composite of cultural and physical characteristics that can be attributed to both individuals and groups.

Evaluation: Judging the worth of an idea or bringing meaning to data, based on predetermined criteria or standards; one of the five components of productive thinking; compare with *assessment.*

Evaluation portfolio: A portfolio of student work used to evaluate students on preselected tasks, using predetermined criteria.

Existential intelligence: An inclination to ask basic questions about existence (Who are we? Where did we come from? Why do we die?); one of the multiple intelligences described by Howard Gardner.

Explicit curriculum: The "official," written-down curriculum.

Family Educational Rights and Privacy Act (Buckley Amendment): A law that ensures that parents of students under the age of eighteen have the right to see and control their children's school records.

Flexibility: Seeing things from a different point of view or breaking away from habitual patterns of thought; one of the five components of productive thinking.

Fluency: Generating many possibilities or producing lots of ideas; values quantity over quality; one of the five components of productive thinking.

Foster care: State-arranged care for children in homes other than those of their biological parents.

Germinal phase: The first stage in the development of most new ideas; characterized by *creative thinking*.

Goal: A general outcome a teacher plans to achieve in his or her practice.

Goals 2000: Educate America Act: Major recent legislation emphasizing school-home partnerships.

Group investigation: A grouping strategy in which each member of a heterogeneous group pursues an in-depth investigation of an aspect of a topic; then group members synthesize the results of their individual investigations, plan and execute a group presentation of their findings, and evaluate both the group's investigation process and its finished product.

Hidden curriculum: Unofficial instructional influences that support or weaken goal attainment.

Holistic learning experiences: Learning opportunities that connect several different curriculum components.

Holistic rubric: A *rubric* that results in one score that represents an evaluation of the total performance or product; compare with *analytic rubric*.

Horizontal relevance: Appropriate integration of curricular activities across a particular grade level.

Immigrant families: Families that have recently moved to the United States from a foreign country.

Implicit curriculum: Learning that takes place because students are part of the school culture (such as learning to provide the teacher with what the teacher wants or expects).

Inclusion: The practice of providing for learners' special needs within a regular classroom environment.

Individualized instruction: A strategy in which a student receives one-on-one instruction.

Instructional decision making: The complex process of selecting appropriate instruction and reflecting on one's teaching practice to provide optimum performance as a teacher.

Instructional guidance: An alternative approach to classroom management that goes beyond conventional classroom discipline, which focuses on controlling learners; requires a positive learning environment that is developmentally appropriate and culturally responsive; teaches learners the life skills they need as citizens of a democracy.

Instructional objectives: Statements that describe teachers' intentions for students' growth and change.

Integrated curriculum: A curriculum that incorporates the interrelationships or connections between different developmental domains and content areas; the larger notion from which *integrative units* are derived.

Integrated therapy team (ITT): A group of professionals from different disciplines (teachers, doctors, social services providers, and so on) who work collaboratively to address the social, physical, and psychological issues that affect children, families, and communities, without duplicating services or getting in one another's way.

Integrative unit: A collection of lessons, activities, and resources connected by a unifying concept or topic that is contextualized in a real-life framework, promotes active learning, and interrelates development as learners acquire knowledge, performances (skills), and dispositions.

Interactive planning phase: The second phase of instructional planning and decision making; consists of presenting, questioning, assisting, providing for skills practice, making transitions, and guiding learners.

Intercultural marriages: Marriages between individuals from different cultural groups.

Interdisciplinary instruction: Instruction that makes use of an *integrated curriculum* and *integrative units;* instruction that includes a range of disciplines.

Interest groups: A grouping strategy in which small groups are formed on the basis of students' interests.

Interethnic marriages: Marriages between individuals from different ethnic groups.

Interpersonal skills: The ability to work with and through people to achieve desired results; the most crucial group of leadership skills teachers must master.

Interstate certification contract: A program that enables teachers and other education professionals to have their credentials recognized in other states.

Interstate New Teachers Assessment and Support Consortium (INTASC): A group that has created a set of performance standards for beginning teacher licensure and an assessment process for measuring beginning teachers' performance against those standards.

Jigsaw groups: A grouping strategy in which each member of a heterogeneous study team studies one aspect of a topic, instructs members of other teams in what he or she has learned and in turn learns about what they've studied, and then rejoins his or her original team to teach the team members what was learned from the other teams.

KWL strategy: An instructional strategy that takes account of learners' existing schemata ("What do you *know*?"), considers what they're interested in learning ("What do you *want* to know?"), and measures what they learn as a result of instruction ("What did you *learn*?").

Laissez-faire parenting style: A parenting style characterized by an "anything goes" approach, neglectful parents, an environment in which no one cares, and withdrawal from parental responsibilities.

Leadership: A part of or corollary to decision making; in the context of teacher leadership refers to assisting people in accomplishing goals that represent their own values as well as one's own; also see *decision making.*

Learning center: A learning station; a place in the classroom where materials related to a specific curriculum component are available for students to use on their own.

Learning environments: The setting for learning; includes the classroom and all places where learning occurs, encompassing both incidental and planned learning.

Legal guardians: The adults who have legal guardianship rights and responsibilities in relation to a given child; frequently but not always the child's biological or adoptive parents.

Literature-based instruction: Instruction that is centered around trade books rather than textbooks.

Literature circles: A grouping strategy similar to adult book discussion groups, in which students choose their own books and discussion partners, establish a reading and meeting schedule, and determine how they will share their reading with one another.

Logical consequences: An instructional guidance approach designed not to punish students but to change their behavior by making clear the connection between a learner's behavior and a resulting action.

Long-range planning: Planning that identifies the general curriculum content and its sequence over the long term (generally a year); the most comprehensive type of instructional planning; compare with *mid-range planning* and *short-range planning.*

Management: An inherent element of leadership and a prerequisite of effective teaching; entails nine "executive functions," including planning; communicating

goals; regulating activities; and motivating, supervising, and evaluating other people.

Mentoring: A relationship in which a more experienced professional (such as a teacher) instructs and serves as a role model for a less experienced colleague.

Metacognition: Thinking about thinking; learners' considering their own thought processes and choosing learning strategies that are appropriate for specific tasks.

Mid-range planning: Term and unit planning; compare with *long-range planning* and *short-range planning.*

Migrant families: Families that must move frequently, usually because of employment requirements.

Multiple intelligences theory: A way of thinking about intelligence, proposed by Howard Gardner in 1983, that defines intelligence as the ability to solve problems and create products valued in a particular cultural setting; includes the premises that there is more than one kind of intelligence, intelligence can be taught, a brain is as unique as a fingerprint, and intelligences are forever changing throughout life.

National Board for Professional Teaching Standards (NBPTS): A group established to develop rigorous standards and assessments for certifying highly experienced and accomplished teachers.

National Council for Accreditation of Teacher Education (NCATE): A collaborative, nongovernmental, nonprofit enterprise that provides accreditation of U.S. teacher preparation programs.

Nation at Risk, A: A report released by the National Commission on Excellence in Education in 1983 that became a watershed event in education; called for higher standards for learning and teaching, increased funding for education, more leadership from government and from schools, longer school days, a longer school year, stricter attendance policies, stricter conduct policies, more homework, and academic performance prerequisites for extracurricular activities.

Natural consequences: An instructional guidance approach based on the principle that reality can influence students' behavior more than teachers can; "teachable moments" that provide authentic and natural contexts for learning.

Nonlinear instructional planning model: Planning process in which the teacher begins by developing instructional activities, then connects those activities to the outcomes they will produce, and then identifies the goals to which the outcomes relate; the "ready-fire-aim" approach.

Norm-referenced assessment: Comparing students to one another; compare with *criterion-referenced assessment.*

Null curriculum: The curriculum that does not exist; what schools *do not* teach.

Objective: A specific outcome a teacher plans to achieve in his or her practice.

Official curriculum: The written curriculum.

Operational curriculum: What teachers actually teach and how teachers communicate to students the importance of what is taught.

Organizational change: A disruption to the status quo of an organization; introducing an innovation that those in charge believe will lead to enhanced performance or improvements of some sort.

Organizational culture: The basic assumptions that operate within an organization, revealed by the behavior of organizational members as well as by certain value-led outward manifestations of those assumptions, such as the organizational structure, the management style of the organization's leaders, and the organization's physical setting; includes an emotional dimension and reflects the importance of having a sense of identification and meaning; acts as a kind of social glue that connects and holds together an organization's different parts.

Organizational environment: The everyday social and physical surroundings in which people do most or all of their work.

Organizational structures: The way in which teachers organize people, time, space, resources, curricula, and materials; can directly affect learner success.

Originality: Seeing in a unique way or thinking in a new or novel pattern; one of the five components of productive thinking.

Parenting styles: The general approach or style a parent has in raising his or her children; may be effective or ineffective.

Pedagogy: The methods, art, and science of educating people; knowledge and scholarship related to the teaching profession.

Peer assessment: An assessment method in which either an individual student or a small group of three or four students are called on to evaluate the work of one or more peers.

Peer response and editing groups: A grouping strategy in which three to five students meet regularly to offer one another feedback and advice on their writing.

Performance assessment: An assessment method in which students demonstrate their competencies or knowledge by creating an answer or developing a product.

Performances: Teaching skills teachers must display and apply as effective practitioners.

Performance standards: One of three types of standards that education reform initiatives typically center around; focus on student work and assessment; compare with *content standards* and *school delivery standards*.

Physical neglect: Failure by parents to provide their children with necessities such as adequate shelter, care and supervision, food, clothing, protection, and medical care.

Portfolio: A collection of materials that demonstrate a preservice or inservice teacher's knowledge base and instructional experience and philosophy.

Portfolio assessment: An assessment method that uses collections of selected student work which may or may not represent authentic tasks.

Positive discipline: A learner-centered approach to *instructional guidance* that emphasizes supporting students in reaching their goal of belonging and contributing.

Postinstructional planning phase: The last phase of instructional planning and decision making, consisting of checking for understanding, providing feedback, assessing and evaluating student performance, and communicating the learning outcomes to students and parents.

Practical phase: The second stage in the development of most new ideas; characterized by *critical thinking*.

Preinstructional planning phase: The first phase of instructional planning and decision making; includes choosing content, choosing an instructional approach, allocating time and space, determining structures, and determining motivation.

Presentation model: An instructional strategy often used to help students learn and retain declarative knowledge; typically includes four steps: present objectives and establish set, present an advance organizer, present learning materials, and check for understanding and strengthen learner thinking.

Principles of best practice: A synopsis, developed by Zemelman, Daniels, and Hyde (1998) of what researchers and practitioners know about effective teaching and learning.

Procedural knowledge: Knowledge about how to do something; compare with *declarative knowledge* and *conditional knowledge*.

Process portfolio: A collection of items and artifacts demonstrating work that typically is a part of a larger project.

Productive thinking: A combination of creative and critical thinking; includes *divergent* and *convergent thinking,* soft and hard thinking, *germinal* and *practical thinking.*

Professional development plan (PDP): The objectives, rationales, procedures, materials, and assessment and evaluation strategies a teacher defines and develops to guide her or his professional development.

Professional development schools (PDSs): An educational innovation designed to simultaneously restructure and renew PreK–12 schooling and teacher preparation.

Professional ethics: Moral guidelines that direct one's judgment and actions; the manifestations of a teacher's beliefs and values in his or her practice.

Professional teaching portfolio (product or showcase portfolio): A portfolio developed by a preservice or inservice teacher to showcase his or her achievements; sometimes required to complete a teacher preparation program.

Program articulation: Describing the ways in which programs and curricula within or across grade levels connect with one another.

Project: An investigation undertaken by a student or group of students to learn more about a topic.

Project Approach: An approach to instruction that involves students in in-depth investigations of topics.

Psychomotor domain: The domain of learning that involves physical movement, ranging from the lowest level, simple manipulation of materials, to the higher level of communicating ideas and finally the highest level, creative performance.

Public Law 100-297 (Stafford-Hawkins Act): Legislation passed in 1988 that established the National Assessment Governing Board and set provisions for developing a national examination.

Question-and-answer relationships (QARs): Relationships that exist among the kinds of questions asked, a piece of text, and the reader's *schema* or prior knowledge.

Rational-linear instructional planning model: A planning approach in which the teacher first defines goals and objectives and then plans instructional activities to satisfy those objectives; the dominant perspective on instructional planning.

Reality therapy model: A learner-centered approach to *instructional guidance* in which teachers help students identify inappropriate behavior and plan more desirable behavior.

Reciprocity: An agreement by which teaching credentials from one state are honored by other states' credentialing agencies; may be regional or among several states.

Reflect: To think about learning processes and outcomes and analyze one's own thinking and performance as a learner.

Reflection: Self-analysis of one's teaching practice; consists of assessing the attitudes, dispositions, knowledge base, and performances that together make up the whole picture of how effective one is as a teacher.

Reflective educator: An individual who carefully examines his or her own and others' professional practice and engages in school-based action research with fellow *researcher-teachers.*

Reflective practitioners: Teachers who engage in reflection.

Reggio Emilia Approach: An approach to curricular integration in which children learn through cooperating with other children and their teachers in long-term projects based on children's interests and centered around the creative arts.

Relational concepts: Concepts that describe relationships between two or more other concepts; compare with *disjunctive concepts* and *conjunctive concepts.*

Reliability: The accuracy of students' scores or outcomes on an assessment; the degree to which similar scores are likely to be produced in subsequent administrations of a given test or alternative assessment.

Researcher-teacher: A teacher who systematically analyzes his or her teaching and his or her students' learning to find out if certain strategies are making a difference in the students' achievement and performance.

Resource interdependence: A type of positive interdependence for use in cooperative learning; exists when group members need to share one set of materials and subdivide them so each member is responsible for a certain resource; also called a resource jigsaw.

Resource unit: A group of learning centers organized to promote independent, small group, or self-directed study.

Responsible classroom management model: A learner-centered approach to *instructional guidance* that considers learners as individuals to be treated fairly, but not necessarily identically.

Retention: The practice of having students repeat a grade.

Reward interdependence: A type of positive interdependence for use in cooperative learning; exists when group members learn new material together, are assessed individually, and then are rewarded on the basis of a performance ratio, such as 50 percent credit for every problem they solve correctly and 50 percent of the group members' average performance.

Rites and rituals: Activities that demonstrate for an organization's members its values, expectations, or accepted operating procedures; can be mundane and part of the daily routine of the organization (such as meetings) or extravagant, powerful events (such as awards ceremonies).

Role interdependence: A type of positive interdependence for use in cooperative learning; created when group members have complementary, interconnected roles.

Rote rehearsal: A rehearsal strategy; repeating out loud or subvocalizing information learners wish to remember; used to remember short lists, phone numbers, directions, and other simple information.

Round robin reading: The practice of having one student read aloud while other students follow along in their books; an example of a teaching practice that has not kept pace with theory and research on learning.

Rubric: A scoring guide that helps establish uniformity in evaluation of a student.

Schema: A model or pattern, based on a person's prior experience, used to make sense of a situation or concept.

Schema theory: A theory of knowledge that concerns the manner in which information is organized by the brain, encoded into memory, and retrieved from memory.

School-based action research: Systematic attempts to assess the effectiveness of one's teaching (see *researcher-teacher*).

School culture: The organizational culture of a school.

School delivery standards: One of three types of standards that education reform initiatives typically center around; focus on resources and support for school, teacher, and children; compare with *content standards* and *performance standards*.

School-family compacts: Agreements made between families and schools that declare their mutual responsibility for children's learning.

School volunteers: Unpaid personnel who usually work on a temporary basis and perform tasks that supplement, but do not take the place of, the work of paid staff members.

Screening: A method often used to determine students' readiness for school or specific programs; provides an opportunity to look at the developmental skills of a large number of students in a limited amount of time.

Self-assessment: A strategy for promoting in-depth learning with a focus on continual growth and improvement.

Self-control: The management of one's own behavior based, in part, on information generated through *self-monitoring*.

Self-monitoring: Consistently tracking, recording, and evaluating one's own behavior over time.

Sexual harassment: Unwelcome verbal or physical conduct of a sexual nature imposed by one individual on another.

Shared values: The basic beliefs that provide a sense of common direction for organization members and provide guidelines for their day-to-day behavior; the basis for an *organizational culture*.

Short-range planning: Weekly and daily lesson planning; compare with *mid-range planning* and *long-range planning*.

Showcase portfolio: A collection of work that both a student and his or her teacher believe represents that student's best efforts.

Simulation model: An instructional strategy that allows students to learn from self-generated feedback, by playing out specific situations within a controlled environment and then modifying their behavior based on their reactions and performances.

Single-parent family: A family in which a mother or father is single-handedly raising dependent children living in the same household; also called a one-parent, lone-parent, or solo-parent family.

Situational leadership: Determining whether group or individual leadership is preferable in a specific circumstance; considers the characteristics and needs of individual followers.

Skills groups: A grouping strategy in which a heterogeneous mix of students who share a common instructional need are brought together.

Stafford-Hawkins Act: See *Public Law 100-297*.

Student-teacher conference: A meeting in which the teacher talks with a student to help the student reflect on her or his work.

Suchman inquiry model: An approach for teaching problem solving through discovery and questioning; based on the belief that the strategies scientists use to solve problems and explore the unknown can be taught and learned and that people learn best those things that puzzle and intrigue them.

Survey: An instrument that asks students to respond to questions or rate items; used to learn about student attitudes toward specific subject matter, to determine their history with particular subjects, and to communicate to students that their ideas are valued.

Task interdependence: A type of positive interdependence for use in cooperative learning; arises when a division of labor is created and the actions of one group member must be completed if the next group member is to complete his or her responsibilities.

Taxonomy: A classification system that divides things into ordered categories.

Teacher effectiveness training: A learner-centered approach to *instructional guidance* in which each individual is supported in gaining confidence in his or her abilities by using open communication.

Teacher efficacy: The belief of teachers who see themselves as teacher leaders that they can make a positive difference in students' achievement; encourages teachers to place less blame on factors beyond their control.

Teacher induction: A rite of passage into the culture of teaching; the period during which a new teacher becomes socialized into the culture of the teaching profession.

Teaching credo: A succinct articulation of a teacher's fundamental beliefs about teaching and learning.

Technical skills: One of the three groups of skills required for teacher leadership and decision making; includes knowledge of both technology and pedagogy; see also *interpersonal skills* and *conceptual skills*.

Think-aloud: An instructional strategy in which teachers talk out loud to model the thinking they are using to approach a problem or answer a question.

Tracking: The practice of assigning students to different curricula (steering them toward specific course sequences, such as vocational or college preparatory courses) or different classes based on ability levels; can take many forms, including retention, acceleration, ability grouping, educational sorting, and the use of reading groups.

Traditional model: A teacher-centered approach to classroom management in which the teacher uses praise and rewards to correct student misbehavior.

Transactional leadership: When one person takes the initiative to contact others for the purpose of exchanging something of value.

Transescence: The transition phase between childhood and adolescence.

Transforming leadership: When leader and follower interact in such a way that both are raised to a higher level of motivation and morality; has the potential to raise the moral level of human conduct and the ethical aspirations of both the leader and the led.

Triangulated assessment: An assessment tool that provides three windows or modes for evaluating students' competencies.

Unit: A collection of lessons, activities, and resources connected by a unifying concept or topic.

Validity: How closely a test or alternative assessment measures what it is intended to measure.

Vertical articulation: The overall learning continuum that begins in pre-K and extends through the twelfth-grade curriculum.

Whole language: A philosophy that proposes that instruction should keep language whole and involve children in using it purposefully and functionally.

Whole learner: A complete picture of a learner; accounts for a learner's attitudes, values, and emotions as well as his or her social, physical, and cognitive development.

Zone of proximal development (ZPD): The area between an individual's actual and potential development; described by Vygotsky.

REFERENCES

Aaronsohn, E. (1996). *Going against the grain*. Thousand Oaks, CA: Corwin Press.

AAUW Educational Foundation. (1992). *The AAUW report: How schools shortchange girls*. Washington, DC: Author.

Abdal-Haqq, I. (1994). Culturally responsive curriculum. *ERIC Digest, EDO-SP 93/5.*

Abdal-Haqq, I. (1995). Professional standards development: Teacher involvement. *ERIC Digest, EDO-SP-93-8*, 3–4.

Ackland, R. (1991). A review of the peer coaching literature. *Journal of Staff Development, 12*(1), 22–27.

Akin, G., & Hopelain, D. (1986). Finding the culture of productivity. *Organizational Dynamics, 14*(3), 19–32.

Alexander, K. L., Entwisle, D. R., & Dauber, S. L. (1994). *On the success of failure: A reassessment of the effects of retention in the primary grades*. New York: Cambridge University Press.

Allen, S. (1997a). *Improving school climate: Creating a circle of communication between educators and families*. (ERIC Document Reproduction Service No. ED 408 094)

Allen, S. (1997b). *What teachers want from parents and what parents want from teachers: Similarities and differences*. (ERIC Document Reproduction Service No. ED 408 097)

Altwerger, B., Edelsky, C., & Flores, B. (1987). Whole language: What's new? *The Reading Teacher, 41*, 144–155.

Amabile, T. M. (1983). *The social psychology of creativity*. New York: Springer-Verlag.

Amabile, T. M., Burnside, R. M., & Gryskiewicz, S. S. (1995). *KEYS: Assessing the climate for creativity*. Greensboro, NC: Center for Creative Leadership.

Ambert, A. (1986). Being a stepparent: Live-in and visiting stepchildren. *Journal of Marriage and the Family, 48*(4), 795–804.

American Humane Association. (1992a, July). *Fact sheet: Shaken baby syndrome*. Englewood, CO: Author.

American Humane Association. (1992b, October). *Fact sheet: Child abuse and neglect data*. Englewood, CO: Author.

Ames, C. (1993). How school-to-home communications influence parent beliefs and perceptions. *Equity and Choice, 9*, 44–49.

Anderson, B., & Ellis, D. (1992). *Does a national test/examination system support or undermine higher student learning?* (ERIC Reproduction Document Number 346 162)

Anderson, E., Linder, M., & Bennion, L. (1992). The effect of family relationships on adolescent development during family reorganization. In E. M. Hetherington & G. Clingempeel (Eds.), Coping with marital transitions. *Monographs of the Society for Research in Child Development, 57*(2–3), 178–199.

Anderson, E. M., & Shannon, A. L. (1988). Toward a conceptualization of mentoring. *Journal of Teacher Education, 39*(1), 38–42.

Anderson, S., Rolheiser, C., & Gordon, K. (1998). Preparing teachers to be leaders. *Educational Leadership, 55*(5), 59–61.

Anthony, R., Johnson, T., Mickelson, N., & Preece, A. (1988). *Evaluation: A perspective for change*. Brisbane, Australia: International Reading Association.

Arends, R. I. (1997). *Classroom instruction and management*. New York: McGraw-Hill.

Arends, R. I. (1998). *Learning to teach* (4th ed.). New York: McGraw-Hill.

Argys, L. M., Rees, D. I., & Brewer, D. J. (1996). Detracking America's schools: Equity at zero cost? *Journal of Policy Analysis and Management, 15*(4), 623–645.

Asayesh, G. (1993). Ten years after *A Nation at Risk. The School Administrator, 50*(4), 8–14.

Baker, A. (1997). Improving parent involvement programs and practice: A qualitative study of parent perceptions. *The School Community Journal, 7*(1), 9–35.

Baratz-Snowden, J. (1993). Assessment of teachers: A view from the National Board for Professional Teaching Standards. *Theory into Practice, 32*(2), 82–85.

Baratz-Snowden, J., Shapiro, B. C., & Streeter, K. R. (1993). The National Board for Professional Teaching Standards: Making a profession. *Middle School Journal, 25*(2), 68–71.

Barbour, C., & Barbour, N. (1997). *Families, schools, and communities: Building partnerships for educating children*. Upper Saddle River, NJ: Prentice-Hall.

Barclay, K., Benelli, C., Campbell, P., & Kleine, L. (1995). Dream or nightmare? Planning for a year without textbooks. *Journal of the Association for Childhood Education International, 71*(4), 205–211.

Barlow, D. H., Hayes, S. C., & Nelson, R. O. (1984). *The scientist practitioner: Research and accountability in clinical and educational settings*. Elmsford, NY: Pergamon.

Baron, E. B. (1992). *Discipline strategies for teachers: Fastback 344*. Bloomington, IN: Phi Delta Kappa Educational Foundation.

Barrera, R. (1992). The cultural gap in literature-based literacy instruction. *Education and Urban Society, 24*(2), 227–243.

Barringer, M.D. (1993). How the National Board builds professionalism. *Educational Leadership, 50*(6), 18–22.

Bartell, C. A. (1995). Shaping teacher induction policy in California. *Teacher Education Quarterly, 22*(4), 27–43.

Bartlett, C. (1994). *Developing medical and educational partnerships in school settings to meet health-related and educational needs of students who are medically fragile: How can rural schools catch that elusive rainbow?* (ERIC Document Reproduction Service No. 369 613)

Batenburg, M. (1995). *Community agency and school collaboration: Going in with your eyes open*. (ERIC Document Reproduction Service No. 383 901)

Beane, J. (1995). Curriculum integration and the disciplines of knowledge. *Phi Delta Kappan, 76*(8), 616-622.

Behrmann, M. M. (1998). Assistive technology for young children in special education. In C. Dede (Ed.), *ASCD year book 1998: Learning with technology* (pp. 73–93). Alexandria, VA: Association for Supervision and Curriculum Development.

Bell, T. H. (1993). Reflections one decade after *A Nation at Risk*. *Phi Delta Kappan, 74*(8), 592–597.

Bennett, C. (1995). *Teacher perspectives as a tool for reflection, partnerships, and professional growth*. (ERIC Document Reproduction Service No. 390 833)

Bergen, D. (1992). Teaching strategies: Using humor to facilitate learning. *Childhood Education, 69*(2), 105.

Berger, E. H. (1995). *Parents as partners in education: Schools and families working together* (4th ed.). Englewood Cliffs, NJ: Prentice-Hall.

Bergin, D. A., Osburn, V. L., & Cryan, J. R. (1996). Influence of child independence, gender, and birthdate on kindergarten teachers' recommendations for retention. *Journal of Research in Childhood Education, 10*(2), 152–159.

Berliner, D. (1983). The executive functions of teaching. *Instructor, 43*(2), 28–40.

Berliner, D. (1985). Effective classroom teaching: The necessary but not sufficient condition for developing exemplary schools. In *Research on exemplary schools*. Orlando, FL: Academic Press, 127–154.

Berliner, D. (1986). In pursuit of the expert pedagogue. *Educational Researcher, 15*(3), 5–15.

Berliner, D. C., & Biddle, B. J. (1995). *The manufactured crisis: Myths, fraud, and the attack on America's public schools*. Reading, MA: Addison-Wesley.

Berman, D. M. (1994). Becoming a teacher: The teacher internship as a rite of passage. *Teaching Education, 6*(1), 41–56.

Berreth, D., & Berman, S. (1997). The moral dimensions of schools. *Educational Leadership, 54*(8), 24–27.

Besharov, D. J. (1990). *Recognizing child abuse*. New York: Free Press.

Bey, T. M. (1990). A new knowledge base for an old practice. In T. M. Bey & C. T. Holmes (Eds.), *Mentoring: Developing successful new teachers* (pp. 51–73). Reston, VA: Association of Teacher Educators.

Bey, T. M. , & Holmes, T. C. (Eds.). (1990). *Mentoring: Developing successful new teachers*. Reston, VA: Association of Teacher Educators.

Beyer, B. K. (1985). Teaching critical thinking: A direct approach. *Social Education, 49*, 297–303.

Beyer, B. K., & Backes, J. D. (1990). Integrating thinking skills into the curriculum. *PRINCIPAL, 69*(3), 18–21.

Bigenho, F. W. (1992). *Conceptual developments in schema theory*. (ERIC Document Reproduction Service No. ED 351 392)

Bisson, C., & Luckner, J. (1996). Fun in learning: The pedagogical role of fun in adventure education. *The Journal of Experiential Education, 19*(2), 108–113.

Bloom, B. S. (1956). *Taxonomy of educational objectives: The classification of educational goals. Handbook 1: Cognitive domain*. New York: McKay.

Bloom, B. S. (Ed.). (1984). *Taxonomy of educational objectives, Book I: Cognitive domain*. White Plains, NY: Longman.

Bolman, L., & Deal, T. (1993). *The path to school leadership: A portable mentor*. Thousand Oaks, CA: Corwin Press.

Bondy, E. (1985). *Classroom influences on children's conceptions of reading*. Paper presented at the National Association for the Education of Young Children Conference, New Orleans, LA.

Borgia, E. (1996). Learning through projects. *Scholastic Early Childhood Today, 10*(6), 22–29.

Borich, G. (1996). *Effective teaching methods* (3rd ed.). Englewood Cliffs, NJ: Prentice-Hall.

Borko, H., & Livingston, C. (1989). Cognition and improvisation: Differences in mathematics instruction by expert and novice teachers. *American Educational Research Journal, 26*(4), 473–498.

Bova, B. M., & Phillips, R. R . (1984). Mentoring as a learning experience for adults. *Journal of Teacher Education, 35*(3), 16–20.

Bowman, B. (1992). Reaching potentials of minority children through developmentally and culturally appropriate programs. In S. Bredekamp & T. Rosegrant (Eds.), *Reaching potentials: Appropriate curriculum and assessment of young children* (pp. 128–138). Washington, DC: National Association for the Education of Young Children.

Boyer, E. L. (1991). *Ready to learn: A mandate for the nation*. Princeton, NJ: Carnegie Foundation for the Advancement of Teaching.

Bracey, G. W. (1994). *Transforming America's schools: An Rx for getting past blame*. Arlington, VA: American Association of School Administrators.

Brazelton, T. (1992). *Heart start: The emotional foundations of school readiness*. Arlington, VA: National Center for Clinical Infant Programs.

Bredekamp, S. (1987). *Developmentally appropriate practice in early childhood programs serving children from birth through age 8*. Washington, DC: National Association for the Education of Young Children.

Bredekamp, S., & Copple, C. (Eds.). (1997). *Developmentally appropriate practice in early childhood program*. (Rev. ed.). Washington, DC: National Association for the Education of Young Children.

Brodzinsky, D. (1993). Long-term outcomes in adoption. *The Future of Children: Adoption, 3*(1), 153–166.

Brooks, J. G., & Brooks, M. G. (1993). *In search of understanding: The case for constructivist classrooms*. Alexandria, VA: Association for Supervision and Curriculum Development.

Brooks, M. G. (1984). A constructivist approach to staff development. *Educational Leadership, 42*(3), 23–27.

Brooks, M. G., & Brooks, J. G. (1987). Becoming a teacher for thinking: Constructivism, change, and consequence. *The Journal of Staff Development, 8*(3), 16–20.

Brown, P., & Goren, P. (1993). *Ability grouping and tracking*. Washington, DC: National Governors' Association.

Brown, R. S. (1993). *School acceleration: What does the research say?* (ERIC Document Reproduction Service No. ED 367 120)

Brubacher, J. W., Case, C. W., & Reagan, T. G. (1994). *Becoming a reflective educator: How to build a culture of inquiry in the schools*. Newbury Park, CA: Corwin.

Bruner, J. (1960). *The process of education*. Cambridge, MA: Harvard University Press.

Bruner, J. (1986). *Actual minds, possible worlds*. Cambridge, England: Cambridge University Press.

Bruner, J. (1990). *Acts of meaning*. Cambridge, MA: Harvard University Press.

Buday, M. C., & Kelly, J. A. (1996). National Board Certification and the teaching profession's commitment to quality assurance. *Phi Delta Kappan, 78*(3), 215–219.

Buehler, C. (1988). The social and emotional well-being of divorced residential parents. *Sex Roles, 18*(5–6), 247–257.

Bull, B. (1994). *Professional development and teacher time: Principles, guidelines, and policy options for Indiana*. (ERIC Document Reproduction Service No. ED 408 094)

Bullough, R., Jr. (1990). Supervision, mentoring, and self-discovery: A case study of a first-year teacher. *Journal of Curriculum and Supervision, 5*(4), 338–360.

Burnette, J. (1996). Including students with disabilities in general education classrooms: From policy to practice. *ERIC Review, 4*(3), 2–11.

Burns, J. M. (1995). Transactional and transforming leadership. In J. T. Wren (Ed.), *Leader's companion: Insights on leadership through the ages* (pp. 100–107). New York: Free Press.

Caccia, P. F. (1996). Linguistic coaching: Helping beginning teachers defeat discouragement. *Educational Leadership, 53*(6), 17–20.

Cairney, T. (1988). The purpose of basals: What children think. *The Reading Teacher, 41*, 420–428.

Caldwell, B. M. (1990). Educare: A new professional identity. *Dimensions of Early Childhood, 18*(4), 3–6.

Calhoun, E. F. (1993). Action research: Three approaches. *Educational Leadership, 51*(2), 62–65.

Callahan, C. (1986). The special needs of gifted girls. *Journal of Children in Contemporary Society, 18*(3, 4), 105–117.

Cambourne, B. (1988). *The whole story: Natural learning and the acquisition of literacy in the classroom*. Richmond Hill, Ontario: Scholastic-TAB.

Campbell, D. M. (1974). *If you don't know where you're going, you'll probably end up somewhere else*. Allen, TX: Argus Communications.

Campbell, D. M. (1980). *If I'm in charge here why is everybody laughing?* Allen, TX: Argus Communications.

Campbell, D. M., Cignetti, P. B., Melenyzer, B. J., Nettles, D. H., & Wyman, R. M., Jr. (1997). *How to develop a professional portfolio: A manual for teachers*. Boston: Allyn & Bacon.

Campbell, P. B., & Storo, J. N. (1996). *Teacher strategies that work for girls and boys: Math and science for the coed classroom*. (ERIC Document Reproduction Service No. ED 409 248)

Cangelosi, J. S. (1990). *Cooperation in the classroom: Students and teachers together*. (2nd ed.). Washington, DC: National Education Association of the United States.

Canter, L., & Canter, M. (1976). *Assertive discipline: A take charge approach for today's educator*. Santa Monica, CA: Canter and Associates.

Canter, L., & Canter, M. (1985). *Assertive discipline*. Santa Monica, CA: Canter and Associates.

Canter, L., & Canter, M. (1993). *Succeeding with difficult students*. Santa Monica, CA: Canter and Associates.

Carlson, P. M., & Peterson, R. L. (1995). What is humor and why is it important? *Reclaiming Children and Youth: Journal of Emotional and Behavioral Problems, 4*(3), 6–12.

Carlson, R. V. (1996.). *Reframing & reform*. White Plains, NY: Longman.

Carnegie Corporation of New York. (1986). *A nation prepared: Teachers for the 21st century*. New York: Author.

Carter, K., Sabers, D., Cushing, K., Pinnegar, S., & Berliner, D. (1988). Expert-novice differences in perceiving and processing visual classroom stimuli. *Journal of Teacher Education, 39*(3), 25–31.

Cascio, C. (1995). National Board for Professional Teaching Standards: Changing teaching through teachers. *The Clearing House, 68*(4), 211–214.

Casey, M. B., & Tucker, E. C. (1994). Problem-centered classrooms: Creating lifelong learners. *Phi Delta Kappan, 76*(2), 139–143.

Castle, K. (1997). Constructing knowledge of constructivism. *Journal of Early Childhood Teacher Education, 18*(1), 55–67.

Cavaliere, F. (1995, July). Society appears more open to gay parenting. *APA Monitor*, p. 51.

Cavanaugh, R., & Dellar, G. B. (1997, March). *School culture: A quantitative perspective on a subjective phenomenon*. Paper presented at the annual meeting of the American Educational Research Association, Chicago.

Chapman, C. (1993). *If the shoe fits . . . : How to develop multiple intelligences in the classroom*. Arlington Heights, IL: IRI/Skylight Training and Publishing.

Charbonneau, M., & Reider, B. (1995). *The integrated elementary classroom: A developmental model for the 21st century*. Needham Heights, MA: Allyn & Bacon.

Chard, S. (1992). *The project approach: A practical guide for teachers*. Edmonton: University of Alberta Printing Services.

Charters, W., Jr. (1970). Some factors affecting teacher survival in school districts. *American Educational Research Journal, 7*, 1–27.

Checkley, K. (1997). The first seven . . . and the eighth: A conversation with Howard Gardner. *Educational Leadership, 55*(1), 8–13.

Chester, M. D., & Beaudin, B. Q. (1996). Efficacy beliefs of newly hired teachers in urban schools. *American Educational Research Journal, 33*(1), 233–257.

Children's Defense Fund. (1992). *The state of America's children yearbook*. Washington, DC: Author.

Children's Defense Fund. (1994). *Wasting America's Future: The Children's Defense Fund report on the costs of child poverty*. Washington, DC: Author.

Children's Defense Fund. (1995). *The state of America's children yearbook*. Washington, DC: Author.

Children's Defense Fund. (1998). *The state of America's children yearbook*. Washington, DC: Author.

Chrispeels, J. H. (1996). Evaluating teachers' relationships with families: A case study of one district. *The Elementary School Journal, 97*, 179–200.

Chuska, K. R. (1995). *Improving classroom questions*. Bloomington, IN: Phi Delta Kappa Educational Foundation.

Clark, F. L. (1993). Preparing teachers to implement strategy instruction. *Preventing School Failure, 38*(1), 50–51.

Clinchy, E. (1995). Why are we restructuring? *New Schools, New Communities, 11*(3), 7–12.

Cochren, J. R. (1996). Tracking: An affront to American idealism. *International Journal of Educational Reform, 5*(2), 179–185.

Cody, W. S. (1998). The value of NCATE. *NCATE Quality Teaching, 7*(2), 4–5.

Coleman, J., Campbell, E., Hobson, C., McPartland, J., Mood, A., Weinfield, F., & York, R. (1966). *Equality of educational opportunity.* Washington, DC: U.S. Government Printing Office.

Coleman, M. (1997). Families and schools: In search of common ground. *Young Children, 52*(5), 14–21.

Coleman, M., & Ganong, L. (1991). Remarriage and stepfamily research in the 1980s: Increased interest in an old family form. In A. Booth (Ed.), *Contemporary families: Looking forward, looking back* (pp. 192–206). Minneapolis: National Council on Family Relations.

Collins, C. (1991). Don your critical thinking caps: Ways to help students think better. *The School Administrator, 48*(1), 8–13.

Comer, J. P., & Haynes, N. M. (1991). Parent involvement in schools: An ecological approach. *The Elementary School Journal, 91,* 271–278.

Cooper, J. M. (1994). Teacher as a decision maker. In J. M. Cooper (Ed.), *Classroom teaching skills* (5th ed., p. 9). Lexington, MA: Heath.

Costa, A. (1985). Teacher behaviors that enable student thinking. In A. Costa (Ed.), *Developing minds: A resource book for teaching thinking.* Alexandria, VA: Association for Supervision and Curriculum Development, pp. 125–137.

Coutinho, M., & Malouf, D. (1993). Performance assessment and children with disabilities: Issues and possibilities. *Teaching Exceptional Children, 25*(4), 62–67.

Covert, J. R. (1986). *A study of the quality of teaching of beginning teachers.* (ERIC Document Reproduction Service No. 273 604)

Covey, S. R. (1989). *The seven habits of highly effective people.* New York: Simon & Schuster.

Coyle, M. (1997). Teacher leadership vs. school management: Flatten the hierarchies. *Clearing House, 70*(5), 236–239.

Crosbie-Burnett, M., & Helmbrecht, L. (1993). A descriptive empirical study of gay male stepfamilies. *Family Relations, 42,* 256–262.

Crosby, A. (1968). *Creativity and performance in industrial organizations.* London: Tavistock Publications.

Crosby, E. A. (1993). The "at-risk" decade. *Phi Delta Kappan, 74*(8), 598–604.

Cummings, C., & Hagerty, K. (1997). Raising healthy children. *Educational Leadership, 54*(8), 28–30.

Curwin, R. L., & Mendler, A. N. (1988). *Discipline with dignity.* Alexandria, VA: Association for Supervision and Curriculum Development.

Daniel, L. G., & Ferrell, C. M. (1991). *Clarifying reasons why people aspire to teach: An application of Q-Methodology.* (ERIC Document Reproduction Service No. 341 671)

Daniels, E., & Gatto, M. (1996). *The cooperative companion digest (No. 1-4), Thinking about the nature and power of cooperative learning.* (ERIC Document Reproduction Service No. 402 038)

Daniels, H. (1996). The best practice project: Building. *Educational Leadership, 53*(7), 38–43.

Daniels, H., & Bizar, M. (1998). *Methods that matter: Six structures for best practice classrooms.* York, ME: Stenhouse Publishers.

Dardick, G. (1990). Learning to laugh on the job. *Principal, 69*(5), 32–34.

Darling, E. (1994). A tale of two schools. Ohlone: An open door. *Palo Alto Weekly, 15*(5), 20–24.

Darling-Hammond, L. (1988). The futures of teaching. *Educational Leadership, 46*(3), 4–10.

Darling-Hammond, L. (1990). Teachers and teaching: Signs of a changing profession. In W. R. Houston (Ed.), *Handbook of research on teacher education* (pp. 267–290). New York: MacMillan.

Darling-Hammond, L. (Ed.), (1994). *Professional development schools: Schools for developing a profession.* New York: Teachers College Press.

Darling-Hammond, L. (1993a). Reframing the school reform agenda. *Phi Delta Kappan, 74,* 752–762.

Darling-Hammond, L. (1993b). Teachers and teaching: Signs of a changing profession. In W. R. Houston (Ed.), *The handbook of research on teacher education* (pp. 267–290). New York: Macmillan.

Darling-Hammond, L. (1995). Changing conceptions of teaching and teacher development. *Teacher Education Quarterly, 22*(4), 9–26.

Davis, C., & Shade, D. (1994). *Integrate, don't isolate!—Computers in the early childhood curriculum. ERIC Digest,* EDO-PS-94-17.

Deal, T. E., & Kennedy, A. A. (1982). *Corporate cultures.* Reading, MA: Addison-Wesley.

Dearden, R. (1984). *Theory and practice in education.* London: Routledge & Kegan Paul.

Dede, C. (Ed.). (1998). *ASCD year book 1998: Learning with technology.* Alexandria, VA: Association for Supervision and Curriculum Development.

DeFelice, L. (1989). The bibbidibobbidiboo factor in teaching. *Phi Delta Kappan, 70*(8), 639–641.

Delgado-Gaitin, C. (1991). Involving parents in the schools: A process of empowerment. *American Journal of Education, 100*(1), 20–46.

Delpit, L. D. (1988). The silenced dialogue: Power and pedagogy in educating other people's children. *Harvard Educational Review, 58*(3), 280–287.

DeVries, R., & Kohlberg, L. (1987). *Programs of early education: The constructivist view.* New York: Longman.

DeVries, R., & Zan, B. (1994). *Moral classroom, moral children.* New York: Teachers College Press.

Dickmeyer, S. G. (1993). *Humor as an instructional practice: A longitudinal content analysis of humor use in the classroom.* (ERIC Document Reproduction Service No. ED 359 587)

Dodd, A. W. (1997). Creating a climate for learning: Making the classroom more like an ideal home. *The National Association of Secondary School Principals Bulletin, 81*(589), 10–16.

Doll, R. C. (1996). *Curriculum improvement* (9th ed.). Needham Heights, MA: Allyn & Bacon.

Dollard, N., Christensen, L., Colucci, K., & Epanchin, B. (1996). Constructive classroom management. *Focus on Exceptional Children, 29*(2), 1–12.

Donaldson, G. A., Jr., & Marnik, G. F. (1995). *Becoming better leaders: The challenge of improving student learning.* Thousand Oaks, CA: Corwin Press.

Donaldson, G. A., & Sanderson, D. (1996). *Working together in schools: A guide for educators.* (ERIC Document Reproduction Service No. 399 679)

Downing, J. E., & Gifford, V. (1996). An investigation of preservice teachers' science process skills and questioning strategies used during a demonstration science discovery lesson. *Journal of Elementary Science Education, 8*(1), 64–75.

Doyle, D. P., & Hartle, T. W. (1985). Leadership in education. Governors, legislators, and teachers. *Phi Delta Kappan, 67*(1), 21–27.

Dreikurs, R., Grunwald, B. B., & Pepper, F. C. (1982). *Maintaining sanity in the classroom* (2nd ed.). New York: Harper & Row.

Dryfoos, J. (1994). *Full-service schools: A revolution in health and social services for children, youth and families.* San Francisco: Jossey-Bass.

Dryfoos, J. (1996). Full-service schools. *Educational Leadership, 53*(7), 18–23.

DuFour, R., & Berkey, T. (1995). The principal as staff developer. *Journal of Staff Development, 16*(4), 2–6.

Duis, M. (1995). Making time for authentic teaching and learning. *Kappa Delta Pi Record, 30*(3), 136–138.

Duis, M. (1996). Using schema theory to teach American history. *Social Education, 60*(3), 144–146.

Dukewits, P., & Gowan, L. (1996). Creating successful collaborative teams. *Journal of Staff Development, 17*(4), 12–16.

Dunifon, W. S. (1985). *Excellence in secondary education: The induction of teachers.* Paper presented at Secondary Education Conference Excellence Week, Normal, IL.

Dunn, L., & Kontos, S. (1997). What have we learned about developmentally appropriate practice? *Young Children, 52*(5), 4–13.

Dunn, R. (1996). 19 easy-to-try ways to turn on students. *Teaching K-8, 27*(3), 50, 51.

Dunn, R., & Dunn, K. (1978). *Teaching students through their individual learning styles: A practical approach.* Reston, VA: Reston Publishing.

Durkin, D. (1961). Children who read before grade one. *The Reading Teacher, 14*, 163–166.

Durkin, D. (1989). *Teaching them to read* (5th ed.). Needham Heights, MA: Allyn & Bacon.

Dyson, A. (1990). Research currents: Diversity, social responsibility and the story of literacy development. *Language Arts, 67*, 192–205.

Eaton, M. (1997). Positive discipline: Fostering the self-esteem of young children. *Young Children, 52*(6), 43–46.

Eberle, R. E. (1971). *Scamper: Games for imagination development.* Buffalo, NY: D.O.K. Publishers.

Eby, J. W., & Kujawa, E. (1994). *Reflective planning, teaching, and evaluation: K–12.* New York: Merrill.

Edwards, C. H. (1997). *Classroom discipline & management* (2nd ed.). Upper Saddle River, NJ: Prentice-Hall.

Edwards, C. H., & Allred, W. E. (1993). More on *A Nation at Risk*: Have the recommendations been implemented? *The Clearing House, 67*(2), 85–87.

Eggen, P., & Kauchak, D. (1992). *Educational psychology: Classroom connections.* New York: Merrill.

Eisner, E. W. (1994). *The educational imagination: On the design and evaluation of school programs* (3rd ed.). New York: Macmillan.

Elias, M., Bruene-Butler, L., Blum. L, & Schuyler, T. (1997). How to launch a social and emotional learning program. *Educational Leadership, 54*(8), 15–19.

Elias, M., Gara, M., Schuyler, T. Brandon-Muller, L., & Sayette, M. (1991). The promotion of social competence: Longitudinal study of a preventive school-based program. *American Journal of Orthopsychiatry, 61*(3), 409–417.

Elias, M., Zins, J., Weissberg, R., Frey, K., Greenberg, M., Haynes, N., Kessler, R., Schwab-Stone, M., & Shriver, T. (1997). *Promoting social and emotional learning: Guidelines for educators.* Alexandria, VA: Association for Supervision and Curriculum Development.

Elliott, S. (1994). *Creating meaningful performance assessments: Fundamental concepts.* Reston, VA: Council for Exceptional Children.

Ellis, N. (1990). Collaborative interaction for improvement of teaching. *Teaching and Teacher Education, 6*(3), 267–277.

Emmer, E. T., Evertson, C. M., Clements, B. S., & Worsham, M. E. (1994). *Classroom management for secondary teachers* (3rd ed.). Needham Heights, MA: Allyn & Bacon.

Epstein, A. S. (1993). *Training for quality: Improving early childhood programs through systematic inservice training.* Monographs of the High/Scope Educational Research Foundation, Number Nine. Ypsilanti, MI: High/Scope Educational Research Foundation.

Epstein, J. L. (1987). Parent involvement. *Education and Urban Society, 19*(2), 119–136.

Epstein, J. L. (1991). Paths to partnership: What we can learn from federal, state, district, and school initiatives. *Phi Delta Kappan, 72*, 344–349.

Epstein, J. L. (1995). School/family/community partnerships: Caring for the children we share. *Phi Delta Kappan, 76*, 701–712.

Epstein, J. L., & Dauber, S. L. (1991). School programs and teacher practices of parent involvement in inner-city elementary and middle schools. *The Elementary School Journal, 91*, 289–306.

Estrada, L. F. (1993). The dynamic demographic mosaic called America: Implications for education. *Education and Urban Society, 25*(3), 231–245.

Estrin, E. (1993). *Alternative assessment: Issues in language, culture, and equity.* (ERIC Document Reproduction Service No. ED 373 082)

Evans, S. (1996). Heterogeneous grouping: Is it an effective instructional arrangement for all students? *Southern Social Studies Journal, 22*(1), 3–16.

Faber, A., Maxlish, E., Nyberg, L., & Templeton, R. A. (1995). *How to talk so kids can learn at home and in school.* New York: Simon & Schuster.

Fairbanks, C. (1995). Teaching reflection: A conceptual model. *Teacher Education and Practice, 1*(2), 28–40.

Farwest Laboratory for Educational Research and Development. (1995). *Draft framework of knowledge, skills and abilities for beginning teachers.* San Francisco: Author.

Feiman-Nemser, S. F. (1983). Learning to teach. In L. S. Shulman & G. Sykes (Eds.), *Handbook of teaching and policy.* New York: Longman.

Feiman-Nemser, S. F., & Parker, M. B. (1992, Spring). *Mentoring in context: A comparison of two U.S. programs for beginning teachers* (NCTRL special report). East Lansing, MI: National Center for Research on Teacher Learning, Michigan State University.

Feldhusen, J. (1994). Developing units of instruction, in J. Van Tassel-Baska (Ed.). *Comprehensive curriculum for gifted learners* (2nd ed.). Needham Heights, MA: Allyn & Bacon.

Feuer, M., & Fulton, K. (1993). The many faces of performance assessment. *Phi Delta Kappan, 74*(6), 478–479.

Field, M., & Spangler, K. (1995). *Let's begin reading right: Developmentally appropriate beginning literacy* (3rd ed.). Englewood Cliffs, NJ: Merrill.

Fine, M., & Fine, D. (1992). Recent changes in laws affecting stepfamilies: Suggestions for legal reform. *Family Relations, 41*(3), 334–340.

Firestone, W. A., & Pennell, J. R. (1993). Changing the cosmology of the school schedule. In L. W. Anderson & H. J. Walberg (Eds.), *Time piece: Extending and enhancing learning time* (pp. 23–29). Reston, VA: National Association of Secondary School Principals.

Fisher, B. (1991). *Joyful learning: A whole language kindergarten.* Portsmouth, NH: Heinemann.

Fisher, D. L., Fraser, B. J., & Bassett, J. (1995). Using a classroom environment instrument in an early childhood classroom. *Australian Journal of Early Childhood, 20*(3), 10–15.

Fisher, D. L., & Waldrip, B. G. (1997). Assessing culturally sensitive factors in the learning environment of science classrooms. *Research in Science Education, 27*(1), 41–49.

Floden, R., & Buchmann, M. (1992). *Between routines and anarchy: Preparing teachers for uncertainty.* (ERIC Document Reproduction Service No. 346 065)

Foster, S. M. (1994). Successful parent meetings. *Young Children, 50*(1), 78–80.

Fouse, B., Beidelman, V., & Morrison, J. A. (1994). Conflict resolution for parents and teachers of gifted and talented students. *Gifted Child Today, 17*(6), 39–41.

Fowell, N., & Lawton, J. (1993). Beyond polar descriptions and developmentally appropriate practice: A reply to Bredekamp. *Early Childhood Research Quarterly, 8*(1), 53–73.

Francis, R., & Hord, S. (1995). *Designing scoring tools for authentic & alternative assessments: A common sense method.* (ERIC Document Reproduction Service No. ED 392 804)

Fraser, B. J., & Fisher, D. L. (1983). Student achievement as a function of person-environment fit: A regression surface analysis. *British Journal of Educational Psychology, 53*(1), 89–99.

Fraser, B. J., & Tobin, K. (1992). Combining qualitative and quantitative methods in the study of learning environments. In H. C. Waxman and C. D. Ellet (Eds.), *The Study of Learning Environments* (Vol. 5). Houston, TX: University of Houston.

Fredericks, A. D., & Rasinski, T. V. (1990). Conferencing with parents: Successful approaches. *The Reading Teacher, 44*(2), 174–176.

French, V. W. (1997). Teachers must be learners, too: Professional development and national teaching standards. *The National Association of Secondary School Principals Bulletin, 81*(585), 38–44.

Friend, M., & Cook, L. (1996). *Interactions: Collaboration skills for school professionals* (2nd ed.). White Plains, NY: Longman.

Fullan, M. G. (1991). *The new meaning of educational change* (2nd ed.). New York: Teachers College Press.

Fullan, M. G. (1993). *Change forces.* New York: Falmer.

Gable, R. A., & Manning, M. L. (1997). The role of teacher collaboration in school reform. *Childhood Education: Infancy Through Early Adolescence, 73*(4), 219–223.

Gage, J., & Workman, S. (1994). Creating family support systems: In Head Start and beyond. *Young Children, 50*(1), 74–77.

Galda, L., Cullinan, B., & Strickland, D. S. (1993). *Language, literacy and the child.* Fort Worth, TX: Harcourt Brace Jovanovich.

Gallup, G., Jr., & Gallup, A.M. (1986). *The great American success story.* Homewood, IL: Dow Jones-Irwin.

Ganong, L., & Coleman, M. (1989). Preparing for remarriage: Anticipating the issues, seeking solutions. *Family Relations 38*(1), 28–33.

Ganser, T. (1996). *Teacher effectiveness: Views of preservice and inservice teachers.* (ERIC Document Reproduction Service No. 401 265)

Gardner, H. (1983). *Frames of mind: The theory of multiple intelligences.* New York: Basic Books.

Gardner, H. (1996). *Leading minds: An anatomy of leadership.* New York: Harper-Collins.

Gardner, J. (1989). *On leadership.* New York: Free Press.

Garfield, C. (1986). *Peak performers.* New York: Avon Books.

Gartrell, D. (1997). Beyond discipline to guidance. *Young Children, 52*(6), 34–42.

Geertz, C. (1973). *The interpretation of cultures.* New York: Basic Books.

Gehrenbeck, H. (1994). *First-grade language report.* Normal, IL: Metcalf School.

Ghaye, T., Cuthbert, S., Danai, K., & Dennis, D. (1996). *Learning through critical reflective practice: Self-supported learning experiences for health care professionals.* Newcastle upon Tyne, England: Pentaxion, Ltd.

Giddings, L. (1991). Literature-based reading instruction: Understanding the holistic perspective. *Contemporary Issues in Reading, 6*(2), 69–74.

Gilbert, L. C. (1940). Effect on silent reading of attempting to follow oral reading. *Elementary School Journal, 40*, 614–621.

Giles-Sims, J., & Crosbie-Burnett, M. (1989). Stepfamily research: Implications for policy, clinical interventions, and further research. *Family Relations, 38*(1), 19–23.

Giroux, H. A., & McLaren, P. (1986). Teacher education and

the politics of engagement: The case of democratic schooling. *Harvard Educational Review, 56,* 213–238.

Giroux, H. A., & Simon, R. (1989). Schooling, popular culture, and a pedagogy of possibility. *Journal of Education, 170*(1), 9–26.

Glasser, W. G. (1969). *Schools without failure.* New York: Harper & Row.

Glasser, W. G. (1986). *Control theory in the classroom.* New York: Harper & Row.

Glasser, W. G. (1992). *The quality school: Managing students without coercion* (2nd ed.). New York: Harper & Row.

Glatthorn, A. A. (1993). Teacher planning: A foundation for effective instruction. *NASSP Bulletin, 77*(551), 1–7.

Glatthorn, A. A. (1994). *Developing a quality curriculum.* Alexandria, VA. Association for Supervision and Curriculum Development.

Glazer, S. (1995). Are those alternatives to grades honest alternatives? *Teaching K–8, 25*(8), 98–101.

Glover, D. C. (1992). An investigation of criteria used by parents and community in judgment of school quality. *Educational Research, 34,* 35–44.

Goetz, E. (1985). In defense of curriculum themes. *Day Care and Early Education, 13*(1), 12–13.

Goh, S. C., & Fraser, B. J. (1995, April). *Learning environment and student outcomes in primary mathematics classrooms in Singapore.* Paper presented at the annual meeting of the American Educational Research Association, San Francisco.

Goldberg, M., & Renton, A. M. (1993). Heeding the call to arms in a "Nation at Risk." *The School Administrator, 50*(4), 16–18, 20–23.

Goleman, D. (1995). *Emotional intelligence.* New York: Bantam Books.

Golombok, S., & Tasker, F. (1996). Do parents influence the sexual orientation of their children? Findings from a longitudinal study of lesbian families. *Developmental Psychology, 32*(1), 3–11.

Good, T. L., & Brophy, J. E. (1994). *Looking in classrooms* (6th ed.). New York: HarperCollins.

Goodman, K. (1986). *What's whole in whole language?* Portsmouth, NH: Heinemann.

Goodman, K. (1994). Standards not! *Education Week, 7,* 39.

Gordon, E. (1993). *Human diversity, equity, and educational assessment.* Paper presented at 1993 CRESST Assessment Conference.

Gordon, H., & Gordon, R. (Trans.) (1951). *The education of man.* New York: Philosophical Library.

Gordon, J. (1993). *Why did you select teaching as a career? Teachers of color tell their stories.* (ERIC Document Reproduction Service No. 383 653)

Gordon, J. (1994). Why students of color are not entering teaching: Reflections from minority teachers. *Journal of Teacher Education, 45*(5), 346–353.

Gordon, S. P. (1991). *How to help beginning teachers succeed.* Alexandria, VA: Association for Supervision and Curriculum Development.

Gordon, T. (1974). *T.E.T. Teacher effectiveness training.* New York: Peter H. Wyden.

Graves, D. (1983). *Writing: Teachers and children at work.* Portsmouth, NH: Heinemann.

Graves, D. (1994). *A fresh look at writing.* Portsmouth, NH: Heinemann.

Green, J. E., & Weaver, R. A. (1992). Who aspires to teach? A descriptive study of preservice teachers. *Contemporary Education, 63*(3), 234–238.

Gregorc, A. (1984). Style as symptom. *Theory into Practice, 23*(1), 51–55.

Grene, M., & Campbell, C. (1993). *Becoming a teacher: The contribution of teacher education.* (ERIC Document Reproduction Service No. 369 769)

Griffith, J. (1996). Relation of parental involvement, empowerment, and school traits to student academic performance. *The Journal of Educational Research, 90,* 33–41.

Grissmer, D., & Kirby, S. (1987). *Teacher attrition: The uphill climb to staff the nation's schools.* Santa Monica, CA: Rand.

Griswold, P. A. (1993). *Total Quality Schools implementation evaluation: A concerns-based approach.* (ERIC Document Reproduction Service No. ED 385 007)

Gronlund, N. E. (1995). *How to write and use instructional objectives* (5th ed.). Englewood Cliffs, NJ: Merrill.

Gross, M. U. M. (1994). Radical acceleration. *The Journal of Secondary Gifted Education, 5*(4), 27–34.

Gullat, D. E. (1997). Taking the lead. *Schools in the Middle, 6*(5), 12–14.

Gunter, M. A., Estes, T. H., & Schwab, J. (1995). *Instruction: A models approach* (2nd ed.). Needham Heights, MA: Allyn & Bacon.

Habgood, M. (1993). Alternative assessment practices as new rules in the whole-language game. *The International Journal of Social Education, 8*(2), 81–87.

Hagans, , K. B., & Case, J. (1988). *When your child has been molested: A parent's guide to healing and recovery.* Lexington, MA: Lexington Books.

Hall, G. E. (1974). *The Concerns-Based Adoption Model: A developmental conceptualization of the adoption process within educational institutions.* Austin, TX: Research and Development Center for Teacher Education, University of Texas.

Hammer, T. J., & Turner, P. H. (1996). *Parenting in contemporary society* (3rd ed.). Needham Heights, MA: Allyn & Bacon.

Hancock, J., & Hill, S. (Eds.). (1987). *Literature-based reading programs at work.* Portsmouth, NH: Heinemann.

Hange, J., & Rolfe, H. (1994). *Creating and implementing alternative assessments: Moving toward a moving target.* (ERIC Document Reproduction Service No. ED 375 171)

Hanson, M. J., & Lynch, E. W. (1995). *Early intervention: Implementing child and family services for infants and toddlers who are at risk or disabled* (2nd ed.). Austin, TX: PRO-ED.

Hanson, S., & Sporakowski, M. (1986). Single parent families. *Family Relations, 35*(1), 3–8.

Hargreaves, A., & Dawe, R. (1990). Paths of professional development: Contrived collegiality, collaborative culture, and the case of peer coaching. *Teaching & Teacher Education, 6*(3), 227–241.

Harmin, M. (1994). *Inspiring active learning: A handbook for teachers.* Alexandria, VA: Association for Supervision and Curriculum Development.

Harris and Associates, Inc. (1991). *The Metropolitan Life survey of the American teacher, 1991. The first year: New teachers' expectations and ideals.* New York: Author.

Harris, J. J. (1997). From minority to majority: The students and faculty of tomorrow. *School Business Affairs, 63*(4), 13–18.

Harrow, A. (1977). *Taxonomy of the psychomotor domain.* New York: Longman.

Haseloff, W. (1990). The efficacy of the parent-teacher partnership of the 1990s. *Early Child Development and Care, 58,* 51–55.

Hatton, N., & Smith, D. (1994). *Facilitating reflection: Issues and research.* (ERIC Document Reproduction Service No. 375 110)

Henderson, J. G. (1996). *Reflective teaching: The study of your constructivist practices* (2nd ed.). Englewood Cliffs, NJ: Merrill.

Hendrick, J. (1992). *The whole child* (5th ed.) New York: Merrill.

Hersey, P., Blanchard, K., & Johnson, D. E. (1996). *Management of organizational behavior: Utilizing human resources* (7th ed.). Englewood Cliffs, NJ: Prentice-Hall.

Hetherington, E. M. (1992). Coping with marital transitions: A family systems perspective. In E. M. Hetherington & G. Clingempeel (Eds.), Coping with marital transitions. *Monographs of the Society for Research in Child Development, 57*(2-3), 1–14.

Hewit, J. S., & Whittier, K. S. (1997). *Teaching methods for today's schools: Collaboration and inclusion.* Needham Heights, MA: Allyn & Bacon.

Hickman, J. (1977). What do fluent readers do? *Theory into Practice, 16,* 372–375.

Hiebert, E. (1983). An examination of ability grouping for reading instruction. *Reading Research Quarterly, 18,* 231–255.

Hiebert, E., & Colt, J. (1989). Patterns of literature-based reading instruction. *The Reading Teacher, 43,* 14–20.

Hoberman, M. A. (1978). *A house is a house for me.* New York: Viking.

Hoffman, J., Roser, H., & Farest, C. (1988). Literature sharing strategies in classrooms serving students from economically disadvantaged and language different homes environments. In J. E. Readence & R. S. Baldwin (Eds.), *Dialogues in literacy research.* 37th yearbook of the National Reading Conference (pp. 331–338). Chicago: National Reading Conference.

Holdaway, D. (1979). *The foundations of literacy.* Portsmouth, NH: Heinemann.

Holden, J. (Ed.). (1995). *Mentoring frameworks for Texas Teachers* (Rev. ed.). Austin: Texas Education Agency.

Holmes Group. (1986). *Tomorrow's teachers: A report of the Holmes Group.* East Lansing, MI: Author.

Holmes, S. (1994, July 20). Birthrate for unwed women up 70% since '83, study says. *The New York Times,* pp. A1, A7.

Holt-Reynold, D. (1991). *Practicing what we teach.* (ERIC Document Reproduction Service No. 337 460)

Hoover, H., & Bray, G. (1995, April). *The research and development phase: Can a performance assessment be cost-effective?* Paper presented at the annual meeting of the American Educational Research Association, San Francisco.

Hoover, R. L., & Kindsvatter, R. (1997). *Democratic discipline: Foundation & practice.* Upper Saddle River, NJ: Prentice-Hall.

Hoover, S. P., & Achilles, C. M. (1996, March). *The problem is only part of the problem.* Paper presented at the annual meeting of the American Association of School Administrators, San Diego, CA.

Hope, W. C. (1995). *Microcomputer technology: Its impact on teachers in an elementary school.* (ERIC Document Reproduction Service No. ED 384 336)

Hornstein, S. (1992). *Whole language goes to college.* (ERIC Document Reproduction Service No. 341 960).

Hoskisson, K. (1979). Learning to read naturally. *Language Arts, 56,* 489–496.

Huang, S. L., & Waxman, H. C. (1996, April). *Learning environment differences between high- and low-achieving minority students in urban middle schools.* Paper presented at the annual meeting of the American Educational Research Association, New York.

Huang, S. L., Waxman, H. C., & Houston, W. R. (1993). Comparing school-level work environment of first-year and experienced-support teachers in inner-city schools. In D. L. Fisher (Ed.), *The study of learning environments* (Vol. 7). Perth, Australia: Curtin University of Technology.

Huffman, L., Benson, M., Gebelt, J., & Phelps, H. (1996). *Family intervention makes a difference: The positive effect of the Trenton Transition Project on parental involvement, attendance, and academic achievement.* Paper presented at the third annual Head Start Research Conference, Washington, DC.

Huling-Austin, L. (1987). Teacher induction. In D. M. Brooks (Ed.), *Teacher induction: A new beginning.* Reston, VA: Association of Teacher Educators.

Huling-Austin, L. (1990a). Squishy business. In T. M. Bey & T. C. Holmes (Ed.), *Mentoring: Developing successful new teachers* (pp. 39–50). Reston, VA: Association of Teacher Educators.

Huling-Austin, L. (1990b). Teacher induction programs and internships. In W. R. Houston (Ed.), *Handbook of research on teacher education* (pp. 535–548). New York: Macmillan.

Huling-Austin, L., Putnam, S., & Glavez-Hjornevik, C. (1986). *Model teacher induction project study findings* (Report No. 7212). Austin: Research & Development Center for Teacher Education, University of Texas.

Hunt, S. L., & Staton, A. Q. (1996). The communication of education reform. *Communication Education, 45*(4), 271–292.

IASCD Early Childhood Committee. (1989). *Early childhood screening.* Normal: Illinois Association for Supervision and Curriculum Development, Illinois State University.

Interstate New Teacher Assessment and Support Consortium. (1992). *Model standards for beginning teacher licensing and development: A resource for state dialogue.* Washington, DC: Council of Chief State School Officers.

Isaaksen, S. G. (1995). *Some recent developments on assessing the climate for creativity and change.* Paper presented at the International Conference on Climate for Creativity and Change, Buffalo, NY.

Isaksen, S. G., Dorval, K. B., & Treffinger, D. J. (1994). *Creative approaches to problem solving.* Dubuque, IA: Kendall/Hunt.

Isbell, R. (1995). *The complete learning center book.* Beltsville, MD: Gryphon House.

Isenberg, J. (1992). Early childhood teachers: A profile. In L. R. Williams & D. P. Fromberg (Eds.), *Encyclopedia of early childhood education* (pp. 426–428). New York: Garland Publishers.

Jacobs, G. M. (1997, March). *Four or more eyes are better than two: Using cooperative learning to maximize the success of group activities in reading.* Paper presented at the Singapore Symposium on Reading for Success, Singapore.

Jacobson, M. G., & Lombard, R. H. (1992). Effective school climate: Roles for peers, practitioners, and principals. *Rural Research Report, 3*(4).

Jaffe, M. (1997). *Understanding parenting* (2nd ed.). Needham Heights, MA: Allyn & Bacon.

James, B. (1995). School violence and the law. *Momentum, 26*(1), 31–34.

Javaid, G. A. (1993). The children of homosexual and heterosexual single mothers. *Child Psychiatry & Human Development, 23*(4), 235–248.

Jencks, C., Smith, M., Acland, H., Bane, M., Cohen, D., Gintis, H., Heyns, B., & Michelson, S. (1972). *Inequality: A reassessment of the effect of family and schooling in America.* New York: Basic Books.

Jensen, E. (1995). *Brain-based teaching and learning.* Del Mar, CA: Turning Point.

Jensen, E. (1998). *Teaching with the brain in mind.* Alexandria, VA: Association for Supervision and Curriculum Development.

Jensen, E. (1999). Teaching with the brain in mind. Retrieved May 1999 from the World Wide Web: http://www.thebrainstore.com

Jensen, R. A. (1988). *Iowa's young leaders: Characteristics, organizational environment, and career orientations.* Ames: Iowa State University.

Jensen, R. A., & Kiley, T. J. (1997a). *Creating collaborative learning environments for preservice and inservice teachers.* (ERIC Document Reproduction Service No. 407 365)

Jensen, R. A., & Kiley, T. J. (1997b). Significant connections: Mentoring relationships and processes. *Eastern Education Journal, 26*(1), 37–44.

Jensen, R. A., & Kiley, T. J. (1998, April). *Teams or torture: Creating a climate for collaboration.* Paper presented at the annual meeting of the American Educational Research Association, San Diego.

Jensen, R. A., Kiley Shepston, T. J., Killmer, N., & Connor, K. (1994). Student teacher and cooperating teachers' assessments of actual and preferred learning environments: A comparative analysis. In D. L. Fisher (Ed.), *The study of learning environments* (Vol. 8). Perth, Australia: Curtin University of Technology.

Jensen, R., Kiley Shepston, T., Connor, K., & Killmer, N. (1994). *Fear of the known: Using audio-visual technology as a tool for reflection in teacher education.* (ERIC Document Reproduction Service No. 387 482)

Jipson, J. (1991). Developmentally appropriate practice: Culture, curriculum, connections. *Early Education and Development, 2*(2), 120–136.

Johns, J., & Ellis, D. (1976). Reading: Children tell it like it is. *Reading World, 16*, 155–158.

Johnson, B. L. Jr., Ellet, C., & Licata, J. (1993). Analyses of school level learning environments: Centralized decision-making, teacher work alienation, and organizational effectiveness. In D. L. Fisher (Ed.), *The study of learning environments* (Vol. 7). Perth, Australia: Curtin University of Technology.

Johnson, D. W., & Johnson, R. T. (1994). *Learning together and alone* (4th ed.). Boston: Allyn & Bacon.

Johnson, R. W. (1993). Where can teacher research lead? One teacher's daydream. *Educational Leadership, 51*(2), 66–68.

Johnston, J. H. (1990). *The new American family and the school.* Columbus, OH: National Middle School Association.

Johnston, M., & Thomas, J. (1997, March). *Reframing our differences.* Paper presented at the annual meeting of the American Educational Research Association, Chicago.

Jones, V. F., & Jones, L. S. (1995). *Comprehensive classroom management* (4th ed.). Needham Heights, MA: Allyn & Bacon.

Joyce, B. R., Weil, M., & Calhoun, E. (2000). *Models of teaching* (6th ed.). Needham Heights, MA: Allyn & Bacon.

Kagan, S. (1989). Early care and education: Reflecting on options and opportunities. *Phi Delta Kappan, 71*(2), 107–112.

Kagan, S. (1990). Readiness 2000: Rethinking rhetoric and responsibility. *Phi Delta Kappan, 72*(4), 272–279.

Kamii, C., Manning, M., & Manning, G. (Eds.). (1991). *Early literacy: A constructivist foundation for whole language.* Washington, DC: National Education Association.

Karmos, J. S., Greathouse, L. R., & Presley, C. A. (1990). Questioning techniques in the classroom. *Illinois Schools Journal, 69*(2), 20–24.

Kass, M. (1993). *Ohlone School: 1993–94 Report to the Community.* Palo Alto, CA: Palo Alto Unified School District.

Kasten, B. J. (1996). *Helping preservice teachers construct their own philosophies of teaching through reflection.* (ERIC Document Reproduction Service No. 402 072)

Kasten, B. J., & Ferraro, J. (1995). *A case study: Helping preservice teachers internalize the interconnectedness of believing, knowing, seeing, and doing.* (ERIC Document Reproduction Service No. 383 676)

Katz, L. G. (1993). *Dispositions: Definitions and implications for early childhood practices.* Urbana, IL: ERIC Clearinghouse on Elementary and Early Childhood Education.

Katz, L. G. (1994). *The Project Approach*. ERIC DIGEST. EDO-PS-94-6.

Katz, L. G., & Chard, S. (1989). *Engaging children's minds: The Project Approach*. Norwood, NJ: Ablex.

Katz, L. G., & Chard, S. (1993). The Project Approach. In J. Roopnarine & J. Johnson (Eds.), *Approaches to early childhood education* (2nd ed., pp. 209–222). Columbus, OH: Merrill.

Katzenmeyer, M., & Moller, G. (1996). *Awakening the sleeping giant: Leadership development for teachers*. Thousand Oaks, CA: Corwin Press.

Kaufman, D., & Brooks, J. G. (1996). Interdisciplinary collaboration in teacher education: A constructivist approach. *TESOL Quarterly, 30*(2), 231–251.

Keefe, J. W., & Jenkins, J. M. (1997). *Instruction and the learning environment*. Larchmont, NY: Eye On Education.

Kellough, R. D., & Roberts, P. L. (1998). *A resource guide for elementary school teaching: Planning for competence* (4th ed.). Upper Saddle River, NJ: Merrill.

Kempe, C. H., & Kempe, R. (1984). *The common secret: Sexual abuse of children and adults*. San Francisco: W. H. Freeman.

Ketner, C. S., Smith, K. E., & Parnell, M. K. (1997). Relationship between teacher theoretical orientation to reading and endorsement of developmentally appropriate practice. *The Journal of Educational Research, 90*(4), 212–220.

Kiley, T. J., & Jensen, R. A. (1998). Cooperating teacher and student teacher assessments of actual and preferred learning environments: A matched pair analysis. *Learning Environments Research: An International Journal, 1*(2), 181–197.

Kiley Shepston, T. J. (1991). *An analysis of the childrearing expectations of parents of at-risk and non-at-risk preschoolers*. Normal: Illinois State University.

Kiley Shepston, T. J., Jensen, R. A., Alm, M., & Beaver, L. (1997). *Dodging bullets and BMWs: Two tales of teacher induction*. (ERIC Document Reproduction Service No. ED 407 364)

Kilgore, K., Ross, D., & Zbikowski, J. (1990). Understanding the teaching perspectives of first year teachers. *Journal of Teacher Education, 41*(1), 28–38.

King, M. B. (1994). Locking ourselves in: National standards for the teaching profession. *Teaching and Teacher Education, 10*(1), 95–108.

King, S. E. (1986). Inquiry into the hidden curriculum. *Journal of Curriculum and Supervision, 2*(1), 82–90.

Kirkpatrick, S. A., & Locke, E. A. (1995). Leadership: Do traits matter? In J. T. Wren (Ed.), *Leader's companion: Insights on leadership through the ages* (pp. 133–143). New York: Free Press.

Klatzky, R. (1980). *Human memory: Structures and processes*. San Francisco: Freeman.

Klug, B. J., & Salzman, S. A. (1991). Formal induction vs. informal mentoring: Comparative effects and outcomes. *Teaching and Teacher Educaiton, 7*(3), 241–251.

Kohn, A. (1987). Art for art's sake. *Psychology Today, 21*(9), 52–57.

Kohn, A. (1991). Caring kids: The role of the schools. *Phi Delta Kappan, 73*, 496–506.

Kohn, A. (1993a). Choices for children: Why and how to let students decide. *Phi Delta Kappan, 75*(1), 8–19.

Kohn, A. (1993b). *Punished by rewards: The trouble with gold stars, incentive plans, "As," praise, and other bribes*. Boston: Houghton Mifflin.

Kohn, A. (1996a). *Beyond discipline: From compliance to community*. Alexandria, VA: Association for Supervision and Curriculum Development.

Kohn, A. (1996b). What to look for in a classroom. *Educational Leadership, 54*(1), 54, 55.

Koprowicz, C. L. (1994). *What state legislators need to know about the National Board for Professional Teaching Standards*. Denver: National Conference of State Legislatures.

Kotter, J. P. (1995). What leaders really do. In J. T. Wren (Ed.), *Leader's companion: Insights on leadership through the ages* (pp. 114–123). New York: Free Press.

Kotulak, R. (1996). *Inside the brain*. Kansas City, MO: Andrews and McMeel.

Kounin, J. (1970). *Discipline and group management in classrooms*. New York: Holt, Rinehart and Winston.

Kozol, J. (1991). *Savage inequalities: Children in America's schools*. New York: Crown.

Krathwohl, D., Bloom, B., & Masia, B. (1964). *Taxonomy of educational goals. Handbook II: Affective domain*. New York: David McKay.

Kruse, S. D., & Seashore Louis, K. (1995). *An emerging framework for analyzing school-based professional community*. Presentation to Center on Organization and Restructuring of Schools, National Advisory Panel, University of Wisconsin-Madison.

Kull, J. A., & Bailey, J. D. (1993, April). *Perceptions of recent graduates: Leadership and "standing out."* Paper presented at the annual meeting of the American Educational Research Association, Atlanta.

Kundert, D. K., May, D. C., & Brent, D. (1995). A comparison of students who delay kindergarten entry and those who are retained in grades K–5. *Psychology in the schools, 32*, 202–208.

Kyriacou, C. (1993). Research on the development of expertise in classroom teaching during initial training and the first year of teaching. *Educational Review, 45*(1), 79–87.

Labbo, L., & Field, S. (1998). Visiting South Africa through children's literature: Is it worth the trip? South African educators provide the answer. *The Reading Teacher, 51*(6), 464–475.

Lambert, L., Kent, K., Richert, A. E., Collay, M., & Dietz, M. E. (1997). *Who will save our schools? Teachers as constructivist leaders*. Thousand Oaks, CA: Corwin Press.

Lamme, L. (1987). The natural way to learn to read. In B. E. Cullinan (Ed.), *Children's literature in the reading program* (pp. 41–53). Newark, DE: International Reading Association.

Lathlaen, P. (1990). The National Board for Professional Teaching Standards and possible implications for gifted education. *Journal for the Education of the Gifted, 14*(1), 50–65.

Laws, B. B. (1991). Why teachers must play a role in setting national standards. *Educational Leadership, 49*(3), 37–38.

Leahy, R., & Corcoran, C. (1996). Encouraging reflective

practitioners: Connecting classroom to fieldwork. *Journal of Research and Development in Education, 29*(2), 104–114.

Lee, V. E., Groninger, R. G., & Smith, J. B. (1995). *Some summary findings about school organization and restructuring of high schools: Evidence from NELS:88 data.* Presentation to Center on Organization and Restructuring of Schools, National Advisory Panel, University of Wisconsin-Madison.

Leithwood, K. (1997, March). *Distributed leadership in secondary schools.* Paper presented at the annual meeting of the American Educational Research Association, Chicago.

LeNoir, W. D. (1993). Teacher questions and schema activation. *The Clearing House, 66*(6), 349–352.

Lepper, M., & Greene, D. (Eds.). (1978). *The hidden cost of reward.* New York: Halstead Press.

Levin, J., & Nolan, J. F. (1996). *Principles of classroom management* (2nd ed.). Needham Heights, MA: Allyn & Bacon.

Levine, M. (1998). NCATE to field test PDS standards. *NCATE Quality Teaching, 7*(2), 3.

Lieb, B. (Ed.). (1992). *Achieving world class standards: The challenge for educating teachers.* (Office of Educational Research and Improvement Report PIP 93-1217). Washington, DC: U.S. Government Printing Office.

Lieberman, A. (Ed.) (1988). *Building a professional culture in schools.* New York: Teachers College Press.

Lieberman, A. (1995). Practices that support teacher development. *Phi Delta Kappan, 76,* 591–596.

Lieberman, A., & Miller, L. (1992). Teacher development in professional practice schools. In L. Darling-Hammond (Ed.), *Professional development and restructuring.* New York: Teachers College Press.

Light, J. D. (1996). Linking school community members for school improvement. (ERIC Document Reproduction Service No. ED 401 640)

Lindfors, J. (1987). *Children's language and learning* (2nd ed.). Englewood Cliffs, NJ: Prentice-Hall.

Lindle, J. C. (1989). What do parents want from principals and teachers? *Educational Leadership, 47*(2), 12–14.

Lipson, M., Valencia, S., Wixson, K., & Peters, C. (1993). Integration and thematic teaching: Integration to improve teaching and learning. *Language Arts, 70*(4), 252–263.

Little, J. (1989). District policy choices and teachers' professional development opportunities. *Educational Evaluation and Policy Analysis, 11*(2), 165–179.

Little, J. (1990). The "mentor" phenomenon and the social organization of teaching. *Review of Research in Education* (Vol. 16, pp. 297–351). Washington, DC: American Educational Research Association.

Livingston, C., & Borko, H. (1989). Expert-novice differences in teaching: A cognitive analysis and implications for teacher education. *Journal of Teacher Education, 40*(4), 36–42.

Lockwood, A. T. (1996). *Tracking: Conflicts and resolutions.* Thousand Oaks, CA: Corwin Press.

Losen, S., & Diament, B. (1978). *Parent conferences in the schools: Procedures for developing effective partnerships.* Needham Heights, MA: Allyn & Bacon.

Loucks-Horsley, S., Brooks, J. G., Carlson, M. O., Kuerbis, P., Marsh, D., Padilla, M., Pratt, H., & Smith, K. (1990). *Developing and supporting teachers for science education in the middle years.* Andover, MA: National Center for Improving Science Education.

Luckowski, J. (1996). *Professional ethics among practicing educators.* (ERIC Document Reproduction Service No. ED 395 926)

Lyman, L., Foyle, H. C., & Azwell, T. S. (1993). *Cooperative learning in the elementary classroom.* Washington, DC: National Education Association.

Lynch, S. J. (1994). Should gifted students be grade-advanced? *ERIC Digest, EDO-ED-93-9.* Reston, VA: ERIC Clearinghouse on Disabilities and Gifted Education.

Mager, R. F. (1984a). *Developing attitude toward learning* (2nd ed.). Belmont, CA: David S. Lake Publishers.

Mager, R. F. (1984b). *Preparing instructional objectives* (Revised 2nd ed.). Belmont, CA: David S. Lake Publishers.

Malone, L. D., & Tulbert, B. L. (1996). Beyond content and pedagogy: Preparing centered teachers. *Contemporary Education, 68*(1), 45–48.

Mantzicopoulos, P. Y., & Neuharth-Pritchett, S. (1996, April). *Head Start to second grade: School competence and parental involvement in a public school Transition Project.* Paper presented at the annual meeting of the American Educational Research Association, New York.

Mark. J. & Anderson, B. (1985). Teacher survival rates in St. Louis, 1969–1982. *American Educational Research Journal, 22*(3), 413–421.

Markoff, A. M. (1992). *Within reach: Academic achievement through parent-teacher communication.* (ERIC Document Reproduction No. ED 350 788)

Marsh, C., & Willis, G. (1995). *Curriculum: Alternative approaches, ongoing issues.* Englewood Cliffs, NJ: Prentice-Hall, Inc.

Marso, R., & Pigge, F. (1994). *Personal and family characteristics associated with reasons given by teacher candidates for becoming teachers in the 1990s: Implications for the recruitment of teachers.* (ERIC Document Reproduction Service No. 379 228)

Marttila & Kiley, Inc. (1995). *A study of attitudes among the parents of primary-school children.* Boston: Author.

Maslow, A. H. (1965). *Eupsychian management.* Homewood, IL: Richard D. Irwin, Inc., & The Dorsey Press.

McDermott, P. (1995, October). *"Should we do it the same way?" Teaching in tracked and untracked high school classes.* Paper presented at the annual meeting of the Northeastern Educational Research Association, Portsmouth, NH.

McGee, L., & Tompkins, G. (1995). Literature-based reading instruction: What's guiding the instruction? *Language Arts, 72,* 405–414.

McGregor, D. (1960). *The human side of enterprise.* New York: McGraw-Hill.

McLanahan, S., & Booth, K. (1991). Mother-only families: Problems, prospects, and politics. In A. Booth (Ed.), *Contemporary families: Looking forward, looking back* (pp.

405–428). Minneapolis: National Council on Family Relations.

McLaughlin, M., & Warren, S. (1994). *Performance assessment and students with disabilities: Usage in outcomes-based accountability systems.* Reston, VA: Council for Exceptional Children.

McLoughlin, M., & Lewis, R. (1994). *Assessing special students* (4th ed.). New York: Merrill/Macmillan.

McNeil, J. (1996). *Curriculum: A comprehensive introduction* (5th ed.). New York: HarperCollins.

Meisels, S. (1987). Uses and abuses of developmental screening and school readiness testing. *Young Children, 4*(2), 67–73.

Meisels, S. (1995). Performance assessment in early childhood education: The Work Sampling System. (ERIC Reproduction Document Service No. ED 382 407)

Merlin, D. S. (1995). Adventures in acceleration: A mother's perspective. *Gifted Child Today, 18*(4), 14–17.

Metcalf-Turner, P., & Fischetti, J. (1996). Professional development schools: Persisting questions and lessons learned. *Journal of Teacher Education, 47*(4), 292–299.

Meyer, M. (1997). The GREENing of learning. Using the eighth intelligence. *Educational Leadership, 55*(1), 32–34.

Miles, B. S., & Simpson, R. (1994). Understanding and preventing acts of aggression and violence in school-age children and youth. *The Clearing House, 68*(1), 55–61.

Mills, C. J., Ablard, K. E., & Gustin, W. C. (1994). Academically talented students' achievement in a flexibly paced mathematics program. *Journal of Research in Mathematics Education, 25*(5), 495–511.

Modigliani, K. (1993). Readings in family child care development: Project-to-project compiled. Boston: Wheelock College Family Child Care Project.

Mooney, T. (1994). *Teachers as leaders: Hope for the future.* (ERIC Document Reproduction Service No. ED 380 407)

Moore, L., & Brown, D. L. (1996). *Head Start parents and public school teachers: Different perspectives on parent-teacher partnerships.* Paper presented at the third annual Head Start Research Conference, Washington, DC.

Morrow, L. (1992). The impact of a literature-based program on literacy achievement, use of literature, and attitudes of children from minority backgrounds. *Reading Research Quarterly, 27*, 250–275.

Morrow, L., O'Connor, E., & Smith, J. (1990). Effects of a story reading program on the literacy development of at risk kindergarten children. *Journal of Reading Behavior, 22*, 255–275.

Mosteller, F., Light, R. J., & Sachs, J. A. (1996). Sustained inquiry in education: Lessons from skill grouping and class size. *Harvard Educational Review, 66*(4), 797–828.

Mulcahy, D. G. (1994, November). *Goals 2000 and the role of the National Education Standards and Improvement Council.* Paper presented at the annual conference of the American Educational Studies Association, Chapel Hill, NC.

Murnane, R., Singer, J., & Willet, J. (1988). The effects of salaries and opportunity costs on duration in teaching: Evidence from Michigan. *Review of Economics and Statistics, 71*, 347–352.

Murnane, R., Singer, J., & Willet, J. (1989). The effects of salaries and opportunity costs on length of stay in teaching: Evidence from North Carolina. *Journal of Human Resources, 25*, 106–124.

Murray, F. (1986). Goals for the reform of teacher education: An executive summary of the Holmes Group report. *Phi Delta Kappan, 68*(1), 28–32.

National Association for the Education of Young Children. (1994). NAEYC position statement: A conceptual framework for early childhood professional development. *Young Children, 49*(3), 68–77.

National Board for Professional Teaching Standards. (1991a). *Toward high and rigorous standards for the teaching profession* (3rd ed.). Detroit: Author.

National Board for Professional Teaching Standards. (1991b). What teachers should know and be able to do. In NBPTS (Eds.), *Towards high and rigorous standards for the teaching profession* (3rd ed., pp. 13–31). Detroit: Author.

National Center for Education Statistics (1993). *The condition of education.* Washington, DC: U.S. Government Printing Office.

National Center for Fair and Open Testing. (1995). *Principles and indicators for student assessment systems.* (ERIC Reproduction Document No. ED 400 334)

National Commission on Excellence in Education. (1983). *A nation at risk: The imperative for educational reform.* Washington, DC: U.S. Government Printing Office.

National Commission on Teaching and America's Future. (1996). *What matters most: Teaching for America's future.* New York: Author.

National Council for Accreditation of Teacher Education. (1997). *Standards, procedures, and policies for the accreditation of professional education units.* Washington, DC: Author.

National Education Association. (1991). *Goals 2000: Mobilizing for action: Achieving the national education goals.* Washington, DC: Author.

National Education Association. (1998). *Tomorrow's teachers, 5.* Washington, DC: Author.

Nelson, J. (1987). *Positive discipline.* New York: Ballantine Books.

New, R. (1994). Cultural variations on developmentally appropriate practice: Challenges to theory and practice. In C. Edwards, L. Gandini, & G. Forman (Eds.), *The hundred languages of children: The Reggio Emilia approach to early childhood* (pp. 215–231). Norwood, NJ: Ablex.

Newman, J. (Ed.). (1985). *Whole language: Theory in use.* Portsmouth, NH: Heinemann.

Nieto, S. (1992). *Affirming diversity: The sociopolitical context of multicultural education.* White Plains, NY: Longman.

Noddings, N. (1992). *The challenge to care in schools: An alternative approach to education.* New York: Teachers College Press.

Northfield, J., & Mitchell, I. (1995, April). *Bringing a research focus into the teaching role.* Paper presented at the annual meeting of the American Educational Research Association, San Francisco.

Oakes, J. (1992). One more thought. *Sociology of Education, 67*, 91.

Okabayashi, H., & Torrance, E. P. (1984). Role of style of learning and thinking and self directed learning readiness in the achievement of gifted students. *Journal of Learning Disabilities, 17*(2), 104–107.

Olmstead, P. P. (1991). Parents' involvement in elementary education: Findings and suggestions from the follow-through program. *The Elementary School Journal, 91*, 221–232.

Olson, M., & Osborne, J. (1991). Learning to teach: The first year. *Teaching and Teacher Education, 7*, 331–343.

Olson, S., & Banyard, V. (1993). Stop the world so I can get off for a while: Sources of daily stress in the lives of low-income single mothers of young children. *Family Relations, 42*(1), 50–56.

Ordovensky, P. (1990). Will national certification fly? *The Executive Educator, 12*(1), 18–20, 30.

Orlich, D. C., Harder, R. J., Callahan, R. C., Kauchak, D. P., & Gibson, H. W. (1994). *Teaching strategies: A guide to better instruction* (4th ed.). Lexington, MA: D. C. Heath.

Otto, P. B. (1991). Finding an answer in questioning strategies. *Science and Children, 28*(7), 44–47.

Ovando, M. N. (1994, October). *Effects of teachers' leadership on their teaching practices.* Paper presented at the annual conference of the University Council of Educational Administration.

Papert, S. (1980). *Mindstorms: Children, computers, and powerful ideas.* New York: Basic Books.

Papert, S. (1993). *The children's machine: Rethinking school in the age of the computer.* New York: Basic Books.

Parnes, S. J. (1981). *The magic of your mind.* Buffalo, NY: Creative Education Foundation.

Partridge, S. (1996). *Detracking discussed.* (ERIC Document Reproduction Service ED 390 034)

Passmore, J. (1982). *The philosophy of teaching.* Cambridge, MA: Harvard University Press.

Patterson, C. J. (1992). Children of lesbian and gay parents. *Child Development, 63*, 1025–1042.

Patterson, J. L. (1993). *Leadership for tomorrow's schools.* Alexandria, VA: Association for Supervision and Curriculum Development.

Paulson, F., Paulson, P., & Meyer, C. (1991). What makes a portfolio a portfolio? *Educational Leadership, 48*(5), 60–63.

Peacock, J. (1986). *The anthropological lens: Harsh light, soft focus.* Cambridge, England: Cambridge University Press.

Pellicer, L. O., & Anderson, L. W. (1995). *A handbook for teacher leaders.* Thousand Oaks, CA: Corwin Press.

Perrone, V. (1990). How did we get here? In C. Kamii (Ed.), *Achievement testing in the early grades: The games grown-ups play* (pp. 1–14). Washington, DC: National Association for the Education of Young Children.

Peterson, K. (1988). *Building curriculum for young children: Deciding on content.* (ERIC Reproduction Document No. ED 297 886.)

Pianta, R. C., Tietbohl, P. J., & Bennett, E. M. (1997). Differences in social adjustment and classroom behavior between children retained in kindergarten and groups of age and grade matched peers. *Early Education & Development, 8*(2), 137–152.

Pickert, S. M. (1992). Using simulations to teach leadership roles. *Teaching Education, 5*(1), 37–42.

Pierce, L., & O'Malley, J. (1992). *Performance and portfolio assessment for language minority students.* Washington, DC: National Clearing House for Bilingual Education.

Pigdon, K., & Woolley, M. (Ed.). (1993). *The big picture: Integrating children's learning.* Portsmouth, NH: Heinemann.

Pollard, A., & Tann, S. (1987). *Reflective teaching in the primary school.* London: Cassell.

Pool, C. (1997). Up with emotional health. *Educational Leadership, 54*(8), 12–14.

Posner, G. (1992). *Analyzing the curriculum.* New York: McGraw-Hill.

Poteet, J., Choate, J., & Stewart, S. (1993). Performance assessment and special education: Practices and prospects. *Focus on Exceptional Children, 26*(1), 1–20.

Powell, D. R. (1991). How schools support families: Critical policy tensions. *The Elementary School Journal, 91*, 307–319.

Prosise, R. (1996). *Beyond rules and consequences for classroom management: Fastback 370.* Bloomington, IN: Phi Delta Kappa Educational Foundation.

Purdy, D. (1998). Teacher Helpline provides valuable link for first year teachers. *Northern Iowa Today, 82*(2), 7.

Putnam, J. (1997). *Cooperative learning in diverse classrooms.* Upper Saddle River, NJ: Prentice-Hall.

Queen, J. A., Blackwelder, B. B., & Mallen, L. P. (1997). *Responsible classroom management for teachers and students.* Upper Saddle River, NJ: Prentice-Hall.

Ragan, T. J., & Smith, P. L. (1994). *Opening the black box: Instructional strategies examined.* (ERIC Reproduction Document No. ED 373 749)

Rahn, M., Stecher, B., Goodman, H., & Alt, M. (1997). Making decisions on assessment methods: Weighing the tradeoffs. *Preventing School Failure, 41*(2), 85–89.

Rainforth, B., & England, J. (1997). Collaborations for inclusion. *Education and Treatment of Children, 20*(1), 85–104.

Randall-David, E. (1989). *Strategies for working with culturally diverse communities and clients.* Bethesda, MD: Association for the Care of Children's Health.

Raphael, T. E. (1986). Teaching question answer relationships, revisited. *The Reading Teacher, 39*(6), 516–522.

Rareshide, S. W. (1993). *Implications for teachers' use of humor in the classroom.* (ERIC Reproduction Document Service No. ED 359 165)

Rasinski, T. (1988). The role of interest, purpose and choice in early literacy. *The Reading Teacher, 41*, 396–400.

Rasinski, T. U. (1995). *Parents and teachers helping children learn to read and write.* Fort Worth, TX: Harcourt Brace College Publishers.

Reagan, T. (1993). Educating the "reflective practitioner": The contribution of philosophy of education. *Journal of Research and Development in Education, 26*(4), 189–196.

Reed, D. (1989). Student teacher problems with classroom

discipline: Implications for program development. *Action in Teacher Education, 11,* 59–65.

Rees, D. I., Argys, L. M., & Brewer, D. J. (1996). Tracking in the United States: Descriptive statistics from NELS. *Economics of Education Review, 15*(1), 83–89.

Reis, S. M., & Westberg, K. L. (1994). An examination of current school district policies: Acceleration of secondary students. *The Journal of Secondary Gifted Education, 5*(4), 7–18.

Reising, B. (1995). What's new in national certification of teachers? *The Clearing House, 68*(6), 332–333.

Reynolds, M. (1990). *A checklist for description of features of programs that aim to effectively accommodate mainstreamed special education students in regular education settings.* (ERIC Document Reproduction Service No. ED 405 696)

Ridgeway, N. (1996, Spring). A village of learning. *Hilltopics,* pp. 16–18.

Riley, R. W. (1995). Turning the corner: From a nation at risk to a nation with a future. *The Technology Teacher, 54*(7), 3–5.

Rimm, S. B., & Lovance, K. J. (1992). The use of subject and grade skipping for the prevention and reversal of underachievement. *Gifted Child Quarterly, 36*(2), 100–105.

Roach, P. B., Bell, D., & Salmeri, E. R. (1989). The home-school link: New dimensions in the middle school preservice curriculum. *Action in Teacher Education, 11*(4), 14–17.

Roberson, S. D. (1983). Now who aspires to teach? *Educational Researcher, 12*(6), 13–21.

Roberts, P., & Kellough, R. (1996). *A guide for developing an interdisciplinary thematic unit.* Englewood Cliffs, NJ: Prentice-Hall.

Robertson, A. S. (1997). When retention is recommended, what should parents do? *ERIC Digest, EDO-PS-97-20.* Washington, DC: ERIC Clearinghouse on Elementary and Early Childhood Education.

Robinson, J. (1996). *Picture what women do: An inquiry learning example.* Indianapolis: Media Action Council of Indiana.

Robinson, N. M., & Noble, K. D. (1992). Acceleration: Valuable high school to college options. *Gifted Child Today, 15*(2), 20–23.

Robinson, N., & Robinson, H. (1976). *The mentally retarded child: A psychological approach* (2nd ed.). New York: McGraw-Hill.

Robison, H., & Spodek, B. (1965). *New direction in the kindergarten.* New York: Teachers College Press.

Rockwell, R., Andre, L., & Hawley, M. (1996). *Parents and teachers as partners: Issues and challenges.* Fort Worth, TX: Harcourt Brace.

Rodd, J. (1996). Towards a typology of leadership for the early childhood professional of the 21st century. *Early Child Development and Care, 120,* 119–126.

Roderick, M. (1995). Grade retention and school dropout: Policy debate and research questions. *Phi Delta Kappa Research Bulletin, 15,* 1–6.

Roeber, E., Bond, L., & van der Ploeg, A. (1993). *State student assessment program data base.* Washington, DC: Council of Chief State School Officers/North Central Regional Education Laboratory.

Rogers, K. B., & Kimpston, R. D. (1992). Acceleration: What

we do vs. what we know. *Educational Leadership, 50*(2), 58–61.

Rosenthal, D. M., & Sawyers, J. Y. (1996). Building successful home/school partnerships: Strategies for parent support and involvement. *Childhood Education, 72*(4), 194–200.

Ross, D., Bondy, E., & Kyle, D. (1993). *Reflective teaching for student empowerment: Elementary curriculum and methods.* New York: Macmillan.

Roth, G. L. (1996). *Learning to learn: Western perspectives.* (ERIC Reproduction Document No. ED 401 408)

Routman, R. (1991). *Invitations: Changing as teachers and learners K-12.* Portsmouth, NH: Heinemann.

Rumelhart, D. E. (1980). Schemata: The building blocks of cognition. In R. J. Spiro, B. C. Bruce, & W. F. Brewer (Eds.), *Theoretical issues in reading comprehension* (pp. 33–58). Hillsdale, NJ: Erlbaum.

Russell, T. (1988). From preservice teacher education to first year of teaching: A study of theory and practice. In J. Calderhead (Ed.), *Teachers' professional learning.* London: Falmer Press.

Russell, T., & Munby, H. (1991). Reframing: The role of experience in developing teachers' professional knowledge. In D. A. Schon (Ed.), *The reflective turn: Case studies in and on educational practice.* New York: Teachers College Press.

Ryan, K., & Cooper, J. (1995). *Those who can, teach* (7th ed.). Boston: Houghton Mifflin.

Sanders, M. G. (1996). Building family partnerships that last. *Educational Leadership, 54*(3), 61–66.

Sapon-Shevin, M. (1994). *Playing favorites: Gifted education and the disruption of community.* Albany: State University of New York Press.

Sattler, J. L., & Jensen, R. A. (1998). Innovation in the College of Education and Health Sciences: Connected learning through redefined disciplines. In *The university as learning community: Tradition, innovation, prospects.* Editor: T. K. Conley. Asst. Editor: D. A. Worley (pp. 89–105). Peoria, IL: Bradley University.

Sayler, M. F., & Brookshire, W. K. (1993). Social, emotional, and behavioral adjustment of accelerated students, students in gifted classes, and regular students in eighth grade. *Gifted Child Quarterly, 37*(4), 150–154.

Schargel, F. (1994). *Transforming education through total quality management: A practitioner's guide.* Princeton, NJ: Eye on Education.

Schein, V. (1995). Would women lead differently? In J. T. Wren (Ed.), *Leader's companion: Insights on leadership through the ages* (pp. 161–167). New York: Free Press.

Schimmel, D. (1997). Traditional rule-making and the subversion of citizenship education. *Social Education, 61*(2), 70–74.

Schulz, C. (1996). What really frightens children in school? *Educational Horizons, 74*(3), 139–144.

Scott, C. C., Gargan, A. M., & Zakierski, M. M. (1997). *Managing diversity-based conflicts among children: Fastback 414.* Bloomington, IN: Phi Delta Kappa Educational Foundation.

Seely, A. (1994). *Portfolio assessment.* Westminster, CA: Teacher Created Materials, Inc.

Seidman, R. H. (1995, April). *National Education "Goals 2000": Some disastrous unintended consequences.* Paper presented at the annual meeting of the American Educational Research Association, San Francisco.

Serow, R. (1994). Called to teach: A study of highly motivated preservice teachers. *Journal of Research and Development in Education, 27*(2), 65–72.

Serow, R., & Forrest, K. (1994). Motives and circumstances: Occupational-change experiences of prospective late-entry teachers. *Teaching and Teacher Education, 10*(5), 555–563.

Shapiro, B. (1994). Assessing America's best and brightest teachers: The National Board for Professional Teaching Standards. *The Professional Educator, 17*(1), 41–48.

Shaw, D. S. (1992). The effects of divorce on children's adjustment. In M. E. Procidano & C. B. Fisher (Eds.), *Contemporary families: A handbook for school professionals.* New York: Teachers College Press.

Short, P. M., & Greer, J. T. (1993). *Empowering students: Helping all students realize success.* (ERIC Reproduction Document No. ED 355 670)

Shulman, L. (1986). Those who understand: Knowledge growth in teaching. *Educational Researcher, 15*(2), 4–14.

Shulman, L. (1987). Knowledge and teaching: Foundations of the new reform. *Harvard Educational Review, 57*, 1–22.

Sirotnik, K. A. (1985). Let's examine the profession, not the teachers. *Educational Leadership, 43*(3), 67–69.

Skinner, B. F. (1968). *The technology of teaching.* New York: Appleton-Century-Crofts.

Skinner, B. F. (1982). *Skinner for the classroom.* Champaign, IL: Research Press.

Slavin, R. E. (1988). *Educational psychology: Theory into practice.* Englewood Cliffs, NJ: Prentice-Hall.

Smith, F. (1971). *Understanding reading: A psycholinguistic analysis of reading and learning to read.* New York: Holt, Rinehart and Winston.

Smolowe, J. (1993). Intermarried, with children. *Time, 147*(21), 65–67.

Snyder, J. F. (1995). *Perceptions of preservice teachers: The job market, why teaching, alternatives to teaching.* (ERIC Document Reproduction Service No. 390 865)

Spagnolo, J. A. (1997). World class educators for the 21st century: Illinois framework for a restructured licensure system. *Action in Teacher Education, 19*(2), 7–16.

Spodek, B. (1988). Conceptualizing today's kindergarten curriculum. *Elementary School Journal, 89*(2), 203–211.

Staley, L. (1997). Teaching strategies: "What does purple smell like?" *Childhood Education, 73*(4), 240–242.

Stamp, L. N., & Groves, M. M. (1994). Strengthening the ethic of care: Planning and supporting family involvement. *Dimensions of Early Childhood, 22*(2), 10–13.

Stecher, B. (1995). *The cost of performance assessment in science.* Paper presented at the annual meeting of the National Council on Measurement in Education, San Francisco.

Sternberg, R., & Kooligian, Jr., J. (Eds.). (1990). *Competence considered.* New Haven, CT: Yale University Press.

Stewart, S., Choate, J., & Poteet, J. (1995). The revolution in assessment within and across educational settings. *Preventing School Failure, 39*(3), 20–24.

Stiggins, R. (1997). *Student-centered classroom assessment* (2nd ed.). Englewood Cliffs, NJ: Prentice-Hall.

Stoddart, T. (1990). *Perspectives on guided practice.* (ERIC Document Reproduction Service No. 330 682)

Stogdill, R. M. (1995). Personal factors associated with leadership. In J. T. Wren (Ed.), *Leader's companion: Insights on leadership through the ages* (pp. 127–132). New York: Free Press.

Stolley, K. (1993). Statistics on adoption in the United States. *The Future of Children: Adoption, 3*(1), 26–42.

Stolp, S., & Smith, S. C. (1995). *Transforming school culture: Stories, symbols, values and the leader's role.* Eugene, OR: ERIC Clearinghouse on Educational Management.

Stone, M. (1997, March). *Commonalities and differences in teacher leadership at the elementary, middle, and high school levels.* Paper presented at the annual meeting of the American Educational Research Association, Chicago.

Su, J. (1994). Who will teach our children? Implications for the teaching profession. *Professional Educator, 16*(2), 1–10.

Supovitz, J. (1994). *Encouraging learning through portfolio assessment.* (ERIC Document Reproduction Service No. ED 390 939)

Swick, K. (1984). Family involvement: An empowerment perspective. *Dimensions of Early Childhood, 22*(2), 10–13.

Tanner, C. K., & Combs, F. E. (1993). Student retention policy: The gap between research and practice. *Journal of Research in Childhood Education, 8*(1), 69–77.

Tanner, D., & Tanner, L. (1995). *Curriculum development: Theory into practice* (3rd ed.). Englewood Cliffs, NJ: Prentice-Hall.

Tasker, F., & Golombok, S. (1995). Adults raised as children in lesbian families. *American Journal of Orthopsychiatry, 65*(2), 203–215.

Tauber, R. T. (1992). Those who can't teach: Dispelling the myth. *NASSP Bulletin, 76*(54), 96–102.

Teachman, J., & Heckert, A. (1985). The impact of age and children on remarriage. *Journal of Family Issues, 6*(2), 185–203.

Teitel, L. (1997). Professional development schools and the transformation of teacher leadership. *Teacher Education Quarterly, 24*(1), 9–22.

Telease, J. A. (1996). *Field-based interns' philosophical perspectives on teaching.* (ERIC Document Reproduction Service No. 402 283)

Templeton, R. A., & Jensen, R. A. (1993). How exemplary teachers perceive their school environments. In D. L. Fisher (Ed.), *The study of learning environments* (Vol. 7). Perth, Australia: Curtin University of Technology.

Theis-Sprinthall, L. M., & Gerler, Jr., E. R. (1990). Support groups for novice teachers. *Journal of Staff Development, 11*(4), 18–22.

Theis-Sprinthall, L. M., & Sprinthall, N. (1987, April). *Experienced teachers: Agents for revitalization and renewal as mentors and teacher educators.* Paper presented at the annual meeting of the American Educational Research Association, Washington, DC.

Thomas, J. A., & Montgomery, P. (1998). On becoming a

good teacher: Reflective practice with regard to children's voices. *Journal of Teacher Education, 49*(5), 372–380.

Thompson, S. (1996). How action research can put teachers and parents on the same team. *Educational Horizons, 74*(2) 70–76.

Thompson, S., Knudson, P., & Wilson, D. (1997). Helping primary children with recess play: A social curriculum. *Young Children, 52*(6), 17–21.

Tindal, G., & Marston, D. (1990). *Classroom-based assessment: Evaluating instructional outcomes.* New York: Merrill.

Tomlinson, C. A. (1994). Middle school and acceleration. *The Journal of Secondary Gifted Education, 5*(4), 42–51.

Townsend, J., Fu, D., & Lamme, L. (1997). Writing assessment: Multiple perspectives, multiple purposes. *Preventing School Failure, 41*(2), 71–76.

Townsend, M. A. R., & Hicks, L. (1995, April). *Classroom goal structures, social satisfaction, and the perceived value of academic tasks.* Paper presented at the annual meeting of the American Educational Research Association, San Francisco.

Trubo, R. (1983). Peak performance. *Success, 30*(4), 30–33, 56.

Trueba, H., Jacobs, L., & Kirton, E. (1990). *Cultural conflict and adaptation: The case of Hmong children in American society.* New York: Falmer.

Tunnell, M., & Jacobs, J. (1989). Using "real books": Research findings on literature-based reading instruction. *The Reading Teacher, 42,* 470–477.

U.S. Bureau of the Census (1992a). *Marital status and living arrangements: March, 1992.* (Current Population Reports, Series P20, No. 468.) Washington, DC: U.S. Governement Printing Office.

U.S. Bureau of the Census. (1992b). *Statistical abstract of the U.S.: 1992* (12th ed.). Washington, DC: U.S. Department of Commerce.

U.S. Department of Education. (1994). *Strong families, strong schools: A research base for family involvement in learning.* Washington, DC: Author.

U.S. Department of Education. (1996). *Introducing Goals 2000: A world-class education for every child.* Washington, DC: Author.

U.S. Department of Health and Human Services. (1992, March.) *Child abuse and neglect: A shared community concern.* Washington, DC: U.S. Government Printing Office.

Unger, R., & Crawford, M. (1992). *Women and gender: A feminist psychology.* New York: McGraw-Hill.

Unsworth, L. (1984). Meeting individual needs through flexible within-class grouping of pupils. *The Reading Teacher, 38,* 298–304.

Urbanski, A., & Nickolaou, M. B. (1997). Reflections on teachers as leaders. *Educational Policy, 11*(2), 243–254.

Vacca, R. T., & Vacca, J. L. (1996). *Content area reading* (5th ed.). New York: HarperCollins.

Vacha, E. F., & McLaughlin, T. F. (1992). The social structural, family, school, and personal characteristics of at-risk students: Policy recommendations for school personnel. *Journal of Education, 74,* 9–24.

Vail, K. (1995). Raising the bar. *The American School Board, 182*(4), 48–49.

Valencia, S., & Calfee, R. (1991). The development and use of literacy portfolios for students, classes, and teachers. *Applied Measurement in Education, 4,* 333–345.

Van Tassel-Baska, J. (1992). Educational decision making on acceleration and grouping. *Gifted Child Quarterly, 36*(2), 68–72.

Vance, P. S. (1991). The initiating-extended-role teacher: Exploring facets of teacher leadership. *Dissertation Abstracts International, 53,* 01A–60.

Veenman, S. (1984). Perceived problems of beginning teachers. *Review of Educational Research, 52*(2), 143–178.

Vickers, H. S. (1994). Young children at risk: Differences in family functioning. *Journal of Educational Research, 87,* 262–270.

Visher, E., & Visher, J. (1989). Parenting coalitions after remarriage: Dynamics and therapeutic guidelines. *Family Relations, 38*(1), 65–70.

von Oech, R. (1983). *A whack on the side of the head.* New York: Warner Books.

von Oech, R. (1986). *A kick in the seat of the pants.* New York: Harper & Row.

Vonk, J. H. C. (1995, April). *Conceptualizing novice teachers' professional development: A base for supervisory interventions.* Paper presented at the annual meeting of the American Educational Research Association, San Francisco.

Vygotsky, L. (1978). *Mind in society: The development of higher psychological processes.* Cambridge, MA: Harvard University Press.

Wakefield, A. P. (1993). Developmentally appropriate practice: "Figuring things out." *The Educational Forum, 57*(2), 134–143.

Wakefield, A. P. (1994). Letting children decide: The benefits of choices. *Dimensions of Early Childhood, 22*(3), 14–16.

Walberg, H. J., & Greenberg, R. C. (1997). Using the learning environment inventory. *Educational Leadership, 54*(8), 45–47.

Walberg, J. J. (1984). Families as partners in educational productionists. *Phi Delta Kappan, 65*(6), 397–400.

Walker, H. M. (1995). *The acting out child* (2nd ed.). Longmont, CO: Sopris West.

Wallinger, L. M. (1997). Don't smile before Christmas: The role of humor in education. *The National Association of Secondary School Principals Bulletin, 81*(589), 27–34.

Ward, B. (1992). *Support component of the California New Teacher Project: Third year evaluation report* (1990–91). Los Alamitos, CA: The Southwest Regional Educatonal Laboratory.

Ward, B., & Dianda, M. (1990). *Support component of the California New Teacher Project: First year evaluation report* (1988–89). Los Alamitos, CA: The Southwest Regional Educational Laboratory.

Waxman, H. C., & Ellet, C. D. (Eds.) (1992). *The study of learning environments* (Vol. 5). Houston, TX: University of Houston.

Weaver, C. (1994). *Reading process and practice: From sociopsycholinguistics to whole language.* Portsmouth, NH: Heinemann.

Weinstein, C. S. (1989). Teacher education students' pre-conceptions of teaching. *Journal of Teacher Education, 40*(2), 53–60.

Weinstein, C. S. (1992). Designing the instructional environment: Focus on seating. *Proceedings of Selected Research and Development Presentations at the Convention of the Association for Educational Communications and Technology and Sponsored by the Research and Theory Division,* IR 015 706.

Weinstein, C. S., & Mignano, A. J., Jr. (1996). *Elementary classroom management: Lessons from research and practice* (2nd ed.). New York: McGraw-Hill.

Weinstein, R. S. (1996). High standards in a tracked system of schooling: For which students and with what educational supports? *Educational Researcher, 25*(8), 16–19.

Weitz, E. (1988). *Hidden curriculum: The elusive side of classroom life in first grade.* (ERIC Document Reproduction Service No. ED 307 991)

Wells, G. (1986). *The meaning makers: Children learning language and using language to learn.* Portsmouth, NH: Heinemann.

Welner, K. G., & Oakes, J. (1996). (Li)ability grouping: The new susceptibility of school tracking systems to legal challenges. *Harvard Educational Review, 66*(3), 451–470.

Wescott Dodd, A. (1996). Involving parents, avoiding gridlock. *Educational Leadership, 53*(7), 44–47.

Westerman, D. A. (1991). Expert and novice teacher decision making. *Journal of Teacher Education, 42*(4), 292–305.

West Virginia Early Childhood Transition Initiative: Operation Tadpole. 1995 report. (1995). (ERIC Document Reproduction Service No. ED 407 057)

Wheelock, A. (1992). *Crossing the tracks: How untracking can save America's schools.* New York: New Press.

Whetten, D. A., & Cameron, K. S. (1995). *Developing management skills* (3rd ed.). New York: HarperCollins.

Wiggins, G. (1989). Teaching to the (authentic) test. *Educational Leadership 46*(6), 41–47.

Wiggins, G. (1994). Toward better report cards. *Educational Leadership, 52*(2), 28–37.

Wiley, T. G. (1990-1991). Planning versus prespecification: The role of premeditation in instruction. *Action in Teacher Education, 12*(4), 47–51.

Willet, J., & Singer, J. (1991). From whether to when: New methods for studying student dropout and teacher attrition. *Review of Educational Research, 61*(4), 407–450.

Willinsky, J. (1990). *The new literacy: Redefining reading and writing in the schools.* New York: Routledge, Chapman & Hall.

Wilson, B., & Clarke, S. (1992). Remarriages: A demographic profile. *Journal of Family Issues, 13*(2), 123–141.

Wilson, S., & Cameron, R. (1996). Student teacher perceptions of effective teaching: A developmental perspective. *Journal of Education for Teaching, 22*(2), 181–195.

Wise, A. E. (1998). NCATE 2000 will emphasize candidate performance. *NCATE Quality Teaching, 7*(2), 1–2.

Wong, A. F., & Fraser, B. J. (1996). Environment-attitude as-sociations in the chemistry laboratory classroom. *Research in Science and Technological Education, 14*(1), 91–102.

Wood, K. (1997). *Interdisciplinary instruction: A practical guide for elementary and middle school teachers.* Upper Saddle River, NJ: Prentice-Hall.

Wortham, S. (1996). *The integrated classroom: The assessment-curriculum link in early childhood education.* Englewood Cliffs, NJ: Prentice-Hall.

Worthen, B. (1993). Crtical issues that will determine the future of alternative assessment. *Phi Delta Kappan, 74*(6), 444–454.

Yosha, P. (1991, March). *The benefits of an induction program: What do mentors and novices say?* Paper presented at the annual meeting of the American Educational Research Association, Chicago.

Young, A. C. (1997). Higher-order learning and thinking: What is it and how is it taught? *Educational Technology, 37*(4), 38–41.

Young, B. (1995). Career plans and work perceptions of pre-service teachers. *Teaching and Teacher Education, 11*(3), 281–292.

Ysseldyke, J., Algozzine, B., & Thurlow, M. (1992). *Critical issues in special education* (2nd ed.). Boston: Houghton Mifflin.

Zapata, J. T. (1988). Early identification and recruitment of Hispanic teacher candidates. *Journal of Teacher Education, 39*(1), 19–23.

Zarrillo, J. (1989). Teachers' interpretations of literature-based reading. *The Reading Teacher, 43,* 22–29.

Zeichner, K. (1983). Individual and institutional factors related to the socialization of beginning teachers. In G. Griffin & H. Hukill (Eds.), *First years of teaching: What are the pertinent issues?* Austin: Research & Development Center for Teacher Education, University of Texas.

Zeldin, S. (1990). The implementation of home-school-community partnerships: Policy from the perspective of principals and teachers. *Equity and Choice, 6,* 56–63.

Zemelman, S., Daniels, H., & Hyde, A. (1998). *Best practice: New standards for teaching and learning in America's schools* (2nd ed.). Portsmouth, NH: Heinemann.

Zimpher, N., & Rieger, S. (1988). Mentoring teachers: What are the issues? *Theory into Practice, 27*(3), 175–182.

Zinn, L. F. (1997, March). *Supports and barriers to teacher leadership: Reports of teacher leaders.* Paper presented at the annual meeting of the American Educational Research Association, Chicago.

Zins, J. E., Maher, C. A., Murphy, J. J., & Wess, B. P. (1988). The peer support group: A means of facilitating professional development. *School Psychology Review, 17*(1), 138–146.

Zins, J. E., Travis, L. F. III, & Freppon, P. A. (1997). Linking research and educational programming to promote social and emotional learning. In P. Salovey and D. Sluyter (Eds.), *Emotional development and emotional intelligence: Implications for educators.* New York: Basic Books.

CREDITS

Chapter 1: p. 21: Teaching perspectives copyright © 1995, American Educational Research Association. Reprinted with permission of AERA.

Chapter 2: p. 32: Figure 2.2 reprinted with permission from the National Association for the Education of Young Children. **p. 52:** Figure 2.7 copyright © 1997 by Allyn & Bacon. Reprinted/adapted by permission.

Chapter 4: p. 86: INTASC list from INTASC (1992) Model Standards for Beginning Teacher Licensing, Assessment and Development: A Resource for State Dialogue. Washington, D.C., Council of Chief State School Officers. **p. 93:** Figure 4.2 adapted by permission of Steven Zemelman, Harvey Daniels, and Arthur Hyde: *Best Practice: New Standards for Teaching and Learning in America's Schools*, 2nd edition (Heinemann, A Division of Reed Elsevier, Portsmouth, NH, 1998). **p. 98:** Figure 4.4 from *Promoting Social and Emotional Learning: Guidelines for Educators*, by Maurice J. Elias, Joseph E. Zims, Roger P. Weissberg, Karin S. Frey, Mark T. Greenberg, Norris M. Haynes, Rachael Kessler, Mary E. Schwab-Stone, and Timothy P. Shriver. Alexandria, VA: Association for Supervision and Curriculum Development. Copyright © 1997 ASCD. Reprinted with permission. All rights reserved. **p. 107:** Figure 4.5 from Zero to Three (1992). *Head Start: The Emotional Foundations of School Readiness*, Arlington, VA: (formerly National Center for Clinical Infant Programs). Reprinted with permission. **p. 114:** Principles for a Moral School Community from Diane Berreth and Sheldon Berman, "The Moral Dimensions of School," *Educational Leadership* 54, 8:24–27. Alexandria, VA: Association for Supervision and Curriculum Development. Copyright © 1997 ASCD. Reprinted with permission. All rights reserved.

Chapter 5: p. 124: Recommendations for home-school partnerships from D. M. Rosenthal and J. Y. Sawyers (1996), "Building Successful Home/School Partnerships: Strategies for Parent Support and Involvement," Childhood Education 72 (4), 194–200. **p. 125:** Five steps to developing school-family partnerships reprinted with permission from the National Association of the Education of Young Children. **p. 147:** Reflect and Respond text reprinted with permission of the Association for the Care of Children's Health, 19 Mantua Road, Mt. Royal, NJ 08061. From *Strategies for Working with Culturally Diverse Communities and Clients*, by E. Randall-David, 1989.

Chapter 7: p. 200: Table 7.1 from J. Levin and J. F. Nolan, *Principles of Classroom Management*. Copyright © 1996 by Allyn & Bacon. Reprinted/adapted by permission.

Chapter 8: p. 250: Figure 8.2 adapted from Eric Jensen with permission. © 1999 at www.thebrainstore.com. **p. 263:** Knowledge base statement from *Developing a Quality Curriculum*, by Allan A. Glatthorn. Alexandria, VA: Association for Supervision and Curriculum Development.

Copyright © 1994 ASCD. Reprinted with permission. All rights reserved.

Chapter 9: p. 281: Figure 9.1 reprinted with permission of Prufrock Press, Inc., Waco, TX. (800) 998-2208. **p. 284:** Table 9.2 from *Taxonomy of Educational Objectives Book I: Cognitive Domain*, by Benjamin Bloom. Copyright 1984. Reprinted with permission of Addison Wesley Longman, Inc. **pp. 306–308:** Excerpts from K. R. Chuska (1995), *Improving Classroom Questions*. Bloomington, IN: Phi Delta Kappa Educational Foundation. **p. 309:** Figure 9.2: from T. E. Raphael (1986, February). Teaching question answer relationships, revisited. *The Reading Teacher*, 39 (6), 516–522. Reprinted with permission of Taffy E. Raphael and the International Reading Association. All rights reserved.

Chapter 10: p. 335: Phases of a project from *Engaging Children's Minds, The Project Approach*, by L. Katz and S. Chard. Copyright © 1989 by Ablex Press. Reprinted with permission. **pp. 335–336:** Quotation and list from L. Katz and S. Chard (1993). "The Project Approach," in J. Roopnarine & J. Johnson (eds.), *Approaches to Early Childhood Education*, 2nd edition, pp. 209–222. Columbus, OH: Merrill. Reprinted with permission of Lilian Katz. **p. 336:** List of project topics adapted from E. Borgia (1996). "Learning Through Projects," Scholastic Early Childhood Today, 10 (6), 22–29. Reprinted with permission. **p. 345:** Figure 10. 7 from *Engaging Children's Minds, The Project Approach*, by L. Katz and S. Chard. Copyright © 1989 by Ablex Press. Reprinted with permission. **p. 346:** Learning centers list from "Why Integrate Learning Centers into Your Classroom Environment?" reprinted with permission from The Complete Learning Center Book by Rebecca Isbell, p. 36. © 1995, Gryphon House, Inc., P.O. Box 207, Beltsville, MD 20704-0207. 1-800-638-0928. **pp. 366–367:** Figure 10.8 reprinted with permission of Calvin K. Claus. **p. 371:** Self-assessment and reflection list from L. O. Pellicer and L. W. Anderson, *A Handbook for Teacher Leaders*. Copyright © 1995 by Corwin Press, Inc. Reprinted with permission of Corwin Press, Inc.

Chapter 11: p. 399: Recommendations from Elise Trumbull, *Alternative Assessment: Issues in Language, Culture, and Equity*. Knowledge Brief Number 11, WestEd, San Francisco, CA. **p. 400:** Alternatives in assessment from *Student-Centered Classroom Assessment*, 2nd edition, by Richard Stiggins. Upper Saddle River, NJ: Prentice-Hall 1997. Reprinted with permission of the Washington Commission on Student Learning. **p. 401:** Figure 11.1 adapted from R. Anthony, T. Johnson, N. Mickelson, and A. Preece, "Evaluation: A Perspective for Change," World Congress on Reading. International Reading Association, 1988. Reprinted with permission of the authors. **p. 404:** Assessment examples adapted from Stewart, S., Choate, J., and Poteet, J. (1995), "The Revolution in Assessment Within and Across Educational Settings." *Preventing School Failure*, 39 (3),

INDEX

FEATURES THROUGHOUT THE BOOK PROMOTE ACTIVE LEARNING AND CREATE OPPORTUNITIES FOR REFLECTION AND RESPONSE.

Reflect & Respond

> "School doesn't have to be the way you remember it."
>
> —Howard Gardner

Everybody remembers something about school. What do you remember? Maybe your positive memories include the special field trip you took to the state capitol at the end of sixth grade, sliding down the fire pole during your visit to the fire station in kindergarten, sharing one of your favorite books with a classmate, or the feeling of satisfaction you experienced when you finally conquered those multiplication tables.

For the first entry in your teaching journal, make a list of positive recollections from your own days as a student. Include the names of at least three teachers who truly made a difference in your life and served as significant role models for you. What did they do that made them so special?

REFLECT & RESPOND ▶
ENCOURAGES REFLECTION AND JOURNAL WRITING ON CHAPTER TOPICS.

New teachers talk

What is most important to you in the teaching/ learning process?

In order for the student to learn, I feel that it is crucial to build a trusting relationship between the student and the teacher. Since people naturally organize information into chunks or groups, I feel that it is necessary to teach in this manner. This means that teachers must provide connections between the material and the children's lives. Authenticity is key and will lead to interest in the learning process.

—KAREN, Preservice Teacher

through a variety of extrinsic motivators to perform, to answer questions, or to complete a task. However, I believe that learning is a choice, and we as educators must empower students to choose to learn, and we must support the enthusiasm that will most certainly accompany the pursuit of knowledge. I believe that "skill" I will ever teach is ho dren need guidance to beco perimenters, anthropologist given these opportunities, long learners by nature.

—SA

◀ NEW TEACHERS TALK
HIGHLIGHTS VIEWPOINTS FROM NEW TEACHERS IN THEIR FIRST YEARS OF PRACTICE, FOLLOWED BY AUTHOR ANALYSIS, AND OPPORTUNITIES FOR READER FEEDBACK. ▼

thi
ity
citem
Learn

about methods of teaching and gain insight as to how to work with children in various situations.

—ANN, Preservice Teacher

I feel the comfort level of my students is most important. I strive to ensure my students feel valued and challenged by the learning environment presented to them. I rely upon humor to create a learning environment that is flexible and student oriented. If the students themselves don't feel comfortable enough to take risks and learn, how is real, authentic learning going to occur?

—MIKE, Third-Year Teacher

Authors' Analysis
We find it interesting—but not surprising—to note that each teacher's response focuses on the emotions

and atti
When st
tant to
also focu
one stud
dents' reflections regarding what they wanted from their teachers all focused on affective characteristics: gentleness, caring, understanding, and a love of fun (Thomas & Montgomery, 1998).

Now It's Your Turn

In your teaching journal, provide your own response to the given question: What is most important to *you* in the teaching/ learning process?